# OpenGL®
## Programming Guide
### Sixth Edition

# OpenGL®
## Programming Guide
### Sixth Edition

*The Official Guide to*
*Learning OpenGL®, Version 2.1*

*OpenGL Architecture Review Board*
*Dave Shreiner   Mason Woo*
*Jackie Neider   Tom Davis*

♦♦Addison-Wesley

Upper Saddle River, NJ • Boston • Indianapolis • San Francisco
New York • Toronto • Montreal • London • Munich • Paris • Madrid
Capetown • Sydney • Tokyo • Singapore • Mexico City

Many of the designations used by manufacturers and sellers to distinguish their products are claimed as trademarks. Where those designations appear in this book, and the publisher was aware of a trademark claim, the designations have been printed with initial capital letters or in all capitals.

The authors and publisher have taken care in the preparation of this book, but make no expressed or implied warranty of any kind and assume no responsibility for errors or omissions. No liability is assumed for incidental or consequential damages in connection with or arising out of the use of the information or programs contained herein.

The publisher offers excellent discounts on this book when ordered in quantity for bulk purchases or special sales, which may include electronic versions and/or custom covers and content particular to your business, training goals, marketing focus, and branding interests. For more information, please contact:

U.S. Corporate and Government Sales
(800) 382-3419
corpsales@pearsontechgroup.com

For sales outside of the U.S., please contact:

International Sales
international@pearsoned.com

Visit us on the Web: www.awprofessional.com

*Library of Congress Cataloging-in-Publication Data*

OpenGL programming guide : the official guide to learning OpenGL, version 2.1 / OpenGL Architecture Review Board, Dave Shreiner ... [et al.]. — 6th ed.
    p. cm.
  Includes index.
  ISBN-13: 978-0-321-48100-9 (pbk. : alk. paper)
  ISBN-10: 0-321-48100-3
  1. Computer graphics. 2. OpenGL. I. Shreiner, Dave. II. OpenGL Architecture Review Board.

T385.O636 2007
006.6'6—dc22                                                  2007023543

ISBN 13: 978-0-321-48100-9
ISBN 10:     0-321-48100-3
Text printed in the United States on recycled paper at Courier in Stoughton, Massachusetts.
2nd printing, January 2008

*For my family—Felicity, Max, Sarah, and Scout.*

*—JLN*

*For my family—Ellyn, Ricky, and Lucy.*

*—TRD*

*To Tom Doeppner and Andy van Dam, who started me along this path.*

*—MW*

*For my family—Vicki, Bonnie, Bob, Phantom, Squiggles, Tuxedo, and Toby.*

*—DRS*

*In memory of Phil Karlton and Celeste Fowler.*

# Contents

# Figures

# Tables

# Examples

# About This Guide

The OpenGL graphics system is a software interface to graphics hardware. (The GL stands for Graphics Library.) It allows you to create interactive programs that produce color images of moving three-dimensional objects. With OpenGL, you can control computer-graphics technology to produce realistic pictures or ones that depart from reality in imaginative ways. This guide explains how to program with the OpenGL graphics system to deliver the visual effect you want.

## What This Guide Contains

This guide has 15 chapters. The first five chapters present basic information that you need to understand to be able to draw a properly colored and lit three-dimensional object on the screen.

- Chapter 1, **"Introduction to OpenGL,"** provides a glimpse into the kinds of things OpenGL can do. It also presents a simple OpenGL program and explains essential programming details you need to know for subsequent chapters.

- Chapter 2, **"State Management and Drawing Geometric Objects,"** explains how to create a three-dimensional geometric description of an object that is eventually drawn on the screen.

- Chapter 3, **"Viewing,"** describes how such three-dimensional models are transformed before being drawn on a two-dimensional screen. You can control these transformations to show a particular view of a model.

- Chapter 4, **"Color,"** describes how to specify the color and shading method used to draw an object.

- Chapter 5, **"Lighting,"** explains how to control the lighting conditions surrounding an object and how that object responds to light (that is, how it reflects or absorbs light). Lighting is an important topic, since objects usually don't look three-dimensional until they're lit.

The remaining chapters explain how to optimize or add sophisticated features to your three-dimensional scene. You might choose not to take advantage of many of these features until you're more comfortable with OpenGL. Particularly advanced topics are noted in the text where they occur.

- Chapter 6, **"Blending, Antialiasing, Fog, and Polygon Offset,"** describes techniques essential to creating a realistic scene—alpha blending (to create transparent objects), antialiasing (to eliminate jagged edges), atmospheric effects (to simulate fog or smog), and polygon offset (to remove visual artifacts when highlighting the edges of filled polygons).

- Chapter 7, **"Display Lists,"** discusses how to store a series of OpenGL commands for execution at a later time. You'll want to use this feature to increase the performance of your OpenGL program.

- Chapter 8, **"Drawing Pixels, Bitmaps, Fonts, and Images,"** discusses how to work with sets of two-dimensional data as bitmaps or images. One typical use for bitmaps is describing characters in fonts.

- Chapter 9, **"Texture Mapping,"** explains how to map one-, two-, and three-dimensional images called *textures* onto three-dimensional objects. Many marvelous effects can be achieved through texture mapping.

- Chapter 10, **"The Framebuffer,"** describes all the possible buffers that can exist in an OpenGL implementation and how you can control them. You can use the buffers for such effects as hidden-surface elimination, stenciling, masking, motion blur, and depth-of-field focusing.

- Chapter 11, **"Tessellators and Quadrics,"** shows how to use the tessellation and quadrics routines in the GLU (OpenGL Utility Library).

- Chapter 12, **"Evaluators and NURBS,"** gives an introduction to advanced techniques for efficient generation of curves or surfaces.

- Chapter 13, **"Selection and Feedback,"** explains how you can use OpenGL's selection mechanism to select an object on the screen. Additionally, the chapter explains the feedback mechanism, which allows you to collect the drawing information OpenGL produces, rather than having it be used to draw on the screen.

- Chapter 14, **"Now That You Know,"** describes how to use OpenGL in several clever and unexpected ways to produce interesting results. These techniques are drawn from years of experience with both OpenGL and the technological precursor to OpenGL, the Silicon Graphics IRIS Graphics Library.

- Chapter 15, **"The OpenGL Shading Language,"** discusses the changes that occurred starting with OpenGL Version 2.0. This includes an introduction to the OpenGL Shading Language, also commonly called the "GLSL," which allows you to take control of portions of OpenGL's processing for *vertices* and *fragments*. This functionality can greatly enhance the image quality and computational power of OpenGL.

In addition, there are several appendices that you will likely find useful:

- Appendix A, **"Order of Operations,"** gives a technical overview of the operations OpenGL performs, briefly describing them in the order in which they occur as an application executes.

- Appendix B, **"State Variables,"** lists the state variables that OpenGL maintains and describes how to obtain their values.

- Appendix C, **"OpenGL and Window Systems,"** briefly describes the routines available in window-system-specific libraries, which are extended to support OpenGL rendering. Window system interfaces to the X Window System, Apple's Mac/OS, IBM OS/2, and Microsoft Windows are discussed here.

- Appendix D, **"Basics of GLUT: The OpenGL Utility Toolkit,"** discusses the library that handles window system operations. GLUT is portable and it makes code examples shorter and more comprehensible.

- Appendix E, **"Calculating Normal Vectors,"** tells you how to calculate normal vectors for different types of geometric objects.

- Appendix F, **"Homogeneous Coordinates and Transformation Matrices,"** explains some of the mathematics behind matrix transformations.

- Appendix G, **"Programming Tips,"** lists some programming tips based on the intentions of the designers of OpenGL that you might find useful.

- Appendix H, **"OpenGL Invariance,"** describes when and where an OpenGL implementation must generate the exact pixel values described in the OpenGL specification.

- Appendix I, **"Built-In OpenGL Shading Language Variables and Functions,"** lists all of the built-in variables and functions available in the OpenGL Shading Language.

Finally, an extensive Glossary defines the key terms used in this guide.

## What's New in This Edition

The sixth edition of the *OpenGL Programming Guide* includes new and updated material covering OpenGL Version 2.1:

- Coverage of the following new core capabilities has been added:
  - Storage of pixel rectangles in buffer objects.
  - Support for sRGB formatted textures. The sRGB color space roughly corresponds to a gamma-corrected RGB space (using a gamma value of 2.2).
  - Specification of nonsquare matrices as uniform variables in OpenGL shading language shader programs.
  - Expanded discussion of the OpenGL shading language, including additions supporting OpenGL Version 2.1 functionality.
- Bug fixes and other clarifications

## What You Should Know Before Reading This Guide

This guide assumes only that you know how to program in the C language and that you have some background in mathematics (geometry, trigonometry, linear algebra, calculus, and differential geometry). Even if you have little or no experience with computer graphics technology, you should be able to follow most of the discussions in this book. Of course, computer graphics is a huge subject, so you may want to enrich your learning experience with supplemental reading:

- *Computer Graphics: Principles and Practice* by James D. Foley, Andries van Dam, Steven K. Feiner, and John F. Hughes (Addison-Wesley, 1990)—This book is an encyclopedic treatment of the subject of computer graphics. It includes a wealth of information but is probably best read after you have some experience with the subject.

- *3D Computer Graphics* by Andrew S. Glassner (The Lyons Press, 1994)—This book is a nontechnical, gentle introduction to computer graphics. It focuses on the visual effects that can be achieved, rather than on the techniques needed to achieve them.

Another great place for all sorts of general information is the Official OpenGL Web Site. This Web site contains software, sample programs, documentation, FAQs, discussion boards, and news. It is always a good place to start any search for answers to your OpenGL questions:

```
http://www.opengl.org/
```

Additionally, full documentation of all the procedures that compose OpenGL Version 2.1 are documented at the Official OpenGL Web site. These Web pages replace the *OpenGL Reference Manual* that was published by the OpenGL Architecture Review Board and Addison-Wesley.

OpenGL is really a hardware-independent specification of a programming interface, and you use a particular implementation of it on a particular kind of hardware. This guide explains how to program with any OpenGL implementation. However, since implementations may vary slightly—in performance and in providing additional, optional features, for example—you might want to investigate whether supplementary documentation is available for the particular implementation you're using. In addition, you might have OpenGL-related utilities, toolkits, programming and debugging support, widgets, sample programs, and demos available to you with your system.

## How to Obtain the Sample Code

This guide contains many sample programs to illustrate the use of particular OpenGL programming techniques. These programs make use of Mark Kilgard's OpenGL Utility Toolkit (GLUT). GLUT is documented in *OpenGL Programming for the X Window System* by Mark Kilgard (Addison-Wesley, 1996). The section "OpenGL-Related Libraries" in Chapter 1 and Appendix D give more information about using GLUT. If you have access to the Internet, you can obtain the source code for both the sample programs and GLUT for free via anonymous ftp (file-transfer protocol).

For the source code examples found in this book, please visit

```
http://www.opengl-redbook.com/code/
```

# Acknowledgments

### The Sixth Edition

As with the seven preceding versions of OpenGL, the guidance of the OpenGL Architecture Review Board was paramount in its evolution and development. Without the ARB's guidance and devotion, OpenGL would surely languish, and once again we express our gratitude for their efforts.

Once again, the staff of Addison-Wesley provided the support and encouragement to have this edition come to fruition. Debra Williams-Cauley, Tyrrell Albaugh, and John Fuller once again worked miracles in producing this manuscript. Thanks once again for an effort second to none.

### The Fifth Edition

OpenGL continued its evolutionary track under the careful guidance of the OpenGL Architecture Review Board and its working groups. The small committees that help unify the various business and technical differences among the ARB's membership deserve our thanks and gratitude. They continue to push OpenGL's success to new levels.

As always, the ever-patient and helpful staff at Addison-Wesley were indispensable. Once again, Mary O'Brien, perhaps OpenGL's most devoted non-programming (at least to our knowledge) proponent, continues to encourage us to update the programming guide for the community. Tyrrell Albaugh and John Fuller worked tirelessly in preparing the manuscript for production. Thanks to you all.

### The Fourth Edition

OpenGL continued its evolution and success with the aid of many individuals. The OpenGL Architecture Review Board, along with its many participants, help to mold OpenGL. Their contributions were much appreciated.

Numerous example programs were written by Stace Peterson. Helpful discussions and clarifications were provided by Maryann Simmons, Patrick Brown, Alan Commike, Brad Grantham, Bob Kuehne, Jon Leech, Benjamin Lipchak, Marc Olano, and Vicki Shreiner.

Once again, the editorial and production staff at Addison-Wesley were extremely helpful. Thanks to Mary O'Brien, John Fuller, and Brenda Mulligan.

**The Third Edition**

The third edition of this book required the support of many individuals.

Special thanks are due to the reviewers who volunteered and trudged through the now seven hundred pages of technical material that constitute the third edition: Bill Armstrong, Bob Beretta, David Blythe, Dan Brokenshire, Norman Chin, Steve Cunningham, Angus Dorbie, Laurence Feldman, Celeste Fowler, Jeffery Galinovsky, Brad Grantham, Eric Haines, David Ishimoto, Mark Kilgard, Dale Kirkland, Jon Leech, Seth Livingston, Chikai Ohazama, Bimal Poddar, Mike Schmit, John Stauffer, R. Scott Thompson, David Yu, and Hansong Zhang. Their careful diligence has greatly improved the quality of this book.

An immeasurable debt of gratitude goes to Laura Cooper, Dany Galgani, and Dan Young for their production support, and to Mary O'Brien, Elizabeth Spainhour, Chanda Leary, and John Fuller of Addison-Wesley. Additionally, Miriam Geller, Shawn Hopwood, Stacy Maller, and David Story were instrumental in the coordination and marketing of this effort.

**The First and Second Editions**

Thanks to the long list of pioneers and past contributors to the success of OpenGL and of this book.

Thanks to the chief architects of OpenGL: Mark Segal and Kurt Akeley. Special recognition goes to the pioneers who heavily contributed to the initial design and functionality of OpenGL: Allen Akin, David Blythe, Jim Bushnell, Dick Coulter, John Dennis, Raymond Drewry, Fred Fisher, Celeste Fowler, Chris Frazier, Momi Furuya, Bill Glazier, Kipp Hickman, Paul Ho, Rick Hodgson, Simon Hui, Lesley Kalmin, Phil Karlton, On Lee, Randi Rost, Kevin P. Smith, Murali Sundaresan, Pierre Tardif, Linas Vepstas, Chuck Whitmer, Jim Winget, and Wei Yen.

The impetus for the second edition began with Paula Womack and Tom McReynolds of Silicon Graphics, who recognized the need for a revision and also contributed some of the new material. John Schimpf, OpenGL Product Manager at Silicon Graphics, was instrumental in getting the revision off and running.

Many thanks go to the people who contributed to the success of the first and second editions of this book: Cindy Ahuna, Kurt Akeley, Bill Armstrong, Otto Berkes, Andy Bigos, Drew Bliss, Patrick Brown, Brian Cabral, Norman Chin, Bill Clifford, Jim Cobb, Dick Coulter, Kathleen Danielson, Suzy Deffeyes, Craig Dunwoody, Fred Fisher, Chris Frazier, Ken Garnett, Kathy Gochenour, Michael Gold, Mike Heck, Paul Ho, Deanna Hohn, Brian Hook, Kevin Hunter, Phil Huxley, Renate Kempf, Mark Kilgard, Dale Kirkland, David Koller, Kevin LeFebvre, Hock San Lee, Zicheng Liu, Rob Mace, Kay Maitz, Tim Misner, Jeremy Morris, Dave Orton, Bimal Poddar, Susan Riley, Randi Rost, Mark Segal, Igor Sinyak, Bill Sweeney, Pierre Tardif, Andy Vesper, Henri Warren, Paula Womack, Gilman Wong, Steve Wright, and David Yu.

The color plates received a major overhaul for this edition. The sequence of plates based on the cover image (Plates 1 through 9) was created by Thad Beier, Seth Katz, and Mason Woo. Plates 10 through 20, 22, and 23 are snapshots of programs created by Mason Woo. Plate 21 was created by Paul Haeberli. Plate 24 was created by Cyril Kardassevitch of the Institue de Recherche en Informatique de Toulouse. Plate 25 was created by Yukari Ito and Keisuke Kirii of Nihon SGI. Plate 26 was created by John Coggi and David Stodden of The Aerospace Company. Plate 27 was created by Rainer Goebel, Max Planck Institute for Brain Research. Plate 28 was created by Stefan Brabec and Wolfgang Heidrich of the Max Planck Institute for Computer Science. Plate 29 was created by Mikko Blomqvist, Mediaclick OY. Plate 30 was created by Bernd Lutz of Fraunhofer IGD. Finally, Plates 31 and 32, screenshots from the Quake series of games, were created by id Software.

For the color plates that appeared in the previous editions, we would like to thank Gavin Bell, Barry Brouillette, Rikk Carey, Sharon Clay, Mark Daly, Alain Dumesny, Ben Garlick, Kevin Goldsmith, Jim Helman, Dave Immel, Paul Isaacs, Michael Jones, Carl Korobkin, Howard Look, David Mott, Craig Phillips, John Rohlf, Linda Roy, Paul Strauss, and Doug Voorhies.

And now, each of the authors would like to take the 15 minutes that have been allotted to them by Andy Warhol to say thank you.

*From the first and second editions:*

I'd like to thank my managers at Silicon Graphics—Dave Larson and Way Ting—and the members of my group—Patricia Creek, Arthur Evans, Beth

Fryer, Jed Hartman, Ken Jones, Robert Reimann, Eve Stratton (aka Margaret-Anne Halse), John Stearns, and Josie Wernecke—for their support during this lengthy process. Last, but surely not least, I want to thank those whose contributions toward this project are too deep and mysterious to elucidate: Yvonne Leach, Kathleen Lancaster, Caroline Rose, Cindy Kleinfeld, and my parents, Florence and Ferdinand Neider.

—JLN

In addition to my parents, Edward and Irene Davis, I'd like to thank the people who taught me most of what I know about computers and computer graphics—Doug Engelbart and Jim Clark.

—TRD

I'd like to thank the many past and current members of Silicon Graphics whose accommodation and enlightenment were essential to my contribution to this book: Gerald Anderson, Wendy Chin, Bert Fornaciari, Bill Glazier, Jill Huchital, Howard Look, Bill Mannel, David Marsland, Dave Orton, Linda Roy, Keith Seto, and Dave Shreiner. Very special thanks to Karrin Nicol, Leilani Gayles, Kevin Dankwardt, Kiyoshi Hasegawa, and Raj Singh for their guidance throughout my career. I also bestow much gratitude to my teammates on the Stanford B ice hockey team for periods of glorious distraction throughout the initial writing of this book. Finally, I'd like to thank my family, especially my mother, Bo, and my late father, Henry.

—MW

*And for the third edition:*

I'd first like to acknowledge Mason, who aside from helping me with this undertaking, has been a great friend and mentor over the years. My knowledge of OpenGL would be nothing without the masters who have patiently answered my questions: Kurt Akeley, Allen Akin, David Blythe, Chris Frazier, Mark Kilgard, Mark Segal, Paula Womack, and David Yu and my current teammates working on OpenGL: Paul Ho, George Kyriazis, Jon Leech, Ken Nicholson, and David Yu. Additionally, I'd like to recognize Doug Doren, Kerwin Dobbs, and Karl Sohlberg, who started me on this odyssey so long ago, and Andrew Walton, John Harechmak, and Alan Dare, who have provided illuminating conversations about graphics over the years. Finally and most important, I'd like to thank Vicki, my loving wife, my parents, Bonnie and Bob, and Squiggles and Phantom, who endlessly encourage me in all that I do and have taught me to enjoy life to the fullest.

—DRS

*And for the fourth edition:*

Once again, I owe Mason a debt of thanks for helping to jump start this project. Without him, we all might be waiting for an update. I'd also like to extend my appreciation to Alan Chalmers, James Gain, Geoff Leach, and their students for their enthusiasm and encouragement. I'd also like to thank ACM/SIGGRAPH, Afrigraph, Seagraph, and SGI for the ample opportunities to talk about OpenGL to wonderful audiences worldwide. Brad Grantham, who's been willing to help out with all my OpenGL escapades, deserves special thanks. A couple of friends who deserve special mention are Eric England and Garth Honhart. The biggest thanks goes to those I love most: Vicki, my folks, and Squiggles, Phantom, and Toby. They continue to make me more successful than I ever imagined.

—DRS

*And for the fifth edition:*

First and foremost, a tremendous thanks goes to Vicki, my wife, who patiently waited the countless hours needed to finish this project, and to the rest of my family: Phantom, Toby, Bonnie, and Bob. I also wish to thank the OpenGL and SIGGRAPH communities, which continue to encourage me in these endeavors. And thanks to Alan Commike, Bob Kuehne, Brad Grantham, and Tom True for their help and support in the various OpenGL activities I coerce them into helping me with.

—DRS

*And for the sixth edition:*

As always, my deepest appreciation goes to Vicki and Phantom who waited patiently while I toiled on this edition, and to my parents: Bonnie and Bob, who still encourage and compliment my efforts (and dig the fact that I actually wound up doing something useful in life). I'd also like to thank the members of the OpenGL ARB Working Group (now part of the Khrons Group) and its Ecosystem Technical Sub-Group for their efforts in making documentation and information about OpenGL all the more accessible.

A great thanks goes to the Graphics group at the University of Cape Town's Visual Computing Laboratory: James Gain, Patrick Marais, Gary Marsden, Bruce Merry, Carl Hultquist, Christopher de Kadt, Ilan Angel, and Shaun Nirenstein; and Jason Moore. Last, but certainly not least, thanks once again to the OpenGL and SIGGRAPH communities for encouraging me to continue this project and providing ever needed feedback. Thanks to you all.

—DRS

## Chapter 1

# Introduction to OpenGL

**Chapter Objectives**

After reading this chapter, you'll be able to do the following:

- Appreciate in general terms what OpenGL does

- Identify different levels of rendering complexity

- Understand the basic structure of an OpenGL program

- Recognize OpenGL command syntax

- Identify the sequence of operations of the OpenGL rendering pipeline

- Understand in general terms how to animate graphics in an OpenGL program

This chapter introduces OpenGL. It has the following major sections:

- "What Is OpenGL?" explains what OpenGL is, what it does and doesn't do, and how it works.

- "A Smidgen of OpenGL Code" presents a small OpenGL program and briefly discusses it. This section also defines a few basic computer-graphics terms.

- "OpenGL Command Syntax" explains some of the conventions and notations used by OpenGL commands.

- "OpenGL as a State Machine" describes the use of state variables in OpenGL and the commands for querying, enabling, and disabling states.

- "OpenGL Rendering Pipeline" shows a typical sequence of operations for processing geometric and image data.

- "OpenGL-Related Libraries" describes sets of OpenGL-related routines, including a detailed introduction to GLUT (Graphics Library Utility Toolkit), a portable toolkit.

- "Animation" explains in general terms how to create pictures on the screen that move.

## What Is OpenGL?

OpenGL is a software interface to graphics hardware. This interface consists of over 700 distinct commands (about 650 in the core OpenGL and another 50 in the OpenGL Utility Library) that you use to specify the objects and operations needed to produce interactive three-dimensional applications.

OpenGL is designed as a streamlined, hardware-independent interface to be implemented on many different hardware platforms. To achieve these qualities, no commands for performing windowing tasks or obtaining user input are included in OpenGL; instead, you must work through whatever windowing system controls the particular hardware you're using. Similarly, OpenGL doesn't provide high-level commands for describing models of three-dimensional objects. Such commands might allow you to specify relatively complicated shapes such as automobiles, parts of the body, air-planes, or molecules. With OpenGL, you must build your desired model from a small set of *geometric primitives*—points, lines, and polygons.

A sophisticated library that provides these features could certainly be built on top of OpenGL. The OpenGL Utility Library (GLU) provides many of the modeling features, such as quadric surfaces and NURBS curves and surfaces. GLU is a standard part of every OpenGL implementation.

Now that you know what OpenGL *doesn't* do, here's what it *does* do. Take a look at the color plates—they illustrate typical uses of OpenGL. They show the scene on the cover of this book, *rendered* (which is to say, drawn) by a computer using OpenGL in successively more complicated ways. The following list describes in general terms how these pictures were made.

- Plate 1 shows the entire scene displayed as a *wireframe* model—that is, as if all the objects in the scene were made of wire. Each *line* of wire corresponds to an edge of a primitive (typically a polygon). For example, the surface of the table is constructed from triangular polygons that are positioned like slices of pie.

  Note that you can see portions of objects that would be obscured if the objects were solid rather than wireframe. For example, you can see the entire model of the hills outside the window even though most of this model is normally hidden by the wall of the room. The globe appears to be nearly solid because it's composed of hundreds of colored blocks, and you see the wireframe lines for all the edges of all the blocks, even those forming the back side of the globe. The way the globe is constructed gives you an idea of how complex objects can be created by assembling lower-level objects.

- Plate 2 shows a *depth-cued* version of the same wireframe scene. Note that the lines farther from the eye are dimmer, just as they would be in real life, thereby giving a visual cue of *depth*. OpenGL uses atmospheric effects (collectively referred to as *fog*) to achieve depth cueing.

- Plate 3 shows an *antialiased* version of the wireframe scene. Antialiasing is a technique for reducing the jagged edges (also known as *jaggies*) created when approximating smooth edges using *pixels*—short for *picture elements*—which are confined to a rectangular grid. Such jaggies are usually the most visible, with near-horizontal or near-vertical lines.

- Plate 4 shows a *flat-shaded, unlit* version of the scene. The objects in the scene are now shown as solid. They appear "flat" in the sense that only one color is used to render each polygon, so they don't appear smoothly rounded. There are no effects from any light sources.

- Plate 5 shows a *lit, smooth-shaded* version of the scene. Note how the scene looks much more realistic and three-dimensional when the objects are shaded to respond to the light sources in the room, as if the objects were smoothly rounded.

- Plate 6 adds *shadows* and *textures* to the previous version of the scene. Shadows aren't an explicitly defined feature of OpenGL (there is no "shadow command"), but you can create them yourself using the techniques described in Chapter 9 and Chapter 14. *Texture mapping* allows you to apply a two-dimensional image onto a three-dimensional object. In this scene, the top on the table surface is the most vibrant example of texture mapping. The wood grain on the floor and table surface are all texture mapped, as well as the wallpaper and the toy top (on the table).

- Plate 7 shows a *motion-blurred* object in the scene. The sphinx (or dog, depending on your Rorschach tendencies) appears to be captured moving forward, leaving a blurred trace of its path of motion.

- Plate 8 shows the scene as it was drawn for the cover of the book from a different viewpoint. This plate illustrates that the image really is a snapshot of models of three-dimensional objects.

- Plate 9 brings back the use of fog, which was shown in Plate 2 to simulate the presence of smoke particles in the air. Note how the same effect in Plate 2 now has a more dramatic impact in Plate 9.

- Plate 10 shows the *depth-of-field effect*, which simulates the inability of a camera lens to maintain all objects in a photographed scene in focus. The camera focuses on a particular spot in the scene. Objects that are significantly closer or farther than that spot are somewhat blurred.

The color plates give you an idea of the kinds of things you can do with the OpenGL graphics system. The following list briefly describes the major graphics operations that OpenGL performs to render an image on the screen. (See "OpenGL Rendering Pipeline" on page 10 for detailed information about this order of operations.)

1. Construct shapes from geometric primitives, thereby creating mathematical descriptions of objects. (OpenGL considers points, lines, polygons, images, and bitmaps to be primitives.)

2. Arrange the objects in three-dimensional space and select the desired vantage point for viewing the composed scene.

3. Calculate the colors of all the objects. The colors might be explicitly assigned by the application, determined from specified lighting conditions, obtained by pasting a texture onto the objects, or some combination of these three actions.

4. Convert the mathematical description of objects and their associated color information to pixels on the screen. This process is called *rasterization*.

During these stages, OpenGL might perform other operations, such as eliminating parts of objects that are hidden by other objects. In addition, after the scene is rasterized but before it's drawn on the screen, you can perform some operations on the pixel data if you want.

In some implementations (such as with the X Window System), OpenGL is designed to work even if the computer that displays the graphics you create isn't the computer that runs your graphics program. This might be the case if you work in a networked computer environment where many computers are connected to one another by a digital network. In this situation, the computer on which your program runs and issues OpenGL drawing commands is called the *client*, and the computer that receives those commands and performs the drawing is called the *server*. The format for transmitting OpenGL commands (called the *protocol*) from the client to the server is always the same, so OpenGL programs can work across a *network* even if the client and server are different kinds of computers. If an OpenGL program isn't running across a network, then there's only one computer, and it is both the client and the server.

## A Smidgen of OpenGL Code

Because you can do so many things with the OpenGL graphics system, an OpenGL program can be complicated. However, the basic structure of a useful program can be simple: its tasks are to initialize certain states that control how OpenGL renders and to specify objects to be rendered.

Before you look at some OpenGL code, let's go over a few terms. *Rendering*, which you've already seen used, is the process by which a computer creates images from models. These *models*, or objects, are constructed from geometric primitives—points, lines, and polygons—that are specified by their *vertices*.

The final rendered image consists of pixels drawn on the screen; a pixel is the smallest visible element the display hardware can put on the screen. Information about the pixels (for instance, what color they're supposed to be) is organized in memory into bitplanes. A *bitplane* is an area of memory that holds one *bit* of information for every pixel on the screen; the bit might indicate how red a particular pixel is supposed to be, for example. The bitplanes are themselves organized into a *framebuffer,* which holds all the information that the graphics display needs to control the color and intensity of all the pixels on the screen.

Now look at what an OpenGL program might look like. Example 1-1 renders a white rectangle on a black background, as shown in Figure 1-1.

**Figure 1-1**     White Rectangle on a Black Background

**Example 1-1**     Chunk of OpenGL Code

```
#include <whateverYouNeed.h>

main() {
    InitializeAWindowPlease();

    glClearColor(0.0, 0.0, 0.0, 0.0);
    glClear(GL_COLOR_BUFFER_BIT);
    glColor3f(1.0, 1.0, 1.0);
    glOrtho(0.0, 1.0, 0.0, 1.0, -1.0, 1.0);
    glBegin(GL_POLYGON);
        glVertex3f(0.25, 0.25, 0.0);
        glVertex3f(0.75, 0.25, 0.0);
        glVertex3f(0.75, 0.75, 0.0);
        glVertex3f(0.25, 0.75, 0.0);
    glEnd();
    glFlush();
    UpdateTheWindowAndCheckForEvents();
}
```

The first line of the **main()** routine initializes a *window* on the screen: The **InitializeAWindowPlease()** routine is meant as a placeholder for window-system-specific routines, which are generally not OpenGL calls. The next two lines are OpenGL commands that clear the window to black: **glClearColor()** establishes what color the window will be cleared to, and **glClear()** actually clears the window. Once the clearing color is set, the window is cleared to that color whenever **glClear()** is called. This clearing color can be changed with another call to **glClearColor()**. Similarly, the **glColor3f()** command establishes what color to use for drawing objects—in this case, the color is white. All objects drawn after this point use this color, until it's changed with another call to set the color.

The next OpenGL command used in the program, **glOrtho()**, specifies the *coordinate system* OpenGL assumes as it draws the final image and how the image is mapped to the screen. The next calls, which are bracketed by **glBegin()** and **glEnd()**, define the object to be drawn—in this example, a polygon with four vertices. The polygon's "corners" are defined by the **glVertex3f()** commands. As you might be able to guess from the arguments, which are (*x, y, z*) coordinates, the polygon is a rectangle on the *z* = 0 plane.

Finally, **glFlush()** ensures that the drawing commands are actually executed, rather than stored in a *buffer* awaiting additional OpenGL commands. The **UpdateTheWindowAndCheckForEvents()** placeholder routine manages the contents of the window and begins event processing.

Actually, this piece of OpenGL code isn't well structured. You may be asking, "What happens if I try to move or resize the window?" or "Do I need to reset the coordinate system each time I draw the rectangle?". Later in this chapter, you will see replacements for both **InitializeAWindowPlease()** and **UpdateTheWindowAndCheckForEvents()** that actually work but require restructuring of the code to make it efficient.

## OpenGL Command Syntax

As you might have observed from the simple program in the preceding section, OpenGL commands use the prefix **gl** and initial capital letters for each word making up the command name (recall **glClearColor()**, for example). Similarly, OpenGL defined constants begin with GL_, use all capital letters, and use underscores to separate words (for example, GL_COLOR_BUFFER_BIT).

You might also have noticed some seemingly extraneous letters appended to some command names (for example, the **3f** in **glColor3f()** and **glVertex3f()**). It's true that the **Color** part of the command name **glColor3f()** is enough to define the command as one that sets the current color. However, more than one such command has been defined so that you can use different types of arguments. In particular, the **3** part of the suffix indicates that three arguments are given; another version of the **Color** command takes four arguments. The **f** part of the suffix indicates that the arguments are floating-point numbers. Having different formats allows OpenGL to accept the user's data in his or her own data format.

Some OpenGL commands accept as many as eight different data types for their arguments. The letters used as suffixes to specify these data types for ISO C implementations of OpenGL are shown in Table 1-1, along with the corresponding OpenGL type definitions. The particular implementation of OpenGL that you're using might not follow this scheme exactly; an implementation in C++ or Ada, for example, wouldn't need to.

| Suffix | Data Type | Typical Corresponding C-Language Type | OpenGL Type Definition |
|--------|-----------|---------------------------------------|------------------------|
| b | 8-bit integer | signed char | GLbyte |
| s | 16-bit integer | short | GLshort |
| i | 32-bit integer | int or long | GLint, GLsizei |
| f | 32-bit floating-point | float | GLfloat, GLclampf |
| d | 64-bit floating-point | double | GLdouble, GLclampd |
| ub | 8-bit unsigned integer | unsigned char | GLubyte, GLboolean |
| us | 16-bit unsigned integer | unsigned short | GLushort |
| ui | 32-bit unsigned integer | unsigned int or unsigned long | GLuint, GLenum, GLbitfield |

**Table 1-1**      Command Suffixes and Argument Data Types

Thus, the two commands

```
glVertex2i(1, 3);
glVertex2f(1.0, 3.0);
```

are equivalent, except that the first specifies the vertex's coordinates as 32-bit integers, and the second specifies them as single-precision floating-point numbers.

**Note:** Implementations of OpenGL have leeway in selecting which C data type to use to represent OpenGL data types. If you resolutely use the OpenGL defined data types throughout your application, you will avoid mismatched types when porting your code between different implementations.

Some OpenGL commands can take a final letter **v**, which indicates that the command takes a pointer to a vector (or array) of values, rather than a series of individual arguments. Many commands have both vector and nonvector versions, but some commands accept only individual arguments and others require that at least some of the arguments be specified as a vector. The following lines show how you might use a vector and a nonvector version of the command that sets the current color:

```
glColor3f(1.0, 0.0, 0.0);

GLfloat color_array[] = {1.0, 0.0, 0.0};
glColor3fv(color_array);
```

Finally, OpenGL defines the type of GLvoid. This is most often used for OpenGL commands that accept pointers to arrays of values.

In the rest of this guide (except in actual code examples), OpenGL commands are referred to by their base names only, and an asterisk is included to indicate that there may be more to the command name. For example, **glColor*()** stands for all variations of the command you use to set the current color. If we want to make a specific point about one version of a particular command, we include the suffix necessary to define that version. For example, **glVertex*v()** refers to all the vector versions of the command you use to specify vertices.

## OpenGL as a State Machine

OpenGL is a state machine. You put it into various states (or modes) that then remain in effect until you change them. As you've already seen, the current color is a state variable. You can set the current color to white, red, or any other color, and thereafter every object is drawn with that color until you set the current color to something else. The current color is only one of many state variables that OpenGL maintains. Others control such things as the current viewing and projection transformations, line and polygon stipple patterns, polygon drawing modes, pixel-packing conventions, positions and characteristics of lights, and material properties of the objects being drawn. Many state variables refer to modes that are enabled or disabled with the command **glEnable()** or **glDisable()**.

Each state variable or mode has a default value, and at any point you can query the system for each variable's current value. Typically, you use one of the six following commands to do this: **glGetBooleanv()**, **glGetDoublev()**, **glGetFloatv()**, **glGetIntegerv()**, **glGetPointerv()**, or **glIsEnabled()**. Which of these commands you select depends on what data type you want the answer to be given in. Some state variables have a more specific query command (such as **glGetLight*()**, **glGetError()**, or **glGetPolygonStipple()**). In addition, you can save a collection of state variables on an attribute stack with **glPushAttrib()** or **glPushClientAttrib()**, temporarily modify them, and later restore the values with **glPopAttrib()** or **glPopClientAttrib()**. For temporary state changes, you should use these commands rather than any of the query commands, as they're likely to be more efficient.

See Appendix B for the complete list of state variables you can query. For each variable, the appendix also lists a suggested **glGet*()** command that returns the variable's value, the attribute class to which it belongs, and the variable's default value.

## OpenGL Rendering Pipeline

Most implementations of OpenGL have a similar order of operations, a series of processing stages called the OpenGL rendering pipeline. This ordering, as shown in Figure 1-2, is not a strict rule about how OpenGL is implemented, but it provides a reliable guide for predicting what OpenGL will do.

If you are new to three-dimensional graphics, the upcoming description may seem like drinking water out of a fire hose. You can skim this now, but come back to Figure 1-2 as you go through each chapter in this book.

The following diagram shows the Henry Ford assembly line approach, which OpenGL takes to processing data. Geometric data (vertices, lines, and polygons) follow the path through the row of boxes that includes evaluators and per-vertex operations, while pixel data (pixels, images, and bitmaps) are treated differently for part of the process. Both types of data undergo the same final steps (rasterization and per-fragment operations) before the final pixel data is written into the framebuffer.

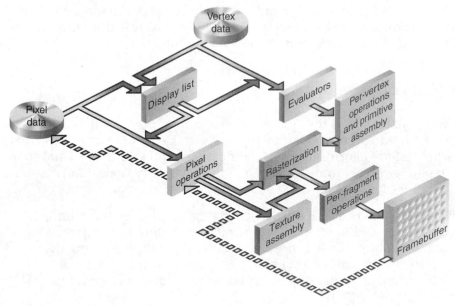

**Figure 1-2**    Order of Operations

Now you'll see more detail about the key stages in the OpenGL rendering pipeline.

## Display Lists

All data, whether it describes geometry or pixels, can be saved in a *display list* for current or later use. (The alternative to retaining data in a display list is processing the data immediately—also known as *immediate mode*.) When a display list is executed, the retained data is sent from the display list just as if it were sent by the application in immediate mode. (See Chapter 7 for more information about display lists.)

## Evaluators

All geometric primitives are eventually described by vertices. Parametric curves and surfaces may be initially described by control points and polynomial functions called *basis functions*. Evaluators provide a method for deriving the vertices used to represent the surface from the control points.

The method is a polynomial mapping, which can produce surface normal, texture coordinates, colors, and spatial coordinate values from the control points. (See Chapter 12 to learn more about evaluators.)

## Per-Vertex Operations

For vertex data, next is the "per-vertex operations" stage, which converts the vertices into primitives. Some types of vertex data (for example, spatial coordinates) are transformed by $4 \times 4$ floating-point matrices. Spatial coordinates are projected from a position in the 3D world to a position on your screen. (See Chapter 3 for details about the transformation matrices.)

If advanced features are enabled, this stage is even busier. If texturing is used, texture coordinates may be generated and transformed here. If lighting is enabled, the lighting calculations are performed using the transformed vertex, surface normal, light source position, material properties, and other lighting information to produce a color value.

## Primitive Assembly

Clipping, a major part of primitive assembly, is the elimination of portions of geometry that fall outside a half-space, defined by a plane. Point clipping simply passes or rejects vertices; line or polygon clipping can add additional vertices depending on how the line or polygon is clipped.

In some cases, this is followed by perspective division, which makes distant geometric objects appear smaller than closer objects. Then viewport and depth ($z$-coordinate) operations are applied. If culling is enabled and the primitive is a polygon, it then may be rejected by a culling test. Depending on the polygon mode, a polygon may be drawn as points or lines. (See "Polygon Details" in Chapter 2.)

The results of this stage are complete geometric primitives, which are the transformed and clipped vertices with related color, depth, and sometimes texture-coordinate values and guidelines for the rasterization step.

## Pixel Operations

While geometric data takes one path through the OpenGL rendering pipeline, pixel data takes a different route. Pixels from an array in system memory are first unpacked from one of a variety of formats into the proper number of components. Next the data is scaled, biased, and processed by a pixel map. The results are clamped and then either written into texture memory or sent to the rasterization step. (See "Imaging Pipeline" in Chapter 8.)

If pixel data is read from the framebuffer, pixel-transfer operations (scale, bias, mapping, and clamping) are performed. Then these results are packed into an appropriate format and returned to an array in system memory.

There are special pixel copy operations for copying data in the framebuffer to other parts of the framebuffer or to the texture memory. A single pass is made through the pixel-transfer operations before the data is written to the texture memory or back to the framebuffer.

## Texture Assembly

OpenGL applications can apply texture images onto geometric objects to make them look more realistic. If several texture images are used, it's wise to put them into texture objects so that you can easily switch among them.

Some OpenGL implementations may have special resources for accelerating texture performance. There may be specialized, high-performance texture memory. If this memory is available, the texture objects may be prioritized to control the use of this limited and valuable resource. (See Chapter 9.)

## Rasterization

Rasterization is the conversion of both geometric and pixel data into *fragments*. Each fragment square corresponds to a pixel in the framebuffer. Line and polygon stipples, line width, point size, shading model, and coverage calculations to support antialiasing are taken into consideration as vertices are connected into lines or the interior pixels are calculated for a filled polygon. Color and depth values are assigned for each fragment square.

## Fragment Operations

Before values are actually stored in the framebuffer, a series of operations are performed that may alter or even throw out fragments. All these operations can be enabled or disabled.

The first operation that may be encountered is texturing, where a *texel* (texture element) is generated from texture memory for each fragment and applied to the fragment. Then fog calculations may be applied, followed by the scissor test, the alpha test, the stencil test, and the depth-buffer test (the depth buffer is for hidden-surface removal). Failing an enabled test may end the continued processing of a fragment's square. Then, blending, dithering, logical operation, and masking by a bitmask may be performed. (See Chapter 6 and Chapter 10.) Finally, the thoroughly processed fragment is drawn into the appropriate buffer, where it has finally become a pixel and achieved its final resting place.

## OpenGL-Related Libraries

OpenGL provides a powerful but primitive set of rendering commands, and all higher-level drawing must be done in terms of these commands. Also, OpenGL programs have to use the underlying mechanisms of the windowing system. Several libraries enable you to simplify your programming tasks, including the following:

- The OpenGL Utility Library (GLU) contains several routines that use lower-level OpenGL commands to perform such tasks as setting up matrices for specific viewing orientations and projections, performing polygon tessellation, and rendering surfaces. This library is provided as part of every OpenGL implementation. Portions of the GLU are described in the *OpenGL Reference Manual*. The more useful GLU routines are described in this guide, where they're relevant to the topic being discussed, such as in all of Chapter 11 and in the section "The GLU NURBS Interface" in Chapter 12. GLU routines use the prefix **glu**.

- For every window system, there is a library that extends the functionality of that window system to support OpenGL rendering. For machines that use the X Window System, the OpenGL Extension to the X Window System (GLX) is provided as an adjunct to OpenGL. GLX routines use the prefix **glX**. For Microsoft Windows, the WGL routines provide the Windows to OpenGL interface. All WGL routines use the prefix **wgl**. For IBM OS/2, the PGL is the Presentation Manager to OpenGL interface, and its routines use the prefix **pgl**. For Apple, the AGL is the interface for systems that support OpenGL, and AGL routines use the prefix **agl**.

  All these window system extension libraries are described in more detail in Appendix C. In addition, the GLX routines are also described in the *OpenGL Reference Manual*.

- The OpenGL Utility Toolkit (GLUT) is a window-system-independent toolkit, written by Mark Kilgard, to hide the complexities of differing window system APIs. GLUT is the subject of the next section, and it's described in more detail in Mark Kilgard's book *OpenGL Programming for the X Window System* (Addison-Wesley, 1996). GLUT routines use the prefix **glut.** To obtain the source code to GLUT, see "How to Obtain the Sample Code" on page xxxix of this book.

## Include Files

For all OpenGL applications, you want to include the gl.h header file in every file. Almost all OpenGL applications use GLU, the aforementioned OpenGL Utility Library, which requires inclusion of the glu.h header file. So almost every OpenGL source file begins with

```
#include <GL/gl.h>
#include <GL/glu.h>
```

**Note:** Microsoft Windows requires that windows.h be included before either gl.h or glu.h, because some macros used internally in the Microsoft Windows version of gl.h and glu.h are defined in windows.h.

The OpenGL library changes all the time. The various vendors that make graphics hardware add new features that may be too new to have been incorporated in gl.h. In order for you to take advantage of these new *extensions* to OpenGL, an additional header file is available, named glext.h. This header contains all of the latest extensions and can usually be found at the Web site of the company that manufactured your graphics hardware, or at the OpenGL Web Site (http://www.opengl.org/). As with any header, you could include it with the following statement:

```
#include "glext.h"
```

You probably noticed the quotes around the filename, as compared to the normal angle brackets. Because glext.h is how graphics card vendors enable access to new extensions, you will probably need to download versions frequently from the Internet, so having a local copy to compile your program is not a bad idea. Additionally, you may not have permission to place the glext.h header file in a system header-file include directory (such as /usr/include on Unix-type systems).

If you are directly accessing a window interface library to support OpenGL, such as GLX, AGL, PGL, or WGL, you must include additional header files.

For example, if you are calling GLX, you may need to add these lines to your code:

```
#include <X11/Xlib.h>
#include <GL/glx.h>
```

In Microsoft Windows, the WGL routines are made accessible with

```
#include <windows.h>
```

If you are using GLUT for managing your window manager tasks, you should include

```
#include <GL/glut.h>
```

**Note:** glut.h guarantees that gl.h and glu.h are properly included for you, so including all three files is redundant. Additionally, glut.h makes sure that any internal operating system dependent macros are properly defined before including gl.h and glu.h. To make your GLUT programs portable, include glut.h and do not explicitly include either gl.h or glu.h.

Most OpenGL applications also use standard C library system calls, so it is common to include header files that are not related to graphics, such as

```
#include <stdlib.h>
#include <stdio.h>
```

We don't include the header file declarations for our examples in this text, so our examples are less cluttered.

## GLUT, the OpenGL Utility Toolkit

As you know, OpenGL contains rendering commands but is designed to be independent of any window system or operating system. Consequently, it contains no commands for opening windows or reading events from the keyboard or mouse. Unfortunately, it's impossible to write a complete graphics program without at least opening a window, and most interesting programs require a bit of user input or other services from the operating system or window system. In many cases, complete programs make the most interesting examples, so this book uses GLUT to simplify opening windows, detecting input, and so on. If you have implementations of OpenGL and GLUT on your system, the examples in this book should run without change when linked with your OpenGL and GLUT libraries.

In addition, since OpenGL drawing commands are limited to those that generate simple geometric primitives (points, lines, and polygons), GLUT includes several routines that create more complicated three-dimensional objects, such as a sphere, a torus, and a teapot. This way, snapshots of program output can be interesting to look at. (Note that the OpenGL Utility Library, GLU, also has quadrics routines that create some of the same three-dimensional objects as GLUT, such as a sphere, cylinder, or cone.)

GLUT may not be satisfactory for full-featured OpenGL applications, but you may find it a useful starting point for learning OpenGL. The rest of this section briefly describes a small subset of GLUT routines so that you can follow the programming examples in the rest of this book. (See Appendix D for more details about this subset of GLUT, or see Chapters 4 and 5 of Kilgard's *OpenGL Programming for the X Window System* for information about the rest of GLUT.)

### Window Management

Five routines perform tasks necessary for initializing a window:

- **glutInit**(int *argc*, char **argv*) initializes GLUT and processes any command line arguments (for X, this would be options such as -display and -geometry). **glutInit**() should be called before any other GLUT routine.

- **glutInitDisplayMode**(unsigned int *mode*) specifies whether to use an *RGBA* or color-index color model. You can also specify whether you want a single- or double-buffered window. (If you're working in color-index mode, you'll want to load certain colors into the color map; use **glutSetColor**() to do this.) Finally, you can use this routine to indicate that you want the window to have an associated depth, stencil, multisampling, and/or accumulation buffer. For example, if you want a window with double buffering, the RGBA color model, and a depth buffer, you might call **glutInitDisplayMode(GLUT_DOUBLE | GLUT_RGBA | GLUT_DEPTH).**

- **glutInitWindowPosition**(int *x*, int *y*) specifies the screen location for the upper-left corner of your window.

- **glutInitWindowSize**(int *width*, int *size*) specifies the size, in pixels, of your window.

- int **glutCreateWindow**(char *string*) creates a window with an OpenGL context. It returns a unique identifier for the new window. Be warned: until **glutMainLoop**() is called, the window is not yet displayed.

### The Display Callback

**glutDisplayFunc**(void (*func*)(void)) is the first and most important event callback function you will see. Whenever GLUT determines that the contents of the window need to be redisplayed, the callback function registered by **glutDisplayFunc()** is executed. Therefore, you should put all the routines you need to redraw the scene in the display callback function.

If your program changes the contents of the window, sometimes you will have to call **glutPostRedisplay()**, which gives **glutMainLoop()** a nudge to call the registered display callback at its next opportunity.

### Running the Program

The very last thing you must do is call **glutMainLoop()**. All windows that have been created are now shown, and rendering to those windows is now effective. Event processing begins, and the registered display callback is triggered. Once this loop is entered, it is never exited!

Example 1-2 shows how you might use GLUT to create the simple program shown in Example 1-1. Note the restructuring of the code. To maximize efficiency, operations that need to be called only once (setting the background color and coordinate system) are now in a procedure called **init()**. Operations to render (and possibly re-render) the scene are in the **display()** procedure, which is the registered GLUT display callback.

**Example 1-2**     Simple OpenGL Program Using GLUT: hello.c

```
void display(void)
{
/*  clear all pixels  */
    glClear(GL_COLOR_BUFFER_BIT);

/*  draw white polygon (rectangle) with corners at
 *  (0.25, 0.25, 0.0) and (0.75, 0.75, 0.0)
 */
    glColor3f(1.0, 1.0, 1.0);
    glBegin(GL_POLYGON);
        glVertex3f(0.25, 0.25, 0.0);
        glVertex3f(0.75, 0.25, 0.0);
        glVertex3f(0.75, 0.75, 0.0);
        glVertex3f(0.25, 0.75, 0.0);
    glEnd();

/*  don't wait!
 *  start processing buffered OpenGL routines
 */
    glFlush();
}
```

```
void init(void)
{
/*   select clearing (background) color         */
     glClearColor(0.0, 0.0, 0.0, 0.0);

/*   initialize viewing values  */
     glMatrixMode(GL_PROJECTION);
     glLoadIdentity();
     glOrtho(0.0, 1.0, 0.0, 1.0, -1.0, 1.0);
}

/*
 *   Declare initial window size, position, and display mode
 *   (single buffer and RGBA).  Open window with "hello"
 *   in its title bar.  Call initialization routines.
 *   Register callback function to display graphics.
 *   Enter main loop and process events.
 */
int main(int argc, char** argv)
{
     glutInit(&argc, argv);
     glutInitDisplayMode(GLUT_SINGLE | GLUT_RGB);
     glutInitWindowSize(250, 250);
     glutInitWindowPosition(100, 100);
     glutCreateWindow("hello");
     init();
     glutDisplayFunc(display);
     glutMainLoop();
     return 0;    /* ISO C requires main to return int. */
}
```

## Handling Input Events

You can use the following routines to register callback commands that are invoked when specified events occur:

- **glutReshapeFunc**(void (*_func_)(int _w_, int _h_)) indicates what action should be taken when the window is resized.

- **glutKeyboardFunc**(void (*_func_)(unsigned char _key_, int _x_, int _y_)) and **glutMouseFunc**(void (*_func_)(int _button_, int _state_, int _x_, int _y_)) allow you to link a keyboard key or a mouse button with a routine that's invoked when the key or mouse button is pressed or released.

- **glutMotionFunc**(void (*_func_)(int _x_, int _y_)) registers a routine to call back when the mouse is moved while a mouse button is also pressed.

### Managing a Background Process

You can specify a function that's to be executed if no other events are pending—for example, when the event loop would otherwise be idle—with **glutIdleFunc**(void (*func)(void)). This routine takes a pointer to the function as its only argument. Pass in NULL (zero) to disable the execution of the function.

### Drawing Three-Dimensional Objects

GLUT includes several routines for drawing these three-dimensional objects:

| | | |
|---|---|---|
| cone | icosahedron | teapot |
| cube | octahedron | tetrahedron |
| dodecahedron | sphere | torus |

You can draw these objects as wireframes or as solid shaded objects with surface normals defined. For example, the routines for a cube and a sphere are as follows:

void **glutWireCube**(GLdouble *size*);

void **glutSolidCube**(GLdouble *size*);

void **glutWireSphere**(GLdouble *radius*, GLint *slices*, GLint *stacks*);

void **glutSolidSphere**(GLdouble *radius*, GLint *slices,* GLint *stacks*);

All these models are drawn centered at the origin of the world coordinate system. (See Appendix D for information on the prototypes of all these drawing routines.)

## Animation

One of the most exciting things you can do on a graphics computer is draw pictures that move. Whether you're an engineer trying to see all sides of a mechanical part you're designing, a pilot learning to fly an airplane using a simulation, or merely a computer-game aficionado, it's clear that *animation* is an important part of computer graphics.

In a movie theater, motion is achieved by taking a sequence of pictures and projecting them at 24 frames per second on the screen. Each frame is moved into position behind the lens, the shutter is opened, and the frame is displayed. The shutter is momentarily closed while the film is advanced to the next frame, then that frame is displayed, and so on. Although you're watching 24 different frames each second, your brain blends them all into a smooth animation. (The old Charlie Chaplin movies were shot at 16 frames per second and are noticeably jerky.) Computer-graphics screens typically refresh (redraw the picture) approximately 60 to 76 times per second, and some even run at about 120 refreshes per second. Clearly, 60 per second is smoother than 30, and 120 is perceptively better than 60. Refresh rates faster than 120, however, may approach a point of diminishing returns, depending on the limits of perception.

The key reason that motion picture projection works is that each frame is complete when it is displayed. Suppose you try to do computer animation of your million-frame movie with a program such as this:

```
open_window();
for (i = 0; i < 1000000; i++) {
    clear_the_window();
    draw_frame(i);
    wait_until_a_24th_of_a_second_is_over();
}
```

If you add the time it takes for your system to clear the screen and to draw a typical frame, this program gives increasingly poor results, depending on how close to 1/24 second it takes to clear and draw. Suppose the drawing takes nearly a full 1/24 second. Items drawn first are visible for the full 1/24 second and present a solid image on the screen; items drawn toward the end are instantly cleared as the program starts on the next frame. This presents at best a ghostlike image, as for most of the 1/24 second your eye is viewing the cleared background instead of the items that were unlucky enough to be drawn last. The problem is that this program doesn't display completely drawn frames; instead, you watch the drawing as it happens.

Most OpenGL implementations provide *double-buffering*—hardware or software that supplies two complete color buffers. One is displayed while the other is being drawn. When the drawing of a frame is complete, the two buffers are swapped, so the one that was being viewed is now used for drawing, and vice versa. This is like a movie projector with only two frames in a loop; while one is being projected on the screen, an artist is desperately erasing and redrawing the frame that's not visible. As long as the artist is quick enough, the viewer notices no difference between this setup and one in which all the frames are already drawn and the projector is simply displaying them one after the other. With double-buffering, every frame is shown only when the drawing is complete; the viewer never sees a partially drawn frame.

A modified version that displays smoothly animated graphics using double-buffering might look like the following:

```
open_window_in_double_buffer_mode();
for (i = 0; i < 1000000; i++) {
    clear_the_window();
    draw_frame(i);
    swap_the_buffers();
}
```

## The Refresh That Pauses

For some OpenGL implementations, in addition to simply swapping the viewable and drawable buffers, the **swap_the_buffers()** routine waits until the current screen refresh period is over so that the previous buffer is completely displayed. This routine also allows the new buffer to be completely displayed, starting from the beginning. Assuming that your system refreshes the display 60 times per second, this means that the fastest frame rate you can achieve is 60 frames per second (*fps*), and if all your frames can be cleared and drawn in under 1/60 second, your animation will run smoothly at that rate.

What often happens on such a system is that the frame is too complicated to draw in 1/60 second, so each frame is displayed more than once. If, for example, it takes 1/45 second to draw a frame, you get 30 fps, and the graphics are idle for 1/30 − 1/45 = 1/90 second per frame, or one-third of the time.

In addition, the video refresh rate is constant, which can have some unexpected performance consequences. For example, with the 1/60 second per refresh monitor and a constant frame rate, you can run at 60 fps, 30 fps, 20 fps, 15 fps, 12 fps, and so on (60/1, 60/2, 60/3, 60/4, 60/5,...). This means that if you're writing an application and gradually adding features (say it's a flight simulator, and you're adding ground scenery), at first each feature you add has no effect on the overall performance—you still get 60 fps. Then, all of a sudden, you add one new feature, and the system can't quite draw the whole thing in 1/60 of a second, so the animation slows from 60 fps to 30 fps because it misses the first possible buffer-swapping time. A similar thing happens when the drawing time per frame is more than 1/30 second—the animation drops from 30 to 20 fps.

If the scene's complexity is close to any of the magic times (1/60 second, 2/60 second, 3/60 second, and so on in this example), then, because of random variation, some frames go slightly over the time and some slightly under. Then the frame rate is irregular, which can be visually disturbing. In this case, if you can't simplify the scene so that all the frames are fast enough, it might be better to add an intentional, tiny delay to make sure they all miss, giving a constant, slower frame rate. If your frames have drastically different complexities, a more sophisticated approach might be necessary.

## Motion = Redraw + Swap

The structure of real animation programs does not differ very much from this description. Usually, it is easier to redraw the entire buffer from scratch for each frame than to figure out which parts require redrawing. This is especially true with applications such as three-dimensional flight simulators, where a tiny change in the plane's orientation changes the position of everything outside the window.

In most animations, the objects in a scene are simply redrawn with different transformations—the *viewpoint* of the viewer moves, or a car moves down the road a bit, or an object is rotated slightly. If significant recomputation is required for nondrawing operations, the attainable frame rate often slows down. Keep in mind, however, that the idle time after the **swap_the_buffers()** routine can often be used for such calculations.

OpenGL doesn't have a **swap_the_buffers()** command because the feature might not be available on all hardware and, in any case, it's highly dependent on the window system. For example, if you are using the X Window System and accessing it directly, you might use the following GLX routine:

```
void glXSwapBuffers(Display *dpy, Window window);
```

(See Appendix C for equivalent routines for other window systems.)

If you are using the GLUT library, you'll want to call this routine:

```
void glutSwapBuffers(void);
```

Example 1-3 illustrates the use of **glutSwapBuffers()** in drawing a spinning square, as shown in Figure 1-3. This example also shows how to use GLUT to control an input device and turn on and off an idle function. In this example, the mouse buttons toggle the spinning on and off.

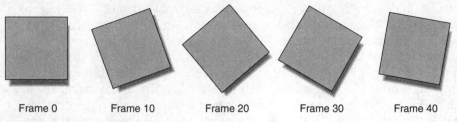

| Frame 0 | Frame 10 | Frame 20 | Frame 30 | Frame 40 |

**Figure 1-3**     Double-Buffered Rotating Square

**Example 1-3**     Double-Buffered Program: double.c

```
static GLfloat spin = 0.0;

void init(void)
{
   glClearColor(0.0, 0.0, 0.0, 0.0);
   glShadeModel(GL_FLAT);
}

void display(void)
{
   glClear(GL_COLOR_BUFFER_BIT);
   glPushMatrix();
   glRotatef(spin, 0.0, 0.0, 1.0);
   glColor3f(1.0, 1.0, 1.0);
   glRectf(-25.0, -25.0, 25.0, 25.0);
   glPopMatrix();
   glutSwapBuffers();
}

void spinDisplay(void)
{
   spin = spin + 2.0;
   if (spin > 360.0)
      spin = spin - 360.0;
   glutPostRedisplay();
}

void reshape(int w, int h)
{
   glViewport(0, 0, (GLsizei) w, (GLsizei) h);
   glMatrixMode(GL_PROJECTION);
```

```
        glLoadIdentity();
        glOrtho(-50.0, 50.0, -50.0, 50.0, -1.0, 1.0);
        glMatrixMode(GL_MODELVIEW);
        glLoadIdentity();
}

void mouse(int button, int state, int x, int y)
{
    switch (button) {
        case GLUT_LEFT_BUTTON:
            if (state == GLUT_DOWN)
                glutIdleFunc(spinDisplay);
            break;

        case GLUT_MIDDLE_BUTTON:
            if (state == GLUT_DOWN)
                glutIdleFunc(NULL);
            break;
        default:
            break;
    }
}

/*
 *  Request double buffer display mode.
 *  Register mouse input callback functions
 */
int main(int argc, char** argv)
{
    glutInit(&argc, argv);
    glutInitDisplayMode(GLUT_DOUBLE | GLUT_RGB);
    glutInitWindowSize(250, 250);
    glutInitWindowPosition(100, 100);
    glutCreateWindow(argv[0]);
    init();
    glutDisplayFunc(display);
    glutReshapeFunc(reshape);
    glutMouseFunc(mouse);
    glutMainLoop();
    return 0;
}
```

## Chapter 2

# State Management and Drawing Geometric Objects

**Chapter Objectives**

After reading this chapter, you'll be able to do the following:

- Clear the window to an arbitrary color

- Force any pending drawing to complete

- Draw with any geometric primitive—point, line, or polygon—in two or three dimensions

- Turn states on and off and query state variables

- Control the display of geometric primitives—for example, draw dashed lines or outlined polygons

- Specify *normal vectors* at appropriate points on the surfaces of solid objects

- Use *vertex arrays* and *buffer objects* to store and access geometric data with fewer function calls

- Save and restore several state variables at once

Although you can draw complex and interesting pictures using OpenGL, they're all constructed from a small number of primitive graphical items. This shouldn't be too surprising—look at what Leonardo da Vinci accomplished with just pencils and paintbrushes.

At the highest level of abstraction, there are three basic drawing operations: clearing the window, drawing a geometric object, and drawing a raster object. Raster objects, which include such things as two-dimensional images, bitmaps, and character fonts, are covered in Chapter 8. In this chapter, you learn how to clear the screen and draw geometric objects, including points, straight lines, and flat polygons.

You might think to yourself, "Wait a minute. I've seen lots of computer graphics in movies and on television, and there are plenty of beautifully shaded curved lines and surfaces. How are those drawn if OpenGL can draw only straight lines and flat polygons?" Even the image on the cover of this book includes a round table and objects on the table that have curved surfaces. It turns out that all the curved lines and surfaces you've seen are approximated by large numbers of little flat polygons or straight lines, in much the same way that the globe on the cover is constructed from a large set of rectangular blocks. The globe doesn't appear to have a smooth surface because the blocks are relatively large compared with the globe. Later in this chapter, we show you how to construct curved lines and surfaces from lots of small geometric primitives.

This chapter has the following major sections:

- "A Drawing Survival Kit" explains how to clear the window and force drawing to be completed. It also gives you basic information about controlling the colors of geometric objects and describing a coordinate system.

- "Describing Points, Lines, and Polygons" shows you the set of primitive geometric objects and how to draw them.

- "Basic State Management" describes how to turn on and off some states (modes) and query state variables.

- "Displaying Points, Lines, and Polygons" explains what control you have over the details of how primitives are drawn—for example, what diameters points have, whether lines are solid or dashed, and whether polygons are outlined or filled.

- "Normal Vectors" discusses how to specify normal vectors for geometric objects and (briefly) what these vectors are for.

- "Vertex Arrays" shows you how to put large amounts of geometric data into just a few arrays and how, with only a few function calls, to render the geometry it describes. Reducing function calls may increase the efficiency and performance of rendering.

- "Buffer Objects" details how to use server-side memory buffers to store vertex array data for more efficient geometric rendering.

- "Attribute Groups" reveals how to query the current value of state variables and how to save and restore several related state values all at once.

- "Some Hints for Building Polygonal Models of Surfaces" explores the issues and techniques involved in constructing polygonal approximations to surfaces.

One thing to keep in mind as you read the rest of this chapter is that with OpenGL, unless you specify otherwise, every time you issue a drawing command, the specified object is drawn. This might seem obvious, but in some systems, you first make a list of things to draw. When your list is complete, you tell the graphics hardware to draw the items in the list. The first style is called *immediate-mode* graphics and is the default OpenGL style. In addition to using immediate mode, you can choose to save some commands in a list (called a *display list*) for later drawing. Immediate-mode graphics are typically easier to program, but display lists are often more efficient. Chapter 7 tells you how to use display lists and why you might want to use them.

Version 1.1 of OpenGL introduced vertex arrays.

In Version 1.2, scaling of surface normals (GL_RESCALE_NORMAL) was added to OpenGL. Also, **glDrawRangeElements**() supplemented vertex arrays.

Version 1.3 marked the initial support for texture coordinates for multiple texture units in the OpenGL core feature set. Previously, multitexturing had been an optional OpenGL extension.

In Version 1.4, fog coordinates and secondary colors may be stored in vertex arrays, and the commands **glMultiDrawArrays**() and **glMultiDrawElements**() may be used to render primitives from vertex arrays.

In Version 1.5, vertex arrays may be stored in buffer objects which may be able to use server memory for storing arrays and potentially accelerating their rendering.

## A Drawing Survival Kit

This section explains how to clear the window in preparation for drawing, set the colors of objects that are to be drawn, and force drawing to be completed. None of these subjects has anything to do with geometric objects in a direct way, but any program that draws geometric objects has to deal with these issues.

## Clearing the Window

Drawing on a computer screen is different from drawing on paper in that the paper starts out white, and all you have to do is draw the picture. On a computer, the memory holding the picture is usually filled with the last picture you drew, so you typically need to clear it to some background color before you start to draw the new scene. The color you use for the background depends on the application. For a word processor, you might clear to white (the color of the paper) before you begin to draw the text. If you're drawing a view from a spaceship, you clear to the black of space before beginning to draw the stars, planets, and alien spaceships. Sometimes you might not need to clear the screen at all; for example, if the image is the inside of a room, the entire graphics window is covered as you draw all the walls.

At this point, you might be wondering why we keep talking about *clearing* the window—why not just draw a rectangle of the appropriate color that's large enough to cover the entire window? First, a special command to clear a window can be much more efficient than a general-purpose drawing command. In addition, as you'll see in Chapter 3, OpenGL allows you to set the coordinate system, viewing position, and viewing direction arbitrarily, so it might be difficult to figure out an appropriate size and location for a window-clearing rectangle. Finally, on many machines, the graphics hardware consists of multiple buffers in addition to the buffer containing colors of the pixels that are displayed. These other buffers must be cleared from time to time, and it's convenient to have a single command that can clear any combination of them. (See Chapter 10 for a discussion of all the possible buffers.)

You must also know how the colors of pixels are stored in the graphics hardware known as *bitplanes*. There are two methods of storage. Either the red, green, blue, and alpha (RGBA) values of a pixel can be directly stored in the bitplanes, or a single index value that references a color lookup table is stored. RGBA color-display mode is more commonly used, so most of the examples in this book use it. (See Chapter 4 for more information about both display modes.) You can safely ignore all references to alpha values until Chapter 6.

As an example, these lines of code clear an RGBA mode window to black:

```
glClearColor(0.0, 0.0, 0.0, 0.0);
glClear(GL_COLOR_BUFFER_BIT);
```

The first line sets the clearing color to black, and the next command clears the entire window to the current clearing color. The single parameter to **glClear()** indicates which buffers are to be cleared. In this case, the program clears only the color buffer, where the image displayed on the screen is kept. Typically, you set the clearing color once, early in your application, and then you clear the buffers as often as necessary. OpenGL keeps track of the current clearing color as a state variable, rather than requiring you to specify it each time a buffer is cleared.

Chapter 4 and Chapter 10 discuss how other buffers are used. For now, all you need to know is that clearing them is simple. For example, to clear both the color buffer and the depth buffer, you would use the following sequence of commands:

```
glClearColor(0.0, 0.0, 0.0, 0.0);
glClearDepth(1.0);
glClear(GL_COLOR_BUFFER_BIT | GL_DEPTH_BUFFER_BIT);
```

In this case, the call to **glClearColor()** is the same as before, the **glClearDepth()** command specifies the value to which every pixel of the depth buffer is to be set, and the parameter to the **glClear()** command now consists of the bitwise logical OR of all the buffers to be cleared. The following summary of **glClear()** includes a table that lists the buffers that can be cleared, their names, and the chapter in which each type of buffer is discussed.

---

void **glClearColor**(GLclampf *red*, GLclampf *green*, GLclampf *blue*, GLclampf *alpha*);

Sets the current clearing color for use in clearing color buffers in RGBA mode. (See Chapter 4 for more information on RGBA mode.) The *red*, *green*, *blue*, and *alpha* values are clamped if necessary to the range [0, 1]. The default clearing color is (0, 0, 0, 0), which is black.

---

void **glClear**(GLbitfield *mask*);

Clears the specified buffers to their current clearing values. The *mask* argument is a bitwise logical OR combination of the values listed in Table 2-1.

| Buffer | Name | Reference |
|---|---|---|
| Color buffer | GL_COLOR_BUFFER_BIT | Chapter 4 |
| Depth buffer | GL_DEPTH_BUFFER_BIT | Chapter 10 |
| Accumulation buffer | GL_ACCUM_BUFFER_BIT | Chapter 10 |
| Stencil buffer | GL_STENCIL_BUFFER_BIT | Chapter 10 |

**Table 2-1**     Clearing Buffers

Before issuing a command to clear multiple buffers, you have to set the values to which each buffer is to be cleared if you want something other than the default RGBA color, depth value, accumulation color, and stencil index. In addition to the **glClearColor()** and **glClearDepth()** commands that set the current values for clearing the color and depth buffers, **glClearIndex()**, **glClearAccum()**, and **glClearStencil()** specify the *color index*, accumulation color, and stencil index used to clear the corresponding buffers. (See Chapter 4 and Chapter 10 for descriptions of these buffers and their uses.)

OpenGL allows you to specify multiple buffers because clearing is generally a slow operation, as every pixel in the window (possibly millions) is touched, and some graphics hardware allows sets of buffers to be cleared simultaneously. Hardware that doesn't support simultaneous clears performs them sequentially. The difference between

```
glClear(GL_COLOR_BUFFER_BIT | GL_DEPTH_BUFFER_BIT);
```

and

```
glClear(GL_COLOR_BUFFER_BIT);
glClear(GL_DEPTH_BUFFER_BIT);
```

is that although both have the same final effect, the first example might run faster on many machines. It certainly won't run more slowly.

## Specifying a Color

With OpenGL, the description of the shape of an object being drawn is independent of the description of its color. Whenever a particular geometric object is drawn, it's drawn using the currently specified coloring scheme. The coloring scheme might be as simple as "draw everything in fire-engine red" or as complicated as "assume the object is made out of blue plastic, that there's a yellow spotlight pointed in such and such a direction, and that there's a general low-level reddish-brown light everywhere else." In general, an OpenGL programmer first sets the color or coloring scheme and then draws the objects. Until the color or coloring scheme is changed, all objects are drawn in that color or using that coloring scheme. This method helps OpenGL achieve higher drawing performance than would result if it didn't keep track of the current color.

For example, the pseudocode

```
set_current_color(red);
draw_object(A);
draw_object(B);
set_current_color(green);
set_current_color(blue);
draw_object(C);
```

draws objects A and B in red, and object C in blue. The command on the fourth line that sets the current color to green is wasted.

Coloring, lighting, and shading are all large topics with entire chapters or large sections devoted to them. To draw geometric primitives that can be seen, however, you need some basic knowledge of how to set the current color; this information is provided in the next few paragraphs. (See Chapter 4 and Chapter 5 for details on these topics.)

To set a color, use the command **glColor3f()**. It takes three parameters, all of which are floating-point numbers between 0.0 and 1.0. The parameters are, in order, the red, green, and blue *components* of the color. You can think of these three values as specifying a "mix" of colors: 0.0 means don't use any of that component, and 1.0 means use all you can of that component. Thus, the code

```
glColor3f(1.0, 0.0, 0.0);
```

makes the brightest red the system can draw, with no green or blue components. All zeros makes black; in contrast, all ones makes white. Setting all three components to 0.5 yields gray (halfway between black and white). Here are eight commands and the colors they would set:

```
glColor3f(0.0, 0.0, 0.0);       /* black */
glColor3f(1.0, 0.0, 0.0);       /* red */
glColor3f(0.0, 1.0, 0.0);       /* green */
glColor3f(1.0, 1.0, 0.0);       /* yellow */
glColor3f(0.0, 0.0, 1.0);       /* blue */
glColor3f(1.0, 0.0, 1.0);       /* magenta */
glColor3f(0.0, 1.0, 1.0);       /* cyan */
glColor3f(1.0, 1.0, 1.0);       /* white */
```

You might have noticed earlier that the routine for setting the clearing color, **glClearColor()**, takes four parameters, the first three of which match the parameters for **glColor3f()**. The fourth parameter is the alpha value; it's covered in detail in "Blending" in Chapter 6. For now, set the fourth parameter of **glClearColor()** to 0.0, which is its default value.

## Forcing Completion of Drawing

As you saw in "OpenGL Rendering Pipeline" in Chapter 1, most modern graphics systems can be thought of as an assembly line. The main central processing unit (CPU) issues a drawing command. Perhaps other hardware does geometric transformations. Clipping is performed, followed by shading and/or texturing. Finally, the values are written into the bitplanes for display. In high-end architectures, each of these operations is performed by a different piece of hardware that's been designed to perform its particular task quickly. In such an architecture, there's no need for the CPU to wait for each drawing command to complete before issuing the next one. While the CPU is sending a vertex down the pipeline, the transformation hardware is working on transforming the last one sent, the one before that is being clipped, and so on. In such a system, if the CPU waited for each command to complete before issuing the next, there could be a huge performance penalty.

In addition, the application might be running on more than one machine. For example, suppose that the main program is running elsewhere (on a machine called the client) and that you're viewing the results of the drawing on your workstation or terminal (the server), which is connected by a network to the client. In that case, it might be horribly inefficient to send each command over the network one at a time, as considerable overhead is often associated with each network transmission. Usually, the client gathers a collection of commands into a single network packet before sending it. Unfortunately, the network code on the client typically has no way of knowing that the graphics program is finished drawing a frame or scene. In the worst case, it waits forever for enough additional drawing commands to fill a packet, and you never see the completed drawing.

For this reason, OpenGL provides the command **glFlush()**, which forces the client to send the network packet even though it might not be full. Where there is no network and all commands are truly executed immediately on the server, **glFlush()** might have no effect. However, if you're writing a program that you want to work properly both with and without a network, include a call to **glFlush()** at the end of each frame or scene. Note that

**glFlush()** doesn't wait for the drawing to complete—it just forces the drawing to begin execution, thereby guaranteeing that all previous commands *execute* in finite time even if no further rendering commands are executed.

There are other situations in which **glFlush()** is useful:

- Software renderers that build images in system memory and don't want to constantly update the screen

- Implementations that gather sets of rendering commands to amortize start-up costs. The aforementioned network transmission example is one instance of this.

---

void **glFlush**(void);

Forces previously issued OpenGL commands to begin execution, thus guaranteeing that they complete in finite time.

A few commands—for example, commands that swap buffers in double-buffer mode—automatically flush pending commands onto the network before they can occur.

If **glFlush()** isn't sufficient for you, try **glFinish()**. This command flushes the network as **glFlush()** does and then waits for notification from the graphics hardware or network indicating that the drawing is complete in the framebuffer. You might need to use **glFinish()** if you want to synchronize tasks—for example, to make sure that your three-dimensional rendering is on the screen before you use Display PostScript to draw labels on top of the rendering. Another example would be to ensure that the drawing is complete before it begins to accept user input. After you issue a **glFinish()** command, your graphics process is blocked until it receives notification from the graphics hardware that the drawing is complete. Keep in mind that excessive use of **glFinish()** can reduce the performance of your application, especially if you're running over a network, because it requires round-trip communication. If **glFlush()** is sufficient for your needs, use it instead of **glFinish()**.

---

void **glFinish**(void);

Forces all previously issued OpenGL commands to complete. This command doesn't return until all effects from previous commands are fully realized.

## Coordinate System Survival Kit

Whenever you initially open a window or later move or resize that window, the window system will send an event to notify you. If you are using GLUT, the notification is automated; whatever routine has been registered to **glutReshapeFunc()** will be called. You must register a callback function that will

- Reestablish the rectangular region that will be the new rendering canvas

- Define the coordinate system to which objects will be drawn

In Chapter 3, you'll see how to define three-dimensional coordinate systems, but right now just create a simple, basic two-dimensional coordinate system into which you can draw a few objects. Call **glutReshapeFunc(reshape)**, where **reshape()** is the following function shown in Example 2-1.

**Example 2-1**    Reshape Callback Function

```
void reshape(int w, int h)
{
   glViewport(0, 0, (GLsizei) w, (GLsizei) h);
   glMatrixMode(GL_PROJECTION);
   glLoadIdentity();
   gluOrtho2D(0.0, (GLdouble) w, 0.0, (GLdouble) h);
}
```

The kernel of GLUT will pass this function two arguments: the width and height, in pixels, of the new, moved, or resized window. **glViewport()** adjusts the pixel rectangle for drawing to be the entire new window. The next three routines adjust the coordinate system for drawing so that the lower left corner is $(0, 0)$ and the upper right corner is $(w, h)$ (see Figure 2-1).

To explain it another way, think about a piece of graphing paper. The $w$ and $h$ values in **reshape()** represent how many columns and rows of squares are on your graph paper. Then you have to put axes on the graph paper. The **gluOrtho2D()** routine puts the origin, $(0, 0)$, in the lowest, leftmost square, and makes each square represent one unit. Now, when you render the points, lines, and polygons in the rest of this chapter, they will appear on this paper in easily predictable squares. (For now, keep all your objects two-dimensional.)

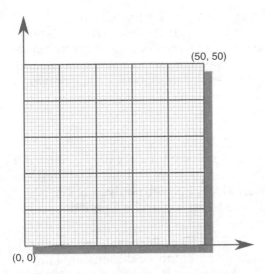

(50, 50)

(0, 0)

**Figure 2-1**  Coordinate System Defined by $w = 50$, $h = 50$

## Describing Points, Lines, and Polygons

This section explains how to describe OpenGL geometric primitives. All geometric primitives are eventually described in terms of their *vertices*—coordinates that define the points themselves, the endpoints of line segments, or the corners of polygons. The next section discusses how these primitives are displayed and what control you have over their display.

### What Are Points, Lines, and Polygons?

You probably have a fairly good idea of what a mathematician means by the terms *point*, *line*, and *polygon*. The OpenGL meanings are similar, but not quite the same.

One difference comes from the limitations of computer-based calculations. In any OpenGL implementation, floating-point calculations are of finite precision, and they have round-off errors. Consequently, the coordinates of OpenGL points, lines, and polygons suffer from the same problems.

A more important difference arises from the limitations of a raster graphics display. On such a display, the smallest displayable unit is a pixel, and although pixels might be less than 1/100 of an inch wide, they are still much larger than the mathematician's concepts of infinitely small (for points) and infinitely thin (for lines). When OpenGL performs calculations, it assumes that points are represented as vectors of floating-point numbers. However, a point is typically (but not always) drawn as a single pixel, and many different points with slightly different coordinates could be drawn by OpenGL on the same pixel.

## Points

A point is represented by a set of floating-point numbers called a *vertex*. All internal calculations are done as if vertices are three-dimensional. Vertices specified by the user as two-dimensional (that is, with only *x*- and *y*-coordinates) are assigned a *z*-coordinate equal to zero by OpenGL.

### Advanced

Advanced

OpenGL works in the *homogeneous coordinates* of three-dimensional projective geometry, so for internal calculations, all vertices are represented with four floating-point coordinates (*x*, *y*, *z*, *w*). If *w* is different from zero, these coordinates correspond to the Euclidean, three-dimensional point (*x/w*, *y/w*, *z/w*). You can specify the *w*-coordinate in OpenGL commands, but this is rarely done. If the *w*-coordinate isn't specified, it is understood to be 1.0. (See Appendix F for more information about homogeneous coordinate systems.)

## Lines

In OpenGL, the term *line* refers to a *line segment*, not the mathematician's version that extends to infinity in both directions. There are easy ways to specify a connected series of line segments, or even a closed, connected series of segments (see Figure 2-2). In all cases, though, the lines constituting the connected series are specified in terms of the vertices at their endpoints.

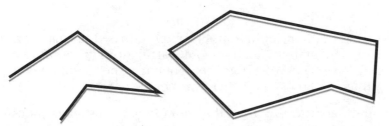

**Figure 2-2**     Two Connected Series of Line Segments

## Polygons

Polygons are the areas enclosed by single closed loops of line segments, where the line segments are specified by the vertices at their endpoints. Polygons are typically drawn with the pixels in the interior filled in, but you can also draw them as outlines or a set of points. (See "Polygon Details" on page 55.)

In general, polygons can be complicated, so OpenGL imposes some strong restrictions on what constitutes a primitive polygon. First, the edges of OpenGL polygons can't intersect (a mathematician would call a polygon satisfying this condition a *simple polygon*). Second, OpenGL polygons must be *convex*, meaning that they cannot have indentations. Stated precisely, a region is convex if, given any two points in the interior, the line segment joining them is also in the interior. See Figure 2-3 for some examples of valid and invalid polygons. OpenGL, however, doesn't restrict the number of line segments making up the boundary of a convex polygon. Note that polygons with holes can't be described. They are *nonconvex*, and they can't be drawn with a boundary made up of a single closed loop. Be aware that if you present OpenGL with a nonconvex filled polygon, it might not draw it as you expect. For instance, on most systems, no more than the *convex hull* of the polygon would be filled. On some systems, less than the convex hull might be filled.

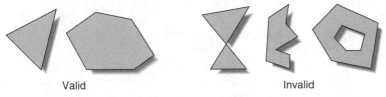

Valid                                                    Invalid

**Figure 2-3**     Valid and Invalid Polygons

The reason for the OpenGL restrictions on valid polygon types is that it's simpler to provide fast polygon-rendering hardware for that restricted class of polygons. Simple polygons can be rendered quickly. The difficult cases are hard to detect quickly, so for maximum performance, OpenGL crosses its fingers and assumes the polygons are simple.

Many real-world surfaces consist of nonsimple polygons, nonconvex polygons, or polygons with holes. Since all such polygons can be formed from unions of simple convex polygons, some routines to build more complex objects are provided in the GLU library. These routines take complex descriptions and tessellate them, or break them down into groups of the simpler OpenGL polygons that can then be rendered. (See "Polygon Tessellation" in Chapter 11 for more information about the *tessellation* routines.)

Since OpenGL vertices are always three-dimensional, the points forming the boundary of a particular polygon don't necessarily lie on the same plane in space. (Of course, they do in many cases—if all the *z*-coordinates are zero, for example, or if the polygon is a *triangle*.) If a polygon's vertices don't lie in the same plane, then after various rotations in space, changes in the viewpoint, and projection onto the display screen, the points might no longer form a simple convex polygon. For example, imagine a four-point *quadrilateral* where the points are slightly out of plane, and look at it almost edge-on. You can get a nonsimple polygon that resembles a bow tie, as shown in Figure 2-4, which isn't guaranteed to be rendered correctly. This situation isn't all that unusual if you approximate curved surfaces by quadrilaterals made of points lying on the true surface. You can always avoid the problem by using triangles, as any three points always lie on a plane.

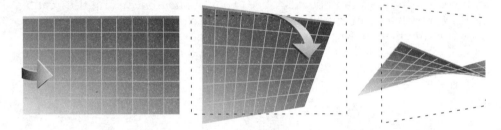

**Figure 2-4**    Nonplanar Polygon Transformed to Nonsimple Polygon

## Rectangles

Since rectangles are so common in graphics applications, OpenGL provides a filled-rectangle drawing primitive, **glRect*()**. You can draw a rectangle as a polygon, as described in "OpenGL Geometric Drawing Primitives" on page 42, but your particular implementation of OpenGL might have optimized **glRect*()** for rectangles.

---

void **glRect**{sifd}(*TYPE x1, TYPE y1, TYPE x2, TYPE y2*);
void **glRect**{sifd}**v**(const *TYPE *v1*, const *TYPE *v2*);

Draws the rectangle defined by the corner points (*x1, y1*) and (*x2, y2*). The rectangle lies in the plane *z* = 0 and has sides parallel to the *x*- and *y*-axes. If the vector form of the function is used, the corners are given by two pointers to arrays, each of which contains an (*x, y*) pair.

---

Note that although the rectangle begins with a particular orientation in three-dimensional space (in the *xy*-plane and parallel to the axes), you can change this by applying rotations or other transformations. (See Chapter 3 for information about how to do this.)

### Curves and Curved Surfaces

Any smoothly curved line or surface can be approximated—to any arbitrary degree of accuracy—by short line segments or small polygonal regions. Thus, subdividing curved lines and surfaces sufficiently and then approximating them with straight line segments or flat polygons makes them appear curved (see Figure 2-5). If you're skeptical that this really works, imagine subdividing until each line segment or polygon is so tiny that it's smaller than a pixel on the screen.

**Figure 2-5**    Approximating Curves

Even though curves aren't geometric primitives, OpenGL provides some direct support for subdividing and drawing them. (See Chapter 12 for information about how to draw curves and curved surfaces.)

## Specifying Vertices

With OpenGL, every geometric object is ultimately described as an ordered set of vertices. You use the **glVertex*()** command to specify a vertex.

---

void **glVertex**[234]{sifd}(*TYPE coords*);
void **glVertex**[234]{sifd}v(const *TYPE* *coords*);

---

Specifies a vertex for use in describing a geometric object. You can supply up to four coordinates (*x, y, z, w*) for a particular vertex or as few as two (*x, y*) by selecting the appropriate version of the command. If you use a version that doesn't explicitly specify *z* or *w*, *z* is understood to be 0 and *w* is understood to be 1. Calls to **glVertex*()** are effective only between a **glBegin()** and **glEnd()** pair.

Example 2-2 provides some examples of using **glVertex\*()**.

**Example 2-2**    Legal Uses of glVertex*()

```
glVertex2s(2, 3);
glVertex3d(0.0, 0.0, 3.1415926535898);
glVertex4f(2.3, 1.0, -2.2, 2.0);

GLdouble dvect[3] = {5.0, 9.0, 1992.0};
glVertex3dv(dvect);
```

The first example represents a vertex with three-dimensional coordinates (2, 3, 0). (Remember that if it isn't specified, the z-coordinate is understood to be 0.) The coordinates in the second example are (0.0, 0.0, 3.1415926535898) (double-precision floating-point numbers). The third example represents the vertex with three-dimensional coordinates (1.15, 0.5, −1.1) as a homogenous coordinate. (Remember that the x-, y-, and z-coordinates are eventually divided by the w-coordinate.) In the final example, *dvect* is a pointer to an array of three double-precision floating-point numbers.

On some machines, the vector form of **glVertex\*()** is more efficient, since only a single parameter needs to be passed to the graphics subsystem. Special hardware might be able to send a whole series of coordinates in a single batch. If your machine is like this, it's to your advantage to arrange your data so that the vertex coordinates are packed sequentially in memory. In this case, there may be some gain in performance by using the vertex array operations of OpenGL. (See "Vertex Arrays" on page 65.)

## OpenGL Geometric Drawing Primitives

Now that you've seen how to specify vertices, you still need to know how to tell OpenGL to create a set of points, a line, or a polygon from those vertices. To do this, you bracket each set of vertices between a call to **glBegin()** and a call to **glEnd()**. The argument passed to **glBegin()** determines what sort of geometric primitive is constructed from the vertices. For instance, Example 2-3 specifies the vertices for the polygon shown in Figure 2-6.

**Example 2-3**    Filled Polygon

```
glBegin(GL_POLYGON);
    glVertex2f(0.0, 0.0);
    glVertex2f(0.0, 3.0);
    glVertex2f(4.0, 3.0);
    glVertex2f(6.0, 1.5);
    glVertex2f(4.0, 0.0);
glEnd();
```

GL_POLYGON                    GL_POINTS

**Figure 2-6**      Drawing a Polygon or a Set of Points

If you had used GL_POINTS instead of GL_POLYGON, the primitive would have been simply the five points shown in Figure 2-6. Table 2-2 in the following function summary for **glBegin**() lists the ten possible arguments and the corresponding types of primitives.

---

void **glBegin**(GLenum *mode*);

Marks the beginning of a vertex-data list that describes a geometric primitive. The type of primitive is indicated by *mode*, which can be any of the values shown in Table 2-2.

---

| Value | Meaning |
| --- | --- |
| GL_POINTS | Individual points |
| GL_LINES | Pairs of vertices interpreted as individual line segments |
| GL_LINE_STRIP | Series of connected line segments |
| GL_LINE_LOOP | Same as above, with a segment added between last and first vertices |
| GL_TRIANGLES | Triples of vertices interpreted as triangles |
| GL_TRIANGLE_STRIP | Linked strip of triangles |
| GL_TRIANGLE_FAN | Linked fan of triangles |
| GL_QUADS | Quadruples of vertices interpreted as four-sided polygons |
| GL_QUAD_STRIP | Linked strip of quadrilaterals |
| GL_POLYGON | Boundary of a simple, convex polygon |

**Table 2-2**      Geometric Primitive Names and Meanings

---

void **glEnd**(void);

Marks the end of a vertex-data list.

Figure 2-7 shows examples of all the geometric primitives listed in Table 2-2, with descriptions of the pixels that are drawn for each of the objects. Note that in addition to points, several types of lines and polygons are defined. Obviously, you can find many ways to draw the same primitive. The method you choose depends on your vertex data.

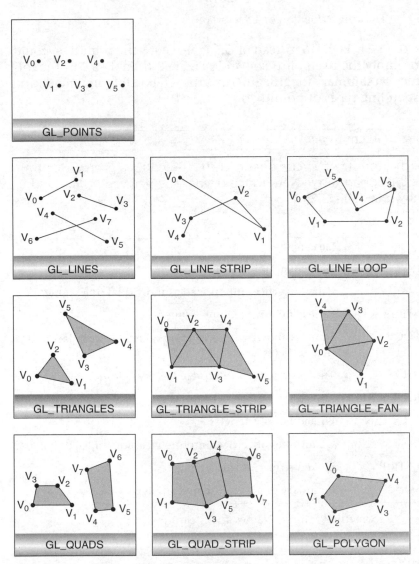

**Figure 2-7**    Geometric Primitive Types

As you read the following descriptions, assume that $n$ vertices ($v_0$, $v_1$, $v_2$, ... , $v_{n-1}$) are described between a **glBegin**() and **glEnd**() pair.

| | |
|---|---|
| GL_POINTS | Draws a point at each of the $n$ vertices. |
| GL_LINES | Draws a series of unconnected line segments. Segments are drawn between $v_0$ and $v_1$, between $v_2$ and $v_3$, and so on. If $n$ is odd, the last segment is drawn between $v_{n-3}$ and $v_{n-2}$, and $v_{n-1}$ is ignored. |
| GL_LINE_STRIP | Draws a line segment from $v_0$ to $v_1$, then from $v_1$ to $v_2$, and so on, finally drawing the segment from $v_{n-2}$ to $v_{n-1}$. Thus, a total of $n-1$ line segments are drawn. Nothing is drawn unless $n$ is larger than 1. There are no restrictions on the vertices describing a line strip (or a line loop); the lines can intersect arbitrarily. |
| GL_LINE_LOOP | Same as GL_LINE_STRIP, except that a final line segment is drawn from $v_{n-1}$ to $v_0$, completing a loop. |
| GL_TRIANGLES | Draws a series of triangles (three-sided polygons) using vertices $v_0$, $v_1$, $v_2$, then $v_3$, $v_4$, $v_5$, and so on. If $n$ isn't a multiple of 3, the final one or two vertices are ignored. |
| GL_TRIANGLE_STRIP | Draws a series of triangles (three-sided polygons) using vertices $v_0$, $v_1$, $v_2$, then $v_2$, $v_1$, $v_3$ (note the order), then $v_2$, $v_3$, $v_4$, and so on. The ordering is to ensure that the triangles are all drawn with the same orientation so that the strip can correctly form part of a surface. Preserving the orientation is important for some operations, such as culling (see "Reversing and Culling Polygon Faces" on page 56). $n$ must be at least 3 for anything to be drawn. |
| GL_TRIANGLE_FAN | Same as GL_TRIANGLE_STRIP, except that the vertices are $v_0$, $v_1$, $v_2$, then $v_0$, $v_2$, $v_3$, then $v_0$, $v_3$, $v_4$, and so on (see Figure 2-7). |

| | |
|---|---|
| GL_QUADS | Draws a series of quadrilaterals (four-sided polygons) using vertices $v_0$, $v_1$, $v_2$, $v_3$, then $v_4$, $v_5$, $v_6$, $v_7$, and so on. If $n$ isn't a multiple of 4, the final one, two, or three vertices are ignored. |
| GL_QUAD_STRIP | Draws a series of quadrilaterals (four-sided polygons) beginning with $v_0$, $v_1$, $v_3$, $v_2$, then $v_2$, $v_3$, $v_5$, $v_4$, then $v_4$, $v_5$, $v_7$, $v_6$, and so on (see Figure 2-7). $n$ must be at least 4 before anything is drawn. If $n$ is odd, the final vertex is ignored. |
| GL_POLYGON | Draws a polygon using the points $v_0$, ... , $v_{n-1}$ as vertices. $n$ must be at least 3, or nothing is drawn. In addition, the polygon specified must not intersect itself and must be convex. If the vertices don't satisfy these conditions, the results are unpredictable. |

**Restrictions on Using glBegin() and glEnd()**

The most important information about vertices is their coordinates, which are specified by the **glVertex*()** command. You can also supply additional vertex-specific data for each vertex—a color, a normal vector, texture coordinates, or any combination of these—using special commands. In addition, a few other commands are valid between a **glBegin()** and **glEnd()** pair. Table 2-3 contains a complete list of such valid commands.

| Command | Purpose of Command | Reference |
|---|---|---|
| glVertex*() | set vertex coordinates | Chapter 2 |
| glColor*() | set RGBA color | Chapter 4 |
| glIndex*() | set color index | Chapter 4 |
| glSecondaryColor*() | set secondary color for post-texturing application | Chapter 9 |
| glNormal*() | set normal vector coordinates | Chapter 2 |
| glMaterial*() | set material properties | Chapter 5 |
| glFogCoord*() | set fog coordinates | Chapter 6 |

**Table 2-3**    Valid Commands between glBegin() and glEnd()

| Command | Purpose of Command | Reference |
| --- | --- | --- |
| glTexCoord*() | set texture coordinates | Chapter 9 |
| glMultiTexCoord*() | set texture coordinates for multitexturing | Chapter 9 |
| glVertexAttrib*() | set generic vertex attribute | Chapter 15 |
| glEdgeFlag*() | control drawing of edges | Chapter 2 |
| glArrayElement() | extract vertex array data | Chapter 2 |
| glEvalCoord*(), glEvalPoint*() | generate coordinates | Chapter 12 |
| glCallList(), glCallLists() | execute display list(s) | Chapter 7 |

**Table 2-3  (continued)**     Valid Commands between glBegin() and glEnd()

No other OpenGL commands are valid between a **glBegin()** and **glEnd()** pair, and making most other OpenGL calls generates an error. Some vertex array commands, such as **glEnableClientState()** and **glVertexPointer()**, when called between **glBegin()** and **glEnd()**, have undefined behavior but do not necessarily generate an error. (Also, routines related to OpenGL, such as **glX*()** routines, have undefined behavior between **glBegin()** and **glEnd()**.) These cases should be avoided, and debugging them may be more difficult.

Note, however, that only OpenGL commands are restricted; you can certainly include other programming-language constructs (except for calls, such as the aforementioned **glX*()** routines). For instance, Example 2-4 draws an outlined circle.

**Example 2-4**     Other Constructs between glBegin() and glEnd()

```
#define PI 3.1415926535898
GLint circle_points = 100;
glBegin(GL_LINE_LOOP);
for (i = 0; i < circle_points; i++) {
   angle = 2*PI*i/circle_points;
   glVertex2f(cos(angle), sin(angle));
}
glEnd();
```

**Note:**  This example isn't the most efficient way to draw a circle, especially if you intend to do it repeatedly. The graphics commands used are typically very fast, but this code calculates an angle and calls the **sin()** and **cos()** routines for each vertex; in addition, there's the loop overhead. (Another way to calculate the vertices of a circle is to use a GLU routine; see "Quadrics: Rendering Spheres, Cylinders, and Disks" in Chapter 11.) If you need to draw numerous circles, calculate the coordinates of the vertices once and save them in an array and create a display list (see Chapter 7), or use vertex arrays to render them.

Unless they are being compiled into a display list, all **glVertex*()** commands should appear between a **glBegin()** and **glEnd()** combination. (If they appear elsewhere, they don't accomplish anything.) If they appear in a display list, they are executed only if they appear between a **glBegin()** and a **glEnd()**. (See Chapter 7 for more information about display lists.)

Although many commands are allowed between **glBegin()** and **glEnd()**, vertices are generated only when a **glVertex*()** command is issued. At the moment **glVertex*()** is called, OpenGL assigns the resulting vertex the current color, texture coordinates, normal vector information, and so on. To see this, look at the following code sequence. The first point is drawn in red, and the second and third ones in blue, despite the extra color commands:

```
glBegin(GL_POINTS);
    glColor3f(0.0, 1.0, 0.0);                      /* green */
    glColor3f(1.0, 0.0, 0.0);                      /* red */
    glVertex(...);
    glColor3f(1.0, 1.0, 0.0);                      /* yellow */
    glColor3f(0.0, 0.0, 1.0);                      /* blue */
    glVertex(...);
    glVertex(...);
glEnd();
```

You can use any combination of the 24 versions of the **glVertex*()** command between **glBegin()** and **glEnd()**, although in real applications all the calls in any particular instance tend to be of the same form. If your vertex-data specification is consistent and repetitive (for example, **glColor***, **glVertex***, **glColor***, **glVertex***,...), you may enhance your program's performance by using vertex arrays. (See "Vertex Arrays" on page 65.)

## Basic State Management

In the preceding section, you saw an example of a state variable, the current RGBA color, and how it can be associated with a primitive. OpenGL maintains many states and state variables. An object may be rendered with lighting, texturing, hidden surface removal, fog, and other states affecting its appearance.

By default, most of these states are initially inactive. These states may be costly to activate; for example, turning on texture mapping will almost certainly slow down the process of rendering a primitive. However, the image will improve in quality and will look more realistic, owing to the enhanced graphics capabilities.

To turn many of these states on and off, use these two simple commands:

> void **glEnable**(GLenum *capability*);
> void **glDisable**(GLenum *capability*);
>
> **glEnable()** turns on a capability, and **glDisable()** turns it off. More than 60 enumerated values can be passed as parameters to **glEnable()** or **glDisable()**. Some examples are GL_BLEND (which controls blending of RGBA values), GL_DEPTH_TEST (which controls depth comparisons and updates to the depth buffer), GL_FOG (which controls fog), GL_LINE_STIPPLE (patterned lines), and GL_LIGHTING (you get the idea).

You can also check whether a state is currently enabled or disabled.

> GLboolean **glIsEnabled**(GLenum *capability*)
>
> Returns GL_TRUE or GL_FALSE, depending on whether or not the queried capability is currently activated.

The states you have just seen have two settings: on and off. However, most OpenGL routines set values for more complicated state variables. For example, the routine **glColor3f()** sets three values, which are part of the GL_CURRENT_COLOR state. There are five querying routines used to find out what values are set for many states:

> void **glGetBooleanv**(GLenum *pname*, GLboolean *\*params*);
> void **glGetIntegerv**(GLenum *pname*, GLint *\*params*);
> void **glGetFloatv**(GLenum *pname*, GLfloat *\*params*);
> void **glGetDoublev**(GLenum *pname*, GLdouble *\*params*);
> void **glGetPointerv**(GLenum *pname*, GLvoid *\*\*params*);

Obtains Boolean, integer, floating-point, double-precision, or pointer state variables. The *pname* argument is a symbolic constant indicating the state variable to return, and *params* is a pointer to an array of the indicated type in which to place the returned data. See the tables in Appendix B for the possible values for *pname*. For example, to get the current RGBA color, a table in Appendix B suggests you use **glGetIntegerv**(GL_CURRENT_COLOR, *params*) or **glGetFloatv**(GL_CURRENT_COLOR, *params*). A type conversion is performed, if necessary, to return the desired variable as the requested data type.

These querying routines handle most, but not all, requests for obtaining state information. (See "The Query Commands" in Appendix B for a list of all of the available OpenGL state querying routines.)

## Displaying Points, Lines, and Polygons

By default, a point is drawn as a single pixel on the screen, a line is drawn solid and 1 pixel wide, and polygons are drawn solidly filled in. The following paragraphs discuss the details of how to change these default display modes.

### Point Details

To control the size of a rendered point, use **glPointSize**() and supply the desired size in pixels as the argument.

void **glPointSize**(GLfloat *size*);

Sets the width in pixels for rendered points; *size* must be greater than 0.0 and by default is 1.0.

The actual collection of pixels on the screen that are drawn for various point widths depends on whether antialiasing is enabled. (Antialiasing is a technique for smoothing points and lines as they're rendered; see "Antialiasing" and "Point Parameters" in Chapter 6 for more detail.) If antialiasing is disabled (the default), fractional widths are rounded to integer widths, and a screen-aligned square region of pixels is drawn. Thus, if the width is 1.0, the square is 1 pixel by 1 pixel; if the width is 2.0, the square is 2 pixels by 2 pixels, and so on.

With antialiasing or multisampling enabled, a circular group of pixels is drawn, and the pixels on the boundaries are typically drawn at less than full intensity to give the edge a smoother appearance. In this mode, noninteger widths aren't rounded.

Most OpenGL implementations support very large point sizes. You can query the minimum and maximum sized for aliased points by using GL_ALIASED_POINT_SIZE_RANGE with **glGetFloatv()**. Likewise, you can obtain the range of supported sizes for antialiased points by passing GL_SMOOTH_POINT_SIZE_RANGE to **glGetFloatv()**. The sizes of supported antialiased points are evenly spaced between the minimum and maximum sizes for the range. Calling **glGetFloatv()** with the parameter GL_SMOOTH_POINT_SIZE_GRANULARITY will return how accurately a given antialiased point size is supported. For example, if you request **glPointSize(2.37)** and the granularity returned is 0.1, then the point size is rounded to 2.4.

## Line Details

With OpenGL, you can specify lines with different widths and lines that are *stippled* in various ways—dotted, dashed, drawn with alternating dots and dashes, and so on.

### Wide Lines

void **glLineWidth**(GLfloat *width*);

Sets the width, in pixels, for rendered lines; *width* must be greater than 0.0 and by default is 1.0.

The actual rendering of lines is affected if either antialiasing or multisampling is enabled. (See "Antialiasing Points or Lines" on page 249 and "Antialiasing Geometric Primitives with Multisampling" on page 255.) Without antialiasing, widths of 1, 2, and 3 draw lines 1, 2, and 3 pixels wide. With antialiasing enabled, noninteger line widths are possible, and pixels on the boundaries are typically drawn at less than full intensity. As with point sizes, a particular OpenGL implementation might limit the width of nonantialiased lines to its maximum antialiased line width, rounded to the nearest integer value. You can obtain the range of supported aliased line widths by using GL_ALIASED_LINE_WIDTH_RANGE with **glGetFloatv()**. To determine the supported minimum and maximum sizes of antialiased line widths, and what granularity your implementation supports, call **glGetFloatv**(), with GL_SMOOTH_LINE_WIDTH_RANGE and GL_SMOOTH_LINE_WIDTH_GRANULARITY.

**Note:** Keep in mind that, by default, lines are 1 pixel wide, so they appear wider on lower-resolution screens. For computer displays, this isn't typically an issue, but if you're using OpenGL to render to a high-resolution plotter, 1-pixel lines might be nearly invisible. To obtain resolution-independent line widths, you need to take into account the physical dimensions of pixels.

**Advanced**

With non-antialiased wide lines, the line width isn't measured perpendicular to the line. Instead, it's measured in the *y*-direction if the absolute value of the slope is less than 1.0; otherwise, it's measured in the *x*-direction. The rendering of an antialiased line is exactly equivalent to the rendering of a filled rectangle of the given width, centered on the exact line.

**Stippled Lines**

To make stippled (dotted or dashed) lines, you use the command **glLineStipple**() to define the *stipple* pattern, and then you enable line stippling with **glEnable**().

```
glLineStipple(1, 0x3F07);
glEnable(GL_LINE_STIPPLE);
```

void **glLineStipple**(GLint *factor*, GLushort *pattern*);

Sets the current stippling pattern for lines. The *pattern* argument is a 16-bit series of 0s and 1s, and it's repeated as necessary to stipple a given line. A 1 indicates that drawing occurs, and a 0 that it does not, on a pixel-by-pixel basis, beginning with the low-order bit of the pattern. The pattern can be stretched out by using *factor*, which multiplies each subseries of consecutive 1s and 0s. Thus, if three consecutive 1s appear in the pattern, they're stretched to six if *factor* is 2. *factor* is clamped to lie between 1 and 256. Line stippling must be enabled by passing GL_LINE_STIPPLE to **glEnable**(); it's disabled by passing the same argument to **glDisable**().

With the preceding example and the pattern 0x3F07 (which translates to 0011111100000111 in binary), a line would be drawn with 3 pixels on, then 5 off, 6 on, and 2 off. (If this seems backward, remember that the low-order bit is used first.) If *factor* had been 2, the pattern would have been elongated: 6 pixels on, 10 off, 12 on, and 4 off. Figure 2-8 shows lines drawn with different patterns and repeat factors. If you don't enable line stippling, drawing proceeds as if *pattern* were 0xFFFF and *factor* were 1. (Use **glDisable()** with GL_LINE_STIPPLE to disable stippling.) Note that stippling can be used in combination with wide lines to produce wide stippled lines.

| PATTERN | FACTOR | |
|---|---|---|
| 0x00FF | 1 | ————   ————   ———— |
| 0x00FF | 2 | ————————————   ———————— |
| 0x0C0F | 1 | ——  —  ——  —  ——  — |
| 0x0C0F | 3 | ————————   ———— |
| 0xAAAA | 1 | - - - - - - - - - - - - - - - - - - - - - |
| 0xAAAA | 2 | — — — — — — — — — — — |
| 0xAAAA | 3 | — — — — — — — — |
| 0xAAAA | 4 | — — — — — — |

**Figure 2-8**    Stippled Lines

One way to think of the stippling is that as the line is being drawn, the pattern is shifted by 1 bit each time a pixel is drawn (or *factor* pixels are drawn, if *factor* isn't 1). When a series of connected line segments is drawn between a single **glBegin()** and **glEnd()**, the pattern continues to shift as one segment turns into the next. This way, a stippling pattern continues across a series of connected line segments. When **glEnd()** is executed, the pattern is reset, and if more lines are drawn before stippling is disabled the stippling restarts at the beginning of the pattern. If you're drawing lines with GL_LINES, the pattern resets for each independent line.

Example 2-5 illustrates the results of drawing with a couple of different stipple patterns and line widths. It also illustrates what happens if the lines are drawn as a series of individual segments instead of a single connected line strip. The results of running the program appear in Figure 2-9.

**Figure 2-9**    Wide Stippled Lines

**Example 2-5**   Line Stipple Patterns: lines.c

```
#define drawOneLine(x1,y1,x2,y2)  glBegin(GL_LINES);  \
   glVertex2f((x1),(y1)); glVertex2f((x2),(y2)); glEnd();

void init(void)
{
   glClearColor(0.0, 0.0, 0.0, 0.0);
   glShadeModel(GL_FLAT);
}

void display(void)
{
   int i;

   glClear(GL_COLOR_BUFFER_BIT);
/* select white for all lines  */
   glColor3f(1.0, 1.0, 1.0);

/* in 1st row, 3 lines, each with a different stipple  */
   glEnable(GL_LINE_STIPPLE);

   glLineStipple(1, 0x0101);  /*  dotted  */
   drawOneLine(50.0, 125.0, 150.0, 125.0);
   glLineStipple(1, 0x00FF);  /*  dashed  */
   drawOneLine(150.0, 125.0, 250.0, 125.0);
   glLineStipple(1, 0x1C47);  /*  dash/dot/dash  */
   drawOneLine(250.0, 125.0, 350.0, 125.0);

/* in 2nd row, 3 wide lines, each with different stipple */
   glLineWidth(5.0);
   glLineStipple(1, 0x0101);  /*  dotted  */
   drawOneLine(50.0, 100.0, 150.0, 100.0);
   glLineStipple(1, 0x00FF);  /*  dashed  */
   drawOneLine(150.0, 100.0, 250.0, 100.0);
   glLineStipple(1, 0x1C47);  /*  dash/dot/dash  */
   drawOneLine(250.0, 100.0, 350.0, 100.0);
   glLineWidth(1.0);

/* in 3rd row, 6 lines, with dash/dot/dash stipple  */
/* as part of a single connected line strip         */
   glLineStipple(1, 0x1C47);  /*  dash/dot/dash  */
   glBegin(GL_LINE_STRIP);
   for (i = 0; i < 7; i++)
      glVertex2f(50.0 + ((GLfloat) i * 50.0), 75.0);
   glEnd();
```

```
/* in 4th row, 6 independent lines with same stipple  */
   for (i = 0; i < 6; i++) {
      drawOneLine(50.0 + ((GLfloat) i * 50.0), 50.0,
                  50.0 + ((GLfloat)(i+1) * 50.0), 50.0);
   }

/* in 5th row, 1 line, with dash/dot/dash stipple    */
/* and a stipple repeat factor of 5                  */
   glLineStipple(5, 0x1C47);  /*  dash/dot/dash  */
   drawOneLine(50.0, 25.0, 350.0, 25.0);

   glDisable(GL_LINE_STIPPLE);
   glFlush();
}

void reshape(int w, int h)
{
   glViewport(0, 0, (GLsizei) w, (GLsizei) h);
   glMatrixMode(GL_PROJECTION);
   glLoadIdentity();
   gluOrtho2D(0.0, (GLdouble) w, 0.0, (GLdouble) h);
}

int main(int argc, char** argv)
{
   glutInit(&argc, argv);
   glutInitDisplayMode(GLUT_SINGLE | GLUT_RGB);
   glutInitWindowSize(400, 150);
   glutInitWindowPosition(100, 100);
   glutCreateWindow(argv[0]);
   init();
   glutDisplayFunc(display);
   glutReshapeFunc(reshape);
   glutMainLoop();
   return 0;
}
```

## Polygon Details

Polygons are typically drawn by filling in all the pixels enclosed within the boundary, but you can also draw them as outlined polygons or simply as points at the vertices. A filled polygon might be solidly filled or stippled with a certain pattern. Although the exact details are omitted here, filled polygons are drawn in such a way that if adjacent polygons share an edge or vertex, the pixels making up the edge or vertex are drawn exactly once—they're included in only one of the polygons. This is done so that partially transparent polygons don't have their edges drawn twice, which would make those edges appear darker (or brighter, depending on what color you're drawing with). Note that it might result in narrow polygons having no filled pixels in one or more rows or columns of pixels.

To antialias filled polygons, multisampling is highly recommended. For details, see "Antialiasing Geometric Primitives with Multisampling" in Chapter 6.

### Polygons as Points, Outlines, or Solids

A polygon has two sides—front and back—and might be rendered differently depending on which side is facing the viewer. This allows you to have cutaway views of solid objects in which there is an obvious distinction between the parts that are inside and those that are outside. By default, both front and back faces are drawn in the same way. To change this, or to draw only outlines or vertices, use **glPolygonMode()**.

---

void **glPolygonMode**(GLenum *face*, GLenum *mode*);

---

Controls the drawing mode for a polygon's front and back faces. The parameter *face* can be GL_FRONT_AND_BACK, GL_FRONT, or GL_BACK; *mode* can be GL_POINT, GL_LINE, or GL_FILL to indicate whether the polygon should be drawn as points, outlined, or filled. By default, both the front and back faces are drawn filled.

For example, you can have the *front faces* filled and the *back faces* outlined with two calls to this routine:

```
glPolygonMode(GL_FRONT, GL_FILL);
glPolygonMode(GL_BACK, GL_LINE);
```

### Reversing and Culling Polygon Faces

By convention, polygons whose vertices appear in counterclockwise order on the screen are called *front-facing*. You can construct the surface of any "reasonable" solid—a mathematician would call such a surface an orientable manifold (spheres, donuts, and teapots are orientable; Klein bottles and Möbius strips aren't)—from polygons of consistent orientation. In other words, you can use all clockwise polygons or all counterclockwise polygons. (This is essentially the mathematical definition of *orientable*.)

Suppose you've consistently described a model of an orientable surface but happen to have the clockwise orientation on the outside. You can swap what OpenGL considers the back face by using the function **glFrontFace()**, supplying the desired orientation for front-facing polygons.

---

void **glFrontFace**(GLenum *mode*);

Controls how front-facing polygons are determined. By default, *mode* is GL_CCW, which corresponds to a counterclockwise orientation of the ordered vertices of a projected polygon in window coordinates. If *mode* is GL_CW, faces with a clockwise orientation are considered front-facing.

**Note:** The orientation (clockwise or counterclockwise) of the vertices is also known as its *winding*.

In a completely enclosed surface constructed from opaque polygons with a consistent orientation, none of the back-facing polygons are ever visible— they're always obscured by the front-facing polygons. If you are outside this surface, you might enable *culling* to discard polygons that OpenGL determines are back-facing. Similarly, if you are inside the object, only back-facing polygons are visible. To instruct OpenGL to discard front- or back-facing polygons, use the command **glCullFace()** and enable culling with **glEnable()**.

---

void **glCullFace**(GLenum *mode*);

Indicates which polygons should be discarded (culled) before they're converted to screen coordinates. The mode is either GL_FRONT, GL_BACK, or GL_FRONT_AND_BACK to indicate front-facing, back-facing, or all polygons. To take effect, culling must be enabled using **glEnable()** with GL_CULL_FACE; it can be disabled with **glDisable()** and the same argument.

**Advanced**

In more technical terms, deciding whether a face of a polygon is front- or back-facing depends on the sign of the polygon's area computed in window coordinates. One way to compute this area is

Advanced

$$a = \frac{1}{2} \sum_{i=0}^{n-1} x_i\, y_{i\oplus 1} - x_{i\oplus 1}\, y_i$$

where $x_i$ and $y_i$ are the $x$ and $y$ window coordinates of the $i$th vertex of the $n$-vertex polygon and

$i \oplus 1$ is $(i+1)$ mod $n$.

Assuming that GL_CCW has been specified, if $a > 0$, the polygon corresponding to that vertex is considered to be front-facing; otherwise, it's back-facing. If GL_CW is specified and if $a < 0$, then the corresponding polygon is front-facing; otherwise, it's back-facing.

**Try This**

Modify Example 2-5 by adding some filled polygons. Experiment with different colors. Try different polygon modes. Also, enable culling to see its effect.

### Stippling Polygons

By default, filled polygons are drawn with a solid pattern. They can also be filled with a 32-bit by 32-bit *window-aligned* stipple pattern, which you specify with **glPolygonStipple()**.

---

void **glPolygonStipple**(const GLubyte *mask);

Defines the current stipple pattern for filled polygons. The argument *mask* is a pointer to a $32 \times 32$ bitmap that's interpreted as a mask of 0s and 1s. Where a 1 appears, the corresponding pixel in the polygon is drawn, and where a 0 appears, nothing is drawn. Figure 2-10 shows how a stipple pattern is constructed from the characters in *mask*. Polygon stippling is enabled and disabled by using **glEnable()** and **glDisable()** with GL_POLYGON_STIPPLE as the argument. The interpretation of the *mask* data is affected by the **glPixelStore*()** GL_UNPACK* modes. (See "Controlling Pixel-Storage Modes" in Chapter 8.)

---

In addition to defining the current polygon stippling pattern, you must enable stippling:

```
glEnable(GL_POLYGON_STIPPLE);
```

Use **glDisable()** with the same argument to disable polygon stippling.

Figure 2-11 shows the results of polygons drawn unstippled and then with two different stippling patterns. The program is shown in Example 2-6. The reversal of white to black (from Figure 2-10 to Figure 2-11) occurs because the program draws in white over a black background, using the pattern in Figure 2-10 as a stencil.

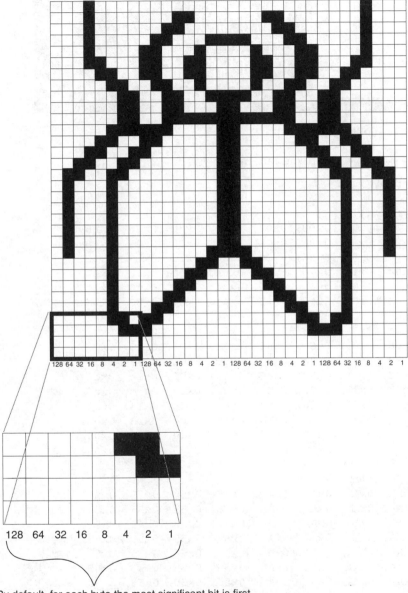

128 64 32 16 8 4 2 1

By default, for each byte the most significant bit is first.
Bit ordering can be changed by calling **glPixelStore*()**.

**Figure 2-10** Constructing a Polygon Stipple Pattern

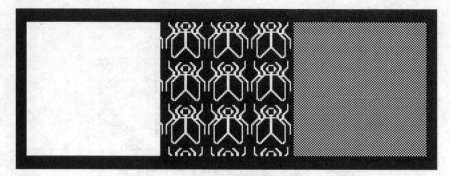

**Figure 2-11**    Stippled Polygons

**Example 2-6**    Polygon Stipple Patterns: polys.c

```
void display(void)
{
    GLubyte fly[] = {
        0x00, 0x00, 0x00, 0x00, 0x00, 0x00, 0x00, 0x00,
        0x03, 0x80, 0x01, 0xC0, 0x06, 0xC0, 0x03, 0x60,
        0x04, 0x60, 0x06, 0x20, 0x04, 0x30, 0x0C, 0x20,
        0x04, 0x18, 0x18, 0x20, 0x04, 0x0C, 0x30, 0x20,
        0x04, 0x06, 0x60, 0x20, 0x44, 0x03, 0xC0, 0x22,
        0x44, 0x01, 0x80, 0x22, 0x44, 0x01, 0x80, 0x22,
        0x44, 0x01, 0x80, 0x22, 0x44, 0x01, 0x80, 0x22,
        0x44, 0x01, 0x80, 0x22, 0x44, 0x01, 0x80, 0x22,
        0x66, 0x01, 0x80, 0x66, 0x33, 0x01, 0x80, 0xCC,
        0x19, 0x81, 0x81, 0x98, 0x0C, 0xC1, 0x83, 0x30,
        0x07, 0xe1, 0x87, 0xe0, 0x03, 0x3f, 0xfc, 0xc0,
        0x03, 0x31, 0x8c, 0xc0, 0x03, 0x33, 0xcc, 0xc0,
        0x06, 0x64, 0x26, 0x60, 0x0c, 0xcc, 0x33, 0x30,
        0x18, 0xcc, 0x33, 0x18, 0x10, 0xc4, 0x23, 0x08,
        0x10, 0x63, 0xC6, 0x08, 0x10, 0x30, 0x0c, 0x08,
        0x10, 0x18, 0x18, 0x08, 0x10, 0x00, 0x00, 0x08};

    GLubyte halftone[] = {
        0xAA, 0xAA, 0xAA, 0xAA, 0x55, 0x55, 0x55, 0x55,
        0xAA, 0xAA, 0xAA, 0xAA, 0x55, 0x55, 0x55, 0x55,
        0xAA, 0xAA, 0xAA, 0xAA, 0x55, 0x55, 0x55, 0x55,
        0xAA, 0xAA, 0xAA, 0xAA, 0x55, 0x55, 0x55, 0x55,
        0xAA, 0xAA, 0xAA, 0xAA, 0x55, 0x55, 0x55, 0x55,
        0xAA, 0xAA, 0xAA, 0xAA, 0x55, 0x55, 0x55, 0x55,
        0xAA, 0xAA, 0xAA, 0xAA, 0x55, 0x55, 0x55, 0x55,
        0xAA, 0xAA, 0xAA, 0xAA, 0x55, 0x55, 0x55, 0x55,
        0xAA, 0xAA, 0xAA, 0xAA, 0x55, 0x55, 0x55, 0x55,
        0xAA, 0xAA, 0xAA, 0xAA, 0x55, 0x55, 0x55, 0x55,
```

```
      0xAA, 0xAA, 0xAA, 0xAA, 0x55, 0x55, 0x55, 0x55,
      0xAA, 0xAA, 0xAA, 0xAA, 0x55, 0x55, 0x55, 0x55,
      0xAA, 0xAA, 0xAA, 0xAA, 0x55, 0x55, 0x55, 0x55,
      0xAA, 0xAA, 0xAA, 0xAA, 0x55, 0x55, 0x55, 0x55,
      0xAA, 0xAA, 0xAA, 0xAA, 0x55, 0x55, 0x55, 0x55,
      0xAA, 0xAA, 0xAA, 0xAA, 0x55, 0x55, 0x55, 0x55};

   glClear(GL_COLOR_BUFFER_BIT);
   glColor3f(1.0, 1.0, 1.0);
/*  draw one solid, unstippled rectangle,      */
/*  then two stippled rectangles               */
   glRectf(25.0, 25.0, 125.0, 125.0);
   glEnable(GL_POLYGON_STIPPLE);
   glPolygonStipple(fly);
   glRectf(125.0, 25.0, 225.0, 125.0);
   glPolygonStipple(halftone);
   glRectf(225.0, 25.0, 325.0, 125.0);
   glDisable(GL_POLYGON_STIPPLE);
   glFlush();
}

void init(void)
{
   glClearColor(0.0, 0.0, 0.0, 0.0);
   glShadeModel(GL_FLAT);
}

void reshape(int w, int h)
{
   glViewport(0, 0, (GLsizei) w, (GLsizei) h);
   glMatrixMode(GL_PROJECTION);
   glLoadIdentity();
   gluOrtho2D(0.0, (GLdouble) w, 0.0, (GLdouble) h);
}

int main(int argc, char** argv)
{
   glutInit(&argc, argv);
   glutInitDisplayMode(GLUT_SINGLE | GLUT_RGB);
   glutInitWindowSize(350, 150);
   glutCreateWindow(argv[0]);
   init();
   glutDisplayFunc(display);
   glutReshapeFunc(reshape);
   glutMainLoop();
   return 0;
}
```

You might want to use display lists to store polygon stipple patterns to maximize efficiency. (See "Display List Design Philosophy" in Chapter 7.)

### Marking Polygon Boundary Edges

Advanced

**Advanced**

OpenGL can render only convex polygons, but many nonconvex polygons arise in practice. To draw these nonconvex polygons, you typically subdivide them into convex polygons—usually triangles, as shown in Figure 2-12—and then draw the triangles. Unfortunately, if you decompose a general polygon into triangles and draw the triangles, you can't really use **glPolygonMode()** to draw the polygon's outline, as you get all the triangle outlines inside it. To solve this problem, you can tell OpenGL whether a particular vertex precedes a boundary edge; OpenGL keeps track of this information by passing along with each vertex a bit indicating whether that vertex is followed by a boundary edge. Then, when a polygon is drawn in GL_LINE mode, the nonboundary edges aren't drawn. In Figure 2-12, the dashed lines represent added edges.

**Figure 2-12**    Subdividing a Nonconvex Polygon

By default, all vertices are marked as preceding a boundary edge, but you can manually control the setting of the *edge flag* with the command **glEdgeFlag*()**. This command is used between **glBegin()** and **glEnd()** pairs, and it affects all the vertices specified after it until the next **glEdgeFlag()** call is made. It applies only to vertices specified for polygons, triangles, and quads, not to those specified for strips of triangles or quads.

---

void **glEdgeFlag**(GLboolean *flag*);
void **glEdgeFlagv**(const GLboolean \**flag*);

---

Indicates whether a vertex should be considered as initializing a boundary edge of a polygon. If *flag* is GL_TRUE, the edge flag is set to TRUE (the default), and any vertices created are considered to precede boundary edges until this function is called again with *flag* being GL_FALSE.

For instance, Example 2-7 draws the outline shown in Figure 2-13.

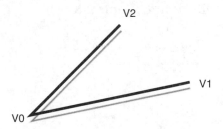

**Figure 2-13**    Outlined Polygon Drawn Using Edge Flags

**Example 2-7**    Marking Polygon Boundary Edges

```
glPolygonMode(GL_FRONT_AND_BACK, GL_LINE);
glBegin(GL_POLYGON);
    glEdgeFlag(GL_TRUE);
    glVertex3fv(V0);
    glEdgeFlag(GL_FALSE);
    glVertex3fv(V1);
    glEdgeFlag(GL_TRUE);
    glVertex3fv(V2);
glEnd();
```

## Normal Vectors

A *normal vector* (or *normal*, for short) is a vector that points in a direction that's perpendicular to a surface. For a flat surface, one perpendicular direction is the same for every point on the surface, but for a general curved surface, the normal direction might be different at each point on the surface. With OpenGL, you can specify a normal for each polygon or for each vertex. Vertices of the same polygon might share the same normal (for a flat surface) or have different normals (for a curved surface). You can't assign normals anywhere other than at the vertices.

An object's normal vectors define the orientation of its surface in space—in particular, its orientation relative to light sources. These vectors are used by OpenGL to determine how much light the object receives at its vertices. Lighting—a large topic by itself—is the subject of Chapter 5, and you might want to review the following information after you've read that chapter. Normal vectors are discussed briefly here because you define normal vectors for an object at the same time you define the object's geometry.

You use **glNormal*()** to set the current normal to the value of the argument passed in. Subsequent calls to **glVertex*()** cause the specified vertices to be assigned the current normal. Often, each vertex has a different normal, which necessitates a series of alternating calls, as in Example 2-8.

**Example 2-8**   Surface Normals at Vertices

```
glBegin (GL_POLYGON);
   glNormal3fv(n0);
   glVertex3fv(v0);
   glNormal3fv(n1);
   glVertex3fv(v1);
   glNormal3fv(n2);
   glVertex3fv(v2);
   glNormal3fv(n3);
   glVertex3fv(v3);
glEnd();
```

void **glNormal3**{bsidf}(*TYPE nx*, *TYPE ny*, *TYPE nz*);
void **glNormal3**{bsidf}**v**(const *TYPE* *v);

Sets the current normal vector as specified by the arguments. The nonvector version (without the **v**) takes three arguments, which specify an (*nx, ny, nz*) vector that's taken to be the normal. Alternatively, you can use the vector version of this function (with the **v**) and supply a single array of three elements to specify the desired normal. The **b**, **s**, and **i** versions scale their parameter values linearly to the range [–1.0, 1.0].

There's no magic to finding the normals for an object—most likely, you have to perform some calculations that might include taking derivatives—but there are several techniques and tricks you can use to achieve certain effects. Appendix E explains how to find normal vectors for surfaces. If you already know how to do this, if you can count on always being supplied with normal vectors, or if you don't want to use the OpenGL lighting facilities, you don't need to read this appendix.

Note that at a given point on a surface, two vectors are perpendicular to the surface, and they point in opposite directions. By convention, the normal is the one that points to the outside of the surface being modeled. (If you get inside and outside reversed in your model, just change every normal vector from $(x, y, z)$ to $(-x, -y, -z)$).

Also, keep in mind that since normal vectors indicate direction only, their lengths are mostly irrelevant. You can specify normals of any length, but eventually they have to be converted to a length of 1 before lighting calculations are performed. (A vector that has a length of 1 is said to be of unit length, or *normalized*.) In general, you should supply normalized normal vectors. To make a normal vector of unit length, divide each of its $x$-, $y$-, $z$-components by the length of the normal:

$$\sqrt{x^2 + y^2 + z^2}$$

Normal vectors remain normalized as long as your model transformations include only rotations and translations. (See Chapter 3 for a discussion of transformations.) If you perform irregular transformations (such as scaling or multiplying by a shear matrix), or if you specify nonunit-length normals, then you should have OpenGL automatically normalize your normal vectors after the transformations. To do this, call **glEnable(GL_NORMALIZE)**.

If you supply unit-length normals, and you perform only uniform scaling (that is, the same scaling value for $x$, $y$, and $z$), you can use **glEnable(GL_RESCALE_NORMAL)** to scale the normals by a constant factor, derived from the modelview transformation matrix, to return them to unit length after transformation.

Note that automatic normalization or rescaling typically requires additional calculations that might reduce the performance of your application. Rescaling normals uniformly with GL_RESCALE_NORMAL is usually less expensive than performing full-fledged normalization with GL_NORMALIZE. By default, both automatic normalizing and rescaling operations are disabled.

## Vertex Arrays

You may have noticed that OpenGL requires many function calls to render geometric primitives. Drawing a 20-sided polygon requires at least 22 function calls: one call to **glBegin()**, one call for each of the vertices, and a final call to **glEnd()**. In the two previous code examples, additional information (polygon boundary edge flags or surface normals) added function calls for each vertex. This can quickly double or triple the number of function calls required for one geometric object. For some systems, function calls have a great deal of overhead and can hinder performance.

An additional problem is the redundant processing of vertices that are shared between adjacent polygons. For example, the cube in Figure 2-14 has six faces and eight shared vertices. Unfortunately, if the standard method of describing this object is used, each vertex has to be specified three times: once for every face that uses it. Therefore, 24 vertices are processed, even though eight would be enough.

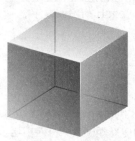

**Figure 2-14**     Six Sides, Eight Shared Vertices

OpenGL has vertex array routines that allow you to specify a lot of vertex-related data with just a few arrays and to access that data with equally few function calls. Using vertex array routines, all 20 vertices in a 20-sided polygon can be put into one array and called with one function. If each vertex also has a surface normal, all 20 surface normals can be put into another array and also called with one function.

Arranging data in vertex arrays may increase the performance of your application. Using vertex arrays reduces the number of function calls, which improves performance. Also, using vertex arrays may allow reuse of already processed shared vertices.

**Note:** Vertex arrays became standard in Version 1.1 of OpenGL. Version 1.4 added support for storing fog coordinates and secondary colors in vertex arrays.

There are three steps to using vertex arrays to render geometry:

1.  Activate (enable) up to eight arrays, each storing a different type of data: vertex coordinates, surface normals, RGBA colors, secondary colors, color indices, fog coordinates, texture coordinates, or polygon edge flags.

2.  Put data into the array or arrays. The arrays are accessed by the addresses of (that is, pointers to) their memory locations. In the client-server model, this data is stored in the client's address space.

3.  Draw geometry with the data. OpenGL obtains the data from all activated arrays by dereferencing the pointers. In the client-server model, the data is transferred to the server's address space. There are three ways to do this:

    *   Accessing individual array elements (randomly hopping around)

    *   Creating a list of individual array elements (methodically hopping around)

    *   Processing sequential array elements

    The dereferencing method you choose may depend on the type of problem you encounter. Version 1.4 added support for multiple array access from a single function call.

Interleaved vertex array data is another common method of organization. Instead of several different arrays, each maintaining a different type of data (color, surface normal, coordinate, and so on), you may have the different types of data mixed into a single array. (See "Interleaved Arrays" on page 78.)

## Step 1: Enabling Arrays

The first step is to call **glEnableClientState()** with an enumerated parameter, which activates the chosen array. In theory, you may need to call this up to eight times to activate the eight available arrays. In practice, you'll probably activate up to six arrays. For example, it is unlikely that you would activate both GL_COLOR_ARRAY and GL_INDEX_ARRAY, as your program's display mode supports either RGBA mode or color-index mode, but probably not both simultaneously.

---

void **glEnableClientState**(GLenum *array*)

Specifies the array to enable. The symbolic constants GL_VERTEX_ARRAY, GL_COLOR_ARRAY, GL_SECONDARY_COLOR_ARRAY, GL_INDEX_ARRAY, GL_NORMAL_ARRAY, GL_FOG_COORDINATE_ARRAY, GL_TEXTURE_COORD_ARRAY, and GL_EDGE_FLAG_ARRAY are acceptable parameters.

If you use lighting, you may want to define a surface normal for every vertex. (See "Normal Vectors" on page 63.) To use vertex arrays for that case, you activate both the surface normal and vertex coordinate arrays:

```
glEnableClientState(GL_NORMAL_ARRAY);
glEnableClientState(GL_VERTEX_ARRAY);
```

Suppose that you want to turn off lighting at some point and just draw the geometry using a single color. You want to call **glDisable()** to turn off lighting states (see Chapter 5). Now that lighting has been deactivated, you also want to stop changing the values of the surface normal state, which is wasted effort. To do this, you call

```
glDisableClientState(GL_NORMAL_ARRAY);
```

void **glDisableClientState**(GLenum *array*);

Specifies the array to disable. It accepts the same symbolic constants as **glEnableClientState()**.

You might be asking yourself why the architects of OpenGL created these new (and long) command names, like **gl\*ClientState()**, for example. Why can't you just call **glEnable()** and **glDisable()**? One reason is that **glEnable()** and **glDisable()** can be stored in a display list, but the specification of vertex arrays cannot, because the data remains on the client's side.

If multitexturing is enabled, enabling and disabling client arrays affects only the active texturing unit. See "Multitexturing" on page 443 for more details.

## Step 2: Specifying Data for the Arrays

There is a straightforward way by which a single command specifies a single array in the client space. There are eight different routines for specifying arrays—one routine for each kind of array. There is also a command that can specify several client-space arrays at once, all originating from a single interleaved array.

---

void **glVertexPointer**(GLint *size*, GLenum *type*, GLsizei *stride*,
                  const GLvoid *\*pointer*);

---

Specifies where spatial coordinate data can be accessed. *pointer* is the memory address of the first coordinate of the first vertex in the array. *type* specifies the data type (GL_SHORT, GL_INT, GL_FLOAT, or GL_DOUBLE) of each coordinate in the array. *size* is the number of coordinates per vertex, which must be 2, 3, or 4. *stride* is the byte offset between consecutive vertices. If *stride* is 0, the vertices are understood to be tightly packed in the array.

To access the other seven arrays, there are seven similar routines:

---

void **glColorPointer**(GLint *size*, GLenum *type*, GLsizei *stride*,
                  const GLvoid *\*pointer*);
void **glSecondaryColorPointer**(GLint *size*, GLenum *type*, GLsizei *stride*,
                  const GLvoid *\*pointer*);
void **glIndexPointer**(GLenum *type*, GLsizei *stride*, const GLvoid *\*pointer*);
void **glNormalPointer**(GLenum *type*, GLsizei *stride*,
                  const GLvoid *\*pointer*);
void **glFogCoordPointer**(GLenum *type*, GLsizei *stride*,
                  const GLvoid *\*pointer*);
void **glTexCoordPointer**(GLint *size*, GLenum *type*, GLsizei *stride*,
                  const GLvoid *\*pointer*);
void **glEdgeFlagPointer**(GLsizei *stride*, const GLvoid *\*pointer*);

---

**Note:** Additional vertex attributes, used by programmable shaders, can be stored in vertex arrays. Because of their association with shaders, they are discussed in Chapter 15, "The OpenGL Shading Language," on page 672.

The main difference among the routines is whether size and type are unique or must be specified. For example, a surface normal always has three components, so it is redundant to specify its size. An edge flag is always a single Boolean, so neither size nor type needs to be mentioned. Table 2-4 displays legal values for size and data types.

For OpenGL implementations that support multitexturing, specifying a texture coordinate array with **glTexCoordPointer()** only affects the currently active texture unit. See "Multitexturing" on page 443 for more information.

Example 2-9 uses vertex arrays for both RGBA colors and vertex coordinates. RGB floating-point values and their corresponding (*x, y*) integer coordinates are loaded into the GL_COLOR_ARRAY and GL_VERTEX_ARRAY.

| Command | Sizes | Values for *type* Argument |
|---|---|---|
| glVertexPointer | 2, 3, 4 | GL_SHORT, GL_INT, GL_FLOAT, GL_DOUBLE |
| glColorPointer | 3, 4 | GL_BYTE, GL_UNSIGNED_BYTE, GL_SHORT, GL_UNSIGNED_SHORT, GL_INT, GL_UNSIGNED_INT, GL_FLOAT, GL_DOUBLE |
| glSecondaryColorPointer | 3 | GL_BYTE, GL_UNSIGNED_BYTE, GL_SHORT, GL_UNSIGNED_SHORT, GL_INT, GL_UNSIGNED_INT, GL_FLOAT, GL_DOUBLE |
| glIndexPointer | 1 | GL_UNSIGNED_BYTE, GL_SHORT, GL_INT, GL_FLOAT, GL_DOUBLE |
| glNormalPointer | 3 | GL_BYTE, GL_SHORT, GL_INT, GL_FLOAT, GL_DOUBLE |
| glFogCoordPointer | 1 | GL_FLOAT, GL_DOUBLE |
| glTexCoordPointer | 1, 2, 3, 4 | GL_SHORT, GL_INT, GL_FLOAT, GL_DOUBLE |
| glEdgeFlagPointer | 1 | no type argument (type of data must be GLboolean) |

**Table 2-4**    Vertex Array Sizes (Values per Vertex) and Data Types

**Example 2-9**    Enabling and Loading Vertex Arrays: varray.c

```
static GLint vertices[] = {25, 25,
                           100, 325,
                           175, 25,
                           175, 325,
                           250, 25,
                           325, 325};
static GLfloat colors[] = {1.0, 0.2, 0.2,
                           0.2, 0.2, 1.0,
                           0.8, 1.0, 0.2,
                           0.75, 0.75, 0.75,
                           0.35, 0.35, 0.35,
                           0.5, 0.5, 0.5};

glEnableClientState(GL_COLOR_ARRAY);
glEnableClientState(GL_VERTEX_ARRAY);

glColorPointer(3, GL_FLOAT, 0, colors);
glVertexPointer(2, GL_INT, 0, vertices);
```

## Stride

The *stride* parameter for the **gl*Pointer()** routines tells OpenGL how to access the data you provide in your pointer arrays. Its value should be the number of bytes between the starts of two successive pointer elements, or zero, which is a special case. For example, suppose you stored both your vertex's RGB and (*x, y, z*) coordinates in a single array, such as the following:

```
static GLfloat intertwined[] =
      {1.0, 0.2, 1.0, 100.0, 100.0, 0.0,
      1.0, 0.2, 0.2,   0.0, 200.0, 0.0,
      1.0, 1.0, 0.2, 100.0, 300.0, 0.0,
      0.2, 1.0, 0.2, 200.0, 300.0, 0.0,
      0.2, 1.0, 1.0, 300.0, 200.0, 0.0,
      0.2, 0.2, 1.0, 200.0, 100.0, 0.0};
```

To reference only the color values in the *intertwined* array, the following call starts from the beginning of the array (which could also be passed as *&intertwined[0]*) and jumps ahead 6 * **sizeof**(GLfloat) bytes, which is the size of both the color and vertex coordinate values. This jump is enough to get to the beginning of the data for the next vertex:

```
glColorPointer(3, GL_FLOAT, 6*sizeof(GLfloat), &intertwined[0]);
```

For the vertex coordinate pointer, you need to start from further in the array, at the fourth element of *intertwined* (remember that C programmers start counting at zero):

```
glVertexPointer(3, GL_FLOAT, 6*sizeof(GLfloat), &intertwined[3]);
```

If your data is stored similar to the *intertwined* array above, you may find "Interleaved Arrays" on page 78 more convenient for storing your data.

With a stride of zero, each type of vertex array (RGB color, color index, vertex coordinate, and so on) must be tightly packed. The data in the array must be homogeneous; that is, the data must be all RGB color values, all vertex coordinates, or all some other data similar in some fashion.

## Step 3: Dereferencing and Rendering

Until the contents of the vertex arrays are dereferenced, the arrays remain on the client side, and their contents are easily changed. In Step 3, contents of the arrays are obtained, sent to the server, and then sent down the graphics processing pipeline for rendering.

You can obtain data from a single array element (indexed location), from an ordered list of array elements (which may be limited to a subset of the entire vertex array data), or from a sequence of array elements.

**Dereferencing a Single Array Element**

---

void **glArrayElement**(GLint *ith*)

---

Obtains the data of one (the *ith*) vertex for all currently enabled arrays. For the vertex coordinate array, the corresponding command would be **glVertex**[*size*][*type*]**v**(), where *size* is one of [2, 3, 4], and *type* is one of [s,i,f,d] for GLshort, GLint, GLfloat, and GLdouble, respectively. Both size and type were defined by **glVertexPointer**(). For other enabled arrays, **glArrayElement**() calls **glEdgeFlagv**(), **glTexCoord**[*size*][*type*]**v**(), **glColor**[*size*][*type*]**v**(), **glSecondaryColor3**[*type*]**v**(), **glIndex**[*type*]**v**(), **glNormal3**[*type*]**v**(), and **glFogCoord**[*type*]**v**(). If the vertex coordinate array is enabled, the **glVertex*v**() routine is executed last, after the execution (if enabled) of up to seven corresponding array values.

---

**glArrayElement**() is usually called between **glBegin**() and **glEnd**(). (If called outside, **glArrayElement**() sets the current state for all enabled arrays, except for vertex, which has no current state.) In Example 2-10, a triangle is drawn using the third, fourth, and sixth vertices from enabled vertex arrays. (Again, remember that C programmers begin counting array locations with zero.)

**Example 2-10**   Using glArrayElement() to Define Colors and Vertices

```
glEnableClientState(GL_COLOR_ARRAY);
glEnableClientState(GL_VERTEX_ARRAY);
glColorPointer(3, GL_FLOAT, 0, colors);
glVertexPointer(2, GL_INT, 0, vertices);

glBegin(GL_TRIANGLES);
glArrayElement(2);
glArrayElement(3);
glArrayElement(5);
glEnd();
```

When executed, the latter five lines of code have the same effect as

```
glBegin(GL_TRIANGLES);
glColor3fv(colors + (2 * 3));
glVertex2iv(vertices + (2 * 2));
glColor3fv(colors + (3 * 3));
```

```
glVertex2iv(vertices + (3 * 2));
glColor3fv(colors + (5 * 3));
glVertex2iv(vertices + (5 * 2));
glEnd();
```

Since **glArrayElement()** is only a single function call per vertex, it may reduce the number of function calls, which increases overall performance.

Be warned that if the contents of the array are changed between **glBegin()** and **glEnd()**, there is no guarantee that you will receive original data or changed data for your requested element. To be safe, don't change the contents of any array element that might be accessed until the primitive is completed.

### Dereferencing a List of Array Elements

**glArrayElement()** is good for randomly "hopping around" your data arrays. Similar routines, **glDrawElements()**, **glMultiDrawElements()**, and **glDrawRangeElements()**, are good for hopping around your data arrays in a more orderly manner.

---

void **glDrawElements**(GLenum *mode*, GLsizei *count*, GLenum *type*,
            const GLvoid *\*indices*);

---

Defines a sequence of geometric primitives using *count* number of elements, whose indices are stored in the array *indices*. *type* must be one of GL_UNSIGNED_BYTE, GL_UNSIGNED_SHORT, or GL_UNSIGNED_INT, indicating the data type of the *indices* array. *mode* specifies what kind of primitives are constructed and is one of the same values that is accepted by **glBegin()**; for example, GL_POLYGON, GL_LINE_LOOP, GL_LINES, GL_POINTS, and so on.

The effect of **glDrawElements()** is almost the same as this command sequence:

```
glBegin(mode);
for (i = 0; i < count; i++)
   glArrayElement(indices[i]);
glEnd();
```

**glDrawElements()** additionally checks to make sure *mode*, *count*, and *type* are valid. Also, unlike the preceding sequence, executing **glDrawElements()** leaves several states indeterminate. After execution of **glDrawElements()**, current RGB color, secondary color, color index, normal coordinates, fog coordinates, texture coordinates, and edge flag are indeterminate if the corresponding array has been enabled.

With **glDrawElements()**, the vertices for each face of the cube can be placed in an array of indices. Example 2-11 shows two ways to use **glDrawElements()** to render the cube. Figure 2-15 shows the numbering of the vertices used in Example 2-11.

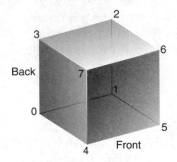

**Figure 2-15**    Cube with Numbered Vertices

**Example 2-11**    Using glDrawElements() to Dereference Several Array Elements

```
static GLubyte frontIndices[] = {4, 5, 6, 7};
static GLubyte rightIndices[] = {1, 2, 6, 5};
static GLubyte bottomIndices[] = {0, 1, 5, 4};
static GLubyte backIndices[] = {0, 3, 2, 1};
static GLubyte leftIndices[] = {0, 4, 7, 3};
static GLubyte topIndices[] = {2, 3, 7, 6};

glDrawElements(GL_QUADS, 4, GL_UNSIGNED_BYTE, frontIndices);
glDrawElements(GL_QUADS, 4, GL_UNSIGNED_BYTE, rightIndices);
glDrawElements(GL_QUADS, 4, GL_UNSIGNED_BYTE, bottomIndices);
glDrawElements(GL_QUADS, 4, GL_UNSIGNED_BYTE, backIndices);
glDrawElements(GL_QUADS, 4, GL_UNSIGNED_BYTE, leftIndices);
glDrawElements(GL_QUADS, 4, GL_UNSIGNED_BYTE, topIndices);
```

**Note:** It is an error to encapsulate **glDrawElements()** between a **glBegin()**/**glEnd()** pair.

With several primitive types (such as GL_QUADS, GL_TRIANGLES, and GL_LINES), you may be able to compact several lists of indices together into a single array. Since the GL_QUADS primitive interprets each group of four vertices as a single polygon, you may compact all the indices used in Example 2-11 into a single array, as shown in Example 2-12:

**Example 2-12**  Compacting Several glDrawElements() Calls into One

```
static GLubyte allIndices[] = {4, 5, 6, 7, 1, 2, 6, 5,
                               0, 1, 5, 4, 0, 3, 2, 1,
                               0, 4, 7, 3, 2, 3, 7, 6};

glDrawElements(GL_QUADS, 24, GL_UNSIGNED_BYTE, allIndices);
```

For other primitive types, compacting indices from several arrays into a single array renders a different result. In Example 2-13, two calls to **glDrawElements()** with the primitive GL_LINE_STRIP render two line strips. You cannot simply combine these two arrays and use a single call to **glDrawElements()** without concatenating the lines into a single strip that would connect vertices #6 and #7. (Note that vertex #1 is being used in both line strips just to show that this is legal.)

**Example 2-13**  Two glDrawElements() Calls That Render Two Line Strips

```
static GLubyte oneIndices[] = {0, 1, 2, 3, 4, 5, 6};
static GLubyte twoIndices[] = {7, 1, 8, 9, 10, 11};

glDrawElements(GL_LINE_STRIP, 7, GL_UNSIGNED_BYTE, oneIndices);
glDrawElements(GL_LINE_STRIP, 6, GL_UNSIGNED_BYTE, twoIndices);
```

The routine **glMultiDrawElements()** was introduced in OpenGL Version 1.4 to enable combining the effects of several **glDrawElements()** calls into a single call.

---

void **glMultiDrawElements**(GLenum *mode*, GLsizei *\*count*,
                          GLenum *type*, const GLvoid **\*\*indices*,
                          GLsizei *primcount*);

Calls a sequence of *primcount* (a number of) **glDrawElements()** commands. *indices* is an array of pointers to lists of array elements. *count* is an array of how many vertices are found in each respective array element list. *mode* (primitive type) and *type* (data type) are the same as they are in **glDrawElements()**.

---

The effect of **glMultiDrawElements()** is the same as

```
for (i = 0; i < primcount; i++) {
   if (count[i] > 0)
      glDrawElements(mode, count[i], type, indices[i]);
}
```

The calls to **glDrawElements()** in Example 2-13 can be combined into a single call of **glMultiDrawElements()**, as shown in Example 2-14:

**Example 2-14**   Use of glMultiDrawElements(): mvarray.c

```
static GLubyte oneIndices[] = {0, 1, 2, 3, 4, 5, 6};
static GLubyte twoIndices[] = {7, 1, 8, 9, 10, 11};
static GLsizei count[] = {7, 6};
static GLvoid * indices[2] = {oneIndices, twoIndices};

glMultiDrawElements(GL_LINE_STRIP, count, GL_UNSIGNED_BYTE,
                    indices, 2);
```

Like **glDrawElements()** or **glMultiDrawElements()**, **glDrawRangeElements()** is also good for hopping around data arrays and rendering their contents. **glDrawRangeElements()** also introduces the added restriction of a range of legal values for its indices, which may increase program performance. For optimal performance, some OpenGL implementations may be able to prefetch (obtain prior to rendering) a limited amount of vertex array data. **glDrawRangeElements()** allows you to specify the range of vertices to be prefetched.

---

void **glDrawRangeElements**(GLenum *mode*, GLuint *start*,
                            GLuint *end*, GLsizei *count*,
                            GLenum *type*, const GLvoid *\*indices*);

Creates a sequence of geometric primitives that is similar to, but more restricted than, the sequence created by **glDrawElements()**. Several parameters of **glDrawRangeElements()** are the same as counterparts in **glDrawElements()**, including *mode* (kind of primitives), *count* (number of elements), *type* (data type), and *indices* (array locations of vertex data). **glDrawRangeElements()** introduces two new parameters: *start* and *end*, which specify a range of acceptable values for *indices*. To be valid, values in the array *indices* must lie between *start* and *end*, inclusive.

---

It is a mistake for vertices in the array *indices* to reference outside the range [*start, end*]. However, OpenGL implementations are not required to find or report this mistake. Therefore, illegal index values may or may not generate an OpenGL error condition, and it is entirely up to the implementation to decide what to do.

You can use **glGetIntegerv()** with GL_MAX_ELEMENTS_VERTICES and GL_MAX_ELEMENTS_INDICES to find out, respectively, the recommended maximum number of vertices to be prefetched and the maximum number of indices (indicating the number of vertices to be rendered) to be referenced. If *end – start + 1* is greater than the recommended maximum of prefetched vertices, or if *count* is greater than the recommended maximum of indices, **glDrawRangeElements**() should still render correctly, but performance may be reduced.

Not all vertices in the range [*start, end*] have to be referenced. However, on some implementations, if you specify a sparsely used range, you may unnecessarily process many vertices that go unused.

With **glArrayElement**(), **glDrawElements**(), **glMultiDrawElements**(), and **glDrawRangeElements**(), it is possible that your OpenGL implementation caches recently processed (meaning transformed, lit) vertices, allowing your application to "reuse" them by not sending them down the transformation pipeline additional times. Take the aforementioned cube, for example, which has six faces (polygons) but only eight vertices. Each vertex is used by exactly three faces. Without **gl*Elements**(), rendering all six faces would require processing 24 vertices, even though 16 vertices are redundant. Your implementation of OpenGL may be able to minimize redundancy and process as few as eight vertices. (Reuse of vertices may be limited to all vertices within a single **glDrawElements**() or **glDrawRangeElements**() call, a single index array for **glMultiDrawElements**(), or, for **glArrayElement**(), within one **glBegin**()/**glEnd**() pair.)

### Dereferencing a Sequence of Array Elements

While **glArrayElement**(), **glDrawElements**(), and **glDrawRangeElements**() "hop around" your data arrays, **glDrawArrays**() plows straight through them.

> void **glDrawArrays**(GLenum *mode*, GLint *first*, GLsizei *count*);
>
> Constructs a sequence of geometric primitives using array elements starting at *first* and ending at *first + count − 1* of each enabled array. *mode* specifies what kinds of primitives are constructed and is one of the same values accepted by **glBegin**(); for example, GL_POLYGON, GL_LINE_LOOP, GL_LINES, GL_POINTS, and so on.

The effect of **glDrawArrays**() is almost the same as this command sequence:

```
glBegin (mode);
for (i = 0; i < count; i++)
   glArrayElement(first + i);
glEnd();
```

As is the case with **glDrawElements**(), **glDrawArrays**() also performs error checking on its parameter values and leaves the current RGB color, secondary color, color index, normal coordinates, fog coordinates, texture coordinates, and edge flag with indeterminate values if the corresponding array has been enabled.

**Try This**

Change the icosahedron drawing routine in Example 2-17 on page 96 to use vertex arrays.

Similar to **glMultiDrawElements**(), the routine **glMultiDrawArrays**() was introduced in OpenGL Version 1.4 to combine several **glDrawArrays**() calls into a single call.

---

void **glMultiDrawArrays**(GLenum *mode*, GLint *\*first*, GLsizei *\*count*
GLsizei *primcount*);

---

Calls a sequence of *primcount* (a number of) **glDrawArray**() commands. *mode* specifies the primitive type with the same values as accepted by **glBegin**(). *first* and *count* contain lists of array locations indicating where to process each list of array elements. Therefore, for the *i*th list of array elements, a geometric primitive is constructed starting at *first[i]* and ending at *first[i] + count[i] – 1*.

The effect of **glMultiDrawArrays**() is the same as

```
for (i = 0; i < primcount; i++) {
    if (count[i] > 0)
        glDrawArrays(mode, first[i], count[i]);
}
```

## Interleaved Arrays

**Advanced**

Earlier in this chapter (see "Stride" on page 71), the special case of interleaved arrays was examined. In that section, the array *intertwined*, which interleaves RGB color and 3D vertex coordinates, was accessed by calls to **glColorPointer**() and **glVertexPointer**(). Careful use of *stride* helped properly specify the arrays:

```
static GLfloat intertwined[] =
       {1.0, 0.2, 1.0, 100.0, 100.0, 0.0,
        1.0, 0.2, 0.2, 0.0, 200.0, 0.0,
```

```
1.0, 1.0, 0.2, 100.0, 300.0, 0.0,
0.2, 1.0, 0.2, 200.0, 300.0, 0.0,
0.2, 1.0, 1.0, 300.0, 200.0, 0.0,
0.2, 0.2, 1.0, 200.0, 100.0, 0.0};
```

There is also a behemoth routine, **glInterleavedArrays()**, that can specify several vertex arrays at once. **glInterleavedArrays()** also enables and disables the appropriate arrays (so it combines "Step 1: Enabling Arrays" on page 67 and "Step 2: Specifying Data for the Arrays" on page 68). The array *intertwined* exactly fits one of the 14 data-interleaving configurations supported by **glInterleavedArrays()**. Therefore, to specify the contents of the array *intertwined* into the RGB color and vertex arrays and enable both arrays, call

```
glInterleavedArrays(GL_C3F_V3F, 0, intertwined);
```

This call to **glInterleavedArrays()** enables GL_COLOR_ARRAY and GL_VERTEX_ARRAY. It disables GL_SECONDARY_COLOR_ARRAY, GL_INDEX_ARRAY, GL_NORMAL_ARRAY, GL_FOG_COORDINATE_ ARRAY, GL_TEXTURE_COORD_ARRAY, and GL_EDGE_FLAG_ARRAY.

This call also has the same effect as calling **glColorPointer()** and **glVertexPointer()** to specify the values for six vertices in each array. Now you are ready for Step 3: calling **glArrayElement()**, **glDrawElements()**, **glDrawRangeElements()**, or **glDrawArrays()** to dereference array elements.

---

void **glInterleavedArrays**(GLenum *format*,
                             GLsizei *stride*, const GLvoid *\*pointer*)

---

Initializes all eight arrays, disabling arrays that are not specified in *format*, and enabling the arrays that are specified. *format* is one of 14 symbolic constants, which represent 14 data configurations; Table 2-5 displays *format* values. *stride* specifies the byte offset between consecutive vertices. If *stride* is 0, the vertices are understood to be tightly packed in the array. *pointer* is the memory address of the first coordinate of the first vertex in the array.

If multitexturing is enabled, **glInterleavedArrays()** affects only the active texture unit. See "Multitexturing" on page 443 for details.

Note that **glInterleavedArrays()** does not support edge flags.

The mechanics of **glInterleavedArrays()** are intricate and require reference to Example 2-15 and Table 2-5. In that example and table, you'll see $e_t$, $e_c$, and $e_n$, which are the Boolean values for the enabled or disabled texture coordinate, color, and normal arrays; and you'll see $s_t$, $s_c$, and $s_v$, which are the sizes (numbers of components) for the texture coordinate, color, and vertex arrays. $t_c$ is the data type for RGBA color, which is the only array that can have nonfloating-point interleaved values. $p_c$, $p_n$, and $p_v$ are the calculated strides for jumping into individual color, normal, and vertex values; and s is the stride (if one is not specified by the user) to jump from one array element to the next.

The effect of **glInterleavedArrays()** is the same as calling the command sequence in Example 2-15 with many values defined in Table 2-5. All pointer arithmetic is performed in units of **sizeof**(GLubyte).

**Example 2-15**   Effect of glInterleavedArrays(format, stride, pointer)

```
int str;
/*  set et, ec, en, st, sc, sv, tc, pc, pn, pv, and s
 *  as a function of Table 2-5 and the value of format
 */

str = stride;
if (str == 0)
   str = s;

glDisableClientState(GL_EDGE_FLAG_ARRAY);
glDisableClientState(GL_INDEX_ARRAY);
glDisableClientState(GL_SECONDARY_COLOR_ARRAY);
glDisableClientState(GL_FOG_COORDINATE_ARRAY);

if (et) {
   glEnableClientState(GL_TEXTURE_COORD_ARRAY);
   glTexCoordPointer(st, GL_FLOAT, str, pointer);
}
else
   glDisableClientState(GL_TEXTURE_COORD_ARRAY);
if (ec) {
   glEnableClientState(GL_COLOR_ARRAY);
   glColorPointer(sc, tc, str, pointer+pc);
}
else
   glDisableClientState(GL_COLOR_ARRAY);
```

```
if (e_n) {
   glEnableClientState(GL_NORMAL_ARRAY);
   glNormalPointer(GL_FLOAT, str, pointer+p_n);
}
else
   glDisableClientState(GL_NORMAL_ARRAY);

glEnableClientState(GL_VERTEX_ARRAY);
glVertexPointer(s_v, GL_FLOAT, str, pointer+p_v);
```

In Table 2-5, T and F are True and False. f is **sizeof**(GLfloat). c is 4 times **sizeof**(GLubyte), rounded up to the nearest multiple of f.

| Format | $e_t$ | $e_c$ | $e_n$ | $s_t$ | $s_c$ | $s_v$ | $t_c$ | $p_c$ | $p_n$ | $p_v$ | s |
|---|---|---|---|---|---|---|---|---|---|---|---|
| GL_V2F | F | F | F | | | 2 | | | | 0 | 2f |
| GL_V3F | F | F | F | | | 3 | | | | 0 | 3f |
| GL_C4UB_V2F | F | T | F | | 4 | 2 | GL_UNSIGNED_BYTE | 0 | | c | c+2f |
| GL_C4UB_V3F | F | T | F | | 4 | 3 | GL_UNSIGNED_BYTE | 0 | | c | c+3f |
| GL_C3F_V3F | F | T | F | | 3 | 3 | GL_FLOAT | 0 | | 3f | 6f |
| GL_N3F_V3F | F | F | T | | | 3 | | | 0 | 3f | 6f |
| GL_C4F_N3F_V3F | F | T | T | | 4 | 3 | GL_FLOAT | 0 | 4f | 7f | 10f |
| GL_T2F_V3F | T | F | F | 2 | | 3 | | | | 2f | 5f |
| GL_T4F_V4F | T | F | F | 4 | | 4 | | | | 4f | 8f |
| GL_T2F_C4UB_V3F | T | T | F | 2 | 4 | 3 | GL_UNSIGNED_BYTE | 2f | | c+2f | c+5f |
| GL_T2F_C3F_V3F | T | T | F | 2 | 3 | 3 | GL_FLOAT | 2f | | 5f | 8f |
| GL_T2F_N3F_V3F | T | F | T | 2 | | 3 | | | 2f | 5f | 8f |
| GL_T2F_C4F_N3F_V3F | T | T | T | 2 | 4 | 3 | GL_FLOAT | 2f | 6f | 9f | 12f |
| GL_T4F_C4F_N3F_V4F | T | T | T | 4 | 4 | 4 | GL_FLOAT | 4f | 8f | 11f | 15f |

**Table 2-5**    Variables That Direct glInterleavedArrays()

Start by learning the simpler formats, GL_V2F, GL_V3F, and GL_C3F_V3F. If you use any of the formats with C4UB, you may have to use a struct data type or do some delicate type casting and pointer math to pack four unsigned bytes into a single 32-bit word.

For some OpenGL implementations, use of interleaved arrays may increase application performance. With an interleaved array, the exact layout of your data is known. You know your data is tightly packed and may be accessed in one chunk. If interleaved arrays are not used, the *stride* and size information has to be examined to detect whether data is tightly packed.

**Note:** **glInterleavedArrays()** only enables and disables vertex arrays and specifies values for the vertex-array data. It does not render anything. You must still complete "Step 3: Dereferencing and Rendering" on page 71 and call **glArrayElement()**, **glDrawElements()**, **glDrawRangeElements()**, or **glDrawArrays()** to dereference the pointers and render graphics.

# Buffer Objects

**Advanced**

Advanced

There are many operations in OpenGL where you send a large block of data to OpenGL, such as passing vertex array data for processing. Transferring that data may be as simple as copying from your system's memory down to your graphics card. However, because OpenGL was designed as a client-server model, any time that OpenGL needs data, it will have to be transferred from the client's memory. If that data doesn't change, or if the client and server reside on different computers (distributed rendering), that data transfer may be slow, or redundant.

*Buffer objects* were added to OpenGL version 1.5 to allow an application to explicitly specify which data it would like to be stored in the graphics server. Vertex arrays could be stored in server-side buffer objects starting with OpenGL version 1.5 and are described in "Using Buffer Objects with Vertex-Array Data" on page 88 of this chapter. Support for storing pixel data in buffer objects was added into OpenGL version 2.1 and is described in "Using Buffer Objects with Pixel Rectangle Data" in Chapter 8.

## Creating Buffer Objects

Any nonzero unsigned integer may used as a buffer object identifier. You may either arbitrarily select representative values or let OpenGL allocate and manage those identifiers for you. Why the difference? By allowing OpenGL to allocate identifiers, you are guaranteed to avoid an already used buffer object identifier. This helps to eliminate the risk of modifying data unintentionally.

To have OpenGL allocate buffer objects identifiers, call **glGenBuffers()**.

---

void **glGenBuffers**(GLsizei *n*, GLuint *\*buffers*);

---

Returns *n* currently unused names for buffer objects in the array *buffers*. The names returned in *buffers* do not have to be a contiguous set of integers.

The names returned are marked as used for the purposes of allocating additional buffer objects, but only acquire a valid state once they have been bound.

Zero is a reserved buffer object name and is never returned as a buffer object by **glGenBuffers()**.

You can also determine whether an identifier is a currently used buffer object identifier by calling **glIsBuffer()**.

---

GLboolean **glIsBuffer**(GLuint *buffer*);

---

Returns GL_TRUE if *buffer* is the name of a buffer object that has been bound, but has not been subsequently deleted. Returns GL_FALSE if *buffer* is zero or if *buffer* is a nonzero value that is not the name of a buffer object.

## Making a Buffer Object Active

To make a buffer object active, it needs to be bound. Binding selects which buffer object future operations will affect, either for initializing data or using that buffer for rendering. That is, if you have more than one buffer object in your application, you'll likely call **glBindBuffer()** multiple times: once to initialize the object and its data, and then subsequent times either to select that object for use in rendering or to update its data.

To disable use of buffer objects, call **glBindBuffer()** with zero as the buffer identifier. This switches OpenGL to the default mode of not using buffer objects.

---

void **glBindBuffer**(GLenum *target*, GLuint *buffer*);

Specifies the current active buffer object. *target* must be set to either GL_ARRAY_BUFFER, GL_ELEMENT_ARRAY_BUFFER, GL_PIXEL_PACK_BUFFER, or GL_PIXEL_UNPACK_BUFFER. *buffer* specifies the buffer object to be bound to.

**glBindBuffer()** does three things: 1. When using *buffer* of an unsigned integer other than zero for the first time, a new buffer object is created and assigned that name. 2. When binding to a previously created buffer object, that buffer object becomes the active buffer object. 3. When binding to a *buffer* value of zero, OpenGL stops using buffer objects.

## Allocating and Initializing Buffer Objects with Data

Once you've bound a buffer object, you need to reserve space for storing your data. This is done by calling **glBufferData()**.

---

void **glBufferData**(GLenum *target*, GLsizeiptr *size*, const GLvoid *\*data*, GLenum *usage*);

Allocates *size* storage units (usually bytes) of OpenGL server memory for storing vertex array data or indices. Any previous data associated with the currently bound object will be deleted.

*target* may be either GL_ARRAY_BUFFER for vertex data, GL_ELEMENT_ARRAY_BUFFER for index data, GL_PIXEL_UNPACK_BUFFER for pixel data being passed into OpenGL, or GL_PIXEL_PACK_BUFFER for pixel data being retrieved from OpenGL.

*size* is the amount of storage required for storing the respective data. This value is generally number of elements in the data multiplied by their respective storage size.

*data* is either a pointer to a client memory that is used to initialize the buffer object or NULL. If a valid pointer is passed, *size* units of storage are copied from the client to the server. If NULL is passed, *size* units of storage are reserved for use, but are left uninitialized.

---

*usage* provides a hint as to how the data will be read and written after allocation. Valid values are GL_STREAM_DRAW, GL_STREAM_READ, GL_STREAM_COPY, GL_STATIC_DRAW, GL_STATIC_READ, GL_STATIC_COPY, GL_DYNAMIC_DRAW, GL_DYNAMIC_READ, GL_DYNAMIC_COPY.

**glBufferData()** will return GL_OUT_OF_MEMORY if the requested *size* exceeds what the server is able to allocate, of a GL_INVALID_VALUE if usage is not one of the permitted values.

**glBufferData()** first allocates memory in the OpenGL server for storing your data. If you request too much memory, a GL_OUT_OF_MEMORY error will be set. Once the storage has been reserved, and if the *data* parameter is not NULL, *size* units of storage (usually bytes) are copied from the client's memory into the buffer object. However, if you need to dynamically load the data at some point after the buffer is created, pass NULL in for the *data* pointer. This will reserve the appropriate storage for your data, but leave it uninitialized.

The final parameter to **glBufferData()**, *usage*, is a performance hint to OpenGL. Based upon the value you specify for *usage*, OpenGL may be able to optimize the data for better performance, or it can choose to ignore the hint. There are three operations that can be done to buffer object data:

1. drawing—the client specifies data that is used for rendering.

2. reading—data values are read from an OpenGL buffer (such as the framebuffer) and used in the application in various computations not immediately related to rendering.

3. copying—data values are read from an OpenGL buffer and then used as data for rendering.

Additionally, depending upon how often you intend to update the data, there are various operational hints for describing how often the data will be read or used in rendering:

• stream mode—it's assumed that you'll be updating the data in the buffer object often, but then only using it a few times in drawing or other operations.

• static mode—you specify the data once, but use the values often.

• dynamic mode—you may update the data often and use the data values in the buffer object many times as well.

Possible values for *usage* are described in Table 2-6.

| Parameter | Meaning |
| --- | --- |
| GL_STREAM_DRAW | Data is specified once and used at most a few times as the source of drawing and image specification commands. |
| GL_STREAM_READ | Data is copied once from an OpenGL buffer and is used at most a few times by the application as data values. |
| GL_STREAM_COPY | Data is copied once from an OpenGL buffer and is used at most a few times as the source for drawing or image specification commands. |
| GL_STATIC_DRAW | Data is specified once and used many times as the source of drawing or image specification commands. |
| GL_STATIC_READ | Data is copied once from an OpenGL buffer and is used many times by the application as data values. |
| GL_STATIC_COPY | Data is copied once from an OpenGL buffer and is used many times as the source for drawing or image specification commands. |
| GL_DYNAMIC_DRAW | Data is specified many times and used many times as the source of drawing and image specification commands. |
| GL_DYNAMIC_READ | Data is copied many times from an OpenGL buffer and is used many times by the application as data values. |
| GL_DYNAMIC_COPY | Data is copied many times from an OpenGL buffer and is used many times as the source for drawing or image specification commands. |

**Table 2-6**     Values for *usage* Parameter of glBufferData()

## Updating Data Values in Buffer Objects

There are two methods for updating data stored in a buffer object. The first method assumes that you have data of the same type prepared in a buffer in your application. **glBufferSubData()** will replace some subset of the data in the bound buffer object with the data you provide.

The second method allows you to more selectively update which data values are replaced. **glMapBuffer()** returns a pointer to the buffer object

void **glBufferSubData**(GLenum *target*, GLintptr *offset*, GLsizeiptr *size*,
const GLvoid *\*data*);

Update *size* bytes starting at *offset* (also measured in bytes) in the currently bound buffer object associated with *target* using the data pointed to by *data*. *target* must be either GL_ARRAY_BUFFER, GL_ELEMENT_ARRAY_ BUFFER, GL_PIXEL_UNPACK_BUFFER, or GL_PIXEL_PACK_BUFFER.

**glBufferSubData**() will generate a GL_INVALID_VALUE error if *size* is less than zero or if *size* + *offset* is greater than the original size specified when the buffer object was created.

memory into which you can write new values (or simply read the data, depending upon your choice of memory access permissions), just as if you were assigning values to an array. When you've completed updating the values in the buffer, you call **glUnmapBuffer**() to signify that you've completed updating the data.

GLvoid *\***glMapBuffer**(GLenum *target*, GLenum *access*);

Returns a pointer to the data storage for the currently bound buffer object associated with *target*, which may be either GL_ARRAY_BUFFER, GL_ELEMENT_ARRAY_BUFFER, GL_PIXEL_PACK_BUFFER, or GL_PIXEL_ UNPACK_BUFFER. *access* must be either GL_READ_ONLY, GL_WRITE_ ONLY, or GL_READ_WRITE, indicating the operations that a client may do on the data.

**glMapBuffer**() will return NULL either if the buffer cannot be mapped (setting the OpenGL error state to GL_OUT_OF_MEMORY) or if the buffer was already mapped previously (where the OpenGL error state will be set to GL_INVALID_OPERATION).

When you've completed accessing the storage, you can unmap the buffer by calling **glUnmapBuffer**().

GLboolean **glUnmapBuffer**(GLenum *target*);

Indicates that updates to the currently bound buffer object are complete, and the buffer may be released. *target* must be either GL_ARRAY_BUFFER or GL_ELEMENT_ARRAY_BUFFER.

As a simple example of how you might selectively update elements of your data, we'll use **glMapBuffer()** to obtain a pointer to the data, and update the values as necessary.

```
GLfloat* data;

data = (GLfloat*) glMapBuffer(GL_ARRAY_BUFFER, GL_READ_WRITE);

if (data != (GLfloat*) NULL) {
    for( i = 0; i < 8; ++i )
        data[3*i+2] *= 2.0;   /* Modify Z values */
    glUnmapBuffer(GL_ARRAY_BUFFER);
} else {
    /* Handle not being able to update data */
}
```

## Cleaning Up Buffer Objects

When you're finished with a buffer object, you can release its resources and make its identifier available by calling **glDeleteBuffers()**. Any bindings to currently bound objects that are deleted are reset to zero.

---

void **glDeleteBuffers**(GLsizei *n*, const GLuint *\*buffers*);

Deletes *n* buffer objects, named by elements in the array *buffers*. The freed buffer objects may now be reused (for example, by **glGenBuffers()**).

If a buffer object is deleted while bound, all bindings to that object are reset to the default buffer object, as if **glBindBuffer()** had been called with zero as the specified buffer object. Attempts to delete nonexistent buffer objects or the buffer object named zero are ignored without generating an error.

---

## Using Buffer Objects with Vertex-Array Data

To store your vertex-array data in buffer objects, you will need to add a few steps to your application.

1.  (Optional) Generate buffer object identifiers.

2.  Bind a buffer object, specifying that it will be used for either storing vertex data or indices.

3. Request storage for your data, and optionally initialize those data elements.

4. Specify offsets relative to the start of the buffer object to initialize the vertex-array functions, such as **glVertexPointer()**.

5. Bind the appropriate buffer object to be utilized in rendering.

6. Render using an appropriate vertex-array rendering function, such as **glDrawArrays()** or **glDrawElements()**.

If you need to initialize multiple buffer objects, you will repeat steps 2 through 4 for each buffer object.

Both "formats" of vertex-array data are available for use in buffer objects. As described in "Step 2: Specifying Data for the Arrays," vertex, color, lighting normal, or any other type of associated vertex data can be stored in a buffer object. Additionally, interleaved vertex array data, as described in "Interleaved Arrays," can also be stored in a buffer object. In either case, you would create a single buffer object to hold all of the data to be used as vertex arrays.

As compared to specifying a memory address in the client's memory where OpenGL should access the vertex-array data, you specify the offset in machine units (usually bytes) to the data in the buffer. To help illustrate computing the offset, and to frustrate the purists in the audience, we'll use the following macro to simplify expressing the offset:

```
#define BUFFER_OFFSET(bytes)   ((GLubyte*) NULL + (bytes))
```

For example, if you had floating-point color and position data for each vertex, perhaps represented as the following array

```
GLfloat vertexData[][6] = {
    { R_0, G_0, B_0, X_0, Y_0, Z_0 },
    { R_1, G_1, B_1, X_1, Y_1, Z_1 },
    ...
    { R_n, G_n, B_n, X_n, Y_n, Z_n }
};
```

that were used to initialize the buffer object, you could specify the data as two separate vertex array calls, one for colors and one for vertices:

```
glColorPointer(3, GL_FLOAT, 6*sizeof(GLfloat),BUFFER_OFFSET(0));
glVertexPointer(3, GL_FLOAT, 6*sizeof(GLfloat),
                BUFFER_OFFSET(3*sizeof(GLfloat)));
glEnableClientState(GL_COLOR_ARRAY);
glEnableClientState(GL_VERTEX_ARRAY);
```

Conversely, since the data in *vertexData* matches a format for an interleaved vertex array, you could use **glInterleavedArrays()** for specifying the vertex-array data:

```
glInterleavedArrays(GL_C3F_V3F, 0, BUFFER_OFFSET(0));
```

Putting this all together, Example 2-16 demonstrates how buffer objects of vertex data might be used. The example creates two buffer objects, one containing vertex data and the other containing index data.

**Example 2-16**   Using Buffer Objects with Vertex Data

```
#define VERTICES      0
#define INDICES       1
#define NUM_BUFFERS   2

GLuint  buffers[NUM_BUFFERS];

GLfloat vertices[][3] = {
    { -1.0, -1.0, -1.0 },
    {  1.0, -1.0, -1.0 },
    {  1.0,  1.0, -1.0 },
    { -1.0,  1.0, -1.0 },
    { -1.0, -1.0,  1.0 },
    {  1.0, -1.0,  1.0 },
    {  1.0,  1.0,  1.0 },
    { -1.0,  1.0,  1.0 }
};

GLubyte indices[][4] = {
    { 0, 1, 2, 3 },
    { 4, 7, 6, 5 },
    { 0, 4, 5, 1 },
    { 3, 2, 6, 7 },
    { 0, 3, 7, 4 },
    { 1, 5, 6, 2 }
};

glGenBuffers(NUM_BUFFERS, buffers);

glBindBuffer(GL_ARRAY_BUFFER, buffers[VERTICES]);
glBufferData(GL_ARRAY_BUFFER, sizeof(vertices), vertices,
             GL_STATIC_DRAW);
glVertexPointer(3, GL_FLOAT, 0, BUFFER_OFFSET(0));
glEnableClientState(GL_VERTEX_ARRAY);
```

```
glBindBuffer(GL_ELEMENT_ARRAY_BUFFER, buffers[INDICES]);
glBufferData(GL_ELEMENT_ARRAY_BUFFER, sizeof(indices), indices
         GL_STATIC_DRAW);

glDrawElements(GL_QUADS, 24, GL_UNSIGNED_BYTE,
          BUFFER_OFFSET(0));
```

# Attribute Groups

In "Basic State Management" you saw how to set or query an individual
state or state variable. You can also save and restore the values of a
collection of related state variables with a single command.

OpenGL groups related state variables into an *attribute group*. For example,
the GL_LINE_BIT attribute consists of five state variables: the line width,
the GL_LINE_STIPPLE enable status, the line stipple pattern, the line
stipple repeat counter, and the GL_LINE_SMOOTH enable status. (See
"Antialiasing" in Chapter 6.) With the commands **glPushAttrib()** and
**glPopAttrib()**, you can save and restore all five state variables at once.

Some state variables are in more than one attribute group. For example,
the state variable GL_CULL_FACE is part of both the polygon and the
enable attribute groups.

In OpenGL Version 1.1, there are now two different attribute stacks. In addition to the original attribute stack (which saves the values of server state
variables), there is also a client attribute stack, accessible by the commands
**glPushClientAttrib()** and **glPopClientAttrib()**.

In general, it's faster to use these commands than to get, save, and restore
the values yourself. Some values might be maintained in the hardware, and
getting them might be expensive. Also, if you're operating on a remote
client, all the attribute data has to be transferred across the network connection and back as it is obtained, saved, and restored. However, your OpenGL
implementation keeps the attribute stack on the server, avoiding unnecessary network delays.

There are about 20 different attribute groups, which can be saved and
restored by **glPushAttrib()** and **glPopAttrib()**. There are two client attribute
groups, which can be saved and restored by **glPushClientAttrib()** and
**glPopClientAttrib()**. For both server and client, the attributes are stored on
a stack, which has a depth of at least 16 saved attribute groups. (The actual

stack depths for your implementation can be obtained using GL_MAX_ATTRIB_STACK_DEPTH and GL_MAX_CLIENT_ATTRIB_STACK_DEPTH with **glGetIntegerv()**.) Pushing a full stack or popping an empty one generates an error.

(See the tables in Appendix B to find out exactly which attributes are saved for particular mask values—that is, which attributes are in a particular attribute group.)

void **glPushAttrib**(GLbitfield *mask*);
void **glPopAttrib**(void);

**glPushAttrib()** saves all the attributes indicated by bits in *mask* by pushing them onto the attribute stack. **glPopAttrib()** restores the values of those state variables that were saved with the last **glPushAttrib()**. Table 2-7 lists the possible mask bits that can be logically ORed together to save any combination of attributes. Each bit corresponds to a collection of individual state variables. For example, GL_LIGHTING_BIT refers to all the state variables related to lighting, which include the current material color; the ambient, diffuse, specular, and emitted light; a list of the lights that are enabled; and the directions of the spotlights. When **glPopAttrib()** is called, all these variables are restored.

The special mask GL_ALL_ATTRIB_BITS is used to save and restore all the state variables in all the attribute groups.

| Mask Bit | Attribute Group |
|----------|-----------------|
| GL_ACCUM_BUFFER_BIT | accum-buffer |
| GL_ALL_ATTRIB_BITS | -- |
| GL_COLOR_BUFFER_BIT | color-buffer |
| GL_CURRENT_BIT | current |
| GL_DEPTH_BUFFER_BIT | depth-buffer |
| GL_ENABLE_BIT | enable |
| GL_EVAL_BIT | eval |

**Table 2-7**    Attribute Groups

| Mask Bit | Attribute Group |
|---|---|
| GL_FOG_BIT | fog |
| GL_HINT_BIT | hint |
| GL_LIGHTING_BIT | lighting |
| GL_LINE_BIT | line |
| GL_LIST_BIT | list |
| GL_MULTISAMPLE_BIT | multisample |
| GL_PIXEL_MODE_BIT | pixel |
| GL_POINT_BIT | point |
| GL_POLYGON_BIT | polygon |
| GL_POLYGON_STIPPLE_BIT | polygon-stipple |
| GL_SCISSOR_BIT | scissor |
| GL_STENCIL_BUFFER_BIT | stencil-buffer |
| GL_TEXTURE_BIT | texture |
| GL_TRANSFORM_BIT | transform |
| GL_VIEWPORT_BIT | viewport |

**Table 2-7** **(continued)** Attribute Groups

---

void **glPushClientAttrib**(GLbitfield *mask*);
void **glPopClientAttrib**(void);

**glPushClientAttrib**() saves all the attributes indicated by bits in *mask* by pushing them onto the client attribute stack. **glPopClientAttrib**() restores the values of those state variables that were saved with the last **glPushClientAttrib**(). Table 2-8 lists the possible mask bits that can be logically ORed together to save any combination of client attributes.

Two client attribute groups, feedback and select, cannot be saved or restored with the stack mechanism.

| Mask Bit | Attribute Group |
|---|---|
| GL_CLIENT_PIXEL_STORE_BIT | pixel-store |
| GL_CLIENT_VERTEX_ARRAY_BIT | vertex-array |
| GL_ALL_CLIENT_ATTRIB_BITS | -- |
| can't be pushed or popped | feedback |
| can't be pushed or popped | select |

**Table 2-8**    Client Attribute Groups

# Some Hints for Building Polygonal Models of Surfaces

Following are some techniques that you can use as you build polygonal approximations of surfaces. You might want to review this section after you've read Chapter 5 on lighting and Chapter 7 on display lists. The lighting conditions affect how models look once they're drawn, and some of the following techniques are much more efficient when used in conjunction with display lists. As you read these techniques, keep in mind that when lighting calculations are enabled, normal vectors must be specified to get proper results.

Constructing polygonal approximations to surfaces is an art, and there is no substitute for experience. This section, however, lists a few pointers that might make it a bit easier to get started.

- Keep polygon orientations (windings) consistent. Make sure that when viewed from the outside, all the polygons on the surface are oriented in the same direction (all clockwise or all counterclockwise). Consistent orientation is important for polygon culling and two-sided lighting. Try to get this right the first time, as it's excruciatingly painful to fix the problem later. (If you use **glScale*()** to reflect geometry around some axis of symmetry, you might change the orientation with **glFrontFace()** to keep the orientations consistent.)

- When you subdivide a surface, watch out for any nontriangular polygons. The three vertices of a triangle are guaranteed to lie on a plane; any polygon with four or more vertices might not. Nonplanar polygons can be viewed from some orientation such that the edges cross each other, and OpenGL might not render such polygons correctly.

- There's always a trade-off between the display speed and the quality of the image. If you subdivide a surface into a small number of polygons, it renders quickly but might have a jagged appearance; if you subdivide it into millions of tiny polygons, it probably looks good but might take a long time to render. Ideally, you can provide a parameter to the subdivision routines that indicates how fine a subdivision you want, and if the object is farther from the eye, you can use a coarser subdivision. Also, when you subdivide, use large polygons where the surface is relatively flat, and small polygons in regions of high curvature.

- For high-quality images, it's a good idea to subdivide more on the silhouette edges than in the interior. If the surface is to be rotated relative to the eye, this is tougher to do, as the silhouette edges keep moving. Silhouette edges occur where the normal vectors are perpendicular to the vector from the surface to the viewpoint—that is, when their vector dot product is zero. Your subdivision algorithm might choose to subdivide more if this dot product is near zero.

- Try to avoid T-intersections in your models (see Figure 2-16). As shown, there's no guarantee that the line segments AB and BC lie on exactly the same pixels as the segment AC. Sometimes they do, and sometimes they don't, depending on the transformations and orientation. This can cause cracks to appear intermittently in the surface.

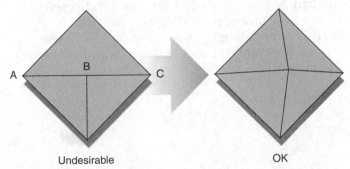

Undesirable        OK

**Figure 2-16**    Modifying an Undesirable T-Intersection

- If you're constructing a closed surface, be sure to use exactly the same numbers for coordinates at the beginning and end of a closed loop, or you can get gaps and cracks due to numerical round-off. Here's an example of bad code for a two-dimensional circle:

```
/* don't use this code */
#define PI 3.14159265
#define EDGES 30


/* draw a circle */
glBegin(GL_LINE_STRIP);
for (i = 0; i <= EDGES; i++)
    glVertex2f(cos((2*PI*i)/EDGES), sin((2*PI*i)/EDGES));
glEnd();
```

The edges meet exactly only if your machine manages to calculate exactly the same values for the sine and cosine of 0 and of (2*PI*EDGES/EDGES). If you trust the floating-point unit on your machine to do this right, the authors have a bridge they'd like to sell you... To correct the code, make sure that when $i$ == EDGES, you use 0 for the sine and cosine, not 2*PI*EDGES/EDGES. (Or simpler still, use GL_LINE_LOOP instead of GL_LINE_STRIP, and change the loop termination condition to $i$ < EDGES.)

## An Example: Building an Icosahedron

To illustrate some of the considerations that arise in approximating a surface, let's look at some example code sequences. This code concerns the vertices of a regular icosahedron (which is a Platonic solid composed of 20 faces that span 12 vertices, the face of each being an equilateral triangle). An icosahedron can be considered a rough approximation of a sphere. Example 2-17 defines the vertices and triangles making up an icosahedron and then draws the icosahedron.

**Example 2-17**   Drawing an Icosahedron

```
#define X .525731112119133606
#define Z .850650808352039932

static GLfloat vdata[12][3] = {
    {-X, 0.0, Z}, {X, 0.0, Z}, {-X, 0.0, -Z}, {X, 0.0, -Z},
    {0.0, Z, X}, {0.0, Z, -X}, {0.0, -Z, X}, {0.0, -Z, -X},
    {Z, X, 0.0}, {-Z, X, 0.0}, {Z, -X, 0.0}, {-Z, -X, 0.0}
};
```

```
static GLuint tindices[20][3] = {
   {1,4,0}, {4,9,0}, {4,5,9}, {8,5,4}, {1,8,4},
   {1,10,8}, {10,3,8}, {8,3,5}, {3,2,5}, {3,7,2},
   {3,10,7}, {10,6,7}, {6,11,7}, {6,0,11}, {6,1,0},
   {10,1,6}, {11,0,9}, {2,11,9}, {5,2,9}, {11,2,7}
};

int i;

glBegin(GL_TRIANGLES);
for (i = 0; i < 20; i++) {
   /* color information here */
   glVertex3fv(&vdata[tindices[i][0]][0]);
   glVertex3fv(&vdata[tindices[i][1]][0]);
   glVertex3fv(&vdata[tindices[i][2]][0]);
}
glEnd();
```

The strange numbers $X$ and $Z$ are chosen so that the distance from the origin to any of the vertices of the icosahedron is 1.0. The coordinates of the 12 vertices are given in the array *vdata[][]*, where the zeroth vertex is {−X, 0.0, Z}, the first is {X, 0.0, Z}, and so on. The array *tindices[][]* tells how to link the vertices to make triangles. For example, the first triangle is made from the zeroth, fourth, and first vertices. If you take the vertices for triangles in the order given, all the triangles have the same orientation.

The line that mentions color information should be replaced by a command that sets the color of the *i*th face. If no code appears here, all faces are drawn in the same color, and it will be impossible to discern the three-dimensional quality of the object. An alternative to explicitly specifying colors is to define surface normals and use lighting, as described in the next subsection.

**Note:**  In all the examples described in this section, unless the surface is to be drawn only once, you should probably save the calculated vertex and normal coordinates so that the calculations don't need to be repeated each time the surface is drawn. This can be done using your own data structures or by constructing display lists (see Chapter 7).

### Calculating Normal Vectors for a Surface

If a surface is to be lit, you need to supply the vector normal to the surface. Calculating the normalized cross product of two vectors on that surface provides their normal vector. With the flat surfaces of an icosahedron, all three vertices defining a surface have the same normal vector. In this case,

the normal needs to be specified only once for each set of three vertices. The
code in Example 2-18 can replace the "color information here" line in
Example 2-17 for drawing the icosahedron.

**Example 2-18**   Generating Normal Vectors for a Surface

```
GLfloat d1[3], d2[3], norm[3];
for (j = 0; j < 3; j++) {
   d1[j] = vdata[tindices[i][0]][j] - vdata[tindices[i][1]][j];
   d2[j] = vdata[tindices[i][1]][j] - vdata[tindices[i][2]][j];
}
normcrossprod(d1, d2, norm);
glNormal3fv(norm);
```

The function **normcrossprod**() produces the normalized cross product of
two vectors, as shown in Example 2-19.

**Example 2-19**   Calculating the Normalized Cross Product of Two Vectors

```
void normalize(float v[3])
{
   GLfloat d = sqrt(v[0]*v[0]+v[1]*v[1]+v[2]*v[2]);
   if (d == 0.0) {
      error("zero length vector");
      return;
   }
   v[0] /= d;
   v[1] /= d;
   v[2] /= d;
}

void normcrossprod(float v1[3], float v2[3], float out[3])
{
   out[0] = v1[1]*v2[2] - v1[2]*v2[1];
   out[1] = v1[2]*v2[0] - v1[0]*v2[2];
   out[2] = v1[0]*v2[1] - v1[1]*v2[0];
   normalize(out);
}
```

If you're using an icosahedron as an approximation for a shaded sphere,
you'll want to use normal vectors that are perpendicular to the true surface
of the sphere, rather than perpendicular to the faces. For a sphere, the normal vectors are simple; each points in the same direction as the vector from

the origin to the corresponding vertex. Since the icosahedron vertex data is for an icosahedron of radius 1, the normal data and vertex data are identical. Here is the code that would draw an icosahedral approximation of a smoothly shaded sphere (assuming that lighting is enabled, as described in Chapter 5):

```
glBegin(GL_TRIANGLES);
for (i = 0; i < 20; i++) {
     glNormal3fv(&vdata[tindices[i][0]][0]);
     glVertex3fv(&vdata[tindices[i][0]][0]);
     glNormal3fv(&vdata[tindices[i][1]][0]);
     glVertex3fv(&vdata[tindices[i][1]][0]);
     glNormal3fv(&vdata[tindices[i][2]][0]);
     glVertex3fv(&vdata[tindices[i][2]][0]);
}
glEnd();
```

## Improving the Model

A 20-sided approximation to a sphere doesn't look good unless the image of the sphere on the screen is quite small, but there's an easy way to increase the accuracy of the approximation. Imagine the icosahedron inscribed in a sphere, and subdivide the triangles as shown in Figure 2-17. The newly introduced vertices lie slightly inside the sphere, so push them to the surface by normalizing them (dividing them by a factor to make them have length 1). This subdivision process can be repeated for arbitrary accuracy. The three objects shown in Figure 2-17 use 20, 80, and 320 approximating triangles, respectively.

**Figure 2-17**      Subdividing to Improve a Polygonal Approximation to a Surface

Example 2-20 performs a single subdivision, creating an 80-sided spherical approximation.

**Example 2-20**  Single Subdivision

```
void drawtriangle(float *v1, float *v2, float *v3)
{
   glBegin(GL_TRIANGLES);
      glNormal3fv(v1);
      glVertex3fv(v1);
      glNormal3fv(v2);
      glVertex3fv(v2);
      glNormal3fv(v3);
      glVertex3fv(v3);
   glEnd();
}



void subdivide(float *v1, float *v2, float *v3)
{
   GLfloat v12[3], v23[3], v31[3];
   GLint i;

   for (i = 0; i < 3; i++) {
      v12[i] = (v1[i]+v2[i])/2.0;
      v23[i] = (v2[i]+v3[i])/2.0;
      v31[i] = (v3[i]+v1[i])/2.0;
   }
   normalize(v12);
   normalize(v23);
   normalize(v31);
   drawtriangle(v1, v12, v31);
   drawtriangle(v2, v23, v12);
   drawtriangle(v3, v31, v23);
   drawtriangle(v12, v23, v31);
}

for (i = 0; i < 20; i++) {
   subdivide(&vdata[tindices[i][0]][0],
             &vdata[tindices[i][1]][0],
             &vdata[tindices[i][2]][0]);
}
```

Example 2-21 is a slight modification of Example 2-20 that recursively sub-divides the triangles to the proper depth. If the depth value is 0, no sub-divisions are performed, and the triangle is drawn as is. If the depth is 1, a single subdivision is performed, and so on.

**Example 2-21**   Recursive Subdivision

```
void subdivide(float *v1, float *v2, float *v3, long depth)
{
    GLfloat v12[3], v23[3], v31[3];
    GLint i;

    if (depth == 0) {
        drawtriangle(v1, v2, v3);
        return;
    }
    for (i = 0; i < 3; i++) {
        v12[i] = (v1[i]+v2[i])/2.0;
        v23[i] = (v2[i]+v3[i])/2.0;
        v31[i] = (v3[i]+v1[i])/2.0;
    }
    normalize(v12);
    normalize(v23);
    normalize(v31);
    subdivide(v1, v12, v31, depth-1);
    subdivide(v2, v23, v12, depth-1);
    subdivide(v3, v31, v23, depth-1);
    subdivide(v12, v23, v31, depth-1);
}
```

## Generalized Subdivision

A recursive subdivision technique such as the one described in Example 2-21 can be used for other types of surfaces. Typically, the recursion ends if either a certain depth is reached or some condition on the curvature is satisfied (highly curved parts of surfaces look better with more subdivision).

To look at a more general solution to the problem of subdivision, consider an arbitrary surface parameterized by two variables, *u[0]* and *u[1]*. Suppose that two routines are provided:

```
void surf(GLfloat u[2], GLfloat vertex[3], GLfloat normal[3]);
float curv(GLfloat u[2]);
```

If *u[]* is passed to **surf()**, the corresponding three-dimensional vertex and normal vectors (of length 1) are returned. If *u[]* is passed to **curv()**, the curvature of the surface at that point is calculated and returned. (See an introductory textbook on differential geometry for more information about measuring surface curvature.)

Example 2-22 shows the recursive routine that subdivides a triangle until either the maximum depth is reached or the maximum curvature at the three vertices is less than some cutoff.

**Example 2-22**   Generalized Subdivision

```
void subdivide(float u1[2], float u2[2], float u3[2],
               float cutoff, long depth)
{
   GLfloat v1[3], v2[3], v3[3], n1[3], n2[3], n3[3];
   GLfloat u12[2], u23[2], u32[2];
   GLint i;

   if (depth == maxdepth || (curv(u1) < cutoff &&
       curv(u2) < cutoff && curv(u3) < cutoff)) {
      surf(u1, v1, n1);
      surf(u2, v2, n2);
      surf(u3, v3, n3);
      glBegin(GL_POLYGON);
         glNormal3fv(n1); glVertex3fv(v1);
         glNormal3fv(n2); glVertex3fv(v2);
         glNormal3fv(n3); glVertex3fv(v3);
      glEnd();
      return;
   }

   for (i = 0; i < 2; i++) {
      u12[i] = (u1[i] + u2[i])/2.0;
      u23[i] = (u2[i] + u3[i])/2.0;
      u31[i] = (u3[i] + u1[i])/2.0;
   }
   subdivide(u1, u12, u31, cutoff, depth+1);
   subdivide(u2, u23, u12, cutoff, depth+1);
   subdivide(u3, u31, u23, cutoff, depth+1);
   subdivide(u12, u23, u31, cutoff, depth+1);
}
```

*Chapter 3*

# Viewing

**Chapter Objectives**

After reading this chapter, you'll be able to do the following:

- View a *geometric model* in any orientation by transforming it in three-dimensional space

- Control the location in three-dimensional space from which the model is viewed

- Clip undesired portions of the model out of the scene that's to be viewed

- Manipulate the appropriate matrix stacks that control model transformation for viewing, and project the model onto the screen

- Combine multiple transformations to mimic sophisticated systems in motion, such as a solar system or an articulated robot arm

- Reverse or mimic the operations of the geometric processing pipeline

Chapter 2 explained how to instruct OpenGL to draw the geometric models you want displayed in your scene. Now you must decide how you want to position the models in the scene, and you must choose a vantage point from which to view the scene. You can use the default positioning and vantage point, but most likely you want to specify them.

Look at the image on the cover of this book. The program that produced that image contained a single geometric description of a building block. Each block was carefully positioned in the scene: some blocks were scattered on the floor, some were stacked on top of each other on the table, and some were assembled to make the globe. Also, a particular viewpoint had to be chosen. Obviously, we wanted to look at the corner of the room containing the globe. But how far away from the scene—and where exactly—should the viewer be? We wanted to make sure that the final image of the scene contained a good view out the window, that a portion of the floor was visible, and that all the objects in the scene were not only visible but presented in an interesting arrangement. This chapter explains how to use OpenGL to accomplish these tasks: how to position and orient models in three-dimensional space and how to establish the location—also in three-dimensional space—of the viewpoint. All of these factors help determine exactly what image appears on the screen.

You want to remember that the point of computer graphics is to create a two-dimensional image of three-dimensional objects (it has to be two-dimensional because it's drawn on a flat screen), but you need to think in three-dimensional coordinates while making many of the decisions that determine what is drawn on the screen. A common mistake people make when creating three-dimensional graphics is to start thinking too soon that the final image appears on a flat, two-dimensional screen. Avoid thinking about which pixels need to be drawn, and instead try to visualize three-dimensional space. Create your models in some three-dimensional universe that lies deep inside your computer, and let the computer do its job of calculating which pixels to color.

A series of three computer operations converts an object's three-dimensional coordinates to pixel positions on the screen:

- Transformations, which are represented by matrix multiplication, include modeling, viewing, and projection operations. Such operations include rotation, translation, scaling, reflecting, orthographic projection, and perspective projection. Generally, you use a combination of several transformations to draw a scene.

- Since the scene is rendered on a rectangular window, objects (or parts of objects) that lie outside the window must be clipped. In three-dimensional computer graphics, clipping occurs by throwing out objects on one side of a clipping plane.

- Finally, a correspondence must be established between the transformed coordinates and screen pixels. This is known as a *viewport* transformation.

This chapter describes all of these operations, and how to control them, in the following major sections:

- "Overview: The Camera Analogy" gives an overview of the transformation process by describing the analogy of taking a photograph with a camera, presents a simple example program that transforms an object, and briefly describes the basic OpenGL transformation commands.

- "Viewing and Modeling Transformations" explains in detail how to specify and imagine the effect of viewing and modeling transformations. These transformations orient the model and the camera relative to each other to obtain the desired final image.

- "Projection Transformations" describes how to specify the shape and orientation of the *viewing volume*. The viewing volume determines how a scene is projected onto the screen (with a perspective or orthographic projection) and which objects or parts of objects are clipped out of the scene.

- "Viewport Transformation" explains how to control the conversion of three-dimensional model coordinates to screen coordinates.

- "Troubleshooting Transformations" presents some tips for discovering why you might not be getting the desired effect from your modeling, viewing, projection, and viewport transformations.

- "Manipulating the Matrix Stacks" discusses how to save and restore certain transformations. This is particularly useful when you're drawing complicated objects that are built from simpler ones.

- "Additional Clipping Planes" describes how to specify additional clipping planes beyond those defined by the viewing volume.

- "Examples of Composing Several Transformations" walks you through a couple of more complicated uses for transformations.

- "Reversing or Mimicking Transformations" shows you how to take a transformed point in window coordinates and reverse the transformation to obtain its original object coordinates. The transformation itself (without reversal) can also be emulated.

In Version 1.3, new OpenGL functions were added to directly support row-major (in OpenGL terms, transposed) matrices.

## Overview: The Camera Analogy

The transformation process used to produce the desired scene for viewing is analogous to taking a photograph with a camera. As shown in Figure 3-1, the steps with a camera (or a computer) might be the following:

1. Set up your tripod and point the camera at the scene (viewing transformation).

2. Arrange the scene to be photographed into the desired composition (modeling transformation).

3. Choose a camera lens or adjust the zoom (projection transformation).

4. Determine how large you want the final photograph to be—for example, you might want it enlarged (viewport transformation).

After these steps have been performed, the picture can be snapped or the scene can be drawn.

Note that these steps correspond to the order in which you specify the desired transformations in your program, not necessarily the order in which the relevant mathematical operations are performed on an object's vertices. The viewing transformations must precede the modeling transformations in your code, but you can specify the projection and viewport transformations at any point before drawing occurs. Figure 3-2 shows the order in which these operations occur on your computer.

With a camera

With a computer

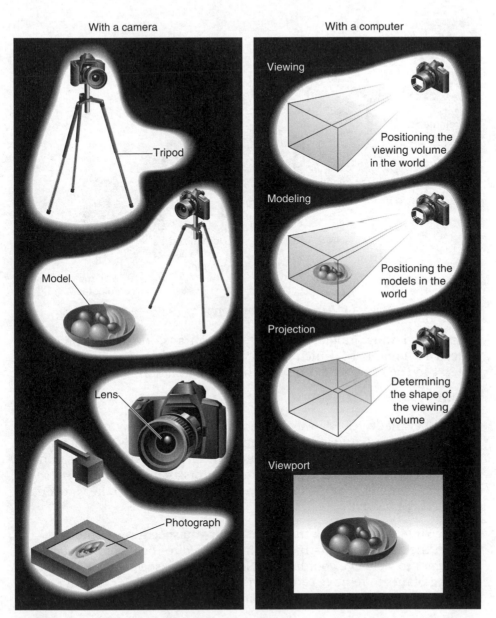

Tripod

Model

Lens

Photograph

Viewing

Positioning the viewing volume in the world

Modeling

Positioning the models in the world

Projection

Determining the shape of the viewing volume

Viewport

**Figure 3-1**    The Camera Analogy

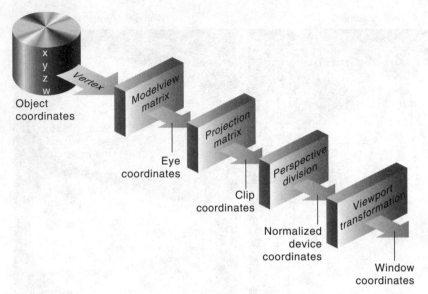

**Figure 3-2**    Stages of Vertex Transformation

To specify viewing, modeling, and projection transformations, you construct a $4 \times 4$ matrix **M**, which is then multiplied by the coordinates of each vertex $v$ in the scene to accomplish the transformation:

$$v' = \mathbf{M}v$$

(Remember that vertices always have four coordinates $(x, y, z, w)$, although in most cases $w$ is 1, and for two-dimensional data, $z$ is 0.) Note that viewing and modeling transformations are automatically applied to surface normal vectors, in addition to vertices. (Normal vectors are used only in *eye coordinates*.) This ensures that the normal vector's relationship to the vertex data is properly preserved.

The viewing and modeling transformations you specify are combined to form the modelview matrix, which is applied to the incoming *object coordinates* to yield eye coordinates. Next, if you've specified additional clipping planes to remove certain objects from the scene or to provide cutaway views of objects, these clipping planes are applied.

After that, OpenGL applies the projection matrix to yield *clip coordinates*. This transformation defines a viewing volume; objects outside this volume are clipped so that they're not drawn in the final scene. After this point, the *perspective division* is performed by dividing coordinate values by $w$, to produce *normalized device coordinates*. (See Appendix F for more information about the meaning of the *w*-coordinate and how it affects matrix transformations.) Finally, the transformed coordinates are converted to *window coordinates* by applying the viewport transformation. You can manipulate the dimensions of the viewport to cause the final image to be enlarged, shrunk, or stretched.

You might correctly suppose that the *x*- and *y*-coordinates are sufficient to determine which pixels need to be drawn on the screen. However, all the transformations are performed on the *z*-coordinates as well. This way, at the end of this transformation process, the *z*-values correctly reflect the depth of a given vertex (measured in distance away from the screen). One use for this depth value is to eliminate unnecessary drawing. For example, suppose two vertices have the same *x*- and *y*-values but different *z*-values. OpenGL can use this information to determine which surfaces are obscured by other surfaces and can then avoid drawing the hidden surfaces. (See Chapter 5 and Chapter 10 for more information about this technique, which is called *hidden-surface removal*.)

As you've probably guessed by now, you need to know a few things about matrix mathematics to get the most out of this chapter. If you want to brush up on your knowledge in this area, you might consult a textbook on linear algebra.

## A Simple Example: Drawing a Cube

Example 3-1 draws a cube that's scaled by a modeling transformation (see Figure 3-3). The viewing transformation, **gluLookAt()**, positions and aims the camera toward where the cube is drawn. A projection transformation and a viewport transformation are also specified. The rest of this section walks you through Example 3-1 and briefly explains the transformation commands it uses. The succeeding sections contain a complete, detailed discussion of all OpenGL transformation commands.

**Figure 3-3**    Transformed Cube

**Example 3-1**   Transformed Cube: cube.c

```c
void init(void)
{
    glClearColor(0.0, 0.0, 0.0, 0.0);
    glShadeModel(GL_FLAT);
}

void display(void)
{
    glClear(GL_COLOR_BUFFER_BIT);
    glColor3f(1.0, 1.0, 1.0);
    glLoadIdentity();             /* clear the matrix */
          /* viewing transformation  */
    gluLookAt(0.0, 0.0, 5.0, 0.0, 0.0, 0.0, 0.0, 1.0, 0.0);
    glScalef(1.0, 2.0, 1.0);      /* modeling transformation */
    glutWireCube(1.0);
    glFlush();
}

void reshape(int w, int h)
{
    glViewport(0, 0, (GLsizei) w, (GLsizei) h);
    glMatrixMode(GL_PROJECTION);
    glLoadIdentity();
    glFrustum(-1.0, 1.0, -1.0, 1.0, 1.5, 20.0);
    glMatrixMode(GL_MODELVIEW);
}

int main(int argc, char** argv)
{
    glutInit(&argc, argv);
    glutInitDisplayMode(GLUT_SINGLE | GLUT_RGB);
    glutInitWindowSize(500, 500);
    glutInitWindowPosition(100, 100);
    glutCreateWindow(argv[0]);
    init();
    glutDisplayFunc(display);
    glutReshapeFunc(reshape);
    glutMainLoop();
    return 0;
}
```

## The Viewing Transformation

Recall that the viewing transformation is analogous to positioning and
aiming a camera. In this code example, before the viewing transformation

can be specified, the *current matrix* is set to the identity matrix with **glLoadIdentity()**. This step is necessary since most of the transformation commands multiply the current matrix by the specified matrix and then set the result to be the current matrix. If you don't clear the current matrix by loading it with the identity matrix, you continue to combine previous transformation matrices with the new one you supply. In some cases, you do want to perform such combinations, but you also need to clear the matrix sometimes.

In Example 3-1, after the matrix is initialized, the viewing transformation is specified with **gluLookAt()**. The arguments for this command indicate where the camera (or eye position) is placed, where it is aimed, and which way is up. The arguments used here place the camera at (0, 0, 5), aim the camera lens toward (0, 0, 0), and specify the *up-vector* as (0, 1, 0). The up-vector defines a unique orientation for the camera.

If **gluLookAt()** was not called, the camera has a default position and orientation. By default, the camera is situated at the origin, points down the negative z-axis, and has an up-vector of (0, 1, 0). Therefore, in Example 3-1, the overall effect is that **gluLookAt()** moves the camera five units along the z-axis. (See "Viewing and Modeling Transformations" on page 117 for more information about viewing transformations.)

### The Modeling Transformation

You use the modeling transformation to position and orient the model. For example, you can rotate, translate, or scale the model—or perform some combination of these operations. In Example 3-1, **glScalef()** is the modeling transformation that is used. The arguments for this command specify how scaling should occur along the three axes. If all the arguments are 1.0, this command has no effect. In Example 3-1, the cube is drawn twice as large in the y-direction. Thus, if one corner of the cube had originally been at (3.0, 3.0, 3.0), that corner would wind up being drawn at (3.0, 6.0, 3.0). The effect of this modeling transformation is to transform the cube so that it isn't a cube but a rectangular box.

### Try This

Try This

Change the **gluLookAt()** call in Example 3-1 to the modeling transformation **glTranslatef()** with parameters (0.0, 0.0, –5.0). The result should look exactly the same as when you used **gluLookAt()**. Why are the effects of these two commands similar?

Note that instead of moving the camera (with a viewing transformation) so that the cube could be viewed, you could have moved the cube away from the camera (with a modeling transformation). This duality in the nature of viewing and modeling transformations is why you need to think about the effects of both types of transformations simultaneously. It doesn't make sense to try to separate the effects, but sometimes it's easier to think about them in one way more than in the other. This is also why modeling and viewing transformations are combined into the *modelview matrix* before the transformations are applied. (See "Viewing and Modeling Transformations" on page 117 for more information about on how to think about modeling and viewing transformations and how to specify them to get the results you want.)

Also note that the modeling and viewing transformations are included in the **display()** routine, along with the call that's used to draw the cube, **glutWireCube()**. In this way, **display()** can be used repeatedly to draw the contents of the window if, for example, the window is moved or uncovered, and you've ensured that the cube is drawn in the desired way each time, with the appropriate transformations. The potential repeated use of **display()** underscores the need to load the identity matrix before performing the viewing and modeling transformations, especially when other transformations might be performed between calls to **display()**.

### The Projection Transformation

Specifying the projection transformation is like choosing a lens for a camera. You can think of this transformation as determining what the field of view or viewing volume is and therefore what objects are inside it and to some extent how they look. This is equivalent to choosing among wide-angle, normal, and telephoto lenses, for example. With a wide-angle lens, you can include a wider scene in the final photograph than you can with a telephoto lens, but a telephoto lens allows you to photograph objects as though they're closer to you than they actually are. In computer graphics, you don't have to pay $10,000 for a 2,000-millimeter telephoto lens; once you've bought your graphics workstation, all you need to do is use a smaller number for your field of view.

In addition to the field-of-view considerations, the projection transformation determines how objects are *projected* onto the screen, as the term suggests. Two basic types of projections are provided for you by OpenGL, along with several corresponding commands for describing the relevant parameters in different ways. One type is the *perspective* projection, which matches how you see things in daily life. Perspective makes objects that are farther away appear smaller; for example, it makes railroad tracks appear to converge in the distance. If you're trying to make realistic pictures, you'll want to choose perspective projection, which is specified with the **glFrustum()** command in Example 3-1.

The other type of projection is *orthographic*, which maps objects directly onto the screen without affecting their relative sizes. Orthographic projection is used in architectural and computer-aided design applications where the final image needs to reflect the measurements of objects, rather than how they might look. Architects create perspective drawings to show how particular buildings or interior spaces look when viewed from various vantage points; the need for orthographic projection arises when blueprint plans or elevations, which are used in the construction of buildings, are generated. (See "Projection Transformations" on page 133 for a discussion of ways to specify both kinds of projection transformations.)

Before **glFrustum()** can be called to set the projection transformation, some preparation is needed. As shown in the **reshape()** routine in Example 3-1, the command called **glMatrixMode()** is used first, with the argument GL_PROJECTION. This indicates that the current matrix specifies the projection transformation and that subsequent transformation calls affect the *projection matrix*. As you can see, a few lines later, **glMatrixMode()** is called again, this time with GL_MODELVIEW as the argument. This indicates that succeeding transformations now affect the modelview matrix instead of the projection matrix. (See "Manipulating the Matrix Stacks" on page 145 for more information about how to control the projection and modelview matrices.)

Note that **glLoadIdentity()** is used to initialize the current projection matrix so that only the specified projection transformation has an effect. Now **glFrustum()** can be called, with arguments that define the parameters of the projection transformation. In this example, both the projection transformation and the viewport transformation are contained in the **reshape()** routine, which is called when the window is first created and whenever the window is moved or reshaped. This makes sense, because both projecting (the width-to-height aspect ratio of the projection viewing volume) and applying the viewport relate directly to the screen, and specifically to the size or aspect ratio of the window on the screen.

**Try This**

Try This

Change the **glFrustum()** call in Example 3-1 to the more commonly used Utility Library routine **gluPerspective()**, with parameters (60.0, 1.0, 1.5, 20.0). Then experiment with different values, especially for *fovy* and *aspect*.

### The Viewport Transformation

Together, the projection transformation and the viewport transformation determine how a scene is mapped onto the computer screen. The projection transformation specifies the mechanics of how the mapping should occur, and the viewport indicates the shape of the available screen area into which the scene is mapped. Since the viewport specifies the region the image occupies on the computer screen, you can think of the viewport transformation as defining the size and location of the final processed photograph—for example, whether the photograph should be enlarged or shrunk.

The arguments for **glViewport**() describe the origin of the available screen space within the window—(0, 0) in this example—and the width and height of the available screen area, all measured in pixels on the screen. This is why this command needs to be called within **reshape**(): if the window changes size, the viewport needs to change accordingly. Note that the width and height are specified using the actual width and height of the window; often, you want to specify the viewport in this way, rather than give an absolute size. (See "Viewport Transformation" on page 138 for more information about how to define the viewport.)

### Drawing the Scene

Once all the necessary transformations have been specified, you can draw the scene (that is, take the photograph). As the scene is drawn, OpenGL transforms each vertex of every object in the scene by the modeling and viewing transformations. Each vertex is then transformed as specified by the projection transformation and clipped if it lies outside the viewing volume described by the projection transformation. Finally, the remaining transformed vertices are divided by $w$ and mapped onto the viewport.

## General-Purpose Transformation Commands

This section discusses some OpenGL commands that you might find useful as you specify desired transformations. You've already seen two of these commands: **glMatrixMode**() and **glLoadIdentity**(). Four commands described here—**glLoadMatrix\***(), **glLoadTransposeMatrix\***(), **glMultMatrix\***(), and **glMultTransposeMatrix\***()—allow you to specify any transformation matrix directly or to multiply the current matrix by that specified matrix. More specific transformation commands—such as **gluLookAt**() and **glScale\***()—are described in later sections.

As described in the preceding section, you need to state whether you want to modify the modelview or projection matrix before supplying a transformation command. You choose the matrix with **glMatrixMode()**. When you use nested sets of OpenGL commands that might be called repeatedly, remember to reset the matrix mode correctly. (The **glMatrixMode()** command can also be used to indicate the *texture matrix*; texturing is discussed in detail in "The Texture Matrix Stack" in Chapter 9.)

---

void **glMatrixMode**(GLenum *mode*);

---

Specifies whether the modelview, projection, or texture matrix will be modified, using the argument GL_MODELVIEW, GL_PROJECTION, or GL_TEXTURE for *mode*. Subsequent transformation commands affect the specified matrix. Note that only one matrix can be modified at a time. By default, the modelview matrix is the one that's modifiable, and all three matrices contain the identity matrix.

You use the **glLoadIdentity()** command to clear the currently modifiable matrix for future transformation commands, as these commands modify the current matrix. Typically, you always call this command before specifying projection or viewing transformations, but you might also call it before specifying a modeling transformation.

---

void **glLoadIdentity**(void);

---

Sets the currently modifiable matrix to the $4 \times 4$ identity matrix.

If you want to specify explicitly a particular matrix to be loaded as the current matrix, use **glLoadMatrix*()** or **glLoadTransposeMatrix*()**. Similarly, use **glMultMatrix*()** or **glMultTransposeMatrix*()** to multiply the current matrix by the matrix passed in as an argument.

---

void **glLoadMatrix**{fd}(const *TYPE* *m*);

---

Sets the 16 values of the current matrix to those specified by *m*.

---

void **glMultMatrix**{fd}(const *TYPE* *m*);

---

Multiplies the matrix specified by the 16 values pointed to by *m* by the current matrix and stores the result as the current matrix.

All matrix multiplication with OpenGL occurs as follows. Suppose the current matrix is **C** and the matrix specified with **glMultMatrix\*()** or any of the transformation commands is **M**. After multiplication, the final matrix is always **CM**. Since matrix multiplication isn't generally commutative, the order makes a difference.

The argument for **glLoadMatrix\*()** and **glMultMatrix\*()** is a vector of 16 values ($m_1$, $m_2$, ... , $m_{16}$) that specifies a matrix **M** stored in column-major order as follows:

$$M = \begin{bmatrix} m_1 & m_5 & m_9 & m_{13} \\ m_2 & m_6 & m_{10} & m_{14} \\ m_3 & m_7 & m_{11} & m_{15} \\ m_4 & m_8 & m_{12} & m_{16} \end{bmatrix}$$

If you're programming in C and you declare a matrix as *m*[4][4], then the element *m[i][j]* is in the *i*th column and *j*th row of the common OpenGL transformation matrix. This is the reverse of the standard C convention in which *m[i][j]* is in row *i* and column *j*. One way to avoid confusion between the column and row is to declare your matrices as *m*[16].

Another way to avoid possible confusion is to call the OpenGL routines **glLoadTransposeMatrix\*()** and **glMultTransposeMatrix\*()**, which use row-major (the standard C convention) matrices as arguments.

---

void **glLoadTransposeMatrix**{fd}(const *TYPE* \**m*);

Sets the 16 values of the current matrix to those specified by *m*, whose values are stored in row-major order. **glLoadTransposeMatrix\*(***m***)** has the same effect as **glLoadMatrix\*(***m^T***)**.

---

void **glMultTransposeMatrix**{fd}(const *TYPE* \**m*);

Multiplies the matrix specified by the 16 values pointed to by *m* by the current matrix and stores the result as the current matrix. **glMultTransposeMatrix\*(***m***)** has the same effect as **glMultMatrix\*(***m^T***)**.

---

You might be able to maximize efficiency by using display lists to store frequently used matrices (and their inverses), rather than recomputing them.

(See "Display List Design Philosophy" in Chapter 7.) OpenGL implementations often must compute the inverse of the modelview matrix so that normals and clipping planes can be correctly transformed to eye coordinates.

## Viewing and Modeling Transformations

Viewing and modeling transformations are inextricably related in OpenGL and are in fact combined into a single modelview matrix. (See "A Simple Example: Drawing a Cube" on page 109.) One of the toughest problems newcomers to computer graphics face is understanding the effects of combined three-dimensional transformations. As you've already seen, there are alternative ways to think about transformations—do you want to move the camera in one direction or move the object in the opposite direction? Each way of thinking about transformations has advantages and disadvantages, but in some cases one way more naturally matches the effect of the intended transformation. If you can find a natural approach for your particular application, it's easier to visualize the necessary transformations and then write the corresponding code to specify the matrix manipulations. The first part of this section discusses how to think about transformations; later, specific commands are presented. For now, we use only the matrix-manipulation commands you've already seen. Finally, keep in mind that you must call **glMatrixMode()** with GL_MODELVIEW as its argument prior to performing modeling or viewing transformations.

### Thinking about Transformations

Let's start with a simple case of two transformations: a 45-degree counterclockwise rotation about the origin around the z-axis and a translation down the x-axis. Suppose that the object you're drawing is small compared with the translation (so that you can see the effect of the translation) and that it's originally located at the origin. If you rotate the object first and then translate it, the rotated object appears on the x-axis. If you translate it down the x-axis first, however, and then rotate about the origin, the object is on the line $y = x$, as shown in Figure 3-4. In general, the order of transformations is critical. If you do transformation A and then transformation B, you almost always get something different than if you do them in the opposite order.

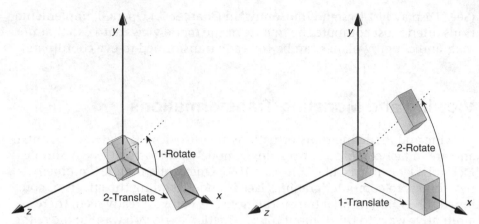

**Figure 3-4**  Rotating First or Translating First

Now let's talk about the order in which you specify a series of transformations. All viewing and modeling transformations are represented as $4 \times 4$ matrices. Each successive **glMultMatrix\*()** or transformation command multiplies a new $4 \times 4$ matrix **M** by the current modelview matrix **C** to yield **CM**. Finally, vertices *v* are multiplied by the current modelview matrix. This process means that the last transformation command called in your program is actually the first one applied to the vertices: **CMv**. Thus, one way of looking at it is to say that you have to specify the matrices in the reverse order. Like many other things, however, once you've gotten used to thinking about this correctly, backward will seem like forward.

Consider the following code sequence, which draws a single point using three transformations:

```
glMatrixMode(GL_MODELVIEW);
glLoadIdentity();
glMultMatrixf(N);                    /* apply transformation N */
glMultMatrixf(M);                    /* apply transformation M */
glMultMatrixf(L);                    /* apply transformation L */
glBegin(GL_POINTS);
glVertex3f(v);                       /* draw transformed vertex v */
glEnd();
```

With this code, the modelview matrix successively contains **I**, **N**, **NM**, and finally **NML**, where **I** represents the identity matrix. The transformed vertex is **NMLv**. Thus, the vertex transformation is **N(M(Lv))**—that is, **v** is multiplied first by **L**, the resulting **Lv** is multiplied by **M**, and the resulting **MLv** is multiplied by **N**. Notice that the transformations to vertex **v** effectively occur in the opposite order than they were specified. (Actually, only a single multiplication of a vertex by the modelview matrix occurs; in this example, the **N**, **M**, and **L** matrices are already multiplied into a single matrix before it's applied to **v**.)

### Grand, Fixed Coordinate System

Thus, if you like to think in terms of a grand, fixed coordinate system—in which matrix multiplications affect the position, orientation, and scaling of your model—you have to think of the multiplications as occurring in the opposite order from how they appear in the code. Using the simple example shown on the left side of Figure 3-4 (a rotation about the origin and a translation along the $x$-axis), if you want the object to appear on the axis after the operations, the rotation must occur first, followed by the translation. To do this, you'll need to reverse the order of operations, so the code looks something like this (where **R** is the rotation matrix and **T** is the translation matrix):

```
glMatrixMode(GL_MODELVIEW);
glLoadIdentity();
glMultMatrixf(T);                  /* translation */
glMultMatrixf(R);                  /* rotation */
draw_the_object();
```

### Moving a Local Coordinate System

Another way to view matrix multiplications is to forget about a grand, fixed coordinate system in which your model is transformed and instead imagine that a local coordinate system is tied to the object you're drawing. All operations occur relative to this changing coordinate system. With this approach, the matrix multiplications now appear in the natural order in the code. (Regardless of which analogy you're using, the code is the same, but how you think about it differs.) To see this in the translation-rotation example, begin by visualizing the object with a coordinate system tied to it. The translation operation moves the object and its coordinate system down the $x$-axis. Then, the rotation occurs about the (now-translated) origin, so the object rotates in place in its position on the axis.

This approach is what you should use for applications such as articulated robot arms, where there are joints at the shoulder, elbow, and wrist, and on each of the fingers. To figure out where the tips of the fingers go relative to the body, you'd like to start at the shoulder, go down to the wrist, and so on, applying the appropriate rotations and translations at each joint. Thinking about it in reverse would be far more confusing.

This second approach can be problematic, however, in cases where scaling occurs, and especially so when the scaling is nonuniform (scaling different amounts along the different axes). After uniform scaling, translations move a vertex by a multiple of what they did before, as the coordinate system is stretched. Non-uniform scaling mixed with rotations may make the axes of the local coordinate system nonperpendicular.

As mentioned earlier, you normally issue viewing transformation commands in your program before any modeling transformations. In this way, a vertex in a model is first transformed into the desired orientation and then transformed by the viewing operation. Since the matrix multiplications must be specified in reverse order, the viewing commands need to come first. Note, however, that you don't need to specify either viewing or modeling transformations if you're satisfied with the default conditions. If there's no viewing transformation, the "camera" is left in the default position at the origin, pointing toward the negative *z*-axis; if there's no modeling transformation, the model isn't moved, and it retains its specified position, orientation, and size.

Since the commands for performing modeling transformations can be used to perform viewing transformations, modeling transformations are *discussed* first, even if viewing transformations are actually *issued* first. This order for discussion also matches the way many programmers think when planning their code. Often, they write all the code necessary to compose the scene, which involves transformations to position and orient objects correctly relative to each other. Next, they decide where they want the viewpoint to be relative to the scene they've composed, and then they write the viewing transformations accordingly.

## Modeling Transformations

The three OpenGL routines for modeling transformations are **glTranslate\*()**, **glRotate\*()**, and **glScale\*()**. As you might suspect, these routines transform an object (or coordinate system, if you're thinking of it in that way) by moving, rotating, stretching, shrinking, or reflecting it. All three commands are equivalent to producing an appropriate translation, rotation, or scaling matrix, and then calling **glMultMatrix\*()** with that matrix as the argument. However, using these three routines might be faster than using **glMultMatrix\*()**. OpenGL automatically computes the matrices for you. (See Appendix F if you're interested in the details.)

In the command summaries that follow, each matrix multiplication is described in terms of what it does to the vertices of a geometric object using the fixed coordinate system approach, and in terms of what it does to the local coordinate system that's attached to an object.

## Translate

void **glTranslate**{fd}(*TYPE x, TYPE y, TYPE z*);

Multiplies the current matrix by a matrix that moves (translates) an object by the given *x*-, *y*-, and *z*-values (or moves the local coordinate system by the same amounts).

Figure 3-5 shows the effect of **glTranslate*()**.

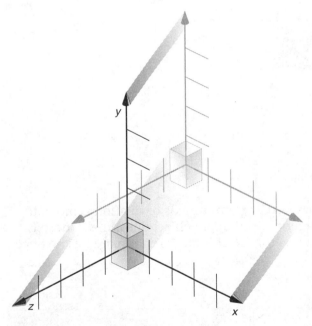

**Figure 3-5**    Translating an Object

Note that using (0.0, 0.0, 0.0) as the argument for **glTranslate*()** is the identity operation—that is, it has no effect on an object or its local coordinate system.

### Rotate

The effect of **glRotatef**(45.0, 0.0, 0.0, 1.0), which is a rotation of 45 degrees about the *z*-axis, is shown in Figure 3-6.

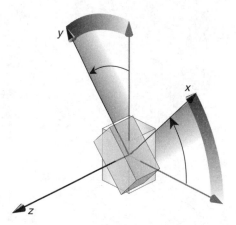

**Figure 3-6**    Rotating an Object

Note that an object that lies farther from the axis of rotation is more dramatically rotated (has a larger orbit) than an object drawn near the axis. Also, if the *angle* argument is zero, the **glRotate*()** command has no effect.

### Scale

Figure 3-7 shows the effect of **glScalef**(2.0, –0.5, 1.0).

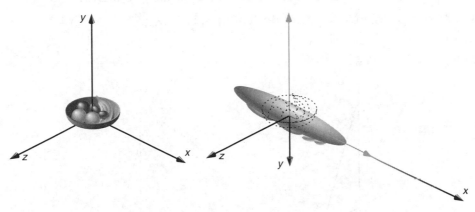

**Figure 3-7**    Scaling and Reflecting an Object

**glScale\*()** is the only one of the three modeling transformations that changes the apparent size of an object: scaling with values greater than 1.0 stretches an object, and using values less than 1.0 shrinks it. Scaling with a –1.0 value reflects an object across an axis. The identity values for scaling are (1.0, 1.0, 1.0). In general, you should limit your use of **glScale\*()** to those cases where it is necessary. Using **glScale\*()** decreases the performance of lighting calculations, because the normal vectors have to be renormalized after transformation.

**Note:** A scale value of zero collapses all object coordinates along that axis to zero. It's usually not a good idea to do this, because such an operation cannot be undone. Mathematically speaking, the matrix cannot be inverted, and inverse matrices are required for certain lighting operations (see Chapter 5). Sometimes collapsing coordinates does make sense; the calculation of shadows on a planar surface is one such application (see "Shadows" in Chapter 14). In general, if a coordinate system is to be collapsed, the projection matrix should be used, rather than the modelview matrix.

## A Modeling Transformation Code Example

Example 3-2 is a portion of a program that renders a triangle four times, as shown in Figure 3-8. These are the four transformed triangles:

- A solid wireframe triangle is drawn with no modeling transformation.

- The same triangle is drawn again, but with a dashed line stipple, and translated (to the left—along the negative x-axis).

- A triangle is drawn with a long dashed line stipple, with its height (*y*-axis) halved and its width (*x*-axis) increased by 50 percent.

- A rotated triangle, made of dotted lines, is drawn.

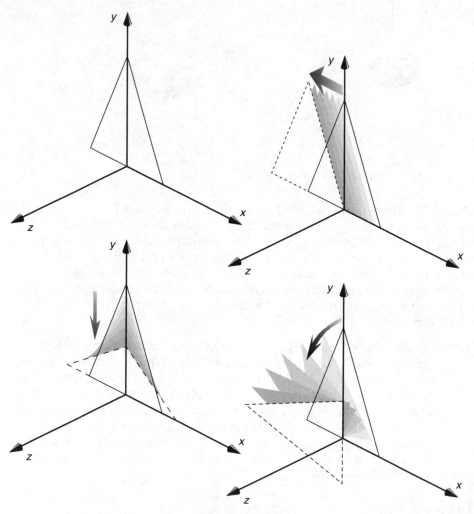

**Figure 3-8**     Modeling Transformation Example

**Example 3-2**    Using Modeling Transformations: model.c

```
glLoadIdentity();
glColor3f(1.0, 1.0, 1.0);
draw_triangle();                        /* solid lines */

glEnable(GL_LINE_STIPPLE);              /* dashed lines */
glLineStipple(1, 0xF0F0);
glLoadIdentity();
glTranslatef(-20.0, 0.0, 0.0);
draw_triangle();

glLineStipple(1, 0xF00F);               /*long dashed lines */
glLoadIdentity();
glScalef(1.5, 0.5, 1.0);
draw_triangle();

glLineStipple(1, 0x8888);               /* dotted lines */
glLoadIdentity();
glRotatef(90.0, 0.0, 0.0, 1.0);
draw_triangle();
glDisable(GL_LINE_STIPPLE);
```

Note the use of **glLoadIdentity()** to isolate the effects of modeling transformations; initializing the matrix values prevents successive transformations from having a cumulative effect. Even though using **glLoadIdentity()** repeatedly has the desired effect, it may be inefficient, because you may have to respecify viewing or modeling transformations. (See "Manipulating the Matrix Stacks" on page 145 for a better way to isolate transformations.)

**Note:** Sometimes, programmers who want a continuously rotating object attempt to achieve this by repeatedly applying a rotation matrix that has small values. The problem with this technique is that because of round-off errors, the product of thousands of tiny rotations gradually drifts away from the value you really want (it might even become something that isn't a rotation). Instead of using this technique, increment the angle and issue a new rotation command with the new angle at each update step.

### Nate Robins' Transformation Tutorial

If you have downloaded Nate Robins' suite of tutorial programs, this is an opportune time to run the **transformation** tutorial. (For information on how and where to download these programs, see "Nate Robins' OpenGL Tutors" on page xl.) With this tutorial, you can experiment with the effects of rotation, translation, and scaling.

## Viewing Transformations

A viewing transformation changes the position and orientation of the viewpoint. If you recall the camera analogy, the viewing transformation positions the camera tripod, pointing the camera toward the model. Just as you move the camera to some position and rotate it until it points in the desired direction, viewing transformations are generally composed of translations and rotations. Also remember that to achieve a certain scene composition in the final image or photograph, you can either move the camera or move all the objects in the opposite direction. Thus, a modeling transformation that rotates an object counterclockwise is equivalent to a viewing transformation that rotates the camera clockwise, for example. Finally, keep in mind that the viewing transformation commands must be called before any modeling transformations are performed, so that the modeling transformations take effect on the objects first.

You can manufacture a viewing transformation in any of several ways, as described next. You can also choose to use the default location and orientation of the viewpoint, which is at the origin, looking down the negative *z*-axis.

- Use one or more modeling transformation commands (that is, **glTranslate\*()** and **glRotate\*()**). You can think of the effect of these transformations as moving the camera position or as moving all the objects in the world, relative to a stationary camera.

- Use the Utility Library routine **gluLookAt()** to define a line of sight. This routine encapsulates a series of rotation and translation commands.

- Create your own utility routine to encapsulate rotations and translations. Some applications might require custom routines that allow you to specify the viewing transformation in a convenient way. For example, you might want to specify the roll, pitch, and heading rotation angles of a plane in flight, or you might want to specify a transformation in terms of polar coordinates for a camera that's orbiting around an object.

### Using glTranslate\*() and glRotate\*()

When you use modeling transformation commands to emulate viewing transformations, you're trying to move the viewpoint in a desired way while keeping the objects in the world stationary. Since the viewpoint is initially located at the origin and since objects are often most easily constructed there as well (see Figure 3-9), you generally have to perform

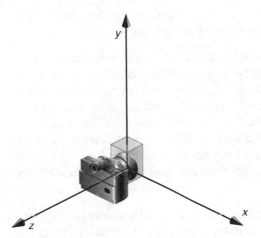

**Figure 3-9**    Object and Viewpoint at the Origin

some transformation so that the objects can be viewed. Note that, as shown in the figure, the camera initially points down the negative $z$-axis. (You're seeing the back of the camera.)

In the simplest case, you can move the viewpoint backward, away from the objects; this has the same effect as moving the objects forward, or away from the viewpoint. Remember that, by default, forward is down the negative $z$-axis; if you rotate the viewpoint, forward has a different meaning. Therefore, to put five units of distance between the viewpoint and the objects by moving the viewpoint, as shown in Figure 3-10, use

```
glTranslatef(0.0, 0.0, -5.0);
```

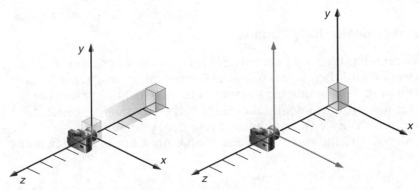

**Figure 3-10**    Separating the Viewpoint and the Object

This routine moves the objects in the scene –5 units along the z-axis. This is also equivalent to moving the camera +5 units along the z-axis.

Now suppose you want to view the objects from the side. Should you issue a rotate command before or after the translate command? If you're thinking in terms of a grand, fixed coordinate system, first imagine both the object and the camera at the origin. You could rotate the object first and then move it away from the camera so that the desired side is visible. You know that with the fixed coordinate system approach, commands have to be issued in the opposite order in which they should take effect, so you know that you need to write the translate command in your code first and follow it with the rotate command.

Now let's use the local coordinate system approach. In this case, think about moving the object and its local coordinate system away from the origin; then, the rotate command is carried out using the now-translated coordinate system. With this approach, commands are issued in the order in which they're applied, so once again the translate command comes first. Thus, the sequence of transformation commands to produce the desired result is

```
glTranslatef(0.0, 0.0, -5.0);
glRotatef(90.0, 0.0, 1.0, 0.0);
```

If you're having trouble keeping track of the effect of successive matrix multiplications, try using both the fixed and local coordinate system approaches and see whether one makes more sense to you. Note that with the fixed coordinate system, rotations always occur about the grand origin, whereas with the local coordinate system, rotations occur about the origin of the local system. You might also try using the **gluLookAt()** utility routine described next.

### Using the gluLookAt() Utility Routine

Often, programmers construct a scene around the origin or some other convenient location and then want to look at it from an arbitrary point to get a good view of it. As its name suggests, the **gluLookAt()** utility routine is designed for just this purpose. It takes three sets of arguments, which specify the location of the viewpoint, define a reference point toward which the camera is aimed, and indicate which direction is up. Choose the viewpoint to yield the desired view of the scene. The reference point is typically somewhere in the middle of the scene. (If you've built your scene at the origin, the reference point is probably the origin.) It might be a little trickier to specify the correct up-vector. Again, if you've built some real-world scene at or around the origin and if you've been taking the positive $y$-axis to point upward, then that's your up-vector for **gluLookAt()**. However, if you're designing a flight simulator, up is the direction perpendicular to the plane's wings, from the plane toward the sky when the plane is right-side-up on the ground.

The **gluLookAt()** routine is particularly useful when you want to pan across a landscape, for instance. With a viewing volume that's symmetric in both $x$ and $y$, the (*eyex, eyey, eyez*) point specified is always in the center of the image on the screen, so you can use a series of commands to move this point slightly, thereby panning across the scene.

---

void **gluLookAt**(GLdouble *eyex*, GLdouble *eyey*, GLdouble *eyez*,
        GLdouble *centerx*, GLdouble *centery*, GLdouble *centerz*,
        GLdouble *upx*, GLdouble *upy*, GLdouble *upz*);

---

Defines a viewing matrix and multiplies it to the right of the current matrix. The desired viewpoint is specified by *eyex*, *eyey*, and *eyez*. The *centerx*, *centery*, and *centerz* arguments specify any point along the desired line of sight, but typically they specify some point in the center of the scene being looked at. The *upx*, *upy*, and *upz* arguments indicate which direction is up (that is, the direction from the bottom to the top of the viewing volume).

In the default position, the camera is at the origin, is looking down the negative $z$-axis, and has the positive $y$-axis as straight up. This is the same as calling

```
gluLookAt(0.0, 0.0, 0.0, 0.0, 0.0, -100.0, 0.0, 1.0, 0.0);
```

The $z$-value of the reference point is –100.0, but could be any negative $z$, because the line of sight will remain the same. In this case, you don't actually want to call **gluLookAt()**, because this is the default (see Figure 3-11) and you are already there. (The lines extending from the camera represent the viewing volume, which indicates its field of view.)

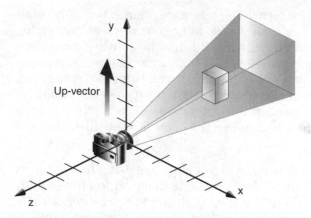

**Figure 3-11**    Default Camera Position

Figure 3-12 shows the effect of a typical **gluLookAt()** routine. The camera position (*eyex, eyey, eyez*) is at (4, 2, 1). In this case, the camera is looking right at the model, so the reference point is at (2, 4, –3). An orientation vector of (2, 2, –1) is chosen to rotate the viewpoint to this 45-degree angle.

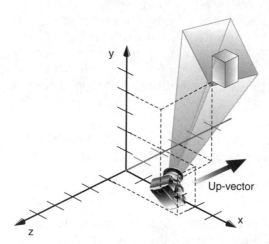

**Figure 3-12**    Using gluLookAt()

Therefore, to achieve this effect, call

```
gluLookAt(4.0, 2.0, 1.0, 2.0, 4.0, -3.0, 2.0, 2.0, -1.0);
```

Note that **gluLookAt()** is part of the Utility Library, rather than the basic OpenGL library. This isn't because it's not useful, but because it encapsulates several basic OpenGL commands—specifically, **glTranslate*()** and **glRotate*()**. To see this, imagine a camera located at an arbitrary viewpoint and oriented according to a line of sight, both as specified with **gluLookAt()** and a scene located at the origin. To "undo" what **gluLookAt()** does, you need to transform the camera so that it sits at the origin and points down the negative z-axis, the default position. A simple translate moves the camera to the origin. You can easily imagine a series of rotations about each of the three axes of a fixed coordinate system that would orient the camera so that it pointed toward negative z-values. Since OpenGL allows rotation about an arbitrary axis, you can accomplish any desired rotation of the camera with a single **glRotate*()** command.

**Note:** You can have only one active viewing transformation. You cannot try to combine the effects of two viewing transformations, any more than a camera can have two tripods. If you want to change the position of the camera, make sure you call **glLoadIdentity()** to erase the effects of any current viewing transformation.

### Nate Robins' Projection Tutorial

If you have Nate Robins' suite of tutorial programs, run the **projection** tutorial. With this tutorial, you can see the effects of changes to the parameters of **gluLookAt()**.

### Advanced

Advanced

To transform any arbitrary vector so that it's coincident with another arbitrary vector (for instance, the negative z-axis), you need to do a little mathematics. The axis about which you want to rotate is given by the cross product of the two normalized vectors. To find the angle of rotation, normalize the initial two vectors. The cosine of the desired angle between the vectors is equal to the dot product of the normalized vectors. The angle of rotation around the axis given by the cross product is always between 0 and 180 degrees. (See Appendix E for definitions of cross and dot products.)

Note that computing the angle between two normalized vectors by taking the inverse cosine of their dot product is not very accurate, especially for small angles, but it should work well enough to get you started.

### Creating a Custom Utility Routine

### Advanced

Advanced

For some specialized applications, you might want to define your own transformation routine. Since this is rarely done and is a fairly advanced topic, it's left mostly as an exercise for the reader. The following exercises suggest two custom viewing transformations that might be useful.

Try This

**Try This**

• Suppose you're writing a flight simulator and you'd like to display the world from the point of view of the pilot of a plane. The world is described in a coordinate system with the origin on the runway and the plane at coordinates (*x*, *y*, *z*). Suppose further that the plane has some *roll*, *pitch*, and *heading* (these are rotation angles of the plane relative to its center of gravity).

Show that the following routine could serve as the viewing transformation:

```
void pilotView{GLdouble planex, GLdouble planey,
            GLdouble planez, GLdouble roll,
            GLdouble pitch, GLdouble heading)
{
    glRotated(roll, 0.0, 0.0, 1.0);
    glRotated(pitch, 0.0, 1.0, 0.0);
    glRotated(heading, 1.0, 0.0, 0.0);
    glTranslated(-planex, -planey, -planez);
}
```

• Suppose your application involves orbiting the camera around an object that's centered at the origin. In this case, you'd like to specify the viewing transformation by using polar coordinates. Let the *distance* variable define the radius of the orbit or how far the camera is from the origin. (Initially, the camera is moved *distance* units along the positive *z*-axis.) The *azimuth* describes the angle of rotation of the camera about the object in the *xy*-plane, measured from the positive *y*-axis. Similarly, *elevation* is the angle of rotation of the camera in the *yz*-plane measured from the positive *z*-axis. Finally, *twist* represents the rotation of the viewing volume around its line of sight.

Show that the following routine could serve as the viewing transformation:

```
void polarView{GLdouble distance, GLdouble twist,
            GLdouble elevation, GLdouble azimuth)
{
    glTranslated(0.0, 0.0, -distance);
    glRotated(-twist, 0.0, 0.0, 1.0);
    glRotated(-elevation, 1.0, 0.0, 0.0);
    glRotated(azimuth, 0.0, 0.0, 1.0);
}
```

# Projection Transformations

The preceding section described how to compose the desired modelview matrix so that the correct modeling and viewing transformations are applied. This section explains how to define the desired projection matrix, which is also used to transform the vertices in your scene. Before you issue any of the transformation commands described in this section, remember to call

```
glMatrixMode(GL_PROJECTION);
glLoadIdentity();
```

so that the commands affect the projection matrix, rather than the model-view matrix, and so that you avoid compound projection transformations. Since each projection transformation command completely describes a particular transformation, typically you don't want to combine a projection transformation with another transformation.

The purpose of the projection transformation is to define a *viewing volume*, which is used in two ways. The viewing volume determines how an object is projected onto the screen (that is, by using a perspective or an orthographic projection), and it defines which objects or portions of objects are clipped out of the final image. You can think of the viewpoint we've been talking about as existing at one end of the viewing volume. At this point, you might want to reread "A Simple Example: Drawing a Cube" on page 109 for its overview of all the transformations, including projection transformations.

## Perspective Projection

The most unmistakable characteristic of perspective projection is *foreshortening*: the farther an object is from the camera, the smaller it appears in the final image. This occurs because the viewing volume for a perspective projection is a *frustum* of a pyramid (a truncated pyramid whose top has been cut off by a plane parallel to its base). Objects that fall within the viewing volume are projected toward the apex of the pyramid, where the camera or viewpoint is. Objects that are closer to the viewpoint appear larger because they occupy a proportionally larger amount of the viewing volume than those that are farther away, in the larger part of the frustum. This method of projection is commonly used for animation, visual simulation, and any other applications that strive for some degree of realism, because it's similar to how our eye (or a camera) works.

The command to define a frustum, **glFrustum()**, calculates a matrix that accomplishes perspective projection and multiplies the current projection matrix (typically the identity matrix) by it. Recall that the viewing volume is used to clip objects that lie outside of it; the four sides of the frustum, its top, and its base correspond to the six clipping planes of the viewing volume, as shown in Figure 3-13. Objects or parts of objects outside these planes are clipped from the final image. Note that **glFrustum()** doesn't require you to define a symmetric viewing volume.

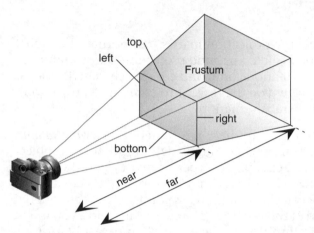

**Figure 3-13**     Perspective Viewing Volume Specified by glFrustum()

---

void **glFrustum**(GLdouble *left*, GLdouble *right*,
            GLdouble *bottom*, GLdouble *top*,
            GLdouble *near*, GLdouble *far*);

---

Creates a matrix for a perspective-view frustum and multiplies the current matrix by it. The frustum's viewing volume is defined by the parameters: (*left, bottom, –near*) and (*right, top, –near*) specify the (*x, y, z*) coordinates of the lower left and upper right corners, respectively, of the near clipping plane; *near* and *far* give the distances from the viewpoint to the near and far clipping planes. They should always be positive.

The frustum has a default orientation in three-dimensional space. You can perform rotations or translations on the projection matrix to alter this orientation, but this is tricky and nearly always avoidable.

### Advanced

The frustum doesn't have to be symmetrical, and its axis isn't necessarily aligned with the *z*-axis. For example, you can use **glFrustum()** to draw a picture as if you were looking through a rectangular window of a house, where the window was above and to the right of you. Photographers use such a viewing volume to create false perspectives. You might use it to have the hardware calculate images at resolutions much higher than normal, perhaps for use on a printer. For example, if you want an image that has twice the resolution of your screen, draw the same picture four times, each time using the frustum to cover the entire screen with one-quarter of the image. After each quarter of the image is rendered, you can read the pixels back to collect the data for the higher-resolution image. (See Chapter 8 for more information about reading pixel data.)

Although it's easy to understand conceptually, **glFrustum()** isn't intuitive to use. Instead, you might try the Utility Library routine **gluPerspective()**. This routine creates a viewing volume of the same shape as **glFrustum()** does, but you specify it in a different way. Rather than specifying corners of the near clipping plane, you specify the angle of the field of view (Θ, or theta, in Figure 3-14) in the *y*-direction and the aspect ratio of the width to the height (*x/y*). (For a square portion of the screen, the aspect ratio is 1.0.) These two parameters are enough to determine an untruncated pyramid along the line of sight, as shown in Figure 3-14. You also specify the distance between the viewpoint and the near and far clipping planes, thereby truncating the pyramid. Note that **gluPerspective()** is limited to creating frustums that are symmetric in both the *x*- and *y*-axes along the line of sight, but this is usually what you want.

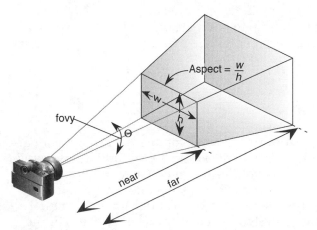

**Figure 3-14**    Perspective Viewing Volume Specified by gluPerspective()

void **gluPerspective**(GLdouble *fovy*, GLdouble *aspect*,
GLdouble *near*, GLdouble *far*);

Creates a matrix for a symmetric perspective-view frustum and multiplies the current matrix by it. *fovy* is the angle of the field of view in the *yz*-plane; its value must be in the range [0.0, 180.0]. *aspect* is the aspect ratio of the frustum, its width divided by its height. *near* and *far* values are the distances between the viewpoint and the clipping planes, along the negative *z*-axis. They should always be positive.

Just as with **glFrustum**(), you can apply rotations or translations to change the default orientation of the viewing volume created by **gluPerspective**(). With no such transformations, the viewpoint remains at the origin, and the line of sight points down the negative *z*-axis.

With **gluPerspective**(), you need to pick appropriate values for the field of view, otherwise the image may look distorted. To get a perfect field of view, figure out how far your eye normally is from the screen and how big the window is, and calculate the angle the window subtends at that size and distance. It's probably smaller than you would guess. Another way to think about it is that a 94-degree field of view with a 35-millimeter camera requires a 20-millimeter lens, which is a very wide-angle lens. (See "Troubleshooting Transformations" on page 142 for more details on how to calculate the desired field of view.)

The preceding paragraph suggests inches and millimeters—do these really have anything to do with OpenGL? The answer is, in a word, no. The projection and other transformations are inherently unitless. If you want to think of the near and far clipping planes as located at 1.0 and 20.0 meters, inches, kilometers, or leagues, it's up to you. The only rule is that you have to use a consistent unit of measurement. Then the resulting image is drawn to scale.

## Orthographic Projection

With an orthographic projection, the viewing volume is a rectangular parallelepiped, or, more informally, a box (see Figure 3-15). Unlike perspective projection, the size of the viewing volume doesn't change from one end to the other, so distance from the camera doesn't affect how large an object appears. This type of projection is used for applications for architectural blueprints and computer-aided design, where it's crucial to maintain the actual sizes of objects and the angles between them as they're projected.

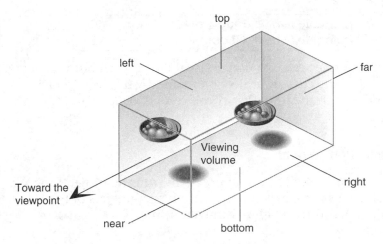

top

left

far

Viewing
volume

right

Toward the
viewpoint

near

bottom

**Figure 3-15**    Orthographic Viewing Volume

The command **glOrtho()** creates an orthographic parallel viewing volume. As with **glFrustum()**, you specify the corners of the near clipping plane and the distance to the far clipping plane.

---

void **glOrtho**(GLdouble *left*, GLdouble *right*,
            GLdouble *bottom*, GLdouble *top*,
            GLdouble *near*, GLdouble *far*);

Creates a matrix for an orthographic parallel viewing volume and multiplies the current matrix by it. (*left, bottom, −near*) and (*right, top, −near*) are points on the near clipping plane that are mapped to the lower left and upper right corners of the viewport window, respectively. (*left, bottom, −far*) and (*right, top, −far*) are points on the far clipping plane that are mapped to the same respective corners of the viewport. Both *near* and *far* may be positive, negative, or even set to zero. However, *near* and *far* should not be the same value.

---

With no other transformations, the direction of projection is parallel to the $z$-axis, and the viewpoint faces toward the negative $z$-axis.

For the special case of projecting a two-dimensional image onto a two-dimensional screen, use the Utility Library routine **gluOrtho2D()**. This routine is identical to the three-dimensional version, **glOrtho()**, except that all the $z$ coordinates for objects in the scene are assumed to lie between −1.0 and 1.0. If you're drawing two-dimensional objects using the two-dimensional vertex commands, all the $z$ coordinates are zero; thus, no object is clipped because of its $z$-value.

---

void **gluOrtho2D**(GLdouble *left*, GLdouble *right*,
              GLdouble *bottom*, GLdouble *top*);

---

Creates a matrix for projecting two-dimensional coordinates onto the screen and multiplies the current projection matrix by it. The clipping region is a rectangle with the lower left corner at (*left, bottom*) and the upper right corner at (*right, top*).

### Nate Robins' Projection Tutorial

If you have Nate Robins' suite of tutorial programs, run the **projection** tutorial once again. This time, experiment with the parameters of the **gluPerspective()**, **glOrtho()**, and **glFrustum()** routines.

## Viewing Volume Clipping

After the vertices of the objects in the scene have been transformed by the modelview and projection matrices, any primitives that lie outside the viewing volume are clipped. The six clipping planes used are those that define the sides and ends of the viewing volume. You can specify additional clipping planes and locate them wherever you choose. (See "Additional Clipping Planes" on page 149 for information about this relatively advanced topic.) Keep in mind that OpenGL reconstructs the edges of polygons that are clipped.

# Viewport Transformation

Recalling the camera analogy, you know that the viewport transformation corresponds to the stage where the size of the developed photograph is chosen. Do you want a wallet-size or a poster-size photograph? Since this is computer graphics, the viewport is the rectangular region of the window where the image is drawn. Figure 3-16 shows a viewport that occupies most of the screen. The viewport is measured in window coordinates, which reflect the positions of pixels on the screen relative to the lower left corner of the window. Keep in mind that all vertices have been transformed by the modelview and projection matrices by this point, and vertices outside the viewing volume have been clipped.

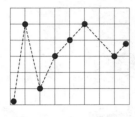

**Figure 3-16**    Viewport Rectangle

## Defining the Viewport

The window system, not OpenGL, is responsible for opening a window on the screen. However, by default, the viewport is set to the entire pixel rectangle of the window that's opened. You use the **glViewport**() command to choose a smaller drawing region; for example, you can subdivide the window to create a split-screen effect for multiple views in the same window.

---

void **glViewport**(GLint *x*, GLint *y*, GLsizei *width*, GLsizei *height*);

Defines a pixel rectangle in the window into which the final image is mapped. The (*x, y*) parameter specifies the lower left corner of the viewport, and *width* and *height* are the size of the viewport rectangle. By default, the initial viewport values are (*0, 0, winWidth, winHeight*), where *winWidth* and *winHeight* specify the size of the window.

---

The aspect ratio of a viewport should generally equal the aspect ratio of the viewing volume. If the two ratios are different, the projected image will be distorted when mapped to the viewport, as shown in Figure 3-17. Note that subsequent changes in the size of the window don't explicitly affect the viewport. Your application should detect window resize events and modify the viewport appropriately.

In Figure 3-17, the left figure shows a projection that maps a square image onto a square viewport using these routines:

```
gluPerspective(fovy, 1.0, near, far);
glViewport(0, 0, 400, 400);
```

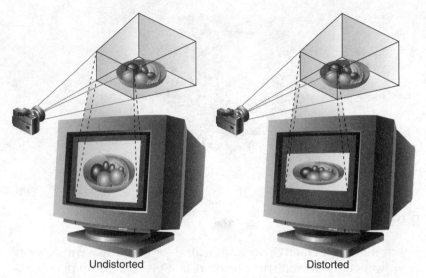

Undistorted         Distorted

**Figure 3-17**  Mapping the Viewing Volume to the Viewport

However, in the right figure, the window has been resized to a nonequilateral rectangular viewport, but the projection is unchanged. The image appears compressed along the *x*-axis:

```
gluPerspective(fovy, 1.0, near, far);
glViewport(0, 0, 400, 200);
```

To avoid the distortion, modify the aspect ratio of the projection to match the viewport:

```
gluPerspective(fovy, 2.0, near, far);
glViewport(0, 0, 400, 200);
```

**Try This**

Modify an existing program so that an object is drawn twice, in different viewports. You might draw the object with different projection and/or viewing transformations for each viewport. To create two side-by-side viewports, you might issue these commands, along with the appropriate modeling, viewing, and projection transformations:

```
glViewport(0, 0, sizex/2, sizey);
            .
            .
            .
glViewport(sizex/2, 0, sizex/2, sizey);
```

Try This

## The Transformed Depth Coordinate

The depth (z) coordinate is encoded during the viewport transformation (and later stored in the depth buffer). You can scale z-values to lie within a desired range with the **glDepthRange**() command. (Chapter 10 discusses the depth buffer and the corresponding uses of the depth coordinate.) Unlike x and y window coordinates, z window coordinates are treated by OpenGL as though they always range from 0.0 to 1.0.

---

void **glDepthRange**(GLclampd *near*, GLclampd *far*);

---

Defines an encoding for z-coordinates that's performed during the viewport transformation. The *near* and *far* values represent adjustments to the minimum and maximum values that can be stored in the depth buffer. By default, they're 0.0 and 1.0, respectively, which work for most applications. These parameters are clamped to lie within [0, 1].

In perspective projection, the transformed depth coordinate (like the x- and y-coordinates) is subject to perspective division by the w-coordinate. As the transformed depth coordinate moves farther away from the near clipping plane, its location becomes increasingly less precise. (See Figure 3-18.)

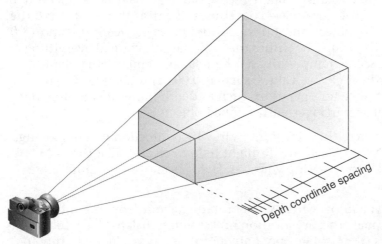

**Figure 3-18**    Perspective Projection and Transformed Depth Coordinates

Therefore, perspective division affects the accuracy of operations that rely on the transformed depth coordinate, especially depth-buffering, which is used for hidden-surface removal.

## Troubleshooting Transformations

It's pretty easy to get a camera pointed in the right direction, but in computer graphics, you have to specify position and direction with coordinates and angles. As we can attest, it's all too easy to achieve the well-known black-screen effect. Although any number of things can go wrong, often you get this effect—which results in absolutely nothing being drawn in the window you open on the screen—from incorrectly aiming the "camera" and taking a picture with the model behind you. A similar problem arises if you don't choose a field of view that's wide enough to view your objects but narrow enough so they appear reasonably large.

If you find yourself exerting great programming effort only to create a black window, try these diagnostic steps:

1. Check the obvious possibilities. Make sure your system is plugged in. Make sure you're drawing your objects with a color that's different from the color with which you're clearing the screen. Make sure that whatever states you're using (such as lighting, texturing, alpha blending, logical operations, or antialiasing) are correctly turned on or off, as desired.

2. Remember that with the projection commands, the near and far coordinates measure distance from the viewpoint and that (by default) you're looking down the negative $z$-axis. Thus, if the near value is 1.0 and the far value is 3.0, objects must have $z$-coordinates between $-1.0$ and $-3.0$ in order to be visible. To ensure that you haven't clipped everything out of your scene, temporarily set the near and far clipping planes to some absurdly inclusive values, such as 0.001 and 1000000.0. This alters appearance for operations such as depth-buffering and fog, but it might uncover inadvertently clipped objects.

3. Determine where the viewpoint is, in which direction you're looking, and where your objects are. It might help to create a real three-dimensional space—using your hands, for instance—to figure these things out.

4. Make sure you know where you're rotating about. You might be rotating about some arbitrary location unless you translated back to the origin first. It's OK to rotate about any point unless you're expecting to rotate about the origin.

5. Check your aim. Use **gluLookAt()** to aim the viewing volume at your objects, or draw your objects at or near the origin, and use **glTranslate*()**

as a viewing transformation to move the camera just far enough in the z-direction so that the objects fall within the viewing volume. Once you've managed to make your objects visible, try to change the viewing volume incrementally to achieve the exact result you want, as described next.

6. For perspective transformations, be certain the near clipping plane is not too close to the viewer (camera), otherwise depth-buffering accuracy may be adversely affected.

Even after you've aimed the camera in the correct direction and you can see your objects, they might appear too small or too large. If you're using **gluPerspective()**, you might need to alter the angle defining the field of view by changing the value of the first parameter for this command. You can use trigonometry to calculate the desired field of view given the size of the object and its distance from the viewpoint: the tangent of half the desired angle is half the size of the object divided by the distance to the object (see Figure 3-19). Thus, you can use an arctangent routine to compute half the desired angle. Example 3-3 assumes such a routine, **atan2()**, which calculates the arctangent given the length of the opposite and adjacent sides of a right triangle. This result then needs to be converted from radians to degrees.

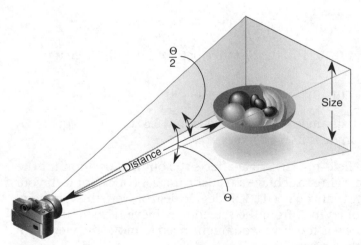

**Figure 3-19**    Using Trigonometry to Calculate the Field of View

**Example 3-3**    Calculating Field of View

```
#define PI 3.1415926535

double calculateAngle(double size, double distance)
{
    double radtheta, degtheta;

    radtheta = 2.0 * atan2 (size/2.0, distance);
    degtheta = (180.0 * radtheta) / PI;
    return degtheta;
}
```

Typically, of course, you don't know the exact size of an object, and only the distance between the viewpoint and a single point in your scene can be determined. To obtain a fairly good approximate value, find the bounding box for your scene by determining the maximum and minimum x-, y-, and z-coordinates of all the objects in your scene. Then calculate the radius of a bounding sphere for that box, and use the center of the sphere to determine the distance and the radius to determine the size.

For example, suppose all the coordinates in your object satisfy the equations $-1 \leq x \leq 3$, $5 \leq y \leq 7$, and $-5 \leq z \leq 5$. The center of the bounding box is (1, 6, 0), and the radius of a bounding sphere is the distance from the center of the box to any corner—say (3, 7, 5)—or

$$\sqrt{(3-1)^2 + (7-6)^2 + (5-0)^2} = \sqrt{30} = 5.477$$

If the viewpoint is at (8, 9, 10), the distance between it and the center is

$$\sqrt{(8-1)^2 + (9-6)^2 + (10-0)^2} = \sqrt{158} = 12.570$$

The tangent of the half-angle is 5.477 divided by 12.570, which equals 0.4357, so the half-angle is 23.54 degrees.

Remember that the field-of-view angle affects the optimal position for the viewpoint, if you're trying to achieve a realistic image. For example, if your calculations indicate that you need a 179-degree field of view, the viewpoint must be a fraction of an inch from the screen to achieve realism. If your calculated field of view is too large, you might need to move the viewpoint farther away from the object.

## Manipulating the Matrix Stacks

The modelview and projection matrices you've been creating, loading, and multiplying have been only the visible tips of their respective icebergs. Each of these matrices is actually the topmost member of a stack of matrices (see Figure 3-20).

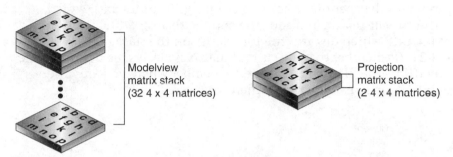

**Figure 3-20**    Modelview and Projection Matrix Stacks

A stack of matrices is useful for constructing hierarchical models, in which complicated objects are constructed from simpler ones. For example, suppose you're drawing an automobile that has four wheels, each of which is attached to the car with five bolts. You have a single routine to draw a wheel and another to draw a bolt, since all the wheels and all the bolts look the same. These routines draw a wheel or a bolt in some convenient position and orientation; for example, centered at the origin with its axis coincident with the z-axis. When you draw the car, including the wheels and bolts, you want to call the wheel-drawing routine four times, with different transformations in effect each time to position the wheels correctly. As you draw each wheel, you want to draw the bolts five times, each time translated appropriately relative to the wheel.

Suppose for a minute that all you have to do is draw the car body and the wheels. The English description of what you want to do might be something like this:

> Draw the car body. Remember where you are, and translate to the right front wheel. Draw the wheel and throw away the last translation so your current position is back at the origin of the car body. Remember where you are, and translate to the left front wheel...

Similarly, for each wheel, you want to draw the wheel, remember where you are, and successively translate to each of the positions where bolts are drawn, throwing away the transformations after each bolt is drawn.

Since the transformations are stored as matrices, a matrix stack provides an ideal mechanism for doing this sort of successive remembering, translating, and throwing away. All the matrix operations that have been described so far (**glLoadMatrix()**, **glLoadTransposeMatrix()**, **glMultMatrix()**, **glMultTransposeMatrix()**, **glLoadIdentity()**, and the commands that create specific transformation matrices) deal with the current matrix or the top matrix on the stack. You can control which matrix is on top with the commands that perform stack operations: **glPushMatrix()**, which copies the current matrix and adds the copy to the top of the stack, and **glPopMatrix()**, which discards the top matrix on the stack, as shown in Figure 3-21. (Remember that the current matrix is always the matrix on the top.) In effect, **glPushMatrix()** means "remember where you are" and **glPopMatrix()** means "go back to where you were."

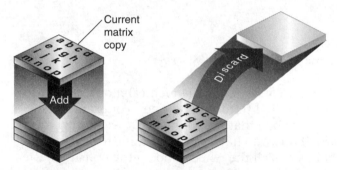

**Figure 3-21**     Pushing and Popping the Matrix Stack

void **glPushMatrix**(void);

Pushes all matrices in the current stack down one level. The current stack is determined by **glMatrixMode()**. The topmost matrix is copied, so its contents are duplicated in both the top and second-from-the-top matrix. If too many matrices are pushed, an error is generated.

void **glPopMatrix**(void);

Pops the top matrix off the stack, destroying the contents of the popped matrix. What was the second-from-the-top matrix becomes the top matrix. The current stack is determined by **glMatrixMode()**. If the stack contains a single matrix, calling **glPopMatrix()** generates an error.

Example 3-4 draws an automobile, assuming the existence of routines that draw the car body, a wheel, and a bolt.

**Example 3-4** Pushing and Popping the Matrix

```
draw_wheel_and_bolts()
{
    int i;

    draw_wheel();
    for(i=0;i<5;i++){
        glPushMatrix();
            glRotatef(72.0*i, 0.0, 0.0, 1.0);
            glTranslatef(3.0, 0.0, 0.0);
            draw_bolt();
        glPopMatrix();
    }
}

draw_body_and_wheel_and_bolts()
{
    draw_car_body();
    glPushMatrix();
        glTranslatef(40, 0, 30);   /*move to first wheel position*/
        draw_wheel_and_bolts();
    glPopMatrix();
    glPushMatrix();
        glTranslatef(40, 0, -30);   /*move to 2nd wheel position*/
        draw_wheel_and_bolts();
    glPopMatrix();
    ...                             /*draw last two wheels similarly*/
}
```

This code assumes that the wheel and bolt axes are coincident with the z-axis; that the bolts are evenly spaced every 72 degrees, 3 units (maybe inches) from the center of the wheel; and that the front wheels are 40 units in front of and 30 units to the right and left of the car's origin.

A stack is more efficient than an individual matrix, especially if the stack is implemented in hardware. When you push a matrix, you don't need to copy the current data back to the main process, and the hardware may be able to copy more than one element of the matrix at a time. Sometimes you might want to keep an identity matrix at the bottom of the stack so that you don't need to call **glLoadIdentity()** repeatedly.

## The Modelview Matrix Stack

As you've seen earlier in "Viewing and Modeling Transformations," the modelview matrix contains the cumulative product of multiplying viewing and modeling transformation matrices. Each viewing or modeling transformation creates a new matrix that multiplies the current modelview matrix; the result, which becomes the new current matrix, represents the composite transformation. The modelview matrix stack contains at least 32 $4 \times 4$ matrices; initially, the topmost matrix is the identity matrix. Some implementations of OpenGL may support more than 32 matrices on the stack. To find the maximum allowable number of matrices, you can use the query command **glGetIntegerv(GL_MAX_MODELVIEW_STACK_DEPTH, GLint *params)**.

## The Projection Matrix Stack

The projection matrix contains a matrix for the projection transformation, which describes the viewing volume. Generally, you don't want to compose projection matrices, so you issue **glLoadIdentity()** before performing a projection transformation. Also for this reason, the projection matrix stack need be only two levels deep; some OpenGL implementations may allow more than two $4 \times 4$ matrices. To find the stack depth, call **glGetIntegerv(GL_MAX_PROJECTION_STACK_DEPTH, GLint *params)**.

One use for a second matrix in the stack would be an application that needs to display a help window with text in it, in addition to its normal window showing a three-dimensional scene. Since text is most easily positioned with an orthographic projection, you could change temporarily to an orthographic projection, display the help, and then return to your previous projection:

```
glMatrixMode(GL_PROJECTION);
glPushMatrix();                    /*save the current projection*/
    glLoadIdentity();
    glOrtho(...);                  /*set up for displaying help*/
    display_the_help();
glPopMatrix();
```

Note that you'd probably also have to change the modelview matrix appropriately.

**Advanced**

Advanced

If you know enough mathematics, you can create custom projection matrices that perform arbitrary projective transformations. For example, OpenGL and its Utility Library have no built-in mechanism for two-point perspective. If you were trying to emulate the drawings in drafting texts, you might need such a projection matrix.

## Additional Clipping Planes

In addition to the six clipping planes of the viewing volume (left, right, bottom, top, near, and far), you can define up to six additional clipping planes for further restriction of the viewing volume, as shown in Figure 3-22. This is useful for removing extraneous objects in a scene—for example, if you want to display a cutaway view of an object.

Each plane is specified by the coefficients of its equation: $Ax + By + Cz + D = 0$. The clipping planes are automatically transformed appropriately by modeling and viewing transformations. The clipping volume becomes the intersection of the viewing volume and all *half-spaces* defined by the additional clipping planes. Remember that polygons that get clipped automatically have their edges reconstructed appropriately by OpenGL.

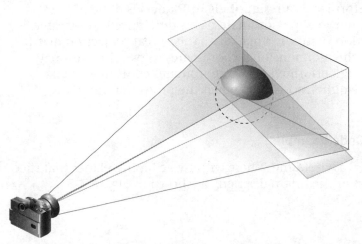

**Figure 3-22**     Additional Clipping Planes and the Viewing Volume

void **glClipPlane**(GLenum *plane*, const GLdouble *\*equation*);

Defines a clipping plane. The *equation* argument points to the four coefficients of the plane equation, $Ax + By + Cz + D = 0$. All points with eye coordinates $(x_e, y_e, z_e, w_e)$ that satisfy $(A\ B\ C\ D)\mathbf{M}^{-1}(x_e\ y_e\ z_e\ w_e)^T >= 0$ lie in the half-space defined by the plane, where **M** is the current modelview matrix at the time **glClipPlane**() is called. All points not in this half-space are clipped away. The *plane* argument is GL_CLIP_PLANE*i*, where *i* is an integer specifying which of the available clipping planes to define. *i* is a number between 0 and one less than the maximum number of additional clipping planes.

You need to enable each additional clipping plane you define:

```
glEnable(GL_CLIP_PLANEi);
```

You can disable a plane with

```
glDisable(GL_CLIP_PLANEi);
```

All implementations of OpenGL must support at least six additional clipping planes, although some implementations may allow more. You can use **glGetIntegerv**() with GL_MAX_CLIP_PLANES to determine how many clipping planes are supported.

**Note:** Clipping performed as a result of **glClipPlane**() is done in eye coordinates, not in clip coordinates. This difference is noticeable if the projection matrix is singular (that is, a real projection matrix that flattens three-dimensional coordinates to two-dimensional ones). Clipping performed in eye coordinates continues to take place in three dimensions even when the projection matrix is singular.

### A Clipping Plane Code Example

Example 3-5 renders a wireframe sphere with two clipping planes that slice away three-quarters of the original sphere, as shown in Figure 3-23.

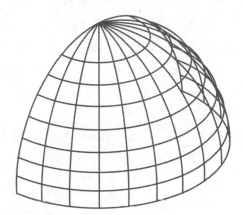

**Figure 3-23**   Clipped Wireframe Sphere

**Example 3-5**   Wireframe Sphere with Two Clipping Planes: clip.c

```
void init(void)
{
   glClearColor(0.0, 0.0, 0.0, 0.0);
   glShadeModel(GL_FLAT);
}
void display(void)
{
   GLdouble eqn[4] = {0.0, 1.0, 0.0, 0.0};
   GLdouble eqn2[4] = {1.0, 0.0, 0.0, 0.0};

   glClear(GL_COLOR_BUFFER_BIT);
   glColor3f(1.0, 1.0, 1.0);
   glPushMatrix();
   glTranslatef(0.0, 0.0, -5.0);

/*    clip lower half -- y < 0             */
   glClipPlane(GL_CLIP_PLANE0, eqn);
   glEnable(GL_CLIP_PLANE0);
/*    clip left half -- x < 0              */
   glClipPlane(GL_CLIP_PLANE1, eqn2);
   glEnable(GL_CLIP_PLANE1);

   glRotatef(90.0, 1.0, 0.0, 0.0);
   glutWireSphere(1.0, 20, 16);
   glPopMatrix();
   glFlush();
}
```

```
void reshape(int w, int h)
{
   glViewport(0, 0, (GLsizei) w, (GLsizei) h);
   glMatrixMode(GL_PROJECTION);
   glLoadIdentity();
   gluPerspective(60.0, (GLfloat) w/(GLfloat) h, 1.0, 20.0);
   glMatrixMode(GL_MODELVIEW);
}

int main(int argc, char** argv)
{
   glutInit(&argc, argv);
   glutInitDisplayMode(GLUT_SINGLE | GLUT_RGB);
   glutInitWindowSize(500, 500);
   glutInitWindowPosition(100, 100);
   glutCreateWindow(argv[0]);
   init();
   glutDisplayFunc(display);
   glutReshapeFunc(reshape);
   glutMainLoop();
   return 0;
}
```

Try This

**Try This**

- Try changing the coefficients that describe the clipping planes in Example 3-5.

- Try calling a modeling transformation, such as **glRotate\*()**, to affect **glClipPlane()**. Make the clipping plane move independently of the objects in the scene.

## Examples of Composing Several Transformations

This section demonstrates how to combine several transformations to achieve a particular result. The two examples discussed are a solar system, in which objects need to rotate on their axes as well as in orbit around each other, and a robot arm, which has several joints that effectively transform coordinate systems as they move relative to each other.

## Building a Solar System

The program described in this section draws a simple solar system with a planet and a sun, both using the same sphere-drawing routine. To write this program, you need to use **glRotate*()** for the revolution of the planet around the sun and for the rotation of the planet around its own axis. You also need **glTranslate*()** to move the planet out to its orbit, away from the origin of the solar system. Remember that you can specify the desired sizes of the two spheres by supplying the appropriate arguments for the **glutWireSphere()** routine.

To draw the solar system, you first want to set up a projection and a viewing transformation. For this example, **gluPerspective()** and **gluLookAt()** are used.

Drawing the sun is straightforward, since it should be located at the origin of the grand, fixed coordinate system, which is where the sphere routine places it. Thus, drawing the sun doesn't require translation; you can use **glRotate*()** to make the sun rotate about an arbitrary axis. Drawing a planet rotating around the sun, as shown in Figure 3-24, requires several modeling transformations. The planet needs to rotate about its own axis once a day; and once a year, the planet completes one revolution around the sun.

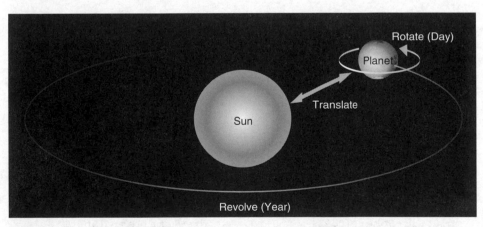

**Figure 3-24**     Planet and Sun

To determine the order of modeling transformations, visualize what happens to the local coordinate system. An initial **glRotate*()** rotates the local coordinate system that initially coincides with the grand coordinate system. Next, **glTranslate*()** moves the local coordinate system to a position on the planet's orbit; the distance moved should equal the radius of the orbit. Thus, the initial **glRotate*()** actually determines where along the orbit the planet is (or what time of year it is).

A second **glRotate*()** rotates the local coordinate system around the local axes, thus determining the time of day for the planet. Once you've issued all these transformation commands, the planet can be drawn.

In summary, the following OpenGL commands draw the sun and planet; the full program is shown in Example 3-6:

```
glPushMatrix();
glutWireSphere(1.0, 20, 16);        /* draw sun */
glRotatef((GLfloat) year, 0.0, 1.0, 0.0);
glTranslatef(2.0, 0.0, 0.0);
glRotatef((GLfloat) day, 0.0, 1.0, 0.0);
glutWireSphere(0.2, 10, 8);         /* draw smaller planet */
glPopMatrix();
```

**Example 3-6**    Planetary System: planet.c

```
static int year = 0, day = 0;

void init(void)
{
    glClearColor(0.0, 0.0, 0.0, 0.0);
    glShadeModel(GL_FLAT);
}

void display(void)
{
    glClear(GL_COLOR_BUFFER_BIT);
    glColor3f(1.0, 1.0, 1.0);

    glPushMatrix();
    glutWireSphere(1.0, 20, 16);    /* draw sun */
    glRotatef((GLfloat) year, 0.0, 1.0, 0.0);
    glTranslatef(2.0, 0.0, 0.0);
    glRotatef((GLfloat) day, 0.0, 1.0, 0.0);
    glutWireSphere(0.2, 10, 8);     /* draw smaller planet */
    glPopMatrix();
    glutSwapBuffers();
}

void reshape(int w, int h)
{
    glViewport(0, 0, (GLsizei) w, (GLsizei) h);
    glMatrixMode(GL_PROJECTION);
```

```
    glLoadIdentity();
    gluPerspective(60.0, (GLfloat) w/(GLfloat) h, 1.0, 20.0);
    glMatrixMode(GL_MODELVIEW);
    glLoadIdentity();
    gluLookAt(0.0, 0.0, 5.0, 0.0, 0.0, 0.0, 0.0, 1.0, 0.0);
}

void keyboard(unsigned char key, int x, int y)
{
    switch (key) {
        case 'd':
            day = (day + 10) % 360;
            glutPostRedisplay();
            break;
        case 'D':
            day = (day - 10) % 360;
            glutPostRedisplay();
            break;
        case 'y':
            year = (year + 5) % 360;
            glutPostRedisplay();
            break;
        case 'Y':
            year = (year - 5) % 360;
            glutPostRedisplay();
            break;
        default:
            break;
    }
}

int main(int argc, char** argv)
{
    glutInit(&argc, argv);
    glutInitDisplayMode(GLUT_DOUBLE | GLUT_RGB);
    glutInitWindowSize(500, 500);
    glutInitWindowPosition(100, 100);
    glutCreateWindow(argv[0]);
    init();
    glutDisplayFunc(display);
    glutReshapeFunc(reshape);
    glutKeyboardFunc(keyboard);
    glutMainLoop();
    return 0;
}
```

**Try This**

- Try adding a moon to the planet, or try several moons and additional planets. Hint: Use **glPushMatrix()** and **glPopMatrix()** to save and restore the position and orientation of the coordinate system at appropriate moments. If you're going to draw several moons around a planet, you need to save the coordinate system prior to positioning each moon and restore the coordinate system after each moon is drawn.

- Try tilting the planet's axis.

## Building an Articulated Robot Arm

This section discusses a program that creates an articulated robot arm with two or more segments. The arm should be connected with pivot points at the shoulder, elbow, or other joints. Figure 3-25 shows a single joint of such an arm.

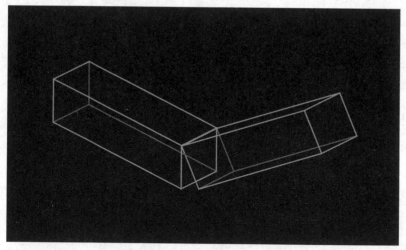

**Figure 3-25**    Robot Arm

You can use a scaled cube as a segment of the robot arm, but first you must call the appropriate modeling transformations to orient each segment. Since the origin of the local coordinate system is initially at the center of the cube, you need to move the local coordinate system to one edge of the cube. Otherwise, the cube rotates about its center, rather than the pivot point.

After you call **glTranslate\*()** to establish the pivot point and **glRotate\*()** to pivot the cube, translate back to the center of the cube. Then the cube is scaled (flattened and widened) before it is drawn. The **glPushMatrix()** and **glPopMatrix()** commands restrict the effect of **glScale\*()**. Here's what your code might look like for this first segment of the arm (the entire program is shown in Example 3-7):

```
glTranslatef(-1.0, 0.0, 0.0);
glRotatef((GLfloat) shoulder, 0.0, 0.0, 1.0);
glTranslatef(1.0, 0.0, 0.0);
glPushMatrix();
glScalef(2.0, 0.4, 1.0);
glutWireCube(1.0);
glPopMatrix();
```

To build a second segment, you need to move the local coordinate system to the next pivot point. Since the coordinate system has previously been rotated, the x-axis is already oriented along the length of the rotated arm. Therefore, translating along the x-axis moves the local coordinate system to the next pivot point. Once it's at that pivot point, you can use the same code to draw the second segment as you used for the first one. This can be continued for an indefinite number of segments (shoulder, elbow, wrist, fingers):

```
glTranslatef(1.0, 0.0, 0.0);
glRotatef((GLfloat) elbow, 0.0, 0.0, 1.0);
glTranslatef(1.0, 0.0, 0.0);
glPushMatrix();
glScalef(2.0, 0.4, 1.0);
glutWireCube(1.0);
glPopMatrix();
```

**Example 3-7**    Robot Arm: robot.c

```
static int shoulder = 0, elbow = 0;

void init(void)
{
   glClearColor(0.0, 0.0, 0.0, 0.0);
   glShadeModel(GL_FLAT);
}

void display(void)
{
   glClear(GL_COLOR_BUFFER_BIT);
   glPushMatrix();
   glTranslatef(-1.0, 0.0, 0.0);
   glRotatef((GLfloat) shoulder, 0.0, 0.0, 1.0);
```

```
      glTranslatef(1.0, 0.0, 0.0);
      glPushMatrix();
      glScalef(2.0, 0.4, 1.0);
      glutWireCube(1.0);
      glPopMatrix();

      glTranslatef(1.0, 0.0, 0.0);
      glRotatef((GLfloat) elbow, 0.0, 0.0, 1.0);
      glTranslatef(1.0, 0.0, 0.0);
      glPushMatrix();
      glScalef(2.0, 0.4, 1.0);
      glutWireCube(1.0);
      glPopMatrix();

      glPopMatrix();
      glutSwapBuffers();
}

void reshape(int w, int h)
{
      glViewport(0, 0, (GLsizei) w, (GLsizei) h);
      glMatrixMode(GL_PROJECTION);
      glLoadIdentity();
      gluPerspective(65.0, (GLfloat) w/(GLfloat) h, 1.0, 20.0);
      glMatrixMode(GL_MODELVIEW);
      glLoadIdentity();
      glTranslatef(0.0, 0.0, -5.0);
}

void keyboard(unsigned char key, int x, int y)
{
      switch (key) {
         case 's':   /*  s key rotates at shoulder  */
            shoulder = (shoulder + 5) % 360;
            glutPostRedisplay();
            break;
         case 'S':
            shoulder = (shoulder - 5) % 360;
            glutPostRedisplay();
            break;
         case 'e':   /*  e key rotates at elbow  */
            elbow = (elbow + 5) % 360;
            glutPostRedisplay();
            break;
```

```
      case 'E':
         elbow = (elbow - 5) % 360;
         glutPostRedisplay();
         break;
      default:
         break;
   }
}

int main(int argc, char** argv)
{
   glutInit(&argc, argv);
   glutInitDisplayMode(GLUT_DOUBLE | GLUT_RGB);
   glutInitWindowSize(500, 500);
   glutInitWindowPosition(100, 100);
   glutCreateWindow(argv[0]);
   init();
   glutDisplayFunc(display);
   glutReshapeFunc(reshape);
   glutKeyboardFunc(keyboard);
   glutMainLoop();
   return 0;
}
```

**Try This**

Try This

- Modify Example 3-7 to add additional segments to the robot arm.

- Modify Example 3-7 to add additional segments at the same position. For example, give the robot arm several "fingers" at the wrist, as shown in Figure 3-26. Hint: Use **glPushMatrix()** and **glPopMatrix()** to save and restore the position and orientation of the coordinate system at the wrist. If you're going to draw fingers at the wrist, you need to save the current matrix prior to positioning each finger, and restore the current matrix after each finger is drawn.

**Figure 3-26**   Robot Arm with Fingers

### Nate Robins' Transformation Tutorial

If you have Nate Robins' suite of tutorial programs, go back to the **transformation** tutorial and run it again. Use the popup menu interface to change the order of **glRotate*()** and **glTranslate()**, and note the effect of swapping the order of these routines.

## Reversing or Mimicking Transformations

The geometric processing pipeline is very good at using viewing and projection matrices and a viewport for clipping to transform the world (or object) coordinates of a vertex into window (or screen) coordinates. However, there are situations in which you want to reverse that process. A common situation is when an application user utilizes the mouse to choose a location in three dimensions. The mouse returns only a two-dimensional value, which is the screen location of the cursor. Therefore, the application will have to reverse the transformation process to determine where in three-dimensional space this screen location originated.

The Utility Library routines **gluUnProject()** and **gluUnProject4()** perform this reversal of the transformations. Given the three-dimensional window coordinates for a transformed vertex and all the transformations that affected it, **gluUnProject()** returns the original world coordinates of that vertex. (Use **gluUnProject4()** if the depth range is other than the default [0, 1].)

int **gluUnProject**(GLdouble *winx*, GLdouble *winy*, GLdouble *winz*,
                const GLdouble *modelMatrix[16]*,
                const GLdouble *projMatrix[16]*,
                const GLint *viewport[4]*,
                GLdouble *\*objx*, GLdouble *\*objy*, GLdouble *\*objz*);

Maps the specified window coordinates (*winx, winy, winz*) into object coordinates, using transformations defined by a modelview matrix (*modelMatrix*), projection matrix (*projMatrix*), and viewport (*viewport*). The resulting object coordinates are returned in *objx, objy,* and *objz*. The function returns GL_TRUE, indicating success, or GL_FALSE, indicating failure (such as a noninvertible matrix). This operation does not attempt to clip the coordinates to the viewport or eliminate depth values that fall outside of **glDepthRange()**.

There are inherent difficulties in trying to reverse the transformation process. A two-dimensional screen location could have originated from anywhere on an entire line in three-dimensional space. To disambiguate the result, **gluUnProject()** requires that a window depth coordinate (*winz*) be provided, specified in terms of **glDepthRange()**. (For more about depth range, see "The Transformed Depth Coordinate" on page 141.) For the default values of **glDepthRange()**, *winz* at 0.0 will request the world coordinates of the transformed point at the near clipping plane, while *winz* at 1.0 will request the point at the far clipping plane.

Example 3-8 demonstrates **gluUnProject()** by reading the mouse position and determining the three-dimensional points at the near and far clipping planes from which the mouse position was transformed. The computed world coordinates are printed to standard output, but the rendered window itself is just black.

**Example 3-8**    Reversing the Geometric Processing Pipeline: unproject.c

```
void display(void)
{
    glClear(GL_COLOR_BUFFER_BIT);
    glFlush();
}

void reshape(int w, int h)
{
    glViewport(0, 0, (GLsizei) w, (GLsizei) h);
    glMatrixMode(GL_PROJECTION);
    glLoadIdentity();
    gluPerspective(45.0, (GLfloat) w/(GLfloat) h, 1.0, 100.0);
    glMatrixMode(GL_MODELVIEW);
    glLoadIdentity();
}

void mouse(int button, int state, int x, int y)
{
    GLint viewport[4];
    GLdouble mvmatrix[16], projmatrix[16];
    GLint realy;  /*  OpenGL y coordinate position  */
    GLdouble wx, wy, wz;  /*  returned world x, y, z coords  */
```

```
        switch (button) {
          case GLUT_LEFT_BUTTON:
            if (state == GLUT_DOWN) {
              glGetIntegerv(GL_VIEWPORT, viewport);
              glGetDoublev(GL_MODELVIEW_MATRIX, mvmatrix);
              glGetDoublev(GL_PROJECTION_MATRIX, projmatrix);
/*  note viewport[3] is height of window in pixels   */
              realy = viewport[3] - (GLint) y - 1;
              printf("Coordinates at cursor are (%4d, %4d)\n",
                 x, realy);
              gluUnProject((GLdouble) x, (GLdouble) realy, 0.0,
                 mvmatrix, projmatrix, viewport, &wx, &wy, &wz);
              printf("World coords at z=0.0 are (%f, %f, %f)\n",
                 wx, wy, wz);
              gluUnProject((GLdouble) x, (GLdouble) realy, 1.0,
                 mvmatrix, projmatrix, viewport, &wx, &wy, &wz);
               printf("World coords at z=1.0 are (%f, %f, %f)\n",
                 wx, wy, wz);
            }
            break;
          case GLUT_RIGHT_BUTTON:
            if (state == GLUT_DOWN)
              exit(0);
            break;
          default:
            break;
      }
}

int main(int argc, char** argv)
{
    glutInit(&argc, argv);
    glutInitDisplayMode(GLUT_SINGLE | GLUT_RGB);
    glutInitWindowSize(500, 500);
    glutInitWindowPosition(100, 100);
    glutCreateWindow(argv[0]);
    glutDisplayFunc(display);
    glutReshapeFunc(reshape);
    glutMouseFunc(mouse);
    glutMainLoop();
    return 0;
}
```

GLU 1.3 introduces a modified version of **gluUnProject()**. **gluUnProject4()**
can handle nonstandard **glDepthRange()** values and also *w*-coordinate
values other than 1.

```
int gluUnProject4(GLdouble winx, GLdouble winy, GLdouble winz,
              GLdouble clipw, const GLdouble modelMatrix[16],
              const GLdouble projMatrix[16],
              const GLint viewport[4],
              GLclampd zNear, GLclampd zFar,
              GLdouble *objx, GLdouble *objy,
              GLdouble *objz, GLdouble *objw);
```

Overall, the operation is similar to **gluUnProject()**. Maps the specified window coordinates (*winx, winy, winz, clipw*) into object coordinates, using transformations defined by a modelview matrix (*modelMatrix*), projection matrix (*projMatrix*), viewport (*viewport*), and the depth range values *zNear* and *zFar*. The resulting object coordinates are returned in *objx, objy, objz*, and *objw*.

**gluProject()** is another Utility Library routine, which is related to **gluUnProject()**. **gluProject()** mimics the actions of the transformation pipeline. Given three-dimensional world coordinates and all the transformations that affect them, **gluProject()** returns the transformed window coordinates.

```
int gluProject(GLdouble objx, GLdouble objy, GLdouble objz,
           const GLdouble modelMatrix[16],
           const GLdouble projMatrix[16],
           const GLint viewport[4],
           GLdouble *winx, GLdouble *winy, GLdouble *winz);
```

Maps the specified object coordinates (*objx, objy, objz*) into window coordinates, using transformations defined by a modelview matrix (*modelMatrix*), projection matrix (*projMatrix*), and viewport (*viewport*). The resulting window coordinates are returned in *winx, winy*, and *winz*. The function returns GL_TRUE, indicating success, or GL_FALSE, indicating failure.

**Note:** The matrices passed to **gluUnProject()**, **gluUnProject4()**, and **gluProject()** are in the OpenGL-standard column-major order. You might use **glGetDoublev()** and **glGetIntegerv()** to obtain the current GL_MODELVIEW_MATRIX, GL_PROJECTION_MATRIX, and GL_VIEWPORT values for use with **gluUnProject()**, **gluUnProject4()**, or **gluProject()**.

*Chapter 4*

# Color

**Chapter Objectives**

After reading this chapter, you'll be able to do the following:

- Decide between using RGBA or color-index mode for your application

- Specify desired colors for drawing objects

- Use smooth shading to draw a single polygon with more than one color

The goal of almost all OpenGL applications is to draw color pictures in a window on the screen. The window is a rectangular array of pixels, each of which contains and displays its own color. Thus, in a sense, the point of all the calculations performed by an OpenGL implementation—calculations that take into account OpenGL commands, state information, and values of parameters—is to determine the final color of every pixel that's to be drawn in the window. This chapter explains the commands for specifying colors and how OpenGL interprets them in the following major sections:

- "Color Perception" discusses how the eye perceives color.

- "Computer Color" describes the relationship between pixels on a computer *monitor* and their colors; it also defines the two display modes: RGBA and color index.

- "RGBA versus Color-Index Mode" explains how the two display modes use graphics hardware and how to decide which mode to use.

- "Specifying a Color and a Shading Model" describes the OpenGL commands you use to specify the desired color or shading model.

## Color Perception

Physically, light is composed of photons—tiny particles of light, each traveling along its own path, and each vibrating at its own frequency (or wavelength or energy—any one of frequency, wavelength, or energy determines the others). A photon is completely characterized by its position, direction, and frequency/wavelength/energy. Photons with wavelengths ranging from about 390 nanometers (nm) (violet) and 720 nm (red) cover the colors of the visible spectrum, forming the colors of a rainbow (violet, indigo, blue, green, yellow, orange, red). However, your eyes perceive lots of colors that aren't in the rainbow—white, black, brown, and pink, for example. How does this happen?

What your eye actually sees is a mixture of photons of different frequencies. Real light sources are characterized by the distribution of photon frequencies they emit. Ideal white light consists of an equal amount of light of all frequencies. Laser light is usually very pure, and all photons are almost identical in frequency (and in direction and phase as well). Light from a sodium-vapor lamp has more light in the yellow frequency. Light from most stars in space has a distribution that depends heavily on their temperatures (black-body radiation). The frequency distribution of light from most sources in your immediate environment is more complicated.

The human eye perceives color when certain cells in the retina (called *cone cells*, or just *cones*) become excited after being struck by photons. The three different kinds of cone cells respond best to three different wavelengths of light: one type of cone cell responds best to red light, one to green light, and the other to blue light. (A person who is color-blind is usually missing one or more types of cone cells.) When a given mixture of photons enters the eye, the cone cells in the retina register different degrees of excitation depending on their types, and if a different mixture of photons happens to excite the three types of cone cells to the same degree, its color is indistinguishable from that of the first mixture.

Since each color is recorded by the eye as the levels of excitation of the cone cells produced by the incoming photons, the eye can perceive colors that aren't in the spectrum produced by a prism or rainbow. For example, if you send a mixture of red and blue photons so that both the red and blue cones in the retina are excited, your eye sees it as magenta, which isn't in the spectrum. Other combinations give browns, turquoises, and mauves, none of which appears in the color spectrum.

A computer-graphics monitor emulates visible colors by lighting pixels with a combination of red, green, and blue light in proportions that excite the red-, green-, and blue-sensitive cones in the retina in such a way that it matches the excitation levels generated by the photon mix it's trying to emulate. If humans had more types of cone cells, some that were yellow-sensitive for example, color monitors would probably have a yellow gun as well, and we'd use RGBY (red, green, blue, yellow) quadruples to specify colors. And if everyone were color-blind in the same way, this chapter would be simpler.

To display a particular color, the monitor sends the right amounts of red, green, and blue (RGB) light to stimulate appropriately the different types of cone cells in your eye. A color monitor can send different proportions of red, green, and blue to each of the pixels, and the eye sees a million or so pinpoints of light, each with its own color.

**Note:** There are many other representations of color, or color models, with acronyms such as HLS, HSV, and CMYK. If your data needs to be in one of these color models, you need to convert to and from RGB. For the formulas to perform these conversions, see Foley, van Dam, et al., *Computer Graphics: Principles and Practice* (Addison-Wesley, 1990).

This section considers only how the eye perceives combinations of photons that enter it. The situation for light bouncing off materials and entering the eye is even more complex—white light bouncing off a red ball will appear red, and yellow light shining through blue glass appears almost black, for example. (See "Real-World and OpenGL Lighting" in Chapter 5 for a discussion of these effects.)

## Computer Color

On a color computer screen, the hardware causes each pixel on the screen to emit different amounts of red, green, and blue light. These are called the R, G, and B values. They're often packed together (sometimes with a fourth value, called alpha, or A), and the packed value is called the RGB (or RGBA) value. (See "Blending" in Chapter 6 for an explanation of the alpha values.) The color information at each pixel can be stored either in *RGBA mode*, in which the R, G, B, and possibly A values are kept for each pixel, or in *color-index mode*, in which a single number (called the *color index*) is stored for each pixel. Each color index indicates an entry in a table that defines a particular set of R, G, and B values. Such a table is called a *color map*.

In color-index mode, you might want to alter the values in the color map. Since color maps are controlled by the window system, there are no OpenGL commands to do this. All the examples in this book initialize the color-display mode at the time the window is opened by using routines from the GLUT library. (See Appendix D for details.)

There is a great deal of variation among the different graphics hardware platforms in both the size of the pixel array and the number of colors that can be displayed at each pixel. On any graphics system, each pixel has the same amount of memory for storing its color, and all the memory for all the pixels is called the *color buffer*. The size of a buffer is usually measured in bits, so an 8-bit buffer could store 8 bits of data (256 possible different colors) for each pixel. The size of the possible buffers varies from machine to machine. (See Chapter 10 for more information.)

The R, G, and B values can range from 0.0 (none) to 1.0 (full intensity). For example, R = 0.0, G = 0.0, and B = 1.0 represents the brightest possible blue. If R, G, and B are all 0.0, the pixel is black; if all are 1.0, the pixel is drawn in the brightest white that can be displayed on the screen. *Blending* green and blue creates shades of cyan. Blue and red combine for magenta. Red and green create yellow. To help you create the colors you want from the R, G, and B components, look at the color cube shown in Plate 12. The axes of this cube represent intensities of red, blue, and green. A black-and-white version of the cube is shown in Figure 4-1.

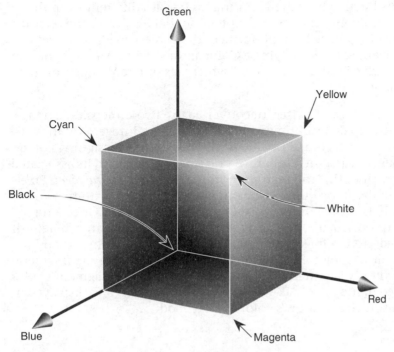

Green

Yellow

Cyan

Black

White

Red

Blue

Magenta

**Figure 4-1**     The Color Cube in Black and White

The commands used to specify a color for an object (in this case, a point) can be as simple as this:

```
glColor3f(1.0, 0.0, 0.0);   /* the current RGB color is red: */
                            /* full red, no green, no blue. */
glBegin(GL_POINTS);
    glVertex3fv(point_array);
glEnd();
```

In certain modes (for example, if lighting or texturing calculations are performed), the assigned color might go through other operations before arriving in the framebuffer as a value representing a color for a pixel. In fact, the color of a pixel is determined by a lengthy sequence of operations.

Early in a program's execution, the color-display mode is set to either RGBA mode or color-index mode. Once the color-display mode is initialized, it can't be changed. As the program executes, a color (either a color index or an RGBA value) is determined on a per-vertex basis for each geometric primitive. This color either is a color you've explicitly specified for a vertex or, if lighting is enabled, is determined from the interaction of the transformation matrices with the surface normals and other material properties. In other words, a red ball with a blue light shining on it looks different from the same ball with no light on it. (See Chapter 5 for details.) After the relevant lighting calculations have been performed, the chosen shading model is applied. As explained in "Specifying a Color and a Shading Model," you can choose flat or smooth shading, each of which has different effects on the eventual color of a pixel.

Next, the primitives are *rasterized*, or converted to a two-dimensional image. Rasterizing involves determining which squares of an integer grid in window coordinates are occupied by the primitive, and then assigning color and other values to each such square. A grid square along with its associated values of color, z (depth), and texture coordinates is called a *fragment*. Pixels are elements of the framebuffer; a fragment comes from a primitive and is combined with its corresponding pixel to yield a new pixel. Once a fragment has been constructed, texturing, fog, and antialiasing are applied—if they're enabled—to the fragments. After that, any specified alpha blending, *dithering*, and bitwise logical operations are carried out using the fragment and the pixel already stored in the framebuffer. Finally, the fragment's color value (either color index or RGBA) is written into the pixel and displayed in the window using the window's color-display mode.

## RGBA versus Color-Index Mode

In either color-index or RGBA mode, a certain amount of color data is stored at each pixel. This amount is determined by the number of bitplanes in the framebuffer. A *bitplane* contains 1 bit of data for each pixel. If there are 8 color bitplanes, there are 8 color bits per pixel, and hence $2^8 = 256$ different values or colors that can be stored at the pixel.

Bitplanes are often divided evenly into storage for R, G, and B components (that is, a 24-bitplane system devotes 8 bits each to red, green, and blue), but this isn't always true. To find out the number of bitplanes available on your system for red, green, blue, alpha, or color-index values, use **glGetIntegerv()** with GL_RED_BITS, GL_GREEN_BITS, GL_BLUE_BITS, GL_ALPHA_BITS, and GL_INDEX_BITS.

**Note:** Color intensities on most computer screens aren't perceived as linear by the human eye. Consider colors consisting of just a red component, with green and blue set at zero. As the intensity varies from 0.0 (off) to 1.0 (full on), the number of electrons striking the pixels increases, but the question is, does 0.5 appear to be halfway between 0.0 and 1.0? To test this, write a program that draws alternate pixels in a checkerboard pattern to intensities 0.0 and 1.0, and compare it with a region drawn solidly in color 0.5. At a reasonable distance from the screen, the two regions should appear to have the same intensity. If they look noticeably different, you need to use whatever correction mechanism is provided on your particular system. For example, many systems have a table to adjust intensities so that 0.5 appears to be halfway between 0.0 and 1.0. The mapping generally used is an exponential one, with the exponent referred to as gamma (hence the term *gamma correction*). Using the same gamma for the red, green, and blue components gives pretty good results, but three different gamma values might give slightly better results. (For more details on this topic, see Foley, van Dam, et al., *Computer Graphics: Principles and Practice*. Addison-Wesley, 1990.)

## RGBA Display Mode

In RGBA mode, the hardware sets aside a certain number of bitplanes for each of the R, G, B, and A components (not necessarily the same number for each component), as shown in Figure 4-2. The R, G, and B values are typically stored as integers, rather than floating-point numbers, and they're scaled to the number of available bits for storage and retrieval. For example, if a system has 8 bits available for the R component, integers between 0 and 255 can be stored; thus, 0, 1, 2, ..., 255 in the bitplanes would correspond to R values of 0/255 = 0.0, 1/255, 2/255, ..., 255/255 = 1.0. Regardless of the number of bitplanes, 0.0 specifies the minimum intensity, and 1.0 specifies the maximum intensity.

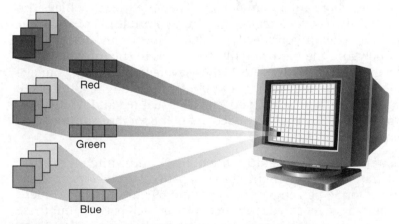

**Figure 4-2**     RGB Values from the Bitplanes

**Note:** The alpha value (the A in RGBA) has no direct effect on the color displayed on the screen. It can be used for many things, including blending and transparency, and it can have an effect on the values of R, G, and B that are written. (See "Blending" in Chapter 6 for more information about alpha values.)

The number of distinct colors that can be displayed at a single pixel depends on the number of bitplanes and the capacity of the hardware to interpret those bitplanes. The number of distinct colors can't exceed $2^n$, where $n$ is the number of bitplanes. Thus, a machine with 24 bitplanes for RGB can display up to 16.77 million distinct colors.

### Dithering

Advanced

Some graphics hardware uses dithering to increase the number of apparent colors. Dithering is the technique of using combinations of some colors to create the effects of other colors. To illustrate how dithering works, suppose your system has only 1 bit each for R, G, and B and thus can display only eight colors: black, white, red, blue, green, yellow, cyan, and magenta. To display a pink region, the hardware can fill the region in a checkerboard manner, alternating red and white pixels. If your eye is far enough away from the screen that it can't distinguish individual pixels, the region appears pink—the average of red and white. Redder pinks can be achieved by filling a higher proportion of the pixels with red, whiter pinks would use more white pixels, and so on.

With this technique, there are no pink pixels. The only way to achieve the effect of "pinkness" is to cover a region consisting of multiple pixels—you can't dither a single pixel. If you specify an RGB value for an unavailable color and fill a polygon, the hardware fills the pixels in the interior of the polygon with a mixture of nearby colors whose average appears to your eye to be the color you want. (Remember, though, that if you're reading pixel information out of the framebuffer, you get the actual red and white pixel values, since there aren't any pink ones. See Chapter 8 for more information about reading pixel values.)

Figure 4-3 illustrates some simple dithering of black and white pixels to make shades of gray. From left to right, the $4 \times 4$ patterns at the top represent dithering patterns for 50 percent, 19 percent, and 69 percent gray. Under each pattern, you can see repeated reduced copies of each pattern, but these black and white squares are still bigger than most pixels. If you look at them from across the room, you can see that they blur together and appear as three levels of gray.

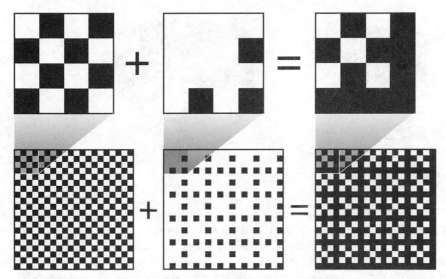

**Figure 4-3**    Dithering Black and White to Create Gray

With about 8 bits each of R, G, and B, you can get a fairly high-quality image without dithering. Just because your machine has 24 color bitplanes, however, doesn't mean that dithering won't be desirable. For example, if you are running in double-buffer mode, the bitplanes might be divided into two sets of 12, so there are really only 4 bits each per R, G, and B component. Without dithering, 4-bit-per-component color can give less than satisfactory results in many situations.

You enable or disable dithering by passing GL_DITHER to **glEnable()** or **glDisable()**. Note that dithering, unlike many other features, is enabled by default.

## Color-Index Display Mode

With color-index mode, OpenGL uses a color map (or *lookup table*), which is similar to using a palette to mix paints to prepare for a paint-by-number scene. A painter's palette provides spaces to mix paints together; similarly, a computer's color map provides indices where the primary red, green, and blue values can be mixed, as shown in Figure 4-4.

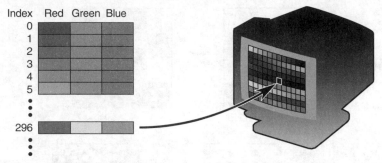

**Figure 4-4**     A Color Map

A painter filling in a paint-by-number scene chooses a color from the color palette and fills the corresponding numbered regions with that color. A computer stores the color index in the bitplanes for each pixel. Then those bitplane values reference the color map, and the screen is painted with the corresponding red, green, and blue values from the color map, as shown in Figure 4-5.

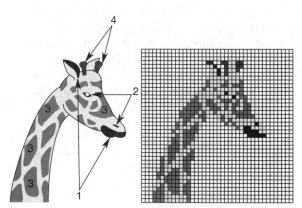

**Figure 4-5**     Using a Color Map to Paint a Picture

In color-index mode, the number of simultaneously available colors is limited by the size of the color map and the number of bitplanes available. The size of the color map is determined by the amount of hardware dedicated to it. The size of the color map is always a power of 2, and typical sizes range from 256 ($2^8$) to 4096 ($2^{12}$), where the exponent is the number of bitplanes being used. If there are $2^n$ indices in the color map and $m$ available bitplanes, the number of usable entries is the smaller of $2^n$ and $2^m$.

With RGBA mode, each pixel's color is independent of other pixels. However, in color-index mode, each pixel with the same index stored in its bitplanes shares the same color-map location. If the contents of an entry in the color map change, then all pixels of that color index change their color.

## Choosing between RGBA and Color-Index Mode

You should base your decision to use RGBA or color-index mode on what hardware is available and on what your application requires. For most systems, more colors can be simultaneously represented with RGBA mode than with color-index mode. Also, for several effects, such as shading, lighting, texture mapping, and fog, RGBA provides more flexibility than color-index mode.

You might prefer to use color-index mode in the following cases:

- If you're porting an existing application that makes significant use of color-index mode, it might be easier not to change to RGBA mode.

- If you have a small number of bitplanes available, RGBA mode may produce noticeably coarse shades of colors. For example, if you have only 8 bitplanes, in RGBA mode you may have only 3 bits for red, 3 bits for green, and 2 bits for blue. You'd have only 8 ($2^3$) shades of red and green, and only 4 shades of blue. The gradients between color shades are likely to be very obvious.

  In this situation, if you have limited shading requirements, you can use the color-lookup table to load more shades of colors. For example, if you need only shades of blue, you can use color-index mode and store up to 256 ($2^8$) shades of blue in the color-lookup table, which is much better than the 4 shades you would have in RGBA mode. Of course, this example would use up your entire color-lookup table, so you would have no shades of red, green, or other combined colors.

- Color-index mode can be useful for various tricks, such as color-map animation and drawing in layers. (See Chapter 14 for more information.)

In general, use RGBA mode wherever possible. It works with texture mapping and works better with lighting, shading, fog, antialiasing, and blending.

## Changing between Display Modes

In the best of all possible worlds, you might want to avoid making a choice between RGBA and color-index display mode. For example, you may want to use color-index mode for a color-map animation effect and then, when needed, immediately change the scene to RGBA mode for texture mapping.

Similarly, you may desire to switch between single and double buffering. For example, you may have very few bitplanes; let's say 8 bitplanes. In single-buffer mode, you'll have 256 ($2^8$) colors, but if you are using double-buffer mode to eliminate flickering from your animated program, you may have only 16 ($2^4$) colors. Perhaps you want to draw a moving object without flicker and are willing to sacrifice colors for using double-buffer mode (maybe the object is moving so fast that the viewer won't notice the details). But when the object comes to rest, you will want to draw it in single-buffer mode so that you can use more colors.

Unfortunately, most window systems won't allow an easy switch. For example, with the X Window System, the color-display mode is an attribute of the X Visual. An X Visual must be specified before the window is created. Once it is specified, it cannot be changed for the life of the window. After you create a window with a double-buffered, RGBA display mode, you're stuck with it.

A tricky solution to this problem is to create more than one window, each with a different display mode. You must control the visibility of each window (for example, mapping or unmapping an X Window, or managing or unmanaging a Motif or Athena widget) and draw the object in the appropriate, visible window.

# Specifying a Color and a Shading Model

OpenGL maintains a current color (in RGBA mode) and a current color index (in color-index mode). Unless you're using a more complicated coloring model such as lighting or texture mapping, each object is drawn using the current color (or color index). Look at the following pseudocode sequence:

```
set_color(RED);
draw_item(A);
draw_item(B);
set_color(GREEN);
set_color(BLUE);
draw_item(C);
```

Items A and B are drawn in red, and item C is drawn in blue. The fourth line, which sets the current color to green, has no effect (except to waste a bit of time). With no lighting or texturing, when the current color is set, all items drawn afterward are drawn in that color until the current color is changed.

## Specifying a Color in RGBA Mode

In RGBA mode, use the **glColor*()** command to select a current color.

void **glColor3**{b s i f d ub us ui}(*TYPE r, TYPE g, TYPE b*);
void **glColor4**{b s i f d ub us ui}(*TYPE r, TYPE g, TYPE b, TYPE a*);
void **glColor3**{b s i f d ub us ui}**v**(const *TYPE *v*);
void **glColor4**{b s i f d ub us ui}**v**(const *TYPE *v*);

Sets the current red, green, blue, and alpha values. This command can have up to three suffixes, which differentiate variations of the parameters accepted. The first suffix is either 3 or 4, to indicate whether you supply an alpha value in addition to the red, green, and blue values. If you don't supply an alpha value, it's automatically set to 1.0. The second suffix indicates the data type for parameters: byte, short, integer, float, double, unsigned byte, unsigned short, or unsigned integer. The third suffix is an optional **v**, which indicates that the argument is a pointer to an array of values of the given data type.

For the versions of **glColor*()** that accept floating-point data types, the values should typically range between 0.0 and 1.0, the minimum and maximum values that can be stored in the framebuffer. Unsigned-integer color components, when specified, are linearly mapped to floating-point values such that the largest representable value maps to 1.0 (full intensity), and zero maps to 0.0 (zero intensity). Signed-integer color components, when specified, are linearly mapped to floating-point values such that the most positive representable value maps to 1.0, and the most negative representable value maps to −1.0 (see Table 4-1).

Neither floating-point nor signed-integer values are clamped to the range [0, 1] before updating the current color or current lighting material parameters. After lighting calculations, resulting color values outside the range [0, 1] are clamped to the range [0, 1] before they are interpolated or written into a color buffer. Even if lighting is disabled, the color components are clamped before rasterization.

| Suffix | Data Type | Minimum Value | Min Value Maps to | Maximum Value | Max Value Maps to |
|---|---|---|---|---|---|
| b | 1-byte integer | −128 | −1.0 | 127 | 1.0 |
| s | 2-byte integer | −32,768 | −1.0 | 32,767 | 1.0 |
| i | 4-byte integer | −2,147,483,648 | −1.0 | 2,147,483,647 | 1.0 |
| ub | unsigned 1-byte integer | 0 | 0.0 | 255 | 1.0 |
| us | unsigned 2-byte integer | 0 | 0.0 | 65,535 | 1.0 |
| ui | unsigned 4-byte integer | 0 | 0.0 | 4,294,967,295 | 1.0 |

**Table 4-1**    Converting Color Values to Floating-Point Numbers

The similar routine **glSecondaryColor*()** is used to specify a color to be applied after texture mapping (if lighting is disabled). For more detail, see "Applying Secondary Color after Texturing" on page 455.

## Specifying a Color in Color-Index Mode

In color-index mode, use the **glIndex*()** command to select a single-valued color index as the current color index.

void **glIndex**{sifd ub}(TYPE *c*);
void **glIndex**{sifd ub}**v**(const TYPE *\*c*);

Sets the current color index to *c*. The first suffix for this command indicates the data type for parameters: short, integer, float, double, or unsigned byte. The second, optional suffix is **v**, which indicates that the argument is an array of values of the given data type (the array contains only one value).

In "Clearing the Window" in Chapter 2, you saw the specification of **glClearColor()**. For color-index mode, there is a corresponding **glClearIndex()**.

> void **glClearIndex**(GLfloat *cindex*);
>
> Sets the current clearing color in color-index mode. In a color-index mode window, a call to **glClear**(GL_COLOR_BUFFER_BIT) will use *cindex* to clear the buffer. The default clearing index is 0.0.

**Note:** OpenGL does not have any routines to load values into the color-lookup table. Window systems typically already have such operations. GLUT has the routine **glutSetColor**() to call the window-system-specific commands.

**Advanced**

The current index is stored as a floating-point value. Integer values are converted directly to floating-point values, with no special mapping. Index values outside the representable range of the color-index buffer aren't clamped. However, before an index is dithered (if enabled) and written to the framebuffer, it's converted to fixed-point format. Any bits in the integer portion of the resulting fixed-point value that don't correspond to bits in the framebuffer are masked out.

Advanced

## Specifying a Shading Model

A line or a filled polygon primitive can be drawn with a single color (flat shading) or with many different colors (smooth shading, also called *Gouraud shading*). You specify the desired shading technique with **glShadeModel**().

> void **glShadeModel**(GLenum *mode*);
>
> Sets the shading model. The mode parameter can be either GL_SMOOTH (the default) or GL_FLAT.

With flat shading, the color of one particular vertex of an independent primitive is duplicated across all the primitive's vertices to render that primitive. With smooth shading, the color at each vertex is treated individually. For a line primitive, the colors along the line segment are interpolated between the vertex colors. For a polygon primitive, the colors for the interior of the polygon are interpolated between the vertex colors. Example 4-1 draws a smooth-shaded triangle, as shown in Plate 11.

**Example 4-1**    Drawing a Smooth-Shaded Triangle: smooth.c

```c
void init(void)
{
   glClearColor(0.0, 0.0, 0.0, 0.0);
   glShadeModel(GL_SMOOTH);
}

void triangle(void)
{
   glBegin(GL_TRIANGLES);
   glColor3f(1.0, 0.0, 0.0);
   glVertex2f(5.0, 5.0);
   glColor3f(0.0, 1.0, 0.0);
   glVertex2f(25.0, 5.0);
   glColor3f(0.0, 0.0, 1.0);
   glVertex2f(5.0, 25.0);
   glEnd();
}

void display(void)
{
   glClear(GL_COLOR_BUFFER_BIT);
   triangle();
   glFlush();
}

void reshape(int w, int h)
{
   glViewport(0, 0, (GLsizei) w, (GLsizei) h);
   glMatrixMode(GL_PROJECTION);
   glLoadIdentity();
   if (w <= h)
      gluOrtho2D(0.0, 30.0, 0.0, 30.0*(GLfloat) h/(GLfloat) w);
   else
      gluOrtho2D(0.0, 30.0*(GLfloat) w/(GLfloat) h, 0.0, 30.0);
   glMatrixMode(GL_MODELVIEW);
}

int main(int argc, char** argv)
{
   glutInit(&argc, argv);
   glutInitDisplayMode(GLUT_SINGLE | GLUT_RGB);
   glutInitWindowSize(500, 500);
   glutInitWindowPosition(100, 100);
   glutCreateWindow(argv[0]);
```

```
    init();
    glutDisplayFunc(display);
    glutReshapeFunc(reshape);
    glutMainLoop();
    return 0;
}
```

With smooth shading, neighboring pixels have slightly different color values. In RGBA mode, adjacent pixels with slightly different values look similar, so the color changes across a polygon appear gradual. In color-index mode, adjacent pixels may reference different locations in the color-index table, which may not have similar colors at all. Adjacent color-index entries may contain wildly different colors, so a smooth-shaded polygon in color-index mode can look psychedelic.

To avoid this problem, you have to create a color ramp of smoothly changing colors among a contiguous set of indices in the color map. Remember that loading colors into a color map is performed through your window system, rather than through OpenGL. If you use GLUT, you can use **glutSetColor()** to load a single index in the color map with specified red, green, and blue values. The first argument for **glutSetColor()** is the index, and the others are the red, green, and blue values. To load 32 contiguous color indices (color indices 16 to 47) with slightly differing shades of yellow, you might call

```
for (i = 0; i < 32; i++) {
    glutSetColor(16+i, 1.0*(i/32.0), 1.0*(i/32.0), 0.0);
}
```

Now, if you render smooth-shaded polygons that use only the colors from indices 16 to 47, those polygons will have gradually differing shades of yellow.

With flat shading, the color of a single vertex defines the color of an entire primitive. For a line segment, the color of the line is the current color when the second (ending) vertex is specified. For a polygon, the color used is the one that's in effect when a particular vertex is specified, as shown in Table 4-2. The table counts vertices and polygons starting from 1. OpenGL follows these rules consistently, but the best way to avoid uncertainty about how a flat-shaded primitive will be drawn is to specify only one color for the primitive.

| Type of Polygon | Vertex Used to Select the Color for the $i$th Polygon |
|---|---|
| single polygon | 1 |
| triangle strip | $i + 2$ |
| triangle fan | $i + 2$ |
| independent triangle | $3i$ |
| quad strip | $2i + 2$ |
| independent quad | $4i$ |

**Table 4-2**    How OpenGL Selects a Color for the $i$th Flat-Shaded Polygon

## Chapter 5

# Lighting

**Chapter Objectives**

After reading this chapter, you'll be able to do the following:

- Understand how real-world lighting conditions are approximated by OpenGL

- Render illuminated objects by defining light source, material, and lighting model properties

- Define the material properties of the objects being illuminated

- Manipulate the matrix stack to control the positions of light sources

As you saw in Chapter 4, OpenGL computes the color of each pixel in a final, displayed scene that's held in the framebuffer. Part of this computation depends on what lighting is used in the scene and on how objects in the scene reflect or absorb that light. As an example of this, recall that the ocean has a different color on a bright, sunny day than it does on a gray, cloudy day. The presence of sunlight or clouds determines whether you see the ocean as bright turquoise or murky gray-green. In fact, most objects don't even look three-dimensional until they're lit. Figure 5-1 shows two versions of the exact same scene (a single sphere), one with lighting and one without.

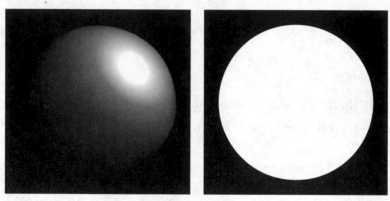

**Figure 5-1**     A Lit and an Unlit Sphere

As you can see, an unlit sphere looks no different from a two-dimensional disk. This demonstrates how critical the interaction between objects and light is in creating a three-dimensional scene.

With OpenGL, you can manipulate the lighting and objects in a scene to create many different kinds of effects. This chapter begins with a primer on hidden-surface removal. Then it explains how to control the lighting in a scene, discusses the OpenGL conceptual model of lighting, and describes in detail how to set the numerous illumination parameters to achieve certain effects. Toward the end of the chapter, the mathematical computations that determine how lighting affects color are presented.

This chapter contains the following major sections:

- "A Hidden-Surface Removal Survival Kit" describes the basics of removing hidden surfaces from view.

- "Real-World and OpenGL Lighting" explains in general terms how light behaves in the world and how OpenGL models this behavior.

- "A Simple Example: Rendering a Lit Sphere" introduces the OpenGL lighting facility by presenting a short program that renders a lit sphere.

- "Creating Light Sources" explains how to define and position light sources.

- "Selecting a Lighting Model" discusses the elements of a lighting model and how to specify them.

- "Defining Material Properties" explains how to describe the properties of objects so that they interact with light in a desired way.

- "The Mathematics of Lighting" presents the mathematical calculations used by OpenGL to determine the effect of lights in a scene.

- "Lighting in Color-Index Mode" discusses the differences between using RGBA mode and color-index mode for lighting.

Lighting calculations typically take place prior to texturing. Version 1.2 introduced a lighting mode (GL_SEPARATE_SPECULAR_COLOR) whereby the calculation of the specular color is done separately from the emissive, ambient, and diffuse components, and then the application of the specular color takes place after texturing. Using a separate specular color often enhances a highlight, making it less influenced by the color of the texture image.

## A Hidden-Surface Removal Survival Kit

With this section, you begin to draw shaded, three-dimensional objects in earnest. With shaded polygons, it becomes very important to draw the objects that are closer to the viewing position and to eliminate objects obscured by others nearer to the eye.

When you draw a scene composed of three-dimensional objects, some of them might obscure all or parts of others. Changing your viewpoint can change the obscuring relationship. For example, if you view the scene from the opposite direction, any object that was previously in front of another is now behind it. To draw a realistic scene, these obscuring relationships must be maintained. Suppose your code works like this:

```
while (1) {
    get_viewing_point_from_mouse_position();
    glClear(GL_COLOR_BUFFER_BIT);
    draw_3d_object_A();
    draw_3d_object_B();
}
```

For some mouse positions, object A might obscure object B. For others, the reverse may hold. If nothing special is done, the preceding code always draws object B second (and thus on top of object A) no matter what viewing position is selected. In a worst-case scenario, if objects A and B intersect one another so that part of object A obscures object B, and part of B obscures A, changing the drawing order does not provide a solution.

The elimination of parts of solid objects that are obscured by others is called *hidden-surface removal*. (Hidden-line removal, which does the same job for objects represented as wireframe skeletons, is a bit trickier and isn't discussed here. See "Hidden-Line Removal" in Chapter 14 for details.) The easiest way to achieve hidden-surface removal is to use the depth buffer (sometimes called a z-buffer). (Also see Chapter 10.)

A depth buffer works by associating a depth, or a distance, from the view plane (usually the near clipping plane), with each pixel on the window. Initially, the depth values for all pixels are set to the largest possible distance (usually the far clipping plane) using the **glClear()** command with GL_DEPTH_BUFFER_BIT. Then the objects in the scene are drawn in any order.

Graphical calculations in hardware or software convert each surface that's drawn to a set of pixels on the window where the surface will appear if it isn't obscured by something else. In addition, the distance from the view plane is computed. With depth-buffering enabled, before each pixel is drawn a comparison is done with the depth value already stored at the pixel. If the new pixel is closer than (in front of) what's there, the new pixel's color and depth values replace those that are currently written into the pixel. If the new pixel's depth is greater than what's currently there, the new pixel is obscured, and the color and depth information for the incoming pixel is discarded.

To use depth-buffering, you need to enable it. This has to be done only once. Before drawing, each time you draw the scene, you need to clear the depth buffer and then draw the objects in the scene in any order.

To convert the preceding code example so that it performs hidden-surface removal, modify it to the following:

```
glutInitDisplayMode(GLUT_DEPTH | .... );
glEnable(GL_DEPTH_TEST);
...
while (1) {
   glClear(GL_COLOR_BUFFER_BIT | GL_DEPTH_BUFFER_BIT);
   get_viewing_point_from_mouse_position();
   draw_3d_object_A();
   draw_3d_object_B();
}
```

The argument for **glClear()** clears both the depth and color buffers.

Depth-buffer testing can affect the performance of your application. Since information is discarded, rather than used for drawing, hidden-surface removal can increase your performance slightly. However, the implementation of your depth buffer probably has the greatest effect on performance. A "software" depth buffer (implemented with processor memory) may be much slower than one implemented with a specialized hardware depth buffer.

## Real-World and OpenGL Lighting

When you look at a physical surface, your eye's perception of the color depends on the distribution of photon energies that arrive and trigger your cone cells. (See "Color Perception" in Chapter 4.) Those photons come from a light source or combination of sources, some of which are absorbed and some of which are reflected by the surface. In addition, different surfaces may have very different properties—some are shiny and preferentially reflect light in certain directions, while others scatter incoming light equally in all directions. Most surfaces are somewhere in between.

OpenGL approximates light and lighting as if light can be broken into red, green, and blue components. Thus, the color of a light source is characterized by the amounts of red, green, and blue light it emits, and the material of a surface is characterized by the percentages of the incoming red, green, and blue components that are reflected in various directions. The OpenGL lighting equations are just approximations, but ones that work fairly well and can be computed relatively quickly. If you want a more accurate (or just different) lighting model, you have to do your own calculations in software. Such software can be enormously complex, as a few hours of reading any optics textbook should convince you.

In the OpenGL lighting model, the light in a scene comes from several light sources that can be individually turned on and off. Some light comes from a particular direction or position, and some light is generally scattered about the scene. For example, when you turn on a lightbulb in a room, most of the light comes from the bulb, but some light results from bouncing off one, two, three, or more walls. This bounced light (called *ambient* light) is assumed to be so scattered that there is no way to tell its original direction, but it disappears if a particular light source is turned off.

Finally, there might be a general ambient light in the scene that comes from no particular source, as if it had been scattered so many times that its original source is impossible to determine.

In the OpenGL model, the light sources have effects only when there are surfaces that absorb and reflect light. Each surface is assumed to be composed of a material with various properties. A material might emit its own light (such as headlights on an automobile), it might scatter some incoming light in all directions, and it might reflect some portion of the incoming light in a preferential direction (such as a mirror or other shiny surface).

The OpenGL lighting model considers the lighting to be divided into four independent components: ambient, diffuse, specular, and emissive. All four components are computed independently and then added together.

## Ambient, Diffuse, Specular, and Emissive Light

*Ambient* illumination is light that's been scattered so much by the environment that its direction is impossible to determine—it seems to come from all directions. Backlighting in a room has a large ambient component, since most of the light that reaches your eye has first bounced off many surfaces. A spotlight outdoors has a tiny ambient component; most of the light travels in the same direction, and since you're outdoors, very little of the light reaches your eye after bouncing off other objects. When ambient light strikes a surface, it's scattered equally in all directions.

The *diffuse* component is the light that comes from one direction, so it's brighter if it comes squarely down on a surface than if it barely glances off the surface. Once it hits a surface, however, it's scattered equally in all directions, so it appears equally bright, no matter where the eye is located. Any light coming from a particular position or direction probably has a diffuse component.

*Specular* light comes from a particular direction, and it tends to bounce off the surface in a preferred direction. A well-collimated laser beam bouncing off a high-quality mirror produces almost 100 percent specular reflection. Shiny metal or plastic has a high specular component, and chalk or carpet has almost none. You can think of specularity as shininess.

In addition to ambient, diffuse, and specular colors, materials may have an *emissive* color, which simulates light originating from an object. In the OpenGL lighting model, the emissive color of a surface adds intensity to the object, but is unaffected by any light sources. Also, the emissive color does not introduce any additional light into the overall scene.

Although a light source delivers a single distribution of frequencies, the ambient, diffuse, and specular components might be different. For example, if you have a white light in a room with red walls, the scattered light tends to be red, although the light directly striking objects is white. OpenGL allows you to set the red, green, and blue values for each component of light independently.

## Material Colors

The OpenGL lighting model approximates a material's color from the percentages of the incoming red, green, and blue light it reflects. For example, a perfectly red ball reflects all the incoming red light and absorbs all the green and blue light that strikes it. If you view such a ball in white light (composed of equal amounts of red, green, and blue light), all the red is reflected, and you see a red ball. If the ball is viewed in pure red light, it also appears to be red. If, however, the red ball is viewed in pure green light, it appears black (all the green is absorbed and there's no incoming red, so no light is reflected).

Like lights, materials have different ambient, diffuse, and specular colors, which determine the ambient, diffuse, and specular reflectances of the material. A material's ambient reflectance is combined with the ambient component of each incoming light source, the diffuse reflectance with the light's diffuse component, and similarly for the specular reflectance and specular component. Ambient and diffuse reflectances define the color of the material and are typically similar if not identical. Specular reflectance is usually white or gray, so that specular highlights end up being the color of the light source's specular intensity. If you think of a white light shining on a shiny red plastic sphere, most of the sphere appears red, but the shiny highlight is white.

## RGB Values for Lights and Materials

The color components specified for lights mean something different than for materials. For a light, the numbers correspond to a percentage of full intensity for each color. If the R, G, and B values for a light's color are all 1.0, the light is the brightest possible white. If the values are 0.5, the color is still white, but only at half intensity, so it appears gray. If R = G = 1 and B = 0 (full red and green with no blue), the light appears yellow.

For materials, the numbers correspond to the reflected proportions of those colors. So if R = 1, G = 0.5, and B = 0 for a material, that material reflects all the incoming red light, half the incoming green light, and none of the incoming blue light. In other words, if an OpenGL light has components (LR, LG, LB), and a material has corresponding components (MR, MG, MB), then, ignoring all other reflectivity effects, the light that arrives at the eye is given by (LR· MR, LG · MG, LB· MB).

Similarly, if you have two lights that send (R1, G1, B1) and (R2, G2, B2) to the eye, OpenGL adds the components, giving (R1 + R2, G1 + G2, B1 + B2). If any of the sums is greater than 1 (corresponding to a color brighter than the equipment can display), the component is clamped to 1.

## A Simple Example: Rendering a Lit Sphere

These are the steps required to add lighting to your scene:

1. Define normal vectors for each vertex of every object. These normals determine the orientation of the object relative to the light sources.

2. Create, select, and position one or more light sources.

3. Create and select a *lighting model*, which defines the level of global ambient light and the effective location of the viewpoint (for the purposes of lighting calculations).

4. Define material properties for the objects in the scene.

Example 5-1 accomplishes these tasks. It displays a sphere illuminated by a single light source, as shown earlier in Figure 5-1.

**Example 5-1**   Drawing a Lit Sphere: light.c

```
void init(void)
{
   GLfloat mat_specular[] = { 1.0, 1.0, 1.0, 1.0 };
   GLfloat mat_shininess[] = { 50.0 };
   GLfloat light_position[] = { 1.0, 1.0, 1.0, 0.0 };
   GLfloat white_light[] = { 1.0, 1.0, 1.0, 1.0 };
   GLfloat lmodel_ambient[] = { 0.1, 0.1, 0.1, 1.0 };
   glClearColor(0.0, 0.0, 0.0, 0.0);
   glShadeModel(GL_SMOOTH);
   glMaterialfv(GL_FRONT, GL_SPECULAR, mat_specular);
   glMaterialfv(GL_FRONT, GL_SHININESS, mat_shininess);
```

```
   glLightfv(GL_LIGHT0, GL_POSITION, light_position);
   glLightfv(GL_LIGHT0, GL_DIFFUSE, white_light);
   glLightfv(GL_LIGHT0, GL_SPECULAR, white_light);
   glLightModelfv(GL_LIGHT_MODEL_AMBIENT, lmodel_ambient);

   glEnable(GL_LIGHTING);
   glEnable(GL_LIGHT0);
   glEnable(GL_DEPTH_TEST);
}

void display(void)
{
   glClear(GL_COLOR_BUFFER_BIT | GL_DEPTH_BUFFER_BIT);
   glutSolidSphere(1.0, 20, 16);
   glFlush();
}

void reshape(int w, int h)
{
   glViewport(0, 0, (GLsizei) w, (GLsizei) h);
   glMatrixMode(GL_PROJECTION);
   glLoadIdentity();
   if (w <= h)
      glOrtho(-1.5, 1.5, -1.5*(GLfloat)h/(GLfloat)w,
         1.5*(GLfloat)h/(GLfloat)w, -10.0, 10.0);
   else
      glOrtho(-1.5*(GLfloat)w/(GLfloat)h,
         1.5*(GLfloat)w/(GLfloat)h, -1.5, 1.5, -10.0, 10.0);
   glMatrixMode(GL_MODELVIEW);
   glLoadIdentity();
}

int main(int argc, char** argv)
{
   glutInit(&argc, argv);
   glutInitDisplayMode(GLUT_SINGLE | GLUT_RGB | GLUT_DEPTH);
   glutInitWindowSize(500, 500);
   glutInitWindowPosition(100, 100);
   glutCreateWindow(argv[0]);
   init();
   glutDisplayFunc(display);
   glutReshapeFunc(reshape);
   glutMainLoop();
   return 0;
}
```

The lighting-related calls are in the **init**() command; they're discussed briefly in the following paragraphs and in more detail later in this chapter. One thing to note about Example 5-1 is that it uses RGBA color mode, not color-index mode. The OpenGL lighting calculation is different for the two modes, and in fact the lighting capabilities are more limited in color-index mode. Thus, RGBA is the preferred mode when doing lighting, and all the examples in this chapter use it. (See "Lighting in Color-Index Mode" on page 226 for more information.)

### Define Normal Vectors for Each Vertex of Every Object

An object's normals determine its orientation relative to the light sources. For each vertex, OpenGL uses the assigned normal to determine how much light that particular vertex receives from each light source. In this example, the normals for the sphere are defined as part of the **glutSolidSphere**() routine.

For proper lighting, surface normals must be of unit length. You must also be careful that the modelview transformation matrix does not scale the surface normal, so that the resulting normal is no longer of unit length. To ensure that normals are of unit length, you may need to call **glEnable**() with GL_NORMALIZE or GL_RESCALE_NORMAL as a parameter.

GL_RESCALE_NORMAL causes each component in a surface normal tobe multiplied by the same value, determined from the modelview transformation matrix. Therefore, it works correctly only if the normal was scaled uniformly and was a unit-length vector to begin with. GL_NORMALIZE is a more thorough operation than GL_RESCALE_NORMAL. When GL_NORMALIZE is enabled, the length of the normal vector is calculated, and then each component of the normal is divided by the calculated length. This operation guarantees that the resulting normal is of unit length, but may be more expensive than simply rescaling normals. (See "Normal Vectors" in Chapter 2 and Appendix E for more details on how to define normals.)

**Note:** Some OpenGL implementations may implement GL_RESCALE_ NORMAL by actually normalizing the normal vectors, not just scaling them. However, you cannot determine whether your implementation does this, nor should you usually rely on this.

## Create, Position, and Enable One or More Light Sources

Example 5-1 uses only one, white light source; its location is specified by the **glLightfv()** call. This example specifies white as the color for light zero (GL_LIGHT0) for calculations of diffuse and specular reflection. If you want a differently colored light, modify **glLight\*()**.

You can also include at least eight different light sources of various colors in your scene. (The particular implementation of OpenGL you're using might allow more than eight.) The default color of lights other than GL_LIGHT0 is black. You can also locate the lights wherever you desire: you can position them near the scene, as a desk lamp would be, or infinitely far away to simulate sunlight, for example. In addition, you can control whether a light produces a narrow, focused beam or a wider beam. Remember that each light source adds significantly to the calculations needed to render the scene, so performance is affected by the number of lights in the scene. (See "Creating Light Sources" on page 194 for more information about how to create lights with the desired characteristics.)

After you've defined the characteristics of the lights you want, you have to turn them on with the **glEnable()** command. You also need to call **glEnable()** with GL_LIGHTING as a parameter to prepare OpenGL to perform lighting calculations. (See "Enabling Lighting" on page 211 for more information.)

## Select a Lighting Model

As you might expect, the **glLightModel\*()** command describes the parameters of a lighting model. In Example 5-1, the only element of the lighting model that's defined explicitly is the global ambient light. The lighting model also defines whether the viewer of the scene should be considered to be infinitely far away or local to the scene, and whether lighting calculations should be performed differently for the front and back surfaces of objects in the scene. Example 5-1 uses the default settings for these two aspects of the model—a viewer infinitely far away ("infinite viewer" mode) and one-sided lighting. Using a local viewer adds significantly to the complexity of the calculations that must be performed, because OpenGL must calculate the angle between the viewpoint and each object. With an infinite viewer, however, the angle is ignored, and the results are slightly less realistic. Further, since in this example the back surface of the sphere is never seen (it's the inside of the sphere), one-sided lighting is sufficient. (See "Selecting a Lighting Model" on page 207 for a more detailed description of the elements of an OpenGL lighting model.)

### Define Material Properties for the Objects in the Scene

An object's material properties determine how it reflects light and therefore of what material it seems to be made. Because the interaction between an object's material surface and incident light is complex, specifying material properties so that an object has a certain desired appearance is an art. You can specify a material's ambient, diffuse, and specular colors and how shiny it is. In this example, only the last two material properties—the specular material color and shininess—are explicitly specified (with the **glMaterialfv()** calls). (See "Defining Material Properties" on page 211 for descriptions and examples of all the material-property parameters.)

### Some Important Notes

As you write your own lighting program, remember that you can use the default values for some lighting parameters, whereas others need to be changed. Also, don't forget to enable whatever lights you define and to enable lighting calculations. Finally, remember that you might be able to use display lists to maximize efficiency as you change lighting conditions. (See "Display List Design Philosophy" in Chapter 7.)

## Creating Light Sources

Light sources have several properties, such as color, position, and direction. The following sections explain how to control these properties and what the resulting light looks like. The command used to specify all properties of lights is **glLight*()**. Its three arguments identify the light whose property is being specified, the property, and the desired value for that property.

---

void **glLight**{if}(GLenum *light*, GLenum *pname*, TYPE *param*);
void **glLight**{if}v(GLenum *light*, GLenum *pname*, const TYPE *\*param*);

---

Creates the light specified by *light*, which can be GL_LIGHT0, GL_LIGHT1, ... , or GL_LIGHT7. The characteristic of the light being set is defined by *pname*, which specifies a named parameter (see Table 5-1). *param* indicates the values to which the *pname* characteristic is set; it's a pointer to a group of values if the vector version is used or the value itself if the nonvector version is used. The nonvector version can be used to set only single-valued light characteristics.

| Parameter Name | Default Values | Meaning |
| --- | --- | --- |
| GL_AMBIENT | (0.0, 0.0, 0.0, 1.0) | ambient intensity of light |
| GL_DIFFUSE | (1.0, 1.0, 1.0, 1.0) or (0.0, 0.0, 0.0, 1.0) | diffuse intensity of light (default for light 0 is white; for other lights, black) |
| GL_SPECULAR | (1.0, 1.0, 1.0, 1.0) or (0.0, 0.0, 0.0, 1.0) | specular intensity of light (default for light 0 is white; for other lights, black) |
| GL_POSITION | (0.0, 0.0, 1.0, 0.0) | $(x, y, z, w)$ position of light |
| GL_SPOT_DIRECTION | (0.0, 0.0, −1.0) | $(x, y, z)$ direction of spotlight |
| GL_SPOT_EXPONENT | 0.0 | spotlight exponent |
| GL_SPOT_CUTOFF | 180.0 | spotlight cutoff angle |
| GL_CONSTANT_ATTENUATION | 1.0 | constant attenuation factor |
| GL_LINEAR_ATTENUATION | 0.0 | linear attenuation factor |
| GL_QUADRATIC_ATTENUATION | 0.0 | quadratic attenuation factor |

**Table 5-1**    Default Values for *pname* Parameter of glLight*()

**Note:** The default values listed for GL_DIFFUSE and GL_SPECULAR in Table 5-1 differ from GL_LIGHT0 to other lights (GL_LIGHT1, GL_LIGHT2, etc.). For GL_LIGHT0, the default value is (1.0, 1.0, 1.0, 1.0) for both GL_DIFFUSE and GL_SPECULAR. For other lights, the default value is (0.0, 0.0, 0.0, 1.0) for the same light source properties.

Example 5-2 shows how to use **glLight*()**:

**Example 5-2**    Defining Colors and Position for a Light Source

```
GLfloat light_ambient[] = { 0.0, 0.0, 0.0, 1.0 };
GLfloat light_diffuse[] = { 1.0, 1.0, 1.0, 1.0 };
GLfloat light_specular[] = { 1.0, 1.0, 1.0, 1.0 };
GLfloat light_position[] = { 1.0, 1.0, 1.0, 0.0 };

glLightfv(GL_LIGHT0, GL_AMBIENT, light_ambient);
glLightfv(GL_LIGHT0, GL_DIFFUSE, light_diffuse);
glLightfv(GL_LIGHT0, GL_SPECULAR, light_specular);
glLightfv(GL_LIGHT0, GL_POSITION, light_position);
```

As you can see, arrays are defined for the parameter values, and **glLightfv()** is called repeatedly to set the various parameters. In this example, the first three calls to **glLightfv()** are superfluous, since they're being used to specify the default values for the GL_AMBIENT, GL_DIFFUSE, and GL_SPECULAR parameters.

**Note:** Remember to turn on each light with **glEnable()**. (See "Enabling Lighting" for more information about how to do this.)

All the parameters for **glLight*()** and their possible values are explained in the following sections. These parameters interact with those that define the overall lighting model for a particular scene and an object's material properties. (See "Selecting a Lighting Model" and "Defining Material Properties" for more information about these two topics. "The Mathematics of Lighting" explains how all these parameters interact mathematically.)

## Color

OpenGL allows you to associate three different color-related parameters—GL_AMBIENT, GL_DIFFUSE, and GL_SPECULAR—with any particular light. The GL_AMBIENT parameter refers to the RGBA intensity of the ambient light that a particular light source adds to the scene. As you can see in Table 5-1, by default there is no ambient light since GL_AMBIENT is (0.0, 0.0, 0.0, 1.0). This value was used in Example 5-1. If this program had specified blue ambient light as

```
GLfloat light_ambient[] = { 0.0, 0.0, 1.0, 1.0};
glLightfv(GL_LIGHT0, GL_AMBIENT, light_ambient);
```

the result would have been as shown on the left side of Plate 13.

The GL_DIFFUSE parameter probably most closely correlates with what you naturally think of as "the color of a light." It defines the RGBA color of the diffuse light that a particular light source adds to a scene. By default, GL_DIFFUSE is (1.0, 1.0, 1.0, 1.0) for GL_LIGHT0, which produces a bright, white light, as shown on the left side of Plate 13. The default value for any other light (GL_LIGHT1, ... , GL_LIGHT7) is (0.0, 0.0, 0.0, 0.0).

The GL_SPECULAR parameter affects the color of the specular highlight on an object. Typically, a real-world object such as a glass bottle has a specular highlight that's the color of the light shining on it (which is often white). Therefore, if you want to create a realistic effect, set the GL_SPECULAR parameter to the same value as the GL_DIFFUSE parameter. By default,

GL_SPECULAR is (1.0, 1.0, 1.0, 1.0) for GL_LIGHT0, and (0.0, 0.0, 0.0, 0.0) for any other light.

**Note:** The alpha component of these colors is not used until blending is enabled (see Chapter 6). Until then, the alpha value can be safely ignored.

## Position and Attenuation

As previously mentioned, you can choose between a light source that's treated as though it's located infinitely far away from the scene and one that's nearer to the scene. The first type is referred to as a *directional* light source; the effect of an infinite location is that the rays of light can be considered parallel by the time they reach an object. An example of a real-world directional light source is the sun. The second type is called a *positional* light source, since its exact position within the scene determines the effect it has on a scene and, specifically, the direction from which the light rays come. A desk lamp is an example of a positional light source. You can see the difference between directional and positional lights in Plate 13. The light used in Example 5-1 is a directional one:

```
GLfloat light_position[] = { 1.0, 1.0, 1.0, 0.0 };
glLightfv(GL_LIGHT0, GL_POSITION, light_position);
```

As shown, you supply a vector of four values ($x, y, z, w$) for the GL_POSITION parameter. If the last value, $w$, is zero, the corresponding light source is a directional one, and the ($x, y, z$) values describe its direction. This direction is transformed by the modelview matrix. By default, GL_POSITION is (0, 0, 1, 0), which defines a directional light that points along the negative $z$-axis. (Note that nothing prevents you from creating a directional light with the direction of (0, 0, 0), but such a light won't help you much.)

If the $w$–value is nonzero, the light is positional, and the ($x, y, z$) values specify the location of the light in homogeneous object coordinates (see Appendix F). This location is transformed by the modelview matrix and stored in eye coordinates. (See "Controlling a Light's Position and Direction" on page 201 for more information about how to control the transformation of the light's location.) Also, by default, a positional light radiates in all directions, but you can restrict it to producing a cone of illumination by defining the light as a spotlight. (See "Spotlights" on page 199 for an explanation of how to define a light as a spotlight.)

**Note:** Remember that the colors across the face of a smooth-shaded polygon are determined by the colors calculated for the vertices. Because of this, you probably want to avoid using large polygons with local lights. If you locate the light near the middle of the polygon, the vertices might be too far away to receive much light, and the whole polygon will look darker than you intended. To avoid this problem, break up the large polygon into smaller ones.

For real-world lights, the intensity of light decreases as distance from the light increases. Since a directional light is infinitely far away, it doesn't make sense to attenuate its intensity over distance, so attenuation is disabled for a directional light. However, you might want to attenuate the light from a positional light. OpenGL attenuates a light source by multiplying the contribution of that source by an attenuation factor:

$$\text{attenuation factor} = \frac{1}{k_c + k_l d + k_q d^2}$$

where

$d$ = distance between the light's position and the vertex

$k_c$ = GL_CONSTANT_ATTENUATION

$k_l$ = GL_LINEAR_ATTENUATION

$k_q$ = GL_QUADRATIC_ATTENUATION

By default, $k_c$ is 1.0 and both $k_l$ and $k_q$ are zero, but you can give these parameters different values:

```
glLightf(GL_LIGHT0, GL_CONSTANT_ATTENUATION, 2.0);
glLightf(GL_LIGHT0, GL_LINEAR_ATTENUATION, 1.0);
glLightf(GL_LIGHT0, GL_QUADRATIC_ATTENUATION, 0.5);
```

Note that the ambient, diffuse, and specular contributions are all attenuated. Only the emission and global ambient values aren't attenuated. Also note that since attenuation requires an additional division (and possibly more math) for each calculated color, using attenuated lights may slow down application performance.

## Spotlights

As previously mentioned, you can have a positional light source act as a spotlight by restricting the shape of the light it emits to a cone. To create a spotlight, you need to determine the spread of the cone of light you desire. (Remember that since spotlights are positional lights, you also have to locate them where you want them. Again, note that nothing prevents you from creating a directional spotlight, but it won't give you the result you want.) To specify the angle between the axis of the cone and a ray along the edge of the cone, use the GL_SPOT_CUTOFF parameter. The angle of the cone at the apex is then twice this value, as shown in Figure 5-2.

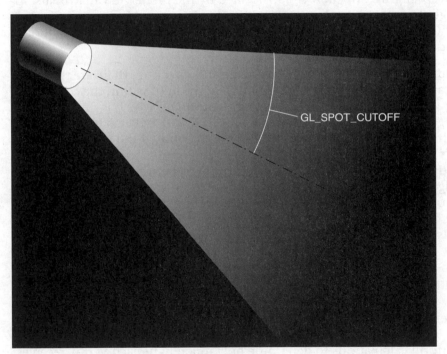

**Figure 5-2**      GL_SPOT_CUTOFF Parameter

Note that no light is emitted beyond the edges of the cone. By default, the spotlight feature is disabled because the GL_SPOT_CUTOFF parameter is 180.0. This value means that light is emitted in all directions (the angle at the cone's apex is 360 degrees, so it isn't a cone at all). The value for

GL_SPOT_CUTOFF is restricted to the range [0.0, 90.0] (unless it has the special value 180.0). The following line sets the cutoff parameter to 45 degrees:

```
glLightf(GL_LIGHT0, GL_SPOT_CUTOFF, 45.0);
```

You also need to specify a spotlight's direction, which determines the axis of the cone of light:

```
GLfloat spot_direction[] = { -1.0, -1.0, 0.0 };
glLightfv(GL_LIGHT0, GL_SPOT_DIRECTION, spot_direction);
```

The direction is specified in object coordinates. By default, the direction is (0.0, 0.0, −1.0), so if you don't explicitly set the value of GL_SPOT_DIRECTION, the light points down the negative z-axis. Also, keep in mind that a spotlight's direction is transformed by the modelview matrix just as though it were a normal vector, and the result is stored in eye coordinates. (See "Controlling a Light's Position and Direction" for more information about such transformations.)

In addition to the spotlight's cutoff angle and direction, there are two ways you can control the intensity distribution of the light within the cone. First, you can set the attenuation factor described earlier, which is multiplied by the light's intensity. You can also set the GL_SPOT_EXPONENT parameter, which by default is zero, to control how concentrated the light is. The light's intensity is highest in the center of the cone. It's attenuated toward the edges of the cone by the cosine of the angle between the direction of the light and the direction from the light to the vertex being lit, raised to the power of the spot exponent. Thus, higher spot exponents result in a more focused light source. (See "The Mathematics of Lighting" for more details on the equations used to calculate light intensity.)

## Multiple Lights

As mentioned, you can have at least eight lights in your scene (possibly more, depending on your OpenGL implementation). Since OpenGL needs to perform calculations to determine how much light each vertex receives from each light source, increasing the number of lights adversely affects performance. The constants used to refer to the eight lights are GL_LIGHT0, GL_LIGHT1, GL_LIGHT2, GL_LIGHT3, and so on. In the preceding discussions, parameters related to GL_LIGHT0 were set. If you want an additional light, you need to specify its parameters; also, remember that the default values are different for these other lights than they are for GL_LIGHT0, as explained in Table 5-1. Example 5-3 defines a white attenuated spotlight.

**Example 5-3**    Second Light Source

```
GLfloat light1_ambient[] = { 0.2, 0.2, 0.2, 1.0 };
GLfloat light1_diffuse[] = { 1.0, 1.0, 1.0, 1.0 };
GLfloat light1_specular[] = { 1.0, 1.0, 1.0, 1.0 };
GLfloat light1_position[] = { -2.0, 2.0, 1.0, 1.0 };
GLfloat spot_direction[] = { -1.0, -1.0, 0.0 };

glLightfv(GL_LIGHT1, GL_AMBIENT, light1_ambient);
glLightfv(GL_LIGHT1, GL_DIFFUSE, light1_diffuse);
glLightfv(GL_LIGHT1, GL_SPECULAR, light1_specular);
glLightfv(GL_LIGHT1, GL_POSITION, light1_position);
glLightf(GL_LIGHT1, GL_CONSTANT_ATTENUATION, 1.5);
glLightf(GL_LIGHT1, GL_LINEAR_ATTENUATION, 0.5);
glLightf(GL_LIGHT1, GL_QUADRATIC_ATTENUATION, 0.2);

glLightf(GL_LIGHT1, GL_SPOT_CUTOFF, 45.0);
glLightfv(GL_LIGHT1, GL_SPOT_DIRECTION, spot_direction);
glLightf(GL_LIGHT1, GL_SPOT_EXPONENT, 2.0);

glEnable(GL_LIGHT1);
```

If these lines were added to Example 5-1, the sphere would be lit with two lights, one directional and one spotlight.

**Try This**

Modify Example 5-1 in the following manner:

Try This

- Change the first light to be a positional colored light, rather than a directional white one.

- Add an additional colored spotlight. Hint: Use some of the code shown in the preceding section.

- Measure how these two changes affect performance.

## Controlling a Light's Position and Direction

OpenGL treats the position and direction of a light source just as it treats the position of a geometric primitive. In other words, a light source is subject to the same matrix transformations as a primitive. More specifically, when **glLight*()** is called to specify the position or the direction of a light source, the position or direction is transformed by the current modelview matrix and stored in eye coordinates. This means you can manipulate a light source's position or direction by changing the contents of the modelview matrix. (The projection matrix has no effect on a light's position or direction.) This section explains how to achieve the following three different effects by changing the point in the program at which the light position is set, relative to modeling or viewing transformations:

- A light position that remains fixed
- A light that moves around a stationary object
- A light that moves along with the viewpoint

## Keeping the Light Stationary

In the simplest example, as in Example 5-1, the light position remains fixed. To achieve this effect, you need to set the light position after whatever viewing and/or modeling transformation you use. Example 5-4 shows how the relevant code from the **init()** and **reshape()** routines might look.

**Example 5-4**    Stationary Light Source

```
glViewport(0, 0, (GLsizei) w, (GLsizei) h);
glMatrixMode(GL_PROJECTION);
glLoadIdentity();
if (w <= h)
    glOrtho(-1.5, 1.5, -1.5*h/w, 1.5*h/w, -10.0, 10.0);
else
    glOrtho(-1.5*w/h, 1.5*w/h, -1.5, 1.5, -10.0, 10.0);
glMatrixMode(GL_MODELVIEW);
glLoadIdentity();

/* later in init() */
GLfloat light_position[] = { 1.0, 1.0, 1.0, 1.0 };
glLightfv(GL_LIGHT0, GL_POSITION, position);
```

As you can see, the viewport and projection matrices are established first. Then, the identity matrix is loaded as the modelview matrix, after which the light position is set. Since the identity matrix is used, the originally specified light position (1.0, 1.0, 1.0) isn't changed by being multiplied by the modelview matrix. Then, since neither the light position nor the modelview matrix is modified after this point, the direction of the light remains (1.0, 1.0, 1.0).

## Independently Moving the Light

Now suppose you want to rotate or translate the light position so that the light moves relative to a stationary object. One way to do this is to set the light position after the modeling transformation, which is itself changed specifically to modify the light position. You can begin with the same series of calls in **init**() early in the program. Then you need to perform the desired modeling transformation (on the modelview stack) and reset the light position, probably in **display**(). Example 5-5 shows what **display**() might be.

**Example 5-5**    Independently Moving Light Source

```
static GLdouble spin;

void display(void)
{
    GLfloat light_position[] = { 0.0, 0.0, 1.5, 1.0 };
    glClear(GL_COLOR_BUFFER_BIT | GL_DEPTH_BUFFER_BIT);

    glPushMatrix();
        gluLookAt(0.0, 0.0, 5.0, 0.0, 0.0, 0.0, 0.0, 1.0, 0.0);
        glPushMatrix();
            glRotated(spin, 1.0, 0.0, 0.0);
            glLightfv(GL_LIGHT0, GL_POSITION, light_position);
        glPopMatrix();
        glutSolidTorus(0.275, 0.85, 8, 15);
    glPopMatrix();
    glFlush();
}
```

*spin* is a global variable and is probably controlled by an input device. **display**() causes the scene to be redrawn with the light rotated *spin* degrees around a stationary torus. Note the two pairs of **glPushMatrix**() and **glPopMatrix**() calls, which are used to isolate the viewing and modeling transformations, all of which occur on the modelview stack. Since in Example 5-5 the viewpoint remains constant, the current matrix is pushed down the stack and then the desired viewing transformation is loaded with **gluLookAt**(). The matrix stack is pushed again before the modeling transformation **glRotated**() is specified. Then the light position is set in the new, rotated coordinate system so that the light itself appears to be rotated from its previous position. (Remember that the light position is stored in eye coordinates, which are obtained after transformation by the modelview matrix.) After the rotated matrix is popped off the stack, the torus is drawn.

Example 5-6 is a program that rotates a light source around an object. When the left mouse button is pressed, the light position rotates an additional 30 degrees. A small, unlit, wireframe cube is drawn to represent the position of the light in the scene.

**Example 5-6**  Moving a Light with Modeling Transformations: movelight.c

```c
static int spin = 0;

void init(void)
{
   glClearColor(0.0, 0.0, 0.0, 0.0);
   glShadeModel(GL_SMOOTH);
   glEnable(GL_LIGHTING);
   glEnable(GL_LIGHT0);
   glEnable(GL_DEPTH_TEST);
}

/*  Here is where the light position is reset after the modeling
 *  transformation (glRotated) is called.  This places the
 *  light at a new position in world coordinates.  The cube
 *  represents the position of the light.
 */
void display(void)
{
   GLfloat position[] = { 0.0, 0.0, 1.5, 1.0 };

   glClear(GL_COLOR_BUFFER_BIT | GL_DEPTH_BUFFER_BIT);
   glPushMatrix();
   glTranslatef(0.0, 0.0, -5.0);

   glPushMatrix();
   glRotated((GLdouble) spin, 1.0, 0.0, 0.0);
   glLightfv(GL_LIGHT0, GL_POSITION, position);

   glTranslated(0.0, 0.0, 1.5);
   glDisable(GL_LIGHTING);
   glColor3f(0.0, 1.0, 1.0);
   glutWireCube(0.1);
   glEnable(GL_LIGHTING);
   glPopMatrix();

   glutSolidTorus(0.275, 0.85, 8, 15);
   glPopMatrix();
   glFlush();
}

void reshape(int w, int h)
{
   glViewport(0, 0, (GLsizei) w, (GLsizei) h);
   glMatrixMode(GL_PROJECTION);
   glLoadIdentity();
```

```
    gluPerspective(40.0, (GLfloat) w/(GLfloat) h, 1.0, 20.0);
    glMatrixMode(GL_MODELVIEW);
    glLoadIdentity();
}

void mouse(int button, int state, int x, int y)
{
    switch (button) {
        case GLUT_LEFT_BUTTON:
            if (state == GLUT_DOWN) {
                spin = (spin + 30) % 360;
                glutPostRedisplay();
            }
            break;
        default:
            break;
    }
}
int main(int argc, char** argv)
{
    glutInit(&argc, argv);
    glutInitDisplayMode(GLUT_SINGLE | GLUT_RGB | GLUT_DEPTH);
    glutInitWindowSize(500, 500);
    glutInitWindowPosition(100, 100);
    glutCreateWindow(argv[0]);
    init();
    glutDisplayFunc(display);
    glutReshapeFunc(reshape);
    glutMouseFunc(mouse);
    glutMainLoop();
    return 0;
}
```

## Moving the Light Source Together with the Viewpoint

To create a light that moves along with the viewpoint, you need to set
the light position before the viewing transformation. Then the viewing
transformation affects both the light and the viewpoint in the same way.
Remember that the light position is stored in eye coordinates, and this is
one of the few times when eye coordinates are critical. In Example 5-7, the
light position is defined in **init**(), which stores the light position at (0, 0, 0)
in eye coordinates. In other words, the light is shining from the lens of the
camera.

**Example 5-7**    Light Source That Moves with the Viewpoint

```
GLfloat light_position[] = { 0.0, 0.0, 0.0, 1.0 };

glViewport(0, 0, (GLint) w, (GLint) h);
glMatrixMode(GL_PROJECTION);
glLoadIdentity();
gluPerspective(40.0, (GLfloat) w/(GLfloat) h, 1.0, 100.0);
glMatrixMode(GL_MODELVIEW);
glLoadIdentity();
glLightfv(GL_LIGHT0, GL_POSITION, light_position);
```

If the viewpoint is now moved, the light will move along with it, maintaining (0, 0, 0) distance, relative to the eye. In the continuation of Example 5-7, which follows next, the global variables (*ex, ey, ez*) control the position of the viewpoint, and (*upx, upy, upz*) control the value of the up-vector. The **display**() routine that's called from the event loop to redraw the scene might be as follows:

```
static GLdouble ex, ey, ez, upx, upy, upz;

void display(void)
{
    glClear(GL_COLOR_BUFFER_BIT | GL_DEPTH_BUFFER_BIT);
    glPushMatrix();
        gluLookAt(ex, ey, ez, 0.0, 0.0, 0.0, upx, upy, upz);
        glutSolidTorus(0.275, 0.85, 8, 15);
    glPopMatrix();
    glFlush();
}
```

When the lit torus is redrawn, both the light position and the viewpoint are moved to the same location. As the values passed to **gluLookAt()** change and the eye moves, the object will never appear dark, because it is always being illuminated from the eye position. Even though you haven't respecified the light position, the light moves because the eye coordinate system has changed.

This method of moving the light can be represented by simulating the illumination from a miner's hat. Another example would be carrying a candle or lantern. The light position specified by the call to **glLightfv(GL_LIGHTi, GL_POSITION, position)** would be the *x*-, *y*-, and *z*-distances from the eye position to the illumination source. Then, as the eye position moves, the light will remain the same relative distance away.

**Try This**

Try This

Modify Example 5-6 in the following manner:

- Make the light translate past the object instead of rotating around it. Hint: Use **glTranslated()** rather than the first **glRotated()** in **display()**, and choose an appropriate value to use instead of *spin*.

- Change the attenuation so that the light decreases in intensity as it is moved away from the object. Hint: Add calls to **glLight*()** to set the desired attenuation parameters.

**Nate Robins' Lightposition Tutorial**

If you have downloaded Nate Robins' suite of tutorial programs, now run the **lightposition** tutorial. (For information on how and where to download these programs, see "Nate Robins' OpenGL Tutors" on page xl.) With this tutorial, you can experiment with the light source position and the effect of the modelview matrix.

# Selecting a Lighting Model

The OpenGL notion of a lighting model has four components:

- The global ambient light intensity

- Whether the viewpoint position is local to the scene or should be considered to be an infinite distance away

- Whether lighting calculations should be performed differently for both the front and back faces of objects

- Whether the specular color should be separated from ambient and diffuse colors and applied after the texturing operation

This section explains how to specify a lighting model. It also discusses how to enable lighting—that is, how to tell OpenGL that you want lighting calculations to be performed.

The command used to specify all properties of the lighting model is **glLightModel*()**. **glLightModel*()** has two arguments: the lighting model property and the desired value for that property.

void **glLightModel**{if}(GLenum *pname*, *TYPE param*);
void **glLightModel**{if}**v**(GLenum *pname*, const *TYPE *param*);

Sets properties of the lighting model. The characteristic of the lighting model being set is defined by *pname*, which specifies a named parameter (see Table 5-2). *param* indicates the values to which the *pname* characteristic is set; it's a pointer to a group of values if the vector version is used or the value itself if the nonvector version is used. The nonvector version can be used to set only single-valued lighting model characteristics, not for GL_LIGHT_MODEL_AMBIENT.

| Parameter Name | Default Value | Meaning |
| --- | --- | --- |
| GL_LIGHT_MODEL_AMBIENT | (0.2, 0.2, 0.2, 1.0) | ambient RGBA intensity of the entire scene |
| GL_LIGHT_MODEL_LOCAL_VIEWER | 0.0 or GL_FALSE | how specular reflection angles are computed |
| GL_LIGHT_MODEL_TWO_SIDE | 0.0 or GL_FALSE | specifies one-sided or two-sided lighting |
| GL_LIGHT_MODEL_COLOR_CONTROL | GL_SINGLE_COLOR | whether specular color is calculated separately from ambient and diffuse |

**Table 5-2**     Default Values for *pname* Parameter of glLightModel*()

## Global Ambient Light

As discussed earlier, each light source can contribute ambient light to a scene. In addition, there can be other ambient light that's not from any particular source. To specify the RGBA intensity of such global ambient light, use the GL_LIGHT_MODEL_AMBIENT parameter as follows:

```
GLfloat lmodel_ambient[] = { 0.2, 0.2, 0.2, 1.0 };
glLightModelfv(GL_LIGHT_MODEL_AMBIENT, lmodel_ambient);
```

In this example, the values used for *lmodel_ambient* are the default values for GL_LIGHT_MODEL_AMBIENT. Since these numbers yield a small amount of white ambient light, even if you don't add a specific light source to your scene, you can still see the objects in the scene. Plate 14 shows the effects of different amounts of global ambient light.

## Local or Infinite Viewpoint

The location of the viewpoint affects the calculations for highlights produced by specular reflectance. More specifically, the intensity of the highlight at a particular vertex depends on the normal at that vertex, the direction from the vertex to the light source, and the direction from the vertex to the viewpoint. Keep in mind that the viewpoint isn't actually being moved by calls to lighting commands (you need to change the projection transformation, as described in "Projection Transformations" in Chapter 3); instead, different assumptions are made for the lighting calculations, as if the viewpoint were moved.

With an infinite viewpoint, the direction between it and any vertex in the scene remains constant. A local viewpoint tends to yield more realistic results, but since the direction has to be calculated for each vertex, overall performance is decreased with a local viewpoint. By default, an infinite viewpoint is assumed. Here's how to change to a local viewpoint:

```
glLightModeli(GL_LIGHT_MODEL_LOCAL_VIEWER, GL_TRUE);
```

This call places the viewpoint at (0, 0, 0) in eye coordinates. To switch back to an infinite viewpoint, pass in GL_FALSE as the argument.

## Two-Sided Lighting

Lighting calculations are performed for all polygons, whether they're front-facing or back-facing. Since you usually set up lighting conditions with the front-facing polygons in mind, however, the back-facing ones typically aren't correctly illuminated. In Example 5-1, where the object is a sphere, only the front faces are ever seen, since they're the ones on the outside of the sphere. Therefore, in this case, it doesn't matter what the back-facing polygons look like. If the sphere is going to be cut away so that its inside surface will be visible, however, you might want to have the inside surface fully lit according to the lighting conditions you've defined; you might also want to supply a different material description for the back faces. When you turn on two-sided lighting with

```
glLightModeli(GL_LIGHT_MODEL_TWO_SIDE, GL_TRUE);
```

OpenGL reverses the surface normals for back-facing polygons; typically, this means that the surface normals of visible back- and front-facing polygons face, rather than point away from, the viewer. As a result, all polygons are illuminated correctly. However, these additional operations usually make two-sided lighting perform more slowly than the default one-sided lighting.

To turn two-sided lighting off, pass in GL_FALSE as the argument in the preceding call. (See "Defining Material Properties" on page 211 for information about how to supply material properties for both faces.) You can also control which faces OpenGL considers to be front-facing with the command **glFrontFace()**. (See "Reversing and Culling Polygon Faces" on page 56 for more information.)

## Secondary Specular Color

For typical lighting calculations, the ambient, diffuse, specular, and emissive contributions are calculated and simply added together. By default, texture mapping is applied after lighting, so specular highlights may appear muted, or texturing may look undesirable in other ways. To delay application of the specular color until after texturing, call

```
glLightModeli(GL_LIGHT_MODEL_COLOR_CONTROL,
              GL_SEPARATE_SPECULAR_COLOR);
```

In this mode, lighting produces two colors per vertex: a primary color, which consists of all nonspecular lighting contributions, and a secondary color, which is a sum of all specular lighting contributions. During texture mapping, only the primary color is combined with the texture colors. After texturing, the secondary color is added to the resulting combination of primary and texture colors (see "Applying Secondary Color after Texturing" on page 455). Objects that are lit and textured using a separate specular color usually have more visible and prominent specular highlights.

To restore the default, call

```
glLightModeli(GL_LIGHT_MODEL_COLOR_CONTROL, GL_SINGLE_COLOR);
```

Once again, the primary color includes all contributing colors: ambient, diffuse, specular, and emissive. Lighting contributions are not added after texturing. (If you are not performing texture mapping, there isn't any reason to separate the specular color from the other lighting components.)

## Enabling Lighting

With OpenGL, you need to enable (or disable) lighting explicitly. If lighting isn't enabled, the current color is simply mapped onto the current vertex, and no calculations concerning normals, light sources, the lighting model, or material properties are performed. Here's how to enable lighting:

```
glEnable(GL_LIGHTING);
```

To disable lighting, call **glDisable()** with GL_LIGHTING as the argument.

You also need explicitly to enable each light source that you define, after you've specified the parameters for that source. Example 5-1 uses only one light, GL_LIGHT0:

```
glEnable(GL_LIGHT0);
```

## Defining Material Properties

You've seen how to create light sources with certain characteristics and how to define the desired lighting model. This section describes how to define the material properties of the objects in the scene: the ambient, diffuse, and specular color, the shininess, and the color of any emitted light. (See "The Mathematics of Lighting" for the equations used in the lighting and material-property calculations.) Most of the material properties are conceptually similar to ones you've already used to create light sources. The mechanism for setting them is similar, except that the command used is called **glMaterial*()**.

void **glMaterial**{if}(GLenum *face*, GLenum *pname*, TYPE *param*);
void **glMaterial**{if}v(GLenum *face*, GLenum *pname*, const TYPE *\*param*);

Specifies a current material property for use in lighting calculations. *face* can be GL_FRONT, GL_BACK, or GL_FRONT_AND_BACK to indicate to which faces of the object the material should be applied. The particular material property being set is identified by *pname*, and the desired values for that property are given by *param*, which is either a pointer to a group of values (if the vector version is used) or the actual value (if the nonvector version is used). The nonvector version works only for setting GL_SHININESS. The possible values for *pname* are shown in Table 5-3. Note that GL_AMBIENT_AND_DIFFUSE allows you to set both the ambient and diffuse material colors simultaneously to the same RGBA value.

| Parameter Name | Default Value | Meaning |
| --- | --- | --- |
| GL_AMBIENT | (0.2, 0.2, 0.2, 1.0) | ambient color of material |
| GL_DIFFUSE | (0.8, 0.8, 0.8, 1.0) | diffuse color of material |
| GL_AMBIENT_AND_DIFFUSE | | ambient and diffuse color of material |
| GL_SPECULAR | (0.0, 0.0, 0.0, 1.0) | specular color of material |
| GL_SHININESS | 0.0 | specular exponent |
| GL_EMISSION | (0.0, 0.0, 0.0, 1.0) | emissive color of material |
| GL_COLOR_INDEXES | (0, 1, 1) | ambient, diffuse, and specular color indices |

**Table 5-3**    Default Values for *pname* Parameter of glMaterial*()

As discussed in "Selecting a Lighting Model," you can choose to have lighting calculations performed differently for the front- and back-facing polygons of objects. If the back faces might indeed be seen, you can supply different material properties for the front and back surfaces by using the *face* parameter of **glMaterial*()**. See Plate 14 for an example of an object drawn with different inside and outside material properties.

To give you an idea of the possible effects you can achieve by manipulating material properties, see Plate 16. This figure shows the same object drawn with several different sets of material properties. The same light source and lighting model are used for the entire figure. The sections that follow discuss the specific properties used to draw each of these spheres.

Note that most of the material properties set with **glMaterial*()** are (R, G, B, A) colors. Regardless of what alpha values are supplied for other parameters, the alpha value at any particular vertex is the diffuse-material alpha value (that is, the alpha value given to GL_DIFFUSE with the **glMaterial*()** command, as described in the next section). (See "Blending" in Chapter 6 for a complete discussion of alpha values.) Also, none of the RGBA material properties apply in color-index mode. (See "Lighting in Color-Index Mode" on page 226 for more information about what parameters are relevant in color-index mode.)

## Diffuse and Ambient Reflection

The GL_DIFFUSE and GL_AMBIENT parameters set with **glMaterial*()** affect the colors of the diffuse and ambient light reflected by an object. Diffuse reflectance plays the most important role in determining what you perceive the color of an object to be. Your perception is affected by the color of the incident diffuse light and the angle of the incident light relative to the normal direction. (It's most intense where the incident light falls perpendicular to the surface.) The position of the viewpoint doesn't affect diffuse reflectance at all.

Ambient reflectance affects the overall color of the object. Because diffuse reflectance is brightest where an object is directly illuminated, ambient reflectance is most noticeable where an object receives no direct illumination. An object's total ambient reflectance is affected by the global ambient light and ambient light from individual light sources. Like diffuse reflectance, ambient reflectance isn't affected by the position of the viewpoint.

For real-world objects, diffuse and ambient reflectance are normally the same color. For this reason, OpenGL provides you with a convenient way of assigning the same value to both simultaneously with **glMaterial*()**:

```
GLfloat mat_amb_diff[] = { 0.1, 0.5, 0.8, 1.0 };
glMaterialfv(GL_FRONT_AND_BACK, GL_AMBIENT_AND_DIFFUSE,
             mat_amb_diff);
```

In this example, the RGBA color (0.1, 0.5, 0.8, 1.0)—a deep blue color—represents the current ambient and diffuse reflectance for both the front- and back-facing polygons.

In Plate 16, the first row of spheres has no ambient reflectance (0.0, 0.0, 0.0, 0.0), and the second row has a significant amount of it (0.7, 0.7, 0.7, 1.0).

## Specular Reflection

Specular reflection from an object produces highlights. Unlike ambient and diffuse reflection, the amount of specular reflection seen by a viewer does depend on the location of the viewpoint—it is brightest along the direct angle of reflection. To see this, imagine looking at a metallic ball outdoors in the sunlight. As you move your head, the highlight created by the sunlight moves with you to some extent. However, if you move your head too much, you lose the highlight entirely.

OpenGL allows you to set the effect that the material has on reflected light (with GL_SPECULAR) and control the size and brightness of the highlight (with GL_SHININESS). You can assign a number in the range [0.0, 128.0] to GL_SHININESS: the higher the value, the smaller and brighter (more focused) the highlight. (See "The Mathematics of Lighting" on page 220 for details about how specular highlights are calculated.)

In Plate 16, the spheres in the first column have no specular reflection. In the second column, GL_SPECULAR and GL_SHININESS are assigned values as follows:

```
GLfloat mat_specular[] = { 1.0, 1.0, 1.0, 1.0 };
GLfloat low_shininess[] = { 5.0 };
glMaterialfv(GL_FRONT, GL_SPECULAR, mat_specular);
glMaterialfv(GL_FRONT, GL_SHININESS, low_shininess);
```

In the third column, the GL_SHININESS parameter is increased to 100.0.

## Emission

By specifying an RGBA color for GL_EMISSION, you can make an object appear to be giving off light of that color. Since most real-world objects (except lights) don't emit light, you'll probably use this feature mostly to simulate lamps and other light sources in a scene. In Plate 16, the spheres in the fourth column have a reddish-gray value for GL_EMISSION:

```
GLfloat mat_emission[] = {0.3, 0.2, 0.2, 0.0};
glMaterialfv(GL_FRONT, GL_EMISSION, mat_emission);
```

Notice that the spheres appear to be slightly glowing; however, they're not actually acting as light sources. You would need to create a light source and position it at the same location as the sphere to create such an effect.

## Changing Material Properties

Example 5-1 uses the same material properties for all vertices of the only object in the scene (the sphere). In other situations, you might want to assign different material properties for different vertices on the same object. More likely, you have more than one object in the scene, and each object has different material properties. For example, the code that produced Plate 16 has to draw 12 different objects (all spheres), each with different material properties. Example 5-8 shows a portion of the code in **display()**.

**Example 5-8**   Different Material Properties: material.c

```
GLfloat no_mat[] = { 0.0, 0.0, 0.0, 1.0 };
GLfloat mat_ambient[] = { 0.7, 0.7, 0.7, 1.0 };
GLfloat mat_ambient_color[] = { 0.8, 0.8, 0.2, 1.0 };
GLfloat mat_diffuse[] = { 0.1, 0.5, 0.8, 1.0 };
GLfloat mat_specular[] = { 1.0, 1.0, 1.0, 1.0 };
GLfloat no_shininess[] = { 0.0 };
GLfloat low_shininess[] = { 5.0 };
GLfloat high_shininess[] = { 100.0 };
GLfloat mat_emission[] = {0.3, 0.2, 0.2, 0.0};

   glClear(GL_COLOR_BUFFER_BIT | GL_DEPTH_BUFFER_BIT);

/* draw sphere in first row, first column
 * diffuse reflection only; no ambient or specular
 */
   glPushMatrix();
   glTranslatef(-3.75, 3.0, 0.0);
   glMaterialfv(GL_FRONT, GL_AMBIENT, no_mat);
   glMaterialfv(GL_FRONT, GL_DIFFUSE, mat_diffuse);
   glMaterialfv(GL_FRONT, GL_SPECULAR, no_mat);
   glMaterialfv(GL_FRONT, GL_SHININESS, no_shininess);
   glMaterialfv(GL_FRONT, GL_EMISSION, no_mat);
   glutSolidSphere(1.0, 16, 16);
   glPopMatrix();

/* draw sphere in first row, second column
 * diffuse and specular reflection; low shininess; no ambient
 */
   glPushMatrix();
   glTranslatef(-1.25, 3.0, 0.0);
   glMaterialfv(GL_FRONT, GL_AMBIENT, no_mat);
   glMaterialfv(GL_FRONT, GL_DIFFUSE, mat_diffuse);
```

```
   glMaterialfv(GL_FRONT, GL_SPECULAR, mat_specular);
   glMaterialfv(GL_FRONT, GL_SHININESS, low_shininess);
   glMaterialfv(GL_FRONT, GL_EMISSION, no_mat);
   glutSolidSphere(1.0, 16, 16);
   glPopMatrix();

/* draw sphere in first row, third column
 * diffuse and specular reflection; high shininess; no ambient
 */
   glPushMatrix();
   glTranslatef(1.25, 3.0, 0.0);
   glMaterialfv(GL_FRONT, GL_AMBIENT, no_mat);
   glMaterialfv(GL_FRONT, GL_DIFFUSE, mat_diffuse);
   glMaterialfv(GL_FRONT, GL_SPECULAR, mat_specular);
   glMaterialfv(GL_FRONT, GL_SHININESS, high_shininess);
   glMaterialfv(GL_FRONT, GL_EMISSION, no_mat);
   glutSolidSphere(1.0, 16, 16);
   glPopMatrix();

/* draw sphere in first row, fourth column
 * diffuse reflection; emission; no ambient or specular refl.
 */
   glPushMatrix();
   glTranslatef(3.75, 3.0, 0.0);
   glMaterialfv(GL_FRONT, GL_AMBIENT, no_mat);
   glMaterialfv(GL_FRONT, GL_DIFFUSE, mat_diffuse);
   glMaterialfv(GL_FRONT, GL_SPECULAR, no_mat);
   glMaterialfv(GL_FRONT, GL_SHININESS, no_shininess);
   glMaterialfv(GL_FRONT, GL_EMISSION, mat_emission);
   glutSolidSphere(1.0, 16, 16);
   glPopMatrix();
```

As you can see, **glMaterialfv()** is called repeatedly to set the desired material property for each sphere. Note that it needs to be called only to change a property that has to be respecified. The second, third, and fourth spheres use the same ambient and diffuse properties as the first sphere, so these properties do not need to be respecified. Since **glMaterial*()** has a performance cost associated with its use, Example 5-8 could be rewritten to minimize material-property changes.

### Nate Robins' Lightmaterial Tutorial

If you have downloaded Nate Robins' suite of tutorial programs, now run the **lightmaterial** tutorial. With this tutorial, you can experiment with the colors of material properties, including ambient, diffuse, and specular colors, as well as the shininess exponent.

## Color Material Mode

Another technique for minimizing performance costs associated with changing material properties is to use **glColorMaterial()**.

---

void **glColorMaterial**(GLenum *face*, GLenum *mode*);

---

Causes the material property (or properties) specified by *mode* of the specified material face (or faces) specified by *face* to track the value of the current color at all times. A change to the current color (using **glColor\*()**) immediately updates the specified material properties. The *face* parameter can be GL_FRONT, GL_BACK, or GL_FRONT_AND_BACK (the default). The *mode* parameter can be GL_AMBIENT, GL_DIFFUSE, GL_SPECULAR, GL_AMBIENT_AND_DIFFUSE (the default), or GL_EMISSION. At any given time, only one mode is active. **glColorMaterial()** has no effect on color-index lighting.

Note that **glColorMaterial()** specifies two independent values: the first determines which face or faces are updated, and the second determines which material property or properties of those faces are updated. OpenGL does *not* maintain separate *mode* variables for each face.

After calling **glColorMaterial()**, you need to call **glEnable()** with GL_COLOR_MATERIAL as the parameter. Then, you can change the current color using **glColor\*()** (or other material properties, using **glMaterial\*()**) as needed as you draw:

```
glEnable(GL_COLOR_MATERIAL);
glColorMaterial(GL_FRONT, GL_DIFFUSE);
/* now glColor* changes diffuse reflection   */
glColor3f(0.2, 0.5, 0.8);
/* draw some objects here */
glColorMaterial(GL_FRONT, GL_SPECULAR);
/* glColor* no longer changes diffuse reflection
 * now glColor* changes specular reflection   */
glColor3f(0.9, 0.0, 0.2);
/* draw other objects here */
glDisable(GL_COLOR_MATERIAL);
```

You should use **glColorMaterial()** whenever you need to change a single material parameter for most vertices in your scene. If you need to change more than one material parameter, as was the case for Plate 16, use **glMaterial\*()**. When you don't need the capabilities of **glColorMaterial()** anymore, be sure to disable it so that you don't get undesired material properties and don't incur the performance cost associated with it. The performance value in using **glColorMaterial**() varies, depending on your OpenGL implementation. Some implementations may be able to optimize the vertex routines so that they can quickly update material properties based on the current color.

Example 5-9 shows an interactive program that uses **glColorMaterial**() to change material parameters. Pressing each of the three mouse buttons changes the color of the diffuse reflection.

**Example 5-9**   Using glColorMaterial(): colormat.c

```
GLfloat diffuseMaterial[4] = { 0.5, 0.5, 0.5, 1.0 };

void init(void)
{
    GLfloat mat_specular[] = { 1.0, 1.0, 1.0, 1.0 };
    GLfloat light_position[] = { 1.0, 1.0, 1.0, 0.0 };

    glClearColor(0.0, 0.0, 0.0, 0.0);
    glShadeModel(GL_SMOOTH);
    glEnable(GL_DEPTH_TEST);
    glMaterialfv(GL_FRONT, GL_DIFFUSE, diffuseMaterial);
    glMaterialfv(GL_FRONT, GL_SPECULAR, mat_specular);
    glMaterialf(GL_FRONT, GL_SHININESS, 25.0);
    glLightfv(GL_LIGHT0, GL_POSITION, light_position);
    glEnable(GL_LIGHTING);
    glEnable(GL_LIGHT0);

    glColorMaterial(GL_FRONT, GL_DIFFUSE);
    glEnable(GL_COLOR_MATERIAL);
}

void display(void)
{
    glClear(GL_COLOR_BUFFER_BIT | GL_DEPTH_BUFFER_BIT);
    glutSolidSphere(1.0, 20, 16);
    glFlush();
}

void reshape(int w, int h)
{
    glViewport(0, 0, (GLsizei) w, (GLsizei) h);
    glMatrixMode(GL_PROJECTION);
    glLoadIdentity();
```

```c
    if (w <= h)
        glOrtho(-1.5, 1.5, -1.5*(GLfloat)h/(GLfloat)w,
            1.5*(GLfloat)h/(GLfloat)w, -10.0, 10.0);
    else
        glOrtho(-1.5*(GLfloat)w/(GLfloat)h,
            1.5*(GLfloat)w/(GLfloat)h, -1.5, 1.5, -10.0, 10.0);
    glMatrixMode(GL_MODELVIEW);
    glLoadIdentity();
}

void mouse(int button, int state, int x, int y)
{
    switch (button) {
        case GLUT_LEFT_BUTTON:
            if (state == GLUT_DOWN) {          /*  change red  */
                diffuseMaterial[0] += 0.1;
                if (diffuseMaterial[0] > 1.0)
                    diffuseMaterial[0] = 0.0;
                glColor4fv(diffuseMaterial);
                glutPostRedisplay();
            }
            break;
        case GLUT_MIDDLE_BUTTON:
            if (state == GLUT_DOWN) {          /*  change green  */
                diffuseMaterial[1] += 0.1;
                if (diffuseMaterial[1] > 1.0)
                    diffuseMaterial[1] = 0.0;
                glColor4fv(diffuseMaterial);
                glutPostRedisplay();
            }
            break;
        case GLUT_RIGHT_BUTTON:
            if (state == GLUT_DOWN) {          /*  change blue  */
                diffuseMaterial[2] += 0.1;
                if (diffuseMaterial[2] > 1.0)
                    diffuseMaterial[2] = 0.0;
                glColor4fv(diffuseMaterial);
                glutPostRedisplay();
            }
            break;
        default:
            break;
    }
}
```

```
int main(int argc, char** argv)
{
    glutInit(&argc, argv);
    glutInitDisplayMode(GLUT_SINGLE | GLUT_RGB | GLUT_DEPTH);
    glutInitWindowSize(500, 500);
    glutInitWindowPosition(100, 100);
    glutCreateWindow(argv[0]);
    init();
    glutDisplayFunc(display);
    glutReshapeFunc(reshape);
    glutMouseFunc(mouse);
    glutMainLoop();
    return 0;
}
```

**Try This**

Modify Example 5-8 in the following manner:

Try This
- Change the global ambient light in the scene. Hint: Alter the value of the GL_LIGHT_MODEL_AMBIENT parameter.

- Change the diffuse, ambient, and specular reflection parameters, the shininess exponent, and the emission color. Hint: Use the **glMaterial*()** command, but avoid making excessive calls.

- Use two-sided materials and add a user-defined clipping plane so that you can see the inside and outside of a row or column of spheres. (See "Additional Clipping Planes" in Chapter 3, if you need to recall user-defined clipping planes.) Hint: Turn on two-sided lighting with GL_LIGHT_MODEL_TWO_SIDE, set the desired material properties, and add a clipping plane.

- Remove the **glMaterialfv()** call for setting the GL_DIFFUSE value, and use the more efficient **glColorMaterial()** calls to achieve the same lighting.

## The Mathematics of Lighting

**Advanced**

Advanced
This section presents the equations used by OpenGL to perform lighting calculations to determine colors when in RGBA mode. (See "The Mathematics of Color-Index Mode Lighting" for corresponding calculations for color-index

mode.) You don't need to read this section if you're willing to experiment to obtain the lighting conditions you want. Even after reading this section, you'll probably have to experiment, but you'll have a better idea of how the values of parameters affect a vertex's color. Remember that if lighting is not enabled, the color of a vertex is simply the current color; if it is enabled, the lighting computations described here are carried out in eye coordinates.

In the following equations, mathematical operations are performed separately on the R, G, and B components. Thus, for example, when three terms are shown as added together, the R values, the G values, and the B values for each term are separately added to form the final RGB color $(R_1 + R_2 + R_3, G_1 + G_2 + G_3, B_1 + B_2 + B_3)$. When three terms are multiplied, the calculation is $(R_1 R_2 R_3, G_1 G_2 G_3, B_1 B_2 B_3)$. (Remember that the final A or alpha component at a vertex is equal to the material's diffuse alpha value at that vertex.)

The color produced by lighting a vertex is computed as follows:

vertex color =     the material emission at that vertex +

the global ambient light scaled by the material's ambient property at that vertex   +

the ambient, diffuse, and specular contributions from all the light sources, properly attenuated

After lighting calculations are performed, the color values are clamped (in RGBA mode) to the range [0, 1].

Note that OpenGL lighting calculations don't take into account the possibility of one object blocking light from another; as a result, shadows aren't automatically created. (See "Shadows" in Chapter 14 for a technique used to create shadows.) Also keep in mind that with OpenGL, illuminated objects don't radiate light onto other objects.

## Material Emission

The material emission term is the simplest. It's the RGB value assigned to the GL_EMISSION parameter.

## Scaled Global Ambient Light

The second term is computed by multiplying the global ambient light (as defined by the GL_LIGHT_MODEL_AMBIENT parameter) by the material's ambient property (GL_AMBIENT value as assigned with **glMaterial\*()**):

$$\text{ambient}_{\text{light model}} * \text{ambient}_{\text{material}}$$

Each of the R, G, and B values for these two parameters are multiplied separately to compute the final RGB value for this term: $(R_1 R_2, G_1 G_2, B_1 B_2)$.

## Contributions from Light Sources

Each light source may contribute to a vertex's color, and these contributions are added together. The equation for computing each light source's contribution is as follows:

contribution = attenuation factor * spotlight effect *

(ambient term + diffuse term + specular term)

### Attenuation Factor

The *attenuation factor* was described in "Position and Attenuation":

$$\text{attenuation factor} = \frac{1}{k_c + k_l d + k_q d^2}$$

where

$d$ = distance between the light's position and the vertex

$k_c$ = GL_CONSTANT_ATTENUATION

$k_l$ = GL_LINEAR_ATTENUATION

$k_q$ = GL_QUADRATIC_ATTENUATION

If the light is a directional one, the attenuation factor is 1.

### Spotlight Effect

The *spotlight effect* evaluates to one of three possible values, depending on whether or not the light is actually a spotlight and whether the vertex lies inside or outside the cone of illumination produced by the spotlight:

- 1 if the light isn't a spotlight (GL_SPOT_CUTOFF is 180.0).

- 0 if the light is a spotlight, but the vertex lies outside the cone of illumination produced by the spotlight.

- $(\max \{\mathbf{v} \cdot \mathbf{d}, 0\})^{\text{GL\_SPOT\_EXPONENT}}$ where:

    $\mathbf{v} = (v_x, v_y, v_z)$ is the unit vector that points from the spotlight (GL_POSITION) to the vertex.

    $\mathbf{d} = (d_x, d_y, d_z)$ is the spotlight's direction (GL_SPOT_DIRECTION), assuming the light is a spotlight and the vertex lies inside the cone of illumination produced by the spotlight.

    The dot product of the two vectors $\mathbf{v}$ and $\mathbf{d}$ varies as the cosine of the angle between them; hence, objects directly in line get maximum illumination, and objects off the axis have their illumination drop as the cosine of the angle.

To determine whether a particular vertex lies within the cone of illumination, OpenGL evaluates $(\max \{\mathbf{v} \cdot \mathbf{d}, 0\})$, where $\mathbf{v}$ and $\mathbf{d}$ are as defined in the preceding discussion. If this value is less than the cosine of the spotlight's cutoff angle (GL_SPOT_CUTOFF), then the vertex lies outside the cone; otherwise, it's inside the cone.

### Ambient Term

The ambient term is simply the ambient color of the light scaled by the ambient material property:

$$\text{ambient}_{\text{light}} * \text{ambient}_{\text{material}}$$

### Diffuse Term

The diffuse term needs to take into account whether or not light falls directly on the vertex, the diffuse color of the light, and the diffuse material property:

$$(\max \{\mathbf{L} \cdot \mathbf{n}, 0\}) * \text{diffuse}_{\text{light}} * \text{diffuse}_{\text{material}}$$

where

$\mathbf{L} = (\mathbf{L}_x, \mathbf{L}_y, \mathbf{L}_z)$ is the unit vector that points from the vertex to the light position (GL_POSITION).

$\mathbf{n} = (\mathbf{n}_x, \mathbf{n}_y, \mathbf{n}_z)$ is the unit normal vector at the vertex.

## Specular Term

The specular term also depends on whether or not light falls directly on the vertex. If $L \cdot n$ is less than or equal to zero, there is no specular component at the vertex. (If it's less than zero, the light is on the wrong side of the surface.) If there's a specular component, it depends on the following:

- The unit normal vector at the vertex $(n_x, n_y, n_z)$

- The sum of the two unit vectors that point between (1) the vertex and the light position (or light direction) and (2) the vertex and the viewpoint (assuming that GL_LIGHT_MODEL_LOCAL_VIEWER is true; if it's not true, the vector (0, 0, 1) is used as the second vector in the sum). This vector sum is normalized (by dividing each component by the magnitude of the vector) to yield $s = (s_x, s_y, s_z)$.

- The specular exponent (GL_SHININESS)

- The specular color of the light (GL_SPECULAR$_{light}$)

- The specular property of the material (GL_SPECULAR$_{material}$)

Using these definitions, here's how OpenGL calculates the specular term:

$$(\max \{s \cdot n, 0\})^{shininess} * specular_{light} * specular_{material}$$

However, if $L \cdot n = 0$, the specular term is 0.

## Putting It All Together

Using the definitions of terms described in the preceding paragraphs, the following represents the entire lighting calculation in RGBA mode:

vertex color = $emission_{material}$ +

$ambient_{light\ model} * ambient_{material}$ +

$$\sum_{i=0}^{n-1} \left( \frac{1}{k_c + k_l d + k_q d^2} \right)_i * (\text{spotlight effect})_i *$$

[$ambient_{light} * ambient_{material}$ +

$(\max \{ L \cdot n , 0\} ) * diffuse_{light} * diffuse_{material}$ +

$(\max \{ s \cdot n , 0\} )^{shininess} * specular_{light} * specular_{material}$ ]$_i$

## Secondary Specular Color

If GL_SEPARATE_SPECULAR_COLOR is the current lighting model color control, then a primary and secondary color are produced for each vertex, which are computed as follows:

primary color =   the material emission at that vertex +

the global ambient light scaled by the material's ambient property at that vertex   +

the ambient and diffuse contributions from all the light sources, properly attenuated

secondary color =   the specular contributions from all the light sources, properly attenuated

The following two equations represent the lighting calculations for the primary and secondary colors:

primary color = $\text{emission}_{\text{material}}$ +

$\text{ambient}_{\text{light model}}$ * $\text{ambient}_{\text{material}}$ +

$$\sum_{i=0}^{n-1} \left(\frac{1}{k_c + k_l d + k_q d^2}\right)_i * (\text{spotlight effect})_i *$$

$[\text{ambient}_{\text{light}}$ * $\text{ambient}_{\text{material}}$ +

$(\max \{ \mathbf{L} \cdot \mathbf{n}, 0 \})$ * $\text{diffuse}_{\text{light}}$ * $\text{diffuse}_{\text{material}}]_i$

secondary color =

$$\sum_{i=0}^{n-1} \left(\frac{1}{k_c + k_l d + k_q d^2}\right)_i * (\text{spotlight effect})_i *$$

$[(\max \{ \mathbf{s} \cdot \mathbf{n}, 0 \})^{\text{shininess}}$ * $\text{specular}_{\text{light}}$ * $\text{specular}_{\text{material}}]_i$

During texture mapping, only the primary color is combined with the texture colors. After the texturing operation, the secondary color is added to the resulting combination of the primary and texture colors.

# Lighting in Color-Index Mode

In color-index mode, the parameters comprising RGBA values either have no effect or have a special interpretation. Since it's much harder to achieve certain effects in color-index mode, you should use RGBA whenever possible. In fact, the only light-source, lighting-model, or material parameters in an RGBA form that are used in color-index mode are the light-source parameters GL_DIFFUSE and GL_SPECULAR and the material parameter GL_SHININESS. GL_DIFFUSE and GL_SPECULAR ($d_l$ and $s_l$, respectively) are used to compute color-index diffuse and specular light intensities ($d_{ci}$ and $s_{ci}$), as follows:

$$d_{ci} = 0.30R(d_l) + 0.59G(d_l) + 0.11B(d_l)$$

$$s_{ci} = 0.30R(s_l) + 0.59G(s_l) + 0.11B(s_l)$$

where $R(x)$, $G(x)$, and $B(x)$ refer to the red, green, and blue components, respectively, of color $x$. The weighting values 0.30, 0.59, and 0.11 reflect the "perceptual" weights that red, green, and blue have for your eye—your eye is most sensitive to green and least sensitive to blue.

To specify material colors in color-index mode, use **glMaterial*()** with the special parameter GL_COLOR_INDEXES, as follows:

```
GLfloat mat_colormap[] = { 16.0, 47.0, 79.0 };
glMaterialfv(GL_FRONT, GL_COLOR_INDEXES, mat_colormap);
```

The three numbers supplied for GL_COLOR_INDEXES specify the color indices for the ambient, diffuse, and specular material colors, respectively. In other words, OpenGL regards the color associated with the first index (16.0 in this example) as the pure ambient color, with the second index (47.0) as the pure diffuse color, and with the third index (79.0) as the pure specular color. (By default, the ambient color index is 0.0, and the diffuse and specular color indices are both 1.0. Note that **glColorMaterial()** has no effect on color-index lighting.)

As it draws a scene, OpenGL uses colors associated with indices between these numbers to shade objects in the scene. Therefore, you must build a color ramp between the indicated indices (in this example, between indices 16 and 47, and then between indices 47 and 79). Often, the color ramp is built smoothly, but you might want to use other formulations to achieve different effects. Here's an example of a smooth color ramp that starts with a black ambient color and goes through a magenta diffuse color to a white specular color:

```
for (i = 0; i < 32; i++) {
    glutSetColor(16 + i, 1.0 * (i/32.0), 0.0, 1.0 * (i/32.0));
    glutSetColor(48 + i, 1.0, 1.0 * (i/32.0), 1.0);
}
```

The GLUT library command **glutSetColor()** takes four arguments. It associates the color index indicated by the first argument with the RGB triplet specified by the last three arguments. When $i = 0$, the color index 16 is assigned the RGB value (0.0, 0.0, 0.0), or black. The color ramp builds smoothly up to the diffuse material color at index 47 (when $i = 31$), which is assigned the pure magenta RGB value (1.0, 0.0, 1.0). The second loop builds the ramp between the magenta diffuse color and the white (1.0, 1.0, 1.0) specular color (index 79). Plate 15 shows the result of using this color ramp with a single lit sphere.

## The Mathematics of Color-Index Mode Lighting

**Advanced**

Advanced

As you might expect, since the allowable parameters are different for color-index mode than for RGBA mode, the calculations are different as well. Since there's no material emission and no ambient light, the only terms of interest from the RGBA equations are the diffuse and specular contributions from the light sources and the shininess. Even these terms need to be modified, however, as explained next.

Begin with the diffuse and specular terms from the RGBA equations. In the diffuse term, instead of diffuse$_{\text{light}}$ * diffuse$_{\text{material}}$, substitute $d_{ci}$ as defined in the preceding section for color-index mode. Similarly, in the specular term, instead of specular$_{\text{light}}$ * specular$_{\text{material}}$, use $s_{ci}$ as defined in the preceding section. (Calculate the attenuation, the spotlight effect, and all other components of these terms as before.) Call these modified diffuse and specular terms $d$ and $s$, respectively. Now, let $s' = \min\{\, s, 1 \,\}$, and then compute

$$c = a_m + d(1 - s')(d_m - a_m) + s'(s_m - a_m)$$

where $a_m$, $d_m$, and $s_m$ are the ambient, diffuse, and specular material indices specified using GL_COLOR_INDEXES. The final color index is

$$c' = \min \{\, c, s_m \,\}$$

After lighting calculations are performed, the color-index values are converted to fixed-point (with an unspecified number of bits to the right of the binary point). Then the integer portion is masked (bitwise ANDed) with $2^n - 1$, where $n$ is the number of bits in a color in the color-index buffer.

## Chapter 6

# Blending, Antialiasing, Fog, and Polygon Offset

**Chapter Objectives**

After reading this chapter, you'll be able to do the following:

- Blend colors to achieve such effects as making objects appear translucent

- Smooth jagged edges of lines and polygons with antialiasing

- Create scenes with realistic atmospheric effects

- Render rounded (antialiased) points with varying sizes, based upon distance from the viewpoint

- Draw geometry at or near the same depth, but avoid unaesthetic artifacts from intersecting geometry

The preceding chapters have given you the basic information you need to create a computer-graphics scene; you've learned how to do the following:

- Draw geometric shapes

- Transform those geometric shapes so that they can be viewed from whatever perspective you wish

- Specify how the geometric shapes in your scene should be colored and shaded

- Add lights and indicate how they should affect the shapes in your scene

Now you're ready to get a little fancier. This chapter discusses five techniques that can add extra detail and polish to your scene. None of these techniques is hard to use—in fact, it's probably harder to explain them than to use them. Each of these techniques is described in its own major section:

- "Blending" tells you how to specify a blending function that combines color values from a source and a destination. The final effect is that parts of your scene appear translucent.

- "Antialiasing" explains this relatively subtle effect that alters colors so that the edges of points, lines, and polygons appear smooth rather than angular and jagged. Multisampling is a powerful technique to antialias all of the primitives in your entire scene.

- "Fog" describes how to create the illusion of depth by computing the color values of an object based on its distance from the viewpoint. Thus, objects that are far away appear to fade into the background, just as they do in real life.

- "Point Parameters" discusses an efficient technique for rendering point primitives with different sizes and color, depending upon distance from the viewpoint. Point parameters can be useful for modeling particle systems.

- If you've tried to draw a wireframe outline atop a shaded object and used the same vertices, you've probably noticed some ugly visual artifacts. "Polygon Offset" shows you how to tweak (offset) depth values to make an outlined, shaded object look beautiful.

OpenGL Version 1.1 added the polygon offset capability.

Version 1.2 of OpenGL introduced a selectable blending equation (**glBlendEquation()**), a constant blending color (**glBlendColor()**), and the blending factors: GL_CONSTANT_COLOR, GL_ONE_MINUS_CONSTANT_COLOR, GL_CONSTANT_ALPHA, and GL_ONE_MINUS_CONSTANT_ALPHA.

In Version 1.2 and 1.3, these features were supported only if the OpenGL implementation supported the imaging subset. In Version 1.4, the blending equation, constant blending color, and constant blending factors became mandatory.

In Version 1.3, multisampling became a core feature of OpenGL.

Version 1.4 also added the following new features, which are covered in this chapter:

- Use of GL_SRC_COLOR and GL_ONE_MINUS_SRC_COLOR as source blending factors. (Prior to Version 1.4, GL_SRC_COLOR and GL_ONE_MINUS_SRC_COLOR had to be destination factors.)

- Use of GL_DST_COLOR and GL_ONE_MINUS_DST_COLOR as destination blending factors. (Prior to Version 1.4, GL_DST_COLOR and GL_ONE_MINUS_DST_COLOR had to be source factors.)

- Explicit specification of fog coordinates

- Point parameters to control characteristics of point primitives

- Capability to blend RGB and alpha color components with separate blending functions

## Blending

What's it all about, alpha? You've already seen alpha values (alpha is the A in RGBA), but they've been ignored until now. Alpha values are specified with **glColor*()** when using **glClearColor()** to specify a clearing color and when specifying certain lighting parameters such as a material property or light source intensity. As you learned in Chapter 4, the pixels on a monitor screen emit red, green, and blue light, which is controlled by the red, green, and blue color values. So how does an alpha value affect what is drawn in a window on the screen?

When blending is enabled, the alpha value is often used to combine the color value of the fragment being processed with that of the pixel already stored in the framebuffer. Blending occurs after your scene has been rasterized and converted to fragments, but just before the final pixels are drawn in the framebuffer. Alpha values can also be used in the alpha test to accept or reject a fragment based on its alpha value. (See Chapter 10 for more information about this process.)

Without blending, each new fragment overwrites any existing color values in the framebuffer, as though the fragment were opaque. With blending, you can control how (and how much of) the existing color value should be combined with the new fragment's value. Thus, you can use alpha blending to create a translucent fragment that lets some of the previously stored color value "show through." Color blending lies at the heart of techniques such as transparency, digital compositing, and painting.

**Note:** Alpha values aren't specified in color-index mode, so blending operations aren't performed in color-index mode.

The most natural way to think of blending operations is to think of the RGB components of a fragment as representing its color, and the alpha component as representing opacity. Transparent or translucent surfaces have lower opacity than opaque ones and, therefore, lower alpha values. For example, if you're viewing an object through green glass, the color you see is partly green from the glass and partly the color of the object. The percentage varies depending on the transmission properties of the glass: if the glass transmits 80 percent of the light that strikes it (that is, has an opacity of 20 percent), the color you see is a combination of 20 percent glass color and 80 percent the color of the object behind it. You can easily imagine situations with multiple translucent surfaces. If you look at an automobile, for instance, its interior has one piece of glass between it and your viewpoint; some objects behind the automobile are visible through two pieces of glass.

## The Source and Destination Factors

During blending, color values of the incoming fragment (the *source*) are combined with the color values of the corresponding currently stored pixel (the *destination*) in a two-stage process. First you specify how to compute source and destination factors. These factors are RGBA quadruplets that are multiplied by each component of the R, G, B, and A values in the source and destination, respectively. Then the corresponding components in the two sets of RGBA quadruplets are combined. To show this mathematically, let the source and destination blending factors be $(S_r, S_g, S_b, S_a)$ and $(D_r, D_g, D_b, D_a)$, respectively, and let the RGBA values of the source and destination be indicated with a subscript of s or d. Then the final, blended RGBA values are given by

$$(R_s S_r + R_d D_r, G_s S_g + G_d D_g, B_s S_b + B_d D_b, A_s S_a + A_d D_a)$$

Each component of this quadruplet is eventually clamped to [0, 1].

The default way to combine the source and destination fragments is to add their values together ($C_sS+C_dD$). See "Combining Pixels Using Blending Equations" on page 235 for how to select other mathematical operations to combine fragments.

You have two different ways to choose the source and destination blending factors. You may call **glBlendFunc()** and choose two blending factors: the first factor for the source RGBA and the second for the destination RGBA. Or, you may use **glBlendFuncSeparate()** and choose four blending factors, which allows you to use one blending operation for RGB and a different one for its corresponding alpha.

---

void **glBlendFunc**(GLenum *srcfactor*, GLenum *destfactor*);

Controls how color values in the fragment being processed (the source) are combined with those already stored in the framebuffer (the destination). The possible values for these arguments are explained in Table 6-1. The argument *srcfactor* indicates how to compute a source blending factor; *destfactor* indicates how to compute a destination blending factor.

The blend factors are assumed to lie in the range [0, 1]. After the color values in the source and destination are combined, they're clamped to the range [0, 1].

---

void **glBlendFuncSeparate**(GLenum *srcRGB*, GLenum *destRGB*,
                              GLenum *srcAlpha*, GLenum *destAlpha*);

Similar to **glBlendFunc()**, **glBlendFuncSeparate()** also controls how source color values (fragment) are combined with destination values (framebuffer). **glBlendFuncSeparate()** also accepts the same arguments (shown in Table 6-1) as **glBlendFunc()**. The argument *srcRGB* indicates the source blending factor for color values; *destRGB* is the destination blending factor for color values. The argument *srcAlpha* indicates the source blending factor for alpha values; *destAlpha* is the destination blending factor for alpha values.

The blend factors are assumed to lie in the range [0, 1]. After the color values in the source and destination are combined, they're clamped to the range [0, 1].

**Note:** In Table 6-1, the RGBA values of the source, destination, and constant colors are indicated with the subscripts s, d, and c, respectively. Subtraction of quadruplets means subtracting them componentwise. GL_SRC_ALPHA_SATURATE may be used only as a source blend factor.

| Constant | RGB Blend Factor | Alpha Blend Factor |
|---|---|---|
| GL_ZERO | $(0, 0, 0)$ | $0$ |
| GL_ONE | $(1, 1, 1)$ | $1$ |
| GL_SRC_COLOR | $(R_s, G_s, B_s)$ | $A_s$ |
| GL_ONE_MINUS_SRC_COLOR | $(1, 1, 1) - (R_s, G_s, B_s)$ | $1 - A_s$ |
| GL_DST_COLOR | $(R_d, G_d, B_d)$ | $A_d$ |
| GL_ONE_MINUS_DST_COLOR | $(1, 1, 1) - (R_d, G_d, B_d)$ | $1 - A_d$ |
| GL_SRC_ALPHA | $(A_s, A_s, A_s)$ | $A_s$ |
| GL_ONE_MINUS_SRC_ALPHA | $(1, 1, 1) - (A_s, A_s, A_s)$ | $1 - A_s$ |
| GL_DST_ALPHA | $(A_d, A_d, A_d)$ | $A_d$ |
| GL_ONE_MINUS_DST_ALPHA | $(1, 1, 1) - (A_d, A_d, A_d)$ | $1 - A_d$ |
| GL_CONSTANT_COLOR | $(R_c, G_c, B_c)$ | $A_c$ |
| GL_ONE_MINUS_CONSTANT_COLOR | $(1, 1, 1) - (R_c, G_c, B_c)$ | $1 - A_c$ |
| GL_CONSTANT_ALPHA | $(A_c, A_c, A_c)$ | $A_c$ |
| GL_ONE_MINUS_CONSTANT_ALPHA | $(1, 1, 1) - (A_c, A_c, A_c)$ | $1 - A_c$ |
| GL_SRC_ALPHA_SATURATE | $(f, f, f); f = \min(A_s, 1 - A_d)$ | $1$ |

**Table 6-1**    Source and Destination Blending Factors

If you use one of the GL*CONSTANT* blending functions, you need to use **glBlendColor()** to specify a constant color.

> void **glBlendColor**(GLclampf *red*, GLclampf *green*, GLclampf *blue*,
>                GLclampf *alpha*);
>
> Sets the current *red*, *green*, *blue*, and *alpha* values for use as the constant color ($R_c$, $G_c$, $B_c$, $A_c$) in blending operations.

## Enabling Blending

No matter how you specify the blending function, you also need to enable blending to have it take effect:

```
glEnable(GL_BLEND);
```

Use **glDisable**() with GL_BLEND to disable blending. Note that using the constants GL_ONE (source) and GL_ZERO (destination) gives the same results as when blending is disabled; these values are the default.

## Combining Pixels Using Blending Equations

With standard blending, colors in the framebuffer are combined (using addition) with incoming fragment colors to produce the new framebuffer color. Either **glBlendEquation**() or **glBlendEquationSeparate**() may be used to select other mathematical operations to compute the difference, minimum, or maximum between color fragments and framebuffer pixels.

> void **glBlendEquation**(GLenum *mode*);
>
> Specifies how framebuffer and source colors are blended together. The allowable values for *mode* are GL_FUNC_ADD (the default), GL_FUNC_SUBTRACT, GL_FUNC_REVERSE_SUBTRACT, GL_MIN, and GL_MAX, of GL_LOGIC_OP. The possible modes are described in Table 6-2.

> void **glBlendEquationSeparate**(GLenum *modeRGB*,
>                         GLenum *modeAlpha*);
>
> Specifies how framebuffer and source colors are blended together, but allows for different blending modes for the rgb and alpha color components. The allowable values for *modeRGB* and *modeAlpha* are identical for the modes accepted by **glBlendEquation**().

In Table 6-2, $C_s$ and $C_d$ represent the source and destination colors. The S and D parameters in the table represent the source and destination blending factors as specified with **glBlendFunc()** or **glBlendFuncSeparate()**. For GL_LOGIC_OP, the logical operator is specified by calling **glLogicOp()**. (See Table 10-4, "Sixteen Logical Operations," on page 489 for the list of supported logical operations.)

| Blending Mode Parameter | Mathematical Operation |
| --- | --- |
| GL_FUNC_ADD | $C_sS + C_dD$ |
| GL_FUNC_SUBTRACT | $C_sS - C_dD$ |
| GL_FUNC_REVERSE_SUBTRACT | $C_dD - C_sS$ |
| GL_MIN | $\min(C_sS, C_dD)$ |
| GL_MAX | $\max(C_sS, C_dD)$ |
| GL_LOGIC_OP | $C_S \ op \ C_D$ |

**Table 6-2**    Blending Equation Mathematical Operations

In Example 6-1, the different blending equation modes are demonstrated. The 'a', 's', 'r', 'm', and 'x' keys are used to select which blending mode to use. A blue square is used for the source color, and the yellow background is used as the destination color. The blending factor for each color is set to GL_ONE using **glBlendFunc()**.

**Example 6-1**    Demonstrating the Blend Equation Modes: blendeqn.c

```
/*  The following keys change the selected blend equation mode
 *
 *       'a'  ->  GL_FUNC_ADD
 *       's'  ->  GL_FUNC_SUBTRACT
 *       'r'  ->  GL_FUNC_REVERSE_SUBTRACT
 *       'm'  ->  GL_MIN
 *       'x'  ->  GL_MAX
 */

void init(void)
{
   glClearColor(1.0, 1.0, 0.0, 0.0);

   glBlendFunc(GL_ONE, GL_ONE);
   glEnable(GL_BLEND);
}
```

```
void display(void)
{
   glClear(GL_COLOR_BUFFER_BIT);
   glColor3f(0.0, 0.0, 1.0);
   glRectf(-0.5, -0.5, 0.5, 0.5);
   glFlush();
}

void keyboard(unsigned char key, int x, int y)
{
   switch (key) {
      case 'a': case 'A':
      /* Colors are added as: (1,1,0) + (0,0,1) = (1,1,1) which
       * will produce a white square on a yellow background. */
         glBlendEquation(GL_FUNC_ADD);
         break;

      case 's': case 'S':
      /* Colors are subtracted as: (0,0,1) - (1,1,0) = (-1,-1,1)
       * which is clamped to (0, 0, 1), producing a blue square
       * on a yellow background. */
         glBlendEquation(GL_FUNC_SUBTRACT);
         break;

      case 'r': case 'R':
      /* Colors are subtracted as: (1,1,0) - (0,0,1) = (1,1,-1)
       * which is clamped to (1, 1, 0). This produces yellow for
       * both the square and the background. */
         glBlendEquation(GL_FUNC_REVERSE_SUBTRACT);
         break;

      case 'm': case 'M':
      /* The minimum of each component is computed, as
       * [min(1,0),min(1,0),min(0,1)] which equates to (0,0,0).
       * This will produce a black square on the yellow
       * background. */
         glBlendEquation(GL_MIN);
         break;

      case 'x': case 'X':
      /* The minimum of each component is computed, as
       * [max(1, 0), max(1, 0), max(0, 1)] which equates to
       * (1, 1, 1).  This will produce a white square on the
       * yellow background. */
         glBlendEquation(GL_MAX);
         break;
```

```
      case 27:
          exit(0);
}         break;

   glutPostRedisplay();
}
```

## Sample Uses of Blending

Not all combinations of source and destination factors make sense. Most applications use a small number of combinations. The following paragraphs describe typical uses for particular combinations of source and destination factors. Some of these examples use only the incoming alpha value, so they work even when alpha values aren't stored in the framebuffer. Note that often there's more than one way to achieve some of these effects.

- One way to draw a picture composed half of one image and half of another, equally blended, is to set the source factor to GL_ONE and the destination factor to GL_ZERO, and draw the first image. Then set the source factor to GL_SRC_ALPHA and the destination factor to GL_ONE_MINUS_SRC_ALPHA, and draw the second image with alpha equal to 0.5. This pair of factors probably represents the most commonly used blending operation. If the picture is supposed to be blended with 0.75 of the first image and 0.25 of the second, draw the first image as before, and draw the second with an alpha of 0.25.

- To blend three different images equally, set the destination factor to GL_ONE and the source factor to GL_SRC_ALPHA. Draw each of the images with alpha equal to 0.3333333. With this technique, each image is only one-third of its original brightness, which is noticeable where the images don't overlap.

- Suppose you're writing a paint program, and you want to have a brush that gradually adds color so that each brush stroke blends in a little more color with whatever is currently in the image (say, 10 percent color with 90 percent image on each pass). To do this, draw the image of the brush with alpha of 10 percent and use GL_SRC_ALPHA (source) and GL_ONE_MINUS_SRC_ALPHA (destination). Note that you can vary the alphas across the brush to make the brush add more of its color in the middle and less on the edges, for an antialiased brush shape (see "Antialiasing"). Similarly, erasers can be implemented by setting the eraser color to the background color.

- The blending functions that use the source or destination colors—GL_DST_COLOR or GL_ONE_MINUS_DST_COLOR for the source factor and GL_SRC_COLOR or GL_ONE_MINUS_SRC_COLOR for the destination factor—effectively allow you to modulate each color component individually. This operation is equivalent to applying a simple filter—for example, multiplying the red component by 80 percent, the green component by 40 percent, and the blue component by 72 percent would simulate viewing the scene through a photographic filter that blocks 20 percent of red light, 60 percent of green, and 28 percent of blue.

- Suppose you want to draw a picture composed of three translucent surfaces, some obscuring others, and all over a solid background. Assume the farthest surface transmits 80 percent of the color behind it, the next transmits 40 percent, and the closest transmits 90 percent. To compose this picture, draw the background first with the default source and destination factors, and then change the blending factors to GL_SRC_ALPHA (source) and GL_ONE_MINUS_SRC_ALPHA (destination). Next, draw the farthest surface with an alpha of 0.2, then the middle surface with an alpha of 0.6, and finally the closest surface with an alpha of 0.1.

- If your system has alpha planes, you can render objects one at a time (including their alpha values), read them back, and then perform interesting matting or compositing operations with the fully rendered objects. (See "Compositing 3D Rendered Images" by Tom Duff, *SIGGRAPH 1985 Proceedings*, pp. 41–44, for examples of this technique.) Note that objects used for picture composition can come from any source—they can be rendered using OpenGL commands, rendered using techniques such as ray-tracing or radiosity that are implemented in another graphics library, or obtained by scanning in existing images.

- You can create the effect of a nonrectangular raster image by assigning different alpha values to individual fragments in the image. In most cases, you would assign an alpha of 0 to each "invisible" fragment and an alpha of 1.0 to each opaque fragment. For example, you can draw a polygon in the shape of a tree and apply a texture map of foliage; the viewer can see through parts of the rectangular texture that aren't part of the tree if you've assigned them alpha values of 0. This method, sometimes called *billboarding*, is much faster than creating the tree out of three-dimensional polygons. An example of this technique is shown in Figure 6-1, in which the tree is a single rectangular polygon that can be rotated about the center of the trunk, as shown by the outlines, so that it's always facing the viewer. (See "Texture Functions" in Chapter 9 for more information about blending textures.)

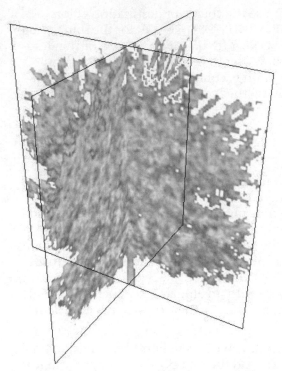

**Figure 6-1**    Creating a Nonrectangular Raster Image

- Blending is also used for *antialiasing*, which is a rendering technique to reduce the jagged appearance of primitives drawn on a raster screen. (See "Antialiasing" for more information.)

## A Blending Example

Example 6-2 draws two overlapping colored triangles, each with an alpha of 0.75. Blending is enabled and the source and destination blending factors are set to GL_SRC_ALPHA and GL_ONE_MINUS_SRC_ALPHA, respectively.

When the program starts up, a yellow triangle is drawn on the left and then a cyan triangle is drawn on the right so that in the center of the window, where the triangles overlap, cyan is blended with the original yellow. You can change which triangle is drawn first by typing 't' in the window.

**Example 6-2**  Blending Example: alpha.c

```
static int leftFirst = GL_TRUE;

/*  Initialize alpha blending function.  */
static void init(void)
{
   glEnable(GL_BLEND);
   glBlendFunc(GL_SRC_ALPHA, GL_ONE_MINUS_SRC_ALPHA);
   glShadeModel(GL_FLAT);
   glClearColor(0.0, 0.0, 0.0, 0.0);
}

static void drawLeftTriangle(void)
{
/* draw yellow triangle on LHS of screen */
   glBegin(GL_TRIANGLES);
      glColor4f(1.0, 1.0, 0.0, 0.75);
      glVertex3f(0.1, 0.9, 0.0);
      glVertex3f(0.1, 0.1, 0.0);
      glVertex3f(0.7, 0.5, 0.0);
   glEnd();
}

static void drawRightTriangle(void)
{
/* draw cyan triangle on RHS of screen */
   glBegin(GL_TRIANGLES);
      glColor4f(0.0, 1.0, 1.0, 0.75);
      glVertex3f(0.9, 0.9, 0.0);
      glVertex3f(0.3, 0.5, 0.0);
      glVertex3f(0.9, 0.1, 0.0);
   glEnd();
}

void display(void)
{
   glClear(GL_COLOR_BUFFER_BIT);

   if (leftFirst) {
      drawLeftTriangle();
      drawRightTriangle();
   }
```

```
        else {
            drawRightTriangle();
            drawLeftTriangle();
        }
        glFlush();
    }

    void reshape(int w, int h)
    {
        glViewport(0, 0, (GLsizei) w, (GLsizei) h);
        glMatrixMode(GL_PROJECTION);
        glLoadIdentity();
        if (w <= h)
            gluOrtho2D(0.0, 1.0, 0.0, 1.0*(GLfloat)h/(GLfloat)w);
        else
            gluOrtho2D(0.0, 1.0*(GLfloat)w/(GLfloat)h, 0.0, 1.0);
    }

    void keyboard(unsigned char key, int x, int y)
    {
        switch (key) {
            case 't':
            case 'T':
                leftFirst = !leftFirst;
                glutPostRedisplay();
                break;
            case 27:  /*  Escape key  */
                exit(0);
                break;
            default:
                break;
        }
    }

    int main(int argc, char** argv)
    {
        glutInit(&argc, argv);
        glutInitDisplayMode(GLUT_SINGLE | GLUT_RGB);
        glutInitWindowSize(200, 200);
        glutCreateWindow(argv[0]);
        init();
        glutReshapeFunc(reshape);
        glutKeyboardFunc(keyboard);
        glutDisplayFunc(display);
        glutMainLoop();
        return 0;
    }
```

The order in which the triangles are drawn affects the color of the overlapping region. When the left triangle is drawn first, cyan fragments (the source) are blended with yellow fragments, which are already in the framebuffer (the destination). When the right triangle is drawn first, yellow is blended with cyan. Because the alpha values are all 0.75, the actual blending factors become 0.75 for the source and $1.0 - 0.75 = 0.25$ for the destination. In other words, the source fragments are somewhat translucent, but they have more effect on the final color than do the destination fragments.

## Three-Dimensional Blending with the Depth Buffer

As you saw in the previous example, the order in which polygons are drawn greatly affects the blended result. When drawing three-dimensional translucent objects, you can get different appearances depending on whether you draw the polygons from back to front or from front to back. You also need to consider the effect of the depth buffer when determining the correct order. (See "A Hidden-Surface Removal Survival Kit" in Chapter 5 for an introduction to the depth buffer. Also see "Depth Test" in Chapter 10 for more information.) The depth buffer keeps track of the distance between the viewpoint and the portion of the object occupying a given pixel in a window on the screen; when another candidate color arrives for that pixel, it's drawn only if its object is closer to the viewpoint, in which case its depth value is stored in the depth buffer. With this method, obscured (or hidden) portions of surfaces aren't necessarily drawn and therefore aren't used for blending.

If you want to render both opaque and translucent objects in the same scene, then you want to use the depth buffer to perform hidden-surface removal for any objects that lie behind the opaque objects. If an opaque object hides either a translucent object or another opaque object, you want the depth buffer to eliminate the more distant object. If the translucent object is closer, however, you want to blend it with the opaque object. You can generally figure out the correct order in which to draw the polygons if everything in the scene is stationary, but the problem can quickly become too hard if either the viewpoint or the object is moving.

The solution is to enable depth buffering but make the depth buffer read-only while drawing the translucent objects. First you draw all the opaque objects, with the depth buffer in normal operation. Then you preserve these depth values by making the depth buffer read-only. When the translucent objects are drawn, their depth values are still compared with the values established by the opaque objects, so they aren't drawn if they're behind the opaque ones. If they're closer to the viewpoint, however, they don't eliminate the opaque objects, since the depth-buffer values can't change. Instead, they're blended with the opaque objects. To control whether the depth buffer is writable, use **glDepthMask()**; if you pass GL_FALSE as the argument, the buffer becomes read-only, whereas GL_TRUE restores the normal, writable operation.

Example 6-3 demonstrates how to use this method to draw opaque and translucent three-dimensional objects. In the program, typing 'a' triggers an animation sequence in which a translucent cube moves through an opaque sphere. Pressing the 'r' key resets the objects in the scene to their initial positions. To get the best results when transparent objects overlap, draw the objects from back to front.

**Example 6-3**   Three-Dimensional Blending: alpha3D.c

```
#define MAXZ 8.0
#define MINZ -8.0
#define ZINC 0.4
static float solidZ = MAXZ;
static float transparentZ = MINZ;
static GLuint sphereList, cubeList;

static void init(void)
{
    GLfloat mat_specular[] = { 1.0, 1.0, 1.0, 0.15 };
    GLfloat mat_shininess[] = { 100.0 };
    GLfloat position[] = { 0.5, 0.5, 1.0, 0.0 };

    glMaterialfv(GL_FRONT, GL_SPECULAR, mat_specular);
    glMaterialfv(GL_FRONT, GL_SHININESS, mat_shininess);
    glLightfv(GL_LIGHT0, GL_POSITION, position);

    glEnable(GL_LIGHTING);
    glEnable(GL_LIGHT0);
    glEnable(GL_DEPTH_TEST);

    sphereList = glGenLists(1);
    glNewList(sphereList, GL_COMPILE);
        glutSolidSphere(0.4, 16, 16);
    glEndList();
    cubeList = glGenLists(1);
    glNewList(cubeList, GL_COMPILE);
        glutSolidCube(0.6);
    glEndList();
}
```

```
void display(void)
{
   GLfloat mat_solid[] = { 0.75, 0.75, 0.0, 1.0 };
   GLfloat mat_zero[] = { 0.0, 0.0, 0.0, 1.0 };
   GLfloat mat_transparent[] = { 0.0, 0.8, 0.8, 0.6 };
   GLfloat mat_emission[] = { 0.0, 0.3, 0.3, 0.6 };

   glClear(GL_COLOR_BUFFER_BIT | GL_DEPTH_BUFFER_BIT);

   glPushMatrix();
      glTranslatef(-0.15, -0.15, solidZ);
      glMaterialfv(GL_FRONT, GL_EMISSION, mat_zero);
      glMaterialfv(GL_FRONT, GL_DIFFUSE, mat_solid);
      glCallList(sphereList);
   glPopMatrix();

   glPushMatrix();
      glTranslatef(0.15, 0.15, transparentZ);
      glRotatef(15.0, 1.0, 1.0, 0.0);
      glRotatef(30.0, 0.0, 1.0, 0.0);
      glMaterialfv(GL_FRONT, GL_EMISSION, mat_emission);
      glMaterialfv(GL_FRONT, GL_DIFFUSE, mat_transparent);
      glEnable(GL_BLEND);
      glDepthMask(GL_FALSE);
      glBlendFunc(GL_SRC_ALPHA, GL_ONE);
      glCallList(cubeList);
      glDepthMask(GL_TRUE);
      glDisable(GL_BLEND);
   glPopMatrix();

   glutSwapBuffers();
}

void reshape(int w, int h)
{
   glViewport(0, 0, (GLint) w, (GLint) h);
   glMatrixMode(GL_PROJECTION);
   glLoadIdentity();
   if (w <= h)
      glOrtho(-1.5, 1.5, -1.5*(GLfloat)h/(GLfloat)w,
              1.5*(GLfloat)h/(GLfloat)w, -10.0, 10.0);
   else
      glOrtho(-1.5*(GLfloat)w/(GLfloat)h,
              1.5*(GLfloat)w/(GLfloat)h, -1.5, 1.5, -10.0, 10.0);
   glMatrixMode(GL_MODELVIEW);
   glLoadIdentity();
}
```

```
void animate(void)
{
   if (solidZ <= MINZ || transparentZ >= MAXZ)
      glutIdleFunc(NULL);
   else {
      solidZ -= ZINC;
      transparentZ += ZINC;
      glutPostRedisplay();
   }
}

void keyboard(unsigned char key, int x, int y)
{
   switch (key) {
      case 'a':
      case 'A':
         solidZ = MAXZ;
         transparentZ = MINZ;
         glutIdleFunc(animate);
         break;
      case 'r':
      case 'R':
         solidZ = MAXZ;
         transparentZ = MINZ;
         glutPostRedisplay();
         break;
      case 27:
         exit(0);
   }   break;
}

int main(int argc, char** argv)
{
   glutInit(&argc, argv);
   glutInitDisplayMode(GLUT_DOUBLE | GLUT_RGB | GLUT_DEPTH);
   glutInitWindowSize(500, 500);
   glutCreateWindow(argv[0]);
   init();
   glutReshapeFunc(reshape);
   glutKeyboardFunc(keyboard);
   glutDisplayFunc(display);
   glutMainLoop();
   return 0;
}
```

# Antialiasing

You might have noticed in some of your OpenGL pictures that lines, especially nearly horizontal and nearly vertical ones, appear jagged. These "jaggies" appear because the ideal line is approximated by a series of pixels that must lie on the pixel grid. The jaggedness is called *aliasing*, and this section describes antialiasing techniques for reducing it. Figure 6-2 shows two intersecting lines, both aliased and antialiased. The pictures have been magnified to show the effect.

**Figure 6-2**  Aliased and Antialiased Lines

Figure 6-3 shows how a diagonal line 1 pixel wide covers more of some pixel squares than others. In fact, when performing antialiasing, OpenGL calculates a *coverage* value for each fragment based on the fraction of the pixel square on the screen that it would cover. Figure 6-3 shows these coverage values for the line. In RGBA mode, OpenGL multiplies the fragment's alpha value by its coverage. You can then use the resulting alpha value to blend the fragment with the corresponding pixel already in the framebuffer. In color-index mode, OpenGL sets the least significant 4 bits of the color index based on the fragment's coverage (0000 for no coverage and 1111 for complete coverage). It's up to you to load your color map and apply it appropriately to take advantage of this coverage information.

The details of calculating coverage values are complex, are difficult to specify in general, and in fact may vary slightly depending on your particular implementation of OpenGL. You can use the **glHint()** command to exercise some control over the trade-off between image quality and speed, but not all implementations will take the hint.

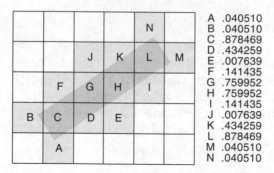

**Figure 6-3**    Determining Coverage Values

void **glHint**(GLenum *target*, GLenum *hint*);

Controls certain aspects of OpenGL behavior. The *target* parameter indicates which behavior is to be controlled; its possible values are shown in Table 6-3. The *hint* parameter can be GL_FASTEST to indicate that the most efficient option should be chosen, GL_NICEST to indicate the highest-quality option, or GL_DONT_CARE to indicate no preference. The interpretation of hints is implementation-dependent; an OpenGL implementation can ignore them entirely. (For more information about the relevant topics, see this section for details about sampling and "Fog" for details about fog.)

The GL_PERSPECTIVE_CORRECTION_HINT target parameter refers to how color values and texture coordinates are interpolated across a primitive: either linearly in screen space (a relatively simple calculation) or in a perspective-correct manner (which requires more computation). Often, systems perform linear color interpolation because the results, while not technically correct, are visually acceptable; however, in most cases, textures require perspective-correct interpolation to be visually acceptable. Thus, an OpenGL implementation can choose to use this parameter to control the method used for interpolation. (See Chapter 3 for a discussion of perspective projection, Chapter 4 for a discussion of color, and Chapter 9 for a discussion of texture mapping.)

| Parameter | Specifies |
|---|---|
| GL_POINT_SMOOTH_HINT, GL_LINE_SMOOTH_HINT, GL_POLYGON_SMOOTH_HINT | sampling quality of points, lines, or polygons during antialiasing operations |
| GL_FOG_HINT | whether fog calculations are done per pixel (GL_NICEST) or per vertex (GL_FASTEST) |
| GL_PERSPECTIVE_CORRECTION_HINT | quality of color and texture-coordinate interpolation |
| GL_GENERATE_MIPMAP_HINT | quality and performance of automatic mipmap level generation |
| GL_TEXTURE_COMPRESSION_HINT | quality and performance of compressing texture images |

**Table 6-3**      Values for Use with glHint()

## Antialiasing Points or Lines

One way to antialias points or lines is to turn on antialiasing with **glEnable()**, passing in GL_POINT_SMOOTH or GL_LINE_SMOOTH, as appropriate. You might also want to provide a quality hint with **glHint()**. (Remember that you can set the size of a point or the width of a line. You can also stipple a line. See "Line Details" in Chapter 2.) Then follow the procedures described in one of the following sections, depending on whether you're in RGBA or color-index mode.

Another way to antialias points or lines is to use multisampling, as described in "Antialiasing Geometric Primitives with Multisampling."

### Antialiasing in RGBA Mode

In RGBA mode, you need to enable blending. The blending factors you most likely want to use are GL_SRC_ALPHA (source) and GL_ONE_MINUS_SRC_ALPHA (destination). Alternatively, you can use GL_ONE for the destination factor to make lines a little brighter where they intersect. Now you're ready to draw whatever points or lines you want antialiased. The antialiased effect is most noticeable if you use a fairly high alpha value. Remember that since you're performing blending, you might need to consider the rendering order as described in "Three-Dimensional Blending with the Depth Buffer."

However, in most cases, the ordering can be ignored without significant adverse effects. Example 6-4 initializes the necessary modes for antialiasing and then draws two intersecting diagonal lines. When you run this program, press the 'r' key to rotate the lines so that you can see the effect of antialiasing on lines of different slopes. Note that the depth buffer isn't enabled in this example.

**Example 6-4**   Antialiased Lines: aargb.c

```
static float rotAngle = 0.;

/*  Initialize antialiasing for RGBA mode, including alpha
 *  blending, hint, and line width.  Print out implementation-
 *  specific info on line width granularity and width.
 */
void init(void)
{
    GLfloat values[2];
    glGetFloatv(GL_LINE_WIDTH_GRANULARITY, values);
    printf("GL_LINE_WIDTH_GRANULARITY value is %3.1f\n",
        values[0]);
    glGetFloatv(GL_LINE_WIDTH_RANGE, values);
    printf("GL_LINE_WIDTH_RANGE values are %3.1f %3.1f\n",
        values[0], values[1]);

    glEnable(GL_LINE_SMOOTH);
    glEnable(GL_BLEND);
    glBlendFunc(GL_SRC_ALPHA, GL_ONE_MINUS_SRC_ALPHA);
    glHint(GL_LINE_SMOOTH_HINT, GL_DONT_CARE);
    glLineWidth(1.5);

    glClearColor(0.0, 0.0, 0.0, 0.0);
}

/* Draw 2 diagonal lines to form an X */
void display(void)
{
    glClear(GL_COLOR_BUFFER_BIT);

    glColor3f(0.0, 1.0, 0.0);
    glPushMatrix();
    glRotatef(-rotAngle, 0.0, 0.0, 0.1);
    glBegin(GL_LINES);
        glVertex2f(-0.5, 0.5);
        glVertex2f(0.5, -0.5);
```

```
    glEnd();
    glPopMatrix();

    glColor3f(0.0, 0.0, 1.0);
    glPushMatrix();
    glRotatef(rotAngle, 0.0, 0.0, 0.1);
    glBegin(GL_LINES);
        glVertex2f(0.5, 0.5);
        glVertex2f(-0.5, -0.5);
    glEnd();
    glPopMatrix();

    glFlush();
}

void reshape(int w, int h)
{
    glViewport(0, 0, (GLint) w, (GLint) h);
    glMatrixMode(GL_PROJECTION);
    glLoadIdentity();
    if (w <= h)
        gluOrtho2D(-1.0, 1.0,
            -1.0*(GLfloat)h/(GLfloat)w, 1.0*(GLfloat)h/(GLfloat)w);
    else
        gluOrtho2D(-1.0*(GLfloat)w/(GLfloat)h,
            1.0*(GLfloat)w/(GLfloat)h, -1.0, 1.0);
    glMatrixMode(GL_MODELVIEW);
    glLoadIdentity();
}

void keyboard(unsigned char key, int x, int y)
{
    switch (key) {
        case 'r':
        case 'R':
            rotAngle += 20.;
            if (rotAngle >= 360.) rotAngle = 0.;
            glutPostRedisplay();
            break;
        case 27:  /*  Escape Key  */
            exit(0);
            break;
        default:
            break;
    }
}
```

```
int main(int argc, char** argv)
{
    glutInit(&argc, argv);
    glutInitDisplayMode(GLUT_SINGLE | GLUT_RGB);
    glutInitWindowSize(200, 200);
    glutCreateWindow(argv[0]);
    init();
    glutReshapeFunc(reshape);
    glutKeyboardFunc(keyboard);
    glutDisplayFunc(display);
    glutMainLoop();
    return 0;
}
```

## Antialiasing in Color-Index Mode

The tricky part about antialiasing in color-index mode is loading and using the color map. Since the last 4 bits of the color index indicate the coverage value, you need to load 16 contiguous indices with a color ramp from the background color to the object's color. (The ramp has to start with an index value that's a multiple of 16.) Then you clear the color buffer to the first of the 16 colors in the ramp and draw your points or lines using colors in the ramp. Example 6-5 demonstrates how to construct the color ramp to draw antialiased lines in color-index mode. In this example, two color ramps are created: one contains shades of green and the other shades of blue.

**Example 6-5**    Antialiasing in Color-Index Mode: aaindex.c

```
#define RAMPSIZE 16
#define RAMP1START 32
#define RAMP2START 48

static float rotAngle = 0.;

/*  Initialize antialiasing for color-index mode,
 *  including loading a green color ramp starting
 *  at RAMP1START and a blue color ramp starting
 *  at RAMP2START. The ramps must be a multiple of 16.
 */
```

```
void init(void)
{
    int i;

    for (i = 0; i < RAMPSIZE; i++) {
        GLfloat shade;
        shade = (GLfloat) i/(GLfloat) RAMPSIZE;
        glutSetColor(RAMP1START+(GLint)i, 0., shade, 0.);
        glutSetColor(RAMP2START+(GLint)i, 0., 0., shade);
    }
    glEnable(GL_LINE_SMOOTH);
    glHint(GL_LINE_SMOOTH_HINT, GL_DONT_CARE);
    glLineWidth(1.5);

    glClearIndex((GLfloat) RAMP1START);
}
/*  Draw 2 diagonal lines to form an X */
void display(void)
{
    glClear(GL_COLOR_BUFFER_BIT);

    glIndexi(RAMP1START);
    glPushMatrix();
    glRotatef(-rotAngle, 0.0, 0.0, 0.1);
    glBegin(GL_LINES);
        glVertex2f(-0.5, 0.5);
        glVertex2f(0.5, -0.5);
    glEnd();
    glPopMatrix();

    glIndexi(RAMP2START);
    glPushMatrix();
    glRotatef(rotAngle, 0.0, 0.0, 0.1);
    glBegin(GL_LINES);
        glVertex2f(0.5, 0.5);
        glVertex2f(-0.5, -0.5);
    glEnd();
    glPopMatrix();

    glFlush();
}

void reshape(int w, int h)
{
    glViewport(0, 0, (GLsizei) w, (GLsizei) h);
    glMatrixMode(GL_PROJECTION);
    glLoadIdentity();
```

```
        if (w <= h)
            gluOrtho2D(-1.0, 1.0,
                -1.0*(GLfloat)h/(GLfloat)w, 1.0*(GLfloat)h/(GLfloat)w);
        else
            gluOrtho2D(-1.0*(GLfloat)w/(GLfloat)h,
                1.0*(GLfloat)w/(GLfloat)h, -1.0, 1.0);
        glMatrixMode(GL_MODELVIEW);
        glLoadIdentity();
    }

    void keyboard(unsigned char key, int x, int y)
    {
        switch (key) {
            case 'r':
            case 'R':
                rotAngle += 20.;
                if (rotAngle >= 360.) rotAngle = 0.;
                glutPostRedisplay();
                break;
            case 27:  /*  Escape Key */
                exit(0);
                break;
            default:
                break;
        }
    }

    int main(int argc, char** argv)
    {
        glutInit(&argc, argv);
        glutInitDisplayMode(GLUT_SINGLE | GLUT_INDEX);
        glutInitWindowSize(200, 200);
        glutCreateWindow(argv[0]);
        init();
        glutReshapeFunc(reshape);
        glutKeyboardFunc(keyboard);
        glutDisplayFunc(display);
        glutMainLoop();
        return 0;
    }
```

Since the color ramp goes from the background color to the object's color, the antialiased lines look correct only in the areas where they are drawn on top of the background. When the blue line is drawn, it erases part of the green line at the point where the lines intersect. To fix this, you would need to redraw the area where the lines intersect using a ramp that goes from green (the color of the line in the framebuffer) to blue (the color of the line being drawn). However, this requires additional calculations, and it is usually not worth the effort since the intersection area is small. Note that this is not a problem in RGBA mode, since the colors of objects being drawn are blended with the color already in the framebuffer.

You may also want to enable the depth test when drawing antialiased points and lines in color-index mode. In this example, the depth test is disabled since both of the lines lie in the same $z$-plane. However, if you want to draw a three-dimensional scene, you should enable the depth buffer so that the resulting pixel colors correspond to the "nearest" objects.

The trick described in "Three-Dimensional Blending with the Depth Buffer" can also be used to mix antialiased points and lines with aliased, depth-buffered polygons. To do this, draw the polygons first, then make the depth buffer read-only and draw the points and lines. The points and lines intersect nicely with each other but will be obscured by nearer polygons.

**Try This**

Take a previous program, such as the robot arm or solar system examples described in "Examples of Composing Several Transformations" in Chapter 3, and draw wireframe objects with antialiasing. Try it in either RGBA or color-index mode. Also try different line widths and point sizes to see their effects.

Try This

## Antialiasing Geometric Primitives with Multisampling

Multisampling is a technique that uses additional color, depth, and stencil information (samples) to antialias OpenGL primitives: points, lines, polygons, bitmaps, and images. Each fragment, instead of having a single color, single depth, and single set of texture coordinates, has multiple colors, depths, and texture coordinate sets, based upon the number of subpixel samples. Calculations aren't at the dead center of each pixel (as they typically are when you have one sample), but are dispersed at several sample locations. Instead of using alpha values to represent how much a primitive covers a pixel, antialiasing coverage values are calculated from the samples saved in a multisample buffer.

Multisampling is especially good for antialiasing the edges of polygons, because sorting isn't needed. (If you are using alpha values to antialias polygons, the order in which translucent objects are drawn affects the color of the results.) Multisampling takes care of traditionally difficult cases, such as intersecting or adjacent polygons.

Multisampling is trivial to add to an application. Just follow these three steps:

1. Obtain a window that supports multisampling. With GLUT, you can ask for one by calling

```
glutInitDisplayMode(GLUT_DOUBLE | GLUT_RGB |
    GLUT_MULTISAMPLE);
```

2. After you've opened a window, you will need to verify that multisampling is available. For instance, GLUT may give you a window with "almost" what you have asked for. If querying the state variable GL_SAMPLE_BUFFERS returns a value of one and GL_SAMPLES returns a value greater than one, then you'll be able to use multisampling. (GL_SAMPLES returns the number of subpixel samples. If there is only one sample, multisampling is effectively disabled.)

```
GLint bufs, samples;
glGetIntegerv(GL_SAMPLE_BUFFERS, &bufs);
glGetIntegerv(GL_SAMPLES, &samples);
```

3. To turn on multisampling, call

```
glEnable(GL_MULTISAMPLE);
```

Example 6-6 displays two sets of primitives side-by-side so that you can see the difference that multisampling makes. **init()** checks the multisampling state variables and then two display lists are compiled: one list with a "pinwheel" of lines of different widths and triangles (filled polygons) and the other with a checkerboard background. In **display()**, the pinwheel is drawn both with multisampling (on the left) and without (right). You should compare the aliasing of the two objects. A contrasting background sometimes accentuates aliasing, and other times it may obscure it. You can press the 'b' key to redraw the scene with or without the checkerboard background.

**Example 6-6**     Enabling Multisampling: multisamp.c

```
static int bgtoggle = 1;

/*
 *  Print out state values related to multisampling.
 *  Create display list with "pinwheel" of lines and
 *  triangles.
 */
void init(void)
{
    GLint buf, sbuf;
    int i, j;
```

```
glClearColor(0.0, 0.0, 0.0, 0.0);
glGetIntegerv(GL_SAMPLE_BUFFERS, &buf);
printf("number of sample buffers is %d\n", buf);
glGetIntegerv(GL_SAMPLES, &sbuf);
printf("number of samples is %d\n", sbuf);

glNewList(1, GL_COMPILE);
for (i = 0; i < 19; i++) {
    glPushMatrix();
    glRotatef(360.0*(float)i/19.0, 0.0, 0.0, 1.0);
    glColor3f (1.0, 1.0, 1.0);
    glLineWidth((i%3)+1.0);
    glBegin(GL_LINES);
        glVertex2f(0.25, 0.05);
        glVertex2f(0.9, 0.2);
    glEnd();
    glColor3f(0.0, 1.0, 1.0);
    glBegin(GL_TRIANGLES);
        glVertex2f(0.25, 0.0);
        glVertex2f(0.9, 0.0);
        glVertex2f(0.875, 0.10);
    glEnd();
    glPopMatrix();
}
glEndList();

glNewList(2, GL_COMPILE);
glColor3f(1.0, 0.5, 0.0);
glBegin(GL_QUADS);
for (i = 0; i < 16; i++) {
    for (j = 0; j < 16; j++) {
        if (((i + j) % 2) == 0) {
            glVertex2f(-2.0 + (i * 0.25), -2.0 + (j * 0.25));
            glVertex2f(-2.0 + (i * 0.25), -1.75 + (j * 0.25));
            glVertex2f(-1.75 + (i * 0.25), -1.75 + (j * 0.25));
            glVertex2f(-1.75 + (i * 0.25), -2.0 + (j * 0.25));
        }
    }
}
glEnd();
glEndList();
}
```

```
    /*  Draw two sets of primitives so that you can
     *  compare the user of multisampling against its absence.
     *
     *  This code enables antialiasing and draws one display list,
     *  and then it disables and draws the other display list.
     */
    void display(void)
    {
        glClear(GL_COLOR_BUFFER_BIT);

        if (bgtoggle)
            glCallList(2);

        glEnable(GL_MULTISAMPLE);
        glPushMatrix();
        glTranslatef(-1.0, 0.0, 0.0);
        glCallList(1);
        glPopMatrix();

        glDisable(GL_MULTISAMPLE);
        glPushMatrix();
        glTranslatef(1.0, 0.0, 0.0);
        glCallList(1);
        glPopMatrix();
        glutSwapBuffers();
    }

    void keyboard(unsigned char key, int x, int y)
    {
        switch (key) {
           case 'b':
           case 'B':
              bgtoggle = !bgtoggle;
              glutPostRedisplay();
              break;
           case 27:   /*  Escape Key  */
              exit(0);
              break;
           default:
              break;
        }

    }
```

With a standard implementation, you can't fine-tune multisampling. You can't change the number of samples or specify (or even query) the subpixel sample locations.

If multisampling is enabled and there's also a multisample buffer, then points, lines, and polygons generate fragments that are intended for antialiasing. For example, a large-sized point primitive is rounded, not square, whether GL_POINT_SMOOTH has been enabled or disabled. The states of GL_LINE_SMOOTH and GL_POLYGON_SMOOTH are similarly ignored. Other primitive attributes, such as point size and line width, are supported during multisampling.

### Alpha and Multisampling Coverage

By default, multisampling calculates fragment coverage values that are independent of alpha. However, if you enable one of the following special modes, then a fragment's alpha value is taken into consideration when calculating the coverage. The special modes are as follows:

- GL_SAMPLE_ALPHA_TO_COVERAGE uses the alpha value of the fragment to compute the final coverage value.

- GL_SAMPLE_ALPHA_TO_ONE sets the fragment's alpha value to one, the maximum alpha value, and then uses that value in the coverage calculation.

- GL_SAMPLE_COVERAGE uses the value set with the **glSampleCoverage()** routine, which is combined (ANDed) with the calculated coverage value. Additionally, this mode can be inverted by setting the *invert* flag with the **glSampleCoverage()** routine.

---

void **glSampleCoverage**(GLclampf *value*, GLboolean *invert*);

Sets parameters to be used to interpret alpha values while computing multisampling coverage. *value* is a temporary coverage value that is used if GL_SAMPLE_COVERAGE or GL_ALPHA_TO_COVERAGE has been enabled. *invert* is a Boolean that indicates whether the temporary coverage value ought to be bitwise inverted before it is used (ANDed) with the fragment coverage.

---

## Antialiasing Polygons

Antialiasing the edges of filled polygons is similar to antialiasing points and lines. When different polygons have overlapping edges, you need to blend the color values appropriately. You can use the method described in this section, or you can use the accumulation buffer to perform antialiasing for your entire scene. Using the accumulation buffer, which is described in

Chapter 10, is easier from your point of view, but it's much more computation-intensive and therefore slower. However, as you'll see, the method described here is rather cumbersome.

**Note:** If you draw your polygons as points at the vertices or as outlines—that is, by passing GL_POINT or GL_LINE to **glPolygonMode()**—point or line antialiasing is applied, if enabled as described earlier. The rest of this section addresses polygon antialiasing when you're using GL_FILL as the polygon mode.

In theory, you can antialias polygons in either RGBA or color-index mode. However, object intersections affect polygon antialiasing more than they affect point or line antialiasing, so rendering order and blending accuracy become more critical. In fact, they're so critical that if you're antialiasing more than one polygon, you need to order the polygons from front to back, and then use **glBlendFunc()** with GL_SRC_ALPHA_SATURATE for the source factor and GL_ONE for the destination factor. Thus, antialiasing polygons in color-index mode normally isn't practical.

To antialias polygons in RGBA mode, you use the alpha value to represent coverage values of polygon edges. You need to enable polygon antialiasing by passing GL_POLYGON_SMOOTH to **glEnable()**. This causes pixels on the edges of the polygon to be assigned fractional alpha values based on their coverage, as though they were lines being antialiased. Also, if you desire, you can supply a value for GL_POLYGON_SMOOTH_HINT.

Now you need to blend overlapping edges appropriately. First, turn off the depth buffer so that you have control over how overlapping pixels are drawn. Then set the blending factors to GL_SRC_ALPHA_SATURATE (source) and GL_ONE (destination). With this specialized blending function, the final color is the sum of the destination color and the scaled source color; the scale factor is the smaller of either the incoming source alpha value or 1 minus the destination alpha value. This means that for a pixel with a large alpha value, successive incoming pixels have little effect on the final color because 1 minus the destination alpha is almost zero. With this method, a pixel on the edge of a polygon might be blended eventually with the colors from another polygon that's drawn later. Finally, you need to sort all the polygons in your scene so that they're ordered from front to back before drawing them.

# Fog

Computer images sometimes seem unrealistically sharp and well defined. Antialiasing makes an object appear more realistic by smoothing its edges. Additionally, you can make an entire image appear more natural by adding *fog*, which makes objects fade into the distance. "Fog" is a general term that describes similar forms of atmospheric effects; it can be used to simulate haze, mist, smoke, or pollution (see Plate 9). Fog is essential in visual-simulation applications, where limited visibility needs to be approximated. It's often incorporated into flight-simulator displays.

When fog is enabled, objects that are farther from the viewpoint begin to fade into the fog color. You can control the density of the fog, which determines the rate at which objects fade as the distance increases, as well as the fog's color. You can also explicitly specify a fog coordinate per-vertex for fog distance calculations, rather than use an automatically calculated depth value.

Fog is available in both RGBA and color-index modes, although the calculations are slightly different in the two modes. Since fog is applied after matrix transformations, lighting, and texturing are performed, it affects transformed, lit, and textured objects. Note that with large simulation programs, fog can improve performance, since you can choose not to draw objects that would be too fogged to be visible.

All types of geometric primitives can be fogged, including points and lines. Using the fog effect on points and lines is also called *depth-cuing* (as shown in Plate 2) and is popular in molecular modeling and other applications.

## Using Fog

Using fog is easy. You enable it by passing GL_FOG to **glEnable()**, and you choose the color and the equation that controls the density with **glFog*()**. If you want, you can supply a value for GL_FOG_HINT with **glHint()**, as described in Table 6-3. Example 6-7 draws five red spheres, each at a different distance from the viewpoint. Pressing the 'f' key selects among the three different fog equations, which are described in the next section.

**Example 6-7**   Five Fogged Spheres in RGBA Mode: fog.c

```
static GLint fogMode;

static void init(void)
{
    GLfloat position[] = { 0.5, 0.5, 3.0, 0.0 };

    glEnable(GL_DEPTH_TEST);

    glLightfv(GL_LIGHT0, GL_POSITION, position);
    glEnable(GL_LIGHTING);
    glEnable(GL_LIGHT0);
    {
        GLfloat mat[3] = {0.1745, 0.01175, 0.01175};
        glMaterialfv(GL_FRONT, GL_AMBIENT, mat);
        mat[0] = 0.61424; mat[1] = 0.04136; mat[2] = 0.04136;
        glMaterialfv(GL_FRONT, GL_DIFFUSE, mat);
        mat[0] = 0.727811; mat[1] = 0.626959; mat[2] = 0.626959;
        glMaterialfv(GL_FRONT, GL_SPECULAR, mat);
        glMaterialf(GL_FRONT, GL_SHININESS, 0.6*128.0);
    }

    glEnable(GL_FOG);
    {
        GLfloat fogColor[4] = {0.5, 0.5, 0.5, 1.0};

        fogMode = GL_EXP;
        glFogi(GL_FOG_MODE, fogMode);
        glFogfv(GL_FOG_COLOR, fogColor);
        glFogf(GL_FOG_DENSITY, 0.35);
        glHint(GL_FOG_HINT, GL_DONT_CARE);
        glFogf(GL_FOG_START, 1.0);
        glFogf(GL_FOG_END, 5.0);
    }
    glClearColor(0.5, 0.5, 0.5, 1.0);  /* fog color */
}

static void renderSphere(GLfloat x, GLfloat y, GLfloat z)
{
    glPushMatrix();
    glTranslatef(x, y, z);
    glutSolidSphere(0.4, 16, 16);
    glPopMatrix();
}
```

```c
/* display() draws 5 spheres at different z positions.
 */
void display(void)
{
    glClear(GL_COLOR_BUFFER_BIT | GL_DEPTH_BUFFER_BIT);
    renderSphere(-2., -0.5, -1.0);
    renderSphere(-1., -0.5, -2.0);
    renderSphere(0., -0.5, -3.0);
    renderSphere(1., -0.5, -4.0);
    renderSphere(2., -0.5, -5.0);
    glFlush();
}

void reshape(int w, int h)
{
    glViewport(0, 0, (GLsizei) w, (GLsizei) h);
    glMatrixMode(GL_PROJECTION);
    glLoadIdentity();
    if (w <= h)
        glOrtho(-2.5, 2.5, -2.5*(GLfloat)h/(GLfloat)w,
            2.5*(GLfloat)h/(GLfloat)w, -10.0, 10.0);
    else
        glOrtho(-2.5*(GLfloat)w/(GLfloat)h,
            2.5*(GLfloat)w/(GLfloat)h, -2.5, 2.5, -10.0, 10.0);
    glMatrixMode(GL_MODELVIEW);
    glLoadIdentity();
}

void keyboard(unsigned char key, int x, int y)
{
    switch (key) {
        case 'f':
        case 'F':
            if (fogMode == GL_EXP) {
                fogMode = GL_EXP2;
                printf("Fog mode is GL_EXP2\n");
            }
            else if (fogMode == GL_EXP2) {
                fogMode = GL_LINEAR;
                printf("Fog mode is GL_LINEAR\n");
            }
            else if (fogMode == GL_LINEAR) {
                fogMode = GL_EXP;
                printf("Fog mode is GL_EXP\n");
            }
```

```
        glFogi(GL_FOG_MODE, fogMode);
        glutPostRedisplay();
        break;
    case 27:
        exit(0);
        break;
    default:
        break;
    }
}

int main(int argc, char** argv)
{
    glutInit(&argc, argv);
    glutInitDisplayMode(GLUT_SINGLE | GLUT_RGB | GLUT_DEPTH);
    glutInitWindowSize(500, 500);
    glutCreateWindow(argv[0]);
    init();
    glutReshapeFunc(reshape);
    glutKeyboardFunc(keyboard);
    glutDisplayFunc(display);
    glutMainLoop();
    return 0;
}
```

## Fog Equations

Fog blends a fog color with an incoming fragment's color using a fog blending factor. This factor, $f$, is computed with one of these three equations and then clamped to the range $[0, 1]$:

$$f = e^{-(density \cdot z)} \quad \text{(GL\_EXP)}$$
$$f = e^{-(density \cdot z)^2} \quad \text{(GL\_EXP2)}$$
$$f = \frac{end - z}{end - start} \quad \text{(GL\_LINEAR)}$$

In these three equations, $z$ is the eye-coordinate distance between the viewpoint and the fragment center. You may have added control over the $z$ eye-coordinate distance with per-vertex fog coordinates, which is described in "Fog Coordinates." The values for *density, start*, and *end* are all specified with **glFog*()**. The $f$ factor is used differently, depending on whether you're in RGBA mode or color-index mode, as explained in the following subsections.

```
void glFog{if}(GLenum pname, TYPE param);
void glFog{if}v(GLenum pname, const TYPE *params);
```

Sets the parameters and function for calculating fog. If *pname* is GL_FOG_MODE, then *param* is GL_EXP (the default), GL_EXP2, or GL_LINEAR to select one of the three fog factors. If *pname* is GL_FOG_DENSITY, GL_FOG_START, or GL_FOG_END, then *param* is (or points to, with the vector version of the command) a value for *density*, *start*, or *end* in the equations. (The default values are 1, 0, and 1, respectively.) In RGBA mode, *pname* can be GL_FOG_COLOR, in which case *params* points to four values that specify the fog's RGBA color values. The corresponding value for *pname* in color-index mode is GL_FOG_INDEX, for which *param* is a single value specifying the fog's color index.

Figure 6-4 plots the fog-density equations for various values of the parameters.

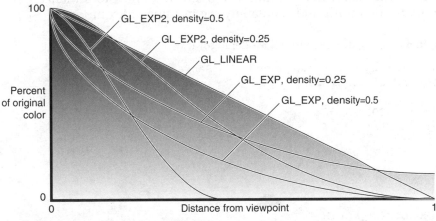

**Figure 6-4**    Fog-Density Equations

### Fog in RGBA Mode

In RGBA mode, the fog factor *f* is used as follows to calculate the final fogged color:

$$C = f\,C_i + (1 - f)\,C_f$$

where $C_i$ represents the incoming fragment's RGBA values and $C_f$ the fog-color values assigned with GL_FOG_COLOR.

## Fog in Color-Index Mode

In color-index mode, the final fogged color index is computed as follows:

$$I = I_i + (1 - f)\, I_f$$

where $I_i$ is the incoming fragment's color index and $I_f$ is the fog's color index as specified with GL_FOG_INDEX.

To use fog in color-index mode, you have to load appropriate values in a color ramp. The first color in the ramp is the color of the object without fog, and the last color in the ramp is the color of the completely fogged object. You probably want to use **glClearIndex()** to initialize the background color index so that it corresponds to the last color in the ramp; this way, totally fogged objects blend into the background. Similarly, before objects are drawn, you should call **glIndex*()** and pass in the index of the first color in the ramp (the unfogged color). Finally, to apply fog to different colored objects in the scene, you need to create several color ramps and call **glIndex*()** before each object is drawn to set the current color index to the start of each color ramp. Example 6-8 illustrates how to initialize appropriate conditions and then apply fog in color-index mode.

**Example 6-8**    Fog in Color-Index Mode: fogindex.c

```
/*  Initialize color map and fog.  Set screen clear color
 *  to end of color ramp.
 */
#define NUMCOLORS 32
#define RAMPSTART 16

static void init(void)
{
   int i;

   glEnable(GL_DEPTH_TEST);

   for (i = 0; i < NUMCOLORS; i++) {
      GLfloat shade;
      shade = (GLfloat) (NUMCOLORS-i)/(GLfloat) NUMCOLORS;
      glutSetColor(RAMPSTART + i, shade, shade, shade);
   }
   glEnable(GL_FOG);

   glFogi(GL_FOG_MODE, GL_LINEAR);
   glFogi(GL_FOG_INDEX, NUMCOLORS);
```

```
    glFogf(GL_FOG_START, 1.0);
    glFogf(GL_FOG_END, 6.0);
    glHint(GL_FOG_HINT, GL_NICEST);
    glClearIndex((GLfloat) (NUMCOLORS+RAMPSTART-1));
}

static void renderSphere(GLfloat x, GLfloat y, GLfloat z)
{
    glPushMatrix();
    glTranslatef(x, y, z);
    glutWireSphere(0.4, 16, 16);
    glPopMatrix();
}

/*  display() draws 5 spheres at different z positions.
 */
void display(void)
{
    glClear(GL_COLOR_BUFFER_BIT | GL_DEPTH_BUFFER_BIT);
    glIndexi(RAMPSTART);

    renderSphere(-2., -0.5, -1.0);
    renderSphere(-1., -0.5, -2.0);
    renderSphere(0., -0.5, -3.0);
    renderSphere(1., -0.5, -4.0);
    renderSphere(2., -0.5, -5.0);

    glFlush();
}

void reshape(int w, int h)
{
    glViewport(0, 0, w, h);
    glMatrixMode(GL_PROJECTION);
    glLoadIdentity();
    if (w <= h)
       glOrtho(-2.5, 2.5, -2.5*(GLfloat)h/(GLfloat)w,
          2.5*(GLfloat)h/(GLfloat)w, -10.0, 10.0);
    else
       glOrtho(-2.5*(GLfloat)w/(GLfloat)h,
          2.5*(GLfloat)w/(GLfloat)h, -2.5, 2.5, -10.0, 10.0);
    glMatrixMode(GL_MODELVIEW);
    glLoadIdentity();
}
```

```
void keyboard(unsigned char key, int x, int y)
{

   switch (key) {
      case 27:
         exit(0);
      }
}

int main(int argc, char** argv)
{
   glutInit(&argc, argv);
   glutInitDisplayMode(GLUT_SINGLE | GLUT_INDEX | GLUT_DEPTH);
   glutInitWindowSize(500, 500);
   glutCreateWindow(argv[0]);
   init();
   glutReshapeFunc(reshape);
   glutKeyboardFunc(keyboard);
   glutDisplayFunc(display);
   glutMainLoop();
   return 0;
}
```

## Fog Coordinates

As discussed earlier, the fog equations use a fog coordinate, $z$, to calculate a color value:

$$f = e^{-(density \cdot z)} \quad \text{(GL\_EXP)}$$
$$f = e^{-(density \cdot z)^2} \quad \text{(GL\_EXP2)}$$
$$f = \frac{end - z}{end - start} \quad \text{(GL\_LINEAR)}$$

By default, $z$ is automatically calculated as the distance from the eye to a fragment, but you may want greater control over how fog is calculated. You may want to simulate a fog equation other than those offered by OpenGL. For example, you might want a flight simulation with "ground-based" fog, so you'll use denser fog closer to sea level.

In OpenGL Version 1.4, you can explicitly specify values for $z$ on a per-vertex basis by calling **glFog(GL_FOG_COORD_SRC, GL_FOG_COORD)**. In explicit fog coordinate mode, you may specify the fog coordinate at each vertex with **glFogCoord*()**.

> void **glFogCoord**{fd}(*TYPE z*);
> void **glFogCoord**{fd}**v**(const *TYPE* *z);
>
> Sets the current fog coordinate to *z*. If GL_FOG_COORD is the current fog coordinate source, the current fog coordinate is used by the current fog equation (GL_LINEAR, GL_EXP, or GL_EXP2) to calculate fog.
>
> Values of *z* should be positive, representing eye-coordinate distance. You should avoid using negative values for fog coordinates, because the calculations may result in strange colors.

Within a geometric primitive, the fog coordinates may be interpolated for each fragment.

The sample program in Example 6-9 renders a triangle and allows you to change the fog coordinate at each vertex by pressing several numerical keys. While in explicit fog coordinate mode, moving the viewpoint forward and backward (pressing the 'f' and 'b' keys) does not transform the fog coordinates and therefore does not affect the colors of the vertices. If you stop using explicit fog coordinates (pressing the 'c' key), moving the viewpoint once again dramatically affects colors calculated for fog.

**Example 6-9**    Fog Coordinates: fogcoord.c

```
static GLfloat f1, f2, f3;

/*  Initialize fog
 */
static void init(void)
{
   GLfloat fogColor[4] = {0.0, 0.25, 0.25, 1.0};
   f1 = 1.0f;
   f2 = 5.0f;
   f3 = 10.0f;

   glEnable(GL_FOG);
   glFogi (GL_FOG_MODE, GL_EXP);
   glFogfv (GL_FOG_COLOR, fogColor);
   glFogf (GL_FOG_DENSITY, 0.25);
   glHint (GL_FOG_HINT, GL_DONT_CARE);
   glFogi(GL_FOG_COORD_SRC, GL_FOG_COORD);
   glClearColor(0.0, 0.25, 0.25, 1.0);  /* fog color */
}
   /* display() draws a triangle at an angle.
 */
```

```
void display(void)
{
    glClear(GL_COLOR_BUFFER_BIT);

    glColor3f(1.0f, 0.75f, 0.0f);
    glBegin(GL_TRIANGLES);
    glFogCoordf(f1);
    glVertex3f(2.0f, -2.0f, 0.0f);
    glFogCoordf(f2);
    glVertex3f(-2.0f, 0.0f, -5.0f);
    glFogCoordf(f3);
    glVertex3f(0.0f, 2.0f, -10.0f);
    glEnd();

    glutSwapBuffers();
}

void keyboard(unsigned char key, int x, int y)
{
    switch (key) {
        case 'c':
            glFogi(GL_FOG_COORD_SRC, GL_FRAGMENT_DEPTH);
            glutPostRedisplay();
            break;
        case 'C':
            glFogi(GL_FOG_COORD_SRC, GL_FOG_COORD);
            glutPostRedisplay();
            break;
        case '1':
            f1 = f1 + 0.25;
            glutPostRedisplay();
            break;
        case '2':
            f2 = f2 + 0.25;
            glutPostRedisplay();
            break;
        case '3':
            f3 = f3 + 0.25;
            glutPostRedisplay();
            break;
        case '8':
            if (f1 > 0.25) {
                f1 = f1 - 0.25;
                glutPostRedisplay();
            }
            break;
```

```
        case '9':
            if (f2 > 0.25) {
                f2 = f2 - 0.25;
                glutPostRedisplay();
            }
            break;
        case '0':
            if (f3 > 0.25) {
                f3 = f3 - 0.25;
                glutPostRedisplay();
            }
            break;
        case 'b':
            glMatrixMode(GL_MODELVIEW);
            glTranslatef(0.0, 0.0, -0.25);
            glutPostRedisplay();
            break;
        case 'f':
            glMatrixMode(GL_MODELVIEW);
            glTranslatef(0.0, 0.0, 0.25);
            glutPostRedisplay();
            break;
        case 27:
            exit(0);
            break;
        default:
            break;
    }
}
```

## Point Parameters

In some situations, you may want to render objects that resemble small circles or spheres, but you don't want to use inefficient, multisided polygonal models. For example, in a flight-simulation application, you may want to model runway landing lights—so as an aircraft approaches a runway, the landing lights appear larger and possibly also brighter. Or, when rendering liquid droplets (such as rain or, for you videogamers, splattered blood), you want to simulate the phenomena using a particle system.

The landing lights or drops of liquid may be rendered as point primitives, but the points may need to be able to change apparent size and brightness. Using **glPointSize()** and **glEnable**(GL_POINT_SMOOTH) to make larger, rounded points is a step toward a solution, possibly using fog to suggest distance. However, **glPointSize()** can't be called within **glBegin()** and **glEnd()**, so it's hard to vary the size of different points. You would have to recalculate the point sizes on the fly and then, for best performance, regroup them by size.

Point parameters are an automated, elegant solution, attenuating the size of point primitives and optionally their brightness, based upon distance to the view point. You use **glPointParameterf*()** to specify the coefficients of the attenuation equation and the alpha component of points (which controls brightness).

void **glPointParameterf**(GLenum *pname*, GLfloat *param*);
void **glPointParameterfv**(GLenum *pname*, const GLfloat *\*param*);

Sets values related to rendering point primitives.

If *pname* is GL_POINT_DISTANCE_ATTENUATION, then *param* is an array of three floating-point values (*a, b, c*), containing the constant, linear, and quadratic coefficients for deriving the size and brightness of a point, based upon eye-coordinate distance, *d*:

$$derivedSize = clamp\left( size \times \sqrt{\left( \frac{1}{a + b \times d + c \times d^2} \right)} \right)$$

If *pname* is set to GL_POINT_SIZE_MIN or GL_POINT_SIZE_MAX, *param* is an absolute limit (either lower or upper bound, respectively) used in the previous equation to clamp the derived point size.

If multisampling is enabled and *pname* is GL_FADE_THRESHOLD_SIZE, then *param* specifies a different lower limit (*threshold*) for the size of a point. If *derivedSize* < *threshold*, then the factor *fade* is computed to modulate the point's alpha, thus diminishing its brightness:

$$fade = \left( \frac{derivedSize}{threshold} \right)^2$$

If *pname* is GL_POINT_SPRITE_COORD_ORIGIN, and *param* is GL_LOWER_LEFT, then the origin for iterated texture coordinates on point sprites is the lower-left fragment, with *t* texture coodinate increasing vertically bottom-to-top across the fragments. Alternatively, if *param* is set to GL_UPPER_LEFT, the *t* texture coordinate decreases from top-to-bottom vertically.

The GL_POINT_DISTANCE_ATTENUATION distance calculation is similar to the math used with the coefficients for attenuated local light sources. In Example 6-10, pressing the 'c', 'l', or 'q' key switches the attenuation equation among constant, linear, and quadratic attenuation. Pressing the 'f' or 'b' key moves the viewer forward or backward, which makes the points appear larger or smaller for the linear and quadratic attenuation modes.

**Example 6-10**   Point Parameters: pointp.c

```
static GLfloat constant[3] = {1.0, 0.0, 0.0};
static GLfloat linear[3] = {0.0, 0.12, 0.0};
static GLfloat quadratic[3] = {0.0, 0.0, 0.01};
...
void keyboard(unsigned char key, int x, int y) {
 switch (key) {
 case 'c':
  glPointParameterfv (GL_POINT_DISTANCE_ATTENUATION, constant);
  glutPostRedisplay();
 break;
 case 'l':
  glPointParameterfv (GL_POINT_DISTANCE_ATTENUATION, linear);
  glutPostRedisplay();
 break;
 case 'q':
  glPointParameterfv (GL_POINT_DISTANCE_ATTENUATION, quadratic);
  glutPostRedisplay();
 break;
 case 'b':
  glMatrixMode (GL_MODELVIEW);
  glTranslatef (0.0, 0.0, -0.5);
  glutPostRedisplay();
 break;
 case 'f':
  glMatrixMode (GL_MODELVIEW);
  glTranslatef (0.0, 0.0, 0.5);
  glutPostRedisplay();
 break;
 ...
```

With the chosen linear and quadratic attenuation coefficients in Example 6-10, moving the eye very close to a point may actually increase the derived point size, by dividing the original point size by a proper fraction. To lessen or prevent this, you can increase the constant attenuation coefficient or add a size limiting value with GL_POINT_SIZE_MAX.

With point parameters, you almost certainly want round, rather than square, points, so you'll have to enable point antialiasing, as described in

"Antialiasing Points or Lines" on page 249. These lines of code will do the trick

```
glEnable(GL_POINT_SMOOTH);
glEnable(GL_BLEND);
glBlendFunc(GL_SRC_ALPHA, GL_ONE_MINUS_SRC_ALPHA);
```

# Polygon Offset

If you want to highlight the edges of a solid object, you might draw the object with polygon mode set to GL_FILL, and then draw it again, but in a different color and with the polygon mode set to GL_LINE. However, because lines and filled polygons are not rasterized in exactly the same way, the depth values generated for the line and polygon edge are usually not the same, even between the same two vertices. The highlighting lines may fade in and out of the coincident polygons, which is sometimes called "stitching" and is visually unpleasant.

This undesirable effect can be eliminated by using polygon offset, which adds an appropriate offset to force coincident $z$-values apart, separating a polygon edge from its highlighting line. (The stencil buffer, described in "Stencil Test" in Chapter 10, can also be used to eliminate stitching. However, polygon offset is almost always faster than stenciling.) Polygon offset is also useful for applying decals to surfaces by rendering images with hidden-line removal. In addition to lines and filled polygons, this technique can also be used with points.

There are three different ways to turn on polygon offset, one for each type of polygon rasterization mode: GL_FILL, GL_LINE, and GL_POINT. You enable the polygon offset by passing the appropriate parameter to **glEnable()**— either GL_POLYGON_OFFSET_FILL, GL_POLYGON_OFFSET_LINE, or GL_POLYGON_OFFSET_POINT. You must also call **glPolygonMode()** to set the current polygon rasterization method.

void **glPolygonOffset**(GLfloat *factor*, GLfloat *units*);

When enabled, the depth value of each fragment is modified by adding a calculated offset value before the depth test is performed. The offset value *offset* is calculated by

$$offset = m \cdot factor + r \cdot units$$

where $m$ is the maximum depth slope of the polygon (computed during rasterization), and $r$ is the smallest value guaranteed to produce a resolvable difference in depth values and is an implementation-specific constant. Both *factor* and *units* may be negative.

To achieve a nice rendering of the highlighted solid object without visual artifacts, you can add either a positive offset to the solid object (push it away from you) or a negative offset to the wireframe (pull it toward you). The big question is: How much offset is enough? Unfortunately, the offset required depends on various factors, including the depth slope of each polygon and the width of the lines in the wireframe.

OpenGL calculates the depth slope (see Figure 6-5), which is the $z$- (depth) value divided by the change in either $x$- or $y$-coordinates as you traverse the polygon. The depth values are clamped to the range [0, 1], and the $x$- and $y$-coordinates are in window coordinates. To estimate the maximum depth slope of a polygon ($m$ in the offset equation), use the formula

$$ m = \sqrt{\left(\frac{\partial z}{\partial x}\right)^2 + \left(\frac{\partial z}{\partial y}\right)^2} \quad \text{(or an implementation may use the approximation } m = max\left(\frac{\partial z}{\partial x}, \frac{\partial z}{\partial y}\right)). $$

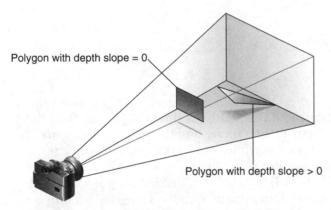

Polygon with depth slope = 0

Polygon with depth slope > 0

**Figure 6-5** Polygons and Their Depth Slopes

For polygons that are parallel to the near and far clipping planes, the depth slope is zero. Those polygons can use a small constant offset, which you can specify by setting *factor* = 0.0 and *units* = 1.0 in your call to **glPolygonOffset()**.

For polygons that are at a great angle to the clipping planes, the depth slope can be significantly greater than zero, and a larger offset may be needed. A small, nonzero value for *factor,* such as 0.75 or 1.0, is probably enough to generate distinct depth values and eliminate the unpleasant visual artifacts.

Example 6-11 shows a portion of code where a display list (which presumably draws a solid object) is first rendered with lighting, the default polygon mode of GL_FILL, and polygon offset with a *factor* value of 1.0 and a *units* value of 1.0. These values ensure that the offset is enough for all polygons in your scene, regardless of depth slope. (These values may actually be a little more offset than the minimum needed, but too much offset is less noticeable than too little.) Then, to highlight the edges of the first object, the object is rendered as an unlit wireframe with the offset disabled.

**Example 6-11**   Polygon Offset to Eliminate Visual Artifacts: polyoff.c

```
glEnable(GL_LIGHT0);
glEnable(GL_LIGHTING);
glPolygonOffset(1.0, 1.0);

glEnable(GL_POLYGON_OFFSET_FILL);
glCallList(list);
glDisable(GL_POLYGON_OFFSET_FILL);

glDisable(GL_LIGHTING);
glDisable(GL_LIGHT0);
glColor3f(1.0, 1.0, 1.0);
glPolygonMode(GL_FRONT_AND_BACK, GL_LINE);
glCallList(list);
glPolygonMode(GL_FRONT_AND_BACK, GL_FILL);
```

In some situations, the simplest values for *factor* and *units* (1.0 and 1.0) aren't the answer. For instance, if the widths of the lines that are highlighting the edges are greater than 1, then increasing the value of *factor* may be necessary. Also, since depth values while using a perspective projection are unevenly transformed into window coordinates (see "The Transformed Depth Coordinate" in Chapter 3), less offset is needed for polygons that are closer to the near clipping plane, and more offset is needed for polygons that are farther away. You may need to experiment with the values you pass to **glPolygonOffset()** to get the result you're looking for.

## Chapter 7

# Display Lists

## Chapter Objectives

After reading this chapter, you'll be able to do the following:

- Understand how display lists can be used along with commands in immediate mode to organize your data and improve performance

- Maximize performance by knowing how and when to use display lists

A *display list* is a group of OpenGL commands that have been stored for later execution. When a display list is invoked, the commands in it are executed in the order in which they were issued. Most OpenGL commands can be either stored in a display list or issued in *immediate mode*, which causes them to be executed immediately. You can freely mix immediate-mode programming and display lists within a single program. The programming examples you've seen so far have used immediate mode. This chapter discusses what display lists are and how best to use them. It has the following major sections:

- "Why Use Display Lists?" explains when to use display lists.

- "An Example of Using a Display List" gives a brief example, showing the basic commands for using display lists.

- "Display List Design Philosophy" explains why certain design choices were made (such as making display lists uneditable) and what performance optimizations you might expect to see when using display lists.

- "Creating and Executing a Display List" discusses in detail the commands for creating, executing, and deleting display lists.

- "Executing Multiple Display Lists" shows how to execute several display lists in succession, using a small character set as an example.

- "Managing State Variables with Display Lists" illustrates how to use display lists to save and restore OpenGL commands that set state variables.

## Why Use Display Lists?

Display lists may improve performance since you can use them to store OpenGL commands for later execution. It is often a good idea to cache commands in a display list if you plan to redraw the same geometry multiple times, or if you have a set of state changes that need to be applied multiple times. Using display lists, you can define the geometry and/or state changes once and execute them multiple times.

To see how you can use display lists to store geometry just once, consider drawing a tricycle. The two wheels on the back are the same size but are offset from each other. The front wheel is larger than the back wheels and also in a different location. An efficient way to render the wheels on the tricycle would be to store the geometry for one wheel in a display list and then execute the list three times. You would need to set the modelview matrix appropriately each time before executing the list to calculate the correct size and location of each wheel.

When running OpenGL programs remotely to another machine on the network, it is especially important to cache commands in a display list. In this case, the server is a machine other than the host. (See "What Is OpenGL?" in Chapter 1 for a discussion of the OpenGL client-server model.) Since display lists are part of the server state and therefore reside on the server machine, you can reduce the cost of repeatedly transmitting that data over a network if you store repeatedly used commands in a display list.

When running locally, you can often improve performance by storing frequently used commands in a display list. Some graphics hardware may store display lists in dedicated memory or may store the data in an optimized form that is more compatible with the graphics hardware or software. (See "Display List Design Philosophy" for a detailed discussion of these optimizations.)

## An Example of Using a Display List

A display list is a convenient and efficient way to name and organize a set of OpenGL commands. For example, suppose you want to draw a torus and view it from different angles. The most efficient way to do this would be to store the torus in a display list. Then, whenever you want to change the view, you would change the modelview matrix and execute the display list to draw the torus. Example 7-1 illustrates this.

**Example 7-1**     Creating a Display List: torus.c

```
GLuint theTorus;

/* Draw a torus */
static void torus(int numc, int numt)
{
    int i, j, k;
    double s, t, x, y, z, twopi;

    twopi = 2 * (double)M_PI;
    for (i = 0; i < numc; i++) {
        glBegin(GL_QUAD_STRIP);
```

```
                for (j = 0; j <= numt; j++) {
                    for (k = 1; k >= 0; k--) {
                        s = (i + k) % numc + 0.5;
                        t = j % numt;

                        x = (1+.1*cos(s*twopi/numc))*cos(t*twopi/numt);
                        y = (1+.1*cos(s*twopi/numc))*sin(t*twopi/numt);
                        z = .1 * sin(s * twopi / numc);
                        glVertex3f(x, y, z);
                    }
                }
            glEnd();
        }
    }

    /* Create display list with Torus and initialize state */
    static void init(void)
    {
        theTorus = glGenLists(1);
        glNewList(theTorus, GL_COMPILE);
        torus(8, 25);
        glEndList();

        glShadeModel(GL_FLAT);
        glClearColor(0.0, 0.0, 0.0, 0.0);
    }

    void display(void)
    {
        glClear(GL_COLOR_BUFFER_BIT);
        glColor3f(1.0, 1.0, 1.0);
        glCallList(theTorus);
        glFlush();
    }

    void reshape(int w, int h)
    {
        glViewport(0, 0, (GLsizei) w, (GLsizei) h);
        glMatrixMode(GL_PROJECTION);
        glLoadIdentity();
        gluPerspective(30, (GLfloat) w/(GLfloat) h, 1.0, 100.0);
        glMatrixMode(GL_MODELVIEW);
        glLoadIdentity();
        gluLookAt(0, 0, 10, 0, 0, 0, 0, 1, 0);
    }
```

```
/* Rotate about x-axis when "x" typed; rotate about y-axis
   when "y" typed; "i" returns torus to original view */
void keyboard(unsigned char key, int x, int y)
{
   switch (key) {
   case 'x':
   case 'X':
      glRotatef(30., 1.0, 0.0, 0.0);
      glutPostRedisplay();
      break;
   case 'y':
   case 'Y':
      glRotatef(30., 0.0, 1.0, 0.0);
      glutPostRedisplay();
      break;
   case 'i':
   case 'I':
      glLoadIdentity();
      gluLookAt(0, 0, 10, 0, 0, 0, 0, 1, 0);
      glutPostRedisplay();
      break;
   case 27:
      exit(0);
      break;
   }
}

int main(int argc, char **argv)
{
   glutInitWindowSize(200, 200);
   glutInit(&argc, argv);
   glutInitDisplayMode(GLUT_SINGLE | GLUT_RGB);
   glutCreateWindow(argv[0]);
   init();
   glutReshapeFunc(reshape);
   glutKeyboardFunc(keyboard);
   glutDisplayFunc(display);
   glutMainLoop();
   return 0;
}
```

Let's start by looking at **init**(). It creates a display list for the torus and
initializes the OpenGL rendering state. Note that the routine for drawing a
torus (**torus**()) is bracketed by **glNewList**() and **glEndList**(), which defines
a display list. The argument *listName* for **glNewList**() is an integer index,
generated by **glGenLists**(), that uniquely identifies this display list.

The user can rotate the torus about the *x*- or *y*-axis by pressing the 'x' or 'y' key when the window has focus. Whenever this happens, the callback function **keyboard()** is called, which concatenates a 30-degree rotation matrix (about the *x*- or *y*-axis) with the current modelview matrix. Then **glutPostRedisplay()** is called, which will cause **glutMainLoop()** to call **display()** and render the torus after other events have been processed. When the 'i' key is pressed, **keyboard()** restores the initial modelview matrix and returns the torus to its original location.

The **display()** function is very simple. It clears the window and then calls **glCallList()** to execute the commands in the display list. If we hadn't used display lists, **display()** would have to reissue the commands to draw the torus each time it was called.

A display list contains only OpenGL commands. In Example 7-1, only the **glBegin()**, **glVertex()**, and **glEnd()** calls are stored in the display list. Their parameters are *evaluated*, and the resulting values are copied into the display list when it is created. All the trigonometry to create the torus is done only once, which should increase rendering performance. However, the values in the display list can't be changed later, and once a command has been stored in a list it is not possible to remove it. Neither can you add any new commands to the list after it has been defined. You can delete the entire display list and create a new one, but you can't edit it.

**Note:** Display lists also work well with GLU commands, since those operations are ultimately broken down into low-level OpenGL commands, which can easily be stored in display lists. Use of display lists with GLU is particularly important for optimizing performance of GLU tessellators (see Chapter 11) and NURBS (see Chapter 12).

## Display List Design Philosophy

To optimize performance, an OpenGL display list is a cache of commands, rather than a dynamic database. In other words, once a display list is created, it can't be modified. If a display list were modifiable, performance could be reduced by the overhead required to search through the display list and perform memory management. As portions of a modifiable display list were changed, memory allocation and deallocation might lead to memory fragmentation. Any modifications that the OpenGL implementation made to the display list commands in order to make them more efficient to render would need to be redone. Also, the display list might be difficult to access, cached somewhere over a network or a system bus.

The way in which the commands in a display list are optimized may vary from implementation to implementation. For example, a command as simple as **glRotate\*()** might show a significant improvement if it's in a display list, since the calculations to produce the rotation matrix aren't trivial (they can involve square roots and trigonometric functions). In the display list, however, only the final rotation matrix needs to be stored, so a display list rotation command can be executed as fast as the hardware can execute **glMultMatrix\*()**. A sophisticated OpenGL implementation might even concatenate adjacent transformation commands into a single matrix multiplication.

Although you're not guaranteed that your OpenGL implementation optimizes display lists for any particular uses, executing display lists is no slower than executing the commands contained within them individually. There is some overhead, however, involved in jumping to a display list. If a particular list is small, this overhead could exceed any execution advantage. The most likely possibilities for optimization are listed next, with references to the chapters in which the topics are discussed:

*   Matrix operations (Chapter 3). Most matrix operations require OpenGL to compute inverses. Both the computed matrix and its inverse might be stored by a particular OpenGL implementation in a display list.

*   Raster bitmaps and images (Chapter 8). The format in which you specify raster data isn't likely to be one that's ideal for the hardware. When a display list is compiled, OpenGL might transform the data into the representation preferred by the hardware. This can have a significant effect on the speed of raster character drawing, since character strings usually consist of a series of small bitmaps.

*   Lights, material properties, and lighting models (Chapter 5). When you draw a scene with complex lighting conditions, you might change the materials for each item in the scene. Setting the materials can be slow, since it might involve significant calculations. If you put the material definitions in display lists, these calculations don't have to be done each time you switch materials, since only the results of the calculations need to be stored; as a result, rendering lit scenes might be faster. (See "Encapsulating Mode Changes" for more details on using display lists to change such values as lighting conditions.)

*   Polygon stipple patterns (Chapter 2).

**Note:** To optimize texture images, you should store texture data in *texture objects* instead of display lists.

Some of the commands used for specifying the properties listed here are context-sensitive, so you need to take this into account to ensure optimum performance. For example, when GL_COLOR_MATERIAL is enabled, some of the material properties will track the current color (see Chapter 5). Any **glMaterial*()** calls that set the same material properties are ignored.

It may improve performance to store state settings with geometry. For example, suppose you want to apply a transformation to some geometric objects and then draw the results. Your code may look like this:

```
glNewList(1, GL_COMPILE);
draw_some_geometric_objects();
glEndList();

glLoadMatrix(M);
glCallList(1);
```

However, if the geometric objects are to be transformed in the same way each time, it is better to store the matrix in the display list. For example, if you write your code as follows, some implementations may be able to improve performance by transforming the objects when they are defined instead of each time they are drawn:

```
glNewList(1, GL_COMPILE);
glLoadMatrix(M);
draw_some_geometric_objects();
glEndList();
glCallList(1);
```

A more likely situation occurs during rendering of images. As you will see in Chapter 8, you can modify pixel-transfer state variables and control the way images and bitmaps are rasterized. If the commands that set these state variables precede the definition of the image or bitmap in the display list, the implementation may be able to perform some of the operations ahead of time and cache the results.

Remember that display lists have some disadvantages. Very small lists may not perform well since there is some overhead when executing a list. Another disadvantage is the immutability of the contents of a display list. To optimize performance, an OpenGL display list can't be changed and its contents can't be read. If the application needs to maintain data separately from the display list (for example, for continued data processing), then a lot of additional memory may be required.

# Creating and Executing a Display List

As you've already seen, **glNewList()** and **glEndList()** are used to begin and end the definition of a display list, which is then invoked by supplying its identifying index with **glCallList()**. In Example 7-2, a display list is created in the **init()** routine. This display list contains OpenGL commands to draw a red triangle. Then, in the **display()** routine, the display list is executed 10 times. In addition, a line is drawn in immediate mode. Note that the display list allocates memory to store the commands and the values of any necessary variables.

**Example 7-2**    Using a Display List: list.c

```
GLuint listName;

static void init(void)
{
   listName = glGenLists(1);
   glNewList(listName, GL_COMPILE);
      glColor3f(1.0, 0.0, 0.0);  /*  current color red  */
      glBegin(GL_TRIANGLES);
      glVertex2f(0.0, 0.0);
      glVertex2f(1.0, 0.0);
      glVertex2f(0.0, 1.0);
      glEnd();
      glTranslatef(1.5, 0.0, 0.0); /*  move position  */
   glEndList();
   glShadeModel(GL_FLAT);
}

static void drawLine(void)
{
   glBegin(GL_LINES);
   glVertex2f(0.0, 0.5);
   glVertex2f(15.0, 0.5);
   glEnd();
}

void display(void)
{
   GLuint i;
```

```
    glClear(GL_COLOR_BUFFER_BIT);
    glColor3f(0.0, 1.0, 0.0);    /*  current color green  */
    for (i = 0; i < 10; i++)     /*  draw 10 triangles   */
        glCallList(listName);
    drawLine();    /* Is this line green?  NO!  */
                   /* Where is the line drawn?  */
    glFlush();
}
```

The **glTranslatef()** routine in the display list alters the position of the next object to be drawn. Without it, calling the display list twice would just draw the triangle on top of itself. The **drawLine()** routine, which is called in immediate mode, is also affected by the 10 **glTranslatef()** calls that precede it. Therefore, if you call transformation commands within a display list, don't forget to take into account the effect those commands will have later in your program.

Only one display list can be created at a time. In other words, you must eventually follow **glNewList()** with **glEndList()** to end the creation of a display list before starting another one. As you might expect, calling **glEndList()** without having started a display list generates the error GL_INVALID_OPERATION. (See "Error Handling" in Chapter 14 for more information about processing errors.)

## Naming and Creating a Display List

Each display list is identified by an integer index. When creating a display list, you want to be careful that you don't accidentally choose an index that's already in use, thereby overwriting an existing display list. To avoid accidental deletions, use **glGenLists()** to generate one or more unused indices.

GLuint **glGenLists**(GLsizei *range*);

Allocates *range* number of contiguous, previously unallocated display list indices. The integer returned is the index that marks the beginning of a contiguous block of empty display list indices. The returned indices are all marked as empty and used, so subsequent calls to **glGenLists()** don't return these indices until they're deleted. Zero is returned if the requested number of indices isn't available, or if *range* is zero.

In the following example, a single index is requested, and if it proves to be available it's used to create a new display list:

```
listIndex = glGenLists(1);
if (listIndex != 0) {
   glNewList(listIndex,GL_COMPILE);
      ...
   glEndList();
}
```

**Note:** Zero is not a valid display list index.

---

void **glNewList**(GLuint *list*, GLenum *mode*);

---

Specifies the start of a display list. OpenGL routines that are called subsequently (until **glEndList()** is called to end the display list) are stored in a display list, except for a few restricted OpenGL routines that can't be stored. (Those restricted routines are executed immediately, during the creation of the display list.) *list* is a nonzero positive integer that uniquely identifies the display list. The possible values for *mode* are GL_COMPILE and GL_COMPILE_AND_EXECUTE. Use GL_COMPILE if you don't want the OpenGL commands executed as they're placed in the display list; to cause the commands to be both executed immediately and placed in the display list for later use, specify GL_COMPILE_AND_EXECUTE.

---

void **glEndList**(void);

---

Marks the end of a display list.

When a display list is created, it is stored with the current OpenGL context. Thus, when the context is destroyed, the display list is also destroyed. Some windowing systems allow multiple contexts to share display lists. In this case, the display list is destroyed when the last context in the *share group* is destroyed.

## What's Stored in a Display List?

When you're building a display list, only the values for expressions are stored in the list. If values in an array are subsequently changed, the display list values don't change. In the following code fragment, the display list contains a command to set the current RGBA color to black (0.0, 0.0, 0.0). The subsequent change of the value of the *color_vector* array to red (1.0, 0.0,

0.0) has no effect on the display list because the display list contains the values that were in effect when it was created:

```
GLfloat color_vector[3] = {0.0, 0.0, 0.0};
glNewList(1, GL_COMPILE);
   glColor3fv(color_vector);
glEndList();
color_vector[0] = 1.0;
```

Not all OpenGL commands can be stored and executed from within a display list. For example, commands that set client state and commands that retrieve state values aren't stored in a display list. (Many of these commands are easily identifiable because they return values in parameters passed by reference or return a value directly.) If these commands are called when making a display list, they're executed immediately.

Table 7-1 enumerates OpenGL commands that cannot be stored in a display list. (Note also that **glNewList()** itself generates an error if it's called while already creating a display list.) Some of these commands haven't been described yet; you can look in the index to see where they're discussed.

| | | |
|---|---|---|
| glAreTexturesResident | glEdgeFlagPointer | glIsShader |
| glAttachShader | glEnableClientState | glIsTexture |
| glBindAttribLocation | glEnableVertexAttribArray | glLinkProgram |
| glBindBuffer | glFeedbackBuffer | glMapBuffer |
| glBufferData | glFinish | glNormalPointer |
| glBufferSubData | glFlush | glPixelStore |
| glClientActiveTexture | glFogCoordPointer | glPopClientAttrib |
| glColorPointer | glFogCoordPointer | glPushClientAttrib |
| glCompileShader | glGenBuffers | glReadPixels |
| glCreateProgram | glGenLists | glRenderMode |
| glCreateShader | glGenQueries | glSecondaryColorPointer |
| glDeleteBuffers | glGenTextures | glSecondaryColorPointer |
| glDeleteLists | glGet* | glSelectBuffer |
| glDeleteProgram | glIndexPointer | glShaderSource |
| glDeleteQueries | glInterleavedArrays | glTexCoordPointer |
| glDeleteShader | glIsBuffer | glUnmapBuffer |
| glDeleteTextures | glIsEnabled | glValidateProgram |
| glDetachShader | glIsList | glVertexAttribPointer |
| glDisableClientState | glIsProgram | glVertexPointer |
| glDisableVertexAttribArray | glIsQuery | |

**Table 7-1**   OpenGL Functions That Cannot Be Stored in Display Lists

To understand more clearly why these commands can't be stored in a display list, remember that when you're using OpenGL across a network, the client may be on one machine and the server on another. After a display list is created, it resides with the server, so the server can't rely on the client for any information related to the display list. If querying commands, such as **glGet\*()** or **glIs\*()**, were allowed in a display list, the calling program would be surprised at random times by data returned over the network. Without parsing the display list as it was sent, the calling program wouldn't know where to put the data. Therefore, any command that returns a value can't be stored in a display list.

Commands that change client state, such as **glPixelStore()**, **glSelectBuffer()**, and the commands to define vertex arrays, can't be stored in a display list. For example, the vertex-array specification routines (such as **glVertexPointer()**, **glColorPointer()**, and **glInterleavedArrays()**) set client state pointers and cannot be stored in a display list. **glArrayElement()**, **glDrawArrays()**, and **glDrawElements()** send data to the server state to construct primitives from elements in the enabled arrays, so these operations can be stored in a display list. (See "Vertex Arrays" in Chapter 2.) The vertex-array data stored in this display list is obtained by dereferencing data from the pointers, not by storing the pointers themselves. Therefore, subsequent changes to the data in the vertex arrays will not affect the definition of the primitive in the display list.

In addition, any commands that use the pixel-storage modes use the modes that are in effect when they are placed in the display list. (See "Controlling Pixel-Storage Modes" in Chapter 8.) Other routines that rely upon client state—such as **glFlush()** and **glFinish()**—can't be stored in a display list because they depend on the client state that is in effect when they are executed.

## Executing a Display List

After you've created a display list, you can execute it by calling **glCallList()**. Naturally, you can execute the same display list many times, and you can mix calls to execute display lists with calls to perform immediate-mode graphics, as you've already seen.

> void **glCallList**(GLuint *list*);
>
> This routine executes the display list specified by *list*. The commands in the display list are executed in the order they were saved, just as if they were issued without using a display list. If *list* hasn't been defined, nothing happens.

You can call **glCallList**() from anywhere within a program, as long as an OpenGL context that can access the display list is active (that is, the context that was active when the display list was created or a context in the same share group). A display list can be created in one routine and executed in a different one, since its index uniquely identifies it. Also, there is no facility for saving the contents of a display list into a data file, nor a facility for creating a display list from a file. In this sense, a display list is designed for temporary use.

## Hierarchical Display Lists

You can create a *hierarchical display list*, which is a display list that executes another display list by calling **glCallList**() between a **glNewList**() and **glEndList**() pair. A hierarchical display list is useful for an object made of components, especially if some of those components are used more than once. For example, this is a display list that renders a bicycle by calling other display lists to render parts of the bicycle:

```
glNewList(listIndex,GL_COMPILE);
    glCallList(handlebars);
    glCallList(frame);
    glTranslatef(1.0, 0.0, 0.0);
    glCallList(wheel);
    glTranslatef(3.0, 0.0, 0.0);
    glCallList(wheel);
glEndList();
```

To avoid infinite recursion, there's a limit on the nesting level of display lists; the limit is at least 64, but it might be higher, depending on the implementation. To determine the nesting limit for your implementation of OpenGL, call

```
glGetIntegerv(GL_MAX_LIST_NESTING, GLint *data);
```

OpenGL allows you to create a display list that calls another list that hasn't been created yet. Nothing happens when the first list calls the second, undefined one.

You can use a hierarchical display list to approximate an editable display list by wrapping a list around several lower-level lists. For example, to put a polygon in a display list while allowing yourself to be able to edit its vertices easily, you could use the code in Example 7-3.

**Example 7-3**  Hierarchical Display List

```
glNewList(1,GL_COMPILE);
    glVertex3fv(v1);
glEndList();
glNewList(2,GL_COMPILE);
    glVertex3fv(v2);
glEndList();
glNewList(3,GL_COMPILE);
    glVertex3fv(v3);
glEndList();

glNewList(4,GL_COMPILE);
    glBegin(GL_POLYGON);
        glCallList(1);
        glCallList(2);
        glCallList(3);
    glEnd();
glEndList();
```

To render the polygon, call display list number 4. To edit a vertex, you need only re-create the single display list corresponding to that vertex. Since an index number uniquely identifies a display list, creating one with the same index as an existing one automatically deletes the old one. Keep in mind that this technique doesn't necessarily provide optimal memory usage or peak performance, but it's acceptable and useful in some cases.

## Managing Display List Indices

So far, we've recommended the use of **glGenLists**() to obtain unused display list indices. If you insist on avoiding **glGenLists**(), then be sure to use **glIsList**() to determine whether a specific index is in use.

GLboolean **glIsList**(GLuint *list*);

Returns GL_TRUE if *list* is already used for a display list, and GL_FALSE otherwise.

You can explicitly delete a specific display list or a contiguous range of lists with **glDeleteLists()**. Using **glDeleteLists()** makes those indices available again.

---

void **glDeleteLists**(GLuint *list*, GLsizei *range*);

Deletes *range* display lists, starting at the index specified by *list*. An attempt to delete a list that has never been created is ignored.

---

## Executing Multiple Display Lists

OpenGL provides an efficient mechanism for executing several display lists in succession. This mechanism requires that you put the display list indices in an array and call **glCallLists()**. An obvious use for such a mechanism occurs when display list indices correspond to meaningful values. For example, if you're creating a font, each display list index might correspond to the ASCII value of a character in that font. To have several such fonts, you would need to establish a different initial display list index for each font. You can specify this initial index by using **glListBase()** before calling **glCallLists()**.

---

void **glListBase**(GLuint *base*);

Specifies the offset that's added to the display list indices in **glCallLists()** to obtain the final display list indices. The default display list base is 0. The list base has no effect on **glCallList()**, which executes only one display list, or on **glNewList()**.

---

void **glCallLists**(GLsizei *n*, GLenum *type*, const GLvoid *\*lists*);

Executes *n* display lists. The indices of the lists to be executed are computed by adding the offset indicated by the current display list base (specified with **glListBase()**) to the signed integer values in the array pointed to by *lists*.

---

The *type* parameter indicates the data type of the values in *lists*. It can be set to GL_BYTE, GL_UNSIGNED_BYTE, GL_SHORT, GL_UNSIGNED_SHORT, GL_INT, GL_UNSIGNED_INT, or GL_FLOAT, indicating that *lists* should be treated as an array of bytes, unsigned bytes, shorts, unsigned shorts, integers, unsigned integers, or floats, respectively. *Type* can also be GL_2_BYTES,

GL_3_BYTES, or GL_4_BYTES, in which case sequences of 2, 3, or 4 bytes are read from *lists* and then shifted and added together, byte by byte, to calculate the display list offset. The following algorithm is used (where *byte[0]* is the start of a byte sequence):

```
/* b = 2, 3, or 4; bytes are numbered 0, 1, 2, 3 in array */
offset = 0;
for (i = 0; i < b; i++) {
   offset = offset << 8;
   offset += byte[i];
}
index = offset + listbase;
```

For multiple-byte data, the highest-order data comes first, as bytes are taken from the array in order.

As an example of the use of multiple display lists, look at the program fragments in Example 7-4 taken from the full program in Example 7-5. This program draws characters with a stroked font (a set of letters made from line segments). The routine **initStrokedFont()** sets up the display list indices for each letter so that they correspond with their ASCII values.

**Example 7-4**   Defining Multiple Display Lists

```
void initStrokedFont(void)
{
   GLuint base;

   base = glGenLists(128);
   glListBase(base);
   glNewList(base+'A', GL_COMPILE);
      drawLetter(Adata); glEndList();
   glNewList(base+'E', GL_COMPILE);
      drawLetter(Edata); glEndList();
   glNewList(base+'P', GL_COMPILE);
      drawLetter(Pdata); glEndList();
   glNewList(base+'R', GL_COMPILE);
      drawLetter(Rdata); glEndList();
   glNewList(base+'S', GL_COMPILE);
      drawLetter(Sdata); glEndList();
   glNewList(base+' ', GL_COMPILE);    /* space character */
      glTranslatef(8.0, 0.0, 0.0);
   glEndList();
}
```

The **glGenLists()** command allocates 128 contiguous display list indices. The first of the contiguous indices becomes the display list base. A display list is made for each letter; each display list index is the sum of the base and the ASCII value of that letter. In this example, only a few letters and the space character are created.

After the display lists have been created, **glCallLists()** can be called to execute the display lists. For example, you can pass a character string to the subroutine **printStrokedString()**:

```
void printStrokedString(GLbyte *s)
{
   GLint len = strlen(s);
   glCallLists(len, GL_BYTE, s);
}
```

The ASCII value for each letter in the string is used as the offset into the display list indices. The current list base is added to the ASCII value of each letter to determine the final display list index to be executed. The output produced by Example 7-5 is shown in Figure 7-1.

**Figure 7-1**     Stroked Font That Defines the Characters A, E, P, R, S

**Example 7-5**     Multiple Display Lists to Define a Stroked Font: stroke.c

```
#define PT 1
#define STROKE 2
#define END 3

typedef struct charpoint {
   GLfloat   x, y;
   int       type;
} CP;

CP Adata[] = {
   { 0, 0, PT}, {0, 9, PT}, {1, 10, PT}, {4, 10, PT},
   {5, 9, PT}, {5, 0, STROKE}, {0, 5, PT}, {5, 5, END}
};

CP Edata[] = {
   {5, 0, PT}, {0, 0, PT}, {0, 10, PT}, {5, 10, STROKE},
   {0, 5, PT}, {4, 5, END}
};
```

```
CP Pdata[] = {
   {0, 0, PT}, {0, 10, PT}, {4, 10, PT}, {5, 9, PT}, {5, 6, PT},
   {4, 5, PT}, {0, 5, END}
};

CP Rdata[] = {
   {0, 0, PT}, {0, 10, PT}, {4, 10, PT}, {5, 9, PT}, {5, 6, PT},
   {4, 5, PT}, {0, 5, STROKE}, {3, 5, PT}, {5, 0, END}
};

CP Sdata[] = {
   {0, 1, PT}, {1, 0, PT}, {4, 0, PT}, {5, 1, PT}, {5, 4, PT},
   {4, 5, PT}, {1, 5, PT}, {0, 6, PT}, {0, 9, PT}, {1, 10, PT},
   {4, 10, PT}, {5, 9, END}
};

/*  drawLetter() interprets the instructions from the array
 *  for that letter and renders the letter with line segments.
 */
static void drawLetter(CP *l)
{
   glBegin(GL_LINE_STRIP);
   while (1) {
      switch (l->type) {
         case PT:
            glVertex2fv(&l->x);
            break;
         case STROKE:
            glVertex2fv(&l->x);
            glEnd();
            glBegin(GL_LINE_STRIP);
            break;
         case END:
            glVertex2fv(&l->x);
            glEnd();
            glTranslatef(8.0, 0.0, 0.0);
            return;
      }
      l++;
   }
}

/*  Create a display list for each of 6 characters. */
static void init(void)
{
   GLuint base;

   glShadeModel(GL_FLAT);
```

```
    base = glGenLists(128);
    glListBase(base);
    glNewList(base+'A', GL_COMPILE);
    drawLetter(Adata);
    glEndList();
    glNewList(base+'E', GL_COMPILE);
    drawLetter(Edata);
    glEndList();
    glNewList(base+'P', GL_COMPILE);
    drawLetter(Pdata);
    glEndList();
    glNewList(base+'R', GL_COMPILE);
    drawLetter(Rdata);
    glEndList();
    glNewList(base+'S', GL_COMPILE);
    drawLetter(Sdata);
    glEndList();
    glNewList(base+' ', GL_COMPILE);
    glTranslatef(8.0, 0.0, 0.0);
    glEndList();
}

char *test1 = "A SPARE SERAPE APPEARS AS";
char *test2 = "APES PREPARE RARE PEPPERS";

static void printStrokedString(char *s)
{
    GLsizei len = strlen(s);
    glCallLists(len, GL_BYTE, (GLbyte *)s);
}

void display(void)
{
    glClear(GL_COLOR_BUFFER_BIT);
    glColor3f(1.0, 1.0, 1.0);
    glPushMatrix();
    glScalef(2.0, 2.0, 2.0);
    glTranslatef(10.0, 30.0, 0.0);
    printStrokedString(test1);
    glPopMatrix();
    glPushMatrix();
    glScalef(2.0, 2.0, 2.0);
    glTranslatef(10.0, 13.0, 0.0);
    printStrokedString(test2);
    glPopMatrix();
    glFlush();
}
```

```
void reshape(int w, int h)
{
    glViewport(0, 0, (GLsizei) w, (GLsizei) h);
    glMatrixMode(GL_PROJECTION);
    glLoadIdentity();
    gluOrtho2D(0.0, (GLdouble) w, 0.0, (GLdouble) h);
}

void keyboard(unsigned char key, int x, int y)
{
    switch (key) {
        case ' ':
            glutPostRedisplay();
            break;
        case 27:
            exit(0);
            break;
    }
}

int main(int argc, char** argv)
{
    glutInit(&argc, argv);
    glutInitDisplayMode(GLUT_SINGLE | GLUT_RGB);
    glutInitWindowSize(440, 120);
    glutCreateWindow(argv[0]);
    init();
    glutReshapeFunc(reshape);
    glutKeyboardFunc(keyboard);
    glutDisplayFunc(display);
    glutMainLoop();
    return 0;
}
```

## Managing State Variables with Display Lists

A display list can contain calls that change the values of OpenGL state variables. These values change as the display list is executed, just as if the commands were called in immediate mode, and the changes persist after execution of the display list is completed. As previously seen in Example 7-2, and as shown in Example 7-6, which follows, the changes in the current color and current matrix made during the execution of the display list remain in effect after it has been called.

**Example 7-6**  Persistence of State Changes after Execution of a Display List

```
glNewList(listIndex,GL_COMPILE);
    glColor3f(1.0, 0.0, 0.0);
    glBegin(GL_POLYGON);
        glVertex2f(0.0, 0.0);
        glVertex2f(1.0, 0.0);
        glVertex2f(0.0, 1.0);
    glEnd();
    glTranslatef(1.5, 0.0, 0.0);
glEndList();
```

If you now call the following sequence, the line drawn after the display list is drawn with red as the current color and translated by an additional (1.5, 0.0, 0.0):

```
glCallList(listIndex);
glBegin(GL_LINES);
    glVertex2f(2.0,-1.0);
    glVertex2f(1.0, 0.0);
glEnd();
```

Sometimes you want state changes to persist, but other times you want to save the values of state variables before executing a display list and then restore these values after the list has been executed. Remember that you cannot use **glGet*()** in a display list, so you must use another way to query and store the values of state variables.

You can use **glPushAttrib()** to save a group of state variables and **glPopAttrib()** to restore the values when you're ready for them. To save and restore the current matrix, use **glPushMatrix()** and **glPopMatrix()** as described in "Manipulating the Matrix Stacks" in Chapter 3. These push and pop routines can be legally cached in a display list. To restore the state variables in Example 7-6, you might use the code shown in Example 7-7.

**Example 7-7**  Restoring State Variables within a Display List

```
glNewList(listIndex,GL_COMPILE);
    glPushMatrix();
    glPushAttrib(GL_CURRENT_BIT);
    glColor3f(1.0, 0.0, 0.0);
    glBegin(GL_POLYGON);
        glVertex2f(0.0, 0.0);
        glVertex2f(1.0, 0.0);
        glVertex2f(0.0, 1.0);
```

```
   glEnd();
   glTranslatef(1.5, 0.0, 0.0);
   glPopAttrib();
   glPopMatrix();
glEndList();
```

If you use the display list from Example 7-7, which restores values, the code in Example 7-8 draws a green, untranslated line. With the display list in Example 7-6, which doesn't save and restore values, the line is drawn red, and its position is translated 10 times (1.5, 0.0, 0.0).

**Example 7-8**     The Display List May or May Not Affect drawLine()

```
void display(void)
{
   GLint i;

   glClear(GL_COLOR_BUFFER_BIT);
   glColor3f(0.0, 1.0, 0.0);   /* set current color to green    */
   for (i = 0; i < 10; i++)
      glCallList(listIndex);   /* display list called 10 times */
   drawLine();             /* how and where does this line appear? */
   glFlush();
}
```

## Encapsulating Mode Changes

You can use display lists to organize and store groups of commands to change various modes or set various parameters. When you want to switch from one group of settings to another, using display lists might be more efficient than making the calls directly, since the settings might be cached in a format that matches the requirements of your graphics system.

Display lists may be more efficient than immediate mode for switching among various lighting, lighting-model, and material-parameter settings. You might also use display lists for stipple patterns, fog parameters, and clipping-plane equations. In general, you'll find that executing display lists is at least as fast as making the relevant calls directly, but remember that some overhead is involved in jumping to a display list.

Example 7-9 shows how to use display lists to switch among three different line stipples. First, you call **glGenLists()** to allocate a display list for each stipple pattern and create a display list for each pattern. Then, you use **glCallList()** to switch from one stipple pattern to another.

**Example 7-9**    Display Lists for Mode Changes

```
GLuint offset;
offset = glGenLists(3);

glNewList(offset, GL_COMPILE);
    glDisable(GL_LINE_STIPPLE);
glEndList();

glNewList(offset+1, GL_COMPILE);
    glEnable(GL_LINE_STIPPLE);
    glLineStipple(1, 0x0F0F);
glEndList();

glNewList(offset+2, GL_COMPILE);
    glEnable(GL_LINE_STIPPLE);
    glLineStipple(1, 0x1111);
glEndList();


#define drawOneLine(x1,y1,x2,y2) glBegin(GL_LINES); \
    glVertex2f((x1),(y1)); glVertex2f((x2),(y2)); glEnd();

glCallList(offset);
drawOneLine(50.0, 125.0, 350.0, 125.0);

glCallList(offset+1);
drawOneLine(50.0, 100.0, 350.0, 100.0);

glCallList(offset+2);
drawOneLine(50.0, 75.0, 350.0, 75.0);
```

## Chapter 8

# Drawing Pixels, Bitmaps, Fonts, and Images

**Chapter Objectives**

After reading this chapter, you'll be able to do the following:

- Position and draw bitmapped data

- Read pixel data (bitmaps and images) from the framebuffer into processor memory and from memory into the framebuffer

- Copy pixel data from one color buffer to another, or to another location in the same buffer

- Magnify or reduce an image as it's written to the framebuffer

- Control pixel data formatting and perform other transformations as the data is moved to and from the framebuffer

- Perform pixel processing using the Imaging Subset

- Use buffer objects for storing pixel data

So far, most of the discussion in this guide has concerned the rendering of geometric data—points, lines, and polygons. Two other important classes of data can be rendered by OpenGL:

- Bitmaps, typically used for characters in fonts

- Image data, which might have been scanned in or calculated

Both bitmaps and image data take the form of rectangular arrays of pixels. One difference between them is that a *bitmap* consists of a single bit of information about each pixel, and image data typically includes several pieces of data per pixel (the complete red, green, blue, and alpha color components, for example). Also, bitmaps are like masks in that they're used to overlay another image, but image data simply overwrites or is blended with whatever data is in the framebuffer.

This chapter describes how to draw pixel data (bitmaps and images) from processor memory to the framebuffer and how to read pixel data from the framebuffer into processor memory. It also describes how to copy pixel data from one position to another, either from one buffer to another or within a single buffer.

**Note:** OpenGL does not support reading or saving pixels and images to files.

This chapter contains the following major sections:

- "Bitmaps and Fonts" describes the commands for positioning and drawing bitmapped data. Such data may describe a font.

- "Images" presents basic information about drawing, reading, and copying pixel data.

- "Imaging Pipeline" describes the operations that are performed on images and bitmaps when they are read from the framebuffer and when they are written to the framebuffer.

- "Reading and Drawing Pixel Rectangles" covers all the details about how pixel data is stored in memory and how to transform it as it's moved into or out of memory.

- "Using Buffer Objects with Pixel Rectangle Data" discusses using server-side buffer objects to store and retrieve pixel data more efficiently.

- "Tips for Improving Pixel Drawing Rates" lists tips for getting better performance when drawing pixel rectangles.

- "Imaging Subset" presents additional pixel processing operations found in this OpenGL extension.

In most cases, the necessary pixel operations are simple, so the first three sections might be all you need to read for your application. However, pixel manipulation can be complex—there are many ways to store pixel data in memory, and you can apply any of several operations to pixels as they're moved to and from the framebuffer. These details are the subject of the fourth section of this chapter. Most likely, you'll want to read this section only when you actually need to make use of the information. "Tips for Improving Pixel Drawing Rates" provides useful tips to get the best performance when rendering bitmaps and images.

OpenGL Version 1.2 added packed (such as GL_UNSIGNED_BYTE_3_3_2 and GL_UNSIGNED_INT_10_10_10_2), BGR, and BGRA pixel formats.

In Version 1.2, a set of Imaging Operations, including color matrix transformations, color lookup tables, histograms, and new blending operations (**glBlendEquation()**, **glBlendColor()**, and several constant blending modes), became an ARB-approved extension named the *Imaging Subset*. In Version 1.4, the blending operations of the Imaging Subset have been promoted to the core OpenGL feature set.

Version 1.4 also introduces use of GL_SRC_COLOR and GL_ONE_MINUS_SRC_COLOR as source blending functions as well as use of GL_DST_COLOR and GL_ONE_MINUS_DST_COLOR as destination blending functions. Version 1.4 also adds **glWindowPos*()** for specifying the raster position in window coordinates.

## Bitmaps and Fonts

A bitmap is a rectangular array of 0s and 1s that serves as a drawing mask for a rectangular portion of the window. Suppose you're drawing a bitmap and the current raster color is red. Wherever there's a 1 in the bitmap, the corresponding pixel in the framebuffer is replaced by a red pixel (or combined with a red pixel, depending on which per-fragment operations are in effect). (See "Testing and Operating on Fragments" in Chapter 10.) If there's a 0 in the bitmap, no fragments are generated, and the contents of the pixel are unaffected. The most common use of bitmaps is for drawing characters on the screen.

OpenGL provides only the lowest level of support for drawing strings of characters and manipulating fonts. The commands **glRasterPos*()** (or alternatively **glWindowPos*()**) and **glBitmap()** position and draw a single bitmap on the screen. In addition, through the display-list mechanism, you can use a sequence of character codes to index into a corresponding series of bitmaps representing those characters. (See Chapter 7 for more information about display lists.) You'll have to write your own routines to provide any other support you need for manipulating bitmaps, fonts, and strings of characters.

Consider Example 8-1, which draws the character F three times on the screen. Figure 8-1 shows the F as a bitmap and its corresponding bitmap data.

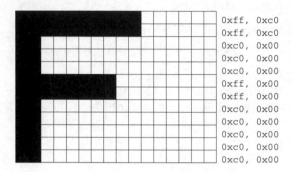

**Figure 8-1**     Bitmapped F and Its Data

**Example 8-1**     Drawing a Bitmapped Character: drawf.c

```
GLubyte rasters[24] = {
    0xc0, 0x00, 0xc0, 0x00, 0xc0, 0x00, 0xc0, 0x00, 0xc0, 0x00,
    0xff, 0x00, 0xff, 0x00, 0xc0, 0x00, 0xc0, 0x00, 0xc0, 0x00,
    0xff, 0xc0, 0xff, 0xc0};

void init(void)
{
    glPixelStorei(GL_UNPACK_ALIGNMENT, 1);
    glClearColor(0.0, 0.0, 0.0, 0.0);
}

void display(void)
{
    glClear(GL_COLOR_BUFFER_BIT);
    glColor3f(1.0, 1.0, 1.0);
    glRasterPos2i(20, 20);
    glBitmap(10, 12, 0.0, 0.0, 11.0, 0.0, rasters);
    glBitmap(10, 12, 0.0, 0.0, 11.0, 0.0, rasters);
    glBitmap(10, 12, 0.0, 0.0, 11.0, 0.0, rasters);
    glFlush();
}
```

In Figure 8-1, note that the visible part of the F character is at most 10 bits wide. Bitmap data is always stored in chunks that are multiples of 8 bits, but the width of the actual bitmap doesn't have to be a multiple of 8. The bits making up a bitmap are drawn starting from the lower left corner: First, the bottom row is drawn, then the next row above it, and so on. As you can tell from the code, the bitmap is stored in memory in this order—the array of rasters begins with 0xc0, 0x00, 0xc0, 0x00 for the bottom two rows of the F and continues to 0xff, 0xc0, 0xff, 0xc0 for the top two rows.

The commands of interest in this example are **glRasterPos2i()** and **glBitmap()**; they're discussed in detail in the next section. For now, ignore the call to **glPixelStorei()**; it describes how the bitmap data is stored in computer memory. (See "Controlling Pixel-Storage Modes" for more information.)

## The Current Raster Position

The *current raster position* is the screen position where the next bitmap (or image) is to be drawn. In the F example, the raster position was set by calling **glRasterPos*()** with coordinates (20, 20), which is where the lower left corner of the F was drawn:

```
glRasterPos2i(20, 20);
```

void **glRasterPos{234}{sifd}**(*TYPE x, TYPE y, TYPE z, TYPE w*);
void **glRasterPos{234}{sifd}v**(const *TYPE *coords*);

Sets the current raster position. The *x, y, z,* and *w* arguments specify the coordinates of the raster position. If the vector form of the function is used, the *coords* array contains the coordinates of the raster position. If **glRasterPos2*()** is used, *z* is implicitly set to zero and *w* is implicitly set to 1; similarly, with **glRasterPos3*()**, *w* is set to 1.

The coordinates of the raster position are transformed to screen coordinates in exactly the same way as coordinates supplied with a **glVertex*()** command (that is, with the modelview and perspective matrices). After transformation, either they define a valid spot in the viewport or they're clipped because the coordinates were outside the viewing volume. If the transformed point is clipped out, the current raster position is invalid.

Prior to Version 1.4, if you wanted to specify the raster position in window (screen) coordinates, you had to set up the modelview and projection matrices for simple 2D rendering, with something like the following sequence of commands, where *width* and *height* are also the size (in pixels) of the viewport:

```
glMatrixMode(GL_PROJECTION);
glLoadIdentity();
gluOrtho2D(0.0, (GLfloat) width, 0.0, (GLfloat) height);
glMatrixMode(GL_MODELVIEW);
glLoadIdentity();
```

In Version 1.4, **glWindowPos*()** was introduced as an alternative to **glRasterPos*()**. **glWindowPos*()** specifies the current raster position in window coordinates, without the transformation of its *x* and *y* coordinates by the modelview or projection matrices, nor clipping to the viewport. **glWindowPos*()** makes it much easier to intermix 2D text and 3D graphics at the same time without the repetitive switching of transformation state.

---

void **glWindowPos{23}{sifd}**(*TYPE x, TYPE y, TYPE z*);
void **glWindowPos{23}{sifd}v**(const *TYPE *coords*);

---

Sets the current raster position using the *x* and *y* arguments as window coordinates without matrix transformation, clipping, lighting, or texture coordinate generation. The *z* value is transformed by (and clamped to) the current near and far values set by **glDepthRange()**. If the vector form of the function is used, the *coords* array contains the coordinates of the raster position. If **glWindowPos2*()** is used, *z* is implicitly set to zero.

To obtain the current raster position (whether set by **glRasterPos*()** or **glWindowPos*()**), you can use the query command **glGetFloatv()** with GL_CURRENT_RASTER_POSITION as the first argument. The second argument should be a pointer to an array that can hold the (*x, y, z, w*) values as floating-point numbers. Call **glGetBooleanv()** with GL_CURRENT_RASTER_POSITION_VALID as the first argument to determine whether the current raster position is valid.

## Drawing the Bitmap

Once you've set the desired raster position, you can use the **glBitmap()** command to draw the data.

---

void **glBitmap**(GLsizei *width*, GLsizei *height*,
         GLfloat $x_{bo}$, GLfloat $y_{bo}$,
         GLfloat $x_{bi}$, GLfloat $y_{bi}$,
         const GLubyte *\*bitmap*);

---

Draws the bitmap specified by *bitmap*, which is a pointer to the bitmap image. The origin of the bitmap is placed at the current raster position. If the current raster position is invalid, nothing is drawn, and the raster position remains invalid. The *width* and *height* arguments indicate the width and height, in pixels, of the bitmap. The width need not be a multiple of 8, although the data is stored in unsigned characters of 8 bits each. (In the F example, it wouldn't matter if there were garbage bits in the data beyond the tenth bit; since **glBitmap**() was called with a width of 10, only 10 bits of the row are rendered.) Use $x_{bo}$ and $y_{bo}$ to define the origin of the bitmap, which is positioned at the current raster position (positive values move the origin up and to the right of the raster position; negative values move it down and to the left); $x_{bi}$ and $y_{bi}$ indicate the $x$ and $y$ increments that are added to the raster position after the bitmap is rasterized (see Figure 8-2).

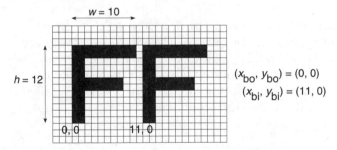

**Figure 8-2**     Bitmap and Its Associated Parameters

Allowing the origin of the bitmap to be placed arbitrarily makes it easy for characters to extend below the origin (typically used for characters with descenders, such as g, j, and y), or to extend beyond the left of the origin (used for various swash characters, which have extended flourishes, or for characters in fonts that lean to the left).

After the bitmap is drawn, the current raster position is advanced by $x_{bi}$ and $y_{bi}$ in the $x$- and $y$-directions, respectively. (If you just want to advance the current raster position without drawing anything, call **glBitmap**() with the *bitmap* parameter set to NULL and the *width* and *height* parameters set to zero.) For standard Latin fonts, $y_{bi}$ is typically 0.0 and $x_{bi}$ is positive (since successive characters are drawn from left to right). For Hebrew, where characters go from right to left, the $x_{bi}$ values would typically be negative. Fonts that draw successive characters vertically in columns would use zero for $x_{bi}$ and nonzero values for $y_{bi}$. In Figure 8-2, each time the F is drawn, the current raster position advances by 11 pixels, allowing a 1-pixel space between successive characters.

Since $x_{bo}$, $y_{bo}$, $x_{bi}$, and $y_{bi}$ are floating-point values, characters need not be an integral number of pixels apart. Actual characters are drawn on exact pixel boundaries, but the current raster position is kept in floating point so that each character is drawn as close as possible to where it belongs. For example, if the code in the F example were modified such that $x_{bi}$ was 11.5 instead of 12, and if more characters were drawn, the space between letters would alternate between 1 and 2 pixels, giving the best approximation to the requested 1.5-pixel space.

**Note:** You can't rotate bitmap fonts because the bitmap is always drawn aligned to the $x$ and $y$ framebuffer axes. Additionally, bitmaps can't be zoomed.

## Choosing a Color for the Bitmap

You are familiar with using **glColor*()** and **glIndex*()** to set the current color or index for drawing geometric primitives. The same commands are used to set different state variables, GL_CURRENT_RASTER_COLOR and GL_CURRENT_RASTER_INDEX, for rendering bitmaps. The raster color state variables are set from the current color when **glRasterPos*()** is called, which can lead to a trap. In the following sequence of code, what is the color of the bitmap?

```
glColor3f(1.0, 1.0, 1.0);   /* white */
glRasterPos3fv(position);
glColor3f(1.0, 0.0, 0.0);   /* red   */
glBitmap(....);
```

Are you surprised to learn that the bitmap is white? The GL_CURRENT_RASTER_COLOR is set to white when **glRasterPos3fv()** is called. The second call to **glColor3f()** changes the value of GL_CURRENT_COLOR for future geometric rendering, but the color used to render the bitmap is unchanged.

To obtain the current raster color or index, you can use the query commands **glGetFloatv()** or **glGetIntegerv()** with GL_CURRENT_RASTER_COLOR or GL_CURRENT_RASTER_INDEX as the first argument.

## Fonts and Display Lists

Display lists are discussed in general terms in Chapter 7. However, a few of the display-list management commands have special relevance for drawing strings of characters. As you read this section, keep in mind that the ideas presented here apply equally well to characters that are drawn using bitmap data and those drawn using geometric primitives (points, lines, and polygons). (See "Executing Multiple Display Lists" in Chapter 7 for an example of a geometric font.)

A font typically consists of a set of characters, where each character has an identifying number (usually the ASCII code) and a drawing method. For a standard ASCII character set, the capital letter A is number 65, B is 66, and so on. The string "DAB" would be represented by the three indices 68, 65, 66. In the simplest approach, display-list number 65 draws an A, number 66 draws a B, and so on. To draw the string 68, 65, 66, just execute the corresponding display lists.

You can use the command **glCallLists()** in just this way:

```
void glCallLists(GLsizei n, GLenum type, const GLvoid *lists);
```

The first argument, *n*, indicates the number of characters to be drawn, *type* is usually GL_BYTE, and *lists* is an array of character codes.

Since many applications need to draw character strings in multiple fonts and sizes, this simplest approach isn't convenient. Instead, you'd like to use 65 as A no matter what font is currently active. You could force font 1 to encode A, B, and C as 1065, 1066, 1067, and font 2 as 2065, 2066, 2067, but then any numbers larger than 256 would no longer fit in an 8-bit byte. A better solution is to add an offset to every entry in the string before choosing the display list. In this case, font 1 has A, B, and C represented by 1065, 1066, and 1067, and in font 2, they might be 2065, 2066, and 2067. To draw characters in font 1, set the offset to 1000 and draw display lists 65, 66, and 67. To draw that same string in font 2, set the offset to 2000 and draw the same lists.

To set the offset, use the command **glListBase()**. For the preceding examples, it should be called with 1000 or 2000 as the (only) argument. Now what you need is a contiguous list of unused display-list numbers, which you can obtain from **glGenLists()**:

```
GLuint glGenLists(GLsizei range);
```

This function returns a block of *range* display-list identifiers. The returned lists are all marked as "used" even though they're empty, so that subsequent calls to **glGenLists()** never return the same lists (unless you've explicitly deleted them previously). Therefore, if you use 4 as the argument and if **glGenLists()** returns 81, you can use display-list identifiers 81, 82, 83, and 84 for your characters. If **glGenLists()** can't find a block of unused identifiers of the requested length, it returns 0. (Note that the command **glDeleteLists()** makes it easy to delete all the lists associated with a font in a single operation.)

Most American and European fonts have a small number of characters (fewer than 256), so it's easy to represent each character with a different code that can be stored in a single byte. Asian fonts, among others, may require much larger character sets, so a byte-per-character encoding is impossible. OpenGL allows strings to be composed of 1-, 2-, 3-, or 4-byte characters through the *type* parameter in **glCallLists()**. This parameter can have any of the following values:

| | |
|---|---|
| GL_BYTE | GL_UNSIGNED_BYTE |
| GL_SHORT | GL_UNSIGNED_SHORT |
| GL_INT | GL_UNSIGNED_INT |
| GL_FLOAT | GL_2_BYTES |
| GL_3_BYTES | GL_4_BYTES |

(See "Executing Multiple Display Lists" in Chapter 7 for more information about these values.)

## Defining and Using a Complete Font

The **glBitmap()** command and the display-list mechanism described in the preceding section make it easy to define a raster font. In Example 8-2, the upper-case characters of an ASCII font are defined. In this example, each character has the same width, but this is not always the case. Once the characters are defined, the program prints the message "THE QUICK BROWN FOX JUMPS OVER A LAZY DOG."

The code in Example 8-2 is similar to the F example, except that each character's bitmap is stored in its own display list. When combined with the offset returned by **glGenLists()**, the display list identifier is equal to the ASCII code for the character.

**Example 8-2**   Drawing a Complete Font: font.c

```
GLubyte space[] =
    {0x00, 0x00, 0x00, 0x00, 0x00, 0x00, 0x00, 0x00, 0x00, 0x00, 0x00, 0x00, 0x00};
GLubyte letters[][13] = {
    {0x00, 0x00, 0xc3, 0xc3, 0xc3, 0xc3, 0xff, 0xc3, 0xc3, 0xc3, 0x66, 0x3c, 0x18},
    {0x00, 0x00, 0xfe, 0xc7, 0xc3, 0xc3, 0xc7, 0xfe, 0xc7, 0xc3, 0xc3, 0xc7, 0xfe},
    {0x00, 0x00, 0x7e, 0xe7, 0xc0, 0xc0, 0xc0, 0xc0, 0xc0, 0xc0, 0xc0, 0xe7, 0x7e},
    {0x00, 0x00, 0xfc, 0xce, 0xc7, 0xc3, 0xc3, 0xc3, 0xc3, 0xc3, 0xc7, 0xce, 0xfc},
    {0x00, 0x00, 0xff, 0xc0, 0xc0, 0xc0, 0xc0, 0xfc, 0xc0, 0xc0, 0xc0, 0xc0, 0xff},
    {0x00, 0x00, 0xc0, 0xc0, 0xc0, 0xc0, 0xc0, 0xc0, 0xfc, 0xc0, 0xc0, 0xc0, 0xff},
    {0x00, 0x00, 0x7e, 0xe7, 0xc3, 0xc3, 0xcf, 0xc0, 0xc0, 0xc0, 0xc0, 0xe7, 0x7e},
    {0x00, 0x00, 0xc3, 0xc3, 0xc3, 0xc3, 0xc3, 0xff, 0xc3, 0xc3, 0xc3, 0xc3, 0xc3},
    {0x00, 0x00, 0x7e, 0x18, 0x18, 0x18, 0x18, 0x18, 0x18, 0x18, 0x18, 0x18, 0x7e},
    {0x00, 0x00, 0x7c, 0xee, 0xc6, 0x06, 0x06, 0x06, 0x06, 0x06, 0x06, 0x06, 0x06},
    {0x00, 0x00, 0xc3, 0xc6, 0xcc, 0xd8, 0xf0, 0xe0, 0xf0, 0xd8, 0xcc, 0xc6, 0xc3},
    {0x00, 0x00, 0xff, 0xc0, 0xc0, 0xc0, 0xc0, 0xc0, 0xc0, 0xc0, 0xc0, 0xc0, 0xc0},
    {0x00, 0x00, 0xc3, 0xc3, 0xc3, 0xc3, 0xc3, 0xc3, 0xdb, 0xff, 0xff, 0xe7, 0xc3},
    {0x00, 0x00, 0xc7, 0xc7, 0xcf, 0xcf, 0xdf, 0xdb, 0xfb, 0xf3, 0xf3, 0xe3, 0xe3},
    {0x00, 0x00, 0x7e, 0xe7, 0xc3, 0xc3, 0xc3, 0xc3, 0xc3, 0xc3, 0xc3, 0xe7, 0x7e},
    {0x00, 0x00, 0xc0, 0xc0, 0xc0, 0xc0, 0xc0, 0xfe, 0xc7, 0xc3, 0xc3, 0xc7, 0xfe},
    {0x00, 0x00, 0x3f, 0x6e, 0xdf, 0xdb, 0xc3, 0xc3, 0xc3, 0xc3, 0xc3, 0x66, 0x3c},
    {0x00, 0x00, 0xc3, 0xc6, 0xcc, 0xd8, 0xf0, 0xfe, 0xc7, 0xc3, 0xc3, 0xc7, 0xfe},
    {0x00, 0x00, 0x7e, 0xe7, 0x03, 0x03, 0x07, 0x7e, 0xe0, 0xc0, 0xc0, 0xe7, 0x7e},
    {0x00, 0x00, 0x18, 0x18, 0x18, 0x18, 0x18, 0x18, 0x18, 0x18, 0x18, 0x18, 0xff},
    {0x00, 0x00, 0x7e, 0xe7, 0xc3, 0xc3, 0xc3, 0xc3, 0xc3, 0xc3, 0xc3, 0xc3, 0xc3},
    {0x00, 0x00, 0x18, 0x3c, 0x3c, 0x66, 0x66, 0xc3, 0xc3, 0xc3, 0xc3, 0xc3, 0xc3},
    {0x00, 0x00, 0xc3, 0xe7, 0xff, 0xff, 0xdb, 0xdb, 0xc3, 0xc3, 0xc3, 0xc3, 0xc3},
    {0x00, 0x00, 0xc3, 0x66, 0x66, 0x3c, 0x3c, 0x18, 0x3c, 0x3c, 0x66, 0x66, 0xc3},
    {0x00, 0x00, 0x18, 0x18, 0x18, 0x18, 0x18, 0x18, 0x3c, 0x3c, 0x66, 0x66, 0xc3},
    {0x00, 0x00, 0xff, 0xc0, 0xc0, 0x60, 0x30, 0x7e, 0x0c, 0x06, 0x03, 0x03, 0xff}
};
GLuint fontOffset;
void makeRasterFont(void)
{
    GLuint i, j;
    glPixelStorei(GL_UNPACK_ALIGNMENT, 1);
    fontOffset = glGenLists(128);
    for (i = 0,j = 'A'; i < 26; i++,j++) {
        glNewList(fontOffset + j, GL_COMPILE);
        glBitmap(8, 13, 0.0, 2.0, 10.0, 0.0, letters[i]);
        glEndList();
    }
    glNewList(fontOffset + ' ', GL_COMPILE);
    glBitmap(8, 13, 0.0, 2.0, 10.0, 0.0, space);
    glEndList();
}
```

```
void init(void)
{
   glShadeModel(GL_FLAT);
   makeRasterFont();
}

void printString(char *s)
{
   glPushAttrib(GL_LIST_BIT);
   glListBase(fontOffset);
   glCallLists(strlen(s), GL_UNSIGNED_BYTE, (GLubyte *) s);
   glPopAttrib();
}

/* Everything above this line could be in a library
 * that defines a font.  To make it work, you've got
 * to call makeRasterFont() before you start making
 * calls to printString().
 */
void display(void)
{
   GLfloat white[3] = { 1.0, 1.0, 1.0 };

   glClear(GL_COLOR_BUFFER_BIT);
   glColor3fv(white);

   glRasterPos2i(20, 60);
   printString("THE QUICK BROWN FOX JUMPS");
   glRasterPos2i(20, 40);
   printString("OVER A LAZY DOG");
   glFlush();
}
```

## Images

An image is similar to a bitmap, but instead of containing only a single bit for each pixel in a rectangular region of the screen, an image can contain much more information. For example, an image can contain a complete (R, G, B, A) color stored at each pixel. Images can come from several sources, such as

- A photograph that's digitized with a scanner

- An image that was first generated on the screen by a graphics program using the graphics hardware and then read back pixel by pixel

- A software program that generated the image in memory pixel by pixel

The images you normally think of as pictures come from the color buffers. However, you can read or write rectangular regions of pixel data from or to the depth buffer or the stencil buffer. (See Chapter 10 for an explanation of these other buffers.)

In addition to simply being displayed on the screen, images can be used for texture maps, in which case they're essentially pasted onto polygons that are rendered on the screen in the normal way. (See Chapter 9 for more information about this technique.)

## Reading, Writing, and Copying Pixel Data

OpenGL provides three basic commands that manipulate image data:

- **glReadPixels()**—Reads a rectangular array of pixels from the framebuffer and stores the data in processor memory.

- **glDrawPixels()**—Writes a rectangular array of pixels from data kept in processor memory into the framebuffer at the current raster position specified by **glRasterPos*()**.

- **glCopyPixels()**—Copies a rectangular array of pixels from one part of the framebuffer to another. This command behaves similarly to a call to **glReadPixels()** followed by a call to **glDrawPixels()**, but the data is never written into processor memory.

For the aforementioned commands, the order of pixel data processing operations is shown in Figure 8-3.

Figure 8-3 presents the basic flow of pixels as they are processed. The coordinates of **glRasterPos*()**, which specify the current raster position used by **glDrawPixels()** and **glCopyPixels()**, are transformed by the geometric processing pipeline. Both **glDrawPixels()** and **glCopyPixels()** are affected by rasterization and per-fragment operations. (But when drawing or copying a pixel rectangle, there's almost never a reason to have fog or texture enabled.)

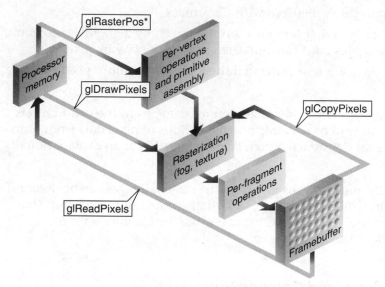

**Figure 8-3** Simplistic Diagram of Pixel Data Flow

However, complications arise because there are many kinds of framebuffer data, many ways to store pixel information in computer memory, and various data conversions that can be performed during the reading, writing, and copying operations. These possibilities translate to many different modes of operation. If all your program does is copy images on the screen or read them into memory temporarily so that they can be copied out later, you can ignore most of these modes. However, if you want your program to modify the data while it's in memory—for example, if you have an image stored in one format but the window requires a different format, or if you want to save image data to a file for future restoration in another session or on another kind of machine with significantly different graphical capabilities—you have to understand the various modes.

The rest of this section describes the basic commands in detail. The following sections discuss the details of the series of imaging operations that comprise the Imaging Pipeline: pixel-storage modes, pixel-transfer operations, and pixel-mapping operations.

## Reading Pixel Data from Framebuffer to Processor Memory

void **glReadPixels**(GLint *x*, GLint *y*, GLsizei *width*, GLsizei *height*,
                     GLenum *format*, GLenum *type*, GLvoid *\*pixels*);

Reads pixel data from the framebuffer rectangle whose lower left corner is at (*x, y*) in window coordinates and whose dimensions are *width* and *height* and stores it in the array pointed to by *pixels*. *format* indicates the kind of pixel data elements that are read (an index value or an R, G, B, or A component value, as listed in Table 8-1), and *type* indicates the data type of each element (see Table 8-2).

If you are using **glReadPixels**() to obtain RGBA or color-index information, you may need to clarify which buffer you are trying to access. For example, if you have a double-buffered window, you need to specify whether you are reading data from the front buffer or back buffer. To control the current read source buffer, call **glReadBuffer**(). (See "Selecting Color Buffers for Writing and Reading" in Chapter 10.)

| format Constant | Pixel Format |
|---|---|
| GL_COLOR_INDEX | a single color index |
| GL_RGB | a red color component, followed by green and blue color components |
| GL_RGBA | a red color component, followed by green, blue, and alpha color components |
| GL_BGR | a blue color component, followed by green and red color components |
| GL_BGRA | a blue color component, followed by green, red, and alpha color components |
| GL_RED | a single red color component |
| GL_GREEN | a single green color component |
| GL_BLUE | a single blue color component |
| GL_ALPHA | a single alpha color component |
| GL_LUMINANCE | a single luminance component |

**Table 8-1**    Pixel Formats for glReadPixels() or glDrawPixels()

| format Constant | Pixel Format |
|---|---|
| GL_LUMINANCE_ALPHA | a luminance component followed by an alpha color component |
| GL_STENCIL_INDEX | a single stencil index |
| GL_DEPTH_COMPONENT | a single depth component |

**Table 8-1    (continued)**    Pixel Formats for glReadPixels() or glDrawPixels()

| type Constant | Data Type |
|---|---|
| GL_UNSIGNED_BYTE | unsigned 8-bit integer |
| GL_BYTE | signed 8-bit integer |
| GL_BITMAP | single bits in unsigned 8-bit integers using the same format as **glBitmap()** |
| GL_UNSIGNED_SHORT | unsigned 16-bit integer |
| GL_SHORT | signed 16-bit integer |
| GL_UNSIGNED_INT | unsigned 32-bit integer |
| GL_INT | signed 32-bit integer |
| GL_FLOAT | single-precision floating point |
| GL_UNSIGNED_BYTE_3_3_2 | packed into unsigned 8-bit integer |
| GL_UNSIGNED_BYTE_2_3_3_REV | packed into unsigned 8-bit integer |
| GL_UNSIGNED_SHORT_5_6_5 | packed into unsigned 16-bit integer |
| GL_UNSIGNED_SHORT_5_6_5_REV | packed into unsigned 16-bit integer |
| GL_UNSIGNED_SHORT_4_4_4_4 | packed into unsigned 16-bit integer |
| GL_UNSIGNED_SHORT_4_4_4_4_REV | packed into unsigned 16-bit integer |
| GL_UNSIGNED_SHORT_5_5_5_1 | packed into unsigned 16-bit integer |
| GL_UNSIGNED_SHORT_1_5_5_5_REV | packed into unsigned 16-bit integer |
| GL_UNSIGNED_INT_8_8_8_8 | packed into unsigned 32-bit integer |

**Table 8-2**    Data Types for glReadPixels() or glDrawPixels()

| type Constant | Data Type |
|---|---|
| GL_UNSIGNED_INT_8_8_8_8_REV | packed into unsigned 32-bit integer |
| GL_UNSIGNED_INT_10_10_10_2 | packed into unsigned 32-bit integer |
| GL_UNSIGNED_INT_2_10_10_10_REV | packed into unsigned 32-bit integer |

**Table 8-2   (continued)**   Data Types for glReadPixels() or glDrawPixels()

**Note:** The GL_*_REV pixel formats are particularly useful on Microsoft's Windows operating systems.

Remember that, depending on the format, anywhere from one to four elements are read (or written). For example, if the format is GL_RGBA and you're reading into 32-bit integers (that is, if *type* is equal to GL_UNSIGNED_INT or GL_INT), then every pixel read requires 16 bytes of storage (four components × four bytes/component).

Each element of the image is stored in memory, as indicated in Table 8-2. If the element represents a continuous value, such as a red, green, blue, or *luminance* component, each value is scaled to fit into the available number of bits. For example, assume the red component is initially specified as a floating-point value between 0.0 and 1.0. If it needs to be packed into an unsigned byte, only 8 bits of precision are kept, even if more bits are allocated to the red component in the framebuffer. GL_UNSIGNED_SHORT and GL_UNSIGNED_INT give 16 and 32 bits of precision, respectively. The signed versions of GL_BYTE, GL_SHORT, and GL_INT have 7, 15, and 31 bits of precision, since the negative values are typically not used.

If the element is an index (a color index or a stencil index, for example), and the type is not GL_FLOAT, the value is simply masked against the available bits in the type. The signed versions—GL_BYTE, GL_SHORT, and GL_INT— have masks with one fewer bit. For example, if a color index is to be stored in a signed 8-bit integer, it's first masked against 0x7f. If the type is GL_FLOAT, the index is simply converted into a single-precision floating-point number (for example, the index 17 is converted to the float 17.0).

For packed data types (denoted by constants that begin with GL_UNSIGNED_BYTE_*, GL_UNSIGNED_SHORT_*, or GL_UNSIGNED_INT_*), all color components of each pixel are squeezed into a single unsigned data type: one of byte, short integer, or standard integer. Valid formats are limited for each type, as indicated in Table 8-3. If an invalid pixel format is used for a packed pixel data type, a GL_INVALID_OPERATION error is generated.

| Packed type Constants | Valid Pixel Formats |
| --- | --- |
| GL_UNSIGNED_BYTE_3_3_2 | GL_RGB |
| GL_UNSIGNED_BYTE_2_3_3_REV | GL_RGB |
| GL_UNSIGNED_SHORT_5_6_5 | GL_RGB |
| GL_UNSIGNED_SHORT_5_6_5_REV | GL_RGB |
| GL_UNSIGNED_SHORT_4_4_4_4 | GL_RGBA, GL_BGRA |
| GL_UNSIGNED_SHORT_4_4_4_4_REV | GL_RGBA, GL_BGRA |
| GL_UNSIGNED_SHORT_5_5_5_1 | GL_RGBA, GL_BGRA |
| GL_UNSIGNED_SHORT_1_5_5_5_REV | GL_RGBA, GL_BGRA |
| GL_UNSIGNED_INT_8_8_8_8 | GL_RGBA, GL_BGRA |
| GL_UNSIGNED_INT_8_8_8_8_REV | GL_RGBA, GL_BGRA |
| GL_UNSIGNED_INT_10_10_10_2 | GL_RGBA, GL_BGRA |
| GL_UNSIGNED_INT_2_10_10_10_REV | GL_RGBA, GL_BGRA |

**Table 8-3**     Valid Pixel Formats for Packed Data Types

The order of color values in bitfield locations of packed pixel data is determined by both the pixel format and whether the type constant contains _REV. Without the _REV suffix, the color components are normally assigned with the first color component occupying the most significant locations. With the _REV suffix, the component packing order is reversed, with the first color component starting with the least significant locations.

To illustrate this, Figure 8-4 shows the bitfield ordering of GL_UNSIGNED_BYTE_3_3_2, GL_UNSIGNED_BYTE_2_3_3_REV, and four valid combinations of GL_UNSIGNED_SHORT_4_4_4_4 (and _REV) data types and the RGBA/BGRA pixel formats. The bitfield organizations for the other 14 valid combinations of packed pixel data types and pixel formats follow similar patterns.

The most significant bit of each color component is always packed in the most significant bit location. Storage of a single component is not affected by any pixel storage modes, although storage of an entire pixel may be affected by the byte swapping mode. (For details on byte swapping, see "Controlling Pixel-Storage Modes" on page 325.)

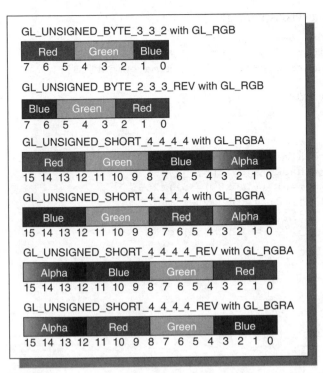

GL_UNSIGNED_BYTE_3_3_2 with GL_RGB

| Red | Green | Blue |
|---|---|---|
| 7 6 5 | 4 3 2 | 1 0 |

GL_UNSIGNED_BYTE_2_3_3_REV with GL_RGB

| Blue | Green | Red |
|---|---|---|
| 7 6 | 5 4 3 | 2 1 0 |

GL_UNSIGNED_SHORT_4_4_4_4 with GL_RGBA

| Red | Green | Blue | Alpha |
|---|---|---|---|
| 15 14 13 12 | 11 10 9 8 | 7 6 5 4 | 3 2 1 0 |

GL_UNSIGNED_SHORT_4_4_4_4 with GL_BGRA

| Blue | Green | Red | Alpha |
|---|---|---|---|
| 15 14 13 12 | 11 10 9 8 | 7 6 5 4 | 3 2 1 0 |

GL_UNSIGNED_SHORT_4_4_4_4_REV with GL_RGBA

| Alpha | Blue | Green | Red |
|---|---|---|---|
| 15 14 13 12 | 11 10 9 8 | 7 6 5 4 | 3 2 1 0 |

GL_UNSIGNED_SHORT_4_4_4_4_REV with GL_BGRA

| Alpha | Red | Green | Blue |
|---|---|---|---|
| 15 14 13 12 | 11 10 9 8 | 7 6 5 4 | 3 2 1 0 |

**Figure 8-4**    Component Ordering for Some Data Types and Pixel Formats

## Writing Pixel Data from Processor Memory to Framebuffer

void **glDrawPixels**(GLsizei *width*, GLsizei *height*, GLenum *format*,
GLenum *type*, const GLvoid *\*pixels*);

Draws a rectangle of pixel data with dimensions *width* and *height*. The pixel rectangle is drawn with its lower left corner at the current raster position. *format* and *type* have the same meaning as with **glReadPixels()**. (For legal values for *format* and *type*, see Tables 8-1 and 8-2.) The array pointed to by *pixels* contains the pixel data to be drawn. If the current raster position is invalid, nothing is drawn, and the raster position remains invalid.

Example 8-3 is a portion of a program that uses **glDrawPixels()** to draw a pixel rectangle in the lower left corner of a window. **makeCheckImage()** creates a 64 × 64 RGB array of a black-and-white checkerboard image. **glRasterPos2i**(0, 0) positions the lower left corner of the image. For now, ignore **glPixelStorei()**.

**Example 8-3**    Use of glDrawPixels(): image.c

```c
#define checkImageWidth 64
#define checkImageHeight 64
GLubyte checkImage[checkImageHeight][checkImageWidth][3];

void makeCheckImage(void)
{
   int i, j, c;

   for (i = 0; i < checkImageHeight; i++) {
      for (j = 0; j < checkImageWidth; j++) {
         c = ((((i&0x8)==0)^((j&0x8))==0))*255;
         checkImage[i][j][0] = (GLubyte) c;
         checkImage[i][j][1] = (GLubyte) c;
         checkImage[i][j][2] = (GLubyte) c;
      }
   }
}

void init(void)
{
   glClearColor(0.0, 0.0, 0.0, 0.0);
   glShadeModel(GL_FLAT);
   makeCheckImage();
   glPixelStorei(GL_UNPACK_ALIGNMENT, 1);
}
void display(void)
{
   glClear(GL_COLOR_BUFFER_BIT);
   glRasterPos2i(0, 0);
   glDrawPixels(checkImageWidth, checkImageHeight, GL_RGB,
                GL_UNSIGNED_BYTE, checkImage);
   glFlush();
}
```

When using **glDrawPixels()** to write RGBA or color-index information, you may need to control the current drawing buffers with **glDrawBuffer()**, which, along with **glReadBuffer()**, is also described in "Selecting Color Buffers for Writing and Reading" in Chapter 10.

## Copying Pixel Data within the Framebuffer

---

void **glCopyPixels**(GLint *x*, GLint *y*, GLsizei *width*, GLsizei *height*,
GLenum *buffer*);

---

Copies pixel data from the framebuffer rectangle whose lower left corner is at (*x, y*) and whose dimensions are *width* and *height*. The data is copied to a new position whose lower left corner is given by the current raster position. *buffer* is either GL_COLOR, GL_STENCIL, or GL_DEPTH, specifying the framebuffer that is used. **glCopyPixels**() behaves similarly to a **glReadPixels**() followed by a **glDrawPixels**(), with the following translation for the *buffer* to *format* parameter:

- If *buffer* is GL_DEPTH or GL_STENCIL, then GL_DEPTH_COMPONENT or GL_STENCIL_INDEX is used, respectively.

- If GL_COLOR is specified, GL_RGBA or GL_COLOR_INDEX is used, depending on whether the system is in RGBA or color-index mode.

Note that there's no need for a *format* or *data* parameter for **glCopyPixels**(), since the data is never copied into processor memory. The read source buffer and the destination buffer of **glCopyPixels**() are specified by **glReadBuffer**() and **glDrawBuffer**(), respectively. Both **glDrawPixels**() and **glCopyPixels**() are used in Example 8-4.

For all three functions, the exact conversions of the data going to or coming from the framebuffer depend on the modes in effect at the time. See the next section for details.


# Imaging Pipeline

This section discusses the complete Imaging Pipeline: the pixel-storage modes and pixel-transfer operations, which include how to set up an arbitrary mapping to convert pixel data. You can also magnify or reduce a pixel rectangle before it's drawn by calling **glPixelZoom**(). The order of these operations is shown in Figure 8-5.

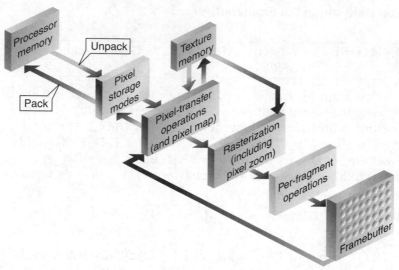

**Figure 8-5**    Imaging Pipeline

When **glDrawPixels()** is called, the data is first unpacked from processor memory according to the pixel-storage modes that are in effect, and then the pixel-transfer operations are applied. The resulting pixels are then rasterized. During rasterization, the pixel rectangle may be zoomed up or down, depending on the current state. Finally, the fragment operations are applied and the pixels are written into the framebuffer. (See "Testing and Operating on Fragments" in Chapter 10 for a discussion of the fragment operations.)

When **glReadPixels()** is called, data is read from the framebuffer, the pixel-transfer operations are performed, and then the resulting data is packed into processor memory.

**glCopyPixels()** applies all the pixel-transfer operations during what would be the **glReadPixels()** activity. The resulting data is written as it would be by **glDrawPixels()**, but the transformations aren't applied a second time. Figure 8-6 shows how **glCopyPixels()** moves pixel data, starting from the framebuffer.

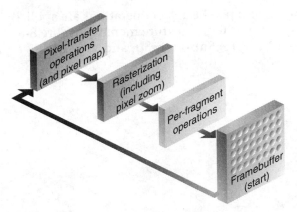

**Figure 8-6**     glCopyPixels() Pixel Path

From "Drawing the Bitmap" and Figure 8-7, you can see that rendering bitmaps is simpler than rendering images. Neither the pixel-transfer operations nor the pixel-zoom operation are applied.

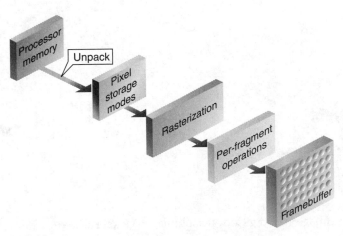

**Figure 8-7**     glBitmap() Pixel Path

Note that the pixel-storage modes and pixel-transfer operations are applied to textures as they are read from or written to texture memory. Figure 8-8 shows the effect on **glTexImage*()**, **glTexSubImage*()**, and **glGetTexImage()**.

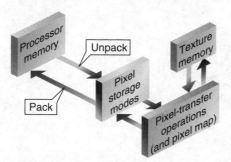

**Figure 8-8**     glTexImage*(), glTexSubImage*(), and glGetTexImage() Pixel Paths

As shown in Figure 8-9, when pixel data is copied from the framebuffer into texture memory (**glCopyTexImage*()** or **glCopyTexSubImage*()**), only pixel-transfer operations are applied. (See Chapter 9 for more information on textures.)

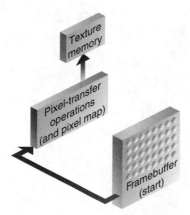

**Figure 8-9**     glCopyTexImage*() and glCopyTexSubImage*() Pixel Paths

## Pixel Packing and Unpacking

Packing and unpacking refer to the way in which pixel data is written to and read from processor memory.

An image stored in memory has between one and four chunks of data, called *elements*. The data might consist of just the color index or the luminance (luminance is the weighted sum of the red, green, and blue values), or it might consist of the red, green, blue, and alpha components for each pixel. The possible arrangements of pixel data, or *formats*, determine the number of elements stored for each pixel and their order.

Some elements (such as a color index or a stencil index) are integers, and others (such as the red, green, blue, and alpha components, or the depth component) are floating-point values, typically ranging between 0.0 and 1.0. Floating-point components are usually stored in the framebuffer with lower resolution than a full floating-point number would require (for example, color components may be stored in 8 bits). The exact number of bits used to represent the components depends on the particular hardware being used. Thus, it's often wasteful to store each component as a full 32-bit floating-point number, especially since images can easily contain a million pixels.

Elements can be stored in memory as various data types, ranging from 8-bit bytes to 32-bit integers or floating-point numbers. OpenGL explicitly defines the conversion of each component in each format to each of the possible data types. Keep in mind that you may lose data if you try to store a high-resolution component in a type represented by a small number of bits.

## Controlling Pixel-Storage Modes

Image data is typically stored in processor memory in rectangular two- or three-dimensional arrays. Often, you want to display or store a subimage that corresponds to a subrectangle of the array. In addition, you might need to take into account that different machines have different byte-ordering conventions. Finally, some machines have hardware that is far more efficient at moving data to and from the framebuffer if the data is aligned on 2-byte, 4-byte, or 8-byte boundaries in processor memory. For such machines, you probably want to control the byte alignment. All the issues raised in this paragraph are controlled as pixel-storage modes, which are discussed in the next subsection. You specify these modes by using **glPixelStore*()**, which you've already seen used in a couple of example programs.

All pixel-storage modes that OpenGL supports are controlled with the **glPixelStore*()** command. Typically, several successive calls are made with this command to set several parameter values.

> void **glPixelStore**{if}(GLenum *pname*, *TYPE param*);
>
> Sets the pixel-storage modes, which affect the operation of **glDrawPixels()**, **glReadPixels()**, **glBitmap()**, **glPolygonStipple()**, **glTexImage1D()**, **glTexImage2D()**, **glTexImage3D()**, **glTexSubImage1D()**, **glTexSubImage2D()**, **glTexSubImage3D()**, **glGetTexImage()**, and, if the Imaging Subset is available (see "Imaging Subset" on page 346), also **glGetColorTable()**, **glGetConvolutionFilter()**, **glGetSeparableFilter()**, **glGetHistogram()**, and **glGetMinmax()**.
>
> The possible parameter names for *pname* are shown in Table 8-4, along with their data types, initial values, and valid ranges of values. The GL_UNPACK* parameters control how data is unpacked from memory by **glDrawPixels()**, **glBitmap()**, **glPolygonStipple()**, **glTexImage1D()**, **glTexImage2D()**, **glTexImage3D()**, **glTexSubImage1D()**, **glTexSubImage2D()**, and **glTexSubImage3D()**. The GL_PACK* parameters control how data is packed into memory by **glReadPixels()** and **glGetTexImage()**, and, if the Imaging Subset is available, also **glGetColorTable()**, **glGetConvolutionFilter()**, **glGetSeparableFilter()**, **glGetHistogram()**, and **glGetMinmax()**.
>
> GL_UNPACK_IMAGE_HEIGHT, GL_PACK_IMAGE_HEIGHT, GL_UNPACK_SKIP_IMAGES, and GL_PACK_SKIP_IMAGES affect only 3D texturing (**glTexImage3D()**, **glTexSubImage3D()**, and **glGetTexImage(GL_TEXTURE_3D,...)**).

| Parameter Name | Type | Initial Value | Valid Range |
|---|---|---|---|
| GL_UNPACK_SWAP_BYTES, GL_PACK_SWAP_BYTES | GLboolean | FALSE | TRUE/FALSE |
| GL_UNPACK_LSB_FIRST, GL_PACK_LSB_FIRST | GLboolean | FALSE | TRUE/FALSE |
| GL_UNPACK_ROW_LENGTH, GL_PACK_ROW_LENGTH | GLint | 0 | any non-negative integer |
| GL_UNPACK_SKIP_ROWS, GL_PACK_SKIP_ROWS | GLint | 0 | any non-negative integer |

**Table 8-4**     glPixelStore() Parameters

| Parameter Name | Type | Initial Value | Valid Range |
|---|---|---|---|
| GL_UNPACK_SKIP_PIXELS, GL_PACK_SKIP_PIXELS | GLint | 0 | any non-negative integer |
| GL_UNPACK_ALIGNMENT, GL_PACK_ALIGNMENT | GLint | 4 | 1, 2, 4, 8 |
| GL_UNPACK_IMAGE_HEIGHT, GL_PACK_IMAGE_HEIGHT | GLint | 0 | any non-negative integer |
| GL_UNPACK_SKIP_IMAGES, GL_PACK_SKIP_IMAGES | GLint | 0 | any non-negative integer |

**Table 8-4    (continued)**    glPixelStore() Parameters

Since the corresponding parameters for packing and unpacking have the same meanings, they're discussed together in the rest of this section and referred to without the GL_PACK or GL_UNPACK prefix. For example, *SWAP_BYTES refers to GL_PACK_SWAP_BYTES and GL_UNPACK_SWAP_BYTES.

If the *SWAP_BYTES parameter is FALSE (the default), the ordering of the bytes in memory is whatever is native for the OpenGL client; otherwise, the bytes are reversed. The byte reversal applies to any size element, but has a meaningful effect only for multibyte elements.

The effect of swapping bytes may differ among OpenGL implementations. If on an implementation, GLubyte has 8 bits, GLushort has 16 bits, and GLuint has 32 bits, then Figure 8-10 illustrates how bytes are swapped for different data types. Note that byte swapping has no effect on single-byte data.

**Note:** As long as your OpenGL application doesn't share images with other machines, you can ignore the issue of byte ordering. If your application must render an OpenGL image that was created on a different machine and the two machines have different byte orders, byte ordering can be swapped using *SWAP_BYTES. However, *SWAP_BYTES does not allow you to reorder elements (for example, to swap red and green).

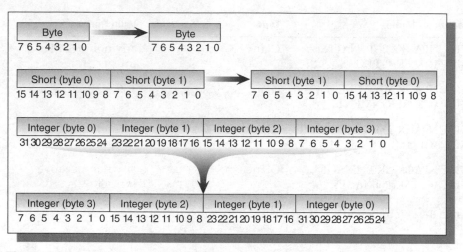

**Figure 8-10** Byte Swap Effect on Byte, Short, and Integer Data

The *LSB_FIRST parameter applies only when drawing or reading 1-bit images or bitmaps for which a single bit of data is saved or restored for each pixel. If *LSB_FIRST is FALSE (the default), the bits are taken from the bytes starting with the most significant bit; otherwise, they're taken in the opposite order. For example, if *LSB_FIRST is FALSE, and the byte in question is 0x31, the bits, in order, are {0, 0, 1, 1, 0, 0, 0, 1}. If *LSB_FIRST is TRUE, the order is {1, 0, 0, 0, 1, 1, 0, 0}.

Sometimes you want to draw or read only a subrectangle of the entire rectangle of image data stored in memory. If the rectangle in memory is larger than the subrectangle that's being drawn or read, you need to specify the actual length (measured in pixels) of the larger rectangle with *ROW_LENGTH. If *ROW_LENGTH is zero (which it is by default), the row length is understood to be the same as the width that's specified with **glReadPixels()**, **glDrawPixels()**, or **glCopyPixels()**. You also need to specify the number of rows and pixels to skip before starting to copy the data for the subrectangle. These numbers are set using the parameters *SKIP_ROWS and *SKIP_PIXELS, as shown in Figure 8-11. By default, both parameters are 0, so you start at the lower left corner.

Often a particular machine's hardware is optimized for moving pixel data to and from memory, if the data is saved in memory with a particular byte alignment. For example, in a machine with 32-bit words, hardware can often retrieve data much faster if it's initially aligned on a 32-bit boundary, which typically has an address that is a multiple of 4. Likewise, 64-bit architectures might work better when the data is aligned to 8-byte boundaries. On some machines, however, byte alignment makes no difference.

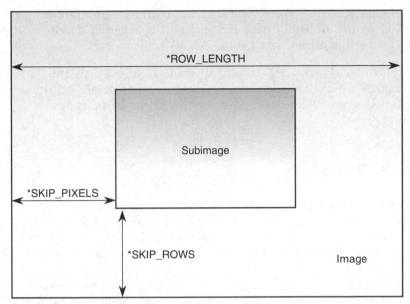

**Figure 8-11**    *SKIP_ROWS, *SKIP_PIXELS, and *ROW_LENGTH Parameters

As an example, suppose your machine works better with pixel data aligned to a 4-byte boundary. Images are most efficiently saved by forcing the data for each row of the image to begin on a 4-byte boundary. If the image is 5 pixels wide and each pixel consists of 1 byte each of red, green, and blue information, a row requires $5 \times 3 = 15$ bytes of data. Maximum display efficiency can be achieved if the first row, and each successive row, begins on a 4-byte boundary, so there is 1 byte of waste in the memory storage for each row. If your data is stored in this way, set the *ALIGNMENT parameter appropriately (to 4, in this case).

If *ALIGNMENT is set to 1, the next available byte is used. If it's 2, a byte is skipped if necessary at the end of each row so that the first byte of the next row has an address that's a multiple of 2. In the case of bitmaps (or 1-bit images), where a single bit is saved for each pixel, the same byte alignment works, although you have to count individual bits. For example, if you're saving a single bit per pixel, if the row length is 75, and if the alignment is 4, then each row requires 75/8, or 9 3/8 bytes. Since 12 is the smallest multiple of 4 that is bigger than 9 3/8, 12 bytes of memory are used for each row. If the alignment is 1, then 10 bytes are used for each row, as 9 3/8 is rounded up to the next byte. (There is a simple use of **glPixelStorei**() shown in Example 8-4.)

**Note:** The default value for *ALIGNMENT is 4. A common programming mistake is assuming that image data is tightly packed and byte aligned (which assumes that *ALIGNMENT is set to 1).

The parameters *IMAGE_HEIGHT and *SKIP_IMAGES affect only the defining and querying of three-dimensional textures. For details on these pixel-storage modes, see "Pixel-Storage Modes for Three-Dimensional Textures" on page 395.

## Pixel-Transfer Operations

As image data is transferred from memory into the framebuffer, or from the framebuffer into memory, OpenGL can perform several operations on it. For example, the ranges of components can be altered—normally, the red component is between 0.0 and 1.0, but you might prefer to keep it in some other range; or perhaps the data you're using from a different graphics system stores the red component in a different range. You can even create maps to perform arbitrary conversions of color indices or color components during pixel transfer. Such conversions performed during the transfer of pixels to and from the framebuffer are called *pixel-transfer operations*. They're controlled with the **glPixelTransfer*()** and **glPixelMap*()** commands.

Be aware that although color, depth, and stencil buffers have many similarities, they don't behave identically, and a few of the modes have special cases. All the mode details are covered in this section and the sections that follow, including all the special cases.

Some of the pixel-transfer function characteristics are set with **glPixelTransfer*()**. The other characteristics are specified with **glPixelMap*()**, which is described in the next section.

void **glPixelTransfer**{if}(GLenum *pname*, *TYPE param*);

Sets pixel-transfer modes that affect the operation of **glDrawPixels()**, **glReadPixels()**, **glCopyPixels()**, **glTexImage1D()**, **glTexImage2D()**, **glTexImage3D()**, **glCopyTexImage1D()**, **glCopyTexImage2D()**, **glTexSubImage1D()**, **glTexSubImage2D()**, **glTexSubImage3D()**, **glCopyTexSubImage1D()**, **glCopyTexSubImage2D()**, **glCopyTexSubImage3D()**, and **glGetTexImage()**. The parameter *pname* must be one of those listed in the first column of Table 8-5, and its value, *param*, must be in the valid range shown.

| Parameter Name | Type | Initial Value | Valid Range |
|---|---|---|---|
| GL_MAP_COLOR | GLboolean | FALSE | TRUE/FALSE |
| GL_MAP_STENCIL | GLboolean | FALSE | TRUE/FALSE |
| GL_INDEX_SHIFT | GLint | 0 | $(-\infty, \infty)$ |
| GL_INDEX_OFFSET | GLint | 0 | $(-\infty, \infty)$ |
| GL_RED_SCALE | GLfloat | 1.0 | $(-\infty, \infty)$ |
| GL_GREEN_SCALE | GLfloat | 1.0 | $(-\infty, \infty)$ |
| GL_BLUE_SCALE | GLfloat | 1.0 | $(-\infty, \infty)$ |
| GL_ALPHA_SCALE | GLfloat | 1.0 | $(-\infty, \infty)$ |
| GL_DEPTH_SCALE | GLfloat | 1.0 | $(-\infty, \infty)$ |
| GL_RED_BIAS | GLfloat | 0.0 | $(-\infty, \infty)$ |
| GL_GREEN_BIAS | GLfloat | 0.0 | $(-\infty, \infty)$ |
| GL_BLUE_BIAS | GLfloat | 0.0 | $(-\infty, \infty)$ |
| GL_ALPHA_BIAS | GLfloat | 0.0 | $(-\infty, \infty)$ |
| GL_DEPTH_BIAS | GLfloat | 0.0 | $(-\infty, \infty)$ |
| GL_POST_CONVOLUTION_RED_SCALE | GLfloat | 1.0 | $(-\infty, \infty)$ |
| GL_POST_CONVOLUTION_GREEN_SCALE | GLfloat | 1.0 | $(-\infty, \infty)$ |
| GL_POST_CONVOLUTION_BLUE_SCALE | GLfloat | 1.0 | $(-\infty, \infty)$ |
| GL_POST_CONVOLUTION_ALPHA_SCALE | GLfloat | 1.0 | $(-\infty, \infty)$ |
| GL_POST_CONVOLUTION_RED_BIAS | GLfloat | 0.0 | $(-\infty, \infty)$ |
| GL_POST_CONVOLUTION_GREEN_BIAS | GLfloat | 0.0 | $(-\infty, \infty)$ |
| GL_POST_CONVOLUTION_BLUE_BIAS | GLfloat | 0.0 | $(-\infty, \infty)$ |
| GL_POST_CONVOLUTION_ALPHA_BIAS | GLfloat | 0.0 | $(-\infty, \infty)$ |

**Table 8-5**    glPixelTransfer*() Parameters

| Parameter Name | Type | Initial Value | Valid Range |
|---|---|---|---|
| GL_POST_COLOR_MATRIX_RED_SCALE | GLfloat | 1.0 | $(-\infty, \infty)$ |
| GL_POST_COLOR_MATRIX_GREEN_SCALE | GLfloat | 1.0 | $(-\infty, \infty)$ |
| GL_POST_COLOR_MATRIX_BLUE_SCALE | GLfloat | 1.0 | $(-\infty, \infty)$ |
| GL_POST_COLOR_MATRIX_ALPHA_SCALE | GLfloat | 1.0 | $(-\infty, \infty)$ |
| GL_POST_COLOR_MATRIX_RED_BIAS | GLfloat | 0.0 | $(-\infty, \infty)$ |
| GL_POST_COLOR_MATRIX_GREEN_BIAS | GLfloat | 0.0 | $(-\infty, \infty)$ |
| GL_POST_COLOR_MATRIX_BLUE_BIAS | GLfloat | 0.0 | $(-\infty, \infty)$ |
| GL_POST_COLOR_MATRIX_ALPHA_BIAS | GLfloat | 0.0 | $(-\infty, \infty)$ |

**Table 8-5    (continued)**    glPixelTransfer*() Parameters

**Caution:**  GL_POST_CONVOLUTION_* and GL_POST_COLOR_MATRIX_*
parameters are present only if the Imaging Subset is supported by
your OpenGL implementation. See "Imaging Subset" on
page 346 for more details.

If the GL_MAP_COLOR or GL_MAP_STENCIL parameter is TRUE, then
mapping is enabled. See the next subsection to learn how the mapping is
done and how to change the contents of the maps. All the other parameters
directly affect the pixel component values.

A scale and bias can be applied to the red, green, blue, alpha, and depth
components. For example, you may wish to scale red, green, and blue components that were read from the framebuffer before converting them to a
luminance format in processor memory. Luminance is computed as the
sum of the red, green, and blue components, so if you use the default value
for GL_RED_SCALE, GL_GREEN_SCALE, and GL_BLUE_SCALE, the components all contribute equally to the final intensity or luminance value. If you
want to convert RGB to luminance, according to the NTSC standard, you
set GL_RED_SCALE to .30, GL_GREEN_SCALE to .59, and GL_BLUE_SCALE
to .11.

Indices (color and stencil) can also be transformed. In the case of indices, a
shift and an offset are applied. This is useful if you need to control which
portion of the color table is used during rendering.

# Pixel Mapping

All the color components, color indices, and stencil indices can be modified by means of a table lookup before they are placed in screen memory. The command for controlling this mapping is **glPixelMap*()**.

> void **glPixelMap**{ui us f}**v**(GLenum *map*, GLint *mapsize*,
>                         const *TYPE* *values*);
>
> Loads the pixel map indicated by *map* with *mapsize* entries, whose values are pointed to by *values*. Table 8-6 lists the map names and values; the default sizes are all 1 and the default values are all 0. Each map's size must be a power of 2.

| Map Name | Address | Value |
|---|---|---|
| GL_PIXEL_MAP_I_TO_I | color index | color index |
| GL_PIXEL_MAP_S_TO_S | stencil index | stencil index |
| GL_PIXEL_MAP_I_TO_R | color index | R |
| GL_PIXEL_MAP_I_TO_G | color index | G |
| GL_PIXEL_MAP_I_TO_B | color index | B |
| GL_PIXEL_MAP_I_TO_A | color index | A |
| GL_PIXEL_MAP_R_TO_R | R | R |
| GL_PIXEL_MAP_G_TO_G | G | G |
| GL_PIXEL_MAP_B_TO_B | B | B |
| GL_PIXEL_MAP_A_TO_A | A | A |

**Table 8-6**    glPixelMap*() Parameter Names and Values

The maximum size of the maps is machine-dependent. You can find the sizes of the pixel maps supported on your machine with **glGetIntegerv()**. Use the query argument GL_MAX_PIXEL_MAP_TABLE to obtain the maximum size for all the pixel map tables, and use GL_PIXEL_MAP_*_TO_*_SIZE to obtain the current size of the specified map. The six maps whose address is a color index or stencil index must always be sized to an integral power of 2. The four RGBA maps can be any size from 1 through GL_MAX_PIXEL_MAP_TABLE.

To understand how a table works, consider a simple example. Suppose that you want to create a 256-entry table that maps color indices to color indices using GL_PIXEL_MAP_I_TO_I. You create a table with an entry for each of the values between 0 and 255 and initialize the table with **glPixelMap*()**. Assume you're using the table for thresholding and want to map indices below 101 (indices 0 to 100) to 0, and all indices 101 and above to 255. In this case, your table consists of 101 0s and 155 255s. The pixel map is enabled using the routine **glPixelTransfer*()** to set the parameter GL_MAP_COLOR to TRUE. Once the pixel map is loaded and enabled, incoming color indices below 101 come out as 0, and incoming pixels from 101 to 255 are mapped to 255. If the incoming pixel is larger than 255, it's first masked by 255, throwing out all the bits above the eighth, and the resulting masked value is looked up in the table. If the incoming index is a floating-point value (say 88.14585), it's rounded to the nearest integer value (giving 88), and that number is looked up in the table (giving 0).

Using pixel maps, you can also map stencil indices or convert color indices to RGB. (See "Reading and Drawing Pixel Rectangles" for information about the conversion of indices.)

## Magnifying, Reducing, or Flipping an Image

After the pixel-storage modes and pixel-transfer operations are applied, images and bitmaps are rasterized. Normally, each pixel in an image is written to a single pixel on the screen. However, you can arbitrarily magnify, reduce, or even flip (reflect) an image by using **glPixelZoom()**.

void **glPixelZoom**(GLfloat $zoom_x$, GLfloat $zoom_y$);

Sets the magnification or reduction factors for pixel-write operations (**glDrawPixels()** and **glCopyPixels()**) in the x- and y-dimensions. By default, $zoom_x$ and $zoom_y$ are 1.0. If they're both 2.0, each image pixel is drawn to 4 screen pixels. Note that fractional magnification or reduction factors are allowed, as are negative factors. Negative zoom factors reflect the resulting image about the current raster position.

During rasterization, each image pixel is treated as a $zoom_x \times zoom_y$ rectangle, and fragments are generated for all the pixels whose centers lie within the rectangle. More specifically, let $(x_{rp}, y_{rp})$ be the current raster position. If a particular group of elements (indices or components) is the $n$th in a row and belongs to the $m$th column, consider the region in window coordinates bounded by the rectangle with corners at

$(x_{rp} + zoom_x \cdot n, y_{rp} + zoom_y \cdot m)$ and $(x_{rp} + zoom_x(n+1), y_{rp} + zoom_y(m+1))$

Any fragments whose centers lie inside this rectangle (or on its bottom or left boundaries) are produced in correspondence with this particular group of elements.

A negative zoom can be useful for flipping an image. OpenGL describes images from the bottom row of pixels to the top (and from left to right). If you have a "top to bottom" image, such as a frame of video, you may want to use **glPixelZoom**(1.0, –1.0) to make the image right side up for OpenGL. Be sure that you reset the current raster position appropriately, if needed.

Example 8-4 shows the use of **glPixelZoom**(). A checkerboard image is initially drawn in the lower left corner of the window. By pressing a mouse button and moving the mouse, you can use **glCopyPixels**() to copy the lower left corner of the window to the current cursor location. (If you copy the image onto itself, it looks wacky!) The copied image is zoomed, but initially it is zoomed by the default value of 1.0, so you won't notice. The 'z' and 'Z' keys increase and decrease the zoom factors by 0.5. Any window damage causes the contents of the window to be redrawn. Pressing the 'r' key resets the image and zoom factors.

**Example 8-4**    Drawing, Copying, and Zooming Pixel Data: image.c

```
#define checkImageWidth 64
#define checkImageHeight 64
GLubyte checkImage[checkImageHeight][checkImageWidth][3];

static GLdouble zoomFactor = 1.0;
static GLint height;

void makeCheckImage(void)
{
    int i, j, c;
```

```
        for (i = 0; i < checkImageHeight; i++) {
            for (j = 0; j < checkImageWidth; j++) {
                c = (((((i&0x8)==0)^((j&0x8))==0))*255;
                checkImage[i][j][0] = (GLubyte) c;
                checkImage[i][j][1] = (GLubyte) c;
                checkImage[i][j][2] = (GLubyte) c;
            }
        }
    }

    void init(void)
    {
        glClearColor(0.0, 0.0, 0.0, 0.0);
        glShadeModel(GL_FLAT);
        makeCheckImage();
        glPixelStorei(GL_UNPACK_ALIGNMENT, 1);
    }

    void display(void)
    {
        glClear(GL_COLOR_BUFFER_BIT);
        glRasterPos2i(0, 0);
        glDrawPixels(checkImageWidth, checkImageHeight, GL_RGB,
                    GL_UNSIGNED_BYTE, checkImage);
        glFlush();
    }

    void reshape(int w, int h)
    {
        glViewport(0, 0, (GLsizei) w, (GLsizei) h);
        height = (GLint) h;
        glMatrixMode(GL_PROJECTION);
        glLoadIdentity();
        gluOrtho2D(0.0, (GLdouble) w, 0.0, (GLdouble) h);
        glMatrixMode(GL_MODELVIEW);
        glLoadIdentity();
    }

    void motion(int x, int y)
    {
        static GLint screeny;

        screeny = height - (GLint) y;
        glRasterPos2i(x, screeny);
```

```
        glPixelZoom(zoomFactor, zoomFactor);
        glCopyPixels(0, 0, checkImageWidth, checkImageHeight,
                     GL_COLOR);
        glPixelZoom(1.0, 1.0);
        glFlush();
}

void keyboard(unsigned char key, int x, int y)
{
    switch (key) {
        case 'r':
        case 'R':
            zoomFactor = 1.0;
            glutPostRedisplay();
            printf("zoomFactor reset to 1.0\n");
            break;
        case 'z':
            zoomFactor += 0.5;
            if (zoomFactor >= 3.0)
                zoomFactor = 3.0;
            printf("zoomFactor is now %4.1f\n", zoomFactor);
            break;
        case 'Z':
            zoomFactor -= 0.5;
            if (zoomFactor <= 0.5)
                zoomFactor = 0.5;
            printf("zoomFactor is now %4.1f\n", zoomFactor);
            break;
        case 27:
            exit(0);
            break;
        default:
            break;
    }
}
```

## Reading and Drawing Pixel Rectangles

This section describes the reading and drawing processes in detail. The pixel conversions performed when going from framebuffer to memory (reading) are similar but not identical to the conversions performed when going in the opposite direction (drawing), as explained in the following sections. You may wish to skip this section the first time through, especially if you do not plan to use the pixel-transfer operations right away.

## The Pixel Rectangle Drawing Process

Figure 8-12 and the following list describe the operation of drawing pixels into the framebuffer.

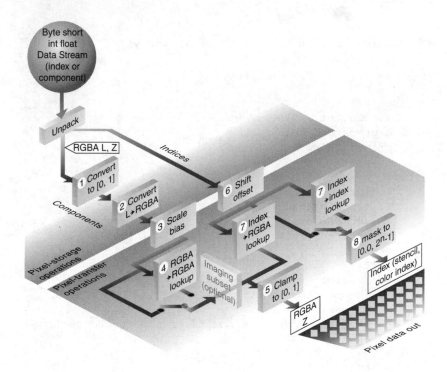

**Figure 8-12**     Drawing Pixels with glDrawPixels()

1.  If the pixels are not indices (that is, if the format isn't GL_COLOR_INDEX or GL_STENCIL_INDEX), the first step is to convert the components to floating-point format if necessary. (See Table 4-1 for the details of the conversion.)

2.  If the format is GL_LUMINANCE or GL_LUMINANCE_ALPHA, the luminance element is converted into R, G, and B by using the luminance value for each of the R, G, and B components. In GL_LUMINANCE_ALPHA format, the alpha value becomes the A value. If GL_LUMINANCE is specified, the A value is set to 1.0.

3. Each component (R, G, B, A, or depth) is multiplied by the appropriate scale, and the appropriate bias is added. For example, the R component is multiplied by the value corresponding to GL_RED_SCALE and added to the value corresponding to GL_RED_BIAS.

4. If GL_MAP_COLOR is TRUE, each of the R, G, B, and A components is clamped to the range [0.0, 1.0], multiplied by an integer 1 less than the table size, truncated, and looked up in the table. (See "Tips for Improving Pixel Drawing Rates" for more details.)

5. Next, the R, G, B, and A components are clamped to [0.0, 1.0], if they weren't already, and are converted to fixed-point with as many bits to the left of the binary point as there are in the corresponding framebuffer component.

6. If you're working with index values (stencil or color indices), then the values are first converted to fixed-point (if they were initially floating-point numbers), with some unspecified bits to the right of the binary point. Indices that were initially fixed-point remain so, and any bits to the right of the binary point are set to zero.

   The resulting index value is then shifted right or left by the absolute value of GL_INDEX_SHIFT bits; the value is shifted left if GL_INDEX_SHIFT > 0, and right otherwise. Finally, GL_INDEX_OFFSET is added to the index.

7. The next step with indices depends on whether you're using RGBA mode or color-index mode. In RGBA mode, a color index is converted to RGBA using the color components specified by GL_PIXEL_MAP_I_TO_R, GL_PIXEL_MAP_I_TO_G, GL_PIXEL_MAP_I_TO_B, and GL_PIXEL_MAP_I_TO_A (see "Pixel Mapping" for details). Otherwise, if GL_MAP_COLOR is GL_TRUE, a color index is looked up through the table GL_PIXEL_MAP_I_TO_I. (If GL_MAP_COLOR is GL_FALSE, the index is unchanged). If the image is made up of stencil indices rather than color indices, and if GL_MAP_STENCIL is GL_TRUE, the index is looked up in the table corresponding to GL_PIXEL_MAP_S_TO_S. If GL_MAP_STENCIL is FALSE, the stencil index is unchanged.

8. Finally, if the indices haven't been converted to RGBA, the indices are then masked to the number of bits of either the color-index or stencil buffer, whichever is appropriate.

### The Pixel Rectangle Reading Process

Many of the conversions done during the pixel rectangle drawing process are also done during the pixel rectangle reading process. The pixel reading process is shown in Figure 8-13 and described in the following list.

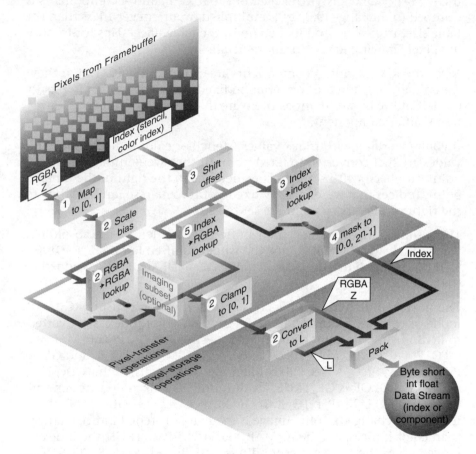

**Figure 8-13**    Reading Pixels with glReadPixels()

1. If the pixels to be read aren't indices (that is, if the format isn't GL_COLOR_INDEX or GL_STENCIL_INDEX), the components are mapped to [0.0, 1.0]—that is, in exactly the opposite way that they are when written.

2. Next, the scales and biases are applied to each component. If GL_MAP_COLOR is GL_TRUE, they're mapped and again clamped to [0.0, 1.0]. If luminance is desired instead of RGB, the R, G, and B components are added (L = R + G + B).

3. If the pixels are indices (color or stencil), they're shifted, offset, and, if GL_MAP_COLOR is GL_TRUE, also mapped.

4. If the storage format is either GL_COLOR_INDEX or GL_STENCIL_INDEX, the pixel indices are masked to the number of bits of the storage type (1, 8, 16, or 32) and packed into memory as previously described.

5. If the storage format is one of the component types (such as luminance or RGB), the pixels are always mapped by the index-to-RGBA maps. Then, they're treated as though they had been RGBA pixels in the first place (including potential conversion to luminance).

6. Finally, for both index and component data, the results are packed into memory according to the GL_PACK* modes set with **glPixelStore*()**.

The scaling, bias, shift, and offset values are the same as those used in drawing pixels, so if you're both reading and drawing pixels, be sure to reset these components to the appropriate values before doing a read or a draw. Similarly, the various maps must be properly reset if you intend to use maps for both reading and drawing.

**Note:** It might seem that luminance is handled incorrectly in both the reading and drawing operations. For example, luminance is not usually equally dependent on the R, G, and B components as it may be assumed from both Figure 8-12 and Figure 8-13. For example, if you want your luminance to be calculated such that the R, G, and B components contribute 30, 59, and 11 percent, respectively, you can set GL_RED_SCALE to 0.30, GL_RED_BIAS to 0.0, and so on. The computed L is then .30R + .59G + .11B.

## Using Buffer Objects with Pixel Rectangle Data

**Advanced**

Advanced

In the same way that storing vertex-array data in buffer objects, as described in "Using Buffer Objects with Vertex-Array Data" in Chapter 2, can increase application performance, storing pixel data in buffer objects can yield similar performance benefits.

By storing pixel rectangles in server-side buffer objects, you can eliminate the need to transfer data from the client's memory to the OpenGL server each frame. You might do this if you render an image as the background, instead of calling **glClear()**, for example.

Compared to vertex-array data in buffer objects, pixel buffer objects can be both read from (just like their vertex counterparts) and written to. Writing to a buffer object occurs when you retrieve pixel data from OpenGL, like when you call **glReadPixels()** or when you retrieve a texture's texels with **glGetTexImage()**.

## Using Buffer Objects to Transfer Pixel Data

OpenGL functions that transfer data from the client application's memory to the OpenGL server, such as **glDrawPixels()**, **glTexImage*D()**, **glCompressedTexImage*D()**, **glPixelMap*()**, and similar functions in the Imaging Subset that take an array of pixels, can use buffer objects for storing pixel data on the server.

To store your pixel rectangle data in buffer objects, you will need to add a few steps to your application.

1. (Optional) Generate buffer object identifiers by calling **glGenBuffers()**.

2. Bind a buffer object for pixel unpacking by calling **glBindBuffer()** with a GL_PIXEL_UNPACK_BUFFER.

3. Request storage for your data and optionally initialize those data elements using **glBufferData()**, once again specifying GL_PIXEL_UNPACK_BUFFER as the *target* parameter.

4. Bind the appropriate buffer object to be used during rendering by once again calling **glBindBuffer()**.

5. Use the data by calling the appropriate function, such as **glDrawPixels()** or **glTexImage2D()**.

If you need to initialize multiple buffer objects, you will repeat steps 2 and 3 for each buffer object.

Example 8-5 modifies the image.c program (shown in Example 8-4) to use pixel buffer objects.

**Example 8-5**    Drawing, Copying, and Zooming Pixel Data Stored in a Buffer Object: pboimage.c

```
#define BUFFER_OFFSET(bytes)  ((GLubyte*) NULL + (bytes))

/*Create checkerboard image*/
#definecheckImageWidth 64
```

```
#definecheckImageHeight 64
GLubyte checkImage[checkImageHeight][checkImageWidth][3];

static GLdouble zoomFactor = 1.0;
static GLint height;
static GLuint pixelBuffer;

void makeCheckImage(void)
{
   int i, j, c;

   for (i = 0; i < checkImageHeight; i++) {
      for (j = 0; j < checkImageWidth; j++) {
         c = ((((i&0x8)==0)^((j&0x8))==0))*255;
         checkImage[i][j][0] = (GLubyte) c;
         checkImage[i][j][1] = (GLubyte) c;
         checkImage[i][j][2] = (GLubyte) c;
      }
   }
}

void init(void)
{
   glewInit();
   glClearColor (0.0, 0.0, 0.0, 0.0);
   glShadeModel(GL_FLAT);
   makeCheckImage();
   glPixelStorei(GL_UNPACK_ALIGNMENT, 1);

   glGenBuffers(1, &pixelBuffer);
   glBindBuffer(GL_PIXEL_UNPACK_BUFFER, pixelBuffer);
   glBufferData(GL_PIXEL_UNPACK_BUFFER,
                3*checkImageWidth*checkImageHeight,
                checkImage, GL_STATIC_DRAW);
}

void display(void)
{
   glClear(GL_COLOR_BUFFER_BIT);
   glRasterPos2i(0, 0);
   glBindBuffer(GL_PIXEL_UNPACK_BUFFER, pixelBuffer);
   glDrawPixels(checkImageWidth, checkImageHeight, GL_RGB,
                GL_UNSIGNED_BYTE, BUFFER_OFFSET(0));
   glFlush();
}
```

## Using Buffer Objects to Retrieve Pixel Data

Pixel buffer objects can also be used as destinations for operations that read pixels from OpenGL buffers and pass those pixels back to the application. Functions like **glReadPixels()** and **glGetTexImage()** can be provided an offset into a currently bound pixel buffer and update the data values in the buffer objects with the retrieved pixels.

Initializing and using a buffer object as the destination for pixel retrieval operations is almost identical to those steps described in "Using Buffer Objects to Transfer Pixel Data," except that the buffer *target* parameter for all buffer object-related calls needs to be GL_PIXEL_PACK_BUFFER.

After the completion of the OpenGL function retrieving the pixels, you can access the data values in the buffer object either by using the **glMapBuffer()** function (described in "Buffer Objects" in Chapter 2) or by **glGetBufferSubData()**. In some cases, **glGetBufferSubData()** may result in a more efficient transfer of data than **glMapBuffer()**.

Example 8-6 demonstrates using a pixel buffer object to store and access the pixels rendered after retrieving the image by calling **glReadPixels()**.

**Example 8-6**   Retrieving Pixel Data Using Buffer Objects

```
#define BUFFER_OFFSET(bytes) ((GLubyte*) NULL + (bytes))

GLuint pixelBuffer;
GLsizei imageWidth;
GLsizei imageHeight;
GLsizei numComponents = 4; /* four components for GL_RGBA */
GLsizei bufferSize;

void
init(void)
{
    bufferSize = imageWidth * imageHeight * numComponents
               * sizeof(GLfloat); /* machine storage size */

    glGenBuffers(1, &pixelBuffer);
    glBindBuffer(GL_PIXEL_PACK_BUFFER, pixelBuffer);
    glBufferData(GL_PIXEL_PACK_BUFFER, bufferSize,
               NULL, /* allocate but don't initialize data */
               GL_STREAM_READ);
}
```

```
void
display(void)
{
    int i;
    GLsizei numPixels = imageWidth * imageHeight;

    /* Draw frame */

    glReadPixels(0, 0, imageWidth, imageHeight, GL_RGBA,
                 GL_FLOAT, BUFFER_OFFSET(0));

    GLfloat *pixels = glMapBuffer(GL_PIXEL_PACK_BUFFER,
                                  GL_READ_ONLY);

    for ( i = 0; i < numPixels; ++i ) {
        /* insert your pixel processing here
            process( &pixels[i*numComponents] );
        */
    }
    glUnmapBuffer(GL_PIXEL_PACK_BUFFER);
}
```

## Tips for Improving Pixel Drawing Rates

As you can see, OpenGL has a rich set of features for reading, drawing, and manipulating pixel data. Although these features are often very useful, they can also decrease performance. Here are some tips for improving pixel draw rates:

- For best performance, set all pixel-transfer parameters to their default values, and set pixel zoom to (1.0, 1.0).

- A series of fragment operations is applied to pixels as they are drawn into the framebuffer. (See "Testing and Operating on Fragments" in Chapter 10.) For optimum performance, disable all necessary fragment operations.

- While performing pixel operations, disable other costly states, such as texture mapping or blending.

- If you use a pixel format and type that match those of the framebuffer, your OpenGL implementation doesn't need to convert the pixels into the format that matches the framebuffer. For example, if you are writing images to an RGB framebuffer with 8 bits per component, call **glDrawPixels()** with *format* set to RGB and *type* set to GL_UNSIGNED_BYTE.

- For many implementations, unsigned image formats are faster to use than signed image formats.

- It is usually faster to draw a large pixel rectangle than to draw several small ones, since the cost of transferring the pixel data can be amortized over many pixels.

- If possible, reduce the amount of data that needs to be copied by using small data types (for example, use GL_UNSIGNED_BYTE) and fewer components (for example, use format GL_LUMINANCE_ALPHA).

- Pixel-transfer operations, including pixel mapping and values for scale, bias, offset, and shift other than the defaults, may decrease performance.

- If you need to render the same image each frame (as a background, for example), render it as a textured quadrilateral, as compared to calling **glDrawPixels()**. Having it stored as a texture requires that the data be downloaded into OpenGL once. See Chapter 9 for a discussion of texture mapping.

## Imaging Subset

The Imaging Subset is a collection of routines that provide additional pixel processing capabilities. With it, you can

- use color lookup tables to replace pixel values

- use convolutions to filter images

- use color matrix transformations to do color space conversions and other linear transformations

- collect histogram statistics and minimum and maximum color component information about images

You should use the Imaging Subset if you need more pixel processing capabilities than those provided by **glPixelTransfer*()** and **glPixelMap*()**.

The Imaging Subset is an extension to OpenGL. If the token *GL_ARB_imaging* is defined, then the subset is present, and all the functionality that is described in the following sections is available for you to use. If the token is not defined, none of the functionality is present in your implementation. To see if your implementation supports the Imaging Subset, see "Extensions to the Standard" on page 605.

Whenever pixels are passed to or read from OpenGL, they are processed by any of the enabled features of the subset. Routines that are affected by the Imaging Subset include functions that

- draw and read pixel rectangles: **glReadPixels()**, **glDrawPixels()**, **glCopyPixels()**

- define textures: **glTexImage1D()**, **glTexImage2D()**, **glCopyTexImage\*D()**, **glSubTexImage1D()**, **glSubTexImage2d()** and **glCopySubTexImage\*D()**

Figure 8-14 illustrates the operations that the Imaging Subset performs on pixels that are passed into or read from OpenGL. Most of the features of the Imaging Subset may be enabled and disabled, with the exception of the color matrix transformation, which is always enabled.

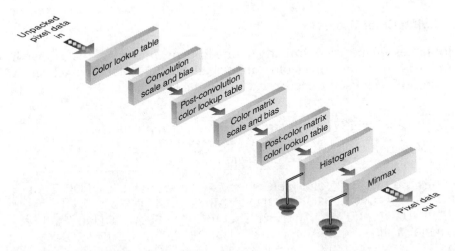

**Figure 8-14**    Imaging Subset Operations

## Color Tables

Color tables are lookup tables used to replace a pixel's color. In applications, color tables may be used for contrast enhancement, filtering, and image equalization.

There are three different color lookup tables available, which operate at different stages of the pixel pipeline. Table 8-7 shows where in the pipeline pixels may be replaced by the respective color table.

| Color Table Parameter | Operates on Pixels |
| --- | --- |
| GL_COLOR_TABLE | when they enter the imaging pipeline |
| GL_POST_CONVOLUTION_COLOR_TABLE | after convolution |
| GL_POST_COLOR_MATRIX_COLOR_TABLE | after the color matrix transformation |

**Table 8-7**     When Color Table Operations Occur in the Imaging Pipeline

Each color table can be enabled separately using **glEnable()** with the respective parameter from Table 8-7.

### Specifying Color Tables

Color tables are specified similarly to one-dimensional images. As shown in Figure 8-14, there are three color tables available for updating pixel values. **glColorTable()** is used to define each color table.

---

void **glColorTable**(GLenum *target*, GLenum *internalFormat*,
              GLsizei *width*, GLenum *format*, GLenum *type*,
              const GLvoid *\*data*);

---

Defines the specified color table when *target* is set to GL_COLOR_TABLE, GL_POST_CONVOLUTION_COLOR_TABLE, or GL_POST_COLOR_ MATRIX_COLOR_TABLE. If *target* is set to GL_PROXY_COLOR_TABLE, GL_PROXY_POST_CONVOLUTION_COLOR_TABLE, or GL_PROXY_ POST_COLOR_MATRIX_COLOR_TABLE, then **glColorTable()** verifies that the specified color table fits into the available resources.

The *internalFormat* variable is used to determine the internal OpenGL representation of *data*. It can be one of the following symbolic constants: GL_ALPHA, GL_ALPHA4, GL_ALPHA8, GL_ALPHA12, GL_ALPHA16, GL_LUMINANCE, GL_LUMINANCE4, GL_LUMINANCE8, GL_LUMINANCE12, GL_LUMINANCE16, GL_LUMINANCE_ALPHA, GL_LUMINANCE4_ALPHA4, GL_LUMINANCE6_ALPHA2, GL_LUMINANCE8_ALPHA8, GL_LUMINANCE12_ALPHA4, GL_LUMINANCE12_ALPHA12, GL_LUMINANCE16_ALPHA16, GL_INTENSITY, GL_INTENSITY4, GL_INTENSITY8, GL_INTENSITY12, GL_INTENSITY16, GL_RGB, GL_R3_G3_B2, GL_RGB4, GL_RGB5, GL_RGB8, GL_RGB10, GL_RGB12, GL_RGB16, GL_RGBA, GL_RGBA2, GL_RGBA4, GL_RGB5_A1, GL_RGBA8, GL_RGB10_A2, GL_RGBA12, and GL_RGBA16.

The *width* parameter, which must be a power of 2, indicates the number of pixels in the color table. The *format* and *type* describe the format and data type of the color table data. They have the same meaning as equivalent parameters of **glDrawPixels()**.

The internal format of the table determines which components of the image's pixels are replaced. For example, if you specify the format to be GL_RGB, then the red, green, and blue components of each incoming pixel are looked up in the appropriate color table and replaced. Table 8-8 describes which pixel components are replaced for a given base internal format.

| Base Internal Format | Red Component | Green Component | Blue Component | Alpha Component |
|---|---|---|---|---|
| GL_ALPHA | Unchanged | Unchanged | Unchanged | $A_t$ |
| GL_LUMINANCE | $L_t$ | $L_t$ | $L_t$ | Unchanged |
| GL_LUMINANCE_ALPHA | $L_t$ | $L_t$ | $L_t$ | $A_t$ |
| GL_INTENSITY | $I_t$ | $I_t$ | $I_t$ | $I_t$ |
| GL_RGB | $R_t$ | $G_t$ | $B_t$ | Unchanged |
| GL_RGBA | $R_t$ | $G_t$ | $B_t$ | $A_t$ |

**Table 8-8**    Color Table Pixel Replacement

In Table 8-8, $L_t$ represents luminance entries in the defined color table, which affect only red, green and blue components. $I_t$ represents intensity entries, which affect red, green, blue, and alpha identically.

After the appropriate color table has been applied to the image, the pixels can be scaled and biased, after which their values are clamped to the range [0, 1]. The GL_COLOR_TABLE_SCALE and GL_COLOR_TABLE_BIAS factors are set for each color table with the **glColorTableParameter*()** routine.

---

void **glColorTableParameter**{if}v(GLenum *target*, GLenum *pname*,
TYPE *\*param);*

---

Sets the GL_COLOR_TABLE_SCALE and GL_COLOR_TABLE_BIAS parameters for each color table. The *target* parameter is one of GL_COLOR_TABLE, GL_POST_CONVOLUTION_COLOR_TABLE, or GL_POST_COLOR_MATRIX_COLOR_TABLE, and it specifies which color table's scale and bias values to set.

The possible values for *pname* are GL_COLOR_TABLE_SCALE and GL_COLOR_TABLE_BIAS.

The value for *param* points to an array of four values, representing the red, green, blue, and alpha modifiers, respectively.

Example 8-7 shows how an image can be inverted using color tables. The color table is set up to replace each color component with its inverse color.

**Example 8-7**    Pixel Replacement Using Color Tables: colortable.c

```
extern GLubyte*  readImage(const char*, GLsizei*, GLsizei* );

GLubyte  *pixels;
GLsizei   width, height;

void init(void)
{
   int   i;
   GLubyte  colorTable[256][3];

   pixels = readImage("Data/leeds.bin", &width, &height);
   glPixelStorei(GL_UNPACK_ALIGNMENT, 1);
   glClearColor(0, 0, 0, 0);
```

```
    /* Set up an inverting color table */
    for (i = 0; i < 256; ++i) {
        colorTable[i][0] = 255 - i;
        colorTable[i][1] = 255 - i;
        colorTable[i][2] = 255 - i;
    }

    glColorTable(GL_COLOR_TABLE, GL_RGB, 256, GL_RGB,
        GL_UNSIGNED_BYTE, colorTable);
    glEnable(GL_COLOR_TABLE);
}

void display(void)
{
    glClear(GL_COLOR_BUFFER_BIT);
    glRasterPos2i(1, 1);
    glDrawPixels(width, height, GL_RGB, GL_UNSIGNED_BYTE,
        pixels);
    glFlush();
}
```

**Note:** Example 8-7 introduces a new function, **readImage()**, which is presented to simplify the example programs. In general, you need to use a routine that can read the image file format that you require. The file format that **readImage()** understands is listed below. The data is listed sequentially in the file.

- width of the image, stored as a *GLsizei*

- height of the image, stored as a *GLsizei*

- *width · height* RGB triples, stored with a *GLubyte* per color component

In addition to specifying a color table explicitly from your application, you may want to use an image created in the framebuffer as the definition for a color table. The **glCopyColorTable()** routine lets you specify a single row of pixels that are read from the framebuffer and used to define a color table.

void **glCopyColorTable**(GLenum *target*, GLenum *internalFormat*,
            GLint *x*, GLint *y*, GLsizei *width*);

Creates a color table using framebuffer data to define the elements of the color table. The pixels are read from the current GL_READ_BUFFER and are processed exactly as if **glCopyPixels()** had been called but stopped before final conversion. The **glPixelTransfer*()** settings are applied.

The *target* parameter must be set to one of the targets of **glColorTable()**. The *internalFormat* parameter uses the same symbolic constants as the *internalFormat* parameter of **glColorTable()**. The color array is defined by the *width* pixels in the row starting at (x, y) in the framebuffer.

### Replacing All or Part of a Color Table

If you would like to replace a part of a color table, then color subtable commands let you reload an arbitrary section of a color table with new values.

---

void **glColorSubTable**(GLenum *target*, GLsizei *start*, GLsizei *count*,
                       GLenum *format*, GLenum *type*,
                       const GLvoid *\*data*);

---

Replaces color table entries *start* to *start* + *count* − 1 with values stored in *data*.

The *target* parameter is GL_COLOR_TABLE, GL_POST_CONVOLUTION_ COLOR_TABLE, or GL_POST_COLOR_MATRIX_COLOR_TABLE. The *format* and *type* parameters are identical to those of **glColorTable()** and describe the pixel values stored in *data*.

---

void **glCopyColorSubTable**(GLenum *target*, GLsizei *start*, GLint *x*,
                             GLint *y*, GLsizei *count*);

---

Replaces color table entries *start* to *start* + *count* − 1 with *count* color pixel values from the row in the framebuffer starting at position (x, y). The pixels are converted into the *internalFormat* of the original color table.

### Querying a Color Table's Values

The pixel values stored in the color tables can be retrieved using the **glGetColorTable()** function. Refer to "The Query Commands" on page 686 for more details.

### Color Table Proxies

Color table proxies provide a way to query OpenGL to see if there are enough resources available to store your color table. If **glColorTable**() is called with one of the following proxy targets:

- GL_PROXY_COLOR_TABLE
- GL_PROXY_POST_CONVOLUTION_COLOR_TABLE
- GL_PROXY_POST_COLOR_MATRIX_COLOR_TABLE

then OpenGL determines if the required color table resources are available. If the color table does not fit, the width, format, and component resolution values are all set to zero. To check if your color table fits, query one of the state values mentioned above. For example:

```
glColorTable(GL_PROXY_COLOR_TABLE, GL_RGB, 1024, GL_RGB,
    GL_UNSIGNED_BYTE, null);
glGetColorTableParameteriv(GL_PROXY_COLOR_TABLE,
    GL_COLOR_TABLE_WIDTH, &width);
if (width == 0)
    /* color table didn't fit as requested */
```

For more details on **glGetColorTableParameter\***(), see "The Query Commands" on page 686.

## Convolutions

Convolutions are pixel filters that replace each pixel with a weighted average of its neighboring pixels and itself. Blurring and sharpening images, finding edges, and adjusting image contrast are examples of how convolutions are used.

Figure 8-15 shows how pixel $P_{00}$ and related pixels are processed by the $3 \times 3$ convolution filter to produce pixel $P'_{11}$.

Convolutions are arrays of pixel weights and operate only on RGBA pixels. A filter, which is also known as a *kernel*, is simply a two-dimensional array of pixel weights. Each pixel in the output image of the convolution process is created by multiplying a set of the input image's pixels by the pixel weights in the convolution kernel and summing the results. For example, in Figure 8-15, pixel $P'_{11}$ is computed by summing the products of the nine pixels from the input image and the nine pixel weights in the convolution filter.

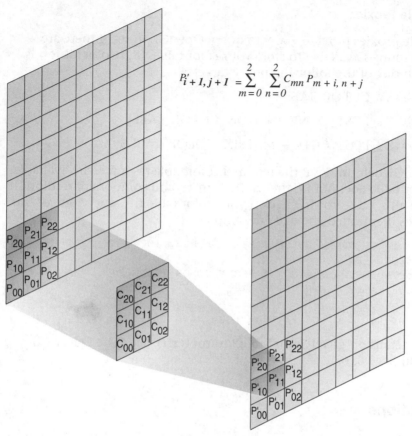

$$P'_{i+1,j+1} = \sum_{m=0}^{2} \sum_{n=0}^{2} C_{mn} P_{m+i,\,n+j}$$

**Figure 8-15**    The Pixel Convolution Operation

---

void **glConvolutionFilter2D**(GLenum *target*, GLenum *internalFormat*,
                      GLsizei *width*, GLsizei *height*,
                      GLenum *format*, GLenum *type*,
                      const GLvoid *\*image*);

---

Defines a two-dimensional convolution filter where the *target* parameter
must be GL_CONVOLUTION_2D.

The *internalFormat* parameter defines which pixel components the
convolution operation is performed on, and can be one of the 38 symbolic
constants that are used for the *internalFormat* parameter for
**glColorTable**().

The *width* and *height* parameters specify the size of the filter in pixels. The maximum width and height for convolution filters may be queried with **glGetConvolutionParameter*()**. Refer to "The Query Commands" on page 686 for more details.

As with **glDrawPixels()**, the *format* and *type* parameters specify the format of the pixels stored in *image*.

Similar to color tables, the internal format of the convolution filter determines which components of the image are operated on. Table 8-9 describes how the different base filter formats affect pixels. $R_s$, $G_s$, $B_s$, and $A_s$ represent the color components of the source pixels. $L_f$ represents the luminance value of a GL_LUMINANCE filter, and $I_f$ corresponds to the intensity value of a GL_INTENSITY filter. Finally, $R_f$, $G_f$, $B_f$, and $A_f$ represent the red, green, blue, and alpha components of the convolution filter.

| Base Filter Format | Red Result | Green Result | Blue Result | Alpha Result |
|---|---|---|---|---|
| GL_ALPHA | Unchanged | Unchanged | Unchanged | $A_s * A_f$ |
| GL_LUMINANCE | $R_s * L_f$ | $G_s * L_f$ | $B_s * L_f$ | Unchanged |
| GL_LUMINANCE_ALPHA | $R_s * L_f$ | $G_s * L_f$ | $B_s * L_f$ | $A_s * A_f$ |
| GL_INTENSITY | $R_s * I_f$ | $G_s * I_f$ | $B_s * I_f$ | $A_s * I_f$ |
| GL_RGB | $R_s * R_f$ | $G_s * G_f$ | $B_s * B_f$ | Unchanged |
| GL_RGBA | $R_s * R_f$ | $G_s * G_f$ | $B_s * B_f$ | $A_s * A_f$ |

**Table 8-9**     How Convolution Filters Affect RGBA Pixel Components

Use **glEnable(GL_CONVOLUTION_2D)** to enable 2D convolution processing.

Example 8-8 demonstrates the use of several $3 \times 3$ GL_LUMINANCE convolution filters to find edges in an RGB image. The 'h', 'l', and 'v' keys change among the various filters.

**Example 8-8**     Using Two-Dimensional Convolution Filters: convolution.c

```
extern GLubyte*  readImage(const char*, GLsizei*, GLsizei*);

GLubyte  *pixels;
GLsizei   width, height;
```

```
/* Define convolution filters */
GLfloat  horizontal[3][3] = {
   { 0, -1, 0 },
   { 0,  1, 0 },
   { 0,  0, 0 }
};

GLfloat  vertical[3][3] = {
   {  0, 0, 0 },
   { -1, 1, 0 },
   {  0, 0, 0 }
};

GLfloat  laplacian[3][3] = {
   { -0.125, -0.125, -0.125 },
   { -0.125,  1.0,   -0.125 },
   { -0.125, -0.125, -0.125 }
};

void display(void)
{
   glClear(GL_COLOR_BUFFER_BIT);
   glRasterPos2i(1, 1);
   glDrawPixels(width, height, GL_RGB, GL_UNSIGNED_BYTE,
      pixels);
   glFlush();
}

void init(void)
{
   pixels = readImage("Data/leeds.bin", &width, &height);
   glPixelStorei(GL_UNPACK_ALIGNMENT, 1);
   glClearColor(0.0, 0.0, 0.0, 0.0);

   printf("Using horizontal filter\n");
   glConvolutionFilter2D(GL_CONVOLUTION_2D, GL_LUMINANCE, 3, 3,
      GL_LUMINANCE, GL_FLOAT, horizontal);
   glEnable(GL_CONVOLUTION_2D);
}

void keyboard(unsigned char key, int x, int y)
{
   switch (key) {
      case 'h' :
         printf("Using horizontal filter\n");
         glConvolutionFilter2D(GL_CONVOLUTION_2D, GL_LUMINANCE,
            3, 3, GL_LUMINANCE, GL_FLOAT, horizontal );
```

```
        break;

    case 'v' :
        printf("Using vertical filter\n" );
        glConvolutionFilter2D( GL_CONVOLUTION_2D, GL_LUMINANCE,
            3, 3, GL_LUMINANCE, GL_FLOAT, vertical );
        break;

    case 'l' :
        printf("Using laplacian filter\n");
        glConvolutionFilter2D(GL_CONVOLUTION_2D, GL_LUMINANCE,
            3, 3, GL_LUMINANCE, GL_FLOAT, laplacian );
        break;

    case 27: /* Escape Key */
        exit(0)
        break;
}
    glutPostRedisplay();
}
```

As with color tables, you may want to specify a convolution filter with pixel
values from the framebuffer. **glCopyConvolutionFilter2D**() copies a
rectangle of pixels from the current GL_READ_BUFFER to use as the
definition of the convolution filter. If GL_LUMINANCE or GL_INTENSITY
is specified for the *internalFormat*, the red component of the pixel is used to
define the convolution filter's value.

---

void **glCopyConvolutionFilter2D**(GLenum *target*,
                                     GLenum *internalFormat*,
                                      GLint *x*, GLint *y*,
                                      GLsizei *width*, GLsizei *height*);

---

Defines a two-dimensional convolution filter initialized with pixels from
the color framebuffer. *target* must be GL_CONVOLUTION_2D, and
*internalFormat* must be set to one of the internal formats defined for
**glConvolutionFilter2D**().

The pixel rectangle with lower left pixel (*x*, *y*) and size *width* by *height* is
read from the framebuffer and converted into the specified *internalFormat*.

### Specifying Separable Two-Dimensional Convolution Filters

Convolution filters are separable if they can be represented by the *outer
product* of two one-dimensional filters.

**glSeparableFilter2D()** is used to specify the two one-dimensional filters that represent the separable two-dimensional convolution filter. As with **glConvolutionFilter2D()**, the internal format of the convolution filter determines how an image's pixels are processed.

---

void **glSeparableFilter2D**(GLenum *target*, GLenum *internalFormat*,
GLsizei *width*, GLsizei *height*, GLenum *format*,
GLenum *type*, const GLvoid *\*row*,
const GLvoid *\*column*);

---

Defines a two-dimensional separable convolution filter. *target* must be set to GL_SEPARABLE_2D. The *internalFormat* parameter uses the same values that are used for **glConvolutionFilter2D()**.

*width* specifies the number of pixels in the *row* array. Likewise, *height* specifies the number of pixels in the *column* array. *type* and *format* define the storage format for *row* and *column* in the same manner as **glConvolutionFilter2D()**.

Use **glEnable(GL_SEPARABLE_2D)** to enable convolutions using a two-dimensional separable convolution filter. GL_CONVOLUTION_2D takes precedence if both GL_CONVOLUTION_2D and GL_SEPARABLE_2D are specified.

A GL_INVALID_OPERATION error is set if an unpack pixel buffer object is bound and the combination of *width, height, format,* and *type*, plus the specified offsets into the bound buffer object would cause a memory access outside of the memory allocated when the buffer object was created.

For example, you might construct a 3 × 3 convolution filter by specifying the one-dimensional filter [ −1/2, 1, −1/2 ] for both *row* and *column* for a GL_LUMINANCE separable convolution filter. OpenGL would compute the convolution of the source image using the two one-dimensional filters in the same manner as if it computed a complete two-dimensional filter by computing the following outer product:

$$
\begin{bmatrix} -1/2 \\ 1 \\ -1/2 \end{bmatrix}
\begin{bmatrix} -1/2 & 1 & -1/2 \end{bmatrix}
=
\begin{bmatrix} 1/4 & -1/2 & 1/4 \\ -1/2 & 1 & -1/2 \\ 1/4 & -1/2 & 1/4 \end{bmatrix}
$$

Using separable convolution filters is computationally more efficient than using a nonseparable two-dimensional convolution filter.

## One-Dimensional Convolution Filters

One-dimensional convolutions are identical to the two-dimensional version except that the filter's *height* parameter is assumed to be 1. However, they affect only the specification of one-dimensional textures (see "One-Dimensional Textures" on page 390 for details).

---

void **glConvolutionFilter1D**(GLenum *target*, GLenum *internalFormat*,
　　　　　　　　　　GLsizei *width*, GLenum *format*,
　　　　　　　　　　GLenum *type*, const GLvoid \**image*);

Specifies a one-dimensional convolution filter. *target* must be set to GL_CONVOLUTION_1D. *width* specifies the number of pixels in the filter. The *internalFormat*, *format*, and *type* have the same meanings as they do for the respective parameters to **glConvolutionFilter2D**(). *image* points to the one-dimensional image to be used as the convolution filter.

Use **glEnable(GL_CONVOLUTION_1D)** to enable one-dimensional convolutions.

You may want to specify the convolution filter with values generated from the framebuffer. **glCopyConvolutionFilter1D**() copies a row of pixels from the current GL_READ_BUFFER, converts them into the specified *internalFormat*, and uses them to define the convolution filter.

A GL_INVALID_OPERATION error is set if an unpack pixel buffer object is bound and the combination of *width*, *format*, and *type*, plus the specified offset into the bound buffer object would cause a memory access outside of the memory allocated when the buffer object was created.

---

void **glCopyConvolutionFilter1D**(GLenum *target*,
　　　　　　　　　　GLenum *internalFormat*, GLint *x*,
　　　　　　　　　　GLint *y*, GLsizei *width*);

Defines a one-dimensional convolution filter with pixel values from the framebuffer. **glCopyConvolutionFilter1D**() copies *width* pixels starting at (*x*, *y*) and converts the pixels into the specified *internalFormat*.

---

When a convolution filter is specified, it can be scaled and biased. The scale and bias values are specified with the **glConvolutionParameter\***(). No clamping of the convolution filter occurs after scaling or biasing.

---

void **glConvolutionParameter**{if}(GLenum *target*, GLenum *pname*, *TYPE param*);

void **glConvolutionParameter**{if}**v**(GLenum *target*, GLenum *pname*, const *TYPE \*params*);

---

Sets parameters that control how a convolution is performed. *target* must be GL_CONVOLUTION_1D, GL_CONVOLUTION_2D, or GL_SEPARABLE_2D.

*pname* must be GL_CONVOLUTION_BORDER_MODE, GL_CONVOLUTION_FILTER_SCALE, or GL_CONVOLUTION_FILTER_ BIAS. Specifying *pname* as GL_CONVOLUTION_BORDER_MODE defines the convolution border mode. In this case, *params* must be GL_REDUCE, GL_CONSTANT_BORDER, or GL_REPLICATE_BORDER. If *pname* is set to either GL_CONVOLUTION_FILTER_SCALE or GL_CONVOLUTION_FILTER_BIAS, then *params* points to an array of four color values for red, green, blue, and alpha, respectively.

**Convolution Border Modes**

The convolutions of pixels at the edges of an image are handled differently from the interior pixels. Their convolutions are modified by the convolution border mode. There are three options for computing border convolutions:

- GL_REDUCE mode causes the resulting image to shrink in each dimension by the size of the convolution filter. The width of the resulting image is *(width – $W_f$)*, and the height of the resulting image is *(height – $H_f$)*, where $W_f$ and $H_f$ are the width and height of the convolution filter, respectively. If this produces an image with zero or negative width or height, no output is generated, nor are any errors.

- GL_CONSTANT_BORDER computes the convolutions of border pixels by using a constant pixel value for pixels outside of the source image. The constant pixel value is set using the **glConvolutionParameter\*()** function. The resulting image's size matches that of the source image.

- GL_REPLICATE_BORDER computes the convolution in the same manner as in GL_CONSTANT_BORDER mode, except the outermost row or column of pixels is used for the pixels that lie outside of the source image. The resulting image's size matches that of the source image.

**Post-Convolution Operations**

After the convolution operation is completed, the pixels of the resulting image may be scaled and biased, and are clamped to the range [0, 1]. The scale and bias values are specified by calling **glPixelTransfer*()**, with either GL_POST_CONVOLUTION_*_SCALE or GL_POST_CONVOLUTION_*_BIAS, respectively. Specifying a GL_POST_CONVOLUTION_COLOR_TABLE with **glColorTable()** allows pixel components to be replaced using a color lookup table.

## Color Matrix

For color space conversions and linear transformations on pixel values, the Imaging Subset supports a 4 × 4 matrix stack, selected by setting **glMatrixMode(GL_COLOR)**. For example, to convert from RGB color space to CMY (cyan, magenta, yellow) color space, you might call

```
GLfloat rgb2cmy[16] = {
    -1,  0,  0, 0,
     0, -1,  0, 0,
     0,  0, -1, 0,
     1,  1,  1, 1
};

glMatrixMode(GL_COLOR);     /* enter color matrix mode */
glLoadMatrixf(rgb2cmy);
glMatrixMode(GL_MODELVIEW);  /* back to modelview mode */
```

**Note:** Recall that OpenGL matrices are stored in a column-major format. See "General-Purpose Transformation Commands" on page 114 for more detail about using matrices with OpenGL.

The color matrix stack has at least two matrix entries. (See "The Query Commands" on page 686 for details on determining the depth of the color matrix stack.) Unlike the other parts of the Imaging Subset, the color matrix transformation is always performed and cannot be disabled.

Example 8-9 illustrates using the color matrix to exchange the red and green color components of an image.

**Example 8-9**     Exchanging Color Components Using the Color Matrix:
           colormatrix.c

```
extern GLubyte*  readImage(const char*, GLsizei*, GLsizei*);

GLubyte  *pixels;
GLsizei   width, height;

void init(void)
{
   /* Specify a color matrix to reorder a pixel's components
    * from RGB to GBR */
   GLfloat  m[16] = {
      0.0, 1.0, 0.0, 0.0,
      0.0, 0.0, 1.0, 0.0,
      1.0, 0.0, 0.0, 0.0,
      0.0, 0.0, 0.0, 1.0
   };

   pixels = readImage("Data/leeds.bin", &width, &height);
   glPixelStorei(GL_UNPACK_ALIGNMENT, 1);
   glClearColor(0.0, 0.0, 0.0, 0.0);

   glMatrixMode(GL_COLOR);
   glLoadMatrixf(m);
   glMatrixMode(GL_MODELVIEW);
}

void display(void)
{
   glClear(GL_COLOR_BUFFER_BIT);
   glRasterPos2i(1, 1);
   glDrawPixels(width, height, GL_RGB, GL_UNSIGNED_BYTE,
      pixels);
   glFlush();
}
```

## Post-Color Matrix Transformation Operations

Similar to the post-convolution operations, pixels can be scaled and biased
after the color matrix step. Calling **glPixelTransfer*()** with either GL_POST_
COLOR_MATRIX_*_SCALE or GL_POST_COLOR_MATRIX_*_BIAS defines the
scale and bias values for the post color matrix operation. Pixel values after
scaling and biasing are clamped to the range [0, 1].

# Histogram

Using the Imaging Subset, you can collect statistics about images. Histogramming determines the distribution of color values in an image, which can be used to determine how to balance an image's contrast, for example.

**glHistogram**() specifies what components of the image you want to histogram, and whether you want only to collect statistics or to continue processing the image. To collect histogram statistics, you must call **glEnable(GL_HISTOGRAM)**.

Similar to color tables as described in "Color Tables" on page 348, a proxy mechanism is available with **glHistogram**() to determine if there are enough resources to store the requested histogram. If resources are not available, the histogram's width, format, and component resolutions are set to zero. You can query the results of a histogram proxy using **glGetHistogramParameter**(), described in "The Query Commands" on page 686.

---

void **glHistogram**(GLenum *target*, GLsizei *width*,
                     GLenum *internalFormat*, GLboolean *sink*);

---

Defines how an image's histogram data should be stored. The *target* parameter must be set to either GL_HISTOGRAM or GL_PROXY_HISTOGRAM. The *width* parameter specifies the number of entries in the histogram table. Its value must be a power of 2.

The *internalFormat* parameter defines how the histogram data should be stored. The allowable values are GL_ALPHA, GL_ALPHA4, GL_ALPHA8, GL_ALPHA12, GL_ALPHA16, GL_LUMINANCE, GL_LUMINANCE4, GL_LUMINANCE8, GL_LUMINANCE12, GL_LUMINANCE16, GL_LUMINANCE_ALPHA, GL_LUMINANCE4_ALPHA4, GL_LUMINANCE6_ALPHA2, GL_LUMINANCE8_ALPHA8, GL_LUMINANCE12_ALPHA4, GL_LUMINANCE12_ALPHA12, GL_LUMINANCE16_ALPHA16, GL_RGB, GL_RGB2, GL_RGB4, GL_RGB5, GL_RGB8, GL_RGB10, GL_RGB12, GL_RGB16, GL_RGBA, GL_RGBA2, GL_RGBA4, GL_RGB5_A1, GL_RGBA8, GL_RGB10_A2, GL_RGBA12, and GL_RGBA16. This list does not include GL_INTENSITY* values. This differs from the list of values accepted by **glColorTable**().

The *sink* parameter indicates whether the pixels should continue to the minmax stage of the pipeline or be discarded.

After you've passed the pixels to the imaging pipeline using **glDrawPixels()**, you can retrieve the results of the histogram using **glGetHistogram()**. In addition to returning the histogram's values, **glGetHistogram()** can be used to reset the histogram's internal storage. The internal storage can also be reset using **glResetHistogram()**, which is described on page 366.

---

void **glGetHistogram**(GLenum *target*, GLboolean *reset*, GLenum *format*, GLenum *type*, GLvoid *\*values*);

---

Returns the collected histogram statistics. *target* must be GL_HISTOGRAM. *reset* specifies if the internal histogram tables should be cleared.

The *format* and *type* parameters specify the storage type of *values*, and how the histogram data should be returned to the application. They accept the same values at their respective parameters in **glDrawPixels()**.

In Example 8-10, the program computes the histogram of an image and plots resulting distributions in the window. The 's' key in the example shows the effect of the *sink* parameter, which controls whether the pixels are passed to the subsequent imaging pipeline operations.

**Example 8-10**   Computing and Diagramming an Image's Histogram: histogram.c

```
#define HISTOGRAM_SIZE  256    /* Must be a power of 2 */

extern GLubyte*  readImage(const char*, GLsizei*, GLsizei*);

GLubyte  *pixels;
GLsizei   width, height;


void init(void)
{
   pixels = readImage("Data/leeds.bin", &width, &height);
   glPixelStorei(GL_UNPACK_ALIGNMENT, 1);
   glClearColor(0.0, 0.0, 0.0, 0.0);

   glHistogram(GL_HISTOGRAM, HISTOGRAM_SIZE, GL_RGB, GL_FALSE);
   glEnable(GL_HISTOGRAM);
}
```

```
void display(void)
{
    int i;
    GLushort values[HISTOGRAM_SIZE][3];

    glClear(GL_COLOR_BUFFER_BIT);
    glRasterPos2i(1, 1);
    glDrawPixels(width, height, GL_RGB, GL_UNSIGNED_BYTE,
        pixels);
    glGetHistogram(GL_HISTOGRAM, GL_TRUE, GL_RGB,
        GL_UNSIGNED_SHORT, values);

    /* Plot histogram */

    glBegin(GL_LINE_STRIP);
    glColor3f(1.0, 0.0, 0.0);
    for (i = 0; i < HISTOGRAM_SIZE; i++)
        glVertex2s(i, values[i][0]);
    glEnd();

    glBegin(GL_LINE_STRIP);
    glColor3f(0.0, 1.0, 0.0);
    for (i = 0; i < HISTOGRAM_SIZE; i++)
        glVertex2s(i, values[i][1]);
    glEnd();

    glBegin(GL_LINE_STRIP);
    glColor3f(0.0, 0.0, 1.0);
    for (i = 0; i < HISTOGRAM_SIZE; i++)
        glVertex2s(i, values[i][2]);
    glEnd();
    glFlush();
}

void keyboard(unsigned char key, int x, int y)
{
    static GLboolean sink = GL_FALSE;

    switch (key) {
        case 's' :
            sink = !sink;
            glHistogram(GL_HISTOGRAM, HISTOGRAM_SIZE, GL_RGB,
                sink);
            break;
```

```
         case 27: /* Escape Key */
             exit(0);
             break;
   }
   glutPostRedisplay();
}
```

**glResetHistogram()** will discard the histogram without retrieving the values.

> void **glResetHistogram**(GLenum *target*);
>
> Resets the histogram counters to zero. The *target* parameter must be GL_HISTOGRAM.

## Minmax

**glMinmax()** computes the minimum and maximum pixel component values for a pixel rectangle. As with **glHistogram()**, you can compute the minimum and maximum values and either render the image or discard the pixels.

> void **glMinmax**(GLenum *target*, GLenum *internalFormat*,
>                 GLboolean *sink*);
>
> Computes the minimum and maximum pixel values for an image. *target* must be GL_MINMAX.
>
> *internalFormat* specifies for which color components the minimum and maximum values should be computed. **glMinmax()** accepts the same values for *internalFormat* as **glHistogram()** accepts.
>
> If GL_TRUE is specified for *sink*, then the pixels are discarded and not written to the framebuffer. GL_FALSE renders the image.

**glGetMinmax()** is used to retrieve the computed minimum and maximum values. Similar to **glHistogram()**, the internal values for the minimum and maximum can be reset when they are accessed.

> void **glGetMinmax**(GLenum *target*, GLboolean *reset*, GLenum *format*,
> GLenum *type*, GLvoid *\*values*);
>
> Returns the results of the minmax operation. *target* must be GL_MINMAX.
> If the *reset* parameter is set to GL_TRUE, the minimum and maximum
> values are reset to their initial values. The *format* and *type* parameters
> describe the format of the minmax data returned in *values*, and use the
> same values as **glDrawPixels**().

Example 8-11 demonstrates the use of **glMinmax**() to compute the minimum and maximum pixel values in GL_RGB format. The minmax operation must be enabled with **glEnable(GL_MINMAX)**.

The minimum and maximum values returned in the array *values* from **glMinmax**() command are grouped by component. For example, if you request GL_RGB values as the *format*, the first three values in the *values* array represent the minimum red, green, and blue values, followed by the maximum red, green, and blue values for the processed pixels.

**Example 8-11**   Computing Minimum and Maximum Pixel Values: minmax.c

```
extern GLubyte*  readImage(const char*, GLsizei*, GLsizei*);

GLubyte  *pixels;
GLsizei   width, height;


void init(void)
{
   pixels = readImage("Data/leeds.bin", &width, &height);
   glPixelStorei(GL_UNPACK_ALIGNMENT, 1);
   glClearColor(0.0, 0.0, 0.0, 0.0);

   glMinmax(GL_MINMAX, GL_RGB, GL_FALSE);
   glEnable(GL_MINMAX);
}

void display(void)
{
   GLubyte  values[6];

   glClear(GL_COLOR_BUFFER_BIT);
   glRasterPos2i(1, 1);
   glDrawPixels(width, height, GL_RGB, GL_UNSIGNED_BYTE,
      pixels);
```

```
    glGetMinmax(GL_MINMAX, GL_TRUE, GL_RGB, GL_UNSIGNED_BYTE,
       values);
    glFlush();
    printf("Red   : min = %d   max = %d\n", values[0], values[3]);
    printf("Green: min = %d   max = %d\n", values[1], values[4]);
    printf("Blue : min = %d   max = %d\n", values[2], values[5]);
}
```

Even though **glGetMinmax()** can reset the minmax values when they are retrieved, you can explicitly reset the internal tables at any time by calling **glResetMinmax()**.

void **glResetMinmax**(GLenum *target*);

Resets the minimum and maximum values to their initial values. The *target* parameter must be GL_MINMAX.

## Chapter 9

# Texture Mapping

**Chapter Objectives**

After reading this chapter, you'll be able to do the following:

- Understand what texture mapping can add to your scene

- Specify texture images in compressed and uncompressed formats

- Control how a texture image is filtered as it is applied to a fragment

- Create and manage texture images in texture objects, and control a high-performance working set of those texture objects

- Specify how the texture and fragment colors are combined

- Supply texture coordinates describing how the texture image should be mapped onto objects in your scene

- Generate texture coordinates automatically to produce effects such as contour maps and environment maps

- Perform complex texture operations in a single pass with multitexturing (sequential texture units)

- Use texture combiner functions to mathematically operate on texture, fragment, and constant color values

- After texturing, process fragments with secondary colors

- Specify textures to be used for processing point sprites

- Transform texture coordinates using the texture matrix

- Render shadowed objects, using depth textures

So far, every geometric primitive has been drawn as either a solid color or smoothly shaded between the colors at its vertices—that is, they've been drawn without texture mapping. If you want to draw a large brick wall without texture mapping, for example, each brick must be drawn as a separate polygon. Without texturing, a large flat wall—which is really a single rectangle—might require thousands of individual bricks, and even then the bricks may appear too smooth and regular to be realistic.

Texture mapping allows you to glue an image of a brick wall (obtained, perhaps, by scanning in a photograph of a real wall) to a polygon and to draw the entire wall as a single polygon. Texture mapping ensures that all the right things happen as the polygon is transformed and rendered. For example, when the wall is viewed in perspective, the bricks may appear smaller as the wall gets farther from the viewpoint. Other uses for texture mapping include depicting vegetation on large polygons representing the ground in flight simulation; wallpaper patterns; and textures that make polygons look like natural substances such as marble, wood, and cloth. The possibilities are endless. Although it's most natural to think of applying textures to polygons, textures can be applied to all primitives—points, lines, polygons, bitmaps, and images. Plates 6, 8, 18–21, and 24–32 all demonstrate the use of textures.

Because there are so many possibilities, texture mapping is a fairly large, complex subject, and you must make several programming choices when using it. For starters, most people intuitively understand a two-dimensional texture, but a texture may be one-dimensional or even three-dimensional. You can map textures to surfaces made of a set of polygons or to curved surfaces, and you can repeat a texture in one, two, or three directions (depending on how many dimensions the texture is described in) to cover the surface. In addition, you can automatically map a texture onto an object in such a way that the texture indicates contours or other properties of the item being viewed. Shiny objects can be textured so that they appear to be in the center of a room or other environment, reflecting the surroundings from their surfaces. Finally, a texture can be applied to a surface in different ways. It can be painted on directly (like a decal placed on a surface), used to modulate the color the surface would have been painted otherwise, or used to blend a texture color with the surface color. If this is your first exposure to texture mapping, you might find that the discussion in this chapter moves fairly quickly. As an additional reference, you might look at the chapter on texture mapping in *3D Computer Graphics* by Alan Watt (Addison-Wesley, 1999).

Textures are simply rectangular arrays of data—for example, color data, luminance data, or color and alpha data. The individual values in a texture array are often called *texels*. What makes texture mapping tricky is that a rectangular texture can be mapped to nonrectangular regions, and this must be done in a reasonable way.

Figure 9-1 illustrates the texture-mapping process. The left side of the figure represents the entire texture, and the black outline represents a quadrilateral shape whose corners are mapped to those spots on the texture. When the quadrilateral is displayed on the screen, it might be distorted by applying various transformations—rotations, translations, scaling, and projections. The right side of the figure shows how the texture-mapped quadrilateral might appear on your screen after these transformations. (Note that this quadrilateral is concave and might not be rendered correctly by OpenGL without prior tessellation. See Chapter 11 for more information about tessellating polygons.)

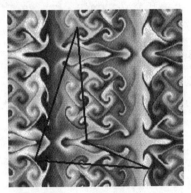

**Figure 9-1**     Texture-Mapping Process

Notice how the texture is distorted to match the distortion of the quadrilateral. In this case, it's stretched in the *x*-direction and compressed in the *y*-direction; there's a bit of rotation and shearing going on as well. Depending on the texture size, the quadrilateral's distortion, and the size of the screen image, some of the texels might be mapped to more than one fragment, and some fragments might be covered by multiple texels. Since the texture is made up of discrete texels (in this case, $256 \times 256$ of them), filtering operations must be performed to map texels to fragments. For example, if many texels correspond to a fragment, they're averaged down to fit; if texel boundaries fall across fragment boundaries, a weighted average of the applicable texels is performed. Because of these calculations, texturing is computationally expensive, which is why many specialized graphics systems include hardware support for texture mapping.

An application may establish texture objects, with each texture object representing a single texture (and possible associated mipmaps). Some implementations of OpenGL can support a special *working set* of texture objects that have better performance than texture objects outside the working set. These high-performance texture objects are said to be *resident* and may have special hardware and/or software acceleration available. You may use OpenGL to create and delete texture objects and to determine which textures constitute your working set.

This chapter covers the OpenGL's texture-mapping facility in the following major sections.

- "An Overview and an Example" gives a brief, broad look at the steps required to perform texture mapping. It also presents a relatively simple example of texture mapping.

- "Specifying the Texture" explains how to specify one-, two-, or three-dimensional textures. It also discusses how to use a texture's borders, how to supply a series of related textures of different sizes, and how to control the filtering methods used to determine how an applied texture is mapped to screen coordinates.

- "Filtering" details how textures are either magnified or minified as they are applied to the pixels of polygons. Minification using special mipmap textures is also explained.

- "Texture Objects" describes how to put texture images into objects so that you can control several textures at one time. With texture objects, you may be able to create a working set of high-performance textures, which are said to be resident. You may also prioritize texture objects to increase or decrease the likelihood that a texture object is resident.

- "Texture Functions" discusses the methods used for painting a texture onto a surface. You can choose to have the texture color values replace those that would be used if texturing were not in effect, or you can have the final color be a combination of the two.

- "Assigning Texture Coordinates" describes how to compute and assign appropriate texture coordinates to the vertices of an object. It also explains how to control the behavior of coordinates that lie outside the default range—that is, how to repeat or clamp textures across a surface.

- "Automatic Texture-Coordinate Generation" shows how to have OpenGL automatically generate texture coordinates so that you can achieve such effects as contour and environment maps.

- "Multitexturing" details how textures may be applied in a serial pipeline of successive texturing operations.

- "Texture Combiner Functions" explains how you can control mathematical operations (multiplication, addition, subtraction, interpolation, and even dot products) on the RGB and alpha values of textures, constant colors, and incoming fragments. Combiner functions expose flexible, programmable fragment processing.

- "Applying Secondary Color after Texturing" shows how secondary colors are applied to fragments after texturing.

- "Point Sprites" discusses how textures can be applied to large points to improve their visual quality.

- "The Texture Matrix Stack" explains how to manipulate the texture matrix stack and use the $q$ texture coordinate.

- "Depth Textures" describes the process for using the values stored in the depth buffer as a texture for use in determining shadowing for a scene.

Version 1.1 of OpenGL introduced several texture-mapping operations:

- Additional internal texture image formats

- Texture proxy, to query whether there are enough resources to accommodate a given texture image

- Texture subimage, to replace all or part of an existing texture image, rather than completely delete and create a texture to achieve the same effect

- Specifying texture data from framebuffer memory (as well as from system memory)

- Texture objects, including resident textures and prioritizing

Version 1.2 added:

- 3D texture images

- A new texture-coordinate wrapping mode, GL_CLAMP_TO_EDGE, which derives texels from the edge of a texture image, not its border

- Greater control over mipmapped textures to represent different levels of detail (LOD)

- Calculating specular highlights (from lighting) after texturing operations

Version 1.3 granted more texture-mapping operations:

- Compressed textures

- Cube map textures

- Multitexturing, which is applying several textures to render a single primitive

- Texture-wrapping mode, GL_CLAMP_TO_BORDER

- Texture environment modes: GL_ADD and GL_COMBINE (including the dot product combination function)

Version 1.4 supplied these texture capabilities:

- Texture-wrapping mode, GL_MIRRORED_REPEAT

- Automatic mipmap generation with GL_GENERATE_MIPMAP

- Texture parameter GL_TEXTURE_LOD_BIAS, which alters selection of the mipmap level of detail

- Application of a secondary color (specified by **glSecondaryColor\*()**) after texturing

- During the texture combine environment mode, the ability to use texture color from different texture units as sources for the texture combine function

- Use of depth (*r* coordinate) as an internal texture format and texturing modes that compare depth texels to decide upon texture application

Version 1.5 added support for:

- Additional texture-comparison modes for use of textures for shadow mapping

Version 2.0 modified texture capabilities by:

- Removing the power-of-two restriction on texture maps

- Iterated texture coordinates across point sprites

Version 2.1 added support for:

- Specifying textures in sRGB format, which accepts gamma-corrected red, green, and blue texture components

- Specifying and retrieving pixel rectangle data in server-side buffer objects. See "Using Buffer Objects with Pixel Rectangle Data" in Chapter 8 for details on using pixel buffer objects.

If you try to use one of these texture-mapping operations and can't find it, check the version number of your implementation of OpenGL to see if it actually supports it. (See "Which Version Am I Using?" in Chapter 14.) In some implementations, a particular feature may be available only as an extension.

For example, in OpenGL Version 1.2, multitexturing was approved by the OpenGL Architecture Review Board (ARB), the governing body for OpenGL, as an optional extension. An implementation of OpenGL 1.2 supporting multitexturing would have function and constant names suffixed with **ARB**, such as **glActiveTextureARB(GL_TEXTURE1_ARB)**. In OpenGL 1.3, multitexturing became mandatory, and the ARB suffix was removed.

# An Overview and an Example

This section gives an overview of the steps necessary to perform texture mapping. It also presents a relatively simple texture-mapping program. Of course, you know that texture mapping can be a very involved process.

## Steps in Texture Mapping

To use texture mapping, you perform the following steps:

1. Create a texture object and specify a texture for that object.
2. Indicate how the texture is to be applied to each pixel.
3. Enable texture mapping.
4. Draw the scene, supplying both texture and geometric coordinates.

Keep in mind that texture mapping works only in RGBA mode. Texture mapping results in color-index mode are undefined.

### Create a Texture Object and Specify a Texture for That Object

A texture is usually thought of as being two-dimensional, like most images, but it can also be one-dimensional or three-dimensional. The data describing a texture may consist of one, two, three, or four elements per texel and may represent an (R, G, B, A) quadruple, a modulation constant, or a depth component.

In Example 9-1, which is very simple, a single texture object is created to maintain a single uncompressed, two-dimensional texture. This example does not find out how much memory is available. Since only one texture is created, there is no attempt to prioritize or otherwise manage a working set of texture objects. Other advanced techniques, such as texture borders, mipmaps, or cube maps, are not used in this simple example.

### Indicate How the Texture Is to Be Applied to Each Pixel

You can choose any of four possible functions for computing the final RGBA value from the fragment color and the texture image data. One possibility is simply to use the texture color as the final color; this is the *replace* mode, in which the texture is painted on top of the fragment, just as a decal would be applied. (Example 9-1 uses *replace* mode.) Another method is to use the texture to *modulate*, or scale, the fragment's color; this technique is useful for combining the effects of lighting with texturing. Finally, a constant color can be blended with that of the fragment, based on the texture value.

### Enable Texture Mapping

You need to enable texturing before drawing your scene. Texturing is enabled or disabled using **glEnable()** or **glDisable()**, with the symbolic constant GL_TEXTURE_1D, GL_TEXTURE_2D, GL_TEXTURE_3D, or GL_TEXTURE_CUBE_MAP for one-, two-, three-dimensional, or cube map texturing, respectively. (If two or all three of the dimensional texturing modes are enabled, the largest dimension enabled is used. If cube map textures are enabled, it trumps all the others. For the sake of clean programs, you should enable only the one you want to use.)

### Draw the Scene, Supplying Both Texture and Geometric Coordinates

You need to indicate how the texture should be aligned relative to the fragments to which it's to be applied before it's "glued on." That is, you need to specify both texture coordinates and geometric coordinates as you specify the objects in your scene. For a two-dimensional texture map, for example, the texture coordinates range from 0.0 to 1.0 in both directions, but the coordinates of the items being textured can be anything. To apply the brick texture to a wall, for example, assuming the wall is square and meant to represent one copy of the texture, the code would probably assign texture coordinates (0, 0), (1, 0), (1, 1), and (0, 1) to the four corners of the wall. If the wall is large, you might want to paint several copies of the texture map on it. If you do so, the texture map must be designed so that the bricks at the left edge match up nicely with the bricks at the right edge, and similarly for the bricks at the top and bottom.

You must also indicate how texture coordinates outside the range [0.0, 1.0] should be treated. Do the textures repeat to cover the object, or are they clamped to a boundary value?

## A Sample Program

One of the problems with showing sample programs to illustrate texture mapping is that interesting textures are large. Typically, textures are read from an image file, since specifying a texture programmatically could take hundreds of lines of code. In Example 9-1, the texture—which consists of alternating white and black squares, like a checkerboard—is generated by the program. The program applies this texture to two squares, which are then rendered in perspective, one of them facing the viewer squarely and the other tilting back at 45 degrees, as shown in Figure 9-2. In object coordinates, both squares are the same size.

**Figure 9-2**     Texture-Mapped Squares

**Example 9-1**     Texture-Mapped Checkerboard: checker.c

```
/*  Create checkerboard texture  */
#define checkImageWidth 64
#define checkImageHeight 64
static GLubyte checkImage[checkImageHeight][checkImageWidth][4];

static GLuint texName;

void makeCheckImage(void)
{
    int i, j, c;

    for (i = 0; i < checkImageHeight; i++) {
```

```
        for (j = 0; j < checkImageWidth; j++) {
            c = (((((i&0x8)==0)^((j&0x8))==0))*255;
            checkImage[i][j][0] = (GLubyte) c;
            checkImage[i][j][1] = (GLubyte) c;
            checkImage[i][j][2] = (GLubyte) c;
            checkImage[i][j][3] = (GLubyte) 255;
        }
    }
}

void init(void)
{
    glClearColor(0.0, 0.0, 0.0, 0.0);
    glShadeModel(GL_FLAT);
    glEnable(GL_DEPTH_TEST);
    makeCheckImage();
    glPixelStorei(GL_UNPACK_ALIGNMENT, 1);

    glGenTextures(1, &texName);
    glBindTexture(GL_TEXTURE_2D, texName);

    glTexParameteri(GL_TEXTURE_2D, GL_TEXTURE_WRAP_S, GL_REPEAT);
    glTexParameteri(GL_TEXTURE_2D, GL_TEXTURE_WRAP_T, GL_REPEAT);
    glTexParameteri(GL_TEXTURE_2D, GL_TEXTURE_MAG_FILTER,
                    GL_NEAREST);
    glTexParameteri(GL_TEXTURE_2D, GL_TEXTURE_MIN_FILTER,
                    GL_NEAREST);
    glTexImage2D(GL_TEXTURE_2D, 0, GL_RGBA, checkImageWidth,
                 checkImageHeight, 0, GL_RGBA, GL_UNSIGNED_BYTE,
                 checkImage);
}

void display(void)
{
    glClear(GL_COLOR_BUFFER_BIT | GL_DEPTH_BUFFER_BIT);
    glEnable(GL_TEXTURE_2D);
    glTexEnvf(GL_TEXTURE_ENV, GL_TEXTURE_ENV_MODE, GL_REPLACE);
    glBindTexture(GL_TEXTURE_2D, texName);
    glBegin(GL_QUADS);
    glTexCoord2f(0.0, 0.0); glVertex3f(-2.0, -1.0, 0.0);
    glTexCoord2f(0.0, 1.0); glVertex3f(-2.0, 1.0, 0.0);
    glTexCoord2f(1.0, 1.0); glVertex3f(0.0, 1.0, 0.0);
    glTexCoord2f(1.0, 0.0); glVertex3f(0.0, -1.0, 0.0);
```

```
    glTexCoord2f(0.0, 0.0); glVertex3f(1.0, -1.0, 0.0);
    glTexCoord2f(0.0, 1.0); glVertex3f(1.0, 1.0, 0.0);
    glTexCoord2f(1.0, 1.0); glVertex3f(2.41421, 1.0, -1.41421);
    glTexCoord2f(1.0, 0.0); glVertex3f(2.41421, -1.0, -1.41421);
    glEnd();
    glFlush();
    glDisable(GL_TEXTURE_2D);
}

void reshape(int w, int h)
{
    glViewport(0, 0, (GLsizei) w, (GLsizei) h);
    glMatrixMode(GL_PROJECTION);
    glLoadIdentity();
    gluPerspective(60.0, (GLfloat) w/(GLfloat) h, 1.0, 30.0);
    glMatrixMode(GL_MODELVIEW);
    glLoadIdentity();
    glTranslatef(0.0, 0.0, -3.6);
}
/*  keyboard() and main() deleted to reduce printing  */
```

The checkerboard texture is generated in the routine **makeCheckImage()**, and all the texture-mapping initialization occurs in the routine **init()**. **glGenTextures()** and **glBindTexture()** name and create a texture object for a texture image. (See "Texture Objects" on page 414.) The single, full-resolution texture map is specified by **glTexImage2D()**, whose parameters indicate the size, type, location, and other properties of the texture image. (See "Specifying the Texture" below for more information about **glTexImage2D()**.)

The four calls to **glTexParameter*()** specify how the texture is to be wrapped and how the colors are to be filtered if there isn't an exact match between texels in the texture and pixels on the screen. (See "Filtering" on page 411 and "Repeating and Clamping Textures" on page 428.)

In **display()**, **glEnable()** turns on texturing. **glTexEnv*()** sets the drawing mode to GL_REPLACE so that the textured polygons are drawn using the colors from the texture map (rather than taking into account the color in which the polygons would have been drawn without the texture).

Then, two polygons are drawn. Note that texture coordinates are specified along with vertex coordinates. The **glTexCoord*()** command behaves similarly to the **glNormal()** command. **glTexCoord*()** sets the current texture coordinates; any subsequent vertex command has those texture coordinates associated with it until **glTexCoord*()** is called again.

**Note:** The checkerboard image on the tilted polygon might look wrong when you compile and run it on your machine—for example, it might look like two triangles with different projections of the checkerboard image on them. If so, try setting the parameter GL_PERSPECTIVE_CORRECTION_HINT to GL_NICEST and running the example again. To do this, use **glHint**().

## Specifying the Texture

The command **glTexImage2D**() defines a two-dimensional texture. It takes several arguments, which are described briefly here and in more detail in the subsections that follow. The related commands for one- and three-dimensional textures, **glTexImage1D**() and **glTexImage3D**(), are described in "One-Dimensional Textures" and "Three-Dimensional Textures," respectively.

void **glTexImage2D**(GLenum *target*, GLint *level*, GLint *internalFormat*,
          GLsizei *width*, GLsizei *height*, GLint *border*,
          GLenum *format*, GLenum *type*, const GLvoid **texels*);

Defines a two-dimensional texture. The *target* parameter is set to one of the constants: GL_TEXTURE_2D, GL_PROXY_TEXTURE_2D, GL_TEXTURE_CUBE_MAP_POSITIVE_X, GL_TEXTURE_CUBE_MAP_NEGATIVE_X, GL_TEXTURE_CUBE_MAP_POSITIVE_Y, GL_TEXTURE_CUBE_MAP_NEGATIVE_Y, GL_TEXTURE_CUBE_MAP_POSITIVE_Z, GL_TEXTURE_CUBE_MAP_NEGATIVE_Z, or GL_PROXY_TEXTURE_CUBE_MAP. (See "Cube Map Textures" for information about use of the GL_*CUBE_MAP* constants with **glTexImage2D** and related functions.) You use the *level* parameter if you're supplying multiple resolutions of the texture map; with only one resolution, *level* should be 0. (See "Mipmaps: Multiple Levels of Detail" for more information about using multiple resolutions.)

The next parameter, *internalFormat*, indicates which components (RGBA, depth, luminance, or intensity) are selected for the texels of an image. The value of *internalFormat* is an integer from 1 to 4, or one of the following symbolic constants: GL_ALPHA, GL_ALPHA4, GL_ALPHA8, GL_ALPHA12, GL_ALPHA16, GL_COMPRESSED_ALPHA, GL_COMPRESSED_LUMINANCE, GL_COMPRESSED_LUMINANCE_ALPHA, GL_COMPRESSED_INTENSITY, GL_COMPRESSED_RGB,

GL_COMPRESSED_RGBA, GL_DEPTH_COMPONENT, GL_DEPTH_COMPONENT16, GL_DEPTH_COMPONENT24, GL_DEPTH_COMPONENT32, GL_INTENSITY, GL_INTENSITY4, GL_INTENSITY8, GL_INTENSITY12, GL_INTENSITY16, GL_LUMINANCE, GL_LUMINANCE4, GL_LUMINANCE8, GL_LUMINANCE12, GL_LUMINANCE16, GL_LUMINANCE_ALPHA, GL_LUMINANCE4_ALPHA4, GL_LUMINANCE6_ALPHA2, GL_LUMINANCE8_ALPHA8, GL_LUMINANCE12_ALPHA4, GL_LUMINANCE12_ALPHA12, GL_LUMINANCE16_ALPHA16, GL_RGB, GL_R3_G3_B2, GL_RGB4, GL_RGB5, GL_RGB8, GL_RGB10, GL_RGB12, GL_RGB16, GL_RGBA, GL_RGBA2, GL_RGBA4, GL_RGB5_A1, GL_RGBA8, GL_RGB10_A2, GL_RGBA12, GL_RGBA16, GL_SRGB, GL_SRGB8, GL_SRGB_ALPHA, GL_SRGB8_ALPHA8, GL_SLUMINANCE_ALPHA, GL_SLUMINANCE8_ALPHA8, GL_SLUMINANCE, GL_SLUMINANCE8, GL_COMPRESSED_SRGB, GL_COMPRESSED_SRGB_ALPHA, GL_COMPRESSED_SLUMINANCE, or GL_COMPRESSED_SLUMINANCE_ALPHA. (See "Texture Functions" for a discussion of how these selected components are applied, and see "Compressed Texture Images" for a discussion of how compressed textures are handled.)

The *internalFormat* may request a specific resolution of components. For example, if *internalFormat* is GL_R3_G3_B2, you are asking that texels be 3 bits of red, 3 bits of green, and 2 bits of blue. But OpenGL is not guaranteed to deliver this; OpenGL is only obligated to choose an internal representation that closely approximates what is requested, but not necessarily an exact match. By definition, GL_INTENSITY, GL_LUMINANCE, GL_LUMINANCE_ALPHA, GL_DEPTH_COMPONENT, GL_RGB, GL_RGBA, GL_SRGB, GL_SRGB_ALPHA, GL_SLUMINANCE, GL_SLUMINANCE_ALPHA, and the compressed forms of the above tokens are lenient, because they do not ask for a specific resolution. (For compatibility with the OpenGL release 1.0, the numeric values 1, 2, 3, and 4 for *internalFormat* are equivalent to the symbolic constants GL_LUMINANCE, GL_LUMINANCE_ALPHA, GL_RGB, and GL_RGBA, respectively.)

The *width* and *height* parameters give the dimensions of the texture image; *border* indicates the width of the border, which is either 0 (no border) or 1. For OpenGL implementations that do not support Version 2.0, both *width* and *height* must have the form $2^m + 2b$, where *m* is a non-negative integer (which can have a different value for *width* than for *height*) and *b* is the value of *border*. The maximum size of a texture map depends on the implementation of OpenGL, but it must be at least 64 × 64 (or 66 × 66 with borders). For OpenGL implementations supporting Version 2.0 and greater, textures may be of any size. The *format* and *type* parameters describe the format and data type of the texture image data. They have the same meaning as they do for **glDrawPixels()**. (See "Imaging Pipeline" in Chapter 8.) In fact, texture data is in the same format as the data used by **glDrawPixels()**, so the settings of **glPixelStore*()** and **glPixelTransfer*()** are applied. (In Example 9-1, the call

```
glPixelStorei(GL_UNPACK_ALIGNMENT, 1);
```

is made because the data in the example isn't padded at the end of each texel row.) The *format* parameter can be GL_COLOR_INDEX, GL_DEPTH_COMPONENT, GL_RGB, GL_RGBA, GL_RED, GL_GREEN, GL_BLUE, GL_ALPHA, GL_LUMINANCE, or GL_LUMINANCE_ALPHA—that is, the same formats available for **glDrawPixels()** with the exception of GL_STENCIL_INDEX.

Similarly, the *type* parameter can be GL_BYTE, GL_UNSIGNED_BYTE, GL_SHORT, GL_UNSIGNED_SHORT, GL_INT, GL_UNSIGNED_INT, GL_FLOAT, GL_BITMAP, or one of the packed pixel data types.

Finally, *texels* contains the texture image data. This data describes the texture image itself as well as its border.

The internal format of a texture image may affect the performance of texture operations. For example, some implementations perform texturing faster with GL_RGBA than with GL_RGB, because the color components align to processor memory better. Since this varies, you should check specific information about your implementation of OpenGL.

The internal format of a texture image also may control how much memory a texture image consumes. For example, a texture of internal format GL_RGBA8 uses 32 bits per texel, while a texture of internal format GL_R3_G3_B2 uses only 8 bits per texel. Of course, there is a corresponding trade-off between memory consumption and color resolution.

A GL_DEPTH_COMPONENT texture stores depth values, as compared to colors, and is most often used for rendering shadows as described in "Depth Textures" on page 459.

Textures specified with an internal format of GL_SRGB, GL_SRGB8, GL_SRGB_ALPHA, GL_SRGB8_ALPHA8, GL_SLUMINANCE_ALPHA,

GL_SLUMINANCE8_ALPHA8, GL_SLUMINANCE, GL_SLUMINANCE8, GL_COMPRESSED_SRGB, GL_COMPRESSED_SRGB_ALPHA, GL_COMPRESSED_SLUMINANCE, or GL_COMPRESSED_SLUMINANCE_ALPHA) are expected to have their red, green, and blue color components specified in the sRGB color space (officially known as the International Electrotechnical Commission IEC standard 61966-2-1). The sRGB color space is approximately the same as the 2.2 gamma-corrected linear RGB color space. For sRGB textures, the alpha values in the texture should not be gamma corrected.

Although texture mapping results in color-index mode are undefined, you can still specify a texture with a GL_COLOR_INDEX image. In that case, pixel-transfer operations are applied to convert the indices to RGBA values by table lookup before they're used to form the texture image.

If your OpenGL implementation supports the *Imaging Subset* and any of its features are enabled, the texture image will be affected by those features. For example, if the two-dimensional convolution filter is enabled, then the convolution will be performed on the texture image. (The convolution may change the image's width and/or height.)

The number of texels for both the width and height of a texture image, not including the optional border, must be a power of 2. If your original image does not have dimensions that fit that limitation, you can use the OpenGL Utility Library routine **gluScaleImage()** to alter the sizes of your textures.

---

int **gluScaleImage**(GLenum *format*, GLint *widthin*, GLint *heightin*, GLenum *typein*, const void *\*datain*, GLint *widthout*, GLint *heightout*, GLenum *typeout*, void *\*dataout*);

---

Scales an image using the appropriate pixel-storage modes to unpack the data from *datain*. The *format*, *typein*, and *typeout* parameters can refer to any of the formats or data types supported by **glDrawPixels()**. The image is scaled using linear interpolation and box filtering (from the size indicated by *widthin* and *heightin* to *widthout* and *heightout*), and the resulting image is written to *dataout*, using the pixel GL_PACK* storage modes. The caller of **gluScaleImage()** must allocate sufficient space for the output buffer. A value of 0 is returned on success, and a GLU error code is returned on failure.

**Note:** In GLU 1.3, **gluScaleImage()** supports packed pixel formats (and their related data types).

The framebuffer itself can also be used as a source for texture data. **glCopyTexImage2D()** reads a rectangle of pixels from the framebuffer and uses that rectangle as texels for a new texture.

---

void **glCopyTexImage2D**(GLenum *target*, GLint *level*,
GLint *internalFormat*,
GLint *x*, GLint *y*, GLsizei *width*, GLsizei *height*,
GLint *border*);

---

Creates a two-dimensional texture, using framebuffer data to define the texels. The pixels are read from the current GL_READ_BUFFER and are processed exactly as if **glCopyPixels()** had been called, but instead of going to the framebuffer, the pixels are placed into texture memory. The settings of **glPixelTransfer*()** and other pixel-transfer operations are applied.

The *target* parameter must be one of the constants GL_TEXTURE_2D, GL_TEXTURE_CUBE_MAP_POSITIVE_X, GL_TEXTURE_CUBE_MAP_NEGATIVE_X, GL_TEXTURE_CUBE_MAP_POSITIVE_Y, GL_TEXTURE_CUBE_MAP_NEGATIVE_Y, GL_TEXTURE_CUBE_MAP_POSITIVE_Z, or GL_TEXTURE_CUBE_MAP_NEGATIVE_Z. (See "Cube Map Textures" on page 441 for information about use of the *CUBE_MAP* constants.) The *level*, *internalFormat*, and *border* parameters have the same effects that they have for **glTexImage2D()**. The texture array is taken from a screen-aligned pixel rectangle with the lower left corner at coordinates specified by the ($x$, $y$) parameters. The *width* and *height* parameters specify the size of this pixel rectangle. For OpenGL implementations that do not support Version 2.0, both *width* and *height* must have the form $2^m+2b$, where $m$ is a non-negative integer (which can have a different value for *width* than for *height*) and $b$ is the value of *border*. For implementations supporting OpenGL Version 2.0 and greater, textures may be of any size.

The next sections give more detail about texturing, including the use of the *target*, *border*, and *level* parameters. The *target* parameter can be used to query accurately the size of a texture (by creating a texture proxy with **glTexImage*D()**) and whether a texture possibly can be used within the texture resources of an OpenGL implementation. Redefining a portion of a texture is described in "Replacing All or Part of a Texture Image" on page 387. One- and three-dimensional textures are discussed in "One-Dimensional Textures" on page 390 and "Three-Dimensional Textures" on page 392, respectively. The texture border, which has its size controlled by the *border* parameter, is detailed in "Compressed Texture Images" on page 397. The *level* parameter is used to specify textures of different resolutions and is incorporated into the special technique of *mipmapping*, which is explained in "Mipmaps: Multiple Levels of Detail" on page 400. Mipmapping requires understanding how to filter textures as they're applied; filtering is covered on page 411.

## Texture Proxy

To an OpenGL programmer who uses textures, size is important. Texture resources are typically limited, and texture format restrictions vary among OpenGL implementations. There is a special texture proxy target to evaluate whether your OpenGL implementation is capable of supporting a particular texture format at a particular texture size.

**glGetIntegerv**(GL_MAX_TEXTURE_SIZE,...) tells you a lower bound on the largest width or height (without borders) of a texture image; typically, the size of the largest square texture supported. For 3D textures, GL_MAX_3D_TEXTURE_SIZE may be used to query the largest allowable dimension (width, height, or depth, without borders) of a 3D texture image. For cube map textures, GL_MAX_CUBE_MAP_TEXTURE_SIZE is similarly used.

However, use of any of the GL_MAX*TEXTURE_SIZE queries does not consider the effect of the internal format or other factors. A texture image that stores texels using the GL_RGBA16 internal format may be using 64 bits per texel, so its image may have to be 16 times smaller than an image with the GL_LUMINANCE4 internal format. Textures requiring borders or mipmaps further reduce the amount of available memory.

A special placeholder, or *proxy*, for a texture image allows the program to query more accurately whether OpenGL can accommodate a texture of a desired internal format.

For instance, to find out whether there are enough resources available for a standard 2D texture, call **glTexImage2D()** with a *target* parameter of GL_PROXY_TEXTURE_2D and the given *level, internalFormat, width, height, border, format,* and *type*. For a proxy, you should pass NULL as the pointer for the *texels* array. (For a cube map, use **glTexImage2D()** with the target GL_PROXY_TEXTURE_CUBE_MAP. For one- or three-dimensional textures, use corresponding 1D or 3D routines and symbolic constants.)

After the texture proxy has been created, query the texture state variables with **glGetTexLevelParameter*()**. If there aren't enough resources to accommodate the texture proxy, the texture state variables for width, height, border width, and component resolutions are set to 0.

---

void **glGetTexLevelParameter**{if}**v**(GLenum *target*, GLint *level*,
GLenum *pname*, TYPE *\*params*);

---

Returns in *params* texture parameter values for a specific level of detail, specified as *level*. *target* defines the target texture and is GL_TEXTURE_1D, GL_TEXTURE_2D, GL_TEXTURE_3D, GL_TEXTURE_CUBE_MAP_ POSITIVE_X, GL_TEXTURE_CUBE_MAP_NEGATIVE_X, GL_TEXTURE_ CUBE_MAP_POSITIVE_Y, GL_TEXTURE_CUBE_MAP_NEGATIVE_Y, GL_TEXTURE_CUBE_MAP_POSITIVE_Z, GL_TEXTURE_CUBE_MAP_ NEGATIVE_Z, GL_PROXY_TEXTURE_1D, GL_PROXY_TEXTURE_2D, GL_PROXY_TEXTURE_3D, or GL_PROXY_TEXTURE_CUBE_MAP. (GL_ TEXTURE_CUBE_MAP is not valid, because it does not specify a particular face of a cube map.) Accepted values for *pname* are GL_TEXTURE_WIDTH, GL_TEXTURE_HEIGHT, GL_TEXTURE_DEPTH, GL_TEXTURE_BORDER, GL_TEXTURE_INTERNAL_FORMAT, GL_TEXTURE_RED_SIZE, GL_ TEXTURE_GREEN_SIZE, GL_TEXTURE_BLUE_SIZE, GL_TEXTURE_ ALPHA_SIZE, GL_TEXTURE_LUMINANCE_SIZE, and GL_TEXTURE_ INTENSITY_SIZE.

Example 9-2 demonstrates how to use the texture proxy to find out if there are enough resources to create a 64 × 64 texel texture with RGBA components with 8 bits of resolution. If this succeeds, then **glGetTexLevelParameteriv()** stores the internal format (in this case, GL_RGBA8) into the variable *format*.

**Example 9-2**    Querying Texture Resources with a Texture Proxy

```
GLint width;

glTexImage2D(GL_PROXY_TEXTURE_2D, 0, GL_RGBA8,
             64, 64, 0, GL_RGBA, GL_UNSIGNED_BYTE, NULL);
glGetTexLevelParameteriv(GL_PROXY_TEXTURE_2D, 0,
                         GL_TEXTURE_WIDTH, &width);
```

**Note:** There is one major limitation with texture proxies: the texture proxy answers the question of whether a texture is capable of being loaded into texture memory. The texture proxy provides the same answer, regardless of how texture resources are currently being used. If other textures are using resources, then the texture proxy query may respond affirmatively, but there may not be enough resources to make your texture resident (that is, part of a possibly high-performance working set of textures). The texture proxy does not answer the question of whether there is sufficient capacity to handle the requested texture. (See "Texture Objects" for more information about managing resident textures.)

## Replacing All or Part of a Texture Image

Creating a texture may be more computationally expensive than modifying an existing one. Often it is better to replace all or part of a texture image with new information, rather than create a new one. This can be helpful for certain applications, such as using real-time, captured video images as texture images. For that application, it makes sense to create a single texture and use **glTexSubImage2D()** to replace repeatedly the texture data with new video images. Also, there are no size restrictions for **glTexSubImage2D()** that force the height or width to be a power of 2. (This is helpful for processing video images, which generally do not have sizes that are powers of 2. However, you must load the video images into an initial, larger image that must have $2^n$ texels for each dimension, and adjust texture coordinates for the subimages.)

---

void **glTexSubImage2D**(GLenum *target*, GLint *level*, GLint *xoffset*,
GLint *yoffset*, GLsizei *width*, GLsizei *height*,
GLenum *format*, GLenum *type*,
const GLvoid *\*texels*);

Defines a two-dimensional texture image that replaces all or part of a contiguous subregion (in 2D, it's simply a rectangle) of the current, existing two-dimensional texture image. The *target* parameter must be set to one of the same options that are available for **glCopyTexImage2D**.

The *level*, *format*, and *type* parameters are similar to the ones used for **glTexImage2D()**. *level* is the mipmap level-of-detail number. It is not an error to specify a width or height of 0, but the subimage will have no effect. *format* and *type* describe the format and data type of the texture image data. The subimage is also affected by modes set by **glPixelStore\*()** and **glPixelTransfer\*()** and other pixel-transfer operations.

*texels* contains the texture data for the subimage. *width* and *height* are the dimensions of the subregion that is replacing all or part of the current texture image. *xoffset* and *yoffset* specify the texel offset in the *x*- and *y*-directions—with (0, 0) at the lower left corner of the texture—and specify where in the existing texture array the subimage should be placed. This region may not include any texels outside the range of the originally defined texture array.

---

In Example 9-3, some of the code from Example 9-1 has been modified so that pressing the 's' key drops a smaller checkered subimage into the existing image. (The resulting texture is shown in Figure 9-3.) Pressing the 'r' key restores the original image. Example 9-3 shows the two routines,

**makeCheckImages()** and **keyboard()**, that have been substantially changed. (See "Texture Objects" for more information about **glBindTexture()**.)

**Figure 9-3**    Texture with Subimage Added

**Example 9-3**    Replacing a Texture Subimage: texsub.c

```
/*  Create checkerboard textures  */
#define checkImageWidth 64
#define checkImageHeight 64
#define subImageWidth 16
#define subImageHeight 16
static GLubyte checkImage[checkImageHeight][checkImageWidth][4];
static GLubyte subImage[subImageHeight][subImageWidth][4];

void makeCheckImages(void)
{
   int i, j, c;

   for (i = 0; i < checkImageHeight; i++) {
      for (j = 0; j < checkImageWidth; j++) {
         c = (((i&0x8)==0) ^ ((j&0x8)==0))*255;
         checkImage[i][j][0] = (GLubyte) c;
         checkImage[i][j][1] = (GLubyte) c;
         checkImage[i][j][2] = (GLubyte) c;
         checkImage[i][j][3] = (GLubyte) 255;
      }
   }
   for (i = 0; i < subImageHeight; i++) {
      for (j = 0; j < subImageWidth; j++) {
         c = (((i&0x4)==0) ^ ((j&0x4)==0))*255;
         subImage[i][j][0] = (GLubyte) c;
         subImage[i][j][1] = (GLubyte) 0;
         subImage[i][j][2] = (GLubyte) 0;
         subImage[i][j][3] = (GLubyte) 255;
      }
   }
```

```
    }

void keyboard(unsigned char key, int x, int y)
{
    switch (key) {
        case 's':
        case 'S':
            glBindTexture(GL_TEXTURE_2D, texName);
            glTexSubImage2D(GL_TEXTURE_2D, 0, 12, 44,
                            subImageWidth, subImageHeight, GL_RGBA,
                            GL_UNSIGNED_BYTE, subImage);
            glutPostRedisplay();
            break;
        case 'r':
        case 'R':
            glBindTexture(GL_TEXTURE_2D, texName);
            glTexImage2D(GL_TEXTURE_2D, 0, GL_RGBA,
                         checkImageWidth, checkImageHeight, 0,
                         GL_RGBA, GL_UNSIGNED_BYTE, checkImage);
            glutPostRedisplay();
            break;
        case 27:
            exit(0);
            break;
        default:
            break;
    }
}
```

Once again, the framebuffer itself can be used as a source for texture data—this time, a texture subimage. **glCopyTexSubImage2D()** reads a rectangle of pixels from the framebuffer and replaces a portion of an existing texture array. (**glCopyTexSubImage2D()** is something of a cross between **glCopyTexImage2D()** and **glTexSubImage2D()**.)

---

void **glCopyTexSubImage2D**(GLenum *target*, GLint *level*, GLint *xoffset*,
               GLint *yoffset*, GLint *x*, GLint *y*,
               GLsizei *width*, GLsizei *height*);

---

Uses image data from the framebuffer to replace all or part of a contiguous subregion of the current, existing two-dimensional texture image. The pixels are read from the current GL_READ_BUFFER and are processed exactly as if **glCopyPixels()** had been called, but instead of going to the framebuffer, the pixels are placed into texture memory. The settings of **glPixelTransfer*()** and other pixel-transfer operations are applied.

The *target* parameter must be set to one of the same options that are available for **glCopyTexImage2D**. *level* is the mipmap level-of-detail number. *xoffset* and *yoffset* specify the texel offset in the *x*- and *y*-directions—with (0, 0) at the lower left corner of the texture—and specify where in the existing texture array the subimage should be placed. The subimage texture array is taken from a screen-aligned pixel rectangle with the lower left corner at coordinates specified by the (*x*, *y*) parameters. The *width* and *height* parameters specify the size of this subimage rectangle.

## One-Dimensional Textures

Sometimes a one-dimensional texture is sufficient—for example, if you're drawing textured bands where all the variation is in one direction. A one-dimensional texture behaves as a two-dimensional one with *height* = 1, and without borders along the top and bottom. All the two-dimensional texture and subtexture definition routines have corresponding one-dimensional routines. To create a simple one-dimensional texture, use **glTexImage1D()**.

---

void **glTexImage1D**(GLenum *target*, GLint *level*, GLint *internalFormat*,
            GLsizei *width*, GLint *border*, GLenum *format*,
            GLenum *type*, const GLvoid *\*texels*);

---

Defines a one-dimensional texture. All the parameters have the same meanings as for **glTexImage2D()**, except that *texels* is now a one-dimensional array. As before, for OpenGL implementations that do not support OpenGL Version 2.0 or greater, the value of *width* is $2^m$ (or $2^m + 2$, if there's a border), where *m* is a non-negative integer. You can supply mipmaps and proxies (set *target* to GL_PROXY_TEXTURE_1D), and the same filtering options are available as well.

For a sample program that uses a one-dimensional texture map, see Example 9-8.

If your OpenGL implementation supports the *Imaging Subset* and if the one-dimensional convolution filter is enabled (GL_CONVOLUTION_1D), then the convolution is performed on the texture image. (The convolution may change the width of the texture image.) Other pixel operations may also be applied.

To replace all or some of the texels of a one-dimensional texture, use **glTexSubImage1D()**.

void **glTexSubImage1D**(GLenum *target*, GLint *level*, GLint *xoffset*,
                 GLsizei *width*, GLenum *format*,
                 GLenum *type*, const GLvoid *\*texels*);

Defines a one-dimensional texture array that replaces all or part of a contiguous subregion (in 1D, a row) of the current, existing one-dimensional texture image. The *target* parameter must be set to GL_TEXTURE_1D.

The *level*, *format*, and *type* parameters are similar to the ones used for **glTexImage1D()**. *level* is the mipmap level-of-detail number. *format* and *type* describe the format and data type of the texture image data. The subimage is also affected by modes set by **glPixelStore\*()**, **glPixclTransfer\*()**, or other pixel-transfer operations.

*texels* contains the texture data for the subimage. *width* is the number of texels that replace part or all of the current texture image. *xoffset* specifies the texel offset in the existing texture array where the subimage should be placed.

To use the framebuffer as the source of a new one-dimensional texture or a replacement for an old one-dimensional texture, use either **glCopyTexImage1D()** or **glCopyTexSubImage1D()**.

void **glCopyTexImage1D**(GLenum *target*, GLint *level*,
                  GLint *internalFormat*, GLivnt *x*, GLint *y*,
                  GLsizei *width*, GLint *border*);

Creates a one-dimensional texture using framebuffer data to define the texels. The pixels are read from the current GL_READ_BUFFER and are processed exactly as if **glCopyPixels()** had been called, but instead of going to the framebuffer, the pixels are placed into texture memory. The settings of **glPixelStore\*()** and **glPixelTransfer\*()** are applied.

The *target* parameter must be set to the constant GL_TEXTURE_1D. The *level*, *internalFormat*, and *border* parameters have the same effects that they have for **glCopyTexImage2D()**. The texture array is taken from a row of pixels with the lower left corner at coordinates specified by the $(x, y)$ parameters. The *width* parameter specifies the number of pixels in this row. For OpenGL implementations that do not support Version 2.0, the value of *width* is $2^m$ (or $2^m + 2$ if there's a border), where $m$ is a non-negative integer.

> void **glCopyTexSubImage1D**(GLenum *target*, GLint *level*, GLint *xoffset*,
>                                GLint *x*, GLint *y*, GLsizei *width*);
>
> Uses image data from the framebuffer to replace all or part of a contiguous
> subregion of the current, existing one-dimensional texture image. The
> pixels are read from the current GL_READ_BUFFER and are processed
> exactly as if **glCopyPixels**() had been called, but instead of going to the
> framebuffer, the pixels are placed into texture memory. The settings of
> **glPixelTransfer*()** and other pixel-transfer operations are applied.
>
> The *target* parameter must be set to GL_TEXTURE_1D. *level* is the mipmap
> level-of-detail number. *xoffset* specifies the texel offset and where to put
> the subimage within the existing texture array. The subimage texture
> array is taken from a row of pixels with the lower left corner at coordinates
> specified by the (*x*, *y*) parameters. The *width* parameter specifies the
> number of pixels in this row.

## Three-Dimensional Textures

**Advanced**

Advanced

Three-dimensional textures are most often used for rendering in medical
and geoscience applications. In a medical application, a three-dimensional
texture may represent a series of layered computed tomography (CT) or
magnetic resonance imaging (MRI) images. To an oil and gas researcher,
a three-dimensional texture may model rock strata. (Three-dimensional
texturing is part of an overall category of applications, called *volume
rendering*. Some advanced volume rendering applications deal with *voxels*,
which represent data as volume-based entities.)

Due to their size, three-dimensional textures may consume a lot of texture
resources. Even a relatively coarse three-dimensional texture may use 16 or
32 times the amount of texture memory that a single two-dimensional texture uses. (Most of the two-dimensional texture and subtexture definition
routines have corresponding three-dimensional routines.)

A three-dimensional texture image can be thought of as layers of two-
dimensional subimage rectangles. In memory, the rectangles are arranged in a
sequence. To create a simple three-dimensional texture, use **glTexImage3D**().

**Note:** There are no three-dimensional convolutions in the *Imaging Subset*.
However, 2D convolution filters may be used to affect three-
dimensional texture images.

void **glTexImage3D**(GLenum *target*, GLint *level*, GLint *internalFormat*,
                GLsizei *width*, GLsizei *height*, GLsizei *depth*,
                GLint *border*, GLenum *format*, GLenum *type*,
                const GLvoid *\*texels*);

Defines a three-dimensional texture. All the parameters have the same
meanings as for **glTexImage2D()**, except that *texels* is now a three-
dimensional array, and the parameter *depth* has been added. Likewise, if the
OpenGL implementation does not support Version 2.0, the value of *depth* is
$2^m$ (or $2^m + 2$, if there's a border), where $m$ is a non-negative integer. For
OpenGL 2.0 implementations, the power-of-two dimension requirement has
been eliminated. You can supply mipmaps and proxies (set *target* to GL_
PROXY_TEXTURE_3D), and the same filtering options are available as well.

For a portion of a program that uses a three-dimensional texture map, see
Example 9-4.

**Example 9-4**    Three-Dimensional Texturing: texture3d.c

```
#define iWidth 16
#define iHeight 16
#define iDepth 16

static GLubyte image [iDepth][iHeight][iWidth][3];
static GLuint texName;

/*  Create a 16x16x16x3 array with different color values in
 *  each array element [r, g, b]. Values range from 0 to 255.
 */
void makeImage(void)
{
   int s, t, r;

   for (s = 0 ; s < 16 ; s++)
      for (t = 0 ; t < 16 ; t++)
         for (r = 0 ; r < 16 ; r++) {
            image[r][t][s][0] = s * 17;
            image[r][t][s][1] = t * 17;
            image[r][t][s][2] = r * 17;
         }
}

/*  Initialize state: the 3D texture object and its image
 */
void init(void)
{
```

```
   glClearColor(0.0, 0.0, 0.0, 0.0);
   glShadeModel(GL_FLAT);
   glEnable(GL_DEPTH_TEST);

   makeImage();
   glPixelStorei(GL_UNPACK_ALIGNMENT, 1);

   glGenTextures(1, &texName);
   glBindTexture(GL_TEXTURE_3D, texName);

   glTexParameteri(GL_TEXTURE_3D, GL_TEXTURE_WRAP_S, GL_CLAMP);
   glTexParameteri(GL_TEXTURE_3D, GL_TEXTURE_WRAP_T, GL_CLAMP);
   glTexParameteri(GL_TEXTURE_3D, GL_TEXTURE_WRAP_R, GL_CLAMP);

   glTexParameteri(GL_TEXTURE_3D, GL_TEXTURE_MAG_FILTER,
                   GL_NEAREST);
   glTexParameteri(GL_TEXTURE_3D, GL_TEXTURE_MIN_FILTER,
                   GL_NEAREST);
   glTexImage3D(GL_TEXTURE_3D, 0, GL_RGB, iWidth, iHeight,
                iDepth, 0, GL_RGB, GL_UNSIGNED_BYTE, image);
}
```

To replace all or some of the texels of a three-dimensional texture, use **glTexSubImage3D()**.

---

void **glTexSubImage3D**(GLenum *target*, GLint *level*, GLint *xoffset*,
 GLint *yoffset*, GLint *zoffset*, GLsizei *width*,
 GLsizei *height*, GLsizei *depth*, GLenum *format*,
 GLenum *type*, const GLvoid *\*texels*);

---

Defines a three-dimensional texture array that replaces all or part of a contiguous subregion of the current, existing three-dimensional texture image. The *target* parameter must be set to GL_TEXTURE_3D.

The *level, format,* and *type* parameters are similar to the ones used for **glTexImage3D()**. *level* is the mipmap level-of-detail number. *format* and *type* describe the format and data type of the texture image data. The subimage is also affected by modes set by **glPixelStore*()**, **glPixelTransfer*()**, and other pixel-transfer operations.

*texels* contains the texture data for the subimage. *width, height,* and *depth* specify the size of the subimage in texels. *xoffset, yoffset,* and *zoffset* specify the texel offset indicating where to put the subimage within the existing texture array.

To use the framebuffer as the source of replacement for a portion of an existing three-dimensional texture, use **glCopyTexSubImage3D()**.

---

void **glCopyTexSubImage3D**(GLenum *target*, GLint *level*, GLint *xoffset*,
                                      GLint *yoffset*, GLint *zoffset*, GLint *x*,
                                      GLint *y*, GLsizei *width*, GLsizei *height*);

---

Uses image data from the framebuffer to replace part of a contiguous subregion of the current, existing three-dimensional texture image. The pixels are read from the current GL_READ_BUFFER and are processed exactly as if **glCopyPixels()** had been called, but instead of going to the framebuffer, the pixels are placed into texture memory. The settings of **glPixelTransfer*()** and other pixel-transfer operations are applied.

The *target* parameter must be set to GL_TEXTURE_3D. *level* is the mipmap level-of-detail number. The subimage texture array is taken from a screen-aligned pixel rectangle with the lower left corner at coordinates specified by the (*x, y*) parameters. The *width* and *height* parameters specify the size of this subimage rectangle. *xoffset, yoffset,* and *zoffset* specify the texel offset indicating where to put the subimage within the existing texture array. Since the subimage is a two-dimensional rectangle, only a single slice of the three-dimensional texture (the slice at *zoffset*) is replaced.

**Pixel-Storage Modes for Three-Dimensional Textures**

Pixel-storage values control the row-to-row spacing of each layer (in other words, of one 2D rectangle). **glPixelStore*()** sets pixel-storage modes, with parameters such as *ROW_LENGTH, *ALIGNMENT, *SKIP_PIXELS, and *SKIP_ROWS (where * is either GL_UNPACK_ or GL_PACK_), which control referencing of a subrectangle of an entire rectangle of pixel or texel data. (These modes were previously described in "Controlling Pixel-Storage Modes" on page 325.)

The aforementioned pixel-storage modes remain useful for describing two of the three dimensions, but additional pixel-storage modes are needed to support referencing of subvolumes of three-dimensional texture image data. New parameters, *IMAGE_HEIGHT and *SKIP_IMAGES, allow the routines **glTexImage3D()**, **glTexSubImage3D()**, and **glGetTexImage()** to delimit and access any desired subvolume.

If the three-dimensional texture in memory is larger than the subvolume that is defined, you need to specify the height of a single subimage with the *IMAGE_HEIGHT parameter. Also, if the subvolume does not start with the very first layer, the *SKIP_IMAGES parameter needs to be set.

*IMAGE_HEIGHT is a pixel-storage parameter that defines the height (number of rows) of a single layer of a three-dimensional texture image. If the *IMAGE_HEIGHT value is zero (a negative number is invalid), then the number of rows in each two-dimensional rectangle is the value of *height*, which is the parameter passed to **glTexImage3D()** or **glTexSubImage3D()**. (This is commonplace because *IMAGE_HEIGHT is zero, by default.) Otherwise, the height of a single layer is the *IMAGE_HEIGHT value.

Figure 9-4 shows how *IMAGE_HEIGHT determines the height of an image (when the parameter *height* determines only the height of the subimage.) This figure shows a three-dimensional texture with only two layers.

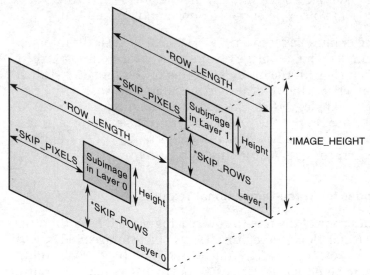

**Figure 9-4**     *IMAGE_HEIGHT Pixel-Storage Mode

*SKIP_IMAGES defines how many layers to bypass before accessing the first data of the subvolume. If the *SKIP_IMAGES value is a positive integer (call the value $n$), then the pointer in the texture image data is advanced that many layers ($n$ * the size of one layer of texels). The resulting subvolume starts at layer $n$ and is several layers deep—how many layers deep is determined by the *depth* parameter passed to **glTexImage3D()** or **glTexSubImage3D()**. If the *SKIP_IMAGES value is zero (the default), then accessing the texel data begins with the very first layer described in the texel array.

Figure 9-5 shows how the *SKIP_IMAGES parameter can bypass several layers to get to where the subvolume is actually located. In this example, *SKIP_IMAGES == 3, and the subvolume begins at layer 3.

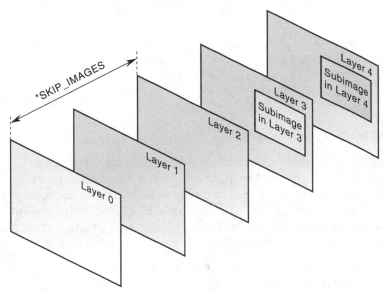

**Figure 9-5**        *SKIP_IMAGES Pixel-Storage Mode

## Compressed Texture Images

Texture maps can be stored internally in a compressed format to possibly reduce the amount of texture memory used. A texture image can either be compressed as it is being loaded or loaded directly in its compressed form.

### Compressing a Texture Image While Loading

To have OpenGL compress a texture image while it's being downloaded, specify one of the GL_COMPRESSED_* enumerants for the *internalformat* parameter. The image will automatically be compressed after the texels have been processed by any active pixel-store (See "Controlling Pixel-Storage Modes") or pixel-transfer modes (See "Pixel-Transfer Operations").

Once the image has been loaded, you can determine if it was compressed, and into which format, using the following:

```
GLboolean compressed;
GLenum    textureFormat;
GLsizei   imageSize;
```

```
glGetTexLevelParameteriv(GL_TEXTURE_2D, GL_TEXTURE_COMPRESSED,
    &compressed);
if (compressed == GL_TRUE) {
    glGetTexLevelParameteriv(GL_TEXTURE_2D,
        GL_TEXTURE_INTERNAL_FORMAT, &textureFormat);
    glGetTexLevelParameteriv(GL_TEXTURE_2D,
        GL_TEXTURE_COMPRESSED_IMAGE_SIZE, &imageSize);
}
```

### Loading a Compressed Texture Images

OpenGL doesn't specify the internal format that should be used for compressed textures; each OpenGL implementation is allowed to specify a set of OpenGL extensions that implement a particular texture compression format. For compressed textures that are to be loaded directly, it's important to know their storage format and to verify that the texture's format is available in your OpenGL implementation.

To load a texture stored in a compressed format, use the **glCompressedTexImage*D()** calls.

---

void **glCompressedTexImage1D**(GLenum *target*, GLint *level*,
                      GLenum *internalformat*, GLsizei *width*,
                      GLint *border*, GLsizei *imageSize*,
                      const GLvoid **texels*);
void **glCompressedTexImage2D**(GLenum *target*, GLint *level*,
                      GLenum *internalformat*, GLsizei *width*,
                      GLsizei *height*, GLint *border*,
                      GLsizei *imageSize*, const GLvoid **texels*);
void **glCompressedTexImage3D**(GLenum *target*, GLint *level*,
                      GLenum *internalformat*, GLsizei *width*,
                      GLsizei *height*, GLsizei *depth*,
                      GLint *border*, GLsizei *imageSize*,
                      const GLvoid **texels*);

---

Defines a one-, two-, or three-dimensional texture from a previously compressed texture image.

Use the *level* parameter if you're supplying multiple resolutions of the texture map; with only one resolution, *level* should be 0. (See "Mipmaps: Multiple Levels of Detail" for more information about using multiple resolutions.)

*internalformat* specifies the format of the compressed texture image. It must be a supported compression format of the implementation loading the texture, otherwise a GL_INVALID_ENUM error is specified. To determine supported compressed texture formats, see Appendix B for details.

*width*, *height*, and *depth* represent the dimensions of the texture image for one-, two-, and three-dimensional texture images, respectively. As with uncompressed textures, *border* indicates the width of the border, which is either 0 (no border) or 1. Each value must have the form $2^m + 2b$, where $m$ is a nonnegative integer and $b$ is the value of *border*. For OpenGL 2.0 implementations, the power-of-two dimension requirement has been eliminated.

Additionally, compressed textures can be used, just like uncompressed texture images, to replace all or part of an already loaded texture. Use the **glCompressedTexSubImage*D()** calls.

---

void **glCompressedTexSubImage1D**(GLenum *target*, GLint *level*, GLint *xoffset*, GLsizei *width*, GLenum *format*, GLsizei *imageSize*, const GLvoid *\*texels*);

void **glCompressedTexSubImage2D**(GLenum *target*, GLint *level*, GLint *xoffset*, GLint *yoffet*, GLsizei *width*, GLsizei *height*, GLsizei *imageSize*, const GLvoid *\*texels*);

void **glCompressedTexSubImage3D**(GLenum *target*, GLint *level*, GLint *xoffset* GLint *yoffset*, GLint *zoffset*, GLsizei *width*, GLsizei *height*, GLsizei *depth*, GLsizei *imageSize*, const GLvoid *\*texels*);

---

Defines a one-, two-, or three-dimensional texture from a previously compressed texture image.

The *xoffset*, *yoffset*, and *zoffset* parameters specify the pixel offsets for the respective texture dimension where to place the new image inside of the texture array.

*width*, *height*, and *depth* specify the size of the one-, two-, or three-dimensional texture image to be used to update the texture image.

*imageSize* specifies the number of bytes stored in the *texels* array.

## Using a Texture's Borders

**Advanced**

If you need to apply a larger texture map than your implementation of OpenGL allows, you can, with a little care, effectively make larger textures by tiling with several different textures. For example, if you need a texture twice as large as the maximum allowed size mapped to a square, draw the square as four subsquares, and load a different texture before drawing each piece.

Since only a single texture map is available at one time, this approach might lead to problems at the edges of the textures, especially if some form of linear filtering is enabled. The texture value to be used for pixels at the edges must be averaged with something beyond the edge, which, ideally, should come from the adjacent texture map. If you define a border for each texture whose texel values are equal to the values of the texels at the edge of the adjacent texture map, then the correct behavior results when linear filtering takes place.

To do this correctly, notice that each map can have eight neighbors—one adjacent to each edge and one touching each corner. The values of the texels in the corner of the border need to correspond with the texels in the texture maps that touch the corners. If your texture is an edge or corner of the whole tiling, you need to decide what values would be reasonable to put in the borders. The easiest reasonable thing to do is to copy the value of the adjacent texel in the texture map with **glTexSubImage2D()**.

A texture's border color is also used if the texture is applied in such a way that it only partially covers a primitive. (See "Repeating and Clamping Textures" on page 428 for more information about this situation.)

## Mipmaps: Multiple Levels of Detail

**Advanced**

Textured objects can be viewed, like any other objects in a scene, at different distances from the viewpoint. In a dynamic scene, as a textured object moves farther from the viewpoint, the texture map must decrease in size along with the size of the projected image. To accomplish this, OpenGL has to filter the texture map down to an appropriate size for mapping onto the object, without introducing visually disturbing artifacts, such as shimmering, flashing, and scintillation. For example, to render a brick wall, you may

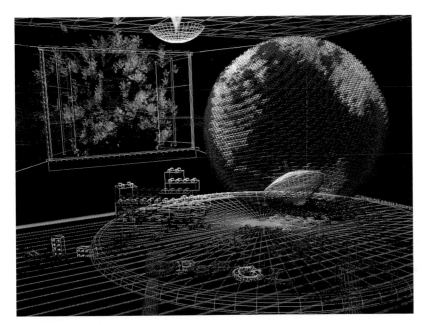

**Plate 1.** The scene from the cover of this book, with the objects rendered as wireframe models. See Chapter 2.

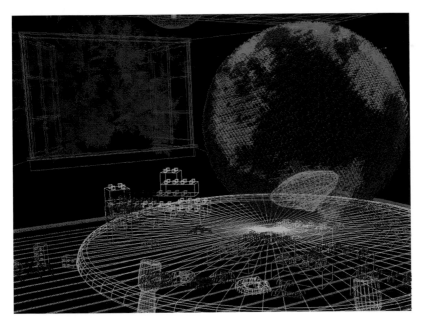

**Plate 2.** The same scene using fog for depth-cueing (lines further from the eye are dimmer). See Chapter 6.

**Plate 3.** The same scene with antialiased lines that smooth the jagged edges. See Chapter 6.

**Plate 4.** The scene drawn with flat-shaded polygons (a single color for each filled polygon). See Chapter 4.

**Plate 5.** The scene rendered with lighting and smooth-shaded polygons. See Chapters 4 and 5.

**Plate 6.** The scene with texture maps and shadows added. See Chapters 9 and 14.

**Plate 7.** The scene drawn with one of the objects motion-blurred. The accumulation buffer is used to compose the sequence of images needed to blur the moving object. See Chapter 10.

**Plate 8.** A close-up shot—the scene is rendered from a new viewpoint. See Chapter 3.

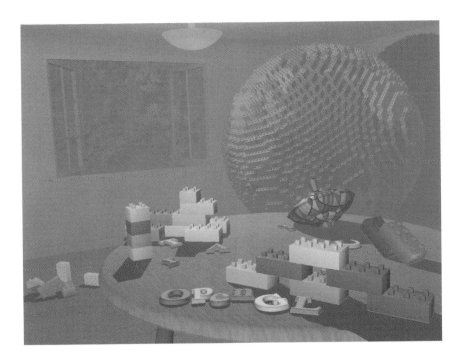

**Plate 9.** The scene drawn using atmospheric effects (fog) to simulate a smoke-filled room. See Chapter 6.

**Plate 10.** Teapots drawn with jittered viewing volumes into the accumulation buffer for a depth-of-field effect. The gold teapot is in sharpest focus. See Chapter 10.

**Plate 11.** A smooth-shaded triangle. The three vertices at the corners are drawn in red, green, and blue; the rest of the triangle is smoothly shaded between these three colors. See Chapter 4.

**Plate 24.** An architectural rendering using OpenGL. This is a rendering of a VRML scene using texture mapping (see Chapter 9) for illumination control and stencil buffering (see Chapter 10). (Image courtesy of Cyril Kardassevitch, Institut de Recherche en Informatique de Toulouse, Toulouse, France)

**Plate 25.** An image representing a manufacturing prototype. Environment mapping is used to enhance the illumination in the scene. See Chapter 9. (Image courtesy of Yukari Ito and Keisuke Kirii, Visual Systems Technology Center, Nihon SGI, Tokyo, Japan)

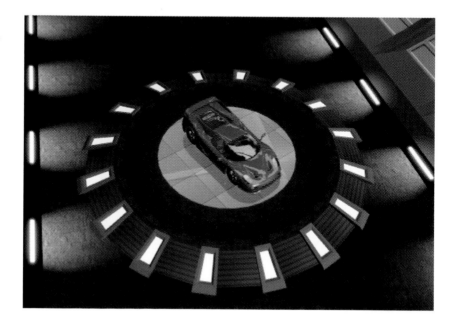

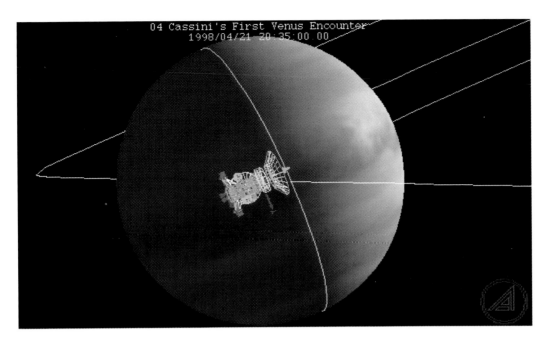

**Plate 26.** Scientific visualization of the interplanetary probe, Cassini, after its initial rendezvous with Venus. (Image courtesy of John Coggi and David Stodden, The Aerospace Company, Los Angeles, California, USA)

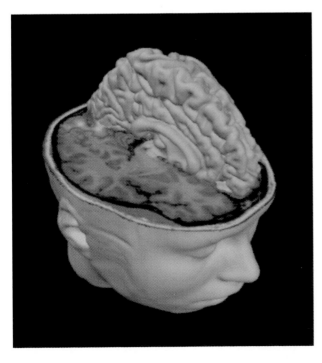

**Plate 27.** Medical visualization based on slices from a magnetic resonance imaging scan. The image is composed of surfaces generated from the slices. (Image courtesy of Rainer Goebel, Max Planck Institute for Brain Research, Frankfurt, Germany)

**Plate 28.** Projected texture mapping. See Chapter 9. (Image courtesy of Stefan Brabec and Wolfgang Heidrich, Max Planck Institute for Computer Science, Saarbrücken, Germany)

**Plate 29.** A synthetic being. The illumination in the scene is augmented using texture mapping. (Image courtesy of Mikko Blomqvist, Mediaclick OY, Tampere, Finland)

**Plate 30.** An image of a virutal oceanarium. Texture mapping and fog are used to generate the underwater effects. See Chapter 6. (Image courtesy of Bernd Lutz, Fraunhofer IGD, Darmstadt, Germany)

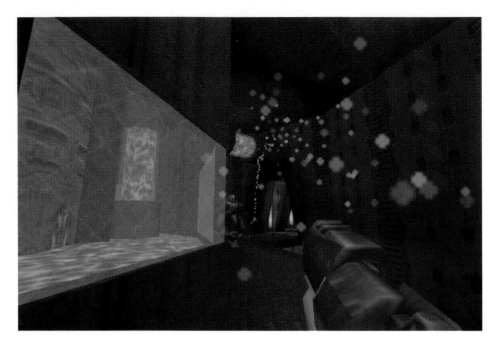

**Plates 31 and 32.** Screen images from Quake II and Quake III Arena, both of which use OpenGL for image generation. Multiple texture mapping passes are used to provide the image quality. Also note the use of fog and alpha blending to increase realism in the scene. (Images courtesy of id Software, Mesquite, Texas, USA)

use a large texture image (say $128 \times 128$ texels) when the wall is close to the viewer. But if the wall is moved farther away from the viewer until it appears on the screen as a single pixel, then the filtered textures may appear to change abruptly at certain transition points.

To avoid such artifacts, you can specify a series of prefiltered texture maps of decreasing resolutions, called *mipmaps*, as shown in Figure 9-6. The term *mipmap* was coined by Lance Williams, when he introduced the idea in his paper "Pyramidal Parametrics" (*SIGGRAPH 1983 Proceedings*). *Mip* stands for the Latin *multum in parvo*, meaning "many things in a small place." Mipmapping uses some clever methods to pack image data into memory.

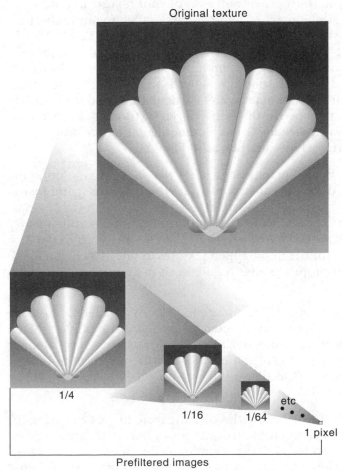

Original texture

1/4

1/16    1/64    etc

1 pixel

Prefiltered images

**Figure 9-6**    Mipmaps

**Note:** To acquire a full understanding of mipmaps, you need to understand minification filters, which are described in "Filtering" on page 411.

When using mipmapping, OpenGL automatically determines which texture map to use based on the size (in pixels) of the object being mapped. With this approach, the level of detail in the texture map is appropriate for the image that's drawn on the screen—as the image of the object gets smaller, the size of the texture map decreases. Mipmapping requires some extra computation and texture storage area; however, when it's not used, textures that are mapped onto smaller objects might shimmer and flash as the objects move.

To use mipmapping, you must provide all sizes of your texture in powers of 2 between the largest size and a $1 \times 1$ map. For example, if your highest-resolution map is $64 \times 16$, you must also provide maps of size $32 \times 8$, $16 \times 4$, $8 \times 2$, $4 \times 1$, $2 \times 1$, and $1 \times 1$. The smaller maps are typically filtered and averaged-down versions of the largest map in which each texel in a smaller texture is an average of the corresponding 4 texels in the higher-resolution texture. (Since OpenGL doesn't require any particular method for calculating the lower-resolution maps, the differently sized textures could be totally unrelated. In practice, unrelated textures would make the transitions between mipmaps extremely noticeable, as in Plate 20.)

To specify these textures, call **glTexImage2D()** once for each resolution of the texture map, with different values for the *level*, *width*, *height*, and *image* parameters. Starting with zero, *level* identifies which texture in the series is specified; with the previous example, the highest-resolution texture of size $64 \times 16$ would be declared with *level* = 0, the $32 \times 8$ texture with *level* = 1, and so on. In addition, for the mipmapped textures to take effect, you need to choose one of the appropriate filtering methods described in "Filtering" on page 411.

**Note:** This description of OpenGL mipmapping avoids detailed discussion of the scale factor (known as $\lambda$) between texel size and polygon size. This description also assumes default values for parameters related to mipmapping. To see an explanation of $\lambda$ and the effects of mipmapping parameters, see "Calculating the Mipmap Level" on page 405 and "Mipmap Level of Detail Control" on page 406.

Example 9-5 illustrates the use of a series of six texture maps decreasing in size from $32 \times 32$ to $1 \times 1$. This program draws a rectangle that extends from the foreground far back in the distance, eventually disappearing at a point, as shown in Plate 20. Note that the texture coordinates range from 0.0 to 8.0, so 64 copies of the texture map are required to tile the rectangle—eight in each direction. To illustrate how one texture map succeeds another, each map has a different color.

**Example 9-5**   Mipmap Textures: mipmap.c

```
GLubyte mipmapImage32[32][32][4];
GLubyte mipmapImage16[16][16][4];
GLubyte mipmapImage8[8][8][4];
GLubyte mipmapImage4[4][4][4];
GLubyte mipmapImage2[2][2][4];
GLubyte mipmapImage1[1][1][4];

static GLuint texName;

void makeImages(void)
{
   int i, j;

   for (i = 0; i < 32; i++) {
      for (j = 0; j < 32; j++) {
         mipmapImage32[i][j][0] = 255;
         mipmapImage32[i][j][1] = 255;
         mipmapImage32[i][j][2] = 0;
         mipmapImage32[i][j][3] = 255;
      }
   }
   for (i = 0; i < 16; i++) {
      for (j = 0; j < 16; j++) {
         mipmapImage16[i][j][0] = 255;
         mipmapImage16[i][j][1] = 0;
         mipmapImage16[i][j][2] = 255;
         mipmapImage16[i][j][3] = 255;
      }
   }
   for (i = 0; i < 8; i++) {
      for (j = 0; j < 8; j++) {
         mipmapImage8[i][j][0] = 255;
         mipmapImage8[i][j][1] = 0;
         mipmapImage8[i][j][2] = 0;
         mipmapImage8[i][j][3] = 255;
      }
   }
   for (i = 0; i < 4; i++) {
      for (j = 0; j < 4; j++) {
         mipmapImage4[i][j][0] = 0;
         mipmapImage4[i][j][1] = 255;
```

```
                        mipmapImage4[i][j][2] = 0;
                        mipmapImage4[i][j][3] = 255;
                }
        }
        for (i = 0; i < 2; i++) {
                for (j = 0; j < 2; j++) {
                        mipmapImage2[i][j][0] = 0;
                        mipmapImage2[i][j][1] = 0;
                        mipmapImage2[i][j][2] = 255;
                        mipmapImage2[i][j][3] = 255;
                }
        }
        mipmapImage1[0][0][0] = 255;
        mipmapImage1[0][0][1] = 255;
        mipmapImage1[0][0][2] = 255;
        mipmapImage1[0][0][3] = 255;
}

void init(void)
{
        glEnable(GL_DEPTH_TEST);
        glShadeModel(GL_FLAT);

        glTranslatef(0.0, 0.0, -3.6);
        makeImages();
        glPixelStorei(GL_UNPACK_ALIGNMENT, 1);

        glGenTextures(1, &texName);
        glBindTexture(GL_TEXTURE_2D, texName);
        glTexParameteri(GL_TEXTURE_2D, GL_TEXTURE_WRAP_S, GL_REPEAT);
        glTexParameteri(GL_TEXTURE_2D, GL_TEXTURE_WRAP_T, GL_REPEAT);
        glTexParameteri(GL_TEXTURE_2D, GL_TEXTURE_MAG_FILTER,
                        GL_NEAREST);
        glTexParameteri(GL_TEXTURE_2D, GL_TEXTURE_MIN_FILTER,
                        GL_NEAREST_MIPMAP_NEAREST);
        glTexImage2D(GL_TEXTURE_2D, 0, GL_RGBA, 32, 32, 0,
                        GL_RGBA, GL_UNSIGNED_BYTE, mipmapImage32);
        glTexImage2D(GL_TEXTURE_2D, 1, GL_RGBA, 16, 16, 0,
                        GL_RGBA, GL_UNSIGNED_BYTE, mipmapImage16);
        glTexImage2D(GL_TEXTURE_2D, 2, GL_RGBA, 8, 8, 0,
                        GL_RGBA, GL_UNSIGNED_BYTE, mipmapImage8);
        glTexImage2D(GL_TEXTURE_2D, 3, GL_RGBA, 4, 4, 0,
                        GL_RGBA, GL_UNSIGNED_BYTE, mipmapImage4);
        glTexImage2D(GL_TEXTURE_2D, 4, GL_RGBA, 2, 2, 0,
                        GL_RGBA, GL_UNSIGNED_BYTE, mipmapImage2);
        glTexImage2D(GL_TEXTURE_2D, 5, GL_RGBA, 1, 1, 0,
                        GL_RGBA, GL_UNSIGNED_BYTE, mipmapImage1);
```

```
    glTexEnvf(GL_TEXTURE_ENV, GL_TEXTURE_ENV_MODE, GL_REPLACE);
    glEnable(GL_TEXTURE_2D);
}

void display(void)
{
    glClear(GL_COLOR_BUFFER_BIT | GL_DEPTH_BUFFER_BIT);
    glBindTexture(GL_TEXTURE_2D, texName);
    glBegin(GL_QUADS);
    glTexCoord2f(0.0, 0.0); glVertex3f(-2.0, -1.0, 0.0);
    glTexCoord2f(0.0, 8.0); glVertex3f(-2.0, 1.0, 0.0);
    glTexCoord2f(8.0, 8.0); glVertex3f(2000.0, 1.0, -6000.0);
    glTexCoord2f(8.0, 0.0); glVertex3f(2000.0, -1.0, -6000.0);
    glEnd();
    glFlush();
}
```

Example 9-5 illustrates mipmapping by making each mipmap a different color so that it's obvious when one map is replaced by another. In a real situation, you define mipmaps such that the transition is as smooth as possible. Thus, the maps of lower resolution are usually filtered versions of an original, high-resolution texture map.

The construction of a series of such mipmaps is a software process, and thus isn't part of OpenGL, which is simply a rendering library. Since mipmap construction is such an important operation, the OpenGL Utility Library contains routines that aid in the manipulation of images to be used as mipmapped textures, as described in "Automated Mipmap Generation."

**Calculating the Mipmap Level**

Computing which level of mipmap to texture a particular polygon depends on the scale factor between the texture image and the size of the polygon to be textured (in pixels). Let's call this scale factor $\rho$ and also define a second value, $\lambda$, where $\lambda = \log_2 \rho + \text{lod}_{\text{bias}}$. (Since texture images can be multidimensional, it is important to clarify that $\rho$ is the maximum scale factor of all dimensions.)

$\text{lod}_{\text{bias}}$ is the level-of-detail bias, a constant value set by **glTexEnv\*()** to adjust $\lambda$. (For information about how to use **glTexEnv\*()** to set level-of-detail bias, see "Texture Functions" on page 421.) By default, $\text{lod}_{\text{bias}} = 0.0$, which has no effect. It's best to start with this default value and adjust in small amounts, if needed.

If $\lambda \leq 0.0$, then the texture is smaller than the polygon, so a magnification filter is used. If $\lambda > 0.0$, then a minification filter is used. If the minification filter selected uses mipmapping, then $\lambda$ indicates the mipmap level. (The minification-to-magnification switchover point is usually at $\lambda = 0.0$, but not always. The choice of mipmapping filter may shift the switchover point.)

For example, if the texture image is $64 \times 64$ texels and the polygon size is $32 \times 32$ pixels, then $\rho = 2.0$ (not 4.0), and therefore $\lambda = 1.0$. If the texture image is $64 \times 32$ texels and the polygon size is $8 \times 16$ pixels, then $\rho = 8.0$ (*x* scales by 8.0, *y* by 2.0; use the maximum value) and therefore $\lambda = 3.0$.

### Mipmap Level of Detail Control

By default, you must provide a mipmap for every level of resolution, down to 1 texel in every dimension. For some techniques, you want to avoid representing your data with very small mipmaps. For instance, you might use a technique called *mosaicing*, where several smaller images are combined on a single texture. One example of mosaicing is shown in Figure 9-7, where many characters are on a single texture, which may be more efficient than creating a texture image for each character. To map only a single letter from the texture, you make smart use of texture coordinates to isolate the letter you want.

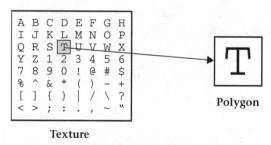

**Texture**

**Figure 9-7**     Using a Mosaic Texture

If you have to supply very small mipmaps, the lower-resolution mipmaps of the mosaic crush together detail from many different letters. Therefore, you may want to set restrictions on how low your resolution can go. Generally, you want the capability to add or remove levels of mipmaps as needed.

Another visible mipmapping problem is *popping*—the sudden transition from using one mipmap to using a radically higher- or lower-resolution mipmap, as a mipmapped polygon becomes larger or smaller.

**Note:** Many mipmapping features were introduced in later versions of OpenGL. Check the version of your implementation to see if a particular feature is supported. In some versions, a particular feature may be available as an extension.

To control mipmapping levels, the constants GL_TEXTURE_BASE_LEVEL, GL_TEXTURE_MAX_LEVEL, GL_TEXTURE_MIN_LOD, and GL_TEXTURE_MAX_LOD are passed to **glTexParameter\*()**. The first two constants (for brevity, shortened to BASE_LEVEL and MAX_LEVEL in the remainder of this section) control which mipmap levels are used and therefore which levels need to be specified. The other two constants (shortened to MIN_LOD and MAX_LOD) control the active range of the aforementioned scale factor $\lambda$.

These texture parameters address several of the previously described problems. Effective use of BASE_LEVEL and MAX_LEVEL may reduce the number of mipmaps that need to be specified and thereby streamline texture resource usage. Selective use of MAX_LOD may preserve the legibility of a mosaic texture, and MIN_LOD may reduce the popping effect with higher-resolution textures.

BASE_LEVEL and MAX_LEVEL are used to set the boundaries for which mipmap levels are used. BASE_LEVEL is the level of the highest-resolution (largest texture) mipmap level that is used. The default value for BASE_LEVEL is 0. However, you may later change the value for BASE_LEVEL, so that you add additional higher-resolution textures "on the fly." Similarly, MAX_LEVEL limits the lowest-resolution mipmap to be used. The default value for MAX_LEVEL is 1000, which almost always means that the smallest-resolution texture is 1 texel.

To set the base and maximum mipmap levels, use **glTexParameter\*()** with the first argument set to GL_TEXTURE_1D, GL_TEXTURE_2D, GL_TEXTURE_3D, or GL_TEXTURE_CUBE_MAP, depending on your textures. The second argument is one of the parameters described in Table 9-1. The third argument denotes the value for the parameter.

| Parameter | Description | Values |
|---|---|---|
| GL_TEXTURE_BASE_LEVEL | level for highest-resolution texture (lowest numbered mipmap level) in use | any non-negative integer |
| GL_TEXTURE_MAX_LEVEL | level for smallest-resolution texture (highest numbered mipmap level) in use | any non-negative integer |

**Table 9-1**     Mipmapping Level Parameter Controls

```
int gluBuild1DMipmaps(GLenum target,
                      GLint internalFormat, GLint width,
                      GLenum format, GLenum type,
                      const void *texels);
int gluBuild2DMipmaps(GLenum target, GLint internalFormat,
                      GLint width, GLint height, GLenum format,
                      GLenum type, const void *texels);
int gluBuild3DMipmaps(GLenum target, GLint internalFormat,
                      GLint width, GLint height, GLint depth,
                      GLenum format, GLenum type, const void *texels);
```

Constructs a series of mipmaps and calls **glTexImage*D()** to load the images. The parameters for *target, internalFormat, width, height, depth, format, type,* and *texels* are exactly the same as those for **glTexImage1D()**, **glTexImage2D()**, and **glTexImage3D()**. A value of 0 is returned if all the mipmaps are constructed successfully; otherwise, a GLU error code is returned.

With increased control over level of detail (using BASE_LEVEL, MAX_LEVEL, MIN_LOD, and MAX_LOD), you may need to create only a subset of the mipmaps defined by **gluBuild*DMipmaps()**. For example, you may want to stop at a 4 × 4 texel image, rather than go all the way to the smallest 1 × 1 texel image. To calculate and load a subset of mipmap levels, you may call **gluBuild*DMipmapLevels()**.

```
int gluBuild1DMipmapLevels(GLenum target, GLint internalFormat,
                           GLint width, GLenum format,
                           GLenum type, GLint level, GLint base,
                           GLint max, const void *texels);
int gluBuild2DMipmapLevels(GLenum target, GLint internalFormat,
                           GLint width, GLint height, GLenum format,
                           GLenum type, GLint level, GLint base,
                           GLint max, const void *texels);
int gluBuild3DMipmapLevels(GLenum target, GLint internalFormat,
                           GLint width, GLint height, GLint depth,
                           GLenum format, GLenum type,
                           GLint level, GLint base, GLint max,
                           const void *texels);
```

Constructs a series of mipmaps and calls **glTexImage*D()** to load the images. *level* indicates the mipmap level of the *texels* image. *base* and *max* determine which mipmap levels will be derived from *texels*. Otherwise, the parameters for *target, internalFormat, width, height, depth, format, type,* and *texels* are exactly the same as those for **glTexImage1D()**, **glTexImage2D()**, and **glTexImage3D()**. A value of 0 is returned if all the mipmaps are constructed successfully; otherwise, a GLU error code is returned.

If you expect that any texels in a mipmapped texture image will change, you will have to replace the complete set of related mipmaps. If you use **glTexParameter*()** to set GL_GENERATE_MIPMAP to GL_TRUE, then any change to the texels (interior or border) of a BASE_LEVEL mipmap will automatically cause all the textures at all mipmap levels from BASE_LEVEL+1 to MAX_LEVEL to be recomputed and replaced. Textures at all other mipmap levels, including at BASE_LEVEL, remain unchanged.

## Filtering

Texture maps are square or rectangular, but after being mapped to a polygon or surface and transformed into screen coordinates, the individual texels of a texture rarely correspond to individual pixels of the final screen image. Depending on the transformations used and the texture mapping applied, a single pixel on the screen can correspond to anything from a tiny portion of a texel (magnification) to a large collection of texels (minification), as shown in Figure 9-8. In either case, it's unclear exactly which texel values should be used and how they should be averaged or interpolated. Consequently, OpenGL allows you to specify any of several filtering options to determine these calculations. The options provide different trade-offs between speed and image quality. Also, you can specify independently the filtering methods for magnification and minification.

In some cases, it isn't obvious whether magnification or minification is called for. If the texture map needs to be stretched (or shrunk) in both the *x*- and *y*- directions, then magnification (or minification) is needed. If the texture map needs to be stretched in one direction and shrunk in the other, OpenGL makes a choice between magnification and minification that in most cases gives the best result possible. It's best to try to avoid these situations by using texture coordinates that map without such distortion. (See "Computing Appropriate Texture Coordinates" on page 427.)

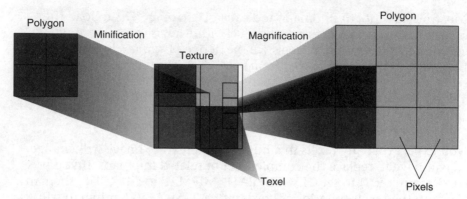

**Figure 9-8**    Texture Magnification and Minification

The following lines are examples of how to use **glTexParameter\*()** to specify the magnification and minification filtering methods:

```
glTexParameteri(GL_TEXTURE_2D, GL_TEXTURE_MAG_FILTER,
                GL_NEAREST);
glTexParameteri(GL_TEXTURE_2D, GL_TEXTURE_MIN_FILTER,
                GL_NEAREST);
```

The first argument to **glTexParameter\*()** is GL_TEXTURE_1D, GL_TEXTURE_2D, GL_TEXTURE_3D, or GL_TEXTURE_CUBE_MAP, whichever is appropriate. For the purposes of this discussion, the second argument is either GL_TEXTURE_MAG_FILTER, or GL_TEXTURE_MIN_FILTER, to indicate whether you're specifying the filtering method for magnification or minification. The third argument specifies the filtering method; Table 9-3 lists the possible values.

| Parameter | Values |
|---|---|
| GL_TEXTURE_MAG_FILTER | GL_NEAREST or GL_LINEAR |
| GL_TEXTURE_MIN_FILTER | GL_NEAREST, GL_LINEAR, GL_NEAREST_MIPMAP_NEAREST, GL_NEAREST_MIPMAP_LINEAR, GL_LINEAR_MIPMAP_NEAREST, or GL_LINEAR_MIPMAP_LINEAR |

**Table 9-3**    Filtering Methods for Magnification and Minification

If you choose GL_NEAREST, the texel with coordinates nearest the center of the pixel is used for both magnification and minification. This can result in aliasing artifacts (sometimes severe). If you choose GL_LINEAR, a weighted linear average of the 2 × 2 array of texels that lie nearest to the center of the pixel is used, again for both magnification and minification. (For three-dimensional textures, it's a 2 × 2 × 2 array; for one-dimensional, it's an average of 2 texels.) When the texture coordinates are near the edge of the texture map, the nearest 2 × 2 array of texels might include some that are outside the texture map. In these cases, the texel values used depend on which wrapping mode is in effect and whether you've assigned a border for the texture. (See "Repeating and Clamping Textures" on page 428.) GL_NEAREST requires less computation than GL_LINEAR and therefore might execute more quickly, but GL_LINEAR provides smoother results.

With magnification, even if you've supplied mipmaps, only the base level texture map is used. With minification, you can choose a filtering method that uses the most appropriate one or two mipmaps, as described in the next paragraph. (If GL_NEAREST or GL_LINEAR is specified with minification, only the base level texture map is used.)

As shown in Table 9-3, four additional filtering options are available when minifying with mipmaps. Within an individual mipmap, you can choose the nearest texel value with GL_NEAREST_MIPMAP_NEAREST, or you can interpolate linearly by specifying GL_LINEAR_MIPMAP_NEAREST. Using the nearest texels is faster but yields less desirable results. The particular mipmap chosen is a function of the amount of minification required, and there's a cutoff point from the use of one particular mipmap to the next. To avoid a sudden transition, use GL_NEAREST_MIPMAP_LINEAR or GL_LINEAR_MIPMAP_LINEAR for linear interpolation of texel values from the two nearest best choices of mipmaps. GL_NEAREST_MIPMAP_LINEAR selects the nearest texel in each of the two maps and then interpolates linearly between these two values. GL_LINEAR_MIPMAP_LINEAR uses linear interpolation to compute the value in each of two maps and then interpolates linearly between these two values. As you might expect, GL_LINEAR_MIPMAP_LINEAR generally produces the highest-quality results, but it requires the most computation and therefore might be the slowest.

**Caution:** If you request a mipmapped texture filter, but you have not supplied a full and consistent set of mipmaps (all correct-sized texture images between GL_TEXTURE_BASE_LEVEL and GL_TEXTURE_MAX_LEVEL), OpenGL will, without any error, implicitly disable texturing. If you are trying to use mipmaps and no texturing appears at all, check the texture images at all your mipmap levels.

Some of these texture filters are known by more popular names. GL_NEAREST is often called *point sampling*. GL_LINEAR is known as *bilinear sampling*, because for two-dimensional textures, a 2 × 2 array of texels is sampled.

GL_LINEAR_MIPMAP_LINEAR is sometimes known as *trilinear sampling*, because it is a linear average between two bilinearly sampled mipmaps.

**Note:** The minification-to-magnification switchover point is usually at $\lambda = 0.0$, but is affected by the type of minification filter you choose. If the current magnification filter is GL_LINEAR and the minification filter is GL_NEAREST_MIPMAP_NEAREST or GL_NEAREST_MIPMAP_LINEAR, then the switch between filters occurs at $\lambda = 0.5$. This prevents the minified texture from looking sharper than its magnified counterpart.

### Nate Robins' Texture Tutorial

If you have downloaded Nate Robins' suite of tutorial programs, now run the **texture** tutorial. (For information on how and where to download these programs, see "Nate Robins' OpenGL Tutors" on page xl.) With this tutorial, you can experiment with the texture-mapping filtering method, switching between GL_NEAREST and GL_LINEAR.

## Texture Objects

A texture object stores texture data and makes it readily available. You may control many textures and go back to textures that have been previously loaded into your texture resources. Using texture objects is usually the fastest way to apply textures, resulting in big performance gains, because it is almost always much faster to bind (reuse) an existing texture object than it is to reload a texture image using **glTexImage*D()**.

Also, some implementations support a limited *working set* of high-performance textures. You can use texture objects to load your most often used textures into this limited area.

To use texture objects for your texture data, take these steps:

1. Generate texture names.

2. Initially bind (create) texture objects to texture data, including the image arrays and texture properties.

3. If your implementation supports a working set of high-performance textures, see if you have enough space for all your texture objects. If there isn't enough space, you may wish to establish priorities for each texture object so that more often used textures stay in the working set.

4. Bind and rebind texture objects, making their data currently available for rendering textured models.

## Naming a Texture Object

Any nonzero unsigned integer may be used as a texture name. To avoid accidentally reusing names, consistently use **glGenTextures()** to provide unused texture names.

void **glGenTextures**(GLsizei *n*, GLuint *\*textureNames*);

Returns *n* currently unused names for texture objects in the array *textureNames*. The names returned in *textureNames* do not have to be a contiguous set of integers.

The names in *textureNames* are marked as used, but they acquire texture state and dimensionality (1D, 2D, or 3D) only when they are first bound.

Zero is a reserved texture name and is never returned as a texture name by **glGenTextures()**.

**glIsTexture()** determines if a texture name is actually in use. If a texture name was returned by **glGenTextures()** but has not yet been bound (calling **glBindTexture()** with the name at least once), then **glIsTexture()** returns GL_FALSE.

GLboolean **glIsTexture**(GLuint *textureName*);

Returns GL_TRUE if *textureName* is the name of a texture that has been bound and has not been subsequently deleted, and returns GL_FALSE if *textureName* is zero or *textureName* is a nonzero value that is not the name of an existing texture.

## Creating and Using Texture Objects

The same routine, **glBindTexture()**, both creates and uses texture objects. When a texture name is initially bound (used with **glBindTexture()**), a new texture object is created with default values for the texture image and texture properties. Subsequent calls to **glTexImage*()**, **glTexSubImage*()**, **glCopyTexImage*()**, **glCopyTexSubImage*()**, **glTexParameter*()**, and **glPrioritizeTextures()** store data in the texture object. The texture object may contain a texture image and associated mipmap images (if any), including associated data such as width, height, border width, internal format, resolution of components, and texture properties. Saved texture properties include minification and magnification filters, wrapping modes, border color, and texture priority.

When a texture object is subsequently bound once again, its data becomes the current texture state. (The state of the previously bound texture is replaced.)

---

void **glBindTexture**(GLenum *target*, GLuint *textureName*);

---

**glBindTexture**() does three things. When using the *textureName* of an unsigned integer other than zero for the first time, a new texture object is created and assigned that name. When binding to a previously created texture object, that texture object becomes active. When binding to a *textureName* value of zero, OpenGL stops using texture objects and returns to the unnamed default texture.

When a texture object is initially bound (that is, created), it assumes the dimensionality of *target*, which is GL_TEXTURE_1D, GL_TEXTURE_2D, GL_TEXTURE_3D, or GL_TEXTURE_CUBE_MAP. Immediately on its initial binding, the state of the texture object is equivalent to the state of the default *target* dimensionality at the initialization of OpenGL. In this initial state, texture properties such as minification and magnification filters, wrapping modes, border color, and texture priority are set to their default values.

In Example 9-7, two texture objects are created in **init**(). In **display**(), each texture object is used to render a different four-sided polygon.

**Example 9-7**    Binding Texture Objects: texbind.c

```
#define checkImageWidth 64
#define checkImageHeight 64
static GLubyte checkImage[checkImageHeight][checkImageWidth][4];
static GLubyte otherImage[checkImageHeight][checkImageWidth][4];

static GLuint texName[2];

void makeCheckImages(void)
{
   int i, j, c;

   for (i = 0; i < checkImageHeight; i++) {
      for (j = 0; j < checkImageWidth; j++) {
         c = (((i&0x8)==0)^((j&0x8)==0))*255;
```

```
            checkImage[i][j][0] = (GLubyte) c;
            checkImage[i][j][1] = (GLubyte) c;
            checkImage[i][j][2] = (GLubyte) c;
            checkImage[i][j][3] = (GLubyte) 255;
            c = (((i&0x10)==0)^((j&0x10)==0))*255;
            otherImage[i][j][0] = (GLubyte) c;
            otherImage[i][j][1] = (GLubyte) 0;
            otherImage[i][j][2] = (GLubyte) 0;
            otherImage[i][j][3] = (GLubyte) 255;
        }
    }
}

void init(void)
{
    glClearColor(0.0, 0.0, 0.0, 0.0);
    glShadeModel(GL_FLAT);
    glEnable(GL_DEPTH_TEST);

    makeCheckImages();
    glPixelStorei(GL_UNPACK_ALIGNMENT, 1);

    glGenTextures(2, texName);
    glBindTexture(GL_TEXTURE_2D, texName[0]);
    glTexParameteri(GL_TEXTURE_2D, GL_TEXTURE_WRAP_S, GL_CLAMP);
    glTexParameteri(GL_TEXTURE_2D, GL_TEXTURE_WRAP_T, GL_CLAMP);
    glTexParameteri(GL_TEXTURE_2D, GL_TEXTURE_MAG_FILTER,
                    GL_NEAREST);
    glTexParameteri(GL_TEXTURE_2D, GL_TEXTURE_MIN_FILTER,
                    GL_NEAREST);
    glTexImage2D(GL_TEXTURE_2D, 0, GL_RGBA, checkImageWidth,
                 checkImageHeight, 0, GL_RGBA, GL_UNSIGNED_BYTE,
                 checkImage);

    glBindTexture(GL_TEXTURE_2D, texName[1]);
    glTexParameteri(GL_TEXTURE_2D, GL_TEXTURE_WRAP_S, GL_CLAMP);
    glTexParameteri(GL_TEXTURE_2D, GL_TEXTURE_WRAP_T, GL_CLAMP);
    glTexParameteri(GL_TEXTURE_2D, GL_TEXTURE_MAG_FILTER,
                    GL_NEAREST);
    glTexParameteri(GL_TEXTURE_2D, GL_TEXTURE_MIN_FILTER,
                    GL_NEAREST);
    glTexEnvf(GL_TEXTURE_ENV, GL_TEXTURE_ENV_MODE, GL_REPLACE);
    glTexImage2D(GL_TEXTURE_2D, 0, GL_RGBA, checkImageWidth,
                 checkImageHeight, 0, GL_RGBA, GL_UNSIGNED_BYTE,
                 otherImage);
    glEnable(GL_TEXTURE_2D);
}
```

```
void display(void)
{
    glClear(GL_COLOR_BUFFER_BIT | GL_DEPTH_BUFFER_BIT);
    glBindTexture(GL_TEXTURE_2D, texName[0]);
    glBegin(GL_QUADS);
    glTexCoord2f(0.0, 0.0); glVertex3f(-2.0, -1.0, 0.0);
    glTexCoord2f(0.0, 1.0); glVertex3f(-2.0, 1.0, 0.0);
    glTexCoord2f(1.0, 1.0); glVertex3f(0.0, 1.0, 0.0);
    glTexCoord2f(1.0, 0.0); glVertex3f(0.0, -1.0, 0.0);
    glEnd();
    glBindTexture(GL_TEXTURE_2D, texName[1]);
    glBegin(GL_QUADS);
    glTexCoord2f(0.0, 0.0); glVertex3f(1.0, -1.0, 0.0);
    glTexCoord2f(0.0, 1.0); glVertex3f(1.0, 1.0, 0.0);
    glTexCoord2f(1.0, 1.0); glVertex3f(2.41421, 1.0, -1.41421);
    glTexCoord2f(1.0, 0.0); glVertex3f(2.41421, -1.0, -1.41421);
    glEnd();
    glFlush();
}
```

Whenever a texture object is bound once again, you may edit the contents of the bound texture object. Any commands you call that change the texture image or other properties change the contents of the currently bound texture object as well as the current texture state.

In Example 9-7, after completion of **display**(), you are still bound to the texture named by the contents of *texName[1]*. Be careful that you don't call a spurious texture routine that changes the data in that texture object.

When mipmaps are used, all related mipmaps of a single texture image must be put into a single texture object. In Example 9-5, levels 0–5 of a mip-mapped texture image are put into a single texture object named *texName*.

## Cleaning Up Texture Objects

As you bind and unbind texture objects, their data still sits around some-where among your texture resources. If texture resources are limited, deleting textures may be one way to free up resources.

void **glDeleteTextures**(GLsizei *n*, const GLuint *\*textureNames*);

Deletes *n* texture objects, named by elements in the array *textureNames*. The freed texture names may now be reused (for example, by **glGenTextures**()).

If a texture that is currently bound is deleted, the binding reverts to the default texture, as if **glBindTexture()** were called with zero for the value of *textureName*. Attempts to delete nonexistent texture names or the texture name of zero are ignored without generating an error.

## A Working Set of Resident Textures

Some OpenGL implementations support a working set of high-performance textures, which are said to be resident. Typically, these implementations have specialized hardware to perform texture operations and a limited hardware cache to store texture images. In this case, using texture objects is recommended, because you are able to load many textures into the working set and then control them.

If all the textures required by the application exceed the size of the cache, some textures cannot be resident. If you want to find out if a single texture is currently resident, bind its object, and then call **glGetTexParameter\*v()** to determine the value associated with the GL_TEXTURE_RESIDENT state. If you want to know about the texture residence status of many textures, use **glAreTexturesResident()**.

GLboolean **glAreTexturesResident**(GLsizei *n*,
                                    const GLuint *\*textureNames*,
                                    GLboolean *\*residences*);

Queries the texture residence status of the *n* texture objects, named in the array *textureNames*. *residences* is an array in which texture residence status is returned for the corresponding texture objects in the array *textureNames*. If all the named textures in *textureNames* are resident, the **glAreTexturesResident()** function returns GL_TRUE, and the contents of the array *residences* are undisturbed. If any texture in *textureNames* is not resident, then **glAreTexturesResident()** returns GL_FALSE, and the elements in *residences*, which correspond to nonresident texture objects in *textureNames*, are also set to GL_FALSE.

Note that **glAreTexturesResident()** returns the current residence status. Texture resources are very dynamic, and texture residence status may change at any time. Some implementations cache textures when they are first used. It may be necessary to draw with the texture before checking residency.

If your OpenGL implementation does not establish a working set of high-performance textures, then the texture objects are always considered resident. In that case, **glAreTexturesResident**() always returns GL_TRUE and basically provides no information.

### Texture Residence Strategies

If you can create a working set of textures and want to get the best texture performance possible, you really have to know the specifics of your implementation and application. For example, with a visual simulation or video game, you have to maintain performance in all situations. In that case, you should never access a nonresident texture. For these applications, you want to load up all your textures on initialization and make them all resident. If you don't have enough texture memory available, you may need to reduce the size, resolution, and levels of mipmaps for your texture images, or you may use **glTexSubImage**\*() to repeatedly reuse the same texture memory.

**Note:** If you have several short-lived textures of the same size, you can use **glTexSubImage**\*() to reload existing texture objects with different images. This technique may be more efficient than deleting textures and reestablishing new textures from scratch.

For applications that create textures "on the fly," nonresident textures may be unavoidable. If some textures are used more frequently than others, you may assign a higher priority to those texture objects to increase their likelihood of being resident. Deleting texture objects also frees up space. Short of that, assigning a lower priority to a texture object may make it first in line for being moved out of the working set, as resources dwindle. **glPrioritizeTextures**() is used to assign priorities to texture objects.

---

void **glPrioritizeTextures**(GLsizei *n*, const GLuint *\*textureNames*,
const GLclampf *\*priorities*);

---

Assigns the *n* texture objects, named in the array *textureNames*, the texture residence priorities in the corresponding elements of the array *priorities*. The priority values in the array *priorities* are clamped to the range [0.0, 1.0] before being assigned. Zero indicates the lowest priority (textures least likely to be resident), and 1 indicates the highest priority.

**glPrioritizeTextures**() does not require that any of the textures in *textureNames* be bound. However, the priority might not have any effect on a texture object until it is initially bound.

**glTexParameter\*()** also may be used to set a single texture's priority, but only if the texture is currently bound. In fact, use of **glTexParameter\*()** is the only way to set the priority of a default texture.

If texture objects have equal priority, typical implementations of OpenGL apply a least recently used (LRU) strategy to decide which texture objects to move out of the working set. If you know that your OpenGL implementation uses this algorithm, then having equal priorities for all texture objects creates a reasonable LRU system for reallocating texture resources.

If your implementation of OpenGL doesn't use an LRU strategy for texture objects of equal priority (or if you don't know how it decides), you can implement your own LRU strategy by carefully maintaining the texture object priorities. When a texture is used (bound), you can maximize its priority, which reflects its recent use. Then, at regular (time) intervals, you can degrade the priorities of all texture objects.

**Note:** Fragmentation of texture memory can be a problem, especially if you're deleting and creating numerous new textures. Although it may be possible to load all the texture objects into a working set by binding them in one sequence, binding them in a different sequence may leave some textures nonresident.

## Texture Functions

In each of the examples presented so far in this chapter, the values in the texture map have been used directly as colors to be painted on the surface being rendered. You can also use the values in the texture map to modulate the color in which the surface would be rendered without texturing or to combine the color in the texture map with the original color of the surface. You choose texturing functions by supplying the appropriate arguments to **glTexEnv\*()**.

---

void **glTexEnv**{if}(GLenum *target*, GLenum *pname*, TYPE *param*);
void **glTexEnv**{if}**v**(GLenum *target*, GLenum *pname*, const TYPE *\*param*);

Sets the current texturing function. *target* must be either GL_TEXTURE_FILTER_CONTROL or GL_TEXTURE_ENV.

If *target* is GL_TEXTURE_FILTER_CONTROL, then *pname* must be GL_TEXTURE_LOD_BIAS, and *param* is a single, floating-point value used to bias the mipmapping level-of-detail parameter.

---

If *target* is GL_TEXTURE_ENV and if *pname* is GL_TEXTURE_ENV_MODE, then *param* is one of GL_DECAL, GL_REPLACE, GL_MODULATE, GL_BLEND, GL_ADD, or GL_COMBINE, which specifies how texture values are combined with the color values of the fragment being processed. If *pname* is GL_TEXTURE_ENV_COLOR, then *param* is an array of 4 floating-point numbers (R, G, B, A) which denotes a color to be used for GL_BLEND operations.

If *target* is GL_POINT_SPRITE and if *pname* is GL_COORD_REPLACE, then setting *param* to GL_TRUE will enable the iteration of texture coordinates across a point sprite. Texture coordinates will remain constant across the primitive if *param* is set to GL_FALSE.

**Note:** This is only a partial list of acceptable values for **glTexEnv*()**, excluding texture combiner functions. For complete details about GL_COMBINE and a complete list of options for *pname* and *param* for **glTexEnv*()**, see "Texture Combiner Functions" on page 449 and Table 9-8.

The combination of the texturing function and the base internal format determines how the textures are applied for each component of the texture. The texturing function operates on selected components of the texture and the color values that would be used with no texturing. (Note that the selection is performed after the pixel-transfer function has been applied.) Recall that when you specify your texture map with **glTexImage*D()**, the third argument is the internal format to be selected for each texel.

There are six base internal formats: GL_ALPHA, GL_LUMINANCE, GL_LUMINANCE_ALPHA, GL_INTENSITY, GL_RGB, and GL_RGBA. Other internal formats (such as GL_LUMINANCE6_ALPHA2 or GL_R3_G3_B2) specify desired resolutions of the texture components and can be matched to one of these six base internal formats.

Texturing calculations are ultimately in RGBA, but some internal formats are not in RGB. Table 9-4 shows how the RGBA color values are derived from different texture formats, including the less obvious derivations.

| Base Internal Format | Derived Source Color (R, G, B, A) |
| --- | --- |
| GL_ALPHA | (0, 0, 0, A) |
| GL_LUMINANCE | (L, L, L, 1) |
| GL_LUMINANCE_ALPHA | (L, L, L, A) |

**Table 9-4** Deriving Color Values from Different Texture Formats

| Base Internal Format | Derived Source Color (R, G, B, A) |
|---|---|
| GL_INTENSITY | $(I, I, I, I)$ |
| GL_RGB | $(R, G, B, 1)$ |
| GL_RGBA | $(R, G, B, A)$ |

**Table 9-4  (continued)**   Deriving Color Values from Different Texture Formats

Table 9-5 and Table 9-6 show how a texturing function (except for GL_COMBINE) and base internal format determine the texturing application formula used for each component of the texture.

In Table 9-5 and Table 9-6, note the following use of subscripts:

- *s* indicates a texture source color, as determined in Table 9-4
- *f* indicates an incoming fragment value
- *c* indicates values assigned with GL_TEXTURE_ENV_COLOR
- no subscript indicates a final, computed value

In these tables, multiplication of a color triple by a scalar means multiplying each of the R, G, and B components by the scalar; multiplying (or adding) two color triples means multiplying (or adding) each component of the second by (or to) the corresponding component of the first.

| Base Internal Format | GL_REPLACE Function | GL_MODULATE Function | GL_DECAL Function |
|---|---|---|---|
| GL_ALPHA | $C = C_f$<br>$A = A_s$ | $C = C_f$<br>$A = A_f A_s$ | undefined |
| GL_LUMINANCE | $C = C_s$<br>$A = A_f$ | $C = C_f C_s$<br>$A = A_f$ | undefined |
| GL_LUMINANCE_ALPHA | $C = C_s$<br>$A = A_s$ | $C = C_f C_s$<br>$A = A_f A_s$ | undefined |
| GL_INTENSITY | $C = C_s$<br>$A = C_s$ | $C = C_f C_s$<br>$A = A_f C_s$ | undefined |
| GL_RGB | $C = C_s$<br>$A = A_f$ | $C = C_f C_s$<br>$A = A_f$ | $C = C_s$<br>$A = A_f$ |
| GL_RGBA | $C = C_s$<br>$A = A_s$ | $C = C_f C_s$<br>$A = A_f A_s$ | $C = C_f(1 - A_s) + C_s A_s$<br>$A = A_f$ |

**Table 9-5**   Replace, Modulate, and Decal Texture Functions

described as an advanced feature in "The $q$-Coordinate." The command to specify texture coordinates, **glTexCoord\*()**, is similar to **glVertex\*()**, **glColor\*()**, and **glNormal\*()**—it comes in similar variations and is used the same way between **glBegin()** and **glEnd()** pairs. Usually, texture-coordinate values range from 0 to 1; values can be assigned outside this range, however, with the results described in "Repeating and Clamping Textures."

---

void **glTexCoord**{1234}{sifd}(*TYPE coords*);
void **glTexCoord**{1234}{sifd}**v**(const *TYPE \*coords*);

Sets the current texture coordinates (*s, t, r, q*). Subsequent calls to **glVertex\*()** result in those vertices being assigned the current texture coordinates. With **glTexCoord1\*()**, the *s*-coordinate is set to the specified value, *t* and *r* are set to 0, and *q* is set to 1. Using **glTexCoord2\*()** allows you to specify *s* and *t*; *r* and *q* are set to 0 and 1, respectively. With **glTexCoord3\*()**, *q* is set to 1 and the other coordinates are set as specified. You can specify all coordinates with **glTexCoord4\*()**. Use the appropriate suffix (s, i, f, or d) and the corresponding value for *TYPE* (GLshort, GLint, GLfloat, or GLdouble) to specify the coordinates' data type. You can supply the coordinates individually, or you can use the vector version of the command to supply them in a single array. Texture coordinates are multiplied by the 4 × 4 texture matrix before any texture mapping occurs. (See "The Texture Matrix Stack" on page 457.) Note that integer texture coordinates are interpreted directly, rather than being mapped to the range [−1, 1] as normal coordinates are.

---

The next subsection discusses how to calculate appropriate texture coordinates. Instead of explicitly assigning them yourself, you can choose to have texture coordinates calculated automatically by OpenGL as a function of the vertex coordinates. (See "Automatic Texture-Coordinate Generation" on page 434.)

### Nate Robins' Texture Tutorial

If you have Nate Robins' **texture** tutorial, run it, and experiment with the parameters of **glTexCoord2f()** for the four different vertices. See how you can map from a portion of the entire texture. (What happens if you make a texture coordinate less than 0 or greater than 1?)

## Computing Appropriate Texture Coordinates

Two-dimensional textures are square or rectangular images that are typically mapped to the polygons that make up a polygonal model. In the simplest case, you're mapping a rectangular texture onto a model that's also rectangular—for example, your texture is a scanned image of a brick wall, and your rectangle represents a brick wall of a building. Suppose the brick wall is square and the texture is square, and you want to map the whole texture to the whole wall. The texture coordinates of the texture square are (0, 0), (1, 0), (1, 1), and (0, 1) in counterclockwise order. When you're drawing the wall, just give those four coordinate sets as the texture coordinates as you specify the wall's vertices in counterclockwise order.

Now suppose that the wall is two-thirds as high as it is wide, and that the texture is again square. To avoid distorting the texture, you need to map the wall to a portion of the texture map so that the aspect ratio of the texture is preserved. Suppose that you decide to use the lower two-thirds of the texture map to texture the wall. In this case, use texture coordinates of (0, 0), (1, 0), (1, 2/3), and (0, 2/3) for the texture coordinates, as the wall vertices are traversed in a counterclockwise order.

As a slightly more complicated example, suppose you'd like to display a tin can with a label wrapped around it on the screen. To obtain the texture, you purchase a can, remove the label, and scan it in. Suppose the label is 4 units tall and 12 units around, which yields an aspect ratio of 3 to 1. Since textures must have aspect ratios of $2^n$ to 1, you can either simply not use the top third of the texture, or you can cut and paste the texture until it has the necessary aspect ratio. Suppose you decide not to use the top third. Now suppose the tin can is a cylinder approximated by 30 polygons of length 4 units (the height of the can) and width 12/30 (1/30 of the circumference of the can). You can use the following texture coordinates for each of the 30 approximating rectangles:

1: (0, 0), (1/30, 0), (1/30, 2/3), (0, 2/3)

2: (1/30, 0), (2/30, 0), (2/30, 2/3), (1/30, 2/3)

3: (2/30, 0), (3/30, 0), (3/30, 2/3), (2/30, 2/3)

. . .

30: (29/30, 0), (1, 0), (1, 2/3), (29/30, 2/3)

Only a few curved surfaces such as cones and cylinders can be mapped to a flat surface without geodesic distortion. Any other shape requires some distortion. In general, the higher the curvature of the surface, the more distortion of the texture is required.

If you don't care about texture distortion, it's often quite easy to find a reasonable mapping. For example, consider a sphere whose surface coordinates are given by $(\cos\theta\cos\phi, \cos\theta\ \sin\phi, \sin\theta)$, where $0 \le \theta \le 2\pi$ and $0 \le \phi \le \pi$. The $\theta$-$\phi$ rectangle can be mapped directly to a rectangular texture map, but the closer you get to the poles, the more distorted the texture is. The entire top edge of the texture map is mapped to the north pole, and the entire bottom edge to the south pole. For other surfaces, such as that of a torus (doughnut) with a large hole, the natural surface coordinates map to the texture coordinates in a way that produces only a little distortion, so it might be suitable for many applications. Figure 9-9 shows two toruses, one with a small hole (and therefore a lot of distortion near the center) and one with a large hole (and only a little distortion).

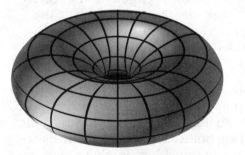 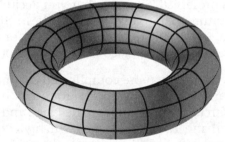

**Figure 9-9**     Texture-Map Distortion

If you're texturing spline surfaces generated with evaluators (see Chapter 12), the *u* and *v* parameters for the surface can sometimes be used as texture coordinates. In general, however, there's a large artistic component to successful mapping of textures to polygonal approximations of curved surfaces.

## Repeating and Clamping Textures

You can assign texture coordinates outside the range [0, 1] and have them either clamp or repeat in the texture map. With repeating textures, if you have a large plane with texture coordinates running from 0.0 to 10.0 in both directions, for example, you'll get 100 copies of the texture tiled together on the screen. During repeating, the integer parts of texture coordinates are ignored, and copies of the texture map tile the surface. For most applications in which the texture is to be repeated, the texels at the top of the texture should match those at the bottom, and similarly for the left and right edges.

A "mirrored" repeat is available, where the surface tiles "flip-flop." For instance, within texture coordinate range [0, 1], a texture may appear oriented from left-to-right (or top-to-bottom or near-to-far), but the "mirrored" repeat wrapping reorients the texture from right-to-left for texture coordinate range [1, 2], then back again to left-to-right for coordinates [2, 3], and so on.

Another possibility is to clamp the texture coordinates: any values greater than 1.0 are set to 1.0, and any values less than 0.0 are set to 0.0. Clamping is useful for applications in which you want a single copy of the texture to appear on a large surface. If the texture coordinates of the surface range from 0.0 to 10.0 in both directions, one copy of the texture appears in the lower left corner of the surface.

If you are using textures with borders or have specified a texture border color, both the wrapping mode and the filtering method (see "Filtering" on page 411) influence whether and how the border information is used.

If you're using the filtering method GL_NEAREST, the closest texel in the texture is used. For most wrapping modes, the border (or border color) is ignored. However, if the texture coordinate is outside the range [0, 1] and the wrapping mode is GL_CLAMP_TO_BORDER, then the nearest border texel is chosen. (If no border is present, the constant border color is used.)

If you've chosen GL_LINEAR as the filtering method, a weighted combination in a $2 \times 2$ array (for two-dimensional textures) of color data is used for texture application. If there is a border or border color, the texture and border colors are used together, as follows:

- For the wrapping mode GL_REPEAT, the border is always ignored. The $2 \times 2$ array of weighted texels wraps to the opposite edge of the texture. Thus, texels at the right edge are averaged with those at the left edge, and top and bottom texels are also averaged.

- For the wrapping mode GL_CLAMP, the texel from the border (or GL_TEXTURE_BORDER_COLOR) is used in the $2 \times 2$ array of weighted texels.

- For the wrapping mode GL_CLAMP_TO_EDGE, the border is always ignored. Texels at or near the edge of the texture are used for texturing calculations, but not the border.

- For the wrapping mode GL_CLAMP_TO_BORDER, if the texture coordinate is outside the range [0, 1], then only border texels (or if no border is present, the constant border color) are used for texture application. Near the edge of texture coordinates, texels from both the border and the interior texture may be sampled in a 2 × 2 array.

If you are using clamping, you can avoid having the rest of the surface affected by the texture. To do this, use alpha values of 0 for the edges (or borders, if they are specified) of the texture. The decal texture function directly uses the texture's alpha value in its calculations. If you are using one of the other texture functions, you may also need to enable blending with good source and destination factors. (See "Blending" in Chapter 6.)

To see the effects of wrapping, you must have texture coordinates that venture beyond [0.0, 1.0]. Start with Example 9-1, and modify the texture coordinates for the squares by mapping the texture coordinates from 0.0 to 4.0, as follows:

```
glBegin(GL_QUADS);
   glTexCoord2f(0.0, 0.0); glVertex3f(-2.0, -1.0, 0.0);
   glTexCoord2f(0.0, 4.0); glVertex3f(-2.0, 1.0, 0.0);
   glTexCoord2f(4.0, 4.0); glVertex3f(0.0, 1.0, 0.0);
   glTexCoord2f(4.0, 0.0); glVertex3f(0.0, -1.0, 0.0);

   glTexCoord2f(0.0, 0.0); glVertex3f(1.0, -1.0, 0.0);
   glTexCoord2f(0.0, 4.0); glVertex3f(1.0, 1.0, 0.0);
   glTexCoord2f(4.0, 4.0); glVertex3f(2.41421, 1.0, -1.41421);
   glTexCoord2f(4.0, 0.0); glVertex3f(2.41421, -1.0, -1.41421);
glEnd();
```

With GL_REPEAT wrapping, the result is as shown in Figure 9-10.

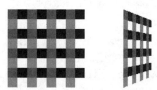

**Figure 9-10**     Repeating a Texture

In this case, the texture is repeated in both the *s*- and *t*- directions, since the following calls are made to **glTexParameter*()**:

```
glTexParameteri(GL_TEXTURE_2D, GL_TEXTURE_WRAP_S, GL_REPEAT);
glTexParameteri(GL_TEXTURE_2D, GL_TEXTURE_WRAP_T, GL_REPEAT);
```

Some OpenGL implementations support GL_MIRRORED_REPEAT wrapping, which reverses orientation at every integer texture coordinate boundary. Figure 9-11 shows the contrast between ordinary repeat wrapping (left) and the mirrored repeat (right).

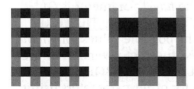

**Figure 9-11**    Comparing GL_REPEAT to GL_MIRRORED_REPEAT

In Figure 9-12, GL_CLAMP is used for each direction. Where the texture coordinate s or t is greater than one, the texel used is from where each texture coordinate is exactly one.

**Figure 9-12**    Clamping a Texture

Wrapping modes are independent for each direction. You can also clamp in one direction and repeat in the other, as shown in Figure 9-13.

**Figure 9-13**    Repeating and Clamping a Texture

You've now seen several arguments for **glTexParameter\*()**, which is summarized as follows.

## Automatic Texture-Coordinate Generation

You can use texture mapping to make contours on your models or to simulate the reflections from an arbitrary environment on a shiny model. To achieve these effects, let OpenGL automatically generate the texture coordinates for you, rather than explicitly assign them with **glTexCoord*()**. To generate texture coordinates automatically, use the command **glTexGen()**.

void **glTexGen**{ifd}(GLenum *coord*, GLenum *pname*, TYPE *param*);
void **glTexGen**{ifd}**v**(GLenum *coord*, GLenum *pname*, const TYPE *\*param*);

Specifies the functions for automatically generating texture coordinates. The first parameter, *coord*, must be GL_S, GL_T, GL_R, or GL_Q to indicate whether texture coordinate *s, t, r,* or *q* is to be generated. The *pname* parameter is GL_TEXTURE_GEN_MODE, GL_OBJECT_PLANE, or GL_EYE_PLANE. If it's GL_TEXTURE_GEN_MODE, *param* is an integer (or, in the vector version of the command, points to an integer) that is one of GL_OBJECT_LINEAR, GL_EYE_LINEAR, GL_SPHERE_MAP, GL_REFLECTION_MAP, or GL_NORMAL_MAP. These symbolic constants determine which function is used to generate the texture coordinate. With either of the other possible values for *pname*, *param* is a pointer to an array of values (for the vector version) specifying parameters for the texture-generation function.

The different methods of texture-coordinate generation have different uses. Specifying the reference plane in object coordinates is best when a texture image remains fixed to a moving object. Thus, GL_OBJECT_LINEAR would be used for putting a wood grain on a tabletop. Specifying the reference plane in eye coordinates (GL_EYE_LINEAR) is best for producing dynamic contour lines on moving objects. GL_EYE_LINEAR may be used by specialists in the geosciences who are drilling for oil or gas. As the drill goes deeper into the ground, the drill may be rendered with different colors to represent the layers of rock at increasing depths. GL_SPHERE_MAP and GL_REFLECTION_MAP are used mainly for spherical environment mapping, and GL_NORMAL_MAP is used for cube maps. (See "Sphere Map" on page 439 and "Cube Map Textures" on page 441.)

## Creating Contours

When GL_TEXTURE_GEN_MODE and GL_OBJECT_LINEAR are specified, the generation function is a linear combination of the object coordinates of the vertex $(x_0, y_0, z_0, w_0)$:

generated coordinate $= p_1 x_0 + p_2 y_0 + p_3 z_0 + p_4 w_0$

The $p_1, ..., p_4$ values are supplied as the *param* argument to **glTexGen\*v**(), with *pname* set to GL_OBJECT_PLANE. With $p_1, ..., p_4$ correctly normalized, this function gives the distance from the vertex to a plane. For example, if $p_2 = p_3 = p_4 = 0$ and $p_1 = 1$, the function gives the distance between the vertex and the plane $x = 0$. The distance is positive on one side of the plane, negative on the other, and zero if the vertex lies on the plane.

Initially, in Example 9-8, equally spaced contour lines are drawn on a teapot; the lines indicate the distance from the plane $x = 0$. The coefficients for the plane $x = 0$ are in this array:

```
static GLfloat xequalzero[] = {1.0, 0.0, 0.0, 0.0};
```

Since only one property is being shown (the distance from the plane), a one-dimensional texture map suffices. The texture map is a constant green color, except that at equally spaced intervals it includes a red mark. Since the teapot is sitting on the *xy*-plane, the contours are all perpendicular to its base. Plate 18 shows the picture drawn by the program.

In the same example, pressing the 's' key changes the parameters of the reference plane to

```
static GLfloat slanted[] = {1.0, 1.0, 1.0, 0.0};
```

The contour stripes are parallel to the plane $x + y + z = 0$, slicing across the teapot at an angle, as shown in Plate 18. To restore the reference plane to its initial value, $x = 0$, press the 'x' key.

**Example 9-8**    Automatic Texture-Coordinate Generation: texgen.c

```
#define stripeImageWidth 32
GLubyte stripeImage[4*stripeImageWidth];

static GLuint texName;

void makeStripeImage(void)
{
    int j;
```

```
        for (j = 0; j < stripeImageWidth; j++) {
            stripeImage[4*j]   = (GLubyte) ((j<=4) ? 255 : 0);
            stripeImage[4*j+1] = (GLubyte) ((j>4) ? 255 : 0);
            stripeImage[4*j+2] = (GLubyte) 0;
            stripeImage[4*j+3] = (GLubyte) 255;
        }
    }

    /*  planes for texture-coordinate generation  */
    static GLfloat xequalzero[] = {1.0, 0.0, 0.0, 0.0};
    static GLfloat slanted[] = {1.0, 1.0, 1.0, 0.0};
    static GLfloat *currentCoeff;
    static GLenum currentPlane;
    static GLint currentGenMode;

    void init(void)
    {
        glClearColor(0.0, 0.0, 0.0, 0.0);
        glEnable(GL_DEPTH_TEST);
        glShadeModel(GL_SMOOTH);

        makeStripeImage();
        glPixelStorei(GL_UNPACK_ALIGNMENT, 1);

        glGenTextures(1, &texName);
        glBindTexture(GL_TEXTURE_1D, texName);
        glTexParameteri(GL_TEXTURE_1D, GL_TEXTURE_WRAP_S, GL_REPEAT);
        glTexParameteri(GL_TEXTURE_1D, GL_TEXTURE_MAG_FILTER,
                        GL_LINEAR);
        glTexParameteri(GL_TEXTURE_1D, GL_TEXTURE_MIN_FILTER,
                        GL_LINEAR);
        glTexImage1D(GL_TEXTURE_1D, 0, GL_RGBA, stripeImageWidth, 0,
                     GL_RGBA, GL_UNSIGNED_BYTE, stripeImage);

        glTexEnvf(GL_TEXTURE_ENV, GL_TEXTURE_ENV_MODE, GL_MODULATE);
        currentCoeff = xequalzero;
        currentGenMode = GL_OBJECT_LINEAR;
        currentPlane = GL_OBJECT_PLANE;
        glTexGeni(GL_S, GL_TEXTURE_GEN_MODE, currentGenMode);
        glTexGenfv(GL_S, currentPlane, currentCoeff);

        glEnable(GL_TEXTURE_GEN_S);
        glEnable(GL_TEXTURE_1D);
        glEnable(GL_CULL_FACE);
        glEnable(GL_LIGHTING);
        glEnable(GL_LIGHT0);
```

```
   glEnable(GL_AUTO_NORMAL);
   glEnable(GL_NORMALIZE);
   glFrontFace(GL_CW);
   glCullFace(GL_BACK);
   glMaterialf(GL_FRONT, GL_SHININESS, 64.0);
}

void display(void)
{
   glClear(GL_COLOR_BUFFER_BIT | GL_DEPTH_BUFFER_BIT);

   glPushMatrix();
   glRotatef(45.0, 0.0, 0.0, 1.0);
   glBindTexture(GL_TEXTURE_1D, texName);
   glutSolidTeapot(2.0);
   glPopMatrix();
   glFlush();
}

void reshape(int w, int h)
{
   glViewport(0, 0, (GLsizei) w, (GLsizei) h);
   glMatrixMode(GL_PROJECTION);
   glLoadIdentity();
   if (w <= h)
       glOrtho(-3.5, 3.5, -3.5*(GLfloat)h/(GLfloat)w,
                3.5*(GLfloat)h/(GLfloat)w, -3.5, 3.5);
   else
       glOrtho(-3.5*(GLfloat)w/(GLfloat)h,
                3.5*(GLfloat)w/(GLfloat)h, -3.5, 3.5, -3.5, 3.5);
   glMatrixMode(GL_MODELVIEW);
   glLoadIdentity();
}

void keyboard(unsigned char key, int x, int y)
{
   switch (key) {
      case 'e':
      case 'E':
         currentGenMode = GL_EYE_LINEAR;
         currentPlane = GL_EYE_PLANE;
         glTexGeni(GL_S, GL_TEXTURE_GEN_MODE, currentGenMode);
         glTexGenfv(GL_S, currentPlane, currentCoeff);
         glutPostRedisplay();
         break;
      case 'o':
      case 'O':
```

```
                    currentGenMode = GL_OBJECT_LINEAR;
                    currentPlane = GL_OBJECT_PLANE;
                    glTexGeni(GL_S, GL_TEXTURE_GEN_MODE, currentGenMode);
                    glTexGenfv(GL_S, currentPlane, currentCoeff);
                    glutPostRedisplay();
                    break;
                case 's':
                case 'S':
                    currentCoeff = slanted;
                    glTexGenfv(GL_S, currentPlane, currentCoeff);
                    glutPostRedisplay();
                    break;
                case 'x':
                case 'X':
                    currentCoeff = xequalzero;
                    glTexGenfv(GL_S, currentPlane, currentCoeff);
                    glutPostRedisplay();
                    break;
                case 27:
                    exit(0);
                    break;
                default:
                    break;
        }
    }

    int main(int argc, char** argv)
    {
        glutInit(&argc, argv);
        glutInitDisplayMode(GLUT_SINGLE | GLUT_RGB | GLUT_DEPTH);
        glutInitWindowSize(256, 256);
        glutInitWindowPosition(100, 100);
        glutCreateWindow(argv[0]);
        init();
        glutDisplayFunc(display);
        glutReshapeFunc(reshape);
        glutKeyboardFunc(keyboard);
        glutMainLoop();
        return 0;
    }
```

You enable texture-coordinate generation for the *s*-coordinate by passing
GL_TEXTURE_GEN_S to **glEnable()**. To generate other coordinates, enable
them with GL_TEXTURE_GEN_T, GL_TEXTURE_GEN_R, or GL_TEXTURE_
GEN_Q. Use **glDisable()** with the appropriate constant to disable coordinate generation. Also note the use of GL_REPEAT to cause the contour lines
to be repeated across the teapot.

The GL_OBJECT_LINEAR function calculates the texture coordinates in the model's coordinate system. Initially, in Example 9-8, the GL_OBJECT_ LINEAR function is used, so the contour lines remain perpendicular to the base of the teapot, no matter how the teapot is rotated or viewed. However, if you press the 'e' key, the texture-generation mode is changed from GL_OBJECT_LINEAR to GL_EYE_LINEAR, and the contour lines are calculated relative to the eye coordinate system. (Pressing the 'o' key restores GL_OBJECT_LINEAR as the texture-generation mode.) If the reference plane is $x = 0$, the result is a teapot with red stripes parallel to the $yz$-plane from the eye's point of view, as shown in Plate 18. Mathematically, you are multiplying the vector $(p_1\ p_2\ p_3\ p_4)$ by the inverse of the modelview matrix to obtain the values used to calculate the distance to the plane. The texture coordinate is generated with the following function:

$$\text{generated coordinate} = p_1'x_e + p_2'y_e + p_3'z_e + p_4'w_e$$

where $(p_1'\ p_2'\ p_3'\ p_4') = (p_1\ p_2\ p_3\ p_4)\mathbf{M}^{-1}$

In this case, $(x_e, y_e, z_e, w_e)$ are the eye coordinates of the vertex, and $p_1, ..., p_4$ are supplied as the *param* argument to **glTexGen\*()**, with *pname* set to GL_EYE_PLANE. The primed values are calculated only at the time they're specified, so this operation isn't as computationally expensive as it looks.

In all these examples, a single texture coordinate is used to generate contours. $s$, $t$, and (if needed) $r$ texture coordinates can be generated independently, however, to indicate the distances to two or three different planes. With a properly constructed two- or three-dimensional texture map, the resulting two or three sets of contours can be viewed simultaneously. For an added level of complexity, you can mix generation functions. For example, you can calculate the $s$-coordinate using GL_OBJECT_LINEAR, and the $t$-coordinate using GL_EYE_LINEAR.

## Sphere Map

### Advanced

Advanced

The goal of environment mapping is to render an object as if it were perfectly reflective, so that the colors on its surface are those reflected to the eye from its surroundings. In other words, if you look at a perfectly polished, perfectly reflective silver object in a room, you see the reflections of the walls, floor, and other items in the room from the object. (A classic example of using environment mapping is the evil, morphing cyborg in the film *Terminator 2*.) The objects whose reflections you see depend on the position of your eye and on the position and surface angles of the silver object. To perform environment mapping, all you have to do is create an appropriate texture map and then have OpenGL generate the texture coordinates for you.

Environment mapping is an approximation based on the assumption that the items in the environment are far away in comparison with the surfaces of the shiny object—that is, it's a small object in a large room. With this assumption, to find the color of a point on the surface, take the ray from the eye to the surface, and reflect the ray off the surface. The direction of the reflected ray completely determines the color to be painted there. Encoding a color for each direction on a flat texture map is equivalent to putting a polished perfect sphere in the middle of the environment and taking a picture of it with a camera that has a lens with a very long focal length placed far away. Mathematically, the lens has an infinite focal length and the camera is infinitely far away. The encoding therefore covers a circular region of the texture map, tangent to the top, bottom, left, and right edges of the map. The texture values outside the circle make no difference, because they are never accessed in environment mapping.

To make a perfectly correct environment texture map, you need to obtain a large silvered sphere, take a photograph of it in some environment with a camera located an infinite distance away and with a lens that has an infinite focal length, and scan in the photograph. To approximate this result, you can use a scanned-in photograph of an environment taken with an extremely wide-angle (or fish-eye) lens. Plate 21 shows a photograph taken with such a lens and the results when that image is used as an environment map.

Once you've created a texture designed for environment mapping, you need to invoke OpenGL's environment-mapping algorithm. This algorithm finds the point on the surface of the sphere with the same tangent surface as that of the point on the object being rendered, and it paints the object's point with the color visible on the sphere at the corresponding point.

To generate automatically the texture coordinates to support environment mapping, use this code in your program:

```
glTexGeni(GL_S, GL_TEXTURE_GEN_MODE, GL_SPHERE_MAP);
glTexGeni(GL_T, GL_TEXTURE_GEN_MODE, GL_SPHERE_MAP);
glEnable(GL_TEXTURE_GEN_S);
glEnable(GL_TEXTURE_GEN_T);
```

The GL_SPHERE_MAP constant creates the proper texture coordinates for the environment mapping. As shown, you need to specify it for both the s- and t-directions. However, you don't have to specify any parameters for the texture-coordinate generation function.

The GL_SPHERE_MAP texture function generates texture coordinates using the following mathematical steps:

1. **u** is the unit vector pointing from the origin to the vertex (in eye coordinates).

2. **n'** is the current normal vector, after transformation to eye coordinates.

3. **r** is the reflection vector, $(r_x\ r_y\ r_z)^T$, which is calculated by $\mathbf{u} - 2\mathbf{n'n'}^T\mathbf{u}$.

4. An interim value, $m$, is calculated by

$$m = 2\sqrt{r_x^2 + r_y^2 + (r_z + 1)^2}$$

5. Finally, the $s$ and $t$ texture coordinates are calculated by

$$s = r_x/m + \frac{1}{2}$$

and

$$t = r_y/m + \frac{1}{2}$$

## Cube Map Textures

### Advanced

Advanced

Cube map textures are a special technique that uses a set of six two-dimensional texture images to form a texture cube centered at the origin. For each fragment, the texture coordinates $(s, t, r)$ are treated as a direction vector, with each texel representing what on the texture cube is "seen" from the origin. Cube maps are ideal for environment, reflection, and lighting effects. Cube maps can also wrap a spherical object with textures, distributing texels relatively evenly on all its sides.

The cube map textures are supplied by calling **glTexImage2D()** six times, with the *target* argument indicating the face of the cube (+X, −X, +Y, −Y, +Z, or −Z). As the name implies, each cube map texture must have the same dimensions so that a cube is formed with the same number of texels on each side, as shown in this code, where *imageSize* has been set to a power of 2:

```
glTexImage2D(GL_TEXTURE_CUBE_MAP_POSITIVE_X, 0, GL_RGBA,
  imageSize, imageSize, 0, GL_RGBA, GL_UNSIGNED_BYTE, image1);
glTexImage2D(GL_TEXTURE_CUBE_MAP_NEGATIVE_X, 0, GL_RGBA,
  imageSize, imageSize, 0, GL_RGBA, GL_UNSIGNED_BYTE, image4);
glTexImage2D(GL_TEXTURE_CUBE_MAP_POSITIVE_Y, 0, GL_RGBA,
  imageSize, imageSize, 0, GL_RGBA, GL_UNSIGNED_BYTE, image2);
glTexImage2D(GL_TEXTURE_CUBE_MAP_NEGATIVE_Y, 0, GL_RGBA,
  imageSize, imageSize, 0, GL_RGBA, GL_UNSIGNED_BYTE, image5);
glTexImage2D(GL_TEXTURE_CUBE_MAP_POSITIVE_Z, 0, GL_RGBA,
  imageSize, imageSize, 0, GL_RGBA, GL_UNSIGNED_BYTE, image3);
glTexImage2D(GL_TEXTURE_CUBE_MAP_NEGATIVE_Z, 0, GL_RGBA,
  imageSize, imageSize, 0, GL_RGBA, GL_UNSIGNED_BYTE, image6);
```

Useful cube map texture images may be generated by setting up a (real or synthetic) camera at the origin of a scene and taking six "snapshots" with 90-degree field-of-view, oriented along the positive and negative axes. The "snapshots" break up the entire 3D space into six frustums, which intersect at the origin.

Cube map functionality is orthogonal to many other texturing operations, so cube maps work with standard texturing features, such as texture borders, mipmaps, copying images, subimages, and multitexturing. There is a special proxy texture target for cube maps (GL_PROXY_TEXTURE_CUBE_MAP) because a cube map generally uses six times as much memory as an ordinary 2D texture. Texture parameters and texture objects should be established for the entire cube map as a whole, not for the six individual cube faces. The following code is an example of setting wrapping and filtering methods with the *target* GL_TEXTURE_CUBE_MAP:

```
glTexParameteri(GL_TEXTURE_CUBE_MAP, GL_TEXTURE_WRAP_S,
                GL_REPEAT);
glTexParameteri(GL_TEXTURE_CUBE_MAP, GL_TEXTURE_WRAP_T,
                GL_REPEAT);
glTexParameteri(GL_TEXTURE_CUBE_MAP, GL_TEXTURE_WRAP_R,
                GL_REPEAT);
glTexParameteri(GL_TEXTURE_CUBE_MAP, GL_TEXTURE_MAG_FILTER,
                GL_NEAREST);
glTexParameteri(GL_TEXTURE_CUBE_MAP, GL_TEXTURE_MIN_FILTER,
                GL_NEAREST);
```

To determine which texture (and texels) to use for a given fragment, the current texture coordinates (*s, t, r*) first select one of the six textures, based upon which of *s*, *t*, and *r* has the largest absolute value (major axis) and its sign (orientation). The remaining two coordinates are divided by the coordinate with the largest value to determine a new $(s', t')$, which is used to look up the corresponding texel(s) in the selected texture of the cube map.

Although you can calculate and specify the texture coordinates explicitly, this is generally laborious and unnecessary. Almost always, you'll want to use **glTexGen\*()** to automatically generate cube map texture coordinates, using one of the two special texture coordinate generation modes: GL_REFLECTION_MAP or GL_NORMAL_MAP.

GL_REFLECTION_MAP uses the same calculations (until step 3 of the sphere-mapping coordinate computation described in "Sphere Map" on page 439) as the GL_SPHERE_MAP texture coordinate generation to determine $(r_x \; r_y \; r_z)$ for use as $(s, t, r)$. The reflection map mode is well-suited for environment mapping as an alternative to sphere mapping.

GL_NORMAL_MAP is particularly useful for rendering scenes with infinite (or distant local) light sources and diffuse reflection. GL_NORMAL_MAP uses the model-view matrix to transform the vertex's normal into eye coordinates. The resulting $(n_x \; n_y \; n_z)$ becomes texture coordinates $(s, t, r)$. In Example 9-9, the normal map mode is used for texture generation and cube map texturing is also enabled.

**Example 9-9**  Generating Cube Map Texture Coordinates: cubemap.c

```
glTexGeni(GL_S, GL_TEXTURE_GEN_MODE, GL_NORMAL_MAP);
glTexGeni(GL_T, GL_TEXTURE_GEN_MODE, GL_NORMAL_MAP);
glTexGeni(GL_R, GL_TEXTURE_GEN_MODE, GL_NORMAL_MAP);
glEnable(GL_TEXTURE_GEN_S);
glEnable(GL_TEXTURE_GEN_T);
glEnable(GL_TEXTURE_GEN_R);
/*  turn on cube map texturing  */
glEnable(GL_TEXTURE_CUBE_MAP);
```

# Multitexturing

During standard texturing, a single texture image is applied once to a polygon. Multitexturing allows several textures to be applied, one by one in a pipeline of texture operations, to the same polygon. There is a series of *texture units*, where each texture unit performs a single texturing operation and successively passes its result onto the next texture unit, until all defined units are completed. Figure 9-14 shows how a fragment might undergo four texturing operations—one for each of four texture units.

Multitexturing enables advanced rendering techniques, such as lighting effects, decals, compositing, and detail textures.

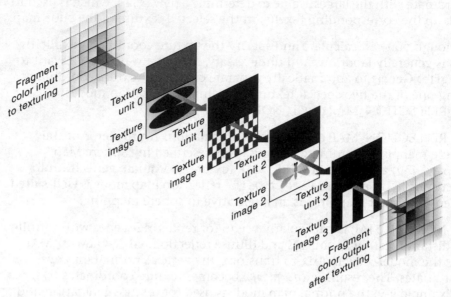

**Figure 9-14**    Multitexture Processing Pipeline

### Steps in Multitexturing

To write code that uses multitexturing, perform the following steps:

>   **Note:** In feedback mode, multitexturing is undefined beyond the first
>   texture unit.

1.  For each texturing unit, establish the texturing state, including texture
    image, filter, environment, coordinate generation, and matrix. Use
    **glActiveTexture()** to change the current texture unit. This is discussed
    further in the next subsection, "Establishing Texture Units." You may
    also call **glGetIntegerv(GL_MAX_TEXTURE_UNITS,...)** to see how
    many texturing units are available on your implementation. In a
    worst-case scenario, there are at least two texture units.

2.  During vertex specification, use **glMultiTexCoord*()** to specify more
    than one texture coordinate per vertex. A different texture coordinate
    may be used for each texturing unit. Each texture coordinate will be
    used during a different texturing pass. Automatic texture-coordinate
    generation and specification of texture coordinates in vertex arrays are
    special cases of this situation. The special cases are described in "Other
    Methods of Texture-Coordinate Specification" on page 448.

## Establishing Texture Units

Multitexturing introduces multiple texture units, which are additional texture application passes. Each texture unit has identical capabilities and houses its own texturing state, including the following:

- Texture image
- Filtering parameters
- Environment application
- Texture matrix stack
- Automatic texture-coordinate generation
- Vertex-array specification (if needed)

Each texture unit combines the previous fragment color with its texture image, according to its texture state. The resulting fragment color is passed onto the next texture unit, if it is active.

To assign texture information to each texture unit, the routine **glActiveTexture()** selects the current texture unit to be modified. After that, calls to **glTexImage*()**, **glTexParameter*()**, **glTexEnv*()**, **glTexGen*()**, and **glBindTexture()** affect only the current texture unit. Queries of these texture states also apply to the current texture unit, as well as queries of the current texture coordinates and current raster texture coordinates.

---

void **glActiveTexture**(GLenum *texUnit*);

Selects the texture unit that is currently modified by texturing routines. *texUnit* is a symbolic constant of the form GL_TEXTURE*i*, where *i* is in the range from 0 to $k - 1$, and $k$ is the maximum number of texture units.

---

If you use texture objects, you can bind a texture to the current texture unit. The current texture unit has the values of the texture state contained within the texture object (including the texture image).

The following code fragment, Example 9-10, has two distinct parts. In the first part, two ordinary texture objects are created (assume the arrays *texels0* and *texels1* define texture images). In the second part, the two texture objects are used to set up two texture units.

**Example 9-10**  Initializing Texture Units for Multitexturing: multitex.c

```
/*  Two ordinary texture objects are created  */
GLuint texNames[2];
glGenTextures(2, texNames);
glBindTexture(GL_TEXTURE_2D, texNames[0]);
glTexImage2D(GL_TEXTURE_2D, 0, GL_RGBA, 32, 32, 0, GL_RGBA,
             GL_UNSIGNED_BYTE, texels0);
glTexParameteri(GL_TEXTURE_2D,GL_TEXTURE_MIN_FILTER,GL_NEAREST);
glTexParameteri(GL_TEXTURE_2D,GL_TEXTURE_MAG_FILTER,GL_NEAREST);
glTexParameteri(GL_TEXTURE_2D, GL_TEXTURE_WRAP_S, GL_REPEAT);
glTexParameteri(GL_TEXTURE_2D, GL_TEXTURE_WRAP_T, GL_REPEAT);
glBindTexture(GL_TEXTURE_2D, texNames[1]);
glTexImage2D(GL_TEXTURE_2D, 0, GL_RGBA, 16, 16, 0, GL_RGBA,
             GL_UNSIGNED_BYTE, texels1);
glTexParameteri(GL_TEXTURE_2D,GL_TEXTURE_MIN_FILTER,GL_LINEAR);
glTexParameteri(GL_TEXTURE_2D,GL_TEXTURE_MAG_FILTER,GL_LINEAR);
glTexParameteri(GL_TEXTURE_2D, GL_TEXTURE_WRAP_S,
                GL_CLAMP_TO_EDGE);
glTexParameteri(GL_TEXTURE_2D, GL_TEXTURE_WRAP_T,
                GL_CLAMP_TO_EDGE);
/*  Use the two texture objects to define two texture units
 *  for use in multitexturing.  */
glActiveTexture(GL_TEXTURE0);
glEnable(GL_TEXTURE_2D);
glBindTexture(GL_TEXTURE_2D, texNames[0]);
glTexEnvi(GL_TEXTURE_ENV, GL_TEXTURE_ENV_MODE, GL_REPLACE);
glMatrixMode(GL_TEXTURE);
   glLoadIdentity();
   glTranslatef(0.5f, 0.5f, 0.0f);
   glRotatef(45.0f, 0.0f, 0.0f, 1.0f);
   glTranslatef(-0.5f, -0.5f, 0.0f);
glMatrixMode(GL_MODELVIEW);
glActiveTexture(GL_TEXTURE1);
glEnable(GL_TEXTURE_2D);
glBindTexture(GL_TEXTURE_2D, texNames[1]);
glTexEnvi(GL_TEXTURE_ENV, GL_TEXTURE_ENV_MODE, GL_MODULATE);
```

When a textured polygon is now rendered, it is rendered with two texturing units. In the first unit, the *texels0* texture image is applied with nearest texel filtering, repeat wrapping, replacement texture environment, and a texture matrix that rotates the texture image. After the first unit is completed, the newly textured polygon is sent onto the second texture unit (GL_TEXTURE1), where it is processed with the *texels1* texture image with linear filtering, edge clamping, modulation texture environment, and the default identity texture matrix.

**Note:** Operations to a texture attribute group (using **glPushAttrib()**, **glPushClientAttrib()**, **glPopAttrib()**, or **glPopClientAttrib()**) save or restore the texture state of *all* texture units (except for the texture matrix stack).

## Specifying Vertices and Their Texture Coordinates

With multitexturing, it isn't enough to have one set of texture coordinates per vertex. You need to have one set for each texture unit for each vertex. Instead of using **glTexCoord*()**, you must use **glMultiTexCoord*()**, which specifies the texture unit, as well as the texture coordinates.

---

void **glMultiTexCoord{1234}{sifd}**(GLenum *texUnit*, *TYPE coords*);
void **glMultiTexCoord{1234}{sifd}v**(GLenum *texUnit*, const *TYPE *coords*);

Sets the texture-coordinate data $(s, t, r, q)$ in *coords* for use with the texture unit *texUnit*. The enumerated values for *texUnit* are the same as for **glActiveTexture()**.

---

In Example 9-11, a triangle is given the two sets of texture coordinates necessary for multitexturing with two active texture units.

**Example 9-11**   Specifying Vertices for Multitexturing

```
glBegin(GL_TRIANGLES);
glMultiTexCoord2f(GL_TEXTURE0, 0.0, 0.0);
glMultiTexCoord2f(GL_TEXTURE1, 1.0, 0.0);
glVertex2f(0.0, 0.0);
glMultiTexCoord2f(GL_TEXTURE0, 0.5, 1.0);
glMultiTexCoord2f(GL_TEXTURE1, 0.5, 0.0);
glVertex2f(50.0, 100.0);
glMultiTexCoord2f(GL_TEXTURE0, 1.0, 0.0);
glMultiTexCoord2f(GL_TEXTURE1, 1.0, 1.0);
glVertex2f(100.0, 0.0);
glEnd();
```

**Note:** If you are multitexturing and you use **glTexCoord*()**, you are setting the texture coordinates for the first texture unit. In other words, using **glTexCoord*()** is equivalent to using **glMultiTexCoord*(GL_TEXTURE0,...)**.

In the rare case that you are multitexturing a bitmap or image rectangle, you need to associate several texture coordinates with each raster position. Therefore, you must call **glMultiTexCoord*()** several times, once for each active texture unit, for each **glRasterPos*()** or **glWindowPos*()** call. (Since

If the texture environment mode is GL_COMBINE, then the GL_COMBINE_RGB, GL_COMBINE_ALPHA, GL_RGB_SCALE, or GL_ALPHA_SCALE parameters are also used. For the GL_COMBINE_RGB function, the GL_SOURCE*i*_RGB and GL_OPERAND*i*_RGB parameters (where *i* is 0, 1, or 2) also may be specified. Similarly for the GL_COMBINE_ALPHA function, GL_SOURCE*i*_ALPHA and GL_OPERAND*i*_ALPHA may be specified.

| glTexEnv pname | glTexEnv param |
|---|---|
| GL_TEXTURE_ENV_MODE | GL_DECAL, GL_REPLACE, GL_MODULATE, GL_BLEND, GL_ADD, or GL_COMBINE |
| GL_TEXTURE_ENV_COLOR | array of 4 floating-point numbers: (R, G, B, A) |
| GL_COMBINE_RGB | GL_REPLACE, GL_MODULATE, GL_ADD, GL_ADD_SIGNED, GL_INTERPOLATE, GL_SUBTRACT, GL_DOT3_RGB, or GL_DOT3_RGBA |
| GL_COMBINE_ALPHA | GL_REPLACE, GL_MODULATE, GL_ADD, GL_ADD_SIGNED, GL_INTERPOLATE, or GL_SUBTRACT |
| GL_SRC*i*_RGB or GL_SRC*i*_ALPHA (where *i* is 0, 1, or 2) | GL_TEXTURE, GL_TEXTURE*n* (where *n* denotes the *n*th texture unit and multitexturing is enabled), GL_CONSTANT, GL_PRIMARY_COLOR, or GL_PREVIOUS |
| GL_OPERAND*i*_RGB (where *i* is 0, 1, or 2) | GL_SRC_COLOR, GL_ONE_MINUS_SRC_COLOR, GL_SRC_ALPHA, or GL_ONE_MINUS_SRC_ALPHA |
| GL_OPERAND*i*_ALPHA (where *i* is 0, 1, or 2) | GL_SRC_ALPHA, or GL_ONE_MINUS_SRC_ALPHA |
| GL_RGB_SCALE | floating-point color scaling factor |
| GL_ALPHA_SCALE | floating-point alpha scaling factor |

**Table 9-8**    Texture Environment Parameters If *target* Is GL_TEXTURE_ENV

Here are the steps for using combiner functions. If you are multitexturing, you may use a different combiner function for every texture unit and thus repeat these steps for each unit.

• To use any combiner function, you must call

```
glTexEnvf(GL_TEXTURE_ENV, GL_TEXTURE_ENV_MODE, GL_COMBINE);
```

- You should specify how you want RGB or alpha values to be combined (see Table 9-9). For instance, Example 9-13 directs the current texture unit to subtract RGB and alpha values of one source from another source.

**Example 9-13** Setting the Programmable Combiner Functions

```
glTexEnvf(GL_TEXTURE_ENV, GL_COMBINE_RGB, GL_SUBTRACT);
glTexEnvf(GL_TEXTURE_ENV, GL_COMBINE_ALPHA, GL_SUBTRACT);
```

| glTexEnv param | Combiner Function |
|---|---|
| GL_REPLACE | $Arg0$ |
| GL_MODULATE (default) | $Arg0 * Arg1$ |
| GL_ADD | $Arg0 + Arg1$ |
| GL_ADD_SIGNED | $Arg0 + Arg1 - 0.5$ |
| GL_INTERPOLATE | $Arg0 * Arg2 + Arg1 * (1 - Arg2)$ |
| GL_SUBTRACT | $Arg0 - Arg1$ |
| GL_DOT3_RGB GL_DOT3_RGBA | $4 * ((Arg0_r - 0.5) * (Arg1_r - 0.5) + (Arg0_g - 0.5) * (Arg1_g - 0.5) + (Arg0_b - 0.5) * (Arg1_b - 0.5))$ |

**Table 9-9**     GL_COMBINE_RGB and GL_COMBINE_ALPHA Functions

**Note:** GL_DOT3_RGB and GL_DOT3_RGBA are used only for GL_COMBINE_RGB and not used for GL_COMBINE_ALPHA.

The GL_DOT3_RGB and GL_DOT3_RGBA modes differ subtly. With GL_DOT3_RGB, the same dot product is placed into all three (R, G, B) values. For GL_DOT3_RGBA, the result is placed into all four (R, G, B, A).

- Specify the source for the $i$th argument of the combiner function with the constant GL_SOURCE$i$_RGB. The number of arguments (up to three) depends upon the type of function chosen. As shown in Table 9-9, GL_SUBTRACT requires two arguments, which may be set with the following code:

**Example 9-14** Setting the Combiner Function Sources

```
glTexEnvf(GL_TEXTURE_ENV, GL_SRC0_RGB, GL_TEXTURE);
glTexEnvf(GL_TEXTURE_ENV, GL_SRC1_RGB, GL_PREVIOUS);
```

When *pname* is GL_SOURCE*i*_RGB, these are your options for *param* along with how the source is determined:

- GL_TEXTURE—the source for the *i*th argument is the texture of the current texture unit

- GL_TEXTURE*n*—the texture associated with texture unit *n*. (If you use this source, texture unit *n* must be enabled and valid, or the result will be undefined.)

- GL_CONSTANT—the constant color set with GL_TEXTURE_ENV_COLOR

- GL_PRIMARY_COLOR—the incoming fragment to texture unit 0, which is the fragment color, prior to texturing

- GL_PREVIOUS—the incoming fragment from the previous texture unit (for texture unit 0, this is the same as GL_PRIMARY_COLOR)

If you suppose that the GL_SUBTRACT combiner code in Example 9-14 is set for texture unit 2, then the output from texture unit 1 (GL_PREVIOUS, *Arg1*) is subtracted from texture unit 2 (GL_TEXTURE, *Arg0*).

- Specify which values (RGB or alpha) of the sources are used and how they are used:

  - GL_OPERAND*i*_RGB matches the corresponding GL_SOURCE*i*_RGB and determines the color values for the current GL_COMBINE_RGB function. If GL_OPERAND*i*_RGB is *pname*, then *param* must be one of GL_SRC_COLOR, GL_ONE_MINUS_SRC_COLOR, GL_SRC_ALPHA, or GL_ONE_MINUS_SRC_ALPHA.

  - Similarly, GL_OPERAND*i*_ALPHA matches the corresponding GL_SOURCE*i*_ALPHA and determines the alpha values for the current GL_COMBINE_ALPHA function. However, *param* is limited to either GL_SRC_ALPHA or GL_ONE_MINUS_SRC_ALPHA.

When GL_SRC_ALPHA is used for the GL_COMBINE_RGB function, the alpha values for the combiner source are interpreted as R, G, B values. In Example 9-15, the three R, G, B components for *Arg2* are (0.4, 0.4, 0.4).

**Example 9-15**  Using an Alpha Value for RGB Combiner Operations

```
static GLfloat constColor[4] = {0.1, 0.2, 0.3, 0.4};
glTexEnvfv(GL_TEXTURE_ENV, GL_TEXTURE_ENV_COLOR, constColor);
glTexEnvf(GL_TEXTURE_ENV, GL_SRC2_RGB, GL_CONSTANT);
glTexEnvf(GL_TEXTURE_ENV, GL_OPERAND2_RGB, GL_SRC_ALPHA);
```

In Example 9-15, if the operand had instead been GL_SRC_COLOR, the RGB components would be (0.1, 0.2, 0.3). For GL_ONE_MINUS* modes, a value's complement (either 1–color or 1–alpha) is used for combiner calculations. In Example 9-15, if the operand is GL_ONE_MINUS_SRC_COLOR, the RGB components are (0.9, 0.8, 0.7). For GL_ONE_MINUS_SRC_ALPHA, the result is (0.6, 0.6, 0.6).

- Optionally choose RGB or alpha scaling factors. The defaults are

```
glTexEnvf(GL_TEXTURE_ENV, GL_RGB_SCALE, 1.0);
glTexEnvf(GL_TEXTURE_ENV, GL_ALPHA_SCALE, 1.0);
```

- Finally draw the geometry, ensuring vertices have associated texture coordinates.

## The Interpolation Combiner Function

The interpolation function helps illustrate texture combiners, because it uses the maximum number of arguments and several source and operand modes. Example 9-16 is a portion of the sample program combiner.c.

**Example 9-16**  Interpolation Combiner Function: combiner.c

```
/* for use as constant texture color */
static GLfloat constColor[4] = {0.0, 0.0, 0.0, 0.0};

constColor[3] = 0.2;
glTexEnvfv(GL_TEXTURE_ENV, GL_TEXTURE_ENV_COLOR, constColor);
glBindTexture(GL_TEXTURE_2D, texName[0]);
glTexEnvf(GL_TEXTURE_ENV, GL_TEXTURE_ENV_MODE, GL_COMBINE);
glTexEnvf(GL_TEXTURE_ENV, GL_COMBINE_RGB, GL_INTERPOLATE);
glTexEnvf(GL_TEXTURE_ENV, GL_SRC0_RGB, GL_TEXTURE);
glTexEnvf(GL_TEXTURE_ENV, GL_OPERAND0_RGB, GL_SRC_COLOR);
glTexEnvf(GL_TEXTURE_ENV, GL_SRC1_RGB, GL_PREVIOUS);
glTexEnvf(GL_TEXTURE_ENV, GL_OPERAND1_RGB, GL_SRC_COLOR);
glTexEnvf(GL_TEXTURE_ENV, GL_SRC2_RGB, GL_CONSTANT);
glTexEnvf(GL_TEXTURE_ENV, GL_OPERAND2_RGB, GL_SRC_ALPHA);

/* geometry is now rendered */
```

In Example 9-16, there is only one active texture unit. Since GL_INTERPOLATE is the combiner function, there are three arguments, and they are combined with the following formula: *(Arg0 \* Arg2) + (Arg1 \* (1 – Arg2))*. The three arguments are as follows:

- *Arg0*, GL_TEXTURE, the texture image associated with the currently bound texture object (*texName[0]*)

- *Arg1*, GL_PREVIOUS, the result of the previous texture unit, but since this is texture unit 0, GL_PREVIOUS is the fragment prior to texturing

- *Arg2*, GL_CONSTANT, a constant color; currently (0.0, 0.0, 0.0, 0.2)

The interpolated result you get is a weighted blending of the texture image and the untextured fragment. Because GL_SRC_ALPHA is specified for GL_OPERAND2_RGB, the alpha value of the constant color (*Arg2*) serves as the weighting.

If you run the sample program combiner.c, you'll see 20 percent of the texture blended with 80 percent of a smooth-shaded polygon. combiner.c also varies the alpha value of the constant color, so you'll see the results of different weightings.

Examining the interpolation function explains why several of the OpenGL default values were chosen. The third argument for interpolation is intended as weight for the two other sources. Since interpolation is the only combiner function to use three arguments, it's safe to make GL_CONSTANT the default for *Arg2*. At first glance, it may seem odd that the default value for GL_OPERAND2_RGB is GL_SRC_ALPHA. But the interpolation weight is usually the same for all three color components, so using a single value makes sense, and taking it from the alpha value of the constant is convenient.

| glTexEnv pname | Initial Value for param |
| --- | --- |
| GL_SRC0_RGB | GL_TEXTURE |
| GL_SRC1_RGB | GL_PREVIOUS |
| GL_SRC2_RGB | GL_CONSTANT |
| GL_OPERAND0_RGB | GL_SRC_COLOR |
| GL_OPERAND1_RGB | GL_SRC_COLOR |
| GL_OPERAND2_RGB | GL_SRC_ALPHA |

**Table 9-10**    Default Values for Some Texture Environment Modes

# Applying Secondary Color after Texturing

While applying a texture to a typical fragment, only a primary color is combined with the texel colors. The primary color may be the result of lighting calculations or **glColor\*()**.

After texturing, but before fog calculations, sometimes a secondary color is also applied to a fragment. Application of a secondary color may result in a more realistic highlight on a textured object.

## Secondary Color When Lighting Is Disabled

If lighting is not enabled and the color sum mode is enabled (by **glEnable(GL_COLOR_SUM)**), then the current secondary color (set by **glSecondaryColor\*()**) is added to the post-texturing fragment color.

---

void **glSecondaryColor3**{b s i f d ub us ui}(*TYPE r, TYPE g, TYPE b*);
void **glSecondaryColor3**{b s i f d ub us ui}**v**(const *TYPE \*values*);

---

Sets the red, green, and blue values for the current secondary color. The first suffix indicates the data type for parameters: byte, short, integer, float, double, unsigned byte, unsigned short, or unsigned integer. If there is a second suffix, **v**, then *values* is a pointer to an array of values of the given data type.

**glSecondaryColor\*()** accepts the same data types and interprets values the same way that **glColor\*()** does. (See Table 4-1 on page 178.) Secondary colors may also be specified in vertex arrays.

## Secondary Specular Color When Lighting Is Enabled

Texturing operations are applied after lighting, but blending specular highlights with a texture's colors usually lessens the effect of lighting. As discussed earlier (in "Selecting a Lighting Model" on page 207), you can calculate two colors per vertex: a primary color, which consists of all nonspecular contributions, and a secondary color, which is a sum of all specular contributions. If specular color is separated, the secondary (specular) color is added to the fragment after the texturing calculation.

**Note:** If lighting is enabled, the secondary specular color is applied, regardless of the GL_COLOR_SUM mode, and any secondary color set by **glSecondaryColor*()** is ignored.

## Point Sprites

While OpenGL supports antialiasing of points with a point size greater than one (as set with **glPointSize()**), the visual results may not be precisely what your application requires. Point *sprites* allow better control over the shading of large points. By default, when point sprites are enabled, every fragment in the sprite is assigned the same state as the vertex that initiated the point's rendering. Point sprites modify how fragment data is generated by iterating texture coordinates across the fragments of the expanded point.

To enable point sprites, call **glEnable()** with a parameter of GL_POINT_SPRITE. This will cause OpenGL to ignore the current settings for point antialiasing. Each fragment in the point will be assigned the associated vertex data, and those values will be used in shading.

To enable the iteration of texture coordinates across the point sprite, you need to call **glTexEnv*(**GL_POINT_SPRITE, GL_COORD_REPLACE, GL_TRUE). This needs to be done for each texture unit with a texture map that you want applied to the sprite. Figure 9-15 illustrates the differences between antialiased points and texture-mapped point sprites. On the left is an image of a 10-pixel antialiased point. The right image is a 10-pixel texture-mapped point sprite.

**Figure 9-15**     Comparison of Antialiased Points and Textured Point Sprites

The texture coordinates for point sprites are automatically assigned by OpenGL during rasterization. Figure 9-16 illustrates how texture coordinates are assigned to the point sprite. The *s* texture coordinate increases from zero to one from left to right across the fragments of the sprite. However, for *t* texture coordinates, values are controlled by where the sprite's texture-coordinate origin is specified. Control of the origin is specified by calling

**glPointParameter()** with GL_POINT_SPRITE_COORD_ORIGIN and setting the value to either GL_LOWER_LEFT or GL_UPPER_LEFT.

When the sprite origin is specified to be the GL_LOWER_LEFT, the *t*-coordinate increases from zero to one going from bottom to top of the sprite. Conversely, when the value is specified to be GL_UPPER_LEFT, the *t*-coordinate increases from zero to one going from top to bottom.

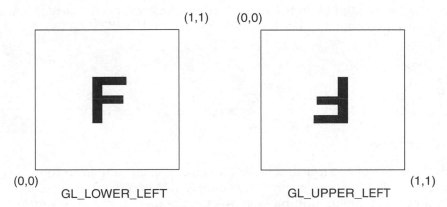

**Figure 9-16**    Assignment of Texture Coordinates Based on the Setting of GL_POINT_SPRITE_COORD_ORIGIN

Example 9-17 demonstrates a 10-pixel-wide point sprite with an applied texture map.

**Example 9-17**    Configuring a Point Sprite for Texture Mapping: sprite.c

```
glPointSize(10.0);
glTexEnvi(GL_POINT_SPRITE, GL_COORD_REPLACE, GL_TRUE);
glPointParameteri(GL_POINT_SPRITE_COORD_ORIGIN, GL_LOWER_LEFT);
glEnable(GL_POINT_SPRITE);
```

## The Texture Matrix Stack

### Advanced

Advanced

Just as your model coordinates are transformed by a matrix before being rendered, texture coordinates are multiplied by a $4 \times 4$ matrix before any texture mapping occurs. By default, the texture matrix is the identity, so the texture coordinates you explicitly assign or those that are automatically generated remain unchanged. By modifying the texture matrix while redrawing an object, however, you can make the texture slide over the surface, rotate around it, stretch and shrink, or any combination of the three. In fact, since the texture matrix is a completely general 4 × 4 matrix, effects such as perspective can be achieved.

The texture matrix is actually the top matrix on a stack, which must have a stack depth of at least two matrices. All the standard matrix-manipulation commands such as **glPushMatrix()**, **glPopMatrix()**, **glMultMatrix()**, and **glRotate*()** can be applied to the texture matrix. To modify the current texture matrix, you need to set the matrix mode to GL_TEXTURE, as follows:

```
glMatrixMode(GL_TEXTURE);  /* enter texture matrix mode */
glRotated(...);
/* ... other matrix manipulations ... */
glMatrixMode(GL_MODELVIEW);  /* back to modelview mode */
```

### The *q*-Coordinate

The mathematics of the fourth texture coordinate, $q$, are similar to the $w$-coordinate of the $(x, y, z, w)$ object coordinates. When the four texture coordinates $(s, t, r, q)$ are multiplied by the texture matrix, the resulting vector $(s', t', r', q')$ is interpreted as homogeneous texture coordinates. In other words, the texture map is indexed by $s'/q'$, $t'/q'$, and $r'/q'$.

You can make use of $q$ in cases where more than one projection or perspective transformation is needed. For example, suppose you want to model a spotlight that has some nonuniform pattern—brighter in the center, perhaps, or noncircular, because of flaps or lenses that modify the shape of the beam. You can emulate shining such a light onto a flat surface by making a texture map that corresponds to the shape and intensity of a light, and then projecting it onto the surface in question using projection transformations. Projecting the cone of light onto surfaces in the scene requires a perspective transformation ($q \neq 1$), since the lights might shine on surfaces that aren't perpendicular to them. A second perspective transformation occurs because the viewer sees the scene from a different (but perspective) point of view. (See Plate 28 for an example; and see "Fast Shadows and Lighting Effects Using Texture Mapping" by Mark Segal, Carl Korobkin, Rolf van Widenfelt, Jim Foran, and Paul Haeberli, SIGGRAPH 1992 Proceedings [*Computer Graphics*, 26:2, July 1992, pp. 249–252] for more details.)

Another example might arise if the texture map to be applied comes from a photograph that itself was taken in perspective. As with spotlights, the final view depends on the combination of two perspective transformations.

### Nate Robins' Texture Tutorial

In Nate Robins' **texture** tutorial, you can use the popup menu to view the $4 \times 4$ texture matrix, make changes in matrix values, and then see their effects.

# Depth Textures

### Advanced

Advanced

After lighting a surface (see Chapter 5), you'll soon notice that OpenGL light sources don't cast shadows. The color at each vertex is calculated without regard to any other objects in the scene. To have shadows, you need to determine and record which surfaces (or portions of the surfaces) are occluded from a direct path to a light source.

A multipass technique using depth textures provides a solution to rendering shadows. If you temporarily move the viewpoint to the light source position, you notice that everything you see is lit—there are no shadows from that perspective. A depth texture provides the mechanism to save the depth values for all "unshadowed" fragments in a *shadow map*. As you render your scene, if you compare each incoming fragment to the corresponding depth value in the shadow map, you can choose what to render, depending upon whether it is or isn't shadowed. The idea is similar to the depth test, except that it's done from the point of view of the light source.

The condensed description is as follows:

1. Render the scene from the point of view of the light source. It doesn't matter how the scene looks; you only want the depth values. Create a shadow map by capturing the depth buffer values and storing them in a texture map (shadow map).

2. Generate texture coordinates with $(s, t)$ coordinates referencing locations within the shadow map, with the third texture coordinate $(r)$, as the distance from the light source. Then draw the scene a second time, comparing the $r$ value with the corresponding depth texture value to determine whether the fragment is lit or in shadow.

The following sections provide a more detailed discussion, along with sample code illustrating each of the steps.

## Creating a Shadow Map

The first step is to create a texture map of depth values. You create this by rendering the scene with the viewpoint positioned at the light source's position. Example 9-18 calls **glGetLightfv()** to obtain the current light source position, calculates an up-vector, and then uses it as the viewing transformation.

Example 9-18 begins by setting the viewport size to match that of the texture map. It then sets up the appropriate projection and viewing matrices. The objects for the scene are rendered, and the resulting depth image is copied into texture memory for use as a shadow map. Finally, the viewport is reset to it's original size and position.

Note a few more points:

- The projection matrix controls the shape of the light's "lampshade." The variables *lightFovy* and *lightAspect* in the **gluPerspective()** control the size of the lampshade. A small *lightFovy* value will be more like a spotlight, and a larger value will be more like a floodlight.

- The near and far clipping planes for the light (*lightNearPlane* and *lightFarPlane*) are used to control the precision of the depth values. Try to keep the separation between the near and far planes as small as possible to maximize the precision of the values.

- After the depth values have been established in the depth buffer, you want to capture them and put them into a GL_DEPTH_COMPONENT format texture map. Example 9-18 uses **glCopyTexImage2D()** to make a texture image from the depth buffer contents. As with any texture, ensure that the image width and height are powers of two.

**Example 9-18**   Rendering Scene with Viewpoint at Light Source: shadowmap.c

```
GLint    viewport[4];
GLfloat  lightPos[4];

glGetLightfv(GL_LIGHT0, GL_POSITION, lightPos);
glGetIntegerv(GL_VIEWPORT, viewport);

glViewport(0, 0, SHADOW_MAP_WIDTH, SHADOW_MAP_HEIGHT);

glClear(GL_COLOR_BUFFER_BIT | GL_DEPTH_BUFFER_BIT);

glMatrixMode(GL_PROJECTION);
glPushMatrix();
```

```
glLoadIdentity();
gluPerspective(lightFovy, lightAspect, lightNearPlane,
               lightFarPlane);
glMatrixMode(GL_MODELVIEW);

glPushMatrix();
glLoadIdentity();
gluLookAt(lightPos[0], lightPos[1], lightPos[2],
    lookat[0], lookat[1], lookat[2],
    up[0], up[1], up[2]);
drawObjects();
glPopMatrix();

glMatrixMode(GL_PROJECTION);
glPopMatrix();
glMatrixMode(GL_MODELVIEW);

glCopyTexImage2D(GL_TEXTURE_2D, 0, GL_DEPTH_COMPONENT, 0, 0,
    SHADOW_MAP_WIDTH, SHADOW_MAP_HEIGHT, 0);

glViewport(viewport[0], viewport[1],
    viewport[2], viewport[3]);
```

## Generating Texture Coordinates and Rendering

Now use **glTexGen*()** to automatically generate texture coordinates that compute the eye-space distance from the light source position. The value of the *r* coordinate should correspond to the distance from the primitives to the light source. You can do this by using the same projection and viewing transformations that you used to create the shadow map. Example 9-19 uses the GL_MODELVIEW matrix stack to do all the matrix computations.

Note that the generated (*s*, *t*, *r*, *q*) texture coordinates and the depth values in the shadow map are not similarly scaled. The texture coordinates are generated in eye coordinates, so they fall in the range [–1, 1]. The depth values in the texels are within [0, 1]. Therefore, an initial translation and scaling maps the texture coordinates into the same range of values as the shadow map.

**Example 9-19**   Calculating Texture Coordinates: shadowmap.c

```
GLfloat  tmpMatrix[16];

glMatrixMode(GL_MODELVIEW);
glPushMatrix();
```

```
glLoadIdentity();
glTranslatef(0.5, 0.5, 0.0);
glScalef(0.5, 0.5, 1.0);
gluPerspective(lightFovy, lightAspect,
    lightNearPlane, lightFarPlane);
gluLookAt(lightPos[0], lightPos[1], lightPos[2],
    lookat[0], lookat[1], lookat[2],
    up[0], up[1], up[2]);
glGetFloatv(GL_MODELVIEW_MATRIX, tmpMatrix);
glPopMatrix();

transposeMatrix(tmpMatrix);

glTexGeni(GL_S, GL_TEXTURE_GEN_MODE, GL_OBJECT_LINEAR);
glTexGeni(GL_T, GL_TEXTURE_GEN_MODE, GL_OBJECT_LINEAR);
glTexGeni(GL_R, GL_TEXTURE_GEN_MODE, GL_OBJECT_LINEAR);
glTexGeni(GL_Q, GL_TEXTURE_GEN_MODE, GL_OBJECT_LINEAR);

glTexGenfv(GL_S, GL_OBJECT_PLANE, &tmpMatrix[0]);
glTexGenfv(GL_T, GL_OBJECT_PLANE, &tmpMatrix[4]);
glTexGenfv(GL_R, GL_OBJECT_PLANE, &tmpMatrix[8]);
glTexGenfv(GL_Q, GL_OBJECT_PLANE, &tmpMatrix[12]);

glEnable(GL_TEXTURE_GEN_S);
glEnable(GL_TEXTURE_GEN_T);
glEnable(GL_TEXTURE_GEN_R);
glEnable(GL_TEXTURE_GEN_Q);
```

In Example 9-20, before the scene is rendered for the second and final time, the texture comparison mode GL_COMPARE_R_TO_TEXTURE instructs OpenGL to compare the fragment's *r*-coordinate with the texel value. If the *r* distance is less than or equal to (the comparison function GL_LEQUAL) the texel value, there is nothing between this fragment and the light source, and it is effectively treated as having a luminance value of one. If the comparison fails, then there is another primitive between this fragment and the light source, so this fragment is shadowed and has an effective luminance of zero.

**Example 9-20**   Rendering Scene Comparing *r* Coordinate: shadowmap.c

```
glTexParameteri(GL_TEXTURE_2D, GL_TEXTURE_WRAP_S,
    GL_CLAMP_TO_EDGE);
glTexParameteri(GL_TEXTURE_2D, GL_TEXTURE_WRAP_T,
    GL_CLAMP_TO_EDGE);
glTexParameteri(GL_TEXTURE_2D, GL_TEXTURE_MIN_FILTER,
    GL_LINEAR);
```

```
glTexParameteri(GL_TEXTURE_2D, GL_TEXTURE_MAG_FILTER,
    GL_LINEAR);
glTexParameteri(GL_TEXTURE_2D, GL_TEXTURE_COMPARE_FUNC,
    GL_LEQUAL);
glTexParameteri(GL_TEXTURE_2D, GL_DEPTH_TEXTURE_MODE,
    GL_LUMINANCE);
glTexParameteri( GL_TEXTURE_2D, GL_TEXTURE_COMPARE_MODE,
    GL_COMPARE_R_TO_TEXTURE);
glEnable(GL_TEXTURE_2D);
```

This technique can produce some unintended visual artifacts:

- Self-shadowing, whereby an object incorrectly casts a shadow upon itself, is a common problem.

- Aliasing of the projected texture, particularly in the regions farthest from the light sources, can occur. Using higher resolution shadow maps can help reduce the aliasing.

- GL_MODULATE mode, when used with depth texturing, may cause sharp transitions between shadowed and unshadowed regions.

Unfortunately, there are no steadfast rules for overcoming these issues. Some experimentation may be required to produce the best-looking image.

*Chapter 10*

# The Framebuffer

**Chapter Objectives**

After reading this chapter, you'll be able to do the following:

• Understand the buffers that make up the framebuffer and how they're used

• Clear selected buffers and enable them for writing

• Control the parameters of the scissor, alpha, stencil, and depth tests that are applied to pixels

• Use occlusion queries to determine if objects will be visible

• Perform dithering and logical operations

• Use the accumulation buffer for such purposes as scene antialiasing

An important goal of almost every graphics program is to draw pictures on the screen. The screen is composed of a rectangular array of pixels, each capable of displaying a tiny square of color at that point in the image. After the rasterization stage (including texturing and fog), the data is not yet pixels, but fragments. Each fragment has coordinate data that corresponds to a pixel, as well as color and depth values. Then each fragment undergoes a series of tests and operations, some of which have been previously described (see "Blending" in Chapter 6), and others that are discussed in this chapter.

If the tests and operations are survived, the fragment values are ready to become pixels. To draw these pixels, you need to know what color they are, which is the information that's stored in the color buffer. Whenever data is stored uniformly for each pixel, such storage for all the pixels is called a *buffer*. Different buffers might contain different amounts of data per pixel, but within a given buffer, each pixel is assigned the same amount of data. A buffer that stores a single bit of information about pixels is called a *bitplane*.

As shown in Figure 10-1, the lower left pixel in an OpenGL window is pixel (0, 0), corresponding to the window coordinates of the lower left corner of the $1 \times 1$ region occupied by this pixel. In general, pixel $(x, y)$ fills the region bounded by $x$ on the left, $x + 1$ on the right, $y$ on the bottom, and $y + 1$ on the top.

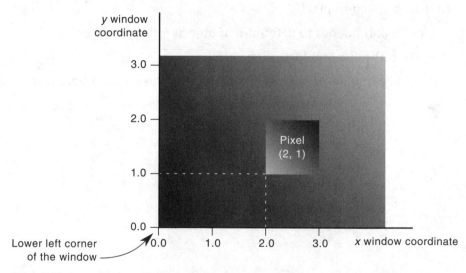

**Figure 10-1**     Region Occupied by a Pixel

As an example of a buffer, let's look more closely at the color buffer, which holds the color information that's to be displayed on the screen. Assume that the screen is 1280 pixels wide and 1024 pixels high and that it's a full 24-bit color screen—in other words, that there are $2^{24}$ (or 16,777,216) different colors that can be displayed. Since 24 bits translates to 3 bytes (8 bits per byte), the color buffer in this example has to store at least 3 bytes of data for each of the 1,310,720 (1280*1024) pixels on the screen. A particular hardware system might have more or fewer pixels on the physical screen as well as more or less color data per pixel. Any particular color buffer, however, has the same amount of data saved for each pixel on the screen.

The color buffer is only one of several buffers that hold information about a pixel. For example, in "A Hidden-Surface Removal Survival Kit" on page 185, you learned that the depth buffer holds depth information for each pixel. The color buffer itself can consist of several subbuffers. The *framebuffer* on a system comprises all of these buffers. With the exception of the color buffer(s), you don't view these other buffers directly; instead, you use them to perform such tasks as hidden-surface elimination, antialiasing of an entire scene, stenciling, drawing smooth motion, and other operations.

This chapter describes all the buffers that can exist in an OpenGL implementation and how they're used. It also discusses the series of tests and pixel operations that are performed before any data is written to the viewable color buffer. Finally, it explains how to use the accumulation buffer, which is used to accumulate images that are drawn into the color buffer. This chapter has the following major sections.

- "Buffers and Their Uses" describes the possible buffers, what they're for, and how to clear them and enable them for writing.

- "Testing and Operating on Fragments" explains the scissor, alpha, stencil, and depth tests that occur after a pixel's position and color have been calculated but before this information is drawn on the screen. Several operations—blending, dithering, and logical operations—can also be performed before a fragment updates the screen.

- "The Accumulation Buffer" describes how to perform several advanced techniques using the accumulation buffer. These techniques include antialiasing an entire scene, using motion blur, and simulating photographic depth of field.

Version 1.4 of OpenGL added

- Stencil operations GL_INCR_WRAP and GL_DECR_WRAP

## Buffers and Their Uses

An OpenGL system can manipulate the following buffers:

- Color buffers: front-left, front-right, back-left, back-right, and any number of auxiliary color buffers

- Depth buffer

- Stencil buffer

- Accumulation buffer

Your particular OpenGL implementation determines which buffers are available and how many bits per pixel each buffer holds. Additionally, you can have multiple visuals, or window types, that have different buffers available. Table 10-1 lists the parameters to use with **glGetIntegerv()** to query your OpenGL system about per-pixel buffer storage for a particular visual.

**Note:** If you're using the X Window System, you're guaranteed, at a minimum, to have a visual with one color buffer for use in RGBA mode, with associated stencil, depth, and accumulation buffers that have color components of nonzero size. Also, if your X Window System implementation supports a Pseudo-Color visual, you are also guaranteed to have one OpenGL visual that has a color buffer for use in color-index mode, with associated depth and stencil buffers. You'll probably want to use **glXGetConfig()** to query your visuals; see Appendix C and the *OpenGL Reference Manual* for more information about this routine.

| Parameter | Meaning |
|---|---|
| GL_RED_BITS, GL_GREEN_BITS, GL_BLUE_BITS, GL_ALPHA_BITS | number of bits per R, G, B, or A component in the color buffers |
| GL_INDEX_BITS | number of bits per index in the color buffers |
| GL_DEPTH_BITS | number of bits per pixel in the depth buffer |
| GL_STENCIL_BITS | number of bits per pixel in the stencil buffer |
| GL_ACCUM_RED_BITS, GL_ACCUM_GREEN_BITS, GL_ACCUM_BLUE_BITS, GL_ACCUM_ALPHA_BITS | number of bits per R, G, B, or A component in the accumulation buffer |

**Table 10-1**    Query Parameters for Per-Pixel Buffer Storage

## Color Buffers

The color buffers are the ones to which you usually draw. They contain either color-index or RGB color data and may also contain alpha values. An OpenGL implementation that supports stereoscopic viewing has left and right color buffers for the left and right stereo images. If stereo isn't supported, only the left buffers are used. Similarly, double-buffered systems have front and back buffers, and a single-buffered system has the front buffers only. Every OpenGL implementation must provide a front-left color buffer.

Optional, nondisplayable auxiliary color buffers may also be supported. OpenGL doesn't specify any particular uses for these buffers, so you can define and use them however you please. For example, you might use them for saving an image that you use repeatedly. Then, rather than redrawing the image, you can just copy it from an auxiliary buffer into the usual color buffers. (See the description of **glCopyPixels()** in "Reading, Writing, and Copying Pixel Data" on page 313 for more information about how to do this.)

You can use GL_STEREO or GL_DOUBLEBUFFER with **glGetBooleanv()** to find out if your system supports stereo (that is, has left and right buffers) or double-buffering (front and back buffers). To find out how many, if any, auxiliary buffers are present, use **glGetIntegerv()** with GL_AUX_BUFFERS.

### Depth Buffer

The depth buffer stores a depth value for each pixel. As described in "A Hidden-Surface Removal Survival Kit" on page 185, depth is usually measured in terms of distance to the eye, so pixels with larger depth-buffer values are overwritten by pixels with smaller values. This is just a useful convention, however, and the depth buffer's behavior can be modified as described in "Depth Test" on page 483. The depth buffer is sometimes called the *z buffer* (the *z* comes from the fact that *x*- and *y*-values measure horizontal and vertical displacement on the screen, and the *z*-value measures distance perpendicular to the screen).

### Stencil Buffer

One use for the stencil buffer is to restrict drawing to certain portions of the screen, just as a cardboard stencil can be used with a can of spray paint to make fairly precise painted images. For example, if you want to draw an image as it would appear through an odd-shaped windshield, you can store an image of the windshield's shape in the stencil buffer, and then draw the entire scene. The stencil buffer prevents anything that wouldn't be visible through the windshield from being drawn. Thus, if your application is a driving simulation, you can draw all the instruments and other items inside the automobile once, and as the car moves, only the outside scene need be updated.

### Accumulation Buffer

The accumulation buffer holds RGBA color data just as the color buffers do in RGBA mode. (The results of using the accumulation buffer in color-index mode are undefined.) It's typically used for accumulating a series of images into a final, composite image. With this method, you can perform operations such as scene antialiasing by supersampling an image and then averaging the samples to produce the values that are finally painted into the pixels of the color buffers. You don't draw directly into the accumulation buffer; accumulation operations are always performed in rectangular blocks, which are usually transfers of data to or from a color buffer.

## Clearing Buffers

In graphics programs, clearing the screen (or any of the buffers) is typically one of the most expensive operations you can perform—on a 1280 × 1024 monitor, it requires touching well over a million pixels. For simple graphics applications, the clear operation can take more time than the rest of the drawing. If you need to clear not only the color buffer but also the depth and stencil buffers, the clear operation can be three times as expensive.

To address this problem, some machines have hardware that can clear more than one buffer at once. The OpenGL clearing commands are structured to take advantage of such architectures. First, you specify the values to be written into each buffer to be cleared. Then you issue a single command to perform the clear operation, passing in a list of all the buffers to be cleared. If the hardware is capable of simultaneous clears, they all occur at once; otherwise, the buffers are cleared sequentially.

The following commands set the clearing values for each buffer:

void **glClearColor**(GLclampf *red*, GLclampf *green*, GLclampf *blue*,
                   GLclampf *alpha*);
void **glClearIndex**(GLfloat *index*);
void **glClearDepth**(GLclampd *depth*);
void **glClearStencil**(GLint *s*);
void **glClearAccum**(GLfloat *red*, GLfloat *green*, GLfloat *blue*,
                   GLfloat *alpha*);

Specifies the current clearing values for the color buffer (in RGBA mode), the color buffer (in color-index mode), the depth buffer, the stencil buffer, and the accumulation buffer. The GLclampf and GLclampd types (clamped GLfloat and clamped GLdouble) are clamped to be between 0.0 and 1.0. The default depth-clearing value is 1.0; all the other default clearing values are 0. The values set with the clear commands remain in effect until they're changed by another call to the same command.

After you've selected your clearing values and you're ready to clear the buffers, use **glClear()**:

void **glClear**(GLbitfield *mask*);

Clears the specified buffers. The value of *mask* is the bitwise logical OR of some combination of GL_COLOR_BUFFER_BIT, GL_DEPTH_BUFFER_BIT, GL_STENCIL_BUFFER_BIT, and GL_ACCUM_BUFFER_BIT to identify which buffers are to be cleared. GL_COLOR_BUFFER_BIT clears either the RGBA color buffer or the color-index buffer, depending on the mode of the system at the time. When you clear the color or color-index buffer, all the color buffers that are enabled for writing (see the next section) are cleared. The pixel ownership test, scissor test, and dithering, if enabled, are applied to the clearing operation. Masking operations, such as **glColorMask()** and **glIndexMask()**, are also effective. The alpha test, stencil test, and depth test do not affect the operation of **glClear()**.

## Selecting Color Buffers for Writing and Reading

The results of a drawing or reading operation can go into or come from any of the color buffers: front, back, front-left, back-left, front-right, back-right, or any of the auxiliary buffers. You can choose an individual buffer to be the drawing or reading target. For drawing, you can also set the target to draw into more than one buffer at the same time. You use **glDrawBuffer()** to select the buffers to be written and **glReadBuffer()** to select the buffer as the source for **glReadPixels()**, **glCopyPixels()**, **glCopyTexImage\*()**, and **glCopyTexSubImage\*()**.

If you are using double-buffering, you usually want to draw only in the back buffer (and swap the buffers when you're finished drawing). In some situations, you might want to treat a double-buffered window as though it were single-buffered by calling **glDrawBuffer()** to enable you to draw to both front and back buffers at the same time.

**glDrawBuffer()** is also used to select buffers to render stereo images (GL\*LEFT and GL\*RIGHT) and to render into auxiliary buffers (GL_AUX*i*).

---

void **glDrawBuffer**(GLenum *mode*);
void **glDrawBuffers**(GLsizei *n*, const GLenum \**buffers*);

---

Selects the color buffers enabled for writing or clearing and disables buffers enabled by previous calls to **glDrawBuffer()**. More than one buffer may be enabled at one time. The value of *mode* can be one of the following:

| | | |
|---|---|---|
| GL_FRONT | GL_FRONT_LEFT | GL_AUX*i* |
| GL_BACK | GL_FRONT_RIGHT | GL_FRONT_AND_BACK |
| GL_LEFT | GL_BACK_LEFT | GL_NONE |
| GL_RIGHT | GL_BACK_RIGHT | |

Arguments that omit LEFT or RIGHT refer to both the left and right stereo buffers; similarly, arguments that omit FRONT or BACK refer to both. The *i* in GL_AUX*i* is a digit identifying a particular auxiliary buffer.

By default, *mode* is GL_FRONT for single-buffered contexts and GL_BACK for double-buffered contexts.

OpenGL 2.0 added the glDrawBuffers() routine, which specifies multiple color buffers capable of recieving color values. *buffers* is an array of buffer enumerates. Only GL_NONE, GL_FRONT_LEFT, GL_FRONT_RIGHT, GL_BACK_LEFT, GL_BACK_RIGHT, and GL_AUX*i* are accepted.

If the fixed-function OpenGL pipeline is utilized for generating fragment colors, each of the specified buffers recieves the same color vaule. If a fragment shader is employed and specifies output to multiple buffers, then each buffer will be written with the color specified in the shader's output. See "Rendering to Multiple Output Buffers" in Chapter 15 for details.

**Note:** You can enable drawing to nonexistent buffers as long as you enable drawing to at least one buffer that does exist. If none of the specified buffers exists, an error results.

---

void **glReadBuffer**(GLenum *mode*);

Selects the color buffer enabled as the source for reading pixels for subsequent calls to **glReadPixels()**, **glCopyPixels()**, **glCopyTexImage\*()**, **glCopyTexSubImage\*()**, and **glCopyConvolutionFilter\*()**, and disables buffers enabled by previous calls to **glReadBuffer()**. The value of *mode* can be one of the following:

| | | |
|---|---|---|
| GL_FRONT | GL_FRONT_LEFT | GL_AUX*i* |
| GL_BACK | GL_FRONT_RIGHT | |
| GL_LEFT | GL_BACK_LEFT | |
| GL_RIGHT | GL_BACK_RIGHT | |

The buffers for **glReadBuffer()** are the same as those described for **glDrawBuffer()**. By default, *mode* is GL_FRONT for single-buffered contexts and GL_BACK for double-buffered contexts.

---

**Note:** You must enable reading from a buffer that exists or an error results.

## Masking Buffers

Before OpenGL writes data into the enabled color, depth, or stencil buffers, a masking operation is applied to the data, as specified with one of the following commands. A bitwise logical AND is performed with each mask and the corresponding data to be written.

---

void **glIndexMask**(GLuint *mask*);
void **glColorMask**(GLboolean *red*, GLboolean *green*, GLboolean *blue*,
             GLboolean *alpha*);
void **glDepthMask**(GLboolean *flag*);
void **glStencilMask**(GLuint *mask*);
void **glStencilMaskSeparate**(GLenum *face*, GLuint *mask*);

---

Sets the masks used to control writing into the indicated buffers. The mask set by **glIndexMask()** applies only in color-index mode. If a 1 appears in *mask*, the corresponding bit in the color-index buffer is written; if a 0 appears, the bit isn't written. Similarly, **glColorMask()** affects drawing in RGBA mode only. The *red*, *green*, *blue*, and *alpha* values control whether the corresponding component is written. (GL_TRUE means it is written.)

If *flag* is GL_TRUE for **glDepthMask()**, the depth buffer is enabled for writing; otherwise, it's disabled. The mask for **glStencilMask()** is used for stencil data in the same way as the mask is used for color-index data in **glIndexMask()**. The default values of all the GLboolean masks are GL_TRUE, and the default values for the two GLuint masks are all 1's.

OpenGL 2.0 includes the **glStencilMaskSeparate()** function that allows separate mask values for front- and back-facing polygons.

You can do plenty of tricks with color masking in color-index mode. For example, you can use each bit in the index as a different layer and set up interactions between arbitrary layers with appropriate settings of the color map. You can create overlays and underlays, and do so-called color-map animations. (See Chapter 14 for examples of using color masking.) Masking in RGBA mode is useful less often, but you can use it for loading separate image files into the red, green, and blue bitplanes, for example.

You've seen one use for disabling the depth buffer in "Three-Dimensional Blending with the Depth Buffer" on page 243. Disabling the depth buffer for writing can also be useful if a common background is desired for a series of frames, and you want to add some features that may be obscured by parts of the background. For example, suppose your background is a forest, and you would like to draw repeated frames with the same trees, but with objects moving among them. After the trees are drawn and their depths recorded in the depth buffer, the image of the trees is saved, and the new items are drawn with the depth buffer disabled for writing. As long as the new items don't overlap each other, the picture is correct. To draw the next frame, restore the image of the trees and continue. You don't need to restore the values in the depth buffer. This trick is most useful if the background is extremely complex—so complex that it's much faster just to recopy the image into the color buffer than to recompute it from the geometry.

Masking the stencil buffer can allow you to use a multiple-bit stencil buffer to hold multiple stencils (one per bit). You might use this technique to perform capping as explained in "Stencil Test" on page 478 or to implement the Game of Life as described in "Life in the Stencil Buffer" on page 627.

**Note:** The mask specified by **glStencilMask()** controls which stencil bit-planes are written. This mask isn't related to the mask that's specified as the third parameter of **glStencilFunc()**, which specifies which bit-planes are considered by the stencil function.

## Testing and Operating on Fragments

When you draw geometry, text, or images on the screen, OpenGL performs several calculations to rotate, translate, scale, determine the lighting, project the object(s) into perspective, figure out which pixels in the window are affected, and determine the colors in which those pixels should be drawn. Many of the earlier chapters in this book provide some information about how to control these operations. After OpenGL determines that an individual fragment should be generated and what its color should be, several processing stages remain that control how and whether the fragment is drawn as a pixel into the framebuffer. For example, if it's outside a rectangular region or if it's farther from the viewpoint than the pixel that's already in the framebuffer, it isn't drawn. In another stage, the fragment's color is blended with the color of the pixel already in the framebuffer.

This section describes both the complete set of tests that a fragment must pass before it goes into the framebuffer and the possible final operations that can be performed on the fragment as it's written. The tests and operations occur in the following order; if a fragment is eliminated in an early test, none of the later tests or operations takes place:

1. Scissor test

2. Alpha test

3. Stencil test

4. Depth test

5. Blending

6. Dithering

7. Logical operations

All of these tests and operations are described in detail in the following subsections.

## Scissor Test

You can define a rectangular portion of your window and restrict drawing to take place within it by using the **glScissor()** command. If a fragment lies inside the rectangle, it passes the scissor test.

---

void **glScissor**(GLint *x*, GLint *y*, GLsizei *width*, GLsizei *height*);

Sets the location and size of the scissor rectangle (also known as the scissor box). The parameters define the lower left corner (*x*, *y*) and the width and height of the rectangle. Pixels that lie inside the rectangle pass the scissor test. Scissoring is enabled and disabled by passing GL_SCISSOR_TEST to **glEnable()** and **glDisable()**. By default, the rectangle matches the size of the window and scissoring is disabled.

---

The scissor test is just a version of a stencil test using a rectangular region of the screen. It's fairly easy to create a blindingly fast hardware implementation of scissoring, while a given system might be much slower at stenciling—perhaps because the stenciling is performed in software.

### Advanced

Advanced An advanced use of scissoring is performing nonlinear projection. First divide the window into a regular grid of subregions, specifying viewport and scissor parameters that limit rendering to one region at a time. Then project the entire scene to each region using a different projection matrix.

To determine whether scissoring is enabled and to obtain the values that define the scissor rectangle, you can use GL_SCISSOR_TEST with **glIsEnabled()** and GL_SCISSOR_BOX with **glGetIntegerv()**.

## Alpha Test

In RGBA mode, the alpha test allows you to accept or reject a fragment based on its alpha value. The alpha test is enabled and disabled by passing GL_ALPHA_TEST to **glEnable()** and **glDisable()**. To determine whether the alpha test is enabled, use GL_ALPHA_TEST with **glIsEnabled()**.

If enabled, the test compares the incoming alpha value with a reference value. The fragment is accepted or rejected depending on the result of the comparison. Both the reference value and the comparison function are set with **glAlphaFunc()**. By default, the reference value is 0, the comparison function is GL_ALWAYS, and the alpha test is disabled. To obtain the alpha comparison function or reference value, use GL_ALPHA_TEST_FUNC or GL_ALPHA_TEST_REF with **glGetIntegerv()**.

---

void **glAlphaFunc**(GLenum *func*, GLclampf *ref*);

Sets the reference value and comparison function for the alpha test. The reference value *ref* is clamped to be between 0 and 1. The possible values for *func* and their meanings are listed in Table 10-2.

| Parameter | Meaning |
| --- | --- |
| GL_NEVER | never accept the fragment |
| GL_ALWAYS | always accept the fragment |
| GL_LESS | accept fragment if fragment alpha < reference alpha |
| GL_LEQUAL | accept fragment if fragment alpha ≤ reference alpha |
| GL_EQUAL | accept fragment if fragment alpha = reference alpha |
| GL_GEQUAL | accept fragment if fragment alpha ≥ reference alpha |
| GL_GREATER | accept fragment if fragment alpha > reference alpha |
| GL_NOTEQUAL | accept fragment if fragment alpha ≠ reference alpha |

**Table 10-2**     glAlphaFunc() Parameter Values

One application for the alpha test is implementation of a transparency algorithm. Render your entire scene twice, the first time accepting only fragments with alpha values of 1, and the second time accepting fragments with alpha values that aren't equal to 1. Turn the depth buffer on during both passes, but disable depth buffer writing during the second pass.

Another use might be to make decals with texture maps whereby you can see through certain parts of the decals. Set the alphas in the decals to 0.0 where you want to see through, set them to 1.0 otherwise, set the reference value to 0.5 (or anything between 0.0 and 1.0), and set the comparison function to GL_GREATER. The decal has see-through parts, and the values in the depth buffer aren't affected. This technique, called *billboarding*, is described in "Sample Uses of Blending" on page 238.

## Stencil Test

The stencil test takes place only if there is a stencil buffer. (If there is no stencil buffer, the stencil test always passes.) Stenciling applies a test that compares a reference value with the value stored at a pixel in the stencil buffer. Depending on the result of the test, the value in the stencil buffer is modified. You can choose the particular comparison function used, the reference value, and the modification performed with the **glStencilFunc()** and **glStencilOp()** commands.

---

void **glStencilFunc**(GLenum *func*, GLint *ref*, GLuint *mask*);
void **glStencilFuncSeparate**(GLenum *face*,
              GLenum *func*, GLint *ref*, GLuint *mask*);

---

Sets the comparison function (*func*), the reference value (*ref*), and a mask (*mask*) for use with the stencil test. The reference value is compared with the value in the stencil buffer using the comparison function, but the comparison applies only to those bits for which the corresponding bits of the mask are 1. The function can be GL_NEVER, GL_ALWAYS, GL_LESS, GL_LEQUAL, GL_EQUAL, GL_GEQUAL, GL_GREATER, or GL_NOTEQUAL. If it's GL_LESS, for example, then the fragment passes if *ref* is less than the value in the stencil buffer. If the stencil buffer contains *s* bitplanes, the low-order *s* bits of *mask* are bitwise ANDed with the value in the stencil buffer and with the reference value before the comparison is performed. The masked values are all interpreted as non-negative values. The stencil test is enabled and disabled by passing GL_STENCIL_TEST to **glEnable()** and **glDisable()**. By default, *func* is GL_ALWAYS, *ref* is 0, *mask* is all 1s, and stenciling is disabled.

OpenGL 2.0 includes the **glStencilFuncSeparate()** function that allows separate stencil function parameters to be specified for front- and back-facing polygons.

---

void **glStencilOp**(GLenum *fail*, GLenum *zfail*, GLenum *zpass*);
void **glStencilOpSeparate**(GLenum *face*, GLenum *fail*, GLenum *zfail*,
              GLenum *zpass*);

---

Specifies how the data in the stencil buffer is modified when a fragment passes or fails the stencil test. The three functions *fail*, *zfail*, and *zpass* can be GL_KEEP, GL_ZERO, GL_REPLACE, GL_INCR, GL_INCR_WRAP, GL_DECR, GL_DECR_WRAP, or GL_INVERT. They correspond to keeping the current value, replacing it with zero, replacing it with the reference value, incrementing it with saturation, incrementing it without saturation, decrementing it with saturation, decrementing it without saturation, and bitwise-inverting it. The result of the increment and decrement functions is clamped to lie between zero and the maximum unsigned integer value ($2^s - 1$ if the stencil buffer holds $s$ bits).

The *fail* function is applied if the fragment fails the stencil test; if it passes, then *zfail* is applied if the depth test fails and *zpass* is applied if the depth test passes, or if no depth test is performed. (See "Depth Test" on page 483.) By default, all three stencil operations are GL_KEEP.

OpenGL 2.0 includes the **glStencilOpSeparate()** function that allows separate stencil tests to be specified for front- and back-facing polygons.

"With saturation" means that the stencil value will clamp to extreme values. If you try to decrement zero with saturation, the stencil value remains zero. "Without saturation" means that going outside the indicated range wraps around. If you try to decrement zero without saturation, the stencil value becomes the maximum unsigned integer value (quite large!).

### Stencil Queries

You can obtain the values for all six stencil-related parameters by using the query function **glGetIntegerv()** and one of the values shown in Table 10-3. You can also determine whether the stencil test is enabled by passing GL_STENCIL_TEST to **glIsEnabled()**.

| Query Value | Meaning |
|---|---|
| GL_STENCIL_FUNC | stencil function |
| GL_STENCIL_REF | stencil reference value |
| GL_STENCIL_VALUE_MASK | stencil mask |
| GL_STENCIL_FAIL | stencil fail action |
| GL_STENCIL_PASS_DEPTH_FAIL | stencil pass and depth buffer fail action |
| GL_STENCIL_PASS_DEPTH_PASS | stencil pass and depth buffer pass action |

**Table 10-3** Query Values for the Stencil Test

```c
void reshape(int w, int h)
{
    glViewport(0, 0, (GLsizei) w, (GLsizei) h);

/* create a diamond shaped stencil area */
    glMatrixMode(GL_PROJECTION);
    glLoadIdentity();
    if (w <= h)
        gluOrtho2D(-3.0, 3.0, -3.0*(GLfloat)h/(GLfloat)w,
                    3.0*(GLfloat)h/(GLfloat)w);
    else
        gluOrtho2D(-3.0*(GLfloat)w/(GLfloat)h,
                    3.0*(GLfloat)w/(GLfloat)h, -3.0, 3.0);
    glMatrixMode(GL_MODELVIEW);
    glLoadIdentity();

    glClear(GL_STENCIL_BUFFER_BIT);
    glStencilFunc(GL_ALWAYS, 0x1, 0x1);
    glStencilOp(GL_REPLACE, GL_REPLACE, GL_REPLACE);
    glBegin(GL_QUADS);
        glVertex2f(-1.0, 0.0);
        glVertex2f(0.0, 1.0);
        glVertex2f(1.0, 0.0);
        glVertex2f(0.0, -1.0);
    glEnd();

    glMatrixMode(GL_PROJECTION);
    glLoadIdentity();
    gluPerspective(45.0, (GLfloat) w/(GLfloat) h, 3.0, 7.0);
    glMatrixMode(GL_MODELVIEW);
    glLoadIdentity();
    glTranslatef(0.0, 0.0, -5.0);
}

/* Main Loop
 * Be certain to request stencil bits.
 */
int main(int argc, char** argv)
{
    glutInit(&argc, argv);
    glutInitDisplayMode(GLUT_SINGLE | GLUT_RGB |
                        GLUT_DEPTH | GLUT_STENCIL);
    glutInitWindowSize(400, 400);
    glutInitWindowPosition(100, 100);
    glutCreateWindow(argv[0]);
    init();
    glutReshapeFunc(reshape);
```

```
   glutDisplayFunc(display);
   glutMainLoop();
   return 0;
}
```

The following examples illustrate other uses of the stencil test. (See
Chapter 14 for additional ideas.)

- Capping—Suppose you're drawing a closed convex object (or several of
  them, as long as they don't intersect or enclose each other) made up of
  several polygons, and you have a clipping plane that may or may not
  slice off a piece of it. Suppose that if the plane does intersect the object,
  you want to cap the object with some constant-colored surface, rather
  than see the inside of it. To do this, clear the stencil buffer to zeros, and
  begin drawing with stenciling enabled and the stencil comparison
  function set always to accept fragments. Invert the value in the stencil
  planes each time a fragment is accepted. After all the objects are drawn,
  regions of the screen where no capping is required have zeros in the
  stencil planes, and regions requiring capping are nonzero. Reset the
  stencil function so that it draws only where the stencil value is nonzero,
  and draw a large polygon of the capping color across the entire screen.

- Overlapping translucent polygons—Suppose you have a translucent
  surface that's made up of polygons that overlap slightly. If you simply
  use alpha blending, portions of the underlying objects are covered by
  more than one transparent surface, which doesn't look right. Use the
  stencil planes to make sure that each fragment is covered by at most
  one portion of the transparent surface. Do this by clearing the stencil
  planes to zeros, drawing only when the stencil plane is zero, and
  incrementing the value in the stencil plane when you draw.

- Stippling—Suppose you want to draw an image with a stipple pattern.
  (See "Displaying Points, Lines, and Polygons" on page 50 for more
  information about stippling.) You can do this by writing the stipple
  pattern into the stencil buffer and then drawing conditionally on
  the contents of the stencil buffer. After the original stipple pattern is
  drawn, the stencil buffer isn't altered while drawing the image, so the
  object is stippled by the pattern in the stencil planes.

## Depth Test

For each pixel on the screen, the depth buffer keeps track of the distance
between the viewpoint and the object occupying that pixel. Then, if the
specified depth test passes, the incoming depth value replaces the value
already in the depth buffer.

The depth buffer is generally used for hidden-surface elimination. If a new candidate color for that pixel appears, it's drawn only if the corresponding object is closer than the previous object. In this way, after the entire scene has been rendered, only objects that aren't obscured by other items remain. Initially, the clearing value for the depth buffer is a value that's as far from the viewpoint as possible, so the depth of any object is nearer than that value. If this is how you want to use the depth buffer, you simply have to enable it by passing GL_DEPTH_TEST to **glEnable()** and remember to clear the depth buffer before you redraw each frame. (See "Clearing Buffers" on page 470.) You can also choose a different comparison function for the depth test with **glDepthFunc()**.

---

void **glDepthFunc**(GLenum *func*);

Sets the comparison function for the depth test. The value for *func* must be GL_NEVER, GL_ALWAYS, GL_LESS, GL_LEQUAL, GL_EQUAL, GL_GEQUAL, GL_GREATER, or GL_NOTEQUAL. An incoming fragment passes the depth test if its *z*-value has the specified relation to the value already stored in the depth buffer. The default is GL_LESS, which means that an incoming fragment passes the test if its *z*-value is less than that already stored in the depth buffer. In this case, the *z*-value represents the distance from the object to the viewpoint, and smaller values mean that the corresponding objects are closer to the viewpoint.

---

## Occlusion Query

**Advanced**

Advanced

The depth buffer determines visiblity on a per-pixel basis. For performance reasons, it would be nice to be able to determine if a geometric object is visible before sending all of its (perhaps complex) geometry for rendering. *Occlusion queries* enable you to determine if a representative set of geometry will be visible after depth testing.

This is particularly useful for complex geometric objects with many polygons. Instead of rendering all of the geometry for a complex object, you might render its bounding box or another simplified representation that require less rendering resources. If OpenGL returns that no fragments or samples would have been modified by rendering that piece of geometry, you know that none of your complex object will be visible for that frame, and you can skip rendering that object for the frame.

The following steps are required to utilize occlusion queries:

1. (Optional) Generate a query id for each occlusion query that you need.

2. Specify the start of an occlusion query by calling **glBeginQuery()**.

3. Render the geometry for the occlusion test.

4. Specify that you've completed the occlusion query by calling **glEndQuery()**.

5. Retrieve the number of samples that passed the depth test.

In order to make the occlusion query process as efficient as possible, you'll want to disable all rendering modes that will increase the rendering time but won't change the visibility of a pixel.

### Generating Query Objects

An occlusion query object identifier is just an unsigned integer. While not strictly necessary, it's a good practice to have OpenGL generate a set of ids for your use. **glGenQueries()** will generate the requested number of unused query ids for your subsequent use.

---

void **glGenQueries**(GLsizei *n*, GLuint *\*ids*);

Returns *n* currently unused names for occlusion query objects in the array *ids* The names returned in *ids* do not have to be a contiguous set of integers.

The names returned are marked as used for the purposes of allocating additional query objects, but only acquire valid state once they have been specified in a call to **glBeginQuery()**.

Zero is a reserved occlusion query object name and is never returned as a valid value by **glGenQueries()**.

---

You can also determine if an identifier is currently being used as an occlusion query by calling **glIsQuery()**.

---

GLboolean **glIsQuery**(GLuint *id*);

Returns GL_TRUE if *id* is the name of an occlusion query object. Returns GL_FLASE if *id* is zero or *id* is a nonzero value that is not the name of a buffer object.

---

### Initiating an Occlusion Query Tes

To specify geometry that's to be used in an occlusion query, merely bracket the rendering operations between calls to **glBeginQuery()** and **glEndQuery()**, as demonstrated in Example 10-2.

**Example 10-2**   Rendering Geometry with Occlusion Query

```
glBeginQuery( GL_SAMPLES_PASSED, occquery );
drawBoundingGeometry();
glEndQuery( GL_SAMPLES_PASSED );
```

All OpenGL operations are available while an occlusion query is active, with the exception of **glGenQueries()** and **glDeleteQueries()**, which will raise a GL_INVALID_OPERATION error.

---

void **glBeginQuery**(GLenum *target*, GLuint *id*);

Specifies the start of an occlusion query operation. *target* must be GL_SAMPLES_PASSED. *id* is an unsigned integer identifier for this occlusion query operation.

---

void **glEndQuery**(GLenum *target*);

Ends an occlusion query. *target* must be GL_SAMPLES_PASSED.

---

### Determining the Results of an Occlusion Query

Once you've completed rendering the geometry for the occlusion query, you need to retrieve the results. This is done with a call to **glGetQueryObject[u]iv()**, as shown in Example 10-3, which will return the number of fragments, or samples, if you're using multisampling (see "Alpha and Multisampling Coverage" on page 259 for details).

---

void **glGetQueryObjectiv**(GLenum *id*, GLenum *pname*,
           GLint *\*params*);
void **glGetQueryObjectuiv**(GLenum *id*, GLenum *pname*,
           GLuint *\*params*);

Queries the state of an occlusion query object. *id* is the name of a query object. If *pname* is GL_QUERY_RESULT, then *params* will contain the number of fragments or samples (if multisampling is enabled) that passed

---

the depth test, with a value of zero representing the object being entirely occluded.

There may be a delay in completing the occlusion query operation. If *pname* is GL_QUERY_RESULT_AVAILABLE, *params* will contain GL_TRUE if the results for query *id* are available, or GL_FALSE otherwise.

**Example 10-3**    Retrieving the Results of an Occlusion Query

```
GLint  samples = 0;
glGetQueryObjectiv( occquery, GL_QUERY_RESULT, &samples );
```

### Cleaning Up Occlusion Query Objects

After you've completed your occlusion query tests, you can release the resources related to those queries by calling **glDeleteQueries()**.

---

void **glDeleteQueries**(GLsizei *n*, const GLuint *\*ids*);

---

Deletes *n* occlusion query objects, named by elements in the array *ids*. The freed query objects may now be reused (for example, by **glGenQueries()**).

## Blending, Dithering, and Logical Operations

Once an incoming fragment has passed all the tests described in "Testing and Operating on Fragments," it can be combined with the current contents of the color buffer in one of several ways. The simplest way, which is also the default, is to overwrite the existing values. Alternatively, if you're using RGBA mode and you want the fragment to be translucent or anti-aliased, you might average its value with the value already in the buffer (blending). On systems with a small number of available colors, you might want to dither color values to increase the number of colors available at the cost of a loss in resolution. In the final stage, you can use arbitrary bitwise logical operations to combine the incoming fragment and the pixel that's already written.

### Blending

Blending combines the incoming fragment's R, G, B, and alpha values with those of the pixel already stored at the location. Different blending operations can be applied, and the blending that occurs depends on the values of the incoming alpha value and the alpha value (if any) stored at the pixel. (See "Blending" on page 231 for an extensive discussion of this topic.)

### Dithering

On systems with a small number of color bitplanes, you can improve the color resolution at the expense of spatial resolution by dithering the color in the image. Dithering is like halftoning in newspapers. Although *The New York Times* has only two colors—black and white—it can show photographs by representing the shades of gray with combinations of black and white dots. Comparing a newspaper image of a photo (having no shades of gray) with the original photo (with grayscale) makes the loss of spatial resolution obvious. Similarly, systems with a small number of color bitplanes may dither values of red, green, and blue on neighboring pixels for the appearance of a wider range of colors.

The dithering operation that takes place is hardware-dependent; all OpenGL allows you to do is to turn it on and off. In fact, on some machines, enabling dithering might do nothing at all, which makes sense if the machine already has high color resolution. To enable and disable dithering, pass GL_DITHER to **glEnable()** and **glDisable()**. Dithering is enabled by default.

Dithering applies in both RGBA and color-index mode. The colors or color indices alternate in some hardware-dependent way between the two nearest possibilities. For example, in color-index mode, if dithering is enabled and the color index to be painted is 4.4, then 60 percent of the pixels may be painted with index 4, and 40 percent of the pixels with index 5. (Many dithering algorithms are possible, but a dithered value produced by any algorithm must depend on only the incoming value and the fragment's $x$- and $y$-coordinates.) In RGBA mode, dithering is performed separately for each component (including alpha). To use dithering in color-index mode, you generally need to arrange the colors in the color map appropriately in ramps; otherwise, bizarre images might result.

### Logical Operations

The final operation on a fragment is the *logical operation*, such as an OR, XOR, or INVERT, which is applied to the incoming fragment values (source) and/or those currently in the color buffer (destination). Such fragment operations are especially useful on bit-blt-type machines, on which the primary graphics operation is copying a rectangle of data from one place in the window to another, from the window to processor memory, or from memory to the window. Typically, the copy doesn't write the data directly into memory but instead allows you to perform an arbitrary logical operation on the incoming data and the data already present; then it replaces the existing data with the results of the operation.

Since this process can be implemented fairly cheaply in hardware, many such machines are available. As an example of using a logical operation, XOR can be used to draw on an image in an undoable way; simply XOR the same drawing again, and the original image is restored. As another example, when using color-index mode, the color indices can be interpreted as bit patterns. Then you can compose an image as combinations of drawings on different layers, use writemasks to limit drawing to different sets of bitplanes, and perform logical operations to modify different layers.

You enable and disable logical operations by passing GL_INDEX_LOGIC_ OP or GL_COLOR_LOGIC_OP to **glEnable()** and **glDisable()** for color-index mode or RGBA mode, respectively. You also must choose among the 16 logical operations with **glLogicOp()**, or you'll just get the effect of the default value, GL_COPY. (For backward compatibility with OpenGL Version 1.0, **glEnable**(GL_LOGIC_OP) also enables logical operation in color-index mode.)

---

void **glLogicOp**(GLenum *opcode*);

Selects the logical operation to be performed, given an incoming (source) fragment and the pixel currently stored in the color buffer (destination). Table 10-4 shows the possible values for *opcode* and their meaning (*s* represents source and *d* destination). The default value is GL_COPY.

---

| Parameter | Operation | Parameter | Operation |
|---|---|---|---|
| GL_CLEAR | 0 | GL_AND | $s \wedge d$ |
| GL_COPY | $s$ | GL_OR | $s \vee d$ |
| GL_NOOP | $d$ | GL_NAND | $\neg(s \wedge d)$ |
| GL_SET | 1 | GL_NOR | $\neg(s \vee d)$ |
| GL_COPY_INVERTED | $\neg s$ | GL_XOR | $s$ XOR $d$ |
| GL_INVERT | $\neg d$ | GL_EQUIV | $\neg(s$ XOR $d)$ |
| GL_AND_REVERSE | $s \wedge \neg d$ | GL_AND_INVERTED | $\neg s \wedge d$ |
| GL_OR_REVERSE | $s \vee \neg d$ | GL_OR_INVERTED | $\neg s \vee d$ |

**Table 10-4**     Sixteen Logical Operations

# The Accumulation Buffer

### Advanced

The accumulation buffer can be used for such things as scene antialiasing, motion blur, simulating photographic depth of field, and calculating the soft shadows that result from multiple light sources. Other techniques are possible, especially in combination with some of the other buffers. (See *The Accumulation Buffer: Hardware Support for High-Quality Rendering* by Paul Haeberli and Kurt Akeley [SIGGRAPH 1990 Proceedings, pp. 309–318] for more information about uses for the accumulation buffer.)

OpenGL graphics operations don't write directly into the accumulation buffer. Typically, a series of images is generated in one of the standard color buffers, and these images are accumulated, one at a time, into the accumulation buffer. When the accumulation is finished, the result is copied back into a color buffer for viewing. To reduce rounding errors, the accumulation buffer may have higher precision (more bits per color) than the standard color buffers. Rendering a scene several times obviously takes longer than rendering it once, but the result is higher quality. You can decide what trade-off between quality and rendering time is appropriate for your application.

You can use the accumulation buffer the same way a photographer can use film for multiple exposures. A photographer typically creates a multiple exposure by taking several pictures of the same scene without advancing the film. If anything in the scene moves, that object appears blurred. Not surprisingly, a computer can do more with an image than a photographer can do with a camera. For example, a computer has exquisite control over the viewpoint, but a photographer can't shake a camera a predictable and controlled amount. (See "Clearing Buffers" on page 470 for information about how to clear the accumulation buffer; use **glAccum()** to control it.)

---

void **glAccum**(GLenum *op*, GLfloat *value*);

---

Controls the accumulation buffer. The *op* parameter selects the operation, and *value* is a number to be used in that operation. The possible operations are GL_ACCUM, GL_LOAD, GL_RETURN, GL_ADD, and GL_MULT:

- GL_ACCUM reads each pixel from the buffer currently selected for reading with **glReadBuffer()**, multiplies the R, G, B, and alpha values by *value*, and adds the resulting values to the accumulation buffer.

- GL_LOAD is the same as GL_ACCUM, except that the values replace those in the accumulation buffer, rather than being added to them.

- GL_RETURN takes values from the accumulation buffer, multiplies them by *value*, and places the results in the color buffer(s) enabled for writing.

- GL_ADD and GL_MULT simply add and multiply, respectively, the value of each pixel in the accumulation buffer to or by *value* and then return it to the accumulation buffer. For GL_MULT, *value* is clamped to be in the range [–1.0, 1.0]. For GL_ADD, no clamping occurs.

## Scene Antialiasing

To perform scene antialiasing, first clear the accumulation buffer and enable the front buffer for reading and writing. Then loop several (say, $n$) times through code that jitters and draws the image (*jittering* is moving the image to a slightly different position), accumulating the data with

```
glAccum(GL_ACCUM, 1.0/n);
```

and finally calling

```
glAccum(GL_RETURN, 1.0);
```

Note that this method is a bit faster if, on the first pass through the loop, GL_LOAD is used and clearing the accumulation buffer is omitted. (See Table 10-5 for possible jittering values.) With this code, the image is drawn $n$ times before the final image is drawn. If you want to avoid showing the user the intermediate images, draw into a color buffer that's not displayed, accumulate from that buffer, and use the GL_RETURN call to draw into a displayed buffer (or into a back buffer that you subsequently swap to the front).

You could instead present a user interface that shows the viewed image improving as each additional piece is accumulated and that allows the user to halt the process when the image is good enough. To accomplish this, in the loop that draws successive images, call **glAccum()** with GL_RETURN after each accumulation, using 16.0/1.0, 16.0/2.0, 16.0/3.0, ... as the second argument. With this technique, after one pass, 1/16 of the final image is shown, after two passes, 2/16 is shown, and so on. After the GL_RETURN, the code should check to see if the user wants to interrupt the process. This interface is slightly slower, since the resultant image must be copied in after each pass.

To decide what *n* should be, you need to trade off speed (the more times you draw the scene, the longer it takes to obtain the final image) and quality (the more times you draw the scene, the smoother it gets, until you make maximum use of the accumulation buffer's resolution). Plate 22 and Plate 23 show improvements made using scene antialiasing.

Example 10-4 defines two routines for jittering that you might find useful: **accPerspective()** and **accFrustum()**. The routine **accPerspective()** is used in place of **gluPerspective()**, and the first four parameters of both routines are the same. To jitter the viewing frustum for scene antialiasing, pass the *x* and *y* jitter values (of less than 1 pixel) to the fifth and sixth parameters of **accPerspective()**. Also, pass 0.0 for the seventh and eighth parameters to **accPerspective()** and a nonzero value for the ninth parameter (to prevent division by zero inside **accPerspective()**). These last three parameters are used for depth-of-field effects, which are described later in this chapter.

**Example 10-4**   Routines for Jittering the Viewing Volume: accpersp.c

```
#define PI_ 3.14159265358979323846

void accFrustum(GLdouble left, GLdouble right, GLdouble bottom,
    GLdouble top, GLdouble zNear, GLdouble zFar, GLdouble pixdx,
    GLdouble pixdy, GLdouble eyedx, GLdouble eyedy,
    GLdouble focus)
{
    GLdouble xwsize, ywsize;
    GLdouble dx, dy;
    GLint viewport[4];

    glGetIntegerv(GL_VIEWPORT, viewport);

    xwsize = right - left;
    ywsize = top - bottom;
    dx = -(pixdx*xwsize/(GLdouble) viewport[2] +
            eyedx*zNear/focus);
    dy = -(pixdy*ywsize/(GLdouble) viewport[3] +
            eyedy*zNear/focus);

    glMatrixMode(GL_PROJECTION);
    glLoadIdentity();
    glFrustum(left + dx, right + dx, bottom + dy, top + dy,
        zNear, zFar);
    glMatrixMode(GL_MODELVIEW);
    glLoadIdentity();
    glTranslatef(-eyedx, -eyedy, 0.0);
}
```

```
void accPerspective(GLdouble fovy, GLdouble aspect,
    GLdouble zNear, GLdouble zFar, GLdouble pixdx,
    GLdouble pixdy, GLdouble eyedx, GLdouble eyedy,
    GLdouble focus)
{
    GLdouble fov2,left,right,bottom,top;
    fov2 = ((fovy*PI_) / 180.0) / 2.0;

    top = zNear / (fcos(fov2) / fsin(fov2));
    bottom = -top;
    right = top * aspect;
    left = -right;

    accFrustum(left, right, bottom, top, zNear, zFar,
        pixdx, pixdy, eyedx, eyedy, focus);
}
```

Example 10-5 uses the two routines in Example 10-4 to perform scene antialiasing.

**Example 10-5**   Scene Antialiasing: accpersp.c

```
void init(void)
{
    GLfloat mat_ambient[] = { 1.0, 1.0, 1.0, 1.0 };
    GLfloat mat_specular[] = { 1.0, 1.0, 1.0, 1.0 };
    GLfloat light_position[] = { 0.0, 0.0, 10.0, 1.0 };
    GLfloat lm_ambient[] = { 0.2, 0.2, 0.2, 1.0 };

    glMaterialfv(GL_FRONT, GL_AMBIENT, mat_ambient);
    glMaterialfv(GL_FRONT, GL_SPECULAR, mat_specular);
    glMaterialf(GL_FRONT, GL_SHININESS, 50.0);
    glLightfv(GL_LIGHT0, GL_POSITION, light_position);
    glLightModelfv(GL_LIGHT_MODEL_AMBIENT, lm_ambient);

    glEnable(GL_LIGHTING);
    glEnable(GL_LIGHT0);
    glEnable(GL_DEPTH_TEST);
    glShadeModel(GL_FLAT);

    glClearColor(0.0, 0.0, 0.0, 0.0);
    glClearAccum(0.0, 0.0, 0.0, 0.0);
}
```

```
void displayObjects(void)
{
    GLfloat torus_diffuse[] = { 0.7, 0.7, 0.0, 1.0 };
    GLfloat cube_diffuse[] = { 0.0, 0.7, 0.7, 1.0 };
    GLfloat sphere_diffuse[] = { 0.7, 0.0, 0.7, 1.0 };
    GLfloat octa_diffuse[] = { 0.7, 0.4, 0.4, 1.0 };

    glPushMatrix();
    glTranslatef(0.0, 0.0, -5.0);
    glRotatef(30.0, 1.0, 0.0, 0.0);

    glPushMatrix();
    glTranslatef(-0.80, 0.35, 0.0);
    glRotatef(100.0, 1.0, 0.0, 0.0);
    glMaterialfv(GL_FRONT, GL_DIFFUSE, torus_diffuse);
    glutSolidTorus(0.275, 0.85, 16, 16);
    glPopMatrix();

    glPushMatrix();
    glTranslatef(-0.75, -0.50, 0.0);
    glRotatef(45.0, 0.0, 0.0, 1.0);
    glRotatef(45.0, 1.0, 0.0, 0.0);
    glMaterialfv(GL_FRONT, GL_DIFFUSE, cube_diffuse);
    glutSolidCube(1.5);
    glPopMatrix();

    glPushMatrix();
    glTranslatef(0.75, 0.60, 0.0);
    glRotatef(30.0, 1.0, 0.0, 0.0);
    glMaterialfv(GL_FRONT, GL_DIFFUSE, sphere_diffuse);
    glutSolidSphere(1.0, 16, 16);
    glPopMatrix();

    glPushMatrix();
    glTranslatef(0.70, -0.90, 0.25);
    glMaterialfv(GL_FRONT, GL_DIFFUSE, octa_diffuse);
    glutSolidOctahedron();
    glPopMatrix();

    glPopMatrix();
}

#define ACSIZE  8

void display(void)
{
```

```
   GLint viewport[4];
   int jitter;

   glGetIntegerv(GL_VIEWPORT, viewport);

   glClear(GL_ACCUM_BUFFER_BIT);
   for (jitter = 0; jitter < ACSIZE; jitter++) {
      glClear(GL_COLOR_BUFFER_BIT | GL_DEPTH_BUFFER_BIT);
      accPerspective(50.0,
         (GLdouble) viewport[2]/(GLdouble) viewport[3],
            1.0, 15.0, j8[jitter].x, j8[jitter].y, 0.0, 0.0, 1.0);
      displayObjects();
      glAccum(GL_ACCUM, 1.0/ACSIZE);
   }
   glAccum(GL_RETURN, 1.0);
   glFlush();
}

void reshape(int w, int h)
{
   glViewport(0, 0, (GLsizei) w, (GLsizei) h);
}

/*  Main Loop
 *  Be certain you request an accumulation buffer.
 */
int main(int argc, char** argv)
{
   glutInit(&argc, argv);
   glutInitDisplayMode(GLUT_SINGLE | GLUT_RGB |
                       GLUT_ACCUM | GLUT_DEPTH);
   glutInitWindowSize(250, 250);
   glutInitWindowPosition(100, 100);
   glutCreateWindow(argv[0]);
   init();
   glutReshapeFunc(reshape);
   glutDisplayFunc(display);
   glutMainLoop();
   return 0;
}
```

You don't have to use a perspective projection to perform scene antialiasing. You can antialias a scene with orthographic projection simply by using **glTranslate*()** to jitter the scene. Keep in mind that **glTranslate*()** operates in world coordinates, but you want the apparent motion of the scene to be less than 1 pixel, measured in screen coordinates. Thus, you must reverse the world-coordinate mapping by calculating the jittering translation values, using its width or height in world coordinates divided by its viewport

Under normal conditions, everything you draw with OpenGL is in focus (unless your monitor is bad; in which case, everything is out of focus). The accumulation buffer can be used to approximate what you would see in a photograph, where items are increasingly blurred as their distance from the plane of perfect focus increases. It isn't an exact simulation of the effects produced in a camera, but the result looks similar to what a camera would produce.

To achieve this result, draw the scene repeatedly using calls with different argument values to **glFrustum()**. Choose the arguments so that the position of the viewpoint varies slightly around its true position and so that each frustum shares a common rectangle that lies in the plane of perfect focus, as shown in Figure 10-3. The results of all the renderings should be averaged in the usual way using the accumulation buffer.

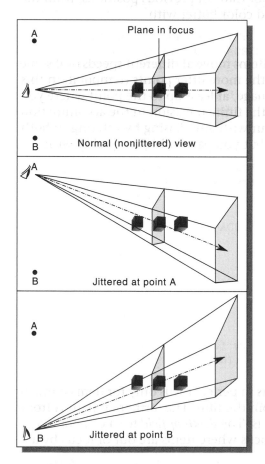

**Figure 10-3**     Jittered Viewing Volume for Depth-of-Field Effects

Plate 10 shows an image of five teapots drawn using the depth-of-field effect. The gold teapot (second from the left) is in focus, and the other teapots get progressively blurrier, depending on their distance from the focal plane (gold teapot). The code used to draw this image is shown in Example 10-7 (which assumes that **accPerspective()** and **accFrustum()** are defined as described in Example 10-4). The scene is drawn eight times, each with a slightly jittered viewing volume, by calling **accPerspective()**. As you recall, with scene antialiasing, the fifth and sixth parameters jitter the viewing volumes in the $x$- and $y$-directions. For the depth-of-field effect, however, you want to jitter the volume while holding it stationary at the focal plane. The focal plane is the depth value defined by the ninth (last) parameter to **accPerspective()**, which is $z = 5.0$ in this example. The amount of blur is determined by multiplying the $x$ and $y$ jitter values (seventh and eighth parameters of **accPerspective()**) by a constant. Determining the constant is not a science; experiment with values until the depth of field is as pronounced as you want. (Note that in Example 10-7, the fifth and sixth parameters to **accPerspective()** are set to 0.0, so scene antialiasing is turned off.)

**Example 10-7**   Depth-of-Field Effect: dof.c

```
void init(void)
{
   GLfloat ambient[] = { 0.0, 0.0, 0.0, 1.0 };
   GLfloat diffuse[] = { 1.0, 1.0, 1.0, 1.0 };
   GLfloat specular[] = { 1.0, 1.0, 1.0, 1.0 };
   GLfloat position[] = { 0.0, 3.0, 3.0, 0.0 };

   GLfloat lmodel_ambient[] = { 0.2, 0.2, 0.2, 1.0 };
   GLfloat local_view[] = { 0.0 };

   glLightfv(GL_LIGHT0, GL_AMBIENT, ambient);
   glLightfv(GL_LIGHT0, GL_DIFFUSE, diffuse);
   glLightfv(GL_LIGHT0, GL_POSITION, position);

   glLightModelfv(GL_LIGHT_MODEL_AMBIENT, lmodel_ambient);
   glLightModelfv(GL_LIGHT_MODEL_LOCAL_VIEWER, local_view);

   glFrontFace(GL_CW);
   glEnable(GL_LIGHTING);
   glEnable(GL_LIGHT0);
   glEnable(GL_AUTO_NORMAL);
   glEnable(GL_NORMALIZE);
   glEnable(GL_DEPTH_TEST);
```

```
      glClearColor(0.0, 0.0, 0.0, 0.0);
      glClearAccum(0.0, 0.0, 0.0, 0.0);
/*  make teapot display list */
      teapotList = glGenLists(1);
      glNewList(teapotList, GL_COMPILE);
      glutSolidTeapot(0.5);
      glEndList();
}

void renderTeapot(GLfloat x, GLfloat y, GLfloat z,
      GLfloat ambr, GLfloat ambg, GLfloat ambb,
      GLfloat difr, GLfloat difg, GLfloat difb,
      GLfloat specr, GLfloat specg, GLfloat specb, GLfloat shine)
{
      GLfloat mat[4];

      glPushMatrix();
      glTranslatef(x, y, z);
      mat[0] = ambr; mat[1] = ambg; mat[2] = ambb; mat[3] = 1.0;
      glMaterialfv(GL_FRONT, GL_AMBIENT, mat);
      mat[0] = difr; mat[1] = difg; mat[2] = difb;
      glMaterialfv(GL_FRONT, GL_DIFFUSE, mat);
      mat[0] = specr; mat[1] = specg; mat[2] = specb;
      glMaterialfv(GL_FRONT, GL_SPECULAR, mat);
      glMaterialf(GL_FRONT, GL_SHININESS, shine*128.0);
      glCallList(teapotList);
      glPopMatrix();
}

void display(void)
{
      int jitter;
      GLint viewport[4];

      glGetIntegerv(GL_VIEWPORT, viewport);
      glClear(GL_ACCUM_BUFFER_BIT);

      for (jitter = 0; jitter < 8; jitter++) {
         glClear(GL_COLOR_BUFFER_BIT | GL_DEPTH_BUFFER_BIT);
         accPerspective(45.0,
            (GLdouble) viewport[2]/(GLdouble) viewport[3],
            1.0, 15.0, 0.0, 0.0,
            0.33*j8[jitter].x, 0.33*j8[jitter].y, 5.0);
```

```
/*        ruby, gold, silver, emerald, and cyan teapots    */
       renderTeapot(-1.1, -0.5, -4.5, 0.1745, 0.01175,
                    0.01175, 0.61424, 0.04136, 0.04136,
                    0.727811, 0.626959, 0.626959, 0.6);
       renderTeapot(-0.5, -0.5, -5.0, 0.24725, 0.1995,
                    0.0745, 0.75164, 0.60648, 0.22648,
                    0.628281, 0.555802, 0.366065, 0.4);
       renderTeapot(0.2, -0.5, -5.5, 0.19225, 0.19225,
                    0.19225, 0.50754, 0.50754, 0.50754,
                    0.508273, 0.508273, 0.508273, 0.4);
       renderTeapot(1.0, -0.5, -6.0, 0.0215, 0.1745, 0.0215,
                    0.07568, 0.61424, 0.07568, 0.633,
                    0.727811, 0.633, 0.6);
       renderTeapot(1.8, -0.5, -6.5, 0.0, 0.1, 0.06, 0.0,
                    0.50980392, 0.50980392, 0.50196078,
                    0.50196078, 0.50196078, .25);
       glAccum(GL_ACCUM, 0.125);
    }
    glAccum(GL_RETURN, 1.0);
    glFlush();
}

void reshape(int w, int h)
{
    glViewport(0, 0, (GLsizei) w, (GLsizei) h);
}

/*  Main Loop
 *  Be certain you request an accumulation buffer.
 */
int main(int argc, char** argv)
{
    glutInit(&argc, argv);
    glutInitDisplayMode(GLUT_SINGLE | GLUT_RGB |
                        GLUT_ACCUM | GLUT_DEPTH);
    glutInitWindowSize(400, 400);
    glutInitWindowPosition(100, 100);
    glutCreateWindow(argv[0]);
    init();
    glutReshapeFunc(reshape);
    glutDisplayFunc(display);
    glutMainLoop();
    return 0;
}
```

## Soft Shadows

To accumulate soft shadows resulting from multiple light sources, render the shadows with one light turned on at a time, and accumulate them together. This can be combined with spatial jittering to antialias the scene at the same time. (See "Shadows" on page 621 for more information about drawing shadows.)

## Jittering

If you need to take 9 or 16 samples to antialias an image, you might think that the best choice of points is an equally spaced grid across the pixel. Surprisingly, this is not necessarily true. In fact, sometimes it's a good idea to take points that lie in adjacent pixels. You might want a uniform distribution or a normalized distribution, clustering toward the center of the pixel. In addition, Table 10-5 shows a few sets of reasonable jittering values to be used for some selected sample counts. Most of the examples in this table are uniformly distributed in the pixel, and all lie within the pixel.

| Count | Values |
|---|---|
| 2 | {0.25, 0.75}, {0.75, 0.25} |
| 3 | {0.5033922635, 0.8317967229}, {0.7806016275, 0.2504380877}, {0.2261828938, 0.4131553612} |
| 4 | {0.375, 0.25}, {0.125, 0.75}, {0.875, 0.25}, {0.625, 0.75} |
| 5 | {0.5, 0.5}, {0.3, 0.1}, {0.7, 0.9}, {0.9, 0.3}, {0.1, 0.7} |
| 6 | {0.4646464646, 0.4646464646}, {0.1313131313, 0.7979797979}, {0.5353535353, 0.8686868686}, {0.8686868686, 0.5353535353}, {0.7979797979, 0.1313131313}, {0.2020202020, 0.2020202020} |
| 8 | {0.5625, 0.4375}, {0.0625, 0.9375}, {0.3125, 0.6875}, {0.6875, 0.8125}, {0.8125, 0.1875}, {0.9375, 0.5625}, {0.4375, 0.0625}, {0.1875, 0.3125} |
| 9 | {0.5, 0.5}, {0.1666666666, 0.9444444444}, {0.5, 0.1666666666}, {0.5, 0.8333333333}, {0.1666666666, 0.2777777777}, {0.8333333333, 0.3888888888}, {0.1666666666, 0.6111111111}, {0.8333333333, 0.7222222222}, {0.8333333333, 0.0555555555} |

**Table 10-5**    Sample Jittering Values

| Count | Values |
|-------|--------|
| 12 | {0.4166666666, 0.625}, {0.9166666666, 0.875}, {0.25, 0.375}, {0.4166666666, 0.125}, {0.75, 0.125}, {0.0833333333, 0.125}, {0.75, 0.625}, {0.25, 0.875}, {0.5833333333, 0.375}, {0.9166666666, 0.375}, {0.0833333333, 0.625}, {0.583333333, 0.875} |
| 16 | {0.375, 0.4375}, {0.625, 0.0625}, {0.875, 0.1875}, {0.125, 0.0625}, {0.375, 0.6875}, {0.875, 0.4375}, {0.625, 0.5625}, {0.375, 0.9375}, {0.625, 0.3125}, {0.125, 0.5625}, {0.125, 0.8125}, {0.375, 0.1875}, {0.875, 0.9375}, {0.875, 0.6875}, {0.125, 0.3125}, {0.625, 0.8125} |

**Table 10-5** **(continued)**     Sample Jittering Values

The OpenGL Library (GL) is designed for low-level operations, both stream-lined and accessible to hardware acceleration. The OpenGL Utility Library (GLU) complements the OpenGL library, supporting higher-level operations. Some of the GLU operations are covered in other chapters. Mipmapping (**gluBuild\*DMipmaps()**) and image scaling (**gluScaleImage()**) are discussed along with other facets of texture mapping in Chapter 9. Several matrix trans-formation GLU routines (**gluOrtho2D()**, **gluPerspective()**, **gluLookAt()**, **gluProject()**, **gluUnProject()**, and **gluUnProject4()**) are described in Chapter 3. The use of **gluPickMatrix()** is explained in Chapter 13. The GLU NURBS facilities, which are built atop OpenGL evaluators, are covered in Chapter 12. Only two GLU topics remain: polygon tessellators and quad-ric surfaces; these topics are discussed in this chapter.

To optimize performance, the basic OpenGL renders only convex polygons, but the GLU contains routines for tessellating concave polygons into con-vex ones, which the basic OpenGL can handle. Where the basic OpenGL operates on simple primitives, such as points, lines, and filled polygons, the GLU can create higher-level objects, such as the surfaces of spheres, cylin-ders, and cones.

This chapter has the following major sections.

- "Polygon Tessellation" explains how to tessellate concave polygons into easier-to-render convex polygons.

- "Quadrics: Rendering Spheres, Cylinders, and Disks" describes how to generate spheres, cylinders, circles and arcs, including data such as surface normals and texture coordinates.

## Polygon Tessellation

As discussed in "Describing Points, Lines, and Polygons" in Chapter 2, OpenGL can directly display only simple convex polygons. A polygon is simple if the edges intersect only at vertices, there are no duplicate vertices, and exactly two edges meet at any vertex. If your application requires the display of concave polygons, polygons containing holes, or polygons with intersecting edges, these polygons must first be subdivided into simple convex polygons before they can be displayed. Such subdivision is called *tessellation*, and the GLU provides a collection of routines that perform tessellation. These routines take as input arbitrary contours, which describe hard-to-render polygons, and they return some combination of triangles, triangle meshes, triangle fans, and lines.

Figure 11-1 shows some contours of polygons that require tessellation: from left to right, a concave polygon, a polygon with a hole, and a self-intersecting polygon.

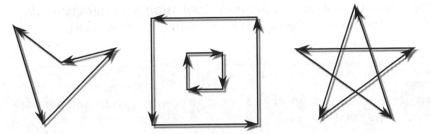

**Figure 11-1**    Contours That Require Tessellation

If you think a polygon may need tessellation, follow these typical steps:

1. Create a new tessellation object with **gluNewTess()**.

2. Use **gluTessCallback()** several times to register callback functions to perform operations during the tessellation. The trickiest case for a callback function is when the tessellation algorithm detects an intersection and must call the function registered for the GLU_TESS_ COMBINE callback.

3. Specify tessellation properties by calling **gluTessProperty()**. The most important property is the winding rule, which determines the regions that should be filled and those that should remain unshaded.

4. Create and render tessellated polygons by specifying the contours of one or more closed polygons. If the data for the object is static, encapsulate the tessellated polygons in a display list. (If you don't have to recalculate the tessellation repeatedly, using display lists is more efficient.)

5. If you need to tessellate something else, you may reuse your tessellation object. If you are forever finished with your tessellation object, you may delete it with **gluDeleteTess()**.

**Note:** The tessellator described here was introduced in Version 1.2 of the GLU. If you are using an older version of the GLU, you must use routines described in "Describing GLU Errors" on page 522. To query which version of GLU you have, use **gluGetString(GLU_VERSION)**, which returns a string with your GLU version number. If you don't seem to have **gluGetString()** in your GLU, then you have GLU 1.0, which did not yet have the **gluGetString()** routine.

## Creating a Tessellation Object

As a complex polygon is being described and tessellated, it has associated data, such as the vertices, edges, and callback functions. All this data is tied to a single tessellation object. To perform tessellation, your program first has to create a tessellation object using the routine **gluNewTess()**.

---

GLUtesselator* **gluNewTess**(void);

Creates a new tessellation object and returns a pointer to it. A null pointer is returned if the creation fails.

---

A single tessellation object can be reused for all your tessellations. This object is required only because library routines might need to do their own tessellations, and they should be able to do so without interfering with any tessellation that your program is doing. It might also be useful to have multiple tessellation objects if you want to use different sets of callbacks for different tessellations. A typical program, however, allocates a single tessellation object and uses it for all its tessellations. There's no real need to free it, because it uses a small amount of memory. On the other hand, it never hurts to be tidy.

## Tessellation Callback Routines

After you create a tessellation object, you must provide a series of callback routines to be called at appropriate times during the tessellation. After specifying the callbacks, you describe the contours of one or more polygons using GLU routines. When the description of the contours is complete, the tessellation facility invokes your callback routines as necessary.

Any functions that are omitted are simply not called during the tessellation, and any information they might have returned to your program is lost. All are specified by the single routine **gluTessCallback()**.

void **gluTessCallback**(GLUtesselator *tessobj*, GLenum *type*, void (*fn*)());

Associates the callback function *fn* with the tessellation object *tessobj*. The type of the callback is determined by the parameter *type*, which can be GLU_TESS_BEGIN, GLU_TESS_BEGIN_DATA, GLU_TESS_EDGE_FLAG, GLU_TESS_EDGE_FLAG_DATA, GLU_TESS_VERTEX, GLU_TESS_VERTEX_DATA, GLU_TESS_END, GLU_TESS_END_DATA, GLU_TESS_COMBINE, GLU_TESS_COMBINE_DATA, GLU_TESS_ERROR, or GLU_TESS_ERROR_DATA. The 12 possible callback functions have the following prototypes:

GLU_TESS_BEGIN                void **begin**(GLenum *type*);

GLU_TESS_BEGIN_DATA           void **begin**(GLenum *type*,
                                      void *\*user_data*);

GLU_TESS_EDGE_FLAG            void **edgeFlag**(GLboolean *flag*);

GLU_TESS_EDGE_FLAG_DATA       void **edgeFlag**(GLboolean *flag*,
                                      void *\*user_data*);

GLU_TESS_VERTEX               void **vertex**(void *\*vertex_data*);

GLU_TESS_VERTEX_DATA          void **vertex**(void *\*vertex_data*,
                                      void *\*user_data*);

GLU_TESS_END                  void **end**(void);

GLU_TESS_END_DATA             void **end**(void *\*user_data*);

GLU_TESS_COMBINE              void **combine**(
                                      GLdouble *coords*[3],
                                      void *\*vertex_data*[4],
                                      GLfloat *weight*[4],
                                      void *\*\*outData*);

GLU_TESS_COMBINE_DATA         void **combine**(
                                      GLdouble *coords*[3],
                                      void *\*vertex_data*[4],
                                      GLfloat *weight*[4],
                                      void *\*\*outData*,
                                      void *\*user_data*);

GLU_TESS_ERROR                void **error**(GLenum *errno*);

GLU_TESS_ERROR_DATA           void **error**(GLenum *errno*,
                                      void *\*user_data*);

To change a callback routine, simply call **gluTessCallback()** with the new routine. To eliminate a callback routine without replacing it with a new one, pass **gluTessCallback()** a null pointer for the appropriate function.

As tessellation proceeds, the callback routines are called in a manner similar to how you use the OpenGL commands **glBegin()**, **glEdgeFlag*()**, **glVertex*()**, and **glEnd()**. (See "Marking Polygon Boundary Edges" in Chapter 2 for more information about **glEdgeFlag*()**.) The combine callback is used to create new vertices where edges intersect. The error callback is invoked during the tessellation only if something goes wrong.

For every tessellator object created, a GLU_TESS_BEGIN callback is invoked with one of four possible parameters: GL_TRIANGLE_FAN, GL_TRIANGLE_STRIP, GL_TRIANGLES, or GL_LINE_LOOP. When the tessellator decomposes the polygons, the tessellation algorithm decides which type of triangle primitive is most efficient to use. (If the GLU_TESS_BOUNDARY_ONLY property is enabled, then GL_LINE_LOOP is used for rendering.)

Since edge flags make no sense in a triangle fan or triangle strip, if there is a callback associated with GLU_TESS_EDGE_FLAG that enables edge flags, the GLU_TESS_BEGIN callback is called only with GL_TRIANGLES. The GLU_TESS_EDGE_FLAG callback works exactly analogously to the OpenGL **glEdgeFlag*()** call.

After the GLU_TESS_BEGIN callback routine is called and before the callback associated with GLU_TESS_END is called, some combination of the GLU_TESS_EDGE_FLAG and GLU_TESS_VERTEX callbacks is invoked (usually by calls to **gluTessVertex()**, which is described on page 519). The associated edge flags and vertices are interpreted exactly as they are in OpenGL between **glBegin()** and the matching **glEnd()**.

If something goes wrong, the error callback is passed a GLU error number. A character string describing the error is obtained using the routine **gluErrorString()**. (See "Describing GLU Errors" on page 522 for more information about this routine.)

Example 11-1 shows a portion of tess.c, in which a tessellation object is created and several callbacks are registered.

**Example 11-1**   Registering Tessellation Callbacks: tess.c

```
#ifndef CALLBACK
#define CALLBACK
#endif
```

```
/*  a portion of init() */

tobj = gluNewTess();
gluTessCallback(tobj, GLU_TESS_VERTEX, glVertex3dv);
gluTessCallback(tobj, GLU_TESS_BEGIN, beginCallback);
gluTessCallback(tobj, GLU_TESS_END, endCallback);
gluTessCallback(tobj, GLU_TESS_ERROR, errorCallback);

/*  the callback routines registered by gluTessCallback() */
void CALLBACK beginCallback(GLenum which)
{
   glBegin(which);
}

void CALLBACK endCallback(void)
{
   glEnd();
}

void CALLBACK errorCallback(GLenum errorCode)
{
   const GLubyte *estring;

   estring = gluErrorString(errorCode);
   fprintf(stderr, "Tessellation Error: %s\n", estring);
   exit(0);
}
```

**Note:** Type casting of callback functions is tricky, especially if you wish to make code that runs equally well on Microsoft Windows and UNIX. To run on Microsoft Windows, programs that declare callback functions, such as tess.c, need the symbol CALLBACK in the declarations of functions. The trick of using an empty definition for CALLBACK (as demonstrated below) allows the code to run well on both Microsoft Windows and UNIX:

```
#ifndef CALLBACK
#define CALLBACK
#endif

void CALLBACK callbackFunction(...) {
   ....
}
```

In Example 11-1, the registered GLU_TESS_VERTEX callback is simply **glVertex3dv()**, and only the coordinates at each vertex are passed along. However, if you want to specify more information at every vertex, such as a color value, a surface normal vector, or a texture coordinate, you'll have to make a more complex callback routine. Example 11-2 shows the start of another tessellated object, further along in program tess.c. The registered function **vertexCallback()** expects to receive a parameter that is a pointer to six double-length floating-point values: the *x*-, *y*-, and *z*-coordinates and the red, green, and blue color values for that vertex.

**Example 11-2**   Vertex and Combine Callbacks: tess.c

```
/*  a different portion of init() */
   gluTessCallback(tobj, GLU_TESS_VERTEX, vertexCallback);
   gluTessCallback(tobj, GLU_TESS_BEGIN, beginCallback);
   gluTessCallback(tobj, GLU_TESS_END, endCallback);
   gluTessCallback(tobj, GLU_TESS_ERROR, errorCallback);
   gluTessCallback(tobj, GLU_TESS_COMBINE, combineCallback);

/*  new callback routines registered by these calls */
void CALLBACK vertexCallback(GLvoid *vertex)
{
   const GLdouble *pointer;

   pointer = (GLdouble *) vertex;
   glColor3dv(pointer+3);
   glVertex3dv(vertex);
}


void CALLBACK combineCallback(GLdouble coords[3],
                   GLdouble *vertex_data[4],
                   GLfloat weight[4], GLdouble **dataOut )
{
   GLdouble *vertex;
   int i;

   vertex = (GLdouble *) malloc(6 * sizeof(GLdouble));
   vertex[0] = coords[0];
   vertex[1] = coords[1];
   vertex[2] = coords[2];
   for (i = 3; i < 6; i++)
      vertex[i] = weight[0] * vertex_data[0][i]
                  + weight[1] * vertex_data[1][i]
                  + weight[2] * vertex_data[2][i]
                  + weight[3] * vertex_data[3][i];
   *dataOut = vertex;
}
```

Example 11-2 also shows the use of the GLU_TESS_COMBINE callback. Whenever the tessellation algorithm examines the input contours, detects an intersection, and decides it must create a new vertex, the GLU_TESS_COMBINE callback is invoked. The callback is also called when the tessellator decides to merge features of two vertices that are very close to one another. The newly created vertex is a linear combination of up to four existing vertices, referenced by *vertex_data*[0..3] in Example 11-2. The coefficients of the linear combination are given by *weight*[0..3]; these weights sum to 1.0. *coords* gives the location of the new vertex.

The registered callback routine must allocate memory for another vertex, perform a weighted interpolation of data using *vertex_data* and *weight*, and return the new vertex pointer as *dataOut*. **combineCallback()** in Example 11-2 interpolates the RGB color value. The function allocates a six-element array, puts the *x*-, *y*-, and *z*-coordinates in the first three elements, and then puts the weighted average of the RGB color values in the last three elements.

### User-Specified Data

Six kinds of callbacks can be registered. Since there are two versions of each kind of callback, there are 12 callbacks in all. For each kind of callback, there is one with user-specified data and one without. The user-specified data is given by the application to **gluTessBeginPolygon()** and is then passed, unaltered, to each *DATA callback routine. With GLU_TESS_BEGIN_DATA, the user-specified data may be used for "per-polygon" data. If you specify both versions of a particular callback, the callback with *user_data* is used, and the other is ignored. Therefore, although there are 12 callbacks, you can have a maximum of six callback functions active at any one time.

For instance, Example 11-2 uses smooth shading, so **vertexCallback()** specifies an RGB color for every vertex. If you want to do lighting and smooth shading, the callback would specify a surface normal for every vertex. However, if you want lighting and flat shading, you might specify only one surface normal for every polygon, not for every vertex. In that case, you might choose to use the GLU_TESS_BEGIN_DATA callback and pass the vertex coordinates and surface normal in the *user_data* pointer.

## Tessellation Properties

Prior to tessellation and rendering, you may use **gluTessProperty()** to set several properties to affect the tessellation algorithm. The most important and complicated of these properties is the winding rule, which determines what is considered "interior" and "exterior."

---

void **gluTessProperty**(GLUtesselator *tessobj*, GLenum *property*, GLdouble *value*);

---

For the tessellation object *tessobj*, the current value of *property* is set to *value*. *property* is GLU_TESS_BOUNDARY_ONLY, GLU_TESS_TOLERANCE, or GLU_TESS_WINDING_RULE.

If *property* is GLU_TESS_BOUNDARY_ONLY, *value* is either GL_TRUE or GL_FALSE. When it is set to GL_TRUE, polygons are no longer tessellated into filled polygons; line loops are drawn to outline the contours that separate the polygon interior and exterior. The default value is GL_FALSE. (See **gluTessNormal**() to see how to control the winding direction of the contours.)

If *property* is GLU_TESS_TOLERANCE, *value* is a distance used to calculate whether two vertices are close enough together to be merged by the GLU_TESS_COMBINE callback. The tolerance value is multiplied by the largest coordinate magnitude of an input vertex to determine the maximum distance any feature can move as a result of a single merge operation. Feature merging may not be supported by your implementation, and the tolerance value is only a hint. The default tolerance value is zero.

The GLU_TESS_WINDING_RULE property determines which parts of the polygon are on the interior and which are on the exterior and should not be filled. *value* can be GLU_TESS_WINDING_ODD (the default), GLU_TESS_WINDING_NONZERO, GLU_TESS_WINDING_POSITIVE, GLU_TESS_WINDING_NEGATIVE, or GLU_TESS_WINDING_ABS_GEQ_TWO.

## Winding Numbers and Winding Rules

For a single contour, the winding number of a point is the signed number of revolutions we make around that point while traveling once around the contour (where a counterclockwise revolution is positive and a clockwise revolution is negative). When there are several contours, the individual winding numbers are summed. This procedure associates a signed integer value with each point in the plane. Note that the winding number is the same for all points in a single region.

Figure 11-2 shows three sets of contours and winding numbers for points inside those contours. In the set at the left, all three contours are counterclockwise, so each nested interior region adds 1 to the winding number. In the middle set, the two interior contours are drawn clockwise, so the winding number decreases and actually becomes negative.

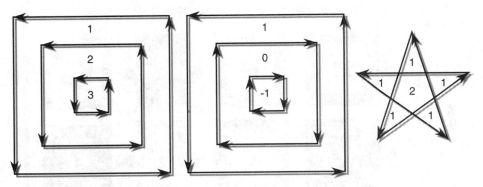

**Figure 11-2**   Winding Numbers for Sample Contours

The winding rule classifies a region as *inside* if its winding number belongs to the chosen category (odd, nonzero, positive, negative, or "absolute value greater than or equal to 2"). The odd and nonzero rules are common ways to define the interior. The positive, negative, and "absolute value ≥ 2" winding rules have some limited use for polygon CSG (computational solid geometry) operations.

The program tesswind.c demonstrates the effects of winding rules. The four sets of contours shown in Figure 11-3 are rendered. The user can then cycle through the different winding rule properties to see their effects. For each winding rule, the dark areas represent interiors. Note the effects of clockwise and counterclockwise winding.

### CSG Uses for Winding Rules

GLU_TESS_WINDING_ODD and GLU_TESS_WINDING_NONZERO are the most commonly used winding rules. They work for the most typical cases of shading.

The winding rules are also designed for CSG operations, making it easy to find the union, difference, or intersection (Boolean operations) of several contours.

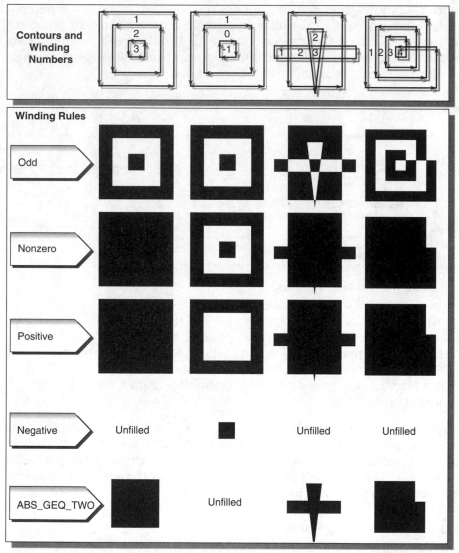

**Figure 11-3** How Winding Rules Define Interiors

First, assume that each contour is defined so that the winding number is 0 for each exterior region and 1 for each interior region. (Each contour must not intersect itself.) Under this model, counterclockwise contours define the outer boundary of the polygon, and clockwise contours define holes. Contours may be nested, but a nested contour must be oriented oppositely from the contour that contains it.

If the original polygons do not satisfy this description, they can be converted to this form by first running the tessellator with the GLU_TESS_BOUNDARY_ONLY property turned on. This returns a list of contours satisfying the restriction just described. By creating two tessellator objects, the callbacks from one tessellator can be fed directly as input to the other.

Given two or more polygons of the preceding form, CSG operations can be implemented as follows:

- UNION—To calculate the union of several contours, draw all input contours as a single polygon. The winding number of each resulting region is the number of original polygons that cover it. The union can be extracted by using the GLU_TESS_WINDING_NONZERO or GLU_TESS_WINDING_POSITIVE winding rule. Note that with the nonzero winding rule, we would get the same result if all contour orientations were reversed.

- INTERSECTION—This works only for two contours at a time. Draw a single polygon using two contours. Extract the result using GLU_TESS_WINDING_ABS_GEQ_TWO.

- DIFFERENCE—Suppose you want to compute A diff (B union C union D). Draw a single polygon consisting of the unmodified contours from A, followed by the contours of B, C, and D, with their vertex order reversed. To extract the result, use the GLU_TESS_WINDING_POSITIVE winding rule. (If B, C, and D are the result of a GLU_TESS_BOUNDARY_ONLY operation, an alternative to reversing the vertex order is to use **gluTessNormal**() to reverse the sign of the supplied normal.)

## Other Tessellation Property Routines

There are also complementary routines, which work alongside **gluTessProperty**(). **gluGetTessProperty**() retrieves the current values of tessellator properties. If the tessellator is being used to generate wireframe outlines instead of filled polygons, **gluTessNormal**() can be used to determine the winding direction of the tessellated polygons.

---

void **gluGetTessProperty**(GLUtesselator *tessobj*, GLenum *property*, GLdouble *value*);

---

For the tessellation object *tessobj*, the current value of *property* is returned to *value*. Values for *property* and *value* are the same as for **gluTessProperty**().

void **gluTessNormal**(GLUtesselator *tessobj*, GLdouble *x*, GLdouble *y*,
            GLdouble *z*);

For the tessellation object *tessobj*, **gluTessNormal**() defines a normal vector, which controls the winding direction of generated polygons. Before tessellation, all input data is projected into a plane perpendicular to the normal. Then, all output triangles are oriented counterclockwise, with respect to the normal. (Clockwise orientation can be obtained by reversing the sign of the supplied normal.) The default normal is (0, 0, 0).

If you have some knowledge about the location and orientation of the input data, then using **gluTessNormal**() can increase the speed of the tessellation. For example, if you know that all polygons lie on the *xy*-plane, call **gluTessNormal**(*tessobj*, 0, 0, 1).

As stated above, the default normal is (0, 0, 0), and its effect is not immediately obvious. In this case, it is expected that the input data lies approximately in a plane, and a plane is fitted to the vertices, no matter how they are truly connected. The sign of the normal is chosen so that the sum of the signed areas of all input contours is non-negative (where a counterclockwise contour has a positive area). Note that if the input data does not lie approximately in a plane, then projection perpendicular to the computed normal may substantially change the geometry.

## Polygon Definition

After all the tessellation properties have been set and the callback actions have been registered, it is finally time to describe the vertices that comprise input contours and tessellate the polygons.

void **gluTessBeginPolygon**(GLUtesselator *tessobj*, void *user_data*);
void **gluTessEndPolygon**(GLUtesselator *tessobj*);

Begins and ends the specification of a polygon to be tessellated and associates a tessellation object, *tessobj*, with it. *user_data* points to a user-defined data structure, which is passed along all the GLU_TESS_*_DATA callback functions that have been bound.

Calls to **gluTessBeginPolygon**() and **gluTessEndPolygon**() surround the definition of one or more contours. When **gluTessEndPolygon**() is called, the tessellation algorithm is implemented, and the tessellated polygons are generated and rendered. The callback functions and tessellation properties that were bound and set to the tessellation object using **gluTessCallback**() and **gluTessProperty**() are used.

---

void **gluTessBeginContour**(GLUtesselator *tessobj*);
void **gluTessEndContour**(GLUtesselator *tessobj*);

---

Begins and ends the specification of a closed contour, which is a portion of a polygon. A closed contour consists of zero or more calls to **gluTessVertex**(), which defines the vertices. The last vertex of each contour is automatically linked to the first.

In practice, a minimum of three vertices is needed for a meaningful contour.

---

void **gluTessVertex**(GLUtesselator *tessobj*, GLdouble *coords*[3],
                void *vertex_data*);

---

Specifies a vertex in the current contour for the tessellation object. *coords* contains the three-dimensional vertex coordinates, and *vertex_data* is a pointer that's sent to the callback associated with GLU_TESS_VERTEX or GLU_TESS_VERTEX_DATA. Typically, *vertex_data* contains vertex coordinates, surface normals, texture coordinates, color information, or whatever else the application may find useful.

In the program tess.c, a portion of which is shown in Example 11-3, two polygons are defined. One polygon is a rectangular contour with a triangular hole inside, and the other is a smooth-shaded, self-intersecting, five-pointed star. For efficiency, both polygons are stored in display lists. The first polygon consists of two contours; the outer one is wound counterclockwise, and the "hole" is wound clockwise. For the second polygon, the *star* array contains both the coordinate and color data, and its tessellation callback, **vertexCallback**(), uses both.

It is important that each vertex is in a different memory location because the vertex data is not copied by **gluTessVertex**(); only the pointer (*vertex_data*) is saved. A program that reuses the same memory for several vertices may not get the desired result.

**Note:** In **gluTessVertex()**, it may seem redundant to specify the vertex coordinate data twice, for both the *coords* and *vertex_data* parameters; however, both are necessary. *coords* refers only to the vertex coordinates. *vertex_data* uses the coordinate data, but may also use other information for each vertex.

**Example 11-3**   Polygon Definition: tess.c

```
GLdouble rect[4][3] = {50.0, 50.0, 0.0,
                       200.0, 50.0, 0.0,
                       200.0, 200.0, 0.0,
                       50.0, 200.0, 0.0};
GLdouble tri[3][3] = {75.0, 75.0, 0.0,
                      125.0, 175.0, 0.0,
                      175.0, 75.0, 0.0};
GLdouble star[5][6] = {250.0, 50.0, 0.0, 1.0, 0.0, 1.0,
                       325.0, 200.0, 0.0, 1.0, 1.0, 0.0,
                       400.0, 50.0, 0.0, 0.0, 1.0, 1.0,
                       250.0, 150.0, 0.0, 1.0, 0.0, 0.0,
                       400.0, 150.0, 0.0, 0.0, 1.0, 0.0};

startList = glGenLists(2);
tobj = gluNewTess();
gluTessCallback(tobj, GLU_TESS_VERTEX, glVertex3dv);
gluTessCallback(tobj, GLU_TESS_BEGIN, beginCallback);
gluTessCallback(tobj, GLU_TESS_END, endCallback);
gluTessCallback(tobj, GLU_TESS_ERROR, errorCallback);

glNewList(startList, GL_COMPILE);
glShadeModel(GL_FLAT);
gluTessBeginPolygon(tobj, NULL);
   gluTessBeginContour(tobj);
      gluTessVertex(tobj, rect[0], rect[0]);
      gluTessVertex(tobj, rect[1], rect[1]);
      gluTessVertex(tobj, rect[2], rect[2]);
      gluTessVertex(tobj, rect[3], rect[3]);
   gluTessEndContour(tobj);
   gluTessBeginContour(tobj);
      gluTessVertex(tobj, tri[0], tri[0]);
      gluTessVertex(tobj, tri[1], tri[1]);
      gluTessVertex(tobj, tri[2], tri[2]);
   gluTessEndContour(tobj);
gluTessEndPolygon(tobj);
glEndList();
```

```
gluTessCallback(tobj, GLU_TESS_VERTEX, vertexCallback);
gluTessCallback(tobj, GLU_TESS_BEGIN, beginCallback);
gluTessCallback(tobj, GLU_TESS_END, endCallback);
gluTessCallback(tobj, GLU_TESS_ERROR, errorCallback);
gluTessCallback(tobj, GLU_TESS_COMBINE, combineCallback);

glNewList(startList + 1, GL_COMPILE);
glShadeModel(GL_SMOOTH);
gluTessProperty(tobj, GLU_TESS_WINDING_RULE,
                GLU_TESS_WINDING_POSITIVE);
gluTessBeginPolygon(tobj, NULL);
   gluTessBeginContour(tobj);
      gluTessVertex(tobj, star[0], star[0]);
      gluTessVertex(tobj, star[1], star[1]);
      gluTessVertex(tobj, star[2], star[2]);
      gluTessVertex(tobj, star[3], star[3]);
      gluTessVertex(tobj, star[4], star[4]);
   gluTessEndContour(tobj);
gluTessEndPolygon(tobj);
glEndList();
```

## Deleting a Tessellation Object

If you no longer need a tessellation object, you can delete it and free all associated memory with **gluDeleteTess()**.

---

void **gluDeleteTess**(GLUtesselator *tessobj*);

Deletes the specified tessellation object, *tessobj*, and frees all associated memory.

---

## Tessellation Performance Tips

For best performance, remember these rules:

- Cache the output of the tessellator in a display list or other user structure. To obtain the post-tessellation vertex coordinates, tessellate the polygons while in feedback mode. (See "Feedback" in Chapter 13.)

- Use **gluTessNormal()** to supply the polygon normal.

- Use the same tessellator object to render many polygons, rather than allocate a new tessellator for each one. (In a multithreaded, multiprocessor environment, you may get better performance using several tessellators.)

## Describing GLU Errors

The GLU provides a routine for obtaining a descriptive string for an error code. This routine is not limited to tessellation but is also used for NURBS and quadrics errors, as well as for errors in the base GL. (See "Error Handling" in Chapter 14 for information about OpenGL's error-handling facility.)

## Backward Compatibility

If you are using the 1.0 or 1.1 version of GLU, you have a much less powerful tessellator. The 1.0/1.1 tessellator handles only simple nonconvex polygons or simple polygons containing holes. It does not properly tessellate intersecting contours (no COMBINE callback) or process per-polygon data. The 1.0/1.1 tessellator still works in either GLU 1.2 or 1.3, but its use is no longer recommended.

The 1.0/1.1 tessellator has some similarities to the current tessellator. **gluNewTess()** and **gluDeleteTess()** are used for both tessellators. The main vertex specification routine remains **gluTessVertex()**. The callback mechanism is controlled by **gluTessCallback()**, although only five callback functions can be registered, a subset of the current 12.

Here are the prototypes for the 1.0/1.1 tessellator:

void **gluBeginPolygon**(GLUtriangulatorObj *tessobj);
void **gluNextContour**(GLUtriangulatorObj *tessobj, GLenum type);
void **gluEndPolygon**(GLUtriangulatorObj *tessobj);

The outermost contour must be specified first, and it does not require an initial call to **gluNextContour()**. For polygons without holes, only one contour is defined, and **gluNextContour()** is not used. If a polygon has multiple contours (that is, holes or holes within holes), the contours are specified one after the other, each preceded by **gluNextContour()**. **gluTessVertex()** is called for each vertex of a contour.

For **gluNextContour**(), *type* can be GLU_EXTERIOR, GLU_INTERIOR, GLU_CCW, GLU_CW, or GLU_UNKNOWN. These serve only as hints to the tessellation. If you get them right, the tessellation might go faster. If you get them wrong, they're ignored, and the tessellation still works. For polygons with holes, one contour is the exterior contour and the other is the interior. The first contour is assumed to be of type GLU_EXTERIOR. Choosing clockwise or counterclockwise orientation is arbitrary in three dimensions; however, there are two different orientations in any plane, and the GLU_CCW and GLU_CW types should be used consistently. Use GLU_UNKNOWN if you don't have a clue.

It is highly recommended that you convert GLU 1.0/1.1 code to the new tessellation interface for GLU 1.2 by following these steps:

1.  Change references to the major data structure type from GLUtriangulatorObj to GLUtesselator. In GLU 1.2, GLUtriangulatorObj and GLUtesselator are defined to be the same type.

2.  Convert **gluBeginPolygon**() to two commands: **gluTessBeginPolygon**() and **gluTessBeginContour**(). All contours must be explicitly started, including the first one.

3.  Convert **gluNextContour**() to both **gluTessEndContour**() and **gluTessBeginContour**(). You have to end the previous contour before starting the next one.

4.  Convert **gluEndPolygon**() to both **gluTessEndContour**() and **gluTessEndPolygon**(). The final contour must be closed.

5.  Change references to constants to **gluTessCallback**(). In GLU 1.2, GLU_BEGIN, GLU_VERTEX, GLU_END, GLU_ERROR, and GLU_EDGE_FLAG are defined as synonyms for GLU_TESS_BEGIN, GLU_TESS_VERTEX, GLU_TESS_END, GLU_TESS_ERROR, and GLU_TESS_EDGE_FLAG.

## Quadrics: Rendering Spheres, Cylinders, and Disks

The base OpenGL Library provides support only for modeling and rendering simple points, lines, and convex filled polygons. Neither 3D objects nor commonly used 2D objects such as circles are directly available.

Throughout this book, you've been using GLUT to create some 3D objects. The GLU also provides routines to model and render tessellated, polygonal approximations for a variety of 2D and 3D shapes (spheres, cylinders, disks, and parts of disks), which can be calculated with quadric equations. This includes routines for drawing the quadric surfaces in a variety of styles and orientations. Quadric surfaces are defined by the following general quadratic equation:

$$a_1x^2 + a_2y^2 + a_3z^2 + a_4xy + a_5yz + a_6xz + a_7x + a_8y + a_9z + a_{10} = 0$$

(See David Rogers' *Procedural Elements for Computer Graphics,* New York, NY: McGraw-Hill, 1985.) Creating and rendering a quadric surface is similar to using the tessellator. To use a quadrics object, follow these steps:

1.  To create a quadrics object, use **gluNewQuadric()**.

2.  Specify the rendering attributes for the quadrics object (unless you're satisfied with the default values).

    a.  Use **gluQuadricOrientation()** to control the winding direction and differentiate the interior from the exterior.

    b.  Use **gluQuadricDrawStyle()** to choose between rendering the object as points, lines, or filled polygons.

    c.  For lit quadrics objects, use **gluQuadricNormals()** to specify one normal per vertex or one normal per face. The default specifies that no normals are generated at all.

    d.  For textured quadrics objects, use **gluQuadricTexture()** if you want to generate texture coordinates.

3.  Prepare for problems by registering an error-handling routine with **gluQuadricCallback()**. Then, if an error occurs during rendering, the routine you've specified is invoked.

4.  Now invoke the rendering routine for the desired type of quadrics object: **gluSphere()**, **gluCylinder()**, **gluDisk()**, or **gluPartialDisk()**. For best performance for static data, encapsulate the quadrics object in a display list.

5.  When you're completely finished with it, destroy this object with **gluDeleteQuadric()**. If you need to create another quadric, it's best to reuse your quadrics object.

## Managing Quadrics Objects

A quadrics object consists of parameters, attributes, and callbacks that are stored in a data structure of type GLUquadricObj. A quadrics object may generate vertices, normals, texture coordinates, and other data, all of which may be used immediately or stored in a display list for later use. The following routines create, destroy, and report errors in a quadrics object.

---

GLUquadricObj* **gluNewQuadric**(void);

---

Creates a new quadrics object and returns a pointer to it. A null pointer is returned if the routine fails.

---

void **gluDeleteQuadric**(GLUquadricObj *qobj);

---

Destroys the quadrics object qobj and frees up any memory used by it.

---

void **gluQuadricCallback**(GLUquadricObj *qobj, GLenum which,
                            void (*fn)());

---

Defines a function fn to be called in special circumstances. GLU_ERROR is the only legal value for which, so fn is called when an error occurs. If fn is NULL, any existing callback is erased.

For GLU_ERROR, fn is called with one parameter, which is the error code. **gluErrorString**() can be used to convert the error code into an ASCII string.

## Controlling Quadrics Attributes

The following routines affect the kinds of data generated by the quadrics routines. Use these routines before you actually specify the primitives.

Example 11-4, quadric.c, on page 529, demonstrates changing the drawing style and the kinds of normals generated as well as creation of quadrics objects, error handling, and drawing the primitives.

---

void **gluQuadricDrawStyle**(GLUquadricObj *qobj, GLenum drawStyle);

---

For the quadrics object qobj, drawStyle controls the rendering style. Legal values for drawStyle are GLU_POINT, GLU_LINE, GLU_SILHOUETTE, and GLU_FILL.

GLU_POINT and GLU_LINE specify that primitives should be rendered as a point at every vertex or a line between each pair of connected vertices.

GLU_SILHOUETTE specifies that primitives are rendered as lines, except that edges separating coplanar faces are not drawn. This is most often used for **gluDisk()** and **gluPartialDisk()**.

GLU_FILL specifies rendering by filled polygons, where the polygons are drawn in a counterclockwise fashion with respect to their normals. This may be affected by **gluQuadricOrientation()**.

---

void **gluQuadricOrientation**(GLUquadricObj *qobj*, GLenum *orientation*);

For the quadrics object *qobj*, *orientation* is either GLU_OUTSIDE (the default) or GLU_INSIDE, which controls the direction in which normals are pointing.

---

For **gluSphere()** and **gluCylinder()**, the definitions of outside and inside are obvious. For **gluDisk()** and **gluPartialDisk()**, the positive *z* side of the disk is considered to be outside.

---

void **gluQuadricNormals**(GLUquadricObj *qobj*, GLenum *normals*);

For the quadrics object *qobj*, *normals* is GLU_NONE (the default), GLU_FLAT, or GLU_SMOOTH.

---

**gluQuadricNormals()** is used to specify when to generate normal vectors. GLU_NONE means that no normals are generated, and is intended for use without lighting. GLU_FLAT generates one normal for each facet, which is often best for lighting with flat shading. GLU_SMOOTH generates one normal for every vertex of the quadric, which is usually best for lighting with smooth shading.

---

void **gluQuadricTexture**(GLUquadricObj *qobj*,
                  GLboolean *textureCoords*);

For the quadrics object *qobj*, *textureCoords* is either GL_FALSE (the default) or GL_TRUE. If the value of *textureCoords* is GL_TRUE, then texture coordinates are generated for the quadrics object. The manner in which the texture coordinates are generated varies, depending on the type of quadrics object rendered.

---

## Quadrics Primitives

The following routines actually generate the vertices and other data that constitute a quadrics object. In each case, *qobj* refers to a quadrics object created by **gluNewQuadric**().

---

void **gluSphere**(GLUquadricObj *qobj*, GLdouble *radius*, GLint *slices*,
    GLint *stacks*);

Draws a sphere of the given *radius*, centered around the origin, (0, 0, 0). The sphere is subdivided around the z-axis into a number of *slices* (similar to longitude) and along the z-axis into a number of *stacks* (latitude).

If texture coordinates are also generated by the quadrics facility, the t-coordinate ranges from 0.0 at $z = -radius$ to 1.0 at $z = radius$, with t increasing linearly along longitudinal lines. Meanwhile, s ranges from 0.0 at the +y axis, to 0.25 at the +x axis, to 0.5 at the −y axis, to 0.75 at the −x axis, and back to 1.0 at the +y axis.

---

void **gluCylinder**(GLUquadricObj *qobj*, GLdouble *baseRadius*,
    GLdouble *topRadius*, GLdouble *height*,
    GLint *slices*, GLint *stacks*);

Draws a cylinder oriented along the z-axis, with the base of the cylinder at $z = 0$ and the top at $z = height$. Like a sphere, the cylinder is subdivided around the z-axis into a number of *slices* and along the z-axis into a number of *stacks*. *baseRadius* is the radius of the cylinder at $z = 0$. *topRadius* is the radius of the cylinder at $z = height$. If *topRadius* is set to 0, then a cone is generated.

If texture coordinates are generated by the quadrics facility, then the t-coordinate ranges linearly from 0.0 at $z = 0$ to 1.0 at $z = height$. The s texture coordinates are generated the same way as they are for a sphere.

---

**Note:** The cylinder is not closed at the top or bottom. The disks at the base and at the top are not drawn.

---

void **gluDisk**(GLUquadricObj *qobj*, GLdouble *innerRadius*,
        GLdouble *outerRadius*, GLint *slices*, GLint *rings*);

---

Draws a disk on the z = 0 plane, with a radius of *outerRadius* and a concentric circular hole with a radius of *innerRadius*. If *innerRadius* is 0, then no hole is created. The disk is subdivided around the z-axis into a number of *slices* (like slices of pizza) and also about the z-axis into a number of concentric *rings*.

With respect to orientation, the +z side of the disk is considered to be "outside"; that is, any normals generated point along the +z axis. Otherwise, the normals point along the −z axis.

If texture coordinates are generated by the quadrics facility, then the texture coordinates are generated linearly such that where R = *outerRadius*, the values for *s* and *t* at (R, 0, 0) are (1, 0.5), at (0, R, 0) they are (0.5, 1), at (−R, 0, 0) they are (0, 0.5), and at (0, −R, 0) they are (0.5, 0).

---

void **gluPartialDisk**(GLUquadricObj *qobj*, GLdouble *innerRadius*,
        GLdouble *outerRadius*, GLint *slices*, GLint *rings*,
        GLdouble *startAngle*, GLdouble *sweepAngle*);

---

Draws a partial disk on the z = 0 plane. A partial disk is similar to a complete disk, in terms of *outerRadius*, *innerRadius*, *slices*, and *rings*. The difference is that only a portion of a partial disk is drawn, starting from *startAngle* through *startAngle* + *sweepAngle* (where *startAngle* and *sweepAngle* are measured in degrees, where 0 degrees is along the +*y* axis, 90 degrees along the +*x* axis, 180 along the −*y* axis, and 270 along the −*x* axis).

A partial disk handles orientation and texture coordinates in the same way as a complete disk.

**Note:**  For all quadrics objects, it's better to use the *\*Radius*, *height*, and similar arguments to scale them, rather than the **glScale\*()** command, so that the unit-length normals that are generated don't have to be renormalized. Set the *rings* and *stacks* arguments to values other than 1 to force lighting calculations at a finer granularity, especially if the material specularity is high.

Example 11-4 shows each of the quadrics primitives being drawn, as well as the effects of different drawing styles.

**Example 11-4**  Quadrics Objects: quadric.c

```c
#ifndef CALLBACK
#define CALLBACK
#endif

GLuint startList;

void CALLBACK errorCallback(GLenum errorCode)
{
    const GLubyte *estring;

    estring = gluErrorString(errorCode);
    fprintf(stderr, "Quadric Error: %s\n", estring);
    exit(0);
}

void init(void)
{
    GLUquadricObj *qobj;
    GLfloat mat_ambient[] = { 0.5, 0.5, 0.5, 1.0 };
    GLfloat mat_specular[] = { 1.0, 1.0, 1.0, 1.0 };
    GLfloat mat_shininess[] = { 50.0 };
    GLfloat light_position[] = { 1.0, 1.0, 1.0, 0.0 };
    GLfloat model_ambient[] = { 0.5, 0.5, 0.5, 1.0 };

    glClearColor(0.0, 0.0, 0.0, 0.0);

    glMaterialfv(GL_FRONT, GL_AMBIENT, mat_ambient);
    glMaterialfv(GL_FRONT, GL_SPECULAR, mat_specular);
    glMaterialfv(GL_FRONT, GL_SHININESS, mat_shininess);
    glLightfv(GL_LIGHT0, GL_POSITION, light_position);
    glLightModelfv(GL_LIGHT_MODEL_AMBIENT, model_ambient);

    glEnable(GL_LIGHTING);
    glEnable(GL_LIGHT0);
    glEnable(GL_DEPTH_TEST);
```

```
/* Create 4 display lists, each with a different quadric object.
 * Different drawing styles and surface normal specifications
 * are demonstrated.
 */
    startList = glGenLists(4);
    qobj = gluNewQuadric();
    gluQuadricCallback(qobj, GLU_ERROR, errorCallback);

    gluQuadricDrawStyle(qobj, GLU_FILL); /* smooth shaded */
    gluQuadricNormals(qobj, GLU_SMOOTH);
    glNewList(startList, GL_COMPILE);
        gluSphere(qobj, 0.75, 15, 10);
    glEndList();

    gluQuadricDrawStyle(qobj, GLU_FILL); /* flat shaded */
    gluQuadricNormals(qobj, GLU_FLAT);
    glNewList(startList+1, GL_COMPILE);
        gluCylinder(qobj, 0.5, 0.3, 1.0, 15, 5);
    glEndList();

    gluQuadricDrawStyle(qobj, GLU_LINE); /* wireframe */
    gluQuadricNormals(qobj, GLU_NONE);
    glNewList(startList+2, GL_COMPILE);
        gluDisk(qobj, 0.25, 1.0, 20, 4);
    glEndList();

    gluQuadricDrawStyle(qobj, GLU_SILHOUETTE);
    gluQuadricNormals(qobj, GLU_NONE);
    glNewList(startList+3, GL_COMPILE);
        gluPartialDisk(qobj, 0.0, 1.0, 20, 4, 0.0, 225.0);
    glEndList();
}

void display(void)
{
    glClear(GL_COLOR_BUFFER_BIT | GL_DEPTH_BUFFER_BIT);
    glPushMatrix();

    glEnable(GL_LIGHTING);
    glShadeModel(GL_SMOOTH);
    glTranslatef(-1.0, -1.0, 0.0);
    glCallList(startList);
```

```
      glShadeModel(GL_FLAT);
      glTranslatef(0.0, 2.0, 0.0);
      glPushMatrix();
      glRotatef(300.0, 1.0, 0.0, 0.0);
      glCallList(startList+1);
      glPopMatrix();

      glDisable(GL_LIGHTING);
      glColor3f(0.0, 1.0, 1.0);
      glTranslatef(2.0, -2.0, 0.0);
      glCallList(startList+2);

      glColor3f(1.0, 1.0, 0.0);
      glTranslatef(0.0, 2.0, 0.0);
      glCallList(startList+3);

      glPopMatrix();
      glFlush();
}

void reshape(int w, int h)
{
   glViewport(0, 0, (GLsizei) w, (GLsizei) h);
   glMatrixMode(GL_PROJECTION);
   glLoadIdentity();
   if (w <= h)
      glOrtho(-2.5, 2.5, -2.5*(GLfloat)h/(GLfloat)w,
         2.5*(GLfloat)h/(GLfloat)w, -10.0, 10.0);
   else
      glOrtho(-2.5*(GLfloat)w/(GLfloat)h,
         2.5*(GLfloat)w/(GLfloat)h, -2.5, 2.5, -10.0, 10.0);
   glMatrixMode(GL_MODELVIEW);
   glLoadIdentity();
}

void keyboard(unsigned char key, int x, int y)
{
   switch (key) {
      case 27:
         exit(0);
         break;
   }
}
```

```
int main(int argc, char** argv)
{
    glutInit(&argc, argv);
    glutInitDisplayMode(GLUT_SINGLE | GLUT_RGB | GLUT_DEPTH);
    glutInitWindowSize(500, 500);
    glutInitWindowPosition(100, 100);
    glutCreateWindow(argv[0]);
    init();
    glutDisplayFunc(display);
    glutReshapeFunc(reshape);
    glutKeyboardFunc(keyboard);
    glutMainLoop();
    return 0;
}
```

*Chapter 12*

# Evaluators and NURBS

## Chapter Objectives

**Advanced**

After reading this chapter, you'll be able to do the following:

Advanced

- Use OpenGL evaluator commands to draw basic curves and surfaces

- Use the GLU's higher-level NURBS facility to draw more complex curves and surfaces and to return data on the vertices of geometric objects, which result from the tessellation of the curves and surfaces

Note that this chapter presumes a number of prerequisites; they're listed in "Prerequisites" on page 535.

At the lowest level, graphics hardware draws points, line segments, and polygons, which are usually triangles and quadrilaterals. Smooth curves and surfaces are drawn by approximating them with large numbers of small line segments or polygons. However, many useful curves and surfaces can be described mathematically by a small number of parameters such as a few *control points*. Saving the 16 control points for a surface requires much less storage than saving 1000 triangles together with the normal vector information at each vertex. In addition, the 1000 triangles only approximate the true surface, but the control points accurately describe the real surface.

Evaluators provide a way to specify points on a curve or surface (or part of one) using only the control points. The curve or surface can then be rendered at any precision. In addition, normal vectors can be calculated for surfaces automatically. You can use the points generated by an evaluator in many ways—to draw dots where the surface would be; to draw a wireframe version of the surface; or to draw a fully lighted, shaded, and even textured version.

You can use evaluators to describe any polynomial or rational polynomial splines or surfaces of any degree. These include almost all splines and spline surfaces in use today, including B-splines, NURBS (Non-Uniform Rational B-Spline) surfaces, Bézier curves and surfaces, and Hermite splines. Since evaluators provide only a low-level description of the points on a curve or surface, they're typically used underneath utility libraries that provide a higher-level interface to the programmer. The GLU's NURBS facility is such a higher-level interface—the NURBS routines encapsulate extensive complicated code. Much of the final rendering is done with evaluators, but for some conditions (trimming curves, for example) the NURBS routines use planar polygons for rendering.

This chapter contains the following major sections:

- "Prerequisites" discusses what knowledge is assumed for this chapter. It also gives several references where you can obtain this information.

- "Evaluators" explains how evaluators work and how to control them using the appropriate OpenGL commands.

- "The GLU NURBS Interface" describes the GLU routines for creating, rendering, and returning the tessellated vertices of NURBS curves and surfaces.

# Prerequisites

Evaluators make splines and surfaces that are based on a Bézier (or Bernstein) basis. The defining formulas for the functions in this basis are given in this chapter, but the discussion doesn't include derivations or even lists of all their interesting mathematical properties. If you want to use evaluators to draw curves and surfaces using other bases, you must know how to convert your basis to a Bézier basis. In addition, when you render a Bézier surface or part of it using evaluators, you need to determine the granularity of your subdivision. Your decision needs to take into account the trade-off between high-quality (highly subdivided) images and high speed. Determining an appropriate subdivision strategy can be quite complicated—too complicated to be discussed here.

Similarly, a complete discussion of NURBS is beyond the scope of this book. The GLU NURBS interface is documented here, and programming examples are provided for readers who already understand the subject. In what follows, you already should know about NURBS control points, knot sequences, and trimming curves.

If you lack some of these prerequisites, the following references will help:

- Farin, Gerald E., *Curves and Surfaces for Computer-Aided Geometric Design, Fourth Edition*. San Diego, CA: Academic Press, 1996.

- Farin, Gerald E., *NURB Curves and Surfaces: from Projective Geometry to Practical Use*. Wellesley, MA: A. K. Peters Ltd., 1995.

- Farin, Gerald E., editor, *NURBS for Curve and Surface Design*, Society for Industrial and Applied Mathematics, Philadelphia, PA, 1991.

- Hoschek, Josef and Dieter Lasser, *Fundamentals of Computer Aided Geometric Design*. Wellesley, MA: A. K. Peters Ltd., 1993.

- Piegl, Les and Wayne Tiller, *The NURBS Book*. New York, NY: Springer-Verlag, 1995.

**Note:** Some terms used in this chapter might have slightly different meanings in other books on spline curves and surfaces, since there isn't total agreement among the practitioners of this art. Generally, the OpenGL meanings are a bit more restrictive. For example, OpenGL evaluators always use Bézier bases; in other contexts, evaluators might refer to the same concept, but with an arbitrary basis.

# Evaluators

A Bézier curve is a vector-valued function of one variable

$$C(u) = [X(u) \quad Y(u) \quad Z(u)]$$

where $u$ varies in some domain (say [0, 1]). A Bézier surface patch is a vector-valued function of two variables

$$S(u,v) = [X(u,v) \quad Y(u,v) \quad Z(u,v)]$$

where $u$ and $v$ can both vary in some domain. The range isn't necessarily three-dimensional as shown here. You might want two-dimensional output for curves on a plane or texture coordinates, or you might want four-dimensional output to specify RGBA information. Even one-dimensional output may make sense for gray levels.

For each $u$ (or $u$ and $v$, in the case of a surface), the formula for C() (or S()) calculates a point on the curve (or surface). To use an evaluator, first define the function C() or S(), enable it, and then use the **glEvalCoord1**() or **glEvalCoord2**() command instead of **glVertex***(). This way, the curve or surface vertices can be used just as any other vertices are used—to form points or lines, for example. In addition, other commands automatically generate a series of vertices that produce a regular mesh uniformly spaced in $u$ (or in $u$ and $v$). One- and two-dimensional evaluators are similar, but the description is somewhat simpler in one dimension, so that case is discussed first.

## One-Dimensional Evaluators

This subsection presents an example of using one-dimensional evaluators to draw a curve. It then describes the commands and equations that control evaluators.

### One-Dimensional Example: A Simple Bézier Curve

The program shown in Example 12-1 draws a cubic Bézier curve using four control points, as shown in Figure 12-1.

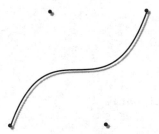

**Figure 12-1**   Bézier Curve

**Example 12-1**   Bézier Curve with Four Control Points: bezcurve.c

```
GLfloat ctrlpoints[4][3] = {
        { -4.0, -4.0, 0.0}, { -2.0, 4.0, 0.0},
        {2.0, -4.0, 0.0}, {4.0, 4.0, 0.0}};

void init(void)
{
   glClearColor(0.0, 0.0, 0.0, 0.0);
   glShadeModel(GL_FLAT);
   glMap1f(GL_MAP1_VERTEX_3, 0.0, 1.0, 3, 4, &ctrlpoints[0][0]);
   glEnable(GL_MAP1_VERTEX_3);
}

void display(void)
{
   int i;

   glClear(GL_COLOR_BUFFER_BIT);
   glColor3f(1.0, 1.0, 1.0);
   glBegin(GL_LINE_STRIP);
      for (i = 0; i <= 30; i++)
         glEvalCoord1f((GLfloat) i/30.0);
   glEnd();
   /* The following code displays the control points as dots. */
   glPointSize(5.0);
   glColor3f(1.0, 1.0, 0.0);
   glBegin(GL_POINTS);
      for (i = 0; i < 4; i++)
         glVertex3fv(&ctrlpoints[i][0]);
   glEnd();
   glFlush();
}
```

```
void reshape(int w, int h)
{
    glViewport(0, 0, (GLsizei) w, (GLsizei) h);
    glMatrixMode(GL_PROJECTION);
    glLoadIdentity();
    if (w <= h)
        glOrtho(-5.0, 5.0, -5.0*(GLfloat)h/(GLfloat)w,
                5.0*(GLfloat)h/(GLfloat)w, -5.0, 5.0);
    else
        glOrtho(-5.0*(GLfloat)w/(GLfloat)h,
                5.0*(GLfloat)w/(GLfloat)h, -5.0, 5.0, -5.0, 5.0);
    glMatrixMode(GL_MODELVIEW);
    glLoadIdentity();
}

int main(int argc, char** argv)
{
    glutInit(&argc, argv);
    glutInitDisplayMode(GLUT_SINGLE | GLUT_RGB);
    glutInitWindowSize(500, 500);
    glutInitWindowPosition(100, 100);
    glutCreateWindow(argv[0]);
    init();
    glutDisplayFunc(display);
    glutReshapeFunc(reshape);
    glutMainLoop();
    return 0;
}
```

A cubic Bézier curve is described by four control points, which appear in this example in the *ctrlpoints[][]* array. This array is one of the arguments for **glMap1f()**. The other arguments for this command are:

| | |
|---|---|
| GL_MAP1_VERTEX_3 | Specifies that three-dimensional control points are provided and that three-dimensional vertices should be produced |
| 0.0 | Low value of parameter $u$ |
| 1.0 | High value of parameter $u$ |
| 3 | The number of floating-point values to advance in the data between one control point and the next |
| 4 | The order of the spline, which is the degree plus 1: in this case, the degree is 3 (since this is a cubic curve) |
| &ctrlpoints[0][0] | Pointer to the first control point's data |

Note that the second and third arguments control the parameterization of the curve—as the variable $u$ ranges from 0.0 to 1.0, the curve goes from one end to the other. The call to **glEnable()** enables the one-dimensional evaluator for three-dimensional vertices.

The curve is drawn in the routine **display()** between the **glBegin()** and **glEnd()** calls. Since the evaluator is enabled, giving the command **glEvalCoord1f()** is just like issuing a **glVertex()** command with the coordinates of a vertex on the curve corresponding to the input parameter $u$.

### Defining and Evaluating a One-Dimensional Evaluator

The Bernstein polynomial of degree $n$ (or order $n + 1$) is given by

$$B_i^n(u) = \binom{n}{i} u^i (1-u)^{n-i}$$

If $P_i$ represents a set of control points (one-, two-, three-, or even four-dimensional), then the equation

$$C(u) = \sum_{i=0}^{n} B_i^n(u) P_i$$

represents a Bézier curve as $u$ varies from 0.0 to 1.0. To represent the same curve but allowing $u$ to vary between $u_1$ and $u_2$ instead of 0.0 and 1.0, evaluate

$$C\left(\frac{u - u_1}{u_2 - u_1}\right)$$

The command **glMap1()** defines a one-dimensional evaluator that uses these equations.

void **glMap1**{fd}(GLenum *target*, TYPE *u1*, TYPE *u2*, GLint *stride*,
GLint *order*, const TYPE **points*);

Defines a one-dimensional evaluator. The *target* parameter specifies what the control points represent, as shown in Table 12-1, and therefore how many values need to be supplied in *points*. The points can represent vertices, RGBA color data, normal vectors, or texture coordinates. For example, with GL_MAP1_COLOR_4, the evaluator generates color data along a curve in four-dimensional (RGBA) color space. You also use the parameter values listed in Table 12-1 to enable each defined evaluator before you invoke it. Pass the appropriate value to **glEnable**() or **glDisable**() to enable or disable the evaluator.

The second two parameters for **glMap1***(), *u1* and *u2*, indicate the range for the variable *u*. The variable *stride* is the number of single- or double-precision values (as appropriate) in each block of storage. Thus, it's an offset value between the beginning of one control point and the beginning of the next.

The *order* is the degree plus 1, and it should agree with the number of control points. The *points* parameter points to the first coordinate of the first control point. Using the example data structure for **glMap1***(), use the following for *points*:

```
(GLfloat *)(&ctlpoints[0].x)
```

| Parameter | Meaning |
| --- | --- |
| GL_MAP1_VERTEX_3 | *x, y, z* vertex coordinates |
| GL_MAP1_VERTEX_4 | *x, y, z, w* vertex coordinates |
| GL_MAP1_INDEX | color index |
| GL_MAP1_COLOR_4 | R, G, B, A |
| GL_MAP1_NORMAL | normal coordinates |
| GL_MAP1_TEXTURE_COORD_1 | *s* texture coordinates |
| GL_MAP1_TEXTURE_COORD_2 | *s, t* texture coordinates |
| GL_MAP1_TEXTURE_COORD_3 | *s, t, r* texture coordinates |
| GL_MAP1_TEXTURE_COORD_4 | *s, t, r, q* texture coordinates |

**Table 12-1**     Types of Control Points for glMap1*()

More than one evaluator can be evaluated at a time. If you have both a GL_MAP1_VERTEX_3 and a GL_MAP1_COLOR_4 evaluator defined and enabled, for example, then calls to **glEvalCoord1**() generate both a position and a color. Only one of the vertex evaluators can be enabled at a time, although you might have defined both of them. Similarly, only one of the texture evaluators can be active. Otherwise, however, evaluators can be used to generate any combination of vertex, normal, color, and texture-coordinate data. If you define and enable more than one evaluator of the same type, the one of highest dimension is used.

Use **glEvalCoord1\***() to evaluate a defined and enabled one-dimensional map.

> void **glEvalCoord1**{fd}(*TYPE u*);
> void **glEvalCoord1**{fd}**v**(const *TYPE \*u*);
>
> Causes evaluation of the enabled one-dimensional maps. The argument *u* is the value (or a pointer to the value, in the vector version of the command) of the domain coordinate.

For evaluated vertices, generation of values for color, color index, normal vectors, and texture coordinates is done by evaluation. Calls to **glEvalCoord\***() do not use the current values for color, color index, normal vectors, and texture coordinates. **glEvalCoord\***() also leaves those values unchanged.

### Defining Evenly Spaced Coordinate Values in One Dimension

You can use **glEvalCoord1**() with any values of *u*, but by far the most common practice is to use evenly spaced values, as shown previously in Example 12-1. To obtain evenly spaced values, define a one-dimensional grid using **glMapGrid1\***() and then apply it using **glEvalMesh1**().

> void **glMapGrid1**{fd}(GLint *n, TYPE u1, TYPE u2*);
>
> Defines a grid that goes from *u1* to *u2* in *n* steps, which are evenly spaced.

```
void glEvalMesh1(GLenum mode, GLint p1, GLint p2);
```

Applies the currently defined map grid to all enabled evaluators. The *mode* can be either GL_POINT or GL_LINE, depending on whether you want to draw points or a connected line along the curve. The call has exactly the same effect as issuing a **glEvalCoord1()** for each of the steps from *p1* to *p2*, inclusive, where $0 \le p1, p2 \le n$. Programmatically, it's equivalent to

```
glBegin(GL_POINTS);       /* OR glBegin(GL_LINE_STRIP); */
   for (i = p1; i <= p2; i++)
      glEvalCoord1(u1 + i*(u2-u1)/n);
glEnd();
```

except that if $i = 0$ or $i = n$, then **glEvalCoord1()** is called with exactly *u1* or *u2* as its parameter.

## Two-Dimensional Evaluators

In two dimensions, everything is similar to the one-dimensional case, except that all the commands must take two parameters, *u* and *v*, into account. Points, colors, normals, or texture coordinates must be supplied over a surface instead of a curve. Mathematically, the definition of a Bézier surface patch is given by

$$S\,(u,\,v) = \sum_{i\,=\,0}^{n} \sum_{j\,=\,0}^{m} B_i^n\,(u)\;B_j^m\,(v)\;P_{ij}$$

where the $P_{ij}$ values are a set of $m \cdot n$ control points, and the $B_i$ functions are the same Bernstein polynomials for one dimension. As before, the $P_{ij}$ values can represent vertices, normals, colors, or texture coordinates.

The procedure for using two-dimensional evaluators is similar to the procedure for one dimension:

1.   Define the evaluator(s) with **glMap2*()**.

2.   Enable them by passing the appropriate value to **glEnable()**.

3.   Invoke them either by calling **glEvalCoord2()** between a **glBegin()** and **glEnd()** pair or by specifying and then applying a mesh with **glMapGrid2()** and **glEvalMesh2()**.

## Defining and Evaluating a Two-Dimensional Evaluator

Use **glMap2\*()** and **glEvalCoord2\*()** to define and then invoke a two-dimensional evaluator.

---

void **glMap2**{fd}(GLenum *target*, TYPE *u1*, TYPE *u2*, GLint *ustride*,
  GLint *uorder*, TYPE *v1*, TYPE *v2*, GLint *vstride*,
  GLint *vorder*, TYPE *points*);

---

The *target* parameter can have any of the values in Table 12-1, except that the string MAP1 is replaced with MAP2. As before, these values are also used with **glEnable**() to enable the corresponding evaluator. Minimum and maximum values for both *u* and *v* are provided as *u1*, *u2*, *v1*, and *v2*. The parameters *ustride* and *vstride* indicate the numbers of single- and double-precision values (as appropriate) between independent settings for these values, allowing users to select a subrectangle of control points out of a much larger array. For example, if the data appears in the form

```
GLfloat ctlpoints[100][100][3];
```

and you want to use the 4 × 4 subset beginning at ctlpoints[20][30], choose *ustride* to be 100*3 and *vstride* to be 3. The starting point, *points*, should be set to &ctlpoints[20][30][0]. Finally, the order parameters, *uorder* and *vorder*, can be different—allowing patches that are cubic in one direction and quadratic in the other, for example.

---

void **glEvalCoord2**{fd}(TYPE *u*, TYPE *v*);
void **glEvalCoord2**{fd}**v**(const TYPE *\*values*);

---

Causes evaluation of the enabled two-dimensional maps. The arguments *u* and *v* are the values (or a pointer to the *values u* and *v*, in the vector version of the command) for the domain coordinates. If either of the vertex evaluators is enabled (GL_MAP2_VERTEX_3 or GL_MAP2_VERTEX_4), then the normal to the surface is computed analytically. This normal is associated with the generated vertex if automatic normal generation has been enabled by passing GL_AUTO_NORMAL to **glEnable**(). If it's disabled, the corresponding enabled normal map is used to produce a normal. If no such map exists, the current normal is used.

## Two-Dimensional Example: A Bézier Surface

Example 12-2 draws a wireframe Bézier surface using evaluators, as shown in Figure 12-2. In this example, the surface is drawn with nine curved lines in each direction. Each curve is drawn as 30 segments. To get the whole program, add the **reshape()** and **main()** routines from Example 12-1.

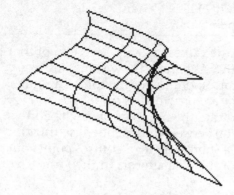

**Figure 12-2**     Bézier Surface

**Example 12-2**     Bézier Surface: bezsurf.c

```
GLfloat ctrlpoints[4][4][3] = {
   {{-1.5, -1.5, 4.0}, {-0.5, -1.5, 2.0},
    {0.5, -1.5, -1.0}, {1.5, -1.5, 2.0}},
   {{-1.5, -0.5, 1.0}, {-0.5, -0.5, 3.0},
    {0.5, -0.5, 0.0}, {1.5, -0.5, -1.0}},
   {{-1.5, 0.5, 4.0}, {-0.5, 0.5, 0.0},
    {0.5, 0.5, 3.0}, {1.5, 0.5, 4.0}},
   {{-1.5, 1.5, -2.0}, {-0.5, 1.5, -2.0},
    {0.5, 1.5, 0.0}, {1.5, 1.5, -1.0}}
};

void display(void)
{
   int i, j;

   glClear(GL_COLOR_BUFFER_BIT | GL_DEPTH_BUFFER_BIT);
   glColor3f(1.0, 1.0, 1.0);
   glPushMatrix();
   glRotatef(85.0, 1.0, 1.0, 1.0);
   for (j = 0; j <= 8; j++) {
      glBegin(GL_LINE_STRIP);
      for (i = 0; i <= 30; i++)
         glEvalCoord2f((GLfloat)i/30.0, (GLfloat)j/8.0);
```

```
        glEnd();
        glBegin(GL_LINE_STRIP);
        for (i = 0; i <= 30; i++)
            glEvalCoord2f((GLfloat)j/8.0, (GLfloat)i/30.0);
        glEnd();
    }
    glPopMatrix();
    glFlush();
}

void init(void)
{
    glClearColor(0.0, 0.0, 0.0, 0.0);
    glMap2f(GL_MAP2_VERTEX_3, 0, 1, 3, 4,
            0, 1, 12, 4, &ctrlpoints[0][0][0]);
    glEnable(GL_MAP2_VERTEX_3);
    glMapGrid2f(20, 0.0, 1.0, 20, 0.0, 1.0);
    glEnable(GL_DEPTH_TEST);
    glShadeModel(GL_FLAT);
}
```

## Defining Evenly Spaced Coordinate Values in Two Dimensions

In two dimensions, the **glMapGrid2\*()** and **glEvalMesh2()** commands
are similar to the one-dimensional versions, except that both *u* and *v*
information must be included.

---

void **glMapGrid2**{fd}(GLint *nu, TYPE u1, TYPE u2,*
              GLint *nv, TYPE v1, TYPE v2);*
void **glEvalMesh2**(GLenum *mode, GLint i1,*
              GLint *i2, GLint j1, GLint j2);*

---

Defines a two-dimensional map grid that goes from *u1* to *u2* in *nu* evenly
spaced steps, goes from *v1* to *v2* in *nv* steps (**glMapGrid2\*()**), and then
applies this grid to all enabled evaluators (**glEvalMesh2()**). The only significant difference from the one-dimensional versions of these two commands is that in **glEvalMesh2()**, the *mode* parameter can be GL_FILL as
well as GL_POINT or GL_LINE. GL_FILL generates filled polygons using
the quad-mesh primitive. Stated precisely, **glEvalMesh2()** is nearly equivalent to one of the following three code fragments. (It's nearly equivalent
because when *i* is equal to *nu*, or *j* to *nv*, the parameter is exactly equal to
*u2* or *v2*, not to $u1 + nu*(u2 - u1)/nu$, which might be slightly different
due to round-off error.)

```
glBegin(GL_POINTS);                          /* mode == GL_POINT */
for (i = nu1; i <= nu2; i++)
    for (j = nv1; j <= nv2; j++)
        glEvalCoord2(u1 + i*(u2-u1)/nu, v1+j*(v2-v1)/nv);
glEnd();
```

or

```
for (i = nu1; i <= nu2; i++) {       /* mode == GL_LINE */
    glBegin(GL_LINES);
        for (j = nv1; j <= nv2; j++)
            glEvalCoord2(u1 + i*(u2-u1)/nu, v1+j*(v2-v1)/nv);
    glEnd();
}
for (j = nv1; j <= nv2; j++) {
    glBegin(GL_LINES);
    for (i = nu1; i <= nu2; i++)
        glEvalCoord2(u1 + i*(u2-u1)/nu, v1+j*(v2-v1)/nv);
    glEnd();
}
```

or

```
for (i = nu1; i < nu2; i++) {        /* mode == GL_FILL */
    glBegin(GL_QUAD_STRIP);
    for (j = nv1; j <= nv2; j++) {
        glEvalCoord2(u1 + i*(u2-u1)/nu, v1+j*(v2-v1)/nv);
        glEvalCoord2(u1 + (i+1)*(u2-u1)/nu, v1+j*(v2-v1)/nv);
    glEnd();
}
```

Example 12-3 shows the differences necessary to draw the same Bézier surface as in Example 12-2, but using **glMapGrid2()** and **glEvalMesh2()** to subdivide the square domain into a uniform 8 × 8 grid. This program also adds lighting and shading, as shown in Figure 12-3.

**Example 12-3**   Lit, Shaded Bézier Surface Using a Mesh: bezmesh.c

```
void initlights(void)
{
   GLfloat ambient[] = {0.2, 0.2, 0.2, 1.0};
   GLfloat position[] = {0.0, 0.0, 2.0, 1.0};
   GLfloat mat_diffuse[] = {0.6, 0.6, 0.6, 1.0};
   GLfloat mat_specular[] = {1.0, 1.0, 1.0, 1.0};
   GLfloat mat_shininess[] = {50.0};

   glEnable(GL_LIGHTING);
   glEnable(GL_LIGHT0);
```

```
      glLightfv(GL_LIGHT0, GL_AMBIENT, ambient);
      glLightfv(GL_LIGHT0, GL_POSITION, position);

      glMaterialfv(GL_FRONT, GL_DIFFUSE, mat_diffuse);
      glMaterialfv(GL_FRONT, GL_SPECULAR, mat_specular);
      glMaterialfv(GL_FRONT, GL_SHININESS, mat_shininess);
}

void display(void)
{
      glClear(GL_COLOR_BUFFER_BIT | GL_DEPTH_BUFFER_BIT);
      glPushMatrix();
      glRotatef(85.0, 1.0, 1.0, 1.0);
      glEvalMesh2(GL_FILL, 0, 20, 0, 20);
      glPopMatrix();
      glFlush();
}

void init(void)
{
      glClearColor(0.0, 0.0, 0.0, 0.0);
      glEnable(GL_DEPTH_TEST);
      glMap2f(GL_MAP2_VERTEX_3, 0, 1, 3, 4,
              0, 1, 12, 4, &ctrlpoints[0][0][0]);
      glEnable(GL_MAP2_VERTEX_3);
      glEnable(GL_AUTO_NORMAL);
      glMapGrid2f(20, 0.0, 1.0, 20, 0.0, 1.0);
      initlights();
}
```

**Figure 12-3**    Lit, Shaded Bézier Surface Drawn with a Mesh

## Using Evaluators for Textures

Example 12-4 enables two evaluators at the same time: the first generates three-dimensional points on the same Bézier surface as in Example 12-3, and the second generates texture coordinates. In this case, the texture coordinates are the same as the *u*- and *v*-coordinates of the surface, but a special flat Bézier patch must be created to do this.

The flat patch is defined over a square with corners at (0, 0), (0, 1), (1, 0), and (1, 1); it generates (0, 0) at corner (0, 0), (0, 1) at corner (0, 1), and so on. Since it's of order 2 (linear degree plus 1), evaluating this texture at the point (*u*, *v*) generates texture coordinates (*s*, *t*). It's enabled at the same time as the vertex evaluator, so both take effect when the surface is drawn (see Plate 19). If you want the texture to repeat three times in each direction, change every 1.0 in the array *texpts[][][]* to 3.0. Since the texture wraps in this example, the surface is rendered with nine copies of the texture map.

**Example 12-4**   Using Evaluators for Textures: texturesurf.c

```
GLfloat ctrlpoints[4][4][3] = {
   {{ -1.5, -1.5, 4.0}, { -0.5, -1.5, 2.0},
    {0.5, -1.5, -1.0}, {1.5, -1.5, 2.0}},
   {{ -1.5, -0.5, 1.0}, { -0.5, -0.5, 3.0},
    {0.5, -0.5, 0.0}, {1.5, -0.5, -1.0}},
   {{ -1.5, 0.5, 4.0}, { -0.5, 0.5, 0.0},
    {0.5, 0.5, 3.0}, {1.5, 0.5, 4.0}},
   {{ -1.5, 1.5, -2.0}, { -0.5, 1.5, -2.0},
    {0.5, 1.5, 0.0}, {1.5, 1.5, -1.0}}
};
GLfloat texpts[2][2][2] = {{{0.0, 0.0}, {0.0, 1.0}},
                           {{1.0, 0.0}, {1.0, 1.0}}};

void display(void)
{
   glClear(GL_COLOR_BUFFER_BIT | GL_DEPTH_BUFFER_BIT);
   glColor3f(1.0, 1.0, 1.0);
   glEvalMesh2(GL_FILL, 0, 20, 0, 20);
   glFlush();
}
#define imageWidth 64
#define imageHeight 64
GLubyte image[3*imageWidth*imageHeight];
```

```c
void makeImage(void)
{
    int i, j;
    float ti, tj;

    for (i = 0; i < imageWidth; i++) {
        ti = 2.0*3.14159265*i/imageWidth;
        for (j = 0; j < imageHeight; j++) {
            tj = 2.0*3.14159265*j/imageHeight;
            image[3*(imageHeight*i+j)] =
                (GLubyte) 127*(1.0+sin(ti));
            image[3*(imageHeight*i+j)+1] =
                (GLubyte) 127*(1.0+cos(2*tj));
            image[3*(imageHeight*i+j)+2] =
                (GLubyte) 127*(1.0+cos(ti+tj));
        }
    }
}

void init(void)
{
    glMap2f(GL_MAP2_VERTEX_3, 0, 1, 3, 4,
            0, 1, 12, 4, &ctrlpoints[0][0][0]);
    glMap2f(GL_MAP2_TEXTURE_COORD_2, 0, 1, 2, 2,
            0, 1, 4, 2, &texpts[0][0][0]);
    glEnable(GL_MAP2_TEXTURE_COORD_2);
    glEnable(GL_MAP2_VERTEX_3);
    glMapGrid2f(20, 0.0, 1.0, 20, 0.0, 1.0);
    makeImage();
    glTexEnvf(GL_TEXTURE_ENV, GL_TEXTURE_ENV_MODE, GL_DECAL);
    glTexParameteri(GL_TEXTURE_2D, GL_TEXTURE_WRAP_S, GL_REPEAT);
    glTexParameteri(GL_TEXTURE_2D, GL_TEXTURE_WRAP_T, GL_REPEAT);
    glTexParameteri(GL_TEXTURE_2D, GL_TEXTURE_MAG_FILTER,
                    GL_NEAREST);
    glTexParameteri(GL_TEXTURE_2D, GL_TEXTURE_MIN_FILTER,
                    GL_NEAREST);
    glTexImage2D(GL_TEXTURE_2D, 0, 3, imageWidth, imageHeight, 0,
                 GL_RGB, GL_UNSIGNED_BYTE, image);
    glEnable(GL_TEXTURE_2D);
    glEnable(GL_DEPTH_TEST);
    glShadeModel(GL_FLAT);
}
```

```
void reshape(int w, int h)
{
    glViewport(0, 0, (GLsizei) w, (GLsizei) h);
    glMatrixMode(GL_PROJECTION);
    glLoadIdentity();
    if (w <= h)
        glOrtho(-4.0, 4.0, -4.0*(GLfloat)h/(GLfloat)w,
                4.0*(GLfloat)h/(GLfloat)w, -4.0, 4.0);
    else
        glOrtho(-4.0*(GLfloat)w/(GLfloat)h,
                4.0*(GLfloat)w/(GLfloat)h, -4.0, 4.0, -4.0, 4.0);
    glMatrixMode(GL_MODELVIEW);
    glLoadIdentity();
    glRotatef(85.0, 1.0, 1.0, 1.0);
}

int main(int argc, char** argv)
{
    glutInit(&argc, argv);
    glutInitDisplayMode(GLUT_SINGLE | GLUT_RGB | GLUT_DEPTH);
    glutInitWindowSize(500, 500);
    glutInitWindowPosition(100, 100);
    glutCreateWindow(argv[0]);
    init();
    glutDisplayFunc(display);
    glutReshapeFunc(reshape);
    glutMainLoop();
    return 0;
}
```

# The GLU NURBS Interface

Although evaluators are the only OpenGL primitives available to draw curves and surfaces directly, and even though they can be implemented very efficiently in hardware, they're often accessed by applications through higher-level libraries. The GLU provides a NURBS interface built on top of the OpenGL evaluator commands.

## A Simple NURBS Example

If you understand NURBS, writing OpenGL code to manipulate NURBS curves and surfaces is relatively easy, even with lighting and texture mapping.

Perform the following steps to draw NURBS curves or untrimmed NURBS surfaces. (See "Trimming a NURBS Surface" on page 565 for information about trimmed surfaces.)

1. If you intend to use lighting with a NURBS surface, call **glEnable()** with GL_AUTO_NORMAL to generate surface normals automatically. (Or you can calculate your own.)

2. Use **gluNewNurbsRenderer()** to create a pointer to a NURBS object, which is referred to when creating your NURBS curve or surface.

3. If desired, call **gluNurbsProperty()** to choose rendering values, such as the maximum size of lines or polygons that are used to render your NURBS object. **gluNurbsProperty()** can also enable a mode, where the tessellated geometric data can be retrieved through the callback interface.

4. Call **gluNurbsCallback()** if you want to be notified when an error is encountered. (Error checking may slightly degrade performance but is still highly recommended.) **gluNurbsCallback()** may also be used to register the functions to call to retrieve the tessellated geometric data.

5. Start your curve or surface by calling **gluBeginCurve()** or **gluBeginSurface()**.

6. Generate and render your curve or surface. Call **gluNurbsCurve()** or **gluNurbsSurface()** at least once with the control points (rational or nonrational), knot sequence, and order of the polynomial basis function for your NURBS object. You might call these functions additional times to specify surface normals and/or texture coordinates.

7. Call **gluEndCurve()** or **gluEndSurface()** to complete the curve or surface.

Example 12-5 renders a NURBS surface in the shape of a symmetrical hill, with control points ranging from −3.0 to 3.0. The basis function is a cubic B-spline, but the knot sequence is nonuniform, with a multiplicity of 4 at each endpoint, causing the basis function to behave as a Bézier curve in each direction. The surface is lighted, with a dark gray diffuse reflection and white specular highlights. Figure 12-4 shows the surface as a lit wireframe.

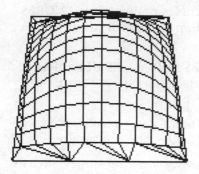

**Figure 12-4**    NURBS Surface

**Example 12-5**    NURBS Surface: surface.c

```
#ifndef CALLBACK
#define CALLBACK
#endif

GLfloat ctlpoints[4][4][3];
int showPoints = 0;

GLUnurbsObj *theNurb;

void init_surface(void)
{
    int u, v;
    for (u = 0; u < 4; u++) {
        for (v = 0; v < 4; v++) {
            ctlpoints[u][v][0] = 2.0*((GLfloat)u - 1.5);
            ctlpoints[u][v][1] = 2.0*((GLfloat)v - 1.5);

            if ( (u == 1 || u == 2) && (v == 1 || v == 2))
                ctlpoints[u][v][2] = 3.0;
            else
                ctlpoints[u][v][2] = -3.0;
        }
    }
}

void CALLBACK nurbsError(GLenum errorCode)
{
    const GLubyte *estring;
```

```c
        estring = gluErrorString(errorCode);
        fprintf(stderr, "Nurbs Error: %s\n", estring);
        exit(0);
}

void init(void)
{
    GLfloat mat_diffuse[] = { 0.7, 0.7, 0.7, 1.0 };
    GLfloat mat_specular[] = { 1.0, 1.0, 1.0, 1.0 };
    GLfloat mat_shininess[] = { 100.0 };

    glClearColor(0.0, 0.0, 0.0, 0.0);
    glMaterialfv(GL_FRONT, GL_DIFFUSE, mat_diffuse);
    glMaterialfv(GL_FRONT, GL_SPECULAR, mat_specular);
    glMaterialfv(GL_FRONT, GL_SHININESS, mat_shininess);

    glEnable(GL_LIGHTING);
    glEnable(GL_LIGHT0);
    glEnable(GL_DEPTH_TEST);
    glEnable(GL_AUTO_NORMAL);
    glEnable(GL_NORMALIZE);

    init_surface();

    theNurb = gluNewNurbsRenderer();
    gluNurbsProperty(theNurb, GLU_SAMPLING_TOLERANCE, 25.0);
    gluNurbsProperty(theNurb, GLU_DISPLAY_MODE, GLU_FILL);
    gluNurbsCallback(theNurb, GLU_ERROR, nurbsError);
}

void display(void)
{
    GLfloat knots[8] = {0.0, 0.0, 0.0, 0.0, 1.0, 1.0, 1.0, 1.0};
    int i, j;

    glClear(GL_COLOR_BUFFER_BIT | GL_DEPTH_BUFFER_BIT);

    glPushMatrix();
    glRotatef(330.0, 1., 0., 0.);
    glScalef(0.5, 0.5, 0.5);

    gluBeginSurface(theNurb);
    gluNurbsSurface(theNurb,
                    8, knots, 8, knots,
                    4 * 3, 3, &ctlpoints[0][0][0],
                    4, 4, GL_MAP2_VERTEX_3);
```

```
        gluEndSurface(theNurb);

        if (showPoints) {
           glPointSize(5.0);
           glDisable(GL_LIGHTING);
           glColor3f(1.0, 1.0, 0.0);
           glBegin(GL_POINTS);
           for (i = 0; i < 4; i++) {
              for (j = 0; j < 4; j++) {
                 glVertex3f(ctlpoints[i][j][0],
                            ctlpoints[i][j][1], ctlpoints[i][j][2]);
              }
           }
           glEnd();
           glEnable(GL_LIGHTING);
        }
        glPopMatrix();
        glFlush();
}

void reshape(int w, int h)
{
        glViewport(0, 0, (GLsizei) w, (GLsizei) h);
        glMatrixMode(GL_PROJECTION);
        glLoadIdentity();
        gluPerspective(45.0, (GLdouble)w/(GLdouble)h, 3.0, 8.0);
        glMatrixMode(GL_MODELVIEW);
        glLoadIdentity();
        glTranslatef(0.0, 0.0, -5.0);
}
void keyboard(unsigned char key, int x, int y)
{
        switch (key) {
           case 'c':
           case 'C':
              showPoints = !showPoints;
              glutPostRedisplay();
              break;
           case 27:
              exit(0);
              break;
           default:
              break;
        }
}
```

```
int main(int argc, char** argv)
{
    glutInit(&argc, argv);
    glutInitDisplayMode(GLUT_SINGLE | GLUT_RGB | GLUT_DEPTH);
    glutInitWindowSize(500, 500);
    glutInitWindowPosition(100, 100);
    glutCreateWindow(argv[0]);
    init();
    glutReshapeFunc(reshape);
    glutDisplayFunc(display);
    glutKeyboardFunc(keyboard);
    glutMainLoop();
    return 0;
}
```

## Managing a NURBS Object

As shown in Example 12-5, **gluNewNurbsRenderer()** returns a new NURBS object, whose type is a pointer to a GLUnurbsObj structure. You must make this object before using any other NURBS routine. When you're done with a NURBS object, you may use **gluDeleteNurbsRenderer**() to free up the memory that was used.

---

GLUnurbsObj* **gluNewNurbsRenderer**(void);

Creates a new NURBS object, *nobj*, and returns a pointer to the new object, or zero, if OpenGL cannot allocate memory for a new NURBS object.

---

void **gluDeleteNurbsRenderer**(GLUnurbsObj *nobj*);

Destroys the NURBS object *nobj*.

---

### Controlling NURBS Rendering Properties

A set of properties associated with a NURBS object affects the way the object is rendered. These properties include how the surface is rasterized (for example, filled or wireframe), whether the tessellated vertices are displayed or returned, and the precision of tessellation.

---

void **gluNurbsProperty**(GLUnurbsObj *nobj*, GLenum *property*,
GLfloat *value*);

---

Controls attributes of a NURBS object, *nobj*. The *property* argument
specifies the property and can be GLU_DISPLAY_MODE, GLU_NURBS_
MODE, GLU_CULLING, GLU_SAMPLING_METHOD, GLU_SAMPLING_
TOLERANCE, GLU_PARAMETRIC_TOLERANCE, GLU_U_STEP, GLU_V_
STEP, or GLU_AUTO_LOAD_MATRIX. The *value* argument indicates what
the property should be.

For the *property* GLU_DISPLAY_MODE, the default *value* is GLU_FILL,
which causes the surface to be rendered as polygons. If GLU_OUTLINE_
POLYGON is used for the display-mode property, only the outlines of
polygons created by tessellation are rendered. GLU_OUTLINE_PATCH
renders the outlines of patches and trimming curves. (See "Creating a
NURBS Curve or Surface" on page 559.)

The *property* GLU_NURBS_MODE controls whether the tessellated vertices
are simply rendered (the default *value*, GLU_NURBS_RENDERER) or
whether the callback interface is activated to allow the tessellated data
to be returned (if *value* is GL_NURBS_TESSELLATOR). For details, see
"Getting Primitives Back from the NURBS Tessellator" on page 561.

GLU_CULLING can speed up performance by not performing tessellation
if the NURBS object falls completely outside the viewing volume; set this
property to GL_TRUE to enable culling (the default is GL_FALSE).

Since a NURBS object is rendered as primitives, it's sampled at different
values of its parameter(s) (*u* and *v*) and broken down into small line
segments or polygons for rendering. If *property* is GLU_SAMPLING_
METHOD, then *value* is set to GLU_PATH_LENGTH (which is the default),
GLU_PARAMETRIC_ERROR, GLU_DOMAIN_DISTANCE, GLU_OBJECT_
PATH_LENGTH, or GLU_OBJECT_PARAMETRIC_ERROR, which specifies
how a NURBS curve or surface should be tessellated. When *value* is set
to GLU_PATH_LENGTH, the surface is rendered so that the maximum
length, in pixels, of the edges of tessellated polygons is no greater than
that specified by GLU_SAMPLING_TOLERANCE. When *value* is set to
GLU_PARAMETRIC_ERROR, then the quantity specified by GLU_
PARAMETRIC_TOLERANCE is the maximum distance, in pixels, between
tessellated polygons and the surfaces they approximate.

A *value* of GLU_OBJECT_PATH_LENGTH is similar to GLU_PATH_LENGTH, except that the maximum length (the value of GLU_SAMPLING_ TOLERANCE) of a tessellated primitive is measured in object space, not pixels. Similarly, GLU_OBJECT_PARAMETRIC_ERROR is related to GLU_PARAMETRIC_ERROR, except that GLU_OBJECT_PARAMETRIC_ TOLERANCE measures the maximum distance between tessellated polygons and the surfaces they approximate, in object space, not in pixels.

When *value* is set to GLU_DOMAIN_DISTANCE, the application specifies, in parametric coordinates, how many sample points per unit length are taken in the *u*- and *v*-dimensions, using the values for GLU_U_STEP and GLU_V_STEP.

If *property* is GLU_SAMPLING_TOLERANCE and the sampling method is GLU_PATH_LENGTH or GLU_OBJECT_PATH_LENGTH, *value* controls the maximum length, in pixels or object space units, respectively, that should be used for tessellated polygons. For example, the default value of 50.0 makes the largest sampled line segment or polygon edge 50.0 pixels long or 50.0 units long in object space. If *property* is GLU_PARAMETRIC_ TOLERANCE and the sampling method is GLU_PARAMETRIC_ERROR or GLU_OBJECT_PARAMETRIC_ERROR, *value* controls the maximum distance, in pixels or object space, respectively, between the tessellated polygons and the surfaces they approximate. For either sampling method, the default value for GLU_PARAMETRIC_TOLERANCE is 0.5. For GLU_PARAMETRIC_ERROR, this value makes the tessellated polygons within one-half pixel of the approximated surface. (For GLU_OBJECT_ PARAMETRIC_ERROR, the default value of 0.5 doesn't have the same obvious meaning.)

If the sampling method is GLU_DOMAIN_DISTANCE and *property* is either GLU_U_STEP or GLU_V_STEP, then *value* is the number of sample points per unit length taken along the *u*- or *v*-dimension, respectively, in parametric coordinates. The default for both GLU_U_STEP and GLU_V_ STEP is 100.

The GLU_AUTO_LOAD_MATRIX property determines whether the projection matrix, modelview matrix, and viewport are downloaded from the OpenGL server (GL_TRUE, the default), or whether the application must supply these matrices with **gluLoadSamplingMatrices()** (GL_FALSE).

**Note:** Several of the NURBS properties (the GLU_NURBS_MODE and its nondefault value GLU_NURBS_TESSELLATOR, and the object space sampling methods GLU_OBJECT_PATH_LENGTH and GLU_OBJECT_PARAMETRIC_ERROR) are introduced in GLU Version 1.3. Prior to GLU 1.3, these NURBS properties existed as vendor-specific extensions, if at all. Make sure you check the GLU version before you attempt to use these properties.

---

void **gluLoadSamplingMatrices**(GLUnurbsObj *nobj,
                        const GLfloat modelMatrix[16],
                        const GLfloat projMatrix[16],
                        const GLint viewport[4]);

---

If the GLU_AUTO_LOAD_MATRIX is turned off, the modelview and projection matrices and the viewport specified in **gluLoadSamplingMatrices()** are used to compute sampling and culling matrices for each NURBS curve or surface.

If you need to query the current value of a NURBS property, you may use **gluGetNurbsProperty()**.

---

void **gluGetNurbsProperty**(GLUnurbsObj *nobj, GLenum property,
                        GLfloat *value);

---

Given the property to be queried for the NURBS object nobj, returns its current value.

### Handling NURBS Errors

Since there are 37 different errors specific to NURBS functions, it's a good idea to register an error callback to let you know if you've stumbled into one of them. In Example 12-5, the callback function was registered with

```
gluNurbsCallback(theNurb, GLU_ERROR, (GLvoid (*)()) nurbsError);
```

> void **gluNurbsCallback**(GLUnurbsObj *nobj*, GLenum *which*,
>                          void (*fn*)(GLenum *errorCode*));
>
> *which* is the type of callback; for error checking, it must be GLU_ERROR.
> When a NURBS function detects an error condition, *fn* is invoked with the
> error code as its only argument. *errorCode* is one of 37 error conditions,
> named GLU_NURBS_ERROR1 through GLU_NURBS_ERROR37. Use
> **gluErrorString()** to describe the meaning of these error codes.

In Example 12-5, the **nurbsError()** routine was registered as the error
callback function:

```
void CALLBACK nurbsError(GLenum errorCode)
{
    const GLubyte *estring;

    estring = gluErrorString(errorCode);
    fprintf(stderr, "Nurbs Error: %s\n", estring);
    exit(0);
}
```

In GLU 1.3, additional NURBS callback functions have been added to return
post-tessellation values back to the program (instead of rendering them).
For more information on these new callbacks, see "Getting Primitives Back
from the NURBS Tessellator" on page 561.

## Creating a NURBS Curve or Surface

To render a NURBS surface, **gluNurbsSurface()** is bracketed by
**gluBeginSurface()** and **gluEndSurface()**. The bracketing routines save and
restore the evaluator state.

> void **gluBeginSurface**(GLUnurbsObj *nobj*);
> void **gluEndSurface**(GLUnurbsObj *nobj*);
>
> After **gluBeginSurface()**, one or more calls to **gluNurbsSurface()** defines
> the attributes of the surface. Exactly one of these calls must have a surface
> type of GL_MAP2_VERTEX_3 or GL_MAP2_VERTEX_4 to generate
> vertices. Use **gluEndSurface()** to end the definition of a surface. Trimming
> of NURBS surfaces is also supported between **gluBeginSurface()** and
> **gluEndSurface()**. (See "Trimming a NURBS Surface" on page 565.)

void **gluNurbsSurface**(GLUnurbsObj *nobj*, GLint *uknot_count*,
 GLfloat *\*uknot*, GLint *vknot_count*, GLfloat *\*vknot*,
 GLint *u_stride*, GLint *v_stride*, GLfloat *\*ctlarray*,
 GLint *uorder*, GLint *vorder*, GLenum *type*);

Describes the vertices (or surface normals or texture coordinates) of a NURBS surface, *nobj*. Several of the values must be specified for both *u* and *v* parametric directions, such as the knot sequences (*uknot* and *vknot*), knot counts (*uknot_count* and *vknot_count*), and the order of the polynomial (*uorder* and *vorder*) for the NURBS surface. Note that the number of control points isn't specified. Instead, it's derived by determining the number of control points along each parameter as the number of knots minus the order. Then, the number of control points for the surface is equal to the number of control points in each parametric direction, multiplied by one another. The *ctlarray* argument points to an array of control points.

The last parameter, *type*, is one of the two-dimensional evaluator types. Commonly, you might use GL_MAP2_VERTEX_3 for nonrational or GL_MAP2_VERTEX_4 for rational control points, respectively. You might also use other types, such as GL_MAP2_TEXTURE_COORD_* or GL_MAP2_NORMAL to calculate and assign texture coordinates or surface normals. For example, to create a lighted (with surface normals) and textured NURBS surface, you may need to call this sequence:

```
gluBeginSurface(nobj);
    gluNurbsSurface(nobj, ..., GL_MAP2_TEXTURE_COORD_2);
    gluNurbsSurface(nobj, ..., GL_MAP2_NORMAL);
    gluNurbsSurface(nobj, ..., GL_MAP2_VERTEX_3);
gluEndSurface(nobj);
```

The *u_stride* and *v_stride* arguments represent the number of floating-point values between control points in each parametric direction. The evaluator type, as well as its order, affects the *u_stride* and *v_stride* values. In Example 12-5, *u_stride* is 12 (4*3) because there are three coordinates for each vertex (set by GL_MAP2_VERTEX_3) and four control points in the parametric *v*-direction; *v_stride* is 3 because each vertex has three coordinates, and the *v* control points are adjacent to one another in memory.

Drawing a NURBS curve is similar to drawing a surface, except that all calculations are done with one parameter, *u*, rather than two. Also, for curves, **gluBeginCurve()** and **gluEndCurve()** are the bracketing routines.

---

void **gluBeginCurve**(GLUnurbsObj *nobj*);
void **gluEndCurve**(GLUnurbsObj *nobj*);

---

After **gluBeginCurve()**, one or more calls to **gluNurbsCurve()** define the attributes of the surface. Exactly one of these calls must have a surface type of GL_MAP1_VERTEX_3 or GL_MAP1_VERTEX_4 to generate vertices. Use **gluEndCurve()** to end the definition of a surface.

---

void **gluNurbsCurve**(GLUnurbsObj *nobj*, GLint *uknot_count*,
                GLfloat *uknot*, GLint *u_stride*, GLfloat *ctlarray*,
                GLint *uorder*, GLenum *type*);

---

Defines a NURBS curve for the object *nobj*. The arguments have the same meaning as those for **gluNurbsSurface()**. Note that this routine requires only one knot sequence and one declaration of the order of the NURBS object. If this curve is defined within a **gluBeginCurve()**/**gluEndCurve()** pair, then the type can be any of the valid one-dimensional evaluator types (such as GL_MAP1_VERTEX_3 or GL_MAP1_VERTEX_4).

### Getting Primitives Back from the NURBS Tessellator

By default, the NURBS tessellator breaks down a NURBS object into geometric lines and polygons, and then renders them. In GLU 1.3, additional callback functions have been added, so instead of rendering the post-tessellation values, they can be returned for use by the application.

To do this, call **gluNurbsProperty()** to set the GLU_NURBS_MODE *property* to the *value* GLU_NURBS_TESSELLATOR. The other necessary step is to call **gluNurbsCallback()** several times to register callback functions, which the NURBS tessellator will now call.

---

| void **gluNurbsCallback**(GLUnurbsObj *nobj*, GLenum *which*, |
|---|
| void (**fn*)()); |

*nobj* is the NURBS object to be tessellated. *which* is the enumerant identifying the callback function. If the *property* GLU_NURBS_MODE is set to GLU_NURBS_TESSELLATOR, then 12 possible callback functions (in addition to GLU_ERROR) are available. (If GLU_NURBS_MODE is set to the default GLU_NURBS_RENDERER value, then only GLU_ERROR is active.) The 12 callbacks have the following enumerants and prototypes:

GLU_NURBS_BEGIN                          void **begin**(GLenum *type*);

GLU_NURBS_BEGIN_DATA                     void **begin**(GLenum *type*,
                                                  void **userData*);

GLU_NURBS_TEXTURE_COORD                  void **texCoord**(
                                                  GLfloat **tCrd*);

GLU_NURBS_TEXTURE_COORD_DATA             void **texCoord**(
                                                  GLfloat **tCrd*,
                                                  void **userData*);

GLU_NURBS_COLOR                          void **color**(GLfloat **color*);

GLU_NURBS_COLOR_DATA                     void **color**(GLfloat **color*,
                                                  void **userData*);

GLU_NURBS_NORMAL                         void **normal**(GLfloat **nml*);

GLU_NURBS_NORMAL_DATA                    void **normal**(GLfloat **nml*,
                                                  void **userData*);

GLU_NURBS_VERTEX                         void **vertex**(GLfloat **vertex*);

GLU_NURBS_VERTEX_DATA                    void **vertex**(GLfloat **vertex*,
                                                  void **userData*);

GLU_NURBS_END                            void **end**(void);

GLU_NURBS_END_DATA                       void **end**(void **userData*);

To change a callback routine, call **gluNurbsCallback**() with the new routine. To eliminate a callback routine without replacing it, pass **gluNurbsCallback**() a null pointer for the appropriate function.

Six of the callback functions allow the user to pass some data to it. To specify that user data, you must call **gluNurbsCallbackData**().

As tessellation proceeds, the callback routines are called in a manner similar
to that in which you use the OpenGL commands **glBegin**(), **glTexCoord\***(),
**glColor\***(), **glNormal\***(), **glVertex\***(), and **glEnd**(). During the GLU_NURBS_
TESSELLATOR mode, the curve or surface is not directly rendered, but you
can capture the vertex data passed as parameters to the callback functions.

To demonstrate these new callbacks, Example 12-6 and Example 12-7 show
portions of surfpoints.c, which is a modification of the earlier surface.c
program. Example 12-6 shows part of the **init**() subroutine, where the
NURBS object is created, GLU_NURBS_MODE is set to perform the
tessellation, and the callback functions are registered.

**Example 12-6**   Registering NURBS Tessellation Callbacks: surfpoints.c

```
void init(void)
{
/* only a portion of init() shown here--several lines deleted */

   theNurb = gluNewNurbsRenderer();
   gluNurbsProperty(theNurb, GLU_NURBS_MODE,
                     GLU_NURBS_TESSELLATOR);
   gluNurbsProperty(theNurb, GLU_SAMPLING_TOLERANCE, 100.0);
   gluNurbsProperty(theNurb, GLU_DISPLAY_MODE, GLU_FILL);
   gluNurbsCallback(theNurb, GLU_ERROR, nurbsError);
   gluNurbsCallback(theNurb, GLU_NURBS_BEGIN, beginCallback);
   gluNurbsCallback(theNurb, GLU_NURBS_VERTEX, vertexCallback);
   gluNurbsCallback(theNurb, GLU_NURBS_NORMAL, normalCallback);
   gluNurbsCallback(theNurb, GLU_NURBS_END, endCallback);
}
```

Example 12-7 shows the callback functions of surfpoints.c. In these
callbacks, **printf**() statements act as diagnostics to show what rendering
directives and vertex data are returned from the tessellator. In addition,
the post-tessellation data is resubmitted to the pipeline for ordinary
rendering.

**Example 12-7**   The NURBS Tessellation Callbacks: surfpoints.c

```c
void CALLBACK beginCallback(GLenum whichType)
{
   glBegin(whichType);  /*  resubmit rendering directive */
   printf("glBegin(");
   switch (whichType) {  /*  print diagnostic message  */
      case GL_LINES:
         printf("GL_LINES)\n"); break;
      case GL_LINE_LOOP:
         printf("GL_LINE_LOOP)\n"); break;
      case GL_LINE_STRIP:
         printf("GL_LINE_STRIP)\n"); break;
      case GL_TRIANGLES:
         printf("GL_TRIANGLES)\n"); break;
      case GL_TRIANGLE_STRIP:
         printf("GL_TRIANGLE_STRIP)\n"); break;
      case GL_TRIANGLE_FAN:
         printf("GL_TRIANGLE_FAN)\n"); break;
      case GL_QUADS:
         printf("GL_QUADS)\n"); break;
      case GL_QUAD_STRIP:
         printf("GL_QUAD_STRIP)\n"); break;
      case GL_POLYGON:
         printf("GL_POLYGON)\n"); break;
      default:
         break;
   }
}
void CALLBACK endCallback()
{
   glEnd();  /*  resubmit rendering directive */
   printf("glEnd()\n");
}

void CALLBACK vertexCallback(GLfloat *vertex)
{
   glVertex3fv(vertex);  /*  resubmit tessellated vertex */
   printf("glVertex3f (%5.3f, %5.3f, %5.3f)\n",
           vertex[0], vertex[1], vertex[2]);
}

void CALLBACK normalCallback(GLfloat *normal)
{
   glNormal3fv(normal);  /*  resubmit tessellated normal */
   printf("glNormal3f (%5.3f, %5.3f, %5.3f) ",
           normal[0], normal[1], normal[2]);
}
```

## Trimming a NURBS Surface

To create a trimmed NURBS surface with OpenGL, start as if you were creating an untrimmed surface. After calling **gluBeginSurface()** and **gluNurbsSurface()** but before calling **gluEndSurface()**, start a trim by calling **gluBeginTrim()**.

---

void **gluBeginTrim**(GLUnurbsObj *nobj);
void **gluEndTrim**(GLUnurbsObj *nobj);

Marks the beginning and end of the definition of a trimming loop. A trimming loop is a set of oriented, trimming curve segments (forming a closed curve) that defines the boundaries of a NURBS surface.

---

You can create two kinds of trimming curves: a piecewise linear curve with **gluPwlCurve()** or a NURBS curve with **gluNurbsCurve()**. A piecewise linear curve doesn't look like what is conventionally called a curve, because it's a series of straight lines. A NURBS curve for trimming must lie within the unit square of parametric $(u, v)$ space. The type for a NURBS trimming curve is usually GLU_MAP1_TRIM2. Less often, the type is GLU_MAP1_TRIM3, where the curve is described in a two-dimensional homogeneous space $(u', v', w')$ by $(u, v) = (u'/w', v'/w')$.

---

void **gluPwlCurve**(GLUnurbsObj *nobj, GLint count, GLfloat *array,
                          GLint stride, GLenum type);

Describes a piecewise linear trimming curve for the NURBS object nobj. There are count points on the curve, and they're given by array. The type can be either GLU_MAP1_TRIM_2 (the most common) or GLU_MAP1_TRIM_3 (($u, v, w$) homogeneous parameter space). The value of type determines whether stride is 2 or 3. stride represents the number of floating-point values to the next vertex in array.

---

You need to consider the orientation of trimming curves—that is, whether they're counterclockwise or clockwise—to make sure you include the desired part of the surface. If you imagine walking along a curve, everything to the left is included and everything to the right is trimmed away. For example, if your trim consists of a single counterclockwise loop, everything inside the loop is included. If the trim consists of two nonintersecting counterclockwise loops with nonintersecting interiors, everything inside either of them is included. If it consists of a counterclockwise loop with two clockwise loops inside it, the trimming region has two holes in it. The outermost trimming curve must be counterclockwise. Often, you run a trimming curve around the entire unit square to include everything within it, which is what you get by default by not specifying any trimming curves.

Trimming curves must be closed and nonintersecting. You can combine trimming curves, as long as the endpoints of the trimming curves meet to form a closed curve. You can nest curves, creating islands that float in space. Be sure to get the curve orientations right. For example, an error results if you specify a trimming region with two counterclockwise curves, one enclosed within the other: the region between the curves is to the left of one and to the right of the other, so it must be both included and excluded, which is impossible. Figure 12-5 illustrates a few valid possibilities.

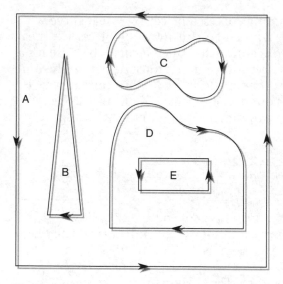

```
gluBeginSurface();
gluNurbsSurface(...);
gluBeginTrim();
gluPwlCurve(...); /* A */
gluEndTrim();
gluBeginTrim();
gluPwlCurve(...); /* B */
gluEndTrim();
gluBeginTrim();
gluNurbsCurve(...); */ C */
gluEndTrim();
gluBeginTrim();
gluNurbsCurve(...); */ D */
gluPwlCurve(...); /* D */
gluEndTrim();
gluBeginTrim();
gluPwlCurve(...); /* E */
gluEndTrim();
gluEndSurface();
```

**Figure 12-5**   Parametric Trimming Curves

Figure 12-6 shows the same small hill shown in Figure 12-4, but with a trimming curve that's a combination of a piecewise linear curve and a NURBS curve. The program that creates this figure is similar to the one shown in Example 12-5; the differences are in the routines shown in Example 12-8.

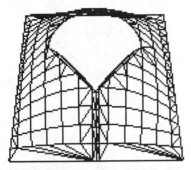

**Figure 12-6**  Trimmed NURBS Surface

**Example 12-8**  Trimming a NURBS Surface: trim.c

```
void display(void)
{
   GLfloat knots[8] = {0.0, 0.0, 0.0, 0.0, 1.0, 1.0, 1.0, 1.0};
   GLfloat edgePt[5][2] = /* counter clockwise */
      {{0.0, 0.0}, {1.0, 0.0}, {1.0, 1.0}, {0.0, 1.0},
       {0.0, 0.0}};
   GLfloat curvePt[4][2] = /* clockwise */
      {{0.25, 0.5}, {0.25, 0.75}, {0.75, 0.75}, {0.75, 0.5}};
   GLfloat curveKnots[8] =
      {0.0, 0.0, 0.0, 0.0, 1.0, 1.0, 1.0, 1.0};
   GLfloat pwlPt[3][2] = /* clockwise */
      {{0.75, 0.5}, {0.5, 0.25}, {0.25, 0.5}};

   glClear(GL_COLOR_BUFFER_BIT | GL_DEPTH_BUFFER_BIT);
   glPushMatrix();
   glRotatef(330.0, 1., 0., 0.);
   glScalef(0.5, 0.5, 0.5);

   gluBeginSurface(theNurb);
   gluNurbsSurface(theNurb, 8, knots, 8, knots,
                   4 * 3, 3, &ctlpoints[0][0][0],
                   4, 4, GL_MAP2_VERTEX_3);
   gluBeginTrim(theNurb);
      gluPwlCurve(theNurb, 5, &edgePt[0][0], 2,
                  GLU_MAP1_TRIM_2);
```

```
        gluEndTrim(theNurb);
        gluBeginTrim(theNurb);
            gluNurbsCurve(theNurb, 8, curveKnots, 2,
                        &curvePt[0][0], 4, GLU_MAP1_TRIM_2);
            gluPwlCurve(theNurb, 3, &pwlPt[0][0], 2,
                        GLU_MAP1_TRIM_2);
        gluEndTrim(theNurb);
        gluEndSurface(theNurb);

        glPopMatrix();
        glFlush();
}
```

In Example 12-8, **gluBeginTrim()** and **gluEndTrim()** bracket each trimming curve. The first trim, with vertices defined by the array *edgePt[][]*, goes counterclockwise around the entire unit square of parametric space. This ensures that everything is drawn, provided it isn't removed by a clockwise trimming curve inside of it. The second trim is a combination of a NURBS trimming curve and a piecewise linear trimming curve. The NURBS curve ends at the points (0.9, 0.5) and (0.1, 0.5), where it is met by the piecewise linear curve, forming a closed clockwise curve.

*Chapter 13*

# Selection and Feedback

**Chapter Objectives**

After reading this chapter, you'll be able to do the following:

- Create applications that allow the user to select a region of the screen or pick an object drawn on the screen

- Use the OpenGL feedback mode to obtain the results of rendering calculations

Some graphics applications simply draw static images of two- and three-dimensional objects. Other applications allow the user to identify objects on the screen and then to move, modify, delete, or otherwise manipulate those objects. OpenGL is designed to support exactly such interactive applications. Since objects drawn on the screen typically undergo multiple rotations, translations, and perspective transformations, it can be difficult for you to determine which object a user is selecting in a three-dimensional scene. To help you, OpenGL provides a selection mechanism that automatically tells you which objects are drawn inside a specified region of the window. You can use this mechanism together with a special utility routine to determine which object within the region the user is specifying, or *picking*, with the cursor.

Selection is actually a mode of operation for OpenGL; feedback is another such mode. In feedback mode, you use your graphics hardware and OpenGL to perform the usual rendering calculations. Instead of using the calculated results to draw an image on the screen, however, OpenGL returns (or feeds back) the drawing information to you. For example, if you want to draw three-dimensional objects on a plotter rather than the screen, you would draw the items in feedback mode, collect the drawing instructions, and then convert them to commands the plotter can understand.

In both selection and feedback modes, drawing information is returned to the application rather than being sent to the framebuffer, as it is in rendering mode. Thus, the screen remains frozen—no drawing occurs—while OpenGL is in selection or feedback mode. In these modes, the contents of the color, depth, stencil, and accumulation buffers are not affected. This chapter explains each of these modes in its own section:

- "Selection" discusses how to use selection mode and related routines to allow a user of your application to pick an object drawn on the screen.

- "Feedback" describes how to obtain information about what would be drawn on the screen and how that information is formatted.

## Selection

Typically, when you're planning to use OpenGL's selection mechanism, you first draw your scene into the framebuffer, and then you enter selection mode and redraw the scene. However, once you're in selection mode, the contents of the framebuffer don't change until you exit selection mode. When you exit selection mode, OpenGL returns a list of the primitives that intersect the viewing volume. (Remember that the viewing volume is defined by the current modelview and projection matrices and any additional clipping planes, as explained in Chapter 3.) Each primitive that intersects the viewing volume causes a selection *hit*. The list of primitives is actually returned as an array of integer-valued *names* and related data—the *hit records*—that correspond to the current contents of the *name stack*. You construct the name stack by loading names onto it as you issue primitive drawing commands while in selection mode. Thus, when the list of names is returned, you can use it to determine which primitives might have been selected on the screen by the user.

In addition to this selection mechanism, OpenGL provides a utility routine designed to simplify selection in some cases by restricting drawing to a small region of the viewport. Typically, you use this routine to determine which objects are drawn near the cursor, so that you can identify which object the user is picking. (You can also delimit a selection region by specifying additional clipping planes. Remember that these planes act in world space, not in screen space.) Since picking is a special case of selection, selection is described first in this chapter, and then picking.

## The Basic Steps

To use the selection mechanism, you need to perform the following steps:

1. Specify the array to be used for the returned hit records with **glSelectBuffer()**.

2. Enter selection mode by specifying GL_SELECT with **glRenderMode()**.

3. Initialize the name stack using **glInitNames()** and **glPushName()**.

4. Define the viewing volume you want to use for selection. Usually this is different from the viewing volume you originally used to draw the scene, so you probably want to save and then restore the current transformation state with **glPushMatrix()** and **glPopMatrix()**.

5. Alternately issue primitive drawing commands and commands to manipulate the name stack so that each primitive of interest is assigned an appropriate name.

6. Exit selection mode and process the returned selection data (the hit records).

The following two paragraphs describe **glSelectBuffer()** and **glRenderMode()**. In the next subsection, the commands for manipulating the name stack are described.

> void **glSelectBuffer**(GLsizei *size*, GLuint *\*buffer*);
>
> Specifies the array to be used for the returned selection data. The *buffer* argument is a pointer to an array of unsigned integers into which the data is put, and *size* indicates the maximum number of values that can be stored in the array. You need to call **glSelectBuffer**() before entering selection mode.

> GLint **glRenderMode**(GLenum *mode*);
>
> Controls whether the application is in rendering, selection, or feedback mode. The *mode* argument can be GL_RENDER (the default), GL_SELECT, or GL_FEEDBACK. The application remains in a given mode until **glRenderMode**() is called again with a different argument. Before selection mode is entered, **glSelectBuffer**() must be called to specify the selection array. Similarly, before feedback mode is entered, **glFeedbackBuffer**() must be called to specify the feedback array. The return value for **glRenderMode**() has meaning if the current render mode (that is, not the *mode* parameter) is either GL_SELECT or GL_FEEDBACK. The return value is the number of selection hits or the number of values placed in the feedback array when either mode is exited; a negative value means that the selection or feedback array has overflowed. You can use GL_RENDER_MODE with **glGetIntegerv**() to obtain the current mode.

## Creating the Name Stack

As mentioned in the preceding subsection, the name stack forms the basis for the selection information that's returned to you. To create the name stack, first initialize it with **glInitNames**(), which simply clears the stack, and then add integer names to it while issuing corresponding drawing commands. As you might expect, the commands to manipulate the stack allow you to push a name onto it (**glPushName**()), pop a name off of it (**glPopName**()), and replace the name at the top of the stack with a different one (**glLoadName**()). Example 13-1 shows what your name-stack manipulation code might look like with these commands.

**Example 13-1**   Creating a Name Stack

```
glInitNames();
glPushName(0);

glPushMatrix();    /* save the current transformation state */

    /* create your desired viewing volume here */

    glLoadName(1);
    drawSomeObject();
    glLoadName(2);
    drawAnotherObject();
    glLoadName(3);
    drawYetAnotherObject();
    drawJustOneMoreObject();

glPopMatrix();    /* restore the previous transformation state*/
```

In this example, the first two objects to be drawn have their own names, and the third and fourth objects share a single name. With this setup, if either or both of the third and fourth objects cause a selection hit, only one hit record is returned to you. You can have multiple objects share the same name if you don't need to differentiate between them when processing the hit records.

---

void **glInitNames**(void);

Clears the name stack so that it's empty.

---

void **glPushName**(GLuint *name*);

Pushes *name* onto the name stack. Pushing a name beyond the capacity of the stack generates the error GL_STACK_OVERFLOW. The name stack's depth can vary among different OpenGL implementations, but it must be able to contain at least 64 names. You can use the parameter GL_NAME_STACK_DEPTH with **glGetIntegerv**() to obtain the depth of the name stack.

---

void **glPopName**(void);

Pops one name off the top of the name stack. Popping an empty stack generates the error GL_STACK_UNDERFLOW.

void **glLoadName**(GLuint *name*);

Replaces the value at the top of the name stack with *name*. If the stack is empty, which it is right after **glInitNames()** is called, **glLoadName()** generates the error GL_INVALID_OPERATION. To avoid this, if the stack is initially empty, call **glPushName()** at least once to put something on the name stack before calling **glLoadName()**.

Calls to **glPushName()**, **glPopName()**, and **glLoadName()** are ignored if you're not in selection mode. You might find that it simplifies your code to use these calls throughout your drawing code, and then use the same drawing code for both selection and normal rendering modes.

## The Hit Record

In selection mode, a primitive that intersects the viewing volume causes a selection hit. Whenever a name-stack manipulation command is executed or **glRenderMode()** is called, OpenGL writes a hit record into the selection array if there's been a hit since the last time the stack was manipulated or **glRenderMode()** was called. With this process, objects that share the same name—for example, an object composed of more than one primitive—don't generate multiple hit records. Also, hit records aren't guaranteed to be written into the array until **glRenderMode()** is called.

**Note:** In addition to geometric primitives, valid raster position coordinates produced by **glRasterPos()** or **glWindowPos()** cause a selection hit. Also, during selection mode, if culling is enabled and a polygon is processed and culled, then no hit occurs.

Each hit record consists of the following four items, in the order shown:

*   The number of names on the name stack when the hit occurred

*   Both the minimum and maximum window-coordinate z-values of all vertices of the primitives that have intersected the viewing volume since the last recorded hit. These two values, which lie in the range [0, 1], are each multiplied by $2^{32} - 1$ and rounded to the nearest unsigned integer.

*   The contents of the name stack at the time of the hit, with the bottommost element first

When you enter selection mode, OpenGL initializes a pointer to the beginning of the selection array. Each time a hit record is written into the array, the pointer is updated accordingly. If writing a hit record would cause the number of values in the array to exceed the *size* argument specified with **glSelectBuffer()**, OpenGL writes as much of the record as will fit in the array and sets an overflow flag. When you exit selection mode with **glRenderMode()**, this command returns the number of hit records that were written (including a partial record if there was one), clears the name stack, resets the overflow flag, and resets the stack pointer. If the overflow flag has been set, the return value is −1.

## A Selection Example

In Example 13-2, four triangles (a green, a red, and two yellow triangles, created by calling **drawTriangle()**) and a wireframe box representing the viewing volume (**drawViewVolume()**) are drawn on the screen. Then the triangles are rendered again (**selectObjects()**), but this time in selection mode. The corresponding hit records are processed in **processHits()**, and the selection array is printed out. The first triangle generates a hit, the second one doesn't, and the third and fourth ones together generate a single hit.

**Example 13-2**   Selection Example: select.c

```
void drawTriangle(GLfloat x1, GLfloat y1, GLfloat x2,
    GLfloat y2, GLfloat x3, GLfloat y3, GLfloat z)
{
   glBegin(GL_TRIANGLES);
   glVertex3f(x1, y1, z);
   glVertex3f(x2, y2, z);
   glVertex3f(x3, y3, z);
   glEnd();
}

void drawViewVolume(GLfloat x1, GLfloat x2, GLfloat y1,
                    GLfloat y2, GLfloat z1, GLfloat z2)
{
   glColor3f(1.0, 1.0, 1.0);
   glBegin(GL_LINE_LOOP);
   glVertex3f(x1, y1, -z1);
   glVertex3f(x2, y1, -z1);
   glVertex3f(x2, y2, -z1);
   glVertex3f(x1, y2, -z1);
   glEnd();
```

```
      glBegin(GL_LINE_LOOP);
      glVertex3f(x1, y1, -z2);
      glVertex3f(x2, y1, -z2);
      glVertex3f(x2, y2, -z2);
      glVertex3f(x1, y2, -z2);
      glEnd();

      glBegin(GL_LINES);  /*  4 lines     */
      glVertex3f(x1, y1, -z1);
      glVertex3f(x1, y1, -z2);
      glVertex3f(x1, y2, -z1);
      glVertex3f(x1, y2, -z2);
      glVertex3f(x2, y1, -z1);
      glVertex3f(x2, y1, -z2);
      glVertex3f(x2, y2, -z1);
      glVertex3f(x2, y2, -z2);
      glEnd();
}

void drawScene(void)
{
   glMatrixMode(GL_PROJECTION);
   glLoadIdentity();
   gluPerspective(40.0, 4.0/3.0, 1.0, 100.0);

   glMatrixMode(GL_MODELVIEW);
   glLoadIdentity();
   gluLookAt(7.5, 7.5, 12.5, 2.5, 2.5, -5.0, 0.0, 1.0, 0.0);
   glColor3f(0.0, 1.0, 0.0);   /*  green triangle      */
   drawTriangle(2.0, 2.0, 3.0, 2.0, 2.5, 3.0, -5.0);
   glColor3f(1.0, 0.0, 0.0);   /*  red triangle       */
   drawTriangle(2.0, 7.0, 3.0, 7.0, 2.5, 8.0, -5.0);
   glColor3f(1.0, 1.0, 0.0);   /*  yellow triangles    */
   drawTriangle(2.0, 2.0, 3.0, 2.0, 2.5, 3.0, 0.0);
   drawTriangle(2.0, 2.0, 3.0, 2.0, 2.5, 3.0, -10.0);
   drawViewVolume(0.0, 5.0, 0.0, 5.0, 0.0, 10.0);
}

void processHits(GLint hits, GLuint buffer[])
{
   unsigned int i, j;
   GLuint names, *ptr;

   printf("hits = %d\n", hits);
   ptr = (GLuint *) buffer;
```

```
   for (i = 0; i < hits; i++) { /*  for each hit  */
      names = *ptr;
      printf(" number of names for hit = %d\n", names); ptr++;
      printf("  z1 is %g;", (float) *ptr/0x7fffffff); ptr++;
      printf(" z2 is %g\n", (float) *ptr/0x7fffffff); ptr++;
      printf("    the name is ");
      for (j = 0; j < names; j++) {       /*  for each name */
         printf("%d ", *ptr); ptr++;
      }
      printf("\n");
   }
}

#define BUFSIZE 512

void selectObjects(void)
{
   GLuint selectBuf[BUFSIZE];
   GLint hits;

   glSelectBuffer(BUFSIZE, selectBuf);
   (void) glRenderMode(GL_SELECT);

   glInitNames();
   glPushName(0);

   glPushMatrix();
   glMatrixMode(GL_PROJECTION);
   glLoadIdentity();
   glOrtho(0.0, 5.0, 0.0, 5.0, 0.0, 10.0);
   glMatrixMode(GL_MODELVIEW);
   glLoadIdentity();
   glLoadName(1);
   drawTriangle(2.0, 2.0, 3.0, 2.0, 2.5, 3.0, -5.0);
   glLoadName(2);
   drawTriangle(2.0, 7.0, 3.0, 7.0, 2.5, 8.0, -5.0);
   glLoadName(3);
   drawTriangle(2.0, 2.0, 3.0, 2.0, 2.5, 3.0, 0.0);
   drawTriangle(2.0, 2.0, 3.0, 2.0, 2.5, 3.0, -10.0);
   glPopMatrix();
   glFlush();

   hits = glRenderMode(GL_RENDER);
   processHits(hits, selectBuf);
}
```

```
void init(void)
{
    glEnable(GL_DEPTH_TEST);
    glShadeModel(GL_FLAT);
}

void display(void)
{
    glClearColor(0.0, 0.0, 0.0, 0.0);
    glClear(GL_COLOR_BUFFER_BIT | GL_DEPTH_BUFFER_BIT);
    drawScene();
    selectObjects();
    glFlush();
}

int main(int argc, char** argv)
{
    glutInit(&argc, argv);
    glutInitDisplayMode(GLUT_SINGLE | GLUT_RGB | GLUT_DEPTH);
    glutInitWindowSize(200, 200);
    glutInitWindowPosition(100, 100);
    glutCreateWindow(argv[0]);
    init();
    glutDisplayFunc(display);
    glutMainLoop();
    return 0;
}
```

## Picking

As an extension of the process described in the preceding section, you can use selection mode to determine if objects are picked. To do this, you use a special picking matrix in conjunction with the projection matrix to restrict drawing to a small region of the viewport, typically near the cursor. Then you allow some form of input, such as clicking a mouse button, to initiate selection mode. With selection mode established and with the special picking matrix used, objects that are drawn near the cursor cause selection hits. Thus, during picking, you're typically determining which objects are drawn near the cursor.

Picking is set up almost exactly the same as regular selection mode with the following major differences:

- Picking is usually triggered by an input device. In the following code examples, pressing the left mouse button invokes a function that performs picking.

- You use the utility routine **gluPickMatrix()** to multiply the current projection matrix by a special picking matrix. This routine should be called prior to multiplying a standard projection matrix (such as **gluPerspective()** or **glOrtho()**). You'll probably want to save the contents of the projection matrix first, so the sequence of operations may look like this:

```
glMatrixMode(GL_PROJECTION);
glPushMatrix();
glLoadIdentity();
gluPickMatrix(...);
gluPerspective, glOrtho, gluOrtho2D, or glFrustum
    /* ... draw scene for picking ; perform picking ... */
glPopMatrix();
```

Another completely different way to perform picking is described in "Object Selection Using the Back Buffer" in Chapter 14. This technique uses color values to identify different components of an object.

---

void **gluPickMatrix**(GLdouble *x*, GLdouble *y*, GLdouble *width*,
        GLdouble *height*, GLint *viewport[4]*);

---

Creates a projection matrix that restricts drawing to a small region of the viewport and multiplies that matrix onto the current matrix stack. The center of the picking region is (*x*, *y*) in window coordinates, typically the cursor location. *width* and *height* define the size of the picking region in screen coordinates. (You can think of the width and height as the sensitivity of the picking device.) *viewport[]* indicates the current viewport boundaries, which can be obtained by calling

```
glGetIntegerv(GL_VIEWPORT, GLint *viewport);
```

**Advanced**

The net result of the matrix created by **gluPickMatrix()** transforms the clipping region into the unit cube $-1 \leq (x, y, z) \leq 1$ (or $-w \leq (wx, wy, wz) \leq w$). The picking matrix effectively performs an orthogonal transformation that maps the clipping region to the unit cube. Since the transformation is arbitrary, you can make picking work for different sorts of regions—for example, for rotated rectangular portions of the window. In certain situations, you might find it easier to specify additional clipping planes to define the picking region.

Example 13-3 illustrates simple picking. It also demonstrates how to use multiple names to identify different components of a primitive; in this case, the row and column of a selected object. A $3 \times 3$ grid of squares is drawn, with each square a different color. The *board*[3][3] array maintains the current amount of blue for each square. When the left mouse button is pressed, the **pickSquares()** routine is called to identify which squares were picked by the mouse. Two names identify each square in the grid—one identifies the row, and the other the column. Also, when the left mouse button is pressed, the colors of all squares under the cursor position change.

**Example 13-3**  Picking Example: picksquare.c

```
int board[3][3];    /* amount of color for each square */

/* Clear color value for every square on the board */
void init(void)
{
   int i, j;
   for (i = 0; i < 3; i++)
      for (j = 0; j < 3; j ++)
         board[i][j] = 0;
   glClearColor(0.0, 0.0, 0.0, 0.0);
}

void drawSquares(GLenum mode)
{
   GLuint i, j;
   for (i = 0; i < 3; i++) {
      if (mode == GL_SELECT)
         glLoadName(i);
      for (j = 0; j < 3; j ++) {
         if (mode == GL_SELECT)
            glPushName(j);
         glColor3f((GLfloat) i/3.0, (GLfloat) j/3.0,
                   (GLfloat) board[i][j]/3.0);
```

```
            glRecti(i, j, i+1, j+1);
            if (mode == GL_SELECT)
                glPopName();
        }
    }
}

/*  processHits prints out the contents of the
 *  selection array.
 */
void processHits(GLint hits, GLuint buffer[])
{
    unsigned int i, j;
    GLuint ii, jj, names, *ptr;

    printf("hits = %d\n", hits);
    ptr = (GLuint *) buffer;
    for (i = 0; i < hits; i++) { /*  for each hit  */
        names = *ptr;
        printf(" number of names for this hit = %d\n", names);
            ptr++;
        printf(" z1 is %g;", (float) *ptr/0x7fffffff); ptr++;
        printf(" z2 is %g\n", (float) *ptr/0x7fffffff); ptr++;
        printf("   names are ");
        for (j = 0; j < names; j++) { /*  for each name */
            printf("%d ", *ptr);
            if (j == 0)  /*  set row and column  */
                ii = *ptr;
            else if (j == 1)
                jj = *ptr;
            ptr++;
        }
        printf("\n");
        board[ii][jj] = (board[ii][jj] + 1) % 3;
    }
}

#define BUFSIZE 512

void pickSquares(int button, int state, int x, int y)
{
    GLuint selectBuf[BUFSIZE];
    GLint hits;
    GLint viewport[4];
```

```
    if (button != GLUT_LEFT_BUTTON || state != GLUT_DOWN)
       return;

    glGetIntegerv(GL_VIEWPORT, viewport);

    glSelectBuffer(BUFSIZE, selectBuf);
    (void) glRenderMode(GL_SELECT);

    glInitNames();
    glPushName(0);

    glMatrixMode(GL_PROJECTION);
    glPushMatrix();
    glLoadIdentity();
/*  create 5x5 pixel picking region near cursor location       */
    gluPickMatrix((GLdouble) x, (GLdouble) (viewport[3] - y),
                  5.0, 5.0, viewport);
    gluOrtho2D(0.0, 3.0, 0.0, 3.0);
    drawSquares(GL_SELECT);

    glMatrixMode(GL_PROJECTION);
    glPopMatrix();
    glFlush();

    hits = glRenderMode(GL_RENDER);
    processHits(hits, selectBuf);
    glutPostRedisplay();
}

void display(void)
{
    glClear(GL_COLOR_BUFFER_BIT);
    drawSquares(GL_RENDER);
    glFlush();
}

void reshape(int w, int h)
{
    glViewport(0, 0, w, h);
    glMatrixMode(GL_PROJECTION);
    glLoadIdentity();
    gluOrtho2D(0.0, 3.0, 0.0, 3.0);
    glMatrixMode(GL_MODELVIEW);
    glLoadIdentity();
}
```

```
int main(int argc, char** argv)
{
    glutInit(&argc, argv);
    glutInitDisplayMode(GLUT_SINGLE | GLUT_RGB);
    glutInitWindowSize(100, 100);
    glutInitWindowPosition(100, 100);
    glutCreateWindow(argv[0]);
    init();
    glutMouseFunc(pickSquares);
    glutReshapeFunc(reshape);
    glutDisplayFunc(display);
    glutMainLoop();
    return 0;
}
```

## Picking with Multiple Names and a Hierarchical Model

Multiple names can also be used to choose parts of a hierarchical object in a scene. For example, if you were rendering an assembly line of automobiles, you might want the user to move the mouse to pick the third bolt on the left front wheel of the third car in line. A different name can be used to identify each level of hierarchy: which car, which wheel, and finally which bolt. As another example, one name can be used to describe a single molecule among other molecules, and additional names can differentiate individual atoms within that molecule.

Example 13-4 is a modification of Figure 3-4, which draws an automobile with four identical wheels, each of which has five identical bolts. Code has been added to manipulate the name stack with the object hierarchy.

**Example 13-4**  Creating Multiple Names

```
draw_wheel_and_bolts()
{
    long i;

    draw_wheel_body();
    for (i = 0; i < 5; i++) {
        glPushMatrix();
            glRotate(72.0*i, 0.0, 0.0, 1.0);
            glTranslatef(3.0, 0.0, 0.0);
            glPushName(i);
                draw_bolt_body();
            glPopName();
        glPopMatrix();
    }
}
```

```
draw_body_and_wheel_and_bolts()
{
    draw_car_body();
    glPushMatrix();
        glTranslate(40, 0, 20);   /* first wheel position*/
        glPushName(1);            /* name of wheel number 1 */
            draw_wheel_and_bolts();
        glPopName();
    glPopMatrix();
    glPushMatrix();
        glTranslate(40, 0, -20); /* second wheel position */
        glPushName(2);            /* name of wheel number 2 */
            draw_wheel_and_bolts();
        glPopName();
    glPopMatrix();

    /* draw last two wheels similarly */
}
```

Example 13-5 uses the routines in Example 13-4 to draw three different cars, numbered 1, 2, and 3.

**Example 13-5**   Using Multiple Names

```
draw_three_cars()
{
    glInitNames();
    glPushMatrix();
        translate_to_first_car_position();
        glPushName(1);
            draw_body_and_wheel_and_bolts();
        glPopName();
    glPopMatrix();

    glPushMatrix();
        translate_to_second_car_position();
        glPushName(2);
            draw_body_and_wheel_and_bolts();
        glPopName();
    glPopMatrix();

    glPushMatrix();
        translate_to_third_car_position();
        glPushName(3);
            draw_body_and_wheel_and_bolts();
        glPopName();
    glPopMatrix();
}
```

Assuming that picking is performed, the following are some possible name-stack return values and their interpretations. In these examples, at most one hit record is returned; also, *d1* and *d2* are depth values.

| | |
|---|---|
| 2 *d1 d2* 2 1 | Car 2, wheel 1 |
| 1 *d1 d2* 3 | Car 3 body |
| 3 *d1 d2* 1 1 0 | Bolt 0 on wheel 1 on car 1 |
| empty | The pick was outside all cars |

The last interpretation assumes that the bolt and wheel don't occupy the same picking region. A user might well pick both the wheel and the bolt, yielding two hits. If you receive multiple hits, you have to decide which hit to process, perhaps by using the depth values to determine which picked object is closest to the viewpoint. The use of depth values is explored further in the next subsection.

### Picking and Depth Values

Example 13-6 demonstrates how to use depth values when picking to determine which object is picked. This program draws three overlapping rectangles in normal rendering mode. When the left mouse button is pressed, the **pickRects()** routine is called. This routine returns the cursor position, enters selection mode, initializes the name stack, and multiplies the picking matrix with the current orthographic projection matrix. A selection hit occurs for each rectangle the cursor is over when the left mouse button is clicked. Finally, the contents of the selection buffer are examined to identify which named objects were within the picking region near the cursor.

The rectangles in this program are drawn at different depth, or *z-*, values. Since only one name is used to identify all three rectangles, only one hit can be recorded. However, if more than one rectangle is picked, that single hit has different minimum and maximum *z*-values.

**Example 13-6**   Picking with Depth Values: pickdepth.c

```
void init(void)
{
    glClearColor(0.0, 0.0, 0.0, 0.0);
    glEnable(GL_DEPTH_TEST);
    glShadeModel(GL_FLAT);
    glDepthRange(0.0, 1.0);   /* The default z mapping */
}
```

```
void drawRects(GLenum mode)
{
    if (mode == GL_SELECT)
        glLoadName(1);
    glBegin(GL_QUADS);
    glColor3f(1.0, 1.0, 0.0);
    glVertex3i(2, 0, 0);
    glVertex3i(2, 6, 0);
    glVertex3i(6, 6, 0);
    glVertex3i(6, 0, 0);
    glEnd();
    if (mode == GL_SELECT)
        glLoadName(2);
    glBegin(GL_QUADS);
    glColor3f(0.0, 1.0, 1.0);
    glVertex3i(3, 2, -1);
    glVertex3i(3, 8, -1);
    glVertex3i(8, 8, -1);
    glVertex3i(8, 2, -1);
    glEnd();
    if (mode == GL_SELECT)
        glLoadName(3);
    glBegin(GL_QUADS);
    glColor3f(1.0, 0.0, 1.0);
    glVertex3i(0, 2, -2);
    glVertex3i(0, 7, -2);
    glVertex3i(5, 7, -2);
    glVertex3i(5, 2, -2);
    glEnd();
}

void processHits(GLint hits, GLuint buffer[])
{
    unsigned int i, j;
    GLuint names, *ptr;

    printf("hits = %d\n", hits);
    ptr = (GLuint *) buffer;
    for (i = 0; i < hits; i++) {  /* for each hit   */
        names = *ptr;
        printf(" number of names for hit = %d\n", names); ptr++;
        printf(" z1 is %g;", (float) *ptr/0x7fffffff); ptr++;
```

```
      printf(" z2 is %g\n", (float) *ptr/0x7fffffff); ptr++;
      printf("   the name is ");
      for (j = 0; j < names; j++) {   /* for each name */
         printf("%d ", *ptr); ptr++;
      }
      printf("\n");
   }
}

#define BUFSIZE 512

void pickRects(int button, int state, int x, int y)
{
   GLuint selectBuf[BUFSIZE];
   GLint hits;
   GLint viewport[4];

   if (button != GLUT_LEFT_BUTTON || state != GLUT_DOWN)
      return;
   glGetIntegerv(GL_VIEWPORT, viewport);

   glSelectBuffer(BUFSIZE, selectBuf);
   (void) glRenderMode(GL_SELECT);

   glInitNames();
   glPushName(0);

   glMatrixMode(GL_PROJECTION);
   glPushMatrix();
   glLoadIdentity();
/* create 5x5 pixel picking region near cursor location */
   gluPickMatrix((GLdouble) x, (GLdouble) (viewport[3] - y),
                 5.0, 5.0, viewport);
   glOrtho(0.0, 8.0, 0.0, 8.0, -0.5, 2.5);
   drawRects(GL_SELECT);
   glPopMatrix();
   glFlush();

   hits = glRenderMode(GL_RENDER);
   processHits(hits, selectBuf);
}
```

```
void display(void)
{
   glClear(GL_COLOR_BUFFER_BIT | GL_DEPTH_BUFFER_BIT);
   drawRects(GL_RENDER);
   glFlush();
}

void reshape(int w, int h)
{
   glViewport(0, 0, (GLsizei) w, (GLsizei) h);
   glMatrixMode(GL_PROJECTION);
   glLoadIdentity();
   glOrtho(0.0, 8.0, 0.0, 8.0, -0.5, 2.5);
   glMatrixMode(GL_MODELVIEW);
   glLoadIdentity();
}

int main(int argc, char **argv)
{
   glutInit(&argc, argv);
   glutInitDisplayMode(GLUT_SINGLE | GLUT_RGB | GLUT_DEPTH);
   glutInitWindowSize(200, 200);
   glutInitWindowPosition(100, 100);
   glutCreateWindow(argv[0]);
   init();
   glutMouseFunc(pickRects);
   glutReshapeFunc(reshape);
   glutDisplayFunc(display);
   glutMainLoop();
   return 0;
}
```

Try This

**Try This**

- Modify Example 13-6 to add additional calls to **glPushName()** so that multiple names are on the stack when the selection hit occurs. What will the contents of the selection buffer be?

- By default, **glDepthRange()** sets the mapping of the $z$-values to [0.0, 1.0]. Try modifying the **glDepthRange()** values and see how these modifications affect the $z$-values that are returned in the selection array.

## Hints for Writing a Program That Uses Selection

Most programs that allow a user to edit geometric objects interactively provide a mechanism for the user to pick items or groups of items for editing. For two-dimensional drawing programs (for example, text editors, page-layout programs, and circuit-design programs), it might be easier to do your own picking calculations instead of using the OpenGL picking mechanism. Often, it's easy to find bounding boxes for two-dimensional objects and to organize them in some hierarchical data structure to speed up searches. For example, picking that uses the OpenGL style in a VLSI layout program containing millions of rectangles can be relatively slow. However, using simple bounding-box information when rectangles are typically aligned with the screen could make picking in such a program extremely fast. The code is probably simpler to write, too.

As another example, since only geometric objects cause hits, you might want to create your own method for picking text. Setting the current raster position is a geometric operation, but it effectively creates only a single pickable point at the current raster position, which is typically at the lower left corner of the text. If your editor needs to manipulate individual characters within a text string, some other picking mechanism must be used. You could draw little rectangles around each character during picking mode, but it's almost certainly easier to handle text as a special case.

If you decide to use OpenGL picking, organize your program and its data structures so that it's easy to draw appropriate lists of objects in either selection or normal drawing mode. This way, when the user picks something, you can use the same data structures for the pick operation that you use to display the items on the screen. Also, consider whether you want to allow the user to select multiple objects. One way to do this is to store a bit for each item, indicating whether it's selected (this method, however, requires you to traverse your entire list of items to find the selected items). You might find it useful to maintain a list of pointers to selected items to speed up this search. It's probably a good idea to keep the selection bit for each item as well, because when you're drawing the entire picture, you might want to draw selected items differently (for example, in a different color or within a selection box). Finally, consider the selection user interface. You might want to allow the user to

- Select an item
- Sweep-select a group of items

- Add an item to the selection

- Add a sweep selection to the current selections

- Delete an item from a selection

- Choose a single item from a group of overlapping items

A typical solution for a two-dimensional drawing program might work as follows:

1. All selection is done by pointing with the mouse cursor and using the left mouse button. In the steps that follow, *cursor* means the cursor tied to the mouse, and *button* means the left mouse button.

2. Clicking on an item selects it and deselects all other currently selected items. If the cursor is on top of multiple items, the smallest is selected. (In three dimensions, there are many other strategies for disambiguating a selection.)

3. Clicking down where there is no item, holding the button down while dragging the cursor, and then releasing the button selects all the items in a screen-aligned rectangle whose corners are determined by the cursor positions when the button went down and where it came up. This is called a *sweep selection*. All items not in the swept-out region are deselected. (You must decide whether an item is selected only if it's completely within the sweep region, or if any part of it falls within the region. The "completely within" strategy usually works best.)

4. If the Shift key is held down and the user clicks on an item that isn't currently selected, that item is added to the selected list. If the clicked-on item is selected, it's deleted from the selection list.

5. If a sweep selection is performed with the Shift key pressed, the items swept out are added to the current selection.

6. In an extremely cluttered region, it's often hard to do a sweep selection. When the button goes down, the cursor might lie on top of some item, and normally that item would be selected. You can make any operation a sweep selection, but a typical user interface interprets a button down on an item plus a mouse motion as a select-plus-drag operation. To solve this problem, you can have an enforced sweep selection by holding down, say, the Alt key. With this procedure, the following set of operations constitutes a sweep selection: Alt button down, sweep, button up. Items under the cursor when the button goes down are ignored.

7. If the Shift key is held during this sweep selection, the items enclosed in the sweep region are added to the current selection.

8. Finally, if the user clicks on multiple items, select just one of them. If the cursor isn't moved (or maybe not moved more than a pixel), and the user clicks again in the same place, deselect the item originally selected, and select a different item under the cursor. Use repeated clicks at the same point to cycle through all the possibilities.

Different rules can apply in particular situations. In a text editor, you probably don't have to worry about characters on top of each other, and selections of multiple characters are always contiguous characters in the document. Thus, you need to mark only the first and last selected characters to identify the complete selection. With text, often the best way to handle selection is to identify the positions between characters, rather than the characters themselves. This allows you to have an empty selection when the beginning and end of the selection are between the same pair of characters; it also allows you to put the cursor before the first character in the document or after the final one with no special-case code.

In a three-dimensional editor, you might provide ways to rotate and zoom between selections, so sophisticated schemes for cycling through the possible selections might be unnecessary. On the other hand, selection in three dimensions is difficult because the cursor's position on the screen usually gives no indication of its depth.

## Feedback

Feedback is similar to selection in that once you're in either mode, no pixels are produced and the screen is frozen. Drawing does not occur; instead, information about primitives that would have been rendered is sent back to the application. The key difference between selection and feedback modes is the information that is sent back. In selection mode, assigned names are returned to an array of integer values. In feedback mode, information about transformed primitives is sent back to an array of floating-point values. The values sent back to the feedback array consist of tokens that specify what type of primitive (point, line, polygon, image, or bitmap) has been processed and transformed, followed by vertex, color, or other data for that primitive. The values returned are fully transformed by lighting and viewing operations. Feedback mode is initiated by calling **glRenderMode()** with GL_FEEDBACK as the argument.

Here's how you enter and exit feedback mode:

1.  Call **glFeedbackBuffer()** to specify the array to hold the feedback information. The arguments for this command describe what type of data and how much of it is written into the array.

2.  Call **glRenderMode()** with GL_FEEDBACK as the argument to enter feedback mode. (For this step, you can ignore the value returned by **glRenderMode()**.) After this point, primitives aren't rasterized to produce pixels until you exit feedback mode, and the contents of the framebuffer don't change.

3.  Draw your primitives. While issuing drawing commands, you can make several calls to **glPassThrough()** to insert markers into the returned feedback data and thus facilitate parsing.

4.  Exit feedback mode by calling **glRenderMode()** with GL_RENDER as the argument if you want to return to normal drawing mode. The integer value returned by **glRenderMode()** is the number of values stored in the feedback array.

5.  Parse the data in the feedback array.

---

void **glFeedbackBuffer**(GLsizei *size*, GLenum *type*, GLfloat *\*buffer*);

---

Establishes a buffer for the feedback data: *buffer* is a pointer to an array where the data is stored. The *size* argument indicates the maximum number of values that can be stored in the array. The *type* argument describes the information fed back for each vertex in the feedback array; its possible values and their meanings are shown in Table 13-1. **glFeedbackBuffer()** must be called before feedback mode is entered. In the table, $k$ is 1 in color-index mode and 4 in RGBA mode.

| *type* Argument | Coordinates | Color | Texture | Total Values |
|---|---|---|---|---|
| GL_2D | x, y | - | - | 2 |
| GL_3D | x, y, z | - | - | 3 |
| GL_3D_COLOR | x, y, z | k | - | 3 + k |
| GL_3D_COLOR_TEXTURE | x, y, z | k | 4 | 7 + k |
| GL_4D_COLOR_TEXTURE | x, y, z, w | k | 4 | 8 + k |

**Table 13-1**    glFeedbackBuffer() *type* Values

**Note:** When multitexturing is supported, feedback returns only the texture coordinates of texture unit 0.

## The Feedback Array

In feedback mode, each primitive that would be rasterized (or each call to **glBitmap()**, **glDrawPixels()**, or **glCopyPixels()**, if the raster position is valid) generates a block of values that's copied into the feedback array. The number of values is determined by the *type* argument of **glFeedbackBuffer()**, as listed in Table 13-1. Use the appropriate value for the type of primitives you're drawing: GL_2D or GL_3D for unlit two- or three-dimensional primitives; GL_3D_COLOR for lit, three-dimensional primitives; and GL_3D_COLOR_TEXTURE or GL_4D_COLOR_TEXTURE for lit, textured, three- or four-dimensional primitives.

Each block of feedback values begins with a code indicating the primitive type, followed by values that describe the primitive's vertices and associated data. Entries are also written for pixel rectangles. In addition, pass-through markers that you've explicitly created can be returned in the array; the next subsection explains these markers in more detail. Table 13-2 shows the syntax for the feedback array; remember that the data associated with each returned vertex is as described in Table 13-1. Note that a polygon can have *n* vertices returned. Also, the *x*-, *y*-, and *z*-coordinates returned by feedback are window coordinates; if *w* is returned, it's in clip coordinates. For bitmaps and pixel rectangles, the coordinates returned are those of the current raster position. In Table 13-2, note that GL_LINE_RESET_TOKEN is returned only when the line stipple is reset for that line segment.

| Primitive Type | Code | Associated Data |
|---|---|---|
| Point | GL_POINT_TOKEN | vertex |
| Line | GL_LINE_TOKEN or GL_LINE_RESET_TOKEN | vertex vertex |
| Polygon | GL_POLYGON_TOKEN | *n* vertex vertex ... vertex |
| Bitmap | GL_BITMAP_TOKEN | vertex |
| Pixel Rectangle | GL_DRAW_PIXEL_TOKEN or GL_COPY_PIXEL_TOKEN | vertex |
| Pass-through | GL_PASS_THROUGH_TOKEN | a floating-point number |

**Table 13-2**    Feedback Array Syntax

## Using Markers in Feedback Mode

Feedback occurs after transformations, lighting, polygon culling, and interpretation of polygons by **glPolygonMode()**. It might also occur after polygons with more than three edges are broken up into triangles (if your particular OpenGL implementation renders polygons by performing this decomposition). Thus, it might be hard for you to recognize the primitives you drew in the feedback data you receive. To help parse the feedback data, call **glPassThrough()** as needed in your sequence of drawing commands to insert a marker. You might use the markers to separate the feedback values returned from different primitives, for example. This command causes GL_PASS_THROUGH_TOKEN to be written into the feedback array, followed by the floating-point value you pass in as an argument.

---

void **glPassThrough**(GLfloat *token*);

---

Inserts a marker into the stream of values written into the feedback array, if called in feedback mode. The marker consists of the code GL_PASS_THROUGH_TOKEN followed by a single floating-point value, *token*. This command has no effect when called outside of feedback mode. Calling **glPassThrough()** between **glBegin()** and **glEnd()** generates a GL_INVALID_OPERATION error.

## A Feedback Example

Example 13-7 demonstrates the use of feedback mode. This program draws a lit, three-dimensional scene in normal rendering mode. Then, feedback mode is entered, and the scene is redrawn. Since the program draws lit, untextured, three-dimensional objects, the type of feedback data is GL_3D_COLOR. Since RGBA mode is used, each unclipped vertex generates seven values for the feedback buffer: $x$, $y$, $z$, $r$, $g$, $b$, and $a$.

In feedback mode, the program draws two lines as part of a line strip and then inserts a pass-through marker. Next, a point is drawn at (–100.0, –100.0, –100.0), which falls outside the orthographic viewing volume and thus doesn't put any values into the feedback array. Finally, another pass-through marker is inserted, and another point is drawn.

**Example 13-7**  Feedback Mode: feedback.c

```c
void init(void)
{
   glEnable(GL_LIGHTING);
   glEnable(GL_LIGHT0);
}

void drawGeometry(GLenum mode)
{
   glBegin(GL_LINE_STRIP);
   glNormal3f(0.0, 0.0, 1.0);
   glVertex3f(30.0, 30.0, 0.0);
   glVertex3f(50.0, 60.0, 0.0);
   glVertex3f(70.0, 40.0, 0.0);
   glEnd();
   if (mode == GL_FEEDBACK)
      glPassThrough(1.0);
   glBegin(GL_POINTS);
   glVertex3f(-100.0, -100.0, -100.0);  /*  will be clipped  */
   glEnd();
   if (mode == GL_FEEDBACK)
      glPassThrough(2.0);
   glBegin(GL_POINTS);
   glNormal3f(0.0, 0.0, 1.0);
   glVertex3f(50.0, 50.0, 0.0);
   glEnd();
   glFlush();
}

void print3DcolorVertex(GLint size, GLint *count,
                        GLfloat *buffer)
{
   int i;

   printf("  ");
   for (i = 0; i < 7; i++) {
      printf("%4.2f ", buffer[size-(*count)]);
      *count = *count - 1;
   }
   printf("\n");
}
```

```
void printBuffer(GLint size, GLfloat *buffer)
{
   GLint count;
   GLfloat token;

   count = size;
   while (count) {
      token = buffer[size-count]; count--;
      if (token == GL_PASS_THROUGH_TOKEN) {
         printf("GL_PASS_THROUGH_TOKEN\n");
         printf("  %4.2f\n", buffer[size-count]);
         count--;
      }
      else if (token == GL_POINT_TOKEN) {
         printf("GL_POINT_TOKEN\n");
         print3DcolorVertex(size, &count, buffer);
      }
      else if (token == GL_LINE_TOKEN) {
         printf("GL_LINE_TOKEN\n");
         print3DcolorVertex(size, &count, buffer);
         print3DcolorVertex(size, &count, buffer);
      }
      else if (token == GL_LINE_RESET_TOKEN) {
         printf("GL_LINE_RESET_TOKEN\n");
         print3DcolorVertex(size, &count, buffer);
         print3DcolorVertex(size, &count, buffer);
      }
   }
}

void display(void)
{
   GLfloat feedBuffer[1024];
   GLint size;

   glMatrixMode(GL_PROJECTION);
   glLoadIdentity();
   glOrtho(0.0, 100.0, 0.0, 100.0, 0.0, 1.0);

   glClearColor(0.0, 0.0, 0.0, 0.0);
   glClear(GL_COLOR_BUFFER_BIT);
   drawGeometry(GL_RENDER);

   glFeedbackBuffer(1024, GL_3D_COLOR, feedBuffer);
   (void) glRenderMode(GL_FEEDBACK);
   drawGeometry(GL_FEEDBACK);
```

```
    size = glRenderMode(GL_RENDER);
    printBuffer(size, feedBuffer);
}

int main(int argc, char** argv)
{
    glutInit(&argc, argv);
    glutInitDisplayMode(GLUT_SINGLE | GLUT_RGB);
    glutInitWindowSize(100, 100);
    glutInitWindowPosition(100, 100);
    glutCreateWindow(argv[0]);
    init();
    glutDisplayFunc(display);
    glutMainLoop();
    return 0;
}
```

Running this program generates the following output:

```
GL_LINE_RESET_TOKEN
  30.00 30.00 0.00 0.84 0.84 0.84 1.00
  50.00 60.00 0.00 0.84 0.84 0.84 1.00
GL_LINE_TOKEN
  50.00 60.00 0.00 0.84 0.84 0.84 1.00
  70.00 40.00 0.00 0.84 0.84 0.84 1.00
GL_PASS_THROUGH_TOKEN
  1.00
GL_PASS_THROUGH_TOKEN
  2.00
GL_POINT_TOKEN
  50.00 50.00 0.00 0.84 0.84 0.84 1.00
```

Thus, the line strip drawn with these commands results in two primitives:

```
glBegin(GL_LINE_STRIP);
    glNormal3f(0.0, 0.0, 1.0);
    glVertex3f(30.0, 30.0, 0.0);
    glVertex3f(50.0, 60.0, 0.0);
    glVertex3f(70.0, 40.0, 0.0);
glEnd();
```

The first primitive begins with GL_LINE_RESET_TOKEN, which indicates that the primitive is a line segment and that the line stipple is reset. The second primitive begins with GL_LINE_TOKEN, so it's also a line segment, but the line stipple isn't reset and hence continues from where the previous line segment left off. Each of the two vertices for these lines generates seven values for the feedback array. Note that the RGBA values for all four vertices in these two lines are (0.84, 0.84, 0.84, 1.0), which is a very light gray color with the maximum alpha value. These color values are a result of the interaction of the surface normal and lighting parameters.

Since no feedback data is generated between the first and second pass-through markers, you can deduce that any primitives drawn between the first two calls to **glPassThrough**() were clipped out of the viewing volume. Finally, the point at (50.0, 50.0, 0.0) is drawn, and its associated data is copied into the feedback array.

**Note:** In both feedback and selection modes, information about objects is returned prior to any fragment tests. Thus, objects that would not be drawn due to failure of the scissor, alpha, depth, or stencil test may still have their data processed and returned in both feedback and selection modes.

Try This

**Try This**

Make changes in Example 13-7 to see how they affect the feedback values that are returned. For example, change the coordinate values of **glOrtho**(). Change the lighting variables, or eliminate lighting altogether and change the feedback type to GL_3D. Or, add more primitives to see what other geometric objects (such as filled polygons) contribute to the feedback array.

## Chapter 14

# Now That You Know

## Chapter Objectives

This chapter doesn't have objectives in the same way that previous chapters do. It's simply a collection of topics that describe ideas you might find useful for your application. Some topics, such as error handling, don't fit into other categories, but are too short for an entire chapter.

OpenGL is a collection of low-level tools; now that you know about those tools, you can use them to implement higher-level functions. This chapter presents several examples of such higher-level capabilities.

This chapter discusses a variety of techniques based on OpenGL commands that illustrate some of the not-so-obvious uses to which you can put these commands. The examples presented are in no particular order and aren't related to each other. The idea is to read the section headings and skip to the examples that you find interesting. For your convenience, the headings are listed and explained briefly here.

**Note:** Most of the examples in the rest of this guide are complete and can be compiled and run as is. In this chapter, however, there are no complete programs, and you have to do a bit of work on your own to make them run.

- "Error Handling" tells you how to check for OpenGL error conditions.

- "Which Version Am I Using?" describes how to find out details about your implementation, including the version number. This can be useful for writing applications that can run on earlier versions of OpenGL.

- "Extensions to the Standard" presents techniques for identifying and using extensions (which are either specific to a vendor or approved by the OpenGL Architecture Review Board) to the OpenGL standard.

- "Cheesy Translucency" explains how to use polygon stippling to achieve translucency; this is particularly useful when no blending hardware is available.

- "An Easy Fade Effect" shows how to use polygon stippling to create the effect of a fade into the background.

- "Object Selection Using the Back Buffer" describes how to use the back buffer in a double-buffered system to handle simple object picking.

- "Cheap Image Transformation" discusses how to draw a distorted version of a bitmapped image by drawing each pixel as a quadrilateral.

- "Displaying Layers" explains how to display multiple layers of different materials and indicate where the materials overlap.

- "Antialiased Characters" describes how to draw smoother fonts.

- "Drawing Round Points" describes how to draw near-round points.

- "Interpolating Images" shows how to blend smoothly from one image to another.

- "Making Decals" explains how to draw two images, where one is a sort of decal that should always appear on top of the other.

- "Drawing Filled, Concave Polygons Using the Stencil Buffer" tells you how to draw concave polygons, nonsimple polygons, and polygons with holes by using the stencil buffer.

- "Finding Interference Regions" describes how to determine where three-dimensional pieces overlap.

- "Shadows" describes how to draw shadows of lit objects.

- "Hidden-Line Removal" discusses how to draw a wireframe object with hidden lines removed by using the stencil buffer.

- "Texture Mapping Applications" describes several clever uses for texture mapping, such as rotating and warping images.

- "Drawing Depth-Buffered Images" tells you how to combine images in a depth-buffered environment.

- "Dirichlet Domains" explains how to find the Dirichlet domain of a set of points using the depth buffer.

- "Life in the Stencil Buffer" explains how to implement the Game of Life using the stencil buffer.

- "Alternative Uses for glDrawPixels() and glCopyPixels()" describes how to use these two commands for such effects as fake video, airbrushing, and transposed images.

## Error Handling

The truth is, your program will make mistakes. Use of error-handling routines is essential during development and is highly recommended for commercially released applications (unless you can give a 100 percent guarantee your program will never generate an OpenGL error condition. Get real!). OpenGL has simple error-handling routines for the base GL and GLU libraries.

When OpenGL detects an error (in either the base GL or GLU), it records a current error code. The command that caused the error is ignored, so it has no effect on the OpenGL state or on the framebuffer contents. (If the error recorded was GL_OUT_OF_MEMORY, however, the results of the command are undefined.) Once recorded, the current error code isn't cleared—that is, additional errors aren't recorded—until you call the query command **glGetError()**, which returns the current error code. After you've queried and cleared the current error code, or if there's no error to begin with, **glGetError()** returns GL_NO_ERROR.

GLenum **glGetError**(void);

Returns the value of the error flag. When an error occurs in either the GL or the GLU, the error flag is set to the appropriate error code value. If GL_NO_ERROR is returned, there has been no detectable error since the last call to **glGetError**() or since the GL was initialized. No other errors are recorded until **glGetError**() is called, the error code is returned, and the flag is reset to GL_NO_ERROR.

It is strongly recommended that you call **glGetError**() at least once in each **display**() routine. Table 14-1 lists the basic defined OpenGL error codes.

| Error Code | Description |
| --- | --- |
| GL_INVALID_ENUM | GLenum argument out of range |
| GL_INVALID_VALUE | numeric argument out of range |
| GL_INVALID_OPERATION | operation illegal in current state |
| GL_STACK_OVERFLOW | command would cause a stack overflow |
| GL_STACK_UNDERFLOW | command would cause a stack underflow |
| GL_OUT_OF_MEMORY | not enough memory left to execute command |

**Table 14-1**     OpenGL Error Codes

There are also 37 GLU NURBS errors (with nondescriptive constant names, GLU_NURBS_ERROR1, GLU_NURBS_ERROR2, and so on); 14 tessellator errors (GLU_TESS_MISSING_BEGIN_POLYGON, GLU_TESS_MISSING_END_POLYGON, GLU_TESS_MISSING_BEGIN_CONTOUR, GLU_TESS_MISSING_END_CONTOUR, GLU_TESS_COORD_TOO_LARGE, GLU_TESS_NEED_COMBINE_CALLBACK, along with eight errors generically named GLU_TESS_ERROR*); and GLU_INCOMPATIBLE_GL_VERSION. Also, the GLU defines the error codes GLU_INVALID_ENUM, GLU_INVALID_VALUE, and GLU_OUT_OF_MEMORY, which have the same meanings as the related OpenGL codes.

To obtain a printable, descriptive string corresponding to either a GL or GLU error code, use the GLU routine **gluErrorString**().

> const GLubyte* **gluErrorString**(GLenum *errorCode*);
>
> Returns a pointer to a descriptive string that corresponds to the OpenGL or GLU error number passed in *errorCode*.

In Example 14-1, a simple error-handling routine is shown.

**Example 14-1**   Querying and Printing an Error

```
GLenum errCode;
const GLubyte *errString;

while ((errCode = glGetError()) != GL_NO_ERROR) {
   errString = gluErrorString(errCode);
   fprintf (stderr, "OpenGL Error: %s\n", errString);
}
```

**Note:**  The string returned by **gluErrorString**() must not be altered or freed by the application.

## Which Version Am I Using?

The portability of OpenGL applications is one of OpenGL's attractive features. However, new versions of OpenGL introduce new features, and if you use new features, you may have problems running your code on older versions of OpenGL. In addition, you may want your application to perform equally well on a variety of implementations. For example, you might make texture mapping the default rendering mode on one machine, but have only flat shading on another. You can use **glGetString**() to obtain release information about your OpenGL implementation.

> const GLubyte* **glGetString**(GLenum *name*);
>
> Returns a pointer to a string that describes an aspect of the OpenGL implementation. *name* can be one of the following: GL_VENDOR, GL_RENDERER, GL_VERSION, or GL_EXTENSIONS.

GL_VENDOR returns the name of the company responsible for the OpenGL implementation. GL_RENDERER returns an identifier of the renderer, which is usually the hardware platform. For more about GL_EXTENSIONS, see the section "Extensions to the Standard."

GL_VERSION returns a string that identifies the version number of your implementation of OpenGL. The version string is laid out as follows:

```
<version number><space><vendor-specific information>
```

The version number is of the form

```
major_number.minor_number
```

or

```
major_number.minor_number.release_number
```

where the numbers all have one or more digits. The vendor-specific information is optional. For example, if this OpenGL implementation is from the fictitious XYZ Corporation, the string returned might be

```
1.2.4 XYZ-OS 3.2
```

which means that this implementation is XYZ's fourth release of an OpenGL library that conforms to the specification for OpenGL Version 1.2. It probably also means that this is release 3.2 of XYZ's proprietary operating system.

Another way to query the OpenGL version number is to use the preprocessor statement #ifdef to look for the symbolic constants named GL_VERSION_1_4, GL_VERSION_1_3, GL_VERSION_1_2, and GL_VERSION_1_1. The absence of the constant GL_VERSION_1_2 means that you have OpenGL Version 1.0 or 1.1. The absence of the constant GL_VERSION_1_1 means that you have OpenGL Version 1.0.

**Note:** If running from client to server, such as when performing indirect rendering with the OpenGL extension to the X Window System, the client and server may be different versions. If your client version is ahead of your server, your client might request an operation that is not supported on your server.

## Utility Library Version

**gluGetString()** is a query function for the Utility Library (GLU) and is similar to **glGetString()**.

> const GLubyte* **gluGetString**(GLenum *name*);
>
> Returns a pointer to a string that describes an aspect of the OpenGL implementation. *name* can be GLU_VERSION or GLU_EXTENSIONS.

Note that **gluGetString**() was not available in GLU 1.0. Another way to query the GLU version number is to look for the symbolic constant GLU_VERSION_1_3. The absence of the constant GLU_VERSION_1_3 means that you have GLU 1.2 or an earlier version. The same principle is true for constants GLU_VERSION_1_1 and GLU_VERSION_1_2.

Also note that GLU extensions are different from OpenGL extensions.

### Window System Extension Versions

For window system extensions for OpenGL, such as GLX, WGL, PGL, and AGL, there are similar routines (such as **glXQueryExtensionString**()) for querying version information. See Appendix C for more information.

(The aforementioned **glXQueryExtensionString**() and related routines were introduced with GLX 1.1 and are not supported with GLX 1.0.)

## Extensions to the Standard

OpenGL has a formal written specification that describes the operations that comprise the library. An individual vendor or a group of vendors may decide to add additional functionality to their released implementation.

Function and symbolic constant names clearly indicate whether a feature is part of the OpenGL standard, a vendor-specific extension, or an OpenGL extension approved by the OpenGL ARB (Architecture Review Board).

To make a vendor-specific name, the vendor appends a company identifier (in uppercase) and, if needed, additional information, such as a machine name. For example, if XYZ Corporation wants to add a new function and symbolic constant, they might be of the form **glCommandXYZ**() and GL_DEFINITION_XYZ. If XYZ Corporation wants to have an extension that is available only on its FooBar graphics board, the names might be **glCommandXYZfb**() and GL_DEFINITION_XYZ_FB.

If two or more vendors agree to implement the same extension, then the functions and constants are suffixed with the more generic EXT (**glCommandEXT()** and GL_DEFINITION_EXT).

Similarly, if the OpenGL ARB approves an extension, the functions and constants are suffixed with ARB (**glCommandARB()** and GL_DEFINITION_ARB).

If you want to know if a specific extension is supported on your implementation, first use **glGetString**(GL_EXTENSIONS), and then use **gluGetString**(GLU_EXTENSIONS). This returns a list of all the extensions in the implementation, separated by spaces.

OpenGL 1.2 introduces the first ARB-approved extensions. If the optional Imaging Subset is supported, then GL_ARB_imaging will be present in the returned extension string. The string GL_ARB_multitexture indicates the presence of the ARB-approved multitexture extension.

If you have GLU 1.3, you can use **gluCheckExtension()** to see if a specified extension is supported.

---

GLboolean **gluCheckExtension**(char *extName,
                                 const GLubyte *extString);

Returns GL_TRUE if *extName* is found in *extString*, or GL_FALSE if it isn't.

---

**gluCheckExtension()** can check OpenGL and GLX extension strings, as well as GLU extension strings.

Prior to GLU 1.3, to find out if a specific extension is supported, use the code in Example 14-2 to search through the list and match the extension name. **QueryExtension()** returns GL_TRUE if the string is found, or GL_FALSE if it isn't.

**Example 14-2**   Determining if an Extension Is Supported (Prior to GLU 1.3)

```
static GLboolean QueryExtension(char *extName)
{
   char *p = (char *) glGetString(GL_EXTENSIONS);
   char *end;
   if (p == NULL)
     return GL_FALSE;
   end = p + strlen(p);
```

```
  while (p < end) {
    int n = strcspn(p, " ");
    if ((strlen(extName)==n) && (strncmp(extName,p,n)==0)) {
      return GL_TRUE;
    }
    p += (n + 1);
  }
  return GL_FALSE;
}
```

## Extensions to the Standard for Microsoft Windows (WGL)

If you need access to an extension function on a Microsoft Windows platform, you should

- create conditional code based on the symbolic constant, which identifies the extension

- query the previously discussed extension string at run-time

- use **wglGetProcAddress()** to locate the pointer to the extension function

Example 14-3 demonstrates how to find a fictitious extension named **glSpecialEXT()**. Note that the conditional code (`#ifdef`) verifies the definition of GL_EXT_special. If the extension is available, a data type (in this case, PFNGLSPECIALEXTPROC) is specifically defined for the function pointer. Finally, **wglGetProcAddress()** obtains the function pointer.

**Example 14-3**  Locating an OpenGL Extension with **wglGetProcAddress()**

```
#ifdef GL_EXT_special
    PFNGLSPECIALEXTPROC glSpecialEXT;
#endif

/* somewhere later in the code */

#ifdef GL_EXT_special
    glSpecialEXT = (PFNGLSPECIALEXTPROC)
                wglGetProcAddress("glSpecialEXT");
    assert(glSpecialEXT != NULL);
#endif
```

## Cheesy Translucency

You can use polygon stippling to simulate a translucent material. This is an especially good solution for systems that don't have blending hardware. Since polygon stipple patterns are 32 × 32 bits, or 1024 bits, you can go from opaque to transparent in 1023 steps. (In practice, that's many more steps than you need.) For example, if you want a surface that lets through 29 percent of the light, simply make up a stipple pattern in which 29 percent (roughly 297) of the pixels in the mask are 0 and the rest are 1. Even if your surfaces have the same translucency, don't use the same stipple pattern for each one, because they cover exactly the same bits on the screen. Make up a different pattern for each surface by randomly selecting the appropriate number of pixels to be 0. (See "Displaying Points, Lines, and Polygons" in Chapter 2 for more information about polygon stippling.)

If you don't like the effect with random pixels turned on, you can use regular patterns, but they don't work as well when transparent surfaces are stacked. This is often not a problem, because most scenes have relatively few translucent regions that overlap. In a picture of an automobile with translucent windows, your line of sight can go through at most two windows, and usually it's only one.

## An Easy Fade Effect

Suppose you have an image that you want to fade gradually to some background color. Define a series of polygon stipple patterns, each of which has more bits turned on so that they represent denser and denser patterns. Then use these patterns repeatedly with a polygon large enough to cover the region over which you want to fade. For example, suppose you want to fade to black in 16 steps. First define 16 different pattern arrays:

```
GLubyte stips[16][4*32];
```

Then load them in such a way that each has one-sixteenth of the pixels in a 32 × 32 stipple pattern turned on and that the bitwise OR of all the stipple patterns is all 1's. After that, the following code does the trick:

```
draw_the_picture();
glColor3f(0.0, 0.0, 0.0);     /* set color to black */
for (i = 0; i < 16; i++) {
    glPolygonStipple(&stips[i][0]);
    draw_a_polygon_large_enough_to_cover_the_whole_region();
}
```

In some OpenGL implementations, you might get better performance by first compiling the stipple patterns into display lists. During your initialization, do something like this:

```
#define STIP_OFFSET 100
for (i = 0; i < 16; i++) {
    glNewList(i+STIP_OFFSET, GL_COMPILE);
    glPolygonStipple(&stips[i][0]);
    glEndList();
}
```

Then, replace this line in the first code fragment

```
glPolygonStipple(&stips[i][0]);
```

with

```
glCallList(i);
```

By compiling the command to set the stipple into a display list, OpenGL might be able to rearrange the data in the *stips[ ][ ]* array into the hardware-specific form required for maximum stipple-setting speed.

Another application for this technique is if you're drawing a changing picture and want to leave some blur behind that gradually fades out to give some indication of past motion. For example, suppose you're simulating a planetary system and you want to leave trails on the planets to show recent portions of their paths. Again, assuming you want to fade in 16 steps, set up the stipple patterns as before (using the display-list version, say), and have the main simulation loop look something like this:

```
current_stipple = 0;
while (1) {                               /* loop forever */
    draw_the_next_frame();
    glCallList(current_stipple++);
    if (current_stipple == 16) current_stipple = 0;
    glColor3f(0.0, 0.0, 0.0);             /* set color to black */
    draw_a_polygon_large_enough_to_cover_the_whole_region();
}
```

Each time through the loop, you clear one-sixteenth of the pixels. Any pixel that hasn't had a planet on it for 16 frames is certain to be cleared to black. Of course, if your system supports blending in hardware, it's easier to blend in a certain amount of background color with each frame. (See "Displaying Points, Lines, and Polygons" in Chapter 2 for polygon stippling details, Chapter 7 for more information about display lists, and "Blending" in Chapter 6 for information about blending.)

## Object Selection Using the Back Buffer

Although the OpenGL selection mechanism (see "Selection" in Chapter 13) is powerful and flexible, it can be cumbersome to use. Often, the situation is simple: your application draws a scene composed of a substantial number of objects; the user points to an object with the mouse, and the application needs to find the item under the tip of the cursor.

One way to do this requires your application to be running in double-buffer mode. When the user picks an object, the application redraws the entire scene in the back buffer, but instead of using the normal colors for objects, it encodes some kind of object identifier for each object's color. The application then simply reads the pixel under the cursor, and the value of that pixel encodes the number of the picked object. If many picks are expected for a single, static picture, you can read the entire color buffer once and look in your copy for each attempted pick, rather than read each pixel individually.

Note that this scheme has an advantage over standard selection in that it picks the object that's in front if multiple objects appear at the same pixel, one behind the other. Since the image with false colors is drawn in the back buffer, the user never sees it; you can redraw the back buffer (or copy it from the front buffer) before swapping the buffers. In color-index mode, the encoding is simple: send the object identifier as the index. In RGBA mode, encode the bits of the identifier into the R, G, and B components.

Be aware that you can run out of identifiers if there are too many objects in the scene. For example, suppose you're running in color-index mode on a system that has 4-bit buffers for color-index information (16 possible different indices) in each of the color buffers, but the scene has thousands of pickable items. To address this issue, the picking can be done in a few passes. To think about this in concrete terms, assume there are fewer than 4096 items, so all the object identifiers can be encoded in 12 bits. In the first pass, draw the scene using indices composed of the 4 high-order bits, and then use the second and third passes to draw the middle 4 bits and the 4 low-order bits. After each pass, read the pixel under the cursor, extract the bits, and pack them together at the end to get the object identifier.

With this method, the picking takes three times as long, but that's often acceptable. Note that after you have the 4 high-order bits, you eliminate 15/16 of all objects, so you really need to draw only 1/16 of them for the second pass. Similarly, after the second pass, 255 of the 256 possible items have been eliminated. The first pass thus takes about as long as drawing a single frame does, but the second and third passes can be up to 16 and 256 times as fast.

If you're trying to write portable code that works on different systems, break up your object identifiers into chunks that fit on the lowest common denominator of those systems. Also, keep in mind that your system might perform automatic dithering in RGB mode. If this is the case, turn off dithering.

## Cheap Image Transformation

If you want to draw a distorted version of a bitmapped image (perhaps simply stretched or rotated, or perhaps drastically modified by some mathematical function), there are many possibilities. You can use the image as a texture map, which allows you to scale, rotate, or otherwise distort the image. If you just want to scale the image, you can use **glPixelZoom()**.

In many cases, you can achieve good results by drawing the image of each pixel as a quadrilateral. Although this scheme doesn't produce images as nice as those you would get by applying a sophisticated filtering algorithm (and it might not be sufficient for sophisticated users), it's a lot quicker.

To make the problem more concrete, assume that the original image is $m$ pixels by $n$ pixels, with coordinates chosen from $[0, m - 1] \times [0, n - 1]$. Let the distortion functions be $x(m, n)$ and $y(m, n)$. For example, if the distortion is simply a zooming by a factor of 3.2, then $x(m, n) = 3.2 \cdot m$ and $y(m, n) = 3.2 \cdot n$. The following code draws the distorted image:

```
glShadeModel(GL_FLAT);
glScale(3.2, 3.2, 1.0);
for (j=0; j < n; j++) {
    glBegin(GL_QUAD_STRIP);
    for (i=0; i <= m; i++) {
        glVertex2i(i,j);
        glVertex2i(i, j+1);
        set_color(i,j);
    }
    glEnd();
}
```

This code draws each transformed pixel in a solid color equal to that pixel's color and scales the image size by 3.2. The routine **set_color()** stands for whatever the appropriate OpenGL command is to set the color of the image pixel.

The following is a slightly more complex version that distorts the image using the functions $x(i, j)$ and $y(i, j)$:

```
glShadeModel(GL_FLAT);
for (j=0; j < n; j++) {
    glBegin(GL_QUAD_STRIP);
    for (i=0; i <= m; i++) {
        glVertex2i(x(i,j), y(i,j));
        glVertex2i(x(i,j+1), y(i,j+1));
        set_color(i,j);
    }
    glEnd();
}
```

An even better distorted image can be drawn with the following code:

```
glShadeModel(GL_SMOOTH);
for (j=0; j < (n-1); j++) {
    glBegin(GL_QUAD_STRIP);
    for (i=0; i < m; i++) {
        set_color(i,j);
        glVertex2i(x(i,j), y(i,j));
        set_color(i,j+1);
        glVertex2i(x(i,j+1), y(i,j+1));
    }
    glEnd();
}
```

This code smoothly interpolates color across each quadrilateral. Note that this version produces one fewer quadrilateral in each dimension than do the flat-shaded versions, because the color image is being used to specify colors at the quadrilateral vertices. In addition, you can antialias the polygons with the appropriate blending function (GL_SRC_ALPHA, GL_ONE) to get an even nicer image.

## Displaying Layers

In some applications, such as semiconductor layout programs, you want to display multiple layers of different materials and indicate where the materials overlap each other.

As a simple example, suppose you have three different substances that can be layered. At any point, eight possible combinations of layers can occur, as shown in Table 14-2.

| | Layer 1 | Layer 2 | Layer 3 | Color |
|---|---------|---------|---------|-------|
| 0 | absent | absent | absent | black |
| 1 | present | absent | absent | red |
| 2 | absent | present | absent | green |
| 3 | present | present | absent | blue |
| 4 | absent | absent | present | pink |
| 5 | present | absent | present | yellow |
| 6 | absent | present | present | white |
| 7 | present | present | present | gray |

**Table 14-2**     Eight Combinations of Layers

You want your program to display eight different colors, depending on the layers present. One arbitrary possibility is shown in the last column of the table. To use this method, use color-index mode and load your color map so that entry 0 is black, entry 1 is red, entry 2 is green, and so on. Note that if the numbers from 0 through 7 are written in binary, the 4 bit is turned on whenever layer 3 appears, the 2 bit whenever layer 2 appears, and the 1 bit whenever layer 1 appears.

To clear the window, set the writemask to 7 (all three layers) and set the clearing color to 0. To draw your image, set the color to 7, and when you want to draw something in layer $n$, set the writemask to $n$. In other types of applications, it might be necessary to erase selectively in a layer, in which case you would use the writemasks just discussed, but set the color to 0 instead of 7. (See "Masking Buffers" in Chapter 10 for more information about writemasks.)

## Antialiased Characters

Using the standard technique for drawing characters with **glBitmap()**, drawing each pixel of a character is an all-or-nothing affair—the pixel is either turned on or not. If you're drawing black characters on a white background, for example, the resulting pixels are either black or white, never a shade of gray. Much smoother, higher-quality images can be achieved if intermediate colors are used when rendering characters (grays, in this example).

Assuming that you're drawing black characters on a white background, imagine a highly magnified picture of the pixels on the screen, with a high-resolution character outline superimposed on it, as shown in the left-hand diagram in Figure 14-1.

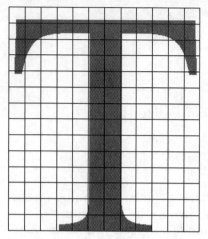

| 0 | 1 | 1 | 1 | 1 | 1 | 1 | 1 | 1 | 1 | 1 | 1 |
|---|---|---|---|---|---|---|---|---|---|---|---|
| 2 | 3 | 2 | 2 | 2 | 3 | 3 | 2 | 2 | 2 | 3 | 2 |
| 2 | 1 | 0 | 0 | 0 | 3 | 3 | 0 | 0 | 0 | 1 | 3 |
| 2 | 0 | 0 | 0 | 0 | 3 | 3 | 0 | 0 | 0 | 0 | 2 |
| 0 | 0 | 0 | 0 | 0 | 3 | 3 | 0 | 0 | 0 | 0 | 0 |
| 0 | 0 | 0 | 0 | 0 | 3 | 3 | 0 | 0 | 0 | 0 | 0 |
| 0 | 0 | 0 | 0 | 0 | 3 | 3 | 0 | 0 | 0 | 0 | 0 |
| 0 | 0 | 0 | 0 | 0 | 3 | 3 | 0 | 0 | 0 | 0 | 0 |
| 0 | 0 | 0 | 0 | 0 | 3 | 3 | 0 | 0 | 0 | 0 | 0 |
| 0 | 0 | 0 | 0 | 0 | 3 | 3 | 0 | 0 | 0 | 0 | 0 |
| 0 | 0 | 0 | 0 | 0 | 3 | 3 | 0 | 0 | 0 | 0 | 0 |
| 0 | 0 | 0 | 0 | 0 | 3 | 3 | 0 | 0 | 0 | 0 | 0 |
| 0 | 0 | 0 | 0 | 0 | 3 | 3 | 0 | 0 | 0 | 0 | 0 |
| 0 | 0 | 0 | 1 | 2 | 3 | 3 | 2 | 1 | 0 | 0 | 0 |

**Figure 14-1**    Antialiased Characters

Notice that some of the pixels are completely enclosed by the character's outline and should be painted black, some pixels are completely outside the outline and should be painted white, but many pixels should ideally be painted some shade of gray, where the darkness of the gray corresponds to the amount of black in the pixel. If this technique is used, the resulting image on the screen looks better.

If speed and memory usage are of no concern, each character can be drawn as a small image instead of as a bitmap. If you're using RGBA mode, however, this method might require up to 32 bits per pixel of the character to be stored and drawn, instead of the 1 bit per pixel for a standard character. Alternatively, you could use one 8-bit index per pixel and convert these indices to RGBA by table lookup during transfer. In many cases, a compromise is possible that allows you to draw the character with a few gray levels between black and white (say, two or three), and the resulting font description requires only 2 or 3 bits per pixel of storage.

The numbers in the right-hand diagram in Figure 14-1 indicate the approximate percentage coverage of each pixel: 0 means approximately empty, 1 means approximately one-third coverage, 2 means two-thirds, and 3 means completely covered. If pixels labeled 0 are painted white, pixels labeled 3 are painted black, and pixels labeled 1 and 2 are painted one-third and two-thirds black, respectively, the resulting character looks quite good. Only 2 bits are required to store the numbers 0, 1, 2, and 3, so for 2 bits per pixel, four levels of gray can be saved.

There are basically two methods of implementing antialiased characters, depending on whether you're in RGBA mode or color-index mode.

In RGBA mode, define three different character bitmaps, corresponding to where 1, 2, and 3 appear in Figure 14-1. Set the color to white, and clear for the background. Set the color to one-third gray (RGB = (0.666, 0.666, 0.666)), and draw all the pixels with a 1 in them. Then set RGB = (0.333, 0.333, 0.333), draw with the 2 bitmap, and use RGB = (0.0, 0.0, 0.0) for the 3 bitmap. What you're doing is defining three different fonts and redrawing the string three times, where each pass fills in the bits of the appropriate color densities.

In color-index mode, you can do exactly the same thing, but if you're willing to set up the color map correctly and use writemasks, you can get away with only two bitmaps per character and two passes per string. In the preceding example, set up one bitmap that has a 1 wherever 1 or 3 appears in the character. Set up a second bitmap that has a 1 wherever 2 or 3 appears. Load the color map so that 0 gives white, 1 gives light gray, 2 gives dark gray, and 3 gives black. Set the color to 3 (11 in binary) and the writemask to 1, and draw the first bitmap. Then change the writemask to 2, and draw the second. Where 0 appears in Figure 14-1, nothing is drawn in the framebuffer. Where 1, 2, and 3 appear, 1, 2, and 3 appear in the framebuffer.

For this example with only four gray levels, the savings are small—two passes instead of three. If eight gray levels were used instead of four, the RGBA method would require seven passes, and the color-map masking technique would require only three. With 16 gray levels, the comparison is 15 passes to four passes. (See "Masking Buffers" in Chapter 10 for more information about writemasks, and "Bitmaps and Fonts" in Chapter 8 for more information about drawing bitmaps.)

### Try This

Try This

- Can you imagine how to do RGBA rendering using no more images than the optimized color-index case?

**Hint:** How are RGB fragments normally merged into the color buffer when antialiasing is desired?

## Drawing Round Points

Draw near-round, aliased points by enabling point antialiasing, turning blending off, and using an alpha function that passes only fragments with alpha greater than 0.5. (See "Antialiasing" and "Blending" in Chapter 6 for more information about these topics.)

## Interpolating Images

Suppose you have a pair of images (where *image* can mean a bitmap image or a picture generated using geometry in the usual way), and you want to blend smoothly from one to the other. This can be done easily using the alpha component and appropriate blending operations. Let's say you want to accomplish the blending in ten steps, where image A is shown in frame 0 and image B is shown in frame 9. The obvious approach is to draw image A with an alpha of $(9 - i)/9$ and image B with an alpha of $i/9$ in frame $i$.

The problem with this method is that both images must be drawn in each frame. A faster approach is to draw image A in frame 0. To get frame 1, blend in 1/9 of image B and 8/9 of what's there. For frame 2, blend in 1/8 of image B with 7/8 of what's there. For frame 3, blend in 1/7 of image B with 6/7 of what's there, and so on. For the last step, you're just drawing 1/1 of image B blended with 0/1 of what's left, yielding image B exactly.

To see that this works, if for frame $i$ you have

$$\frac{(9 - i) A}{9} + \frac{iB}{9}$$

and you blend in $B/(9 - i)$ with $(8 - i)/(9 - i)$ of what's there, you get

$$\frac{B}{9 - i} + \frac{8 - i}{9 - i}\left[\frac{(9 - i) A}{9} + \frac{iB}{9}\right] = \frac{9 - (i + 1) A}{9} + \frac{(i + 1) B}{9}$$

(See "Blending" in Chapter 6.)

## Making Decals

Suppose you're drawing a complex three-dimensional picture using depth-buffering to eliminate the hidden surfaces. Suppose further that one part of your picture is composed of coplanar figures A and B, where figure B is a sort of decal that should always appear on top of figure A.

Your first approach might be to draw figure B after you've drawn figure A, setting the depth-buffering function to replace fragments when their depth is greater than or equal to the value stored in the depth buffer (GL_GEQUAL). Owing to the finite precision of the floating-point representations of the vertices, however, round-off error can cause figure B to be sometimes a bit in front of and sometimes a bit behind figure A. Here's one solution to this problem:

1. Disable the depth buffer for writing, and render A.

2. Enable the depth buffer for writing, and render B.

3. Disable the color buffer for writing, and render A again.

4. Enable the color buffer for writing.

Note that during the entire process, the depth-buffer test is enabled. In Step 1, A is rendered wherever it should be, but none of the depth-buffer values are changed; thus, in Step 2, wherever B appears over A, B is guaranteed to be drawn. Step 3 simply makes sure that all of the depth values under A are updated correctly, but since RGBA writes are disabled, the color pixels are unaffected. Finally, Step 4 returns the system to the default state (writing is enabled in both the depth buffer and the color buffer).

If a stencil buffer is available, the following, simpler technique can be used:

1. Configure the stencil buffer to write 1 if the depth test passes, and 0 otherwise. Render A.

2. Configure the stencil buffer to make no stencil value change, but to render only where stencil values are 1. Disable the depth-buffer test and its update. Render B.

With this method, it's not necessary to initialize the contents of the stencil buffer at any time, because the stencil values of all pixels of interest (that is, those rendered by A) are set when A is rendered. Be sure to reenable the depth test and disable the stencil test before additional polygons are drawn. (See "Selecting Color Buffers for Writing and Reading," "Depth Test," and "Stencil Test" in Chapter 10.)

## Drawing Filled, Concave Polygons Using the Stencil Buffer

Consider the concave polygon 1234567 shown in Figure 14-2. Imagine that it's drawn as a series of triangles: 123, 134, 145, 156, and 167, all of which are shown in the figure. The heavier line represents the original polygon boundary. Drawing all these triangles divides the buffer into nine regions A, B, C, ..., I, where region I is outside all the triangles.

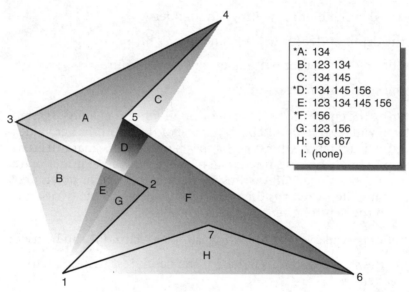

```
*A: 134
 B: 123 134
 C: 134 145
*D: 134 145 156
 E: 123 134 145 156
*F: 156
 G: 123 156
 H: 156 167
 I: (none)
```

**Figure 14-2**    Concave Polygon

In the text of the figure, each of the region names is followed by a list of the triangles that cover it. Regions A, D, and F make up the original polygon; note that these three regions are covered by an odd number of triangles. Every other region is covered by an even number of triangles (possibly zero). Thus, to render the inside of the concave polygon, you need to render only regions that are enclosed by odd numbers of triangles. This can be done using the stencil buffer, with a two-pass algorithm.

First, clear the stencil buffer and disable writing into the color buffer. Next, draw each of the triangles in turn, using the GL_INVERT function in the stencil buffer. (For best performance, use triangle fans.) This flips the value between zero and a nonzero value every time a triangle that covers a pixel is drawn. After all the triangles are drawn, if a pixel is covered an even number of times, the value in the stencil buffers is zero; otherwise, it's nonzero. Finally, draw a large polygon over the whole region (or redraw the triangles), but allow drawing only where the stencil buffer is nonzero.

**Note:** There's a slight generalization of the preceding technique, where you don't need to start with a polygon vertex. In the 1234567 example, let P be any point on or off the polygon. Draw the triangles: P12, P23, P34, P45, P56, P67, and P71. Regions covered by odd numbers of triangles are inside; other regions are outside. This is a generalization in that if P happens to be one of the polygon's edges, one of the triangles is empty.

This technique can be used to fill both nonsimple polygons (polygons whose edges cross each other) and polygons with holes. The following example illustrates how to handle a complicated polygon with two regions, one four-sided and one five-sided. Assume further that there's a triangular hole and a four-sided hole (it doesn't matter in which regions the holes lie). Let the two regions be abcd and efghi, and let the holes be jkl and mnop. Let z be any point in the plane. Draw the following triangles:

zab zbc zcd zda zef zfg zgh zhi zie zjk zkl zlj zmn zno zop zpm

Mark regions covered by odd numbers of triangles as *in*, and those covered by even numbers as *out*. (See "Stencil Test" in Chapter 10 for more information about the stencil buffer.)

# Finding Interference Regions

If you're designing a mechanical part made from smaller three-dimensional pieces, you often want to display regions in which the pieces overlap. In many cases, such regions indicate design errors where parts of a machine interfere with each other. In the case of moving parts, this process can be even more valuable, because a search for interfering regions can be done through a complete mechanical cycle of the design. The method for doing this is complicated, and the description here might be too brief. Complete details can be found in the paper *Interactive Inspection of Solids: Cross-sections and Interferences*, by Jarek Rossignac, Abe Megahed, and Bengt-Olaf Schneider (SIGGRAPH 1992 Proceedings).

The method is related to the capping algorithm described in "Stencil Test" in Chapter 10. The idea is to pass an arbitrary clipping plane through the objects that you want to test for interference, and then determine when a portion of the clipping plane is inside more than one object at a time. For a static image, the clipping plane can be moved manually to highlight interfering regions; for a dynamic image, it might be easier to use a grid of clipping planes to search for all possible interferences.

Draw each of the objects you want to check and clip them against the clipping plane. Note which pixels are inside the object at that clipping plane using an odd-even count in the stencil buffer, as explained in "Drawing Filled, Concave Polygons Using the Stencil Buffer." (For properly formed objects, a point is inside the object if a ray drawn from that point to the eye intersects an odd number of surfaces of the object.) To find interferences, you need to find pixels in the framebuffer where the clipping plane is in the interiors of two or more regions at once; in other words, in the intersection of the interiors of any pair of objects.

If multiple objects need to be tested for mutual intersection, store one bit every time some intersection appears, and another bit wherever the clipping buffer is inside any of the objects (the union of the objects' interiors). For each new object, determine its interior, find the intersection of that interior with the union of the interiors of the objects so far tested, and keep track of the intersection points. Then add the interior points of the new object to the union of the other objects' interiors.

You can perform the operations described in the preceding paragraph by using different bits in the stencil buffer together with various masking operations. Three bits of stencil buffer are required per pixel—one for the toggling to determine the interior of each object, one for the union of all interiors discovered so far, and one for the regions in which interference has occurred so far. To make this discussion more concrete, assume that the 1 bit of the stencil buffer is for toggling between interior and exterior, the 2 bit is the running union, and the 4 bit is for interferences so far. For each object that you're going to render, clear the 1 bit (using a stencil mask of 1 and clearing to 0), then toggle the 1 bit by keeping the stencil mask as 1 and using the GL_INVERT stencil operation.

You can find intersections and unions of the bits in the stencil buffers using the stenciling operations. For example, to make bits in buffer 2 be the union of the bits in buffers 1 and 2, mask the stencil to those 2 bits, and draw something over the entire object with the stencil function set to pass if anything nonzero occurs. This happens if the bits in buffer 1, in buffer 2, or in both are turned on. If the comparison succeeds, write a 1 in buffer 2. Also, make sure that drawing in the color buffer is disabled. An intersection calculation is similar—set the function to pass only if the value in the two buffers is equal to 3 (bits turned on in both buffers 1 and 2). Write the result into the correct buffer. (See "Stencil Test" in Chapter 10.)

# Shadows

Every possible projection of three-dimensional space to three-dimensional space can be achieved with a suitable $4 \times 4$ invertible matrix and homogeneous coordinates. If the matrix isn't invertible but has rank 3, it projects three-dimensional space onto a two-dimensional plane. Every such possible projection can be achieved with a suitable rank-3 $4 \times 4$ matrix. To find the shadow of an arbitrary object on an arbitrary plane from an arbitrary light source (possibly at infinity), you need to find a matrix representing that projection, multiply it on the matrix stack, and draw the object in the shadow color. Keep in mind that you need to project onto each plane that you're calling the "ground."

As a simple illustration, assume the light is at the origin, and the equation of the ground plane is $ax + by + cz + d = 0$. Given a vertex $S = (sx, sy, sz, 1)$, the line from the light through S includes all points $\alpha S$, where $\alpha$ is an arbitrary real number. The point where this line intersects the plane occurs when

$$\alpha(a{\cdot}sx + b{\cdot}sy + c{\cdot}sz) + d = 0,$$

so

$$\alpha = -d/(a{\cdot}sx + b{\cdot}sy + c{\cdot}sz).$$

Plugging this back into the line, we get

$$-d(sx, sy, sz)/(a{\cdot}sx + b{\cdot}sy + c{\cdot}sz)$$

for the point of intersection.

The matrix that maps S to this point for every S is

$$\begin{bmatrix} -d & 0 & 0 & 0 \\ 0 & -d & 0 & 0 \\ 0 & 0 & -d & 0 \\ a & b & c & 0 \end{bmatrix}$$

This matrix can be used if you first translate the world so that the light is at the origin.

If the light is from an infinite source, all you have is a point S and a direction $D = (dx, dy, dz)$. Points along the line are given by

$$S + \alpha D$$

Proceeding as before, the intersection of this line with the plane is given by

$$a(sx + \alpha \cdot dx) + b(sy + \alpha \cdot dy) + c(sz + \alpha \cdot dz) + d = 0$$

Solving for $\alpha$, plugging that back into the equation for a line, and then determining a projection matrix gives

$$\begin{bmatrix} b \times dy + c \times dz & -b \times dx & -c \times dx & -d \times dx \\ -a \times dy & a \times dx + c \times dz & -c \times dy & -d \times dy \\ -a \times dz & -b \times dz & a \times dx + b \times dy & -d \times dz \\ 0 & 0 & 0 & a \times dx + b \times dy + c \times dz \end{bmatrix}$$

This matrix works given the plane and an arbitrary direction vector. There's no need to translate anything first. (See Chapter 3 and Appendix F.)

# Hidden-Line Removal

If you want to draw a wireframe object with hidden lines removed, one approach is to draw the outlines using lines and then fill the interiors of the polygons making up the surface with polygons having the background color. With depth-buffering enabled, this interior fill covers any outlines that would be obscured by faces closer to the eye. This method would work, except that there's no guarantee that the interior of the object falls entirely inside the polygon's outline; in fact, it might overlap it in various places.

There's an easy, two-pass solution using either polygon offset or the stencil buffer. Polygon offset is usually the preferred technique, since polygon offset is almost always faster than stencil buffer. Both methods are described here, so you can see how both approaches to the problem work.

## Hidden-Line Removal with Polygon Offset

To use polygon offset to accomplish hidden-line removal, the object is drawn twice. The highlighted edges are drawn in the foreground color, using filled polygons but with the polygon mode GL_LINE, to rasterize the polygons as wireframe edges. Then the filled polygons are drawn with the default polygon mode, which fills the interior of the wireframe, and with enough polygon offset to nudge the filled polygons a little farther from the eye. With the polygon offset, the interior recedes just enough that the highlighted edges are drawn without unpleasant visual artifacts.

```
glEnable(GL_DEPTH_TEST);
glPolygonMode(GL_FRONT_AND_BACK, GL_LINE);
set_color(foreground);
draw_object_with_filled_polygons();

glPolygonMode(GL_FRONT_AND_BACK, GL_FILL);
glEnable(GL_POLYGON_OFFSET_FILL);
glPolygonOffset(1.0, 1.0);
set_color(background);
draw_object_with_filled_polygons();
glDisable(GL_POLYGON_OFFSET_FILL);
```

You may have to adjust the amount of offset needed (for wider lines, for example). (See "Polygon Offset" in Chapter 6 for more information.)

## Hidden-Line Removal with the Stencil Buffer

Using the stencil buffer for hidden-line removal is a more complicated procedure. For each polygon, you'll need to clear the stencil buffer and then draw the outline in both the framebuffer and the stencil buffer. Then, when you fill the interior, enable drawing only where the stencil buffer is still clear. To avoid doing an entire stencil-buffer clear for each polygon, an easy way to clear it is simply to draw 0's into the buffer using the same polygon outline. In this way, you need to clear the entire stencil buffer only once.

For example, the following code represents the inner loop you might use to perform such hidden-line removal. Each polygon is outlined in the foreground color, filled with the background color, and then outlined again in the foreground color. The stencil buffer is used to keep the fill color of each polygon from overwriting its outline. To optimize performance, the stencil and color parameters are changed only twice per loop by using the same values both times the polygon outline is drawn.

```
glEnable(GL_STENCIL_TEST);
glEnable(GL_DEPTH_TEST);
glClear(GL_STENCIL_BUFFER_BIT);
glStencilFunc(GL_ALWAYS, 0, 1);
glStencilOp(GL_INVERT, GL_INVERT, GL_INVERT);
set_color(foreground);
for (i=0; i < max; i++) {
    outline_polygon(i);
    set_color(background);
    glStencilFunc(GL_EQUAL, 0, 1);
    glStencilOp(GL_KEEP, GL_KEEP, GL_KEEP);
```

```
    fill_polygon(i);
    set_color(foreground);
    glStencilFunc(GL_ALWAYS, 0, 1);
    glStencilOp(GL_INVERT, GL_INVERT, GL_INVERT);
    outline_polygon(i);
}
```

(See "Stencil Test" in Chapter 10.)


## Texture Mapping Applications

Texture mapping is quite powerful, and it can be used in some interesting ways. Here are a few advanced applications of texture mapping:

- Antialiased text—Define a texture map for each character at a relatively high resolution, and then map them onto smaller areas using the filtering provided by texturing. This also makes text appear correctly on surfaces that aren't aligned with the screen, but are tilted and have some perspective distortion.

- Antialiased lines—These can be done like antialiased text: make the line in the texture several pixels wide, and use texture filtering to antialias the lines.

- Image scaling and rotation—If you put an image into a texture map and use that texture to map onto a polygon, rotating and scaling the polygon effectively rotates and scales the image.

- Image warping—Store the image as a texture map, but map it to some spline-defined surface (using evaluators). As you warp the surface, the image follows the warping.

- Projecting images—Put the image in a texture map, and project it as a spotlight, creating a slide projector effect. (See "The q-Coordinate" in Chapter 9 for more information about how to model a spotlight using textures.)

(See Chapter 3 for information about rotating and scaling, Chapter 9 for more information about creating textures, and Chapter 12 for details on evaluators.)

## Drawing Depth-Buffered Images

For complex static backgrounds, the rendering time for the geometric description of the background can be greater than the time it takes to draw a pixel image of the rendered background. If there's a fixed background and a relatively simple changing foreground, you may want to draw the background and its associated depth-buffered version as an image, rather than render it geometrically. The foreground might also consist of items that are time-consuming to render, but whose framebuffer images and depth buffers are available. You can render these items into a depth-buffered environment using a two-pass algorithm.

For example, if you're drawing a model of a molecule made of spheres, you might have an image of a beautifully rendered sphere and its associated depth-buffer values that were calculated using Phong shading or ray-tracing or some other scheme that isn't directly available through OpenGL. To draw a complex model, you might be required to draw hundreds of such spheres, which should be depth-buffered together.

To add a depth-buffered image to the scene, first draw the image's depth-buffer values into the depth buffer using **glDrawPixels()**. Then enable depth-buffering, set the writemask to 0 so that no drawing occurs, and enable stenciling such that the stencil buffers are drawn whenever a write to the depth buffer occurs.

Then draw the image into the color buffer, masked by the stencil buffer you've just written so that writing occurs only when there's a 1 in the stencil buffer. During this write, set the stenciling function to zero out the stencil buffer so that it's automatically cleared when it's time to add the next image to the scene. If the objects are to be moved nearer to or farther from the viewer, you need to use an orthographic projection; in such cases, you use GL_DEPTH_BIAS with **glPixelTransfer*()** to move the depth image. (See "Coordinate System Survival Kit" in Chapter 2, "Depth Test" and "Stencil Test" in Chapter 10, and Chapter 8 for details on **glDrawPixels()** and **glPixelTransfer*()**.)

## Dirichlet Domains

Given a set S of points in a plane, the Dirichlet domain or Voronoi polygon of one of the points is the set of all points in the plane closer to that point than to any other point in the set S. These points provide the solutions to many problems in computational geometry. Figure 14-3 shows outlines of the Dirichlet domains for a set of points.

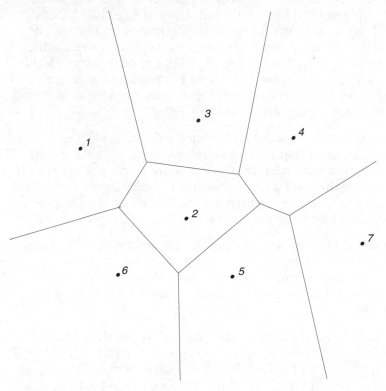

**Figure 14-3**   Dirichlet Domains

If for each point in S, you draw a depth-buffered cone with its apex at the point in a different color than each of the points in S, the Dirichlet domain for each point is drawn in that color. The easiest way to do this is to precompute a cone's depth in an image and use the image as the depth-buffer values as described in the preceding section, "Drawing Depth-Buffered Images." You don't need an image to draw into the framebuffer as in the case of shaded spheres, however. While you're drawing into the depth buffer, use the stencil buffer to record the pixels where drawing should occur by first clearing it and then writing nonzero values wherever the depth test succeeds. To draw the Dirichlet region, draw a polygon over the entire window, but enable drawing only where the stencil buffers are nonzero.

You can do this perhaps more easily by rendering cones of uniform color with a simple depth buffer, but a good cone might require thousands of polygons. The technique described in this section can render higher-quality cones much more quickly. (See "A Hidden-Surface Removal Survival Kit" in Chapter 5 and "Depth Test" in Chapter 10.)

## Life in the Stencil Buffer

The Game of Life, invented by John Conway, is played on a rectangular grid in which each grid location is either "alive" or "dead." To calculate the next generation from the current one, count the number of live neighbors for each grid location (the eight adjacent grid locations are neighbors). A grid location is alive in generation $n + 1$ if it was alive in generation $n$ and has exactly two or three live neighbors, or if it was dead in generation $n$ and has exactly three live neighbors. In all other cases, it is dead in generation $n + 1$. This game generates some incredibly interesting patterns given different initial configurations. (See Martin Gardner, "Mathematical Games," *Scientific American*, vol. 223, no. 4, October 1970, pp. 120–123.) Figure 14-4 shows six generations from a game.

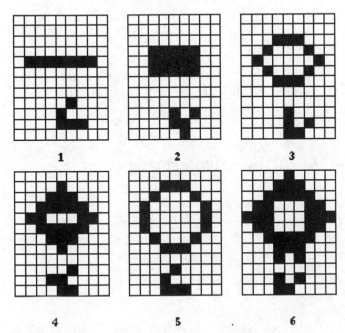

**Figure 14-4**     Six Generations from the Game of Life

One way to create this game using OpenGL is to use a multipass algorithm. Keep the data in the color buffer, one pixel for each grid point. Assume that black (all zeros) is the background color, and that the color of a live pixel is nonzero. Initialize by clearing the depth and stencil buffers to zero, set the depth-buffer writemask to zero, and set the depth comparison function so that it passes on not-equal. To iterate, read the image off the screen, enable drawing into the depth buffer, and set the stencil function so that it increments whenever a depth comparison succeeds but leaves the stencil buffer unchanged otherwise. Disable drawing into the color buffer.

Next, draw the image eight times, and offset one pixel in each vertical, horizontal, and diagonal direction. When you're done, the stencil buffer contains a count of the number of live neighbors for each pixel. Enable drawing to the color buffer, set the color to the color for live cells, and set the stencil function to draw only if the value in the stencil buffer is 3 (three live neighbors). In addition, if this drawing occurs, decrement the value in the stencil buffer. Then draw a rectangle covering the image; this paints each cell that has exactly three live neighbors with the "alive" color.

At this point, the stencil buffers contain 0, 1, 2, 4, 5, 6, 7, and 8, and the values under the 2's are correct. The values under 0, 1, 4, 5, 6, 7, and 8 must be cleared to the "dead" color. Set the stencil function to draw whenever the value is not 2 and to zero the stencil values in all cases. Then draw a large polygon of the "dead" color across the entire image. You're done.

For a usable demonstration program, you might want to zoom the grid up to a size larger than a single pixel; it's hard to see detailed patterns with a single pixel per grid point. (See "Coordinate System Survival Kit" in Chapter 2, and "Depth Test" and "Stencil Test" in Chapter 10.)

## Alternative Uses for glDrawPixels() and glCopyPixels()

You might think of **glDrawPixels**() as a way to draw a rectangular region of pixels to the screen. Although this is often what it's used for, some other interesting uses are outlined here:

- Video—Even if your machine doesn't have special video hardware, you can display short movie clips by repeatedly drawing frames with **glDrawPixels**() in the same region of the back buffer and then swapping the buffers. The size of the frames you can display with reasonable performance using this method depends on your hardware's drawing speed, so you might be limited to $100 \times 100$ pixel movies (or smaller) if you want smooth fake video.

- Airbrush—In a paint program, your airbrush (or paintbrush) shape can be simulated using alpha values. The color of the paint is represented as the color values. To paint with a circular brush in blue, repeatedly draw a blue square with **glDrawPixels()** where the alpha values are largest in the center and taper to zero at the edges of a circle centered in the square. Draw using a blending function that uses alpha of the incoming color and (1 – alpha) of the color already at the pixel. If the alpha values in the brush are all much less than 1, you have to paint over an area repeatedly to get a solid color. If the alpha values are near 1, each brush stroke pretty much obliterates the colors underneath.

- Filtered zooms—If you zoom a pixel image by a nonintegral amount, OpenGL effectively uses a box filter, which can lead to rather severe aliasing effects. To improve the filtering, jitter the resulting image by amounts less than a pixel and redraw it multiple times, using alpha blending to average the resulting pixels. The result is a filtered zoom.

- Transposing images—You can swap same-size images in place with **glCopyPixels()** using the XOR operation. With this method, you can avoid having to read the images back into processor memory. If A and B represent the two images, the operation looks like this:

  a. A = A XOR B

  b. B = A XOR B

  c. A = A XOR B

*Chapter 15*

# The OpenGL Shading Language

**Chapter Objectives**

This chapter discusses the OpenGL Shading Language. GLSL, as the OpenGL Shading Language is commonly called, is a programming language for creating programmable *shaders*. Introduced as a part of OpenGL 2.0, the OpenGL Shading Language enables applications to explicitly specify the operations used in processing vertices and fragments. Additionally, GLSL helps unlock the computation power of modern hardware implementations of OpenGL.

After reading this chapter, you'll be able to do the following:

- Understand the structure and components of programmable shaders written in the OpenGL Shading Language

- Integrate programmable shaders into OpenGL programs

This chapter discusses version 1.20 of the OpenGL Shading Language, which is the required version for OpenGL 2.1 implementations.

# The OpenGL Graphics Pipeline and Programmable Shading

You can think of the internal operation of OpenGL as two machines—one for processing vertices, the other for fragments—with dials and switches on the front of each machine. You control each machine's operation by flipping switches and twisting dials, but the internal operation of the machines is "fixed"; that is, you can't change the order of operations inside of the machine, and you're limited to the features that were built into the machine. This mode of operation for OpenGL is commonly called the *fixed-function pipeline*, and is described in detail in Appendix A, "Order of Operations." Figure 15-1 illustrates the basic architecture of the OpenGL fixed-function pipeline.

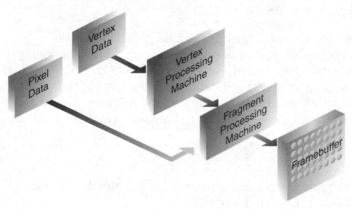

**Figure 15-1**    Overview of the OpenGL Fixed-Function Pipeline

OpenGL 2.0 augmented the fixed-function pipeline approach by adding a *programmable shading pipeline*, where you can control the processing of vertices and fragments with small programs, called *shaders*, written in a special language called *The OpenGL Shading Language*, or *GLSL* for short. In an application, you can use both the fixed-function and programmable pipelines for processing data, but not simultaneously. When you use a shader for processing, the corresponding portion of the fixed-function pipeline is disabled.

While using programmable shaders is not new to computer graphics, its accessibility has only recently become available in interactive graphics libraries such as OpenGL. Just like the field of computer graphics itself, techniques for programmable shaders is a huge subject, and this chapter does not attempt to teach the theory behind programmable shaders. Rather, it covers the language available for authoring shaders available in OpenGL and how to integrate those shaders into an OpenGL application. For more information on programmable shading, you may want to broaden your knowledge of the subject with these supplemental works:

- *The RenderMan Companion: A Programmer's Guide to Realistic Computer Graphics* by Steve Upstill (Addison-Wesley, 1990)—while this text describes Pixar's RenderMan shader language (which is one of the predominant programmable shader languages used for computer-generated images in the movie industry), it describes the basics of programmable shading and presents much of the theory and practice of using shaders to generate images.

- *Real-Time Shading* by John C. Hart, Wolfgang Heidrich, Michael McCool, and Marc Olano (AK Peters, Ltd., 2002)—this modern text describes the latest advancements in programmable shading on graphics hardware and provides a survey of different techniques and implementations of programmable shaders.

- *GPU Gems* and *GPU Gems 2* (Addison-Wesley)—these books describe many shader implementation tricks and techniques.

This section begins with a discussion of how shaders affect the processing of vertices and fragments. We continue describing what's required to integrate shaders to your OpenGL program, and then introduce writing shaders in GLSL. For all of the details on the OpenGL shading language, please see:

- *The OpenGL Shading Language Specification* by John Kessenich, Dave Baldwin, and Randi Rost (available for download from `http://www.opengl.org`)

- *The OpenGL Shading Language* by Randi Rost, John Kessenich, and Barthold Lichtenbelt (Addison-Wesley, 2006)

## Vertex Processing

Figure 15-2 illustrates the processing of a vertex through the OpenGL pipeline. The shaded area indicates the functions of the vertex processing pipeline that are replaced by a vertex shader.

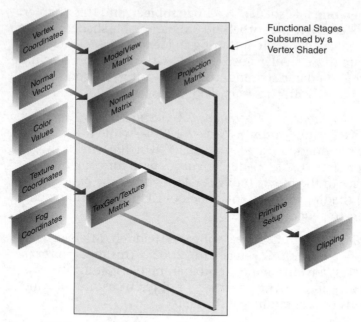

**Figure 15-2**     Vertex Processing Pipeline

When the fixed-function pipeline processes a vertex, it's responsible for providing the following values that are used for rasterization:

- Eye-space coordinates

- Primary and secondary colors

- Texture coordinates

- Fog coordinates

- Point size

Depending upon which features you have enabled, the vertex pipeline may not update all of those values. Those values are computed based on the input of the application through calls like **glVertex*()** and the other vertex data calls.

Not all operations in the vertex pipeline are replaced when you use a shader. After the execution of the shader, the following operations still occur, just as if the vertex were processed by the fixed-function pipeline:

- Perspective division

- Viewport mapping

- Primitive assembly
- Frustum and user clipping
- Backface culling
- Two-sided lighting selection
- Polygon-mode processing
- Polygon offset
- Depth range clamping

## Fragment Processing

Similarly, Figure 15-3 illustrates the pixel processing part of the OpenGL pipeline. Once again, the shaded region indicates the functionality replaced by a fragment shader.

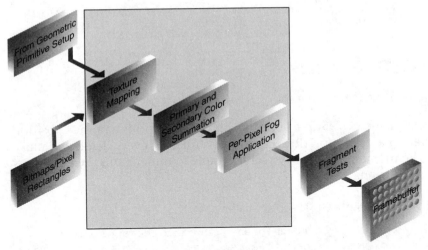

**Figure 15-3**    Fragment Processing Pipeline

Similar to vertex shaders, fragment shaders take over the processing of fragments. The operations subsumed in a fragment shader are:

- Texel retrieval for texture application
- Texture application
- Fogging
- Primary and secondary color summation

The operations that OpenGL does regardless of the application of a fragment shader are:

- Flat or smooth shading (which controls how values are interpolated across fragments)
- Pixel coverage computations
- Pixel ownership tests
- Scissor operations
- Stipple-pattern application
- Alpha test
- Depth test
- Stencil test
- Alpha blending
- Logical operations on pixels
- Dithering of color values
- Color masking

## Using GLSL Shaders

### A Sample Shader

Example 15-1 shows a simple vertex shader. It transforms a point's position by simulating acceleration due to gravity. While not every detail will make sense at the moment, hopefully you'll be able to understand the basic flow of what's going on.

**Example 15-1**   A Sample GLSL Vertex Shader

```
uniform float t;     // Time (passed in from the application)
attribute vec4 vel; // particle velocity

const vec4 g = vec4( 0.0, -9.80, 0.0 );

void main()
{
    vec4 position = gl_Vertex;
    position += t*vel + t*t*g;

    gl_Position = gl_ModelViewProjectionMatrix * position;
}
```

## OpenGL / GLSL Interface

Writing shaders for use with OpenGL programs is similar to using a compiler-based language like "C." You have a compiler analyze your program, check it for errors, and then translate it into object code. Next, a collection of object files are combined together in a linking phase generating an executable program. Using GLSL shaders in your program is a similar process, except that the compiler and linker are part of the OpenGL driver.

Figure 15-4 illustrates the steps required to create GLSL shader objects and link them together to create an executable shader program.

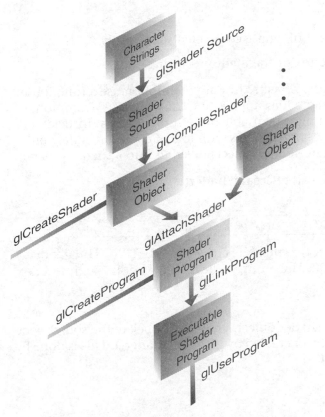

**Figure 15-4**  Shader Creation Flowchart

When you want to use a vertex or fragment shader in your application, you'll need to do the following sequence of steps:

For each shader object:

1. Create a shader object.

2. Compile your shader source into the object.

3. Verify that your shader successfully compiled.

Then, to link multiple shader objects into a shader program, you'll:

1. Create a shader program.

2. Attach the appropriate shader objects to the shader program.

3. Link the shader program.

4. Verify that the shader link phase completed successfully.

5. Use the shader for vertex or fragment processing.

Why create multiple shader objects? Just as you might reuse a function in different programs, the same idea applies to GLSL programs. Common routines that you create might be usable in multiple shaders. Instead of having to compile several large shaders with lots of common code, you'll merely link the appropriate shader objects together into a shader program.

To create a shader object, call **glCreateShader()**.

---

GLuint **glCreateShader**(GLenum *type*);

---

Allocates a shader object. *type* must be either GL_VERTEX_SHADER or GL_FRAGMENT_SHADER. The return value is either a non-zero integer or zero if an error occurred.

---

Once you have created a shader object, you need associate the source code of the shader with that object created by **glCreateShader()**. This is done by calling **glShaderSource()**.

---

void **glShaderSource**(GLuint *shader*, GLsizei *count*,
       const GLchar **\*\*string*, const GLint *\*length*);

---

Associates the source of a shader with a shader object *shader*. *string* is an array of *count* GLchar strings that compose the shader's source. The character strings in *string* may be optionally null-terminated. *length* can be one of three values. If *length* is NULL, then it's assumed that each string provided in *string* is null-terminated. Otherwise, *length* has *count* elements, each of which specifies the length of the corresponding entry in *string*. If the value of an element in the array *length* is a positive integer, the value represents the number of characters in the corresponding *string* element. If the value is negative for particular elements, then that entry in *string* is assumed to be null-terminated.

To compile a shader object's source, use **glCompileShader**().

---

void **glCompileShader**(GLuint *shader*);

---

Compiles the source code for *shader*. The results of the compilation can be queried by calling **glGetShaderiv**() with an argument of GL_COMPILE_STATUS.

---

Similar to when you compile a "C" program, you need to determine if the compilation finished successfully. A call to **glGetShaderiv**(), with an argument of GL_COMPILE_STATUS, will return the status of the compilation phase. If GL_TRUE is returned, the compilation succeeded, and the object can be linked into a shader program. If the compilation failed, you can determine what the error was by retrieving the compilation log. **glGetShaderInfoLog**() will return an implementation-specific set of messages describing the compilation errors. The current size of the error log can be queried by calling **glGetShaderiv**() with an argument of GL_INFO_LOG_LENGTH.

---

void **glGetShaderInfoLog**(GLuint *shader*, GLsizei *bufSize*,
       GLsizei *\*length*, char *\*infoLog*);

---

Returns the log associated with the last compilation of a shader object. *shader* specifies which shader object to query. The log is returned as a null-terminated character string of *length* characters in the buffer *infoLog*. The maximum return size of the log is specified in *bufSize*.

If *length* is NULL, *infoLog*'s length is not returned.

---

Once you have created and compiled all of the necessary shader objects, you will need to link them together to create an executable shader program. This process is similar in nature to creating shader objects. First, you'll need to create a shader program to which you can attach the shader objects. Using **glCreateProgram**(), a shader program will be returned for further processing.

GLuint **glCreateProgram**();

Creates an empty shader program. The return value is either a non-zero integer, or zero if an error occurred.

Once you have your shader program, you'll need to populate it with the necessary shader objects to create the executable program. This is accomplished by attaching a shader object to the program by calling **glAttachShader**().

void **glAttachShader**(GLuint *program*, GLuint *shader*);

Associates the shader object, *shader*, with the shader program, *program*. A shader object can be attached to a shader program at any time, although its functionality will only be available after a successful link of the shader program. A shader object can be attached to multiple shader programs simultaneously.

For parity, if you need to remove a shader object from a program to modify the shader's operation, detach the shader object by calling **glDetachShader**() with the appropriate shader object identifier.

void **glDetachShader**(GLuint *program*, GLuint *shader*);

Removes the association of a shader object, *shader,* from the shader program, *program*. If *shader* is detached from *program* and had been previously marked for deletion (by calling **glDeleteShader**()), it is deleted at that time.

After all the necessary shader objects have been attached to the shader program, you will need to link the objects for an executable program. This is accomplished by calling **glLinkProgram**().

---

void **glLinkProgram**(GLuint *program*);

Processes all shader objects attached to *program* to generate a completed shader program. The result of the linking operation can be queried by calling **glGetProgramiv()** with GL_LINK_STATUS. GL_TRUE is returned for a successful link; GL_FALSE is returned otherwise.

---

As with shader objects, there's a chance that the linking phase may fail due to errors in the attached shader objects. You can query the result of the link operation's success by calling **glGetProgramiv()** with an argument of GL_LINK_STATUS. If GL_TRUE was returned, the link was successful, and you're able to specify the shader program for use in processing vertices or fragments. If the link failed, represented by GL_FALSE being returned, then you can determine the cause of the failure by retrieving the program link information log by calling **glGetProgramLog()**.

---

void **glGetProgramInfoLog**(GLuint *program*, GLsizei *bufSize*, GLsizei *\*length*, char *\*infoLog*);

Returns the log associated with the last compilation of a shader program. *program* specifies which shader program to query. The log is returned as a null-terminated character string of *length* characters in the buffer *infoLog*. The maximum return size of the log is specified in *bufSize*.

If *length* is NULL, *infoLog*'s length is not returned.

---

After a successful program link, you can engage the vertex or fragment program by calling **glUseProgram()** with the program's object handle. To revert back to using the fixed-function pipeline, pass zero as the program object.

---

void **glUseProgram**(GLuint *program*);

Uses *program* for either vertex or fragment processing, depending upon the type of shader created with **glCreateShader()**. If *program* is zero, no shader is used for processing and OpenGL reverts to fixed-function operation.

---

> While a program is in use, it can have new shader objects attached, compile attached shader objects, or detach previously attached objects. It may also be relinked. If the link phase is successful, the newly linked shader program replaces the previously active program. If the link fails, the currently bound shader program remains active and is not replaced until either a new program is specified with **glUseProgram()** or the program is successfully relinked.

Example 15-2 illustrates creating and linking a vertex shader in GLSL. The process is virtually identical for fragment shaders.

**Example 15-2**    Creating and Linking GLSL shaders

```
GLuint shader, program;
GLint  compiled, linked;

const GLchar* shaderSrc[] = {
    "void main()"
    "{"
    "    gl_Position = gl_ModelViewProjectionMatrix * gl_Vertex;"
    "}"
};

shader = glCreateShader(GL_VERTEX_SHADER);

glShaderSource(shader, 1, shaderSrc, NULL);
glCompileShader(shader);

glGetShaderiv(shader, GL_COMPILE_STATUS, &compiled );

if (!compiled) {
    GLint    length;
    GLchar* log;
    glGetShaderiv(shader, GL_INFO_LOG_LENGTH,
        &length );

    log = (GLchar*) malloc(length);
    glGetShaderInfoLog(shader, length, &length, log);
    fprintf(stderr, "compile log = '%s'\n", log);
}

program = glCreateProgram();
```

```
glAttachShader(program, shader);
glLinkProgram(program);

glGetProgramiv(program, GL_LINK_STATUS, &linked );

if (linked) {
    glUseProgram(program);
} else {
    GLint   length;
    GLchar* log;
    glGetProgramiv(progam, GL_INFO_LOG_LENGTH, &length );

    log = (GLchar*) malloc(length);
    glProgramGetInfoLog(program, length, &length, log);
    fprintf(stderr, "link log = '%s'\n", log);
}
```

To release the resources related to shader objects and programs, you can delete those objects by calling the respective deletion function. If either the shader program or object is currently active when it's deleted, the object is only marked for deletion. It is deleted when the program is no longer in use, or the shader object is detached from all shader program objects.

---

void **glDeleteShader**(GLuint *shader*);

---

Deletes *shader*. If *shader* is currently linked to one or more active shader programs, the object is tagged for deletion and deleted once the shader program is no longer being used by any shader program.

---

void **glDeleteProgram**(GLuint *program*);

---

Deletes *program* immediately if not currently in use in any context, or tagged for deletion when the program is no longer in use by any contexts.

To determine if an identifier is currently in use as either a shader program or object, calling **glIsProgram**() or **glIsShader**() will return a boolean value indicating if the identifier is in use.

GLboolean **glIsProgram**(GLuint *program*);

Returns GL_TRUE if *program* is the name of a shader program. If *program* is zero, or non-zero and not the name of a shader object, GL_FALSE is returned.

GLboolean **glIsShader**(GLuint *shader*);

Returns GL_TRUE if *shader* is the name of a shader object. If *shader* is zero, or non-zero and not the name of a shader object, GL_FALSE is returned.

To aid in shader development, the OpenGL call **glValidateProgram**() can help verify that a shader will execute given the current OpenGL state. Depending upon the underlying OpenGL implementation, program validation may also return hints about performance characteristics or other useful information specific to that shader's execution for that OpenGL implementation. You would validate a program in the same manner you would compile it by merely calling **glValidateProgram**() once all of the necessary shader objects were attached to the shader program. Similarly, you can query the results of the validation step by calling **glGetProgramiv**() with an argument of GL_VALIDATE_STATUS.

void **glValidateProgram**(GLuint *program*);

Validates *program* against the current OpenGL state settings. After validation, the value of GL_VALIDATE_STATUS will be set to either GL_TRUE, indicating that the program will execute in the current OpenGL environment, or GL_FALSE otherwise. The value of GL_VALIDATE_STATUS status can be queried by calling **glGetProgramiv**().

## The OpenGL Shading Language

This section provides an overview of the shading language used within OpenGL, commonly called GLSL. GLSL shares many traits with C++ and Java, and is used for authoring both vertex and fragment shaders, although certain features are only available for one type of shader. We will first describe GLSL's requirements, types, and other language constructs that are shared between vertex and fragment shaders, and then discuss the features unique to each type of shader.

# Creating Shaders with GLSL

## The Starting Point

A shader program, just like a "C" program, starts execution in **main()**. Every GLSL shader program begins life as:

```
void
main()
{
    // Your code goes here
}
```

The "//" construct is a comment and terminates at the end of the current line. "C"-type, multi-line comments—the /* and */ type—are also supported. However, unlike ANSI "C," **main()** does not return an integer value; it is declared void.

While this is a perfectly legal GLSL vertex- or fragment-shader program that compiles and even runs, its functionality leaves something to be desired. We will continue by describing variables and their operation.

Also, as with C and its derivative languages, statements are terminated with a semicolon.

## Declaring Variables

GLSL is a strongly typed language; that is, every variable must be declared and have an associated type. Variable names conform to the same rules as those for C: you can use letters, numbers, and the underscore character (_) to compose variable names. A digit cannot be the first character in a variable name.

Table 15-1 shows the three basic types available in GLSL.

| Type | Description |
| --- | --- |
| float | IEEE-like floating-point value |
| int | signed 16-bit integer value |
| bool | boolean value |

**Table 15-1**    Basic Data Types in GLSL

An additional set of types is named *samplers*, which are used as opaque handles for accessing texture maps. The various types of samplers and their uses are discussed in "Accessing Texture Maps in Shaders" on page 653.

> **Note:** An OpenGL implementation is not required to implement these types as stringently as one might like. As long as their operation is semantically and operationally correct, the underlying implementation may vary. For example, integers may be stored in floating-point registers. It is not a good idea to assume particular numeric outcomes, such as the maximum-sized integer value being $2^{15}$, based upon these types.

### Variable Scoping

While all variables must be declared, they may be declared any time before their use (unlike "C," where they must be the first statements in a block of code). The scoping rules of GLSL closely parallel those of C++:

* Variables declared outside of any function definition have global scope and are visible to all functions within the shader program.

* Variables declared within a set of curly braces (e.g., function definition, block following a loop or "if" statement, and so on) exist within the scope of those braces only.

* Loop iteration variables, such as *i* in the loop

```
for (int i = 0; i < 10; ++i) {
    // loop body
}
```

are only scoped for the body of the loop.

### Variable Initialization

Variables may also be initialized when declared. For example:

```
int    i, numParticles = 1500;
float  force, g = -9.8;
bool   falling = true;
```

Integer constants may be expressed as octal, decimal, or hexadecimal values. An optional minus sign before a numeric value negates the constant.

Floating-point values must include a decimal point, unless described in scientific format (e.g., 3E-7), and may optionally include an 'f' or 'F' suffix as in "C."

Boolean values are either *true* or *false*, and can be initialized to either of those values or as the result of a operation that resolves to a boolean expression.

## Constructors

As mentioned, GLSL is a strongly typed language, even more so than C++. In general, there is no implicit conversion between values, except in a few cases. For example,

```
int f = 10.0;
```

will result in a compilation error due to assigning a constant floating-point value to an integer variable. Integer values and vectors will be implicitly converted into the equivalent floating-point value or vector. Any other conversion of values requires using a conversion function (a C++-like constructor). For example,

```
float f = 10.0;
int   ten = int(f);
```

uses the **int()** function to do the conversion. Likewise, the other types also have conversion functions: **float()** and **bool()**. These functions also illustrate another feature of GLSL: operator overloading, whereby each function takes various input types, but all use the same base function name. We will discuss more on functions in a bit.

## Aggregate Types

Three of GLSL's primitive types can be combined to better match core OpenGL's data values and to ease computational operations.

First, GLSL supports vectors of two, three, or four dimensions for each of the primitive types. Also, matrices of floats are available. Table 15-2 lists the valid vector and matrix types.

| Base Type | 2-D vec | 3-D vec | 4-D vec | Matrix Types |
|---|---|---|---|---|
| *float* | *vec2* | *vec3* | *vec4* | *mat2, mat3, mat4*<br>*mat2x2, mat2x3, mat2x4,*<br>*mat3x2, mat3x3, mat3x4*<br>*mat4x2, mat4x3, mat4x4* |
| *int* | *ivec2* | *ivec3* | *ivec4* | — |
| *bool* | *bvec2* | *bvec3* | *bvec4* | — |

**Table 15-2**     GLSL Vector and Matrix Types

Matrix types that list both dimensions, such as *mat4x3*, use the first value to specify the number of columns, the second the number of rows.

Variables declared with these types can be initialized similar to their scalar counterparts:

```
vec3  velocity = vec3(0.0, 2.0, 3.0);
```

and converting between types is equally accessible:

```
ivec3 steps = ivec3(velocity);
```

Vector constructors can also be used to truncate or lengthen a vector. If a longer vector is passed into the constructor of a smaller vector, the vector is truncated to the appropriate length.

```
vec4 color;
vec3 RGB = vec3(color); // now RGB only has three elements
```

Likewise, vectors are lengthened in somewhat the same manner. Scalar values can be promoted to vectors, as in

```
vec3 white = vec3(1.0);   // white = ( 1.0, 1.0, 1.0 )
vec4 translucent = vec4(white, 0.5);
```

Matrices are constructed in the same manner and can be initialized to either a diagonal matrix or a fully populated matrix.

In the case of diagonal matrices, a single value is passed into the constructor, and the diagonal elements of the matrix are set to that value, with all others being set to zero, as in

$$m = mat3(4.0) = \begin{bmatrix} 4.0 & 0.0 & 0.0 \\ 0.0 & 4.0 & 0.0 \\ 0.0 & 0.0 & 4.0 \end{bmatrix}$$

Matrices can also be created by specifying the value of every element in the matrix in the constructor. Values can be specified by combinations of scalars and vectors, as long as enough values are provided, and each column is specified in the same manner. Additionally, matrices are specified in column-major order, meaning the values are used to populate columns before rows (which is the opposite of how "C" initializes two-dimensional arrays).

For example, we could initialize a 3 × 3 matrix in any of the following ways:

```
mat3 M = mat3(1.0,  2.0,  3.0,
              4.0,  5.0,  6.0,
              7.0,  8.0,  9.0 );

vec3 column1 = vec3(1.0,  2.0,  3.0);
vec3 column2 = vec3(4.0,  5.0,  6.0);
vec3 column3 = vec3(7.0,  8.0,  9.0);

mat3 M = mat3(column1, column2, column3);
```

or even

```
vec2 column1 = vec2(1.0,  2.0);
vec2 column2 = vec2(4.0,  5.0);
vec2 column3 = vec2(7.0,  8.0);

mat3 M = mat3(column1, 3.0,
              column2, 6.0,
              column3, 9.0);
```

all yielding the same matrix

$$M = \begin{bmatrix} 1.0 & 4.0 & 7.0 \\ 2.0 & 5.0 & 8.0 \\ 3.0 & 6.0 & 9.0 \end{bmatrix}$$

### Accessing Elements in Vectors and Matrices

The individual elements of vectors and matrices can be accessed and assigned. Vectors support two types of element access: a named-component method and an array-like method. Matrices use a two-dimensional array-like method.

Components of a vector can be accessed by name, as in

```
float red = color.r;
float v_y = velocity.y;
```

or using a zero-based index scheme. The following yield identical results to the above:

```
float red = color[0];
float v_y = velocity[1];
```

In fact, as shown in Table 15-3, there are three sets of component names available, all of which do the same thing. The multiple sets are useful for clarifying the operations that you're doing.

| Component Accessors | Description |
| --- | --- |
| (x, y, z, w) | components associated with positions |
| (r, g, b, a) | components associated with colors |
| (s, t, p, q) | components associated with texture coordinates |

**Table 15-3**    Vector Component Accessors

A common use for component-wise access to vectors is for *swizzling* components, as you might do with colors, perhaps for color space conversion. For example, you could do the following to specify a luminance value based on the red component of an input color:

```
vec3 luminance = color.rrr;
```

Likewise, if you needed to move components around in a vector, you might do:

```
color = color.abgr; // reverse the components of a color
```

The only restriction is that only one set of components can be used with a variable in one statement. That is, you can't do:

```
vec4 color = otherColor.rgz;   // Error: 'z' is from a
                               // different group
```

Also, a compile-time error will be raised if you attempt to access an element that's outside of what the type supports. For example,

```
vec2 pos;
float zPos = pos.z; // Error: no 'z' component in 2D vectors
```

Matrix elements can be accessed using the array notation. Either a single scalar value or an array of elements can be accessed from a matrix:

```
mat4 m = mat4(2.0);
vec4 zVec = m[2];
float yScale = m[1][1]; // or m[1].y works as well
```

## Structures

You can also logically group together collections of different types in a structure. Structures are convenient for passing groups of associated data into functions. When a structure is defined, it automatically creates a new type, and implicitly defines a constructor function that takes the types of the elements of the structure as parameters.

```
struct Particle {
    float lifetime;
    vec3 position;
    vec3 velocity;
};

Particle p = Particle(10.0, pos, vel); // pos, vel arc vec3's
```

Likewise, to reference elements of a structure, use the familiar "dot" notation as you would in "C."

## Arrays

GLSL also supports one-dimensional arrays of any type, including structures. As with "C," arrays are indexed using brackets ([ ]). The range of elements in an array of size *n* is 0 ... *n–1*. Unlike "C," however, negative array indices are not permitted, nor are two-dimensional arrays.

Arrays can be declared sized or unsized. You might use an unsized array as a forward declaration of an array variable and later redeclare it to the appropriate size. Array declarations use the bracket notation, as in:

```
float coeff[3]; // an array of 3 floats
float[3] coeff; // same thing
int   indices[]; // unsized. Redeclare later with a size
```

Arrays are first-class types in GLSL, meaning they have constructors and can be used as function parameters and return types. To statically initialize an array of values, you would use a constructor in the following manner:

```
float coeff[3] = float[3]( 2.38, 3.14, 42.0 );
```

The dimension value on the constructor is optional.

Additionally, similar to Java, GLSL arrays have an implicit method for reporting their number of elements: the **length**() method. If you would like

to operate on all the values in an array, here is an example using the
**length**() method:

```
for ( int i = 0; i < coeff.length(); ++i ) {
    coeff[i] *= 2.0;
}
```

## Storage Qualifiers

Types can also have modifiers that affect their behavior. There are four
modifiers defined in GLSL, as shown in Table 15-4.

| Type Modifier | Description |
| --- | --- |
| const | Labels a variable as a read-only, compile-time constant. |
| attribute | Specifies that the variable is associated with OpenGL vertex attributes set in the application |
| uniform | Specifies that the value is passed to the shader from the application and is constant across a given primitive |
| varying | Specifies that the variable is used both in a vertex and fragment shader program. Varying variables allows data to be passed from vertex programs to fragment programs. |
| centroid varying | The centroid varying version is used when multisampling is enabled and it forces the varying variable's value to be from a sample within the primitive being rendered. |

**Table 15-4**     GLSL Type Modifiers

All storage qualifiers are valid for globally scoped variables. Additionally,
*const* is applicable to local variables and function parameters.

### *Const* Storage Qualifier

Just as with "C," the *const* type modifier indicates that the variable is read-
only. For example, the statement

```
const float Pi = 3.141529
```

sets the variable *Pi* to an approximation of $\pi$. With the addition of the *const*
modifier, it becomes an error to write to a variable after its declaration, so
they must be initialized when declared.

### *Attribute* **Storage Qualifier**

The *attribute* modifier is used only with variables in vertex shaders. They are used for associating shader variables with per-vertex data passed in from the OpenGL application and must be declared global. We discuss the *attribute* modifier in more detail in "User-Defined Attribute Variables" on page 670.

### *Uniform* **Storage Qualifier**

The *uniform* modifier specifies that a variable's value will be specified by the application before the shader's execution and does not change across the primitive being processed. Uniform variables are shared between vertex and fragment shaders and must be declared as global variables. Any type of variable, including structures and arrays, can be specified as uniform.

Consider a shader that uses an additional color in shading a primitive. You might declare a uniform variable to pass that information into your shaders. In the shaders, you would make the declaration:

```
uniform vec4 BaseColor;
```

Within your shaders, you can reference *BaseColor* by name, but to set its value in your application, you need to do a little extra work. The GLSL compiler creates a table of all uniform variables when it links your shader program. To set *BaseColor*'s value from your application, you need to obtain the index of *BaseColor* in the table, which is done using the **glGetUniformLocation()** routine.

---

GLint **glGetUniformLocation**(GLuint *program*, const char *\*name*)

Returns the index of the uniform variable *name* associated with the shader *program*. *name* is a null-terminated character string with no spaces. A value of minus one (–1) is returned if *name* does not correspond to a uniform variable in the active shader *program*, or if a reserved shader variable name (those starting with gl_ prefix) is specified.

*name* can be a single variable name, an element of an array (by including the appropriate index in brackets with the name), or a field of a structure (by specifying *name*, then "." followed by the field name, as you would in the shader program). For arrays of uniform variables, the index of the first element of the array may be queried either by specifying only the array name (for example, "arrayName"), or by specifying the index to the first element of the array (as in "arrayName[0]").

The returned value will not change unless the shader program is relinked (see **glLinkProgram()**).

---

Once you have the associated index for the uniform variable, you can set the value of the uniform variable using the **glUniform\*()** or **glUniformMatrix\*()** routines.

---

void **glUniform**{1234}{if}(GLint *location, TYPE value*);
void **glUniform**{1234}{if}**v**(GLint *location*, GLsizei *count*, const *TYPE \*values*);
void **glUniformMatrix**{234}**fv**(GLint *location*, GLsizei *count*,
      GLboolean *transpose*, const GLfloat *\*values*);
void **glUniformMatrix**{2x3,2x4,3x2,3x4,4x2,4x3}**fv**(GLint *location*,
      GLsizei *count*, GLboolean *transpose*,
      const GLfloat *\*values*);

---

Sets the value for the uniform variable associated with the index *location*
The vector form loads *count* sets of values (from one to four values, depending upon which **glUniform\*()** call is used) into the uniform

variables starting *location*. If location is the start of an array, *count* sequential elements of the array are loaded.

The floating-point forms can be used to load a single float, a floating-point vector, an array of floats, or an array of vectors of floats.

The integer forms can be used to update a single integer, an integer vector, an array of integers, or an array of integer vectors. Additionally, individual and arrays of texture samplers can also be loaded.

For **glUniformMatrix**{234}**fv**(), *count* sets of $2 \times 2$, $3 \times 3$, or $4 \times 4$ matrices are loaded from *values*.

For **glUniformMatrix**{2x3,2x4,3x2,3x4,4x2,4x3}**fv**(), *count* sets of like-dimensioned matrices are loaded from *values*. If *transpose* is GL_TRUE, *values* are specified in row-major order (like arrays in "C"); or if GL_FALSE is specified, *values* are taken to be in column-major order (ordered in the same manner as **glLoadMatrix()**).

Example 15-3 demonstrates obtaining a uniform variable's index and assigning values.

**Example 15-3** Obtaining a Uniform Variable's Index and Assigning Values

```
GLint timeLoc; /* Uniform index for variable "time" in shader */
GLfloat timeValue; /* Application time */

timeLoc = glGetUniformLocation(program, "time");
glUniform1f(timeLoc, timeValue);
```

### *varying* **Storage Qualifier**

Quite often vertex and fragment shaders operate cooperatively. To pass data computed in a vertex shader to its matching fragment shader, or even back to the fixed-function pipeline, we'll use *varying* variables.

Varying variables are written in a vertex shader, and then OpenGL iterates those values across the primitive in a perspective-correct manner. Every time the fragment shader executes, the appropriate iterated values for that fragment are passed into the shader through the varying variables.

OpenGL defines a set of varying variables that are written in a vertex shader for passing data back to OpenGL, and another set of values that are passed into fragment shaders to be read and used in generating the final fragment color and depth values. We discuss the set of vertex varying variables in "Varying Output Variables" on page 674 and in "Input Values" on page 676 for the fragment shader variables.

The types of varying quantities are limited to GLSL's float, vector types (vec*), and matrix types (mat*), or arrays of those types. Integers, booleans, and structures cannot be declared varying.

Similar to uniform variables, varying values must be global variables, and their declaration must match between the vertex and fragment programs. For example,

```
varying float temperature;
```

would need to appear as a global in both the vertex and fragment shaders.

### *centroid varying* **Storage Qualifier**

Varying values are interpolated at pixel centers when multisampling is disabled. However, when multisampling is enabled, the varying value may be interpolated to anywhere within the pixel. This opens up the possibility that the interpolated value may not be within the primitive that invoked the shading of the fragment. To guarantee that the interpolated value lies within both the pixel being shaded and the primitive, the *centroid varying* storage qualifier may be used to qualify a variable. The *centroid* keyboard must immediately proceed the *varying* keyword on the variable's declaration, as in:

```
centroid varying vec2 texCoord;
```

## Computational Invariance

GLSL does not guarantee that two identical computations in different shaders will result in exactly the same value. The situation is no different than for computational applications executing on the CPU, where the order of compiled instructions may result in tiny differences due to the accumulation order of instructions. These tiny errors may be an issue for multipass algorithms that expect positions to be computed exactly the same for each shader pass. GLSL has a method of enforcing this type of invariance between shaders by using the *invariant* keyword.

### *invariant* **Qualifier**

The *invariant* qualifier may be applied to any output varying variables of a vertex shader. The variable may be a built-in variable or a user-defined one. For example:

```
invariant gl_Position;

invariant centroid varying vec3 Color;
```

As you may recall, varying variables are used to pass data from a vertex shader into a fragment shader. Invariant variables must be declared *invariant* in both the vertex and fragment shader. The *invariant* keyword may be applied at any time before use of the variable in the shader and may be used to modify previously declared variables.

For debugging, it may be useful to impose invariance on all varying variables in shader. This can be accomplished by using the vertex shader preprocessor pragma

```
#pragme STDGL invariant(all)
```

Global invariance in this manner is useful for debugging; however, it may likely have an impact on the shader's performance. Guaranteeing invariance usually disables optimizations that may have been performed by the GLSL compiler.

## Statements

The real work in a shader is done by computing values and making decisions. In the same manner as C++, GLSL has a rich set of operators for constructing arithmetic operations for computing values and a standard set of logical constructs for controlling shader execution.

## Arithmetic Operations

No text describing a language is complete without the mandatory table of operator precedence (see Table 15-5). The operators are ordered in decreasing precedence. In general, the types being operated on must be the same, and for vector and matrices, the operands must be of the same dimension.

| Precedence | Operators | Accepted Types | Description |
|---|---|---|---|
| 1 | ( ) | — | Grouping of operations |
| 2 | [] | arrays | Array subscripting |
| | f( ) | functions | Function calls and constructors |
| | . (period) | structures | Structure field or method access |
| | ++ -- | int, float, vec*, mat* | Post-increment and -decrement |
| 3 | ++ -- | int, float, vec*, mat* | Pre-increment and -decrement |
| | + - ! | int, float, vec*, mat* | Unary operations: explicit positive or negative value, negation |
| 4 | * / | int, float, vec*, mat* | Multiplicative operations |
| 5 | + - | int, float, vec*, mat* | Additive operations |
| 6 | < > <= >= | int, float, vec*, mat* | Relational operations |
| 7 | == != | int, float, vec*, mat* | Equality operations |
| 8 | && | bool | Logical and operation |
| 9 | ^^ | bool | Logical exclusive-or operation |
| 10 | \|\| | bool | Logical or operation |
| 11 | a ? b : c | bool int, float, vec*, mat* | Selection operation (inline "if" operation; if (a) then (b) else (c)) |
| 12 | = | int, float, vec*, mat* | Assignment |
| | += -= | | Arithmetic assignment |
| | *= /= | | |
| 13 | , (comma) | — | Sequence of operations |

**Table 15-5** GLSL Operators and Their Precedence

**Note:** This table lists all currently implemented operators of GLSL. Various operations that exist in C++ (%, the modulus operator, for example) are currently reserved but not implemented in GLSL.

## Overload Operators

Most operators in GLSL are *overloaded*, meaning that they operate on a varied set of types. Specifically, arithmetic operations (including pre- and post-increment and -decrement) for vectors and matrices are well-defined in GLSL. For example, to multiply a vector and a matrix (recalling that the order of terms is important—matrix multiplication is non-commutative, for all you math-heads), use the following operation:

```
vec3 v;
mat3 m;
vec3 result = v * m;
```

The normal restrictions apply, that the dimensionality of the matrix and the vector must match. Additionally, scalar multiplication with a vector and matrix will produce the expected result. One notable exception is that the multiplication of two vectors will result in component-wise multiplication of components; however, multiplying two matrices will result in normal matrix multiplication.

```
vec2 a, b, c;
mat2 m, u, v;
c = a * b; //c = ( a.x*b.x, a.y*b.y )
m = u * v; //m = ( u₀₀*v₀₀+u₀₁*v₁₀  u₀₀*v₀₁+u₀₁*v₁₁
                    u₀₁*v₀₀+u₁₁*v₁₀  u₁₀*v₀₁+u₁₁*v₁₁ )
```

Additional common vector operations (e.g., dot and cross products) are supported by function calls, as well as various per-component operations on vectors and matrices.

## Logical Operations

GLSL's only logical control structure is the if-then-else statement. As with "C," the else clause is optional, and multiple statements require a block.

```
if ( truth ) {
    // true clause
} else {
    // false clause
}
```

There is no switch statement as in "C."

## Looping Constructs

GLSL supports the familiar "C" form of **for, while,** and **do ... while** loops.

The **for** loop permits the declaration of the loop iteration variable in the initialization clause of the **for** loop. The scope of iteration variables declared in this manner is only for the lifetime of the loop.

```
for (int i = 0; i < 10; ++i ) {
    . . .
}

while (n < 10) {
    . . .
}

do {
    . . .
} while (n < 10);
```

## Flow Control Statements

Additional control statements beyond conditionals and loops are available in GLSL. Table 15-6 describes available flow-control statements.

| Statement | Description |
| --- | --- |
| break | Terminates execution of the block of a loop, and continues execution after the scope of that block. |
| continue | Terminates the current iteration of the enclosing block of a loop, resuming execution with the next iteration of the loop. |
| return [result] | Returns from the current subroutine, optionally providing a value to be returned from the function (assuming return value matches the return type of the enclosing function). |
| discard | Discards the current fragment and ceases shader execution. Discard statements are only valid in fragment shader programs. |

**Table 15-6**    GLSL Flow-Control Statements

The discard statement is available only in fragment programs. The execution of the fragment shader may be terminated at the execution of the discard statement, but this is implementation dependent.

## Functions

Functions permit you to replace occurrences of common code with a function call. This, of course, allows for smaller code, and less chances for errors. GLSL defines a number of built-in functions, which are listed in Appendix I, "Built-In OpenGL Shading Language Variables and Functions," as well as support for user-defined functions. User-defined functions can be defined in a single shader object, and reused in multiple shader programs.

### Declarations

Function declaration syntax is very similar to "C," with the exception of the access modifiers on variables:

```
returnType functionName([accessModifier] type1 variable1,
                        [accessModifier] type2 varaible2,
                        ... )
{
    // function body
    return returnValue; // unless returnType is void
}
```

Function names can be any combination of letters, numbers, and the underscore character, with the exception that it can neither begin with a digit nor with `gl_`.

Return types can be any built-in GLSL type and user-defined structure; arrays are not available as return values. If a function doesn't return a value, its return type is `void`.

Parameters to functions can be of any type, including arrays (which must specify their size).

Functions must be either declared, or prototyped, before their use. Just as in C++, the compiler must have seen the function's definition before its use or an error will be raised. If a function is used in a shader object other than the one where it's defined, a prototype must be declared. A prototype is merely the function's signature without its accompanying body. Here's a simple example:

```
float HornerEvalPolynomial(float coeff[10], float x);
```

### Parameters Access Modifiers

While functions in GLSL are able to modify and return values after their execution, there's no concept of a pointer or reference, as in "C" or C++.

Rather, parameters of functions have associated access modifiers indicating if the value should be copied into, or out of, a function after execution. Table 15-7 describes the available parameter access modifiers in GLSL.

| Access Modifier | Description |
|---|---|
| in | value copied into a function (default if not specified) |
| const in | read-only value copied into a function |
| out | value copied out of a function (undefined upon entrance into the function) |
| inout | value copied into and out of a function |

**Table 15-7**    GLSL Function Parameter Access Modifiers

The in keyword is optional. If a variable does not include an access modifier, then an "in" modifier is implicitly added to the parameter's declaration. However, if the variable's value needs to be copied out of a function, it must either be tagged with an "out" (for write-only variables) or an "inout" (for read-write variables). Writing to an variable not tagged with one of these modifiers will generate a compile-time error.

Additionally, to verify at compile time that a function doesn't modify an input-only variable, adding a "const in" modifier will cause the compiler to check that the variable is not written to in the function.

## Using OpenGL State Values in GLSL Programs

Almost all values that you set in using the OpenGL API are accessible from within vertex and fragment shader programs. A comprehensive list of GLSL built-in variables is provided in Appendix I, "Built-In OpenGL Shading Language Variables and Functions."

# Accessing Texture Maps in Shaders

GLSL also supports accessing texture maps in both vertex and fragment shaders. Implementations can choose to support texture mapping in vertex shaders (provided the underlying OpenGL implementation supports this functionality), but requires support for fragment shaders.

To access a texture map, GLSL makes an association between an active texture unit (see "Steps in Multitexturing" in Chapter 9) configured in the OpenGL application, and a variable declared in a shader. Such variables use one of the *sampler* data types shown in Table 15-8 to allow the shader program access to the texture map's data. The dimensions of the associated texture map must match the type of the sampler.

| Sampler Name | Description |
| --- | --- |
| sampler1D | Accesses a 1D texture map |
| sampler2D | Accesses a 2D texture map |
| sampler3D | Accesses a 3D texture map |
| samplerCube | Accesses a cube map (for reflection mapping) |
| sampler1DShadow | Accesses a 1D shadow map |
| sampler2DShadow | Accesses a 2D shadow map |

**Table 15-8**    Fragment Shader Texture Sampler Types

Samplers must be declared as uniform variables in the shader and must have their value assigned from within the OpenGL application. Samplers may also be used as parameters in functions, but must be used with samplers of matching type.

Samplers must have a texture unit assigned to them before their use in a shader, and can only be initialized by **glUniform1i()**, or **glUniform1iv()**, with the index of the texture unit that the sampler should use (see Example 15-4).

**Example 15-4**    Associating Texture Units with Sampler Variables

```
GLint texSampler; /* sampler index for shader variable "tex" */

texSampler = glGetUniformLocation(program, "tex");
glUniform1i(texSampler, 2); /* Set "tex" to use GL_TEXTURE2 */
```

### Accessing Textures in GLSL

Sampling a texture map from within a GLSL shader uses the sampler variable that you've declared and associated with a texture unit. There are a number of texture access routines (described in "Texture Lookup Functions" in Appendix I) for accessing all OpenGL supported texture map types.

In Example 15-5, we sample the two-dimensional texture map associated with the sampler2D variable *tex*, and combine the results with the fragment's color, providing the same results as using GL_MODULATE mode for the texture environment mode.

**Example 15-5** Sampling a Texture Within a GLSL Shader

```
uniform sampler2D tex;

void main()
{
    gl_FragColor = gl_Color * texture2D(tex, gl_TexCoord[0].st);
}
```

Even though the example seems simple, that's truly all there is to do. However, much more interesting applications are enabled when the values in a texture map do not necessarily represent colors, but other data used for subsequent computation after retrieving the results from the texture map. Specifically, one application is using the values in one texture map as indices into another, described in "Dependent Texture Reads" on page 655. The same results can be accomplished using the combiner texture environment (see "Texture Combiner Functions" in Chapter 9), but are much simpler to do using shaders.

The results you compute after sampling a texture are controlled by the code you write in your shader, but how the texture map is sampled is still controlled by the state settings in your application. For example, you control whether a texture map contains mipmaps, and how those mipmaps are sampled, as well as the filters used for resolving the returned texel values (basically, the parameters you set with **glTexParameter*()**). From inside the shader, you can control the biasing of mipmap selection, and using projective-texture techniques (see Appendix I for details and suitable functions).

## Dependent Texture Reads

During the execution of a shader that employs texture mapping, you'll use texture coordinates to specify locations in texture maps and retrieve the resulting texel values. While texture coordinates are supplied for each active texture unit, you can use any values you might like as texture coordinates (assuming matching dimensionality) for use with a sampler, including values you may have just sampled from another texture map. Passing the results of one texture access as texture coordinates into another texture access operation is generally termed a *dependent texture read*, indicating that the results of the second operation are dependent on the first operation.

This is easy to implement in GLSL and is illustrated in Example 15-6.

**Example 15-6** Dependent Texture Reads in GLSL

```
uniform sampler1D coords;
uniform sampler3D volume;

void main()
{
    vec3 texCoords = texture1D(coords, gl_TexCoord[0].s);
    vec3 volumeColor = texture3D(volume, texCoords);
    ...
}
```

# Shader Preprocessor

The first step in compilation of a GLSL shader is parsing by the preprocessor. Similar to the "C" preprocessor, there are a number of directives for creating conditional compilation blocks and defining values. However, unlike the "C" preprocessor, there is no file inclusion (`#include`).

## Preprocessor Directives

Table 15-9 lists the preprocessor directives accepted by the GLSL preprocessor and their functions.

| Preprocessor Directive | Description |
| --- | --- |
| `#define`<br>`#undef` | Control the definition of constants and macros similar to the C preprocessor |
| `#if`<br>`#ifdef`<br>`#ifndef` | Conditional code management similar to the C preprocessor, including the **defined** operator. |
| `#else`<br>`#elif`<br>`#endif` | Conditional expressions evaluate integer expressions and defined values (as specified by `#define`) only. |

**Table 15-9**    GLSL Preprocessor Directives

| Preprocessor Directive | Description |
| --- | --- |
| `#error text` | Cause the compiler to insert *text* (up to the first newline character) into the shader information log |
| `#pragma options` | Control compiler specific options |
| `#extension options` | Specify compiler operation with respect to specified GLSL extensions |
| `#version number` | Mandate a specific version of GLSL version support |
| `#line options` | Control diagnostic line numbering |

**Table 15-9** (continued)     GLSL Preprocessor Directives

## Macro Definition

The GLSL preprocessor allows macro definition in much the same manner as the "C" preprocessor, with the exception of the string substitution and concatenation facilities. Macros might define a single value, as in

```
#define NUM_ELEMENTS 10
```

or with parameters like

```
#define LPos(n) gl_LightSource[(n)].position
```

Additionally, there are several predefined macros for aiding in diagnostic messages (that you might issue with the `#error` directive, for example), as shown in Table 15-10.

| Macro | Definition |
| --- | --- |
| \_\_LINE\_\_ | Line number defined by the number of newline characters processed and modified by `#line` directive |
| \_\_FILE\_\_ | Source string number currently being processed |
| \_\_VERSION\_\_ | Integer representation of the OpenGL Shading Language version. |

**Table 15-10**     GLSL Preprocessor Predefined Macros

Likewise, macros (excluding those defined by GLSL) may be undefined by using the #undef directive. For example

```
#undef LPos
```

## Preprocessor Conditionals

Identical to the processing by the "C" preprocessor, the GLSL preprocessor provides conditional code inclusion based on macro definition and integer constant evaluation.

Macro definition may be determined in two ways: Either using the #ifdef directive

```
#ifdef NUM_ELEMENTS
...
#endif
```

or using the **defined** operator with the #if or #elif directives

```
#if defined(NUM_ELEMENTS) && NUM_ELEMENTS > 3
...
#elif NUM_ELEMENTS < 7
...
#endif
```

## Compiler Control

The #pragma directive provides the compiler additional information regarding how you would like your shaders compiled.

### Optimization Compiler Option

The optimize option instructs the compiler to enable or disable optimization of the shader from the point where the directive resides forward in the shader source. You can enable or disable optimization by issuing either

```
#pragma optimize(on)
```

and

```
#pragma optimize(off)
```

respectively. These options may only be issued outside of a function definition. By default, optimization is enabled for all shaders.

### Debug Compiler Option

The `debug` option enables or disables additional diagnostic output of the shader. You can enable or disable debugging by issuing either

```
#pragma debug(on)
```

and

```
#pragma debug(off)
```

respectively. Similar to the `optimize` option, these options may only be issued outside of a function definition, and by default, debugging is disabled for all shaders.

### Global Shader Compilation Option

One final `#pragma` directive is available, `STDGL`. This option is currently used to enable invariance in the output of varying values. See "invariant Qualifier" on page 656 for details.

## Extension Processing

GLSL, like OpenGL itself, may be enhanced by extensions. As vendors may include extensions specific to their OpenGL implementation, it's useful to have some control over shader compilation in light of possible extensions that a shader may use.

The GLSL preprocessor uses the `#extension` directive to provide instructions to the shader compiler regarding how extension availability should be handled during compilation. For any, or all, extensions, you can specify how you would like the compiler to proceed with compilation.

```
#extension extension_name : <directive>
```

where *extensions_name* uses the same extension name returned by calling **glGetString**(GL_EXTENSIONS) or

```
#extension all : <directive>
```

to affect the behavior of all extensions.

The options available are shown in Table 15-11.

| Directive | Description |
| --- | --- |
| require | Flag an error if the extension is not supported, or if the all extension specification is used. |
| enable | Give a warning if the particular extensions specified are not supported, or flag an error if the all extension specification is used. |
| warn | Give a warning if the particular extensions specified are not supported, or give a warning if any extension use is detected during compilation. |
| disable | Disable support for the particular extensions listed (that is, have the compiler act as if the extension is not supported even if it is) or all extensions if all is present, issuing warnings and errors as if the extension were not present. |

**Table 15-11**    GLSL Extension Directive Modifiers

## Vertex Shader Specifics

You can send data from your application into a vertex program using several mechanisms:

- By using the standard OpenGL vertex data interface (those calls that are legal between a **glBegin()** and a **glEnd()**), such as **glVertex*()**, **glNormal*()**, and so on. These values can vary on a per-vertex basis and are considered to be built-in attribute variables.

- By declaring uniform variables. These values remain constant across a geometric primitive.

- By declaring attribute variables, which can be updated on a per-vertex basis, in addition to the standard vertex state.

Likewise, a vertex program must output some data (and optionally update other variables) for continued processing by the remaining vertex processing by the OpenGL pipeline, and possibly an accompanying fragment program.

The outputs that need to be written include:

- `gl_Position`, which must be updated by the vertex program and contain the homogeneous coordinate of the vertex after modelview and projection transformation.

- Various other built-in variables that are declared varying for passing data into the fragment pipeline. These include colors, texture coordinates, and other per-fragment data. They are described in "Varying Output Variables" on page 674.

- User-defined varying variables.

Figure 15-5 illustrates the inputs and outputs of a vertex program.

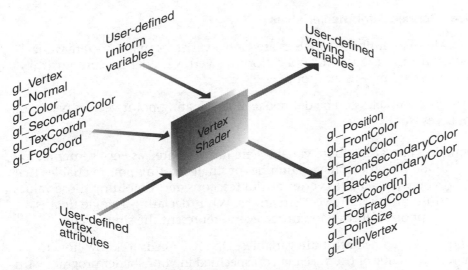

**Figure 15-5**    GLSL Vertex Shader Input and Output Variables

### Built-In Attribute Input Variables

Table 15-12 shows variables representing those that are globally available in a vertex shader. The variables reflect the current OpenGL state, as set by the corresponding routine.

| Variable | Type | Specifying function | Description |
|---|---|---|---|
| gl_Vertex | vec4 | **glVertex** | Vertex's world-space coordinate |
| gl_Color | vec4 | **glColor** | Primary color value |
| gl_SecondaryColor | vec4 | **glSecondaryColor** | Secondary color value |
| gl_Normal | vec4 | **glNormal** | Lighting normal |
| gl_MultiTexCoordn | vec4 | **glMultiTexCoord( $n$, ... );** | Texture unit $n$'s texture coordinates, with $n = 0$ ... 7. |
| gl_FogCoord | float | **glFogCoord** | Fog coordinate |

**Table 15-12**   Vertex Shader Attribute Global Variables

### User-Defined Attribute Variables

User-defined attribute variables are global variables that associate values passed from the OpenGL application to a vertex shader executing within the OpenGL implementation.

Attribute variables can be defined as float, floating-point vectors (vec*), or matrices (mat*).

**Hint:** In general, attribute variables are implemented as vec4's internal to OpenGL. If you have a number of single floating-point variables that you wish to use as vertex attributes, consider combining those values into one or more vec* structures. While declaring a single float is supported, it uses an entire vec4 to represent the single value.

To use user-defined attribute variables, OpenGL needs to know how to match the name of the variable you specified in your shader program with values that you pass into a shader. Similar to how OpenGL handles uniform variables, when a shader program is linked, the linker generates a table of variable names for attribute variables. To determine the maximum number of user-defined vertex attributes, call **glGetIntegerv()** with a parameter of GL_MAX_VERTEX_ATTRIBS.

To determine which index you need to update for the respective variable in the vertex program, you'll call **glGetAttribLocation()**, with the name of your variable, and the index corresponding to that name will be returned.

---

GLint **glGetAttribLocation**(GLuint *program*, const char *\*name*);

Returns the index associated with *name* for the shader *program*. *name* must be a null-terminated character string matching the declaration in *program*. If *name* is not an active variable, or it's the name of a built-in attribute variable, or an error occurs, a value of –1 is returned.

---

For example, in a vertex shader, you might declare

```
varying vec3 displacement;
```

Assuming that the shader compiled and linked appropriately, you would determine the index of "displacement" by calling:

```
int index = glGetAttribLocation(program, "displacement");
```

You can also explicitly set the binding of an attribute variable to an index using the **glBindAttribLocation()** call; however, this must be done before the shader program is linked.

---

void **glBindAttribLocation**(GLint *program*, GLuint *index*,
                              const char *\*name*);

Explicitly specifies which *index* location *name* should be assigned the next time *program* is linked. *index* must be an integer between zero and GL_MAX_VERTEX_ATTRIBS – 1, and *name* must be a null-terminated string. Built-in attribute variables (those beginning with `gl_`) will generate a GL_INVALID_OPERATION error.

---

To set the value associated with the returned index, you'll use a version of the **glVertexAttrib*()** function.

---

void **glVertexAttrib**{1234}{sfd}(GLuint *index*, *TYPE values*);
void **glVertexAttrib**{123}{sfd}**v**(GLuint *index*, const *TYPE *values*);
void **glVertexAttrib4**{bsifd ub us ui}**v**(GLuint *index*, *TYPE values*);
void **glVertexAttrib4Nub**(GLuint *index*, *TYPE values*);
void **glVertexAttrib4N**{bsi ub us ui}**v**(GLuint *index*, const *TYPE *values*);

Specifies the values for vertex attribute variables associated with *index* to *values*. For calls that do not explicitly set all four values, default values of 0.0 will be set for the *y*- and *z*-coordinates, and 1.0 for the *w*-coordinate.

---

Specifying values for *index* zero is identical to calling **glVertex\*()**, with the same values.

The normalized version will convert integer input values into the range zero to one, using the mappings specified in Table 4-1 on page 178.

Matrices are updated by specifying consecutive values for *index*. *values* specified will be used to update the respective columns of the matrix.

While attribute variables are floating point, there's no restriction on the type of input data used to initialize their values. Specifically, integer-type input values can be normalized into the range of zero to one, using **glVertexAttrib4N\*()**, before being assigned into the attribute variable.

Scalar (single-value), vector, and matrix attribute values can be set using **glVertexAttrib\*()**. For the matrix case, multiple calls are required. In particular, for a matrix of dimension *n*, you would call **glVertexAttrib\*()**, with indices: *index, index+1, ..., index+n–1*.

Vertex shaders also augment the vertex array facility (see "Vertex Arrays" on page 65). As with other types of vertex data, values for vertex attribute variables can be stored in vertex arrays and updated by calling **glDrawArrays()**, **glArrayElement()**, and so on. To specify the array to be used to update a variable's value, call **glVertexAttribPointer()**.

---

void **glVertexAttribPointer**(GLuint *index*, GLint *size*, GLenum *type*, GLboolean *normalized*, GLsizei *stride*, const GLvoid\* *pointer*);

---

Specifies where the data values for *index* can be accessed. *pointer* is the memory address of the first set of values in the array. *size* represents the number of components to be updated per vertex. *type* specifies the data type (GL_SHORT, GL_INT, GL_FLOAT, or GL_DOUBLE) of each element in the array. *normalized* indicates that the vertex data should be normalized before being stored (in the same manner as **glVertexAttrib4N\*()**). *stride* is the byte offset between consecutive elements in the array. If *stride* is 0, the data is assumed to be tightly packed.

As with other types of vertex arrays, specifying the array is only one part of the process. Each client-side vertex array needs to be enabled. Compared to using **glEnableClientState()**, arrays of vertex attributes are enabled by calling **glEnableVertexAttribArray()**.

```
void glEnableVertexAttribArray(GLuint index);
void glDisableVertexAttribArray(GLuint index);
```

Specifies that the vertex array associated with variable *index* be enabled or disabled. *index* must be a value between 0 and GL_MAX_VERTEX_ATTRIBS − 1.

## Special Output Variables

The values shown in Table 15-13 are available for writing (and reading after being written) in a vertex shader. gl_Position specifies the vertex's final position upon exit of the vertex shader and is required to be written in the shader.

| Variable Name | Type | Description |
| --- | --- | --- |
| gl_Position | vec4 | Transformed vertex position (in eye coordinates) |
| gl_PointSize | float | Point size of vertex |
| gl_ClipVertex | vec4 | Vertex position to be used with user-defined clipping planes. This value must be in the same coordinate system as the clipping planes: eye-coordinates, or object-coordinates |

**Table 15-13**     Vertex Shader Special Global Variables

While you're able to set the output vertex position to any homogenous coordinate you might like, the final value of gl_Position is usually computed within a vertex program as:

```
gl_Position = gl_ModelViewProjectionMatrix * gl_Vertex;
```

Or, if you're employing a multipass algorithm (one rendering multiple images from the same geometry) that needs to have the results of the vertex shader and fixed function pipeline be consistent, set gl_Position using the following code:

```
gl_Position = ftransform();
```

gl_PointSize controls the output size of a point, similar to **glPointSize()**, but on a per-vertex basis. To control the size of points from within vertex programs, call **glEnable()** with a value of GL_VERTEX_PROGRAM_POINT_SIZE, which overrides any current point size that may have been specified.

User-defined clipping planes, as specified by **glClipPlane()**, can be used by writing a homogeneous coordinate into the `gl_ClipVertex` variable. For clipping to proceed correctly, the clipping plane specified and the coordinate written into `gl_ClipVertex` must be in the same coordinate space. The common space for clipping is eye-coordinates. You can transform the current vertex into eye-coordinates for clipping by executing:

```
gl_ClipVertex = gl_ModelViewMatrix * gl_Vertex;
```

### Varying Output Variables

Table 15-14 represents those variables that can be written to in a vertex shader and have their values readable in a fragment shader. The values in the fragment shader are iterated across the fragments (or samples, if multisampling) of the primitives.

| Variable Name | Type | Description |
|---|---|---|
| gl_FrontColor | vec4 | Primary color to be used for front-facing primitives |
| gl_BackColor | vec4 | Primary color to be used for back-facing primitives |
| gl_FrontSecondaryColor | vec4 | Secondary color to be used for front-facing primitives |
| gl_BackSecondaryColor | vec4 | Secondary color to be used for back-facing primitives |
| gl_TexCoord[$n$] | vec4 | $n^{\text{th}}$ Texture coordinate values |
| gl_FogFragCoord | vec4 | Fragment fog coordinate value |

**Table 15-14**   Vertex Shader Varying Global Variables

A vertex shader has the capability of setting both the front- and back-face color values for a vertex. Be default, regardless of the values set from within a vertex shader, the front-facing color will be chosen. This behavior can be modified by calling **glEnable()**, with a value of GL_VERTEX_PROGRAM_TWO_SIDE, which causes OpenGL to select colors based on the orientation of the underlying primitive.

### Texture Mapping in Vertex Shaders

Texture mapping is available in vertex shaders, but at the time of this writing, it is not a required feature. Nonetheless, using textures in vertex shaders is identical to the process described in "Accessing Textures in GLSL" on page 662 with one minor exception. Automatic mipmap selection is not done in vertex shaders. However, you can manually select which mipmap level using the **texture*Lod** routines in GLSL.

To determine if your implementation is capable of using textures in vertex shaders, query GL_MAX_VERTEX_TEXTURE_IMAGE_UNITS using **glIntegerv()**. If a non-zero value is returned, texturing is supported.

## Fragment Shaders

Like vertex programs, your OpenGL application can send data directly to a fragment program, as well as having OpenGL provide values for use in your program. All of that data, along with the inputs into a fragment shader, result in the final color and depth value of a fragment. After execution of a fragment shader, the computed values continue through the OpenGL fragment pipeline to the fragment test and blending stages.

Figure 15-6 describes the inputs and outputs of a fragment programs.

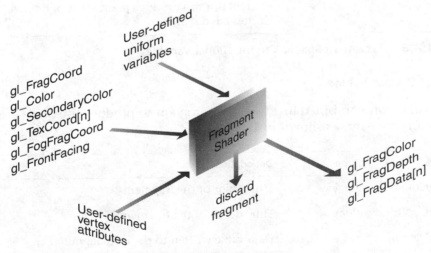

**Figure 15-6**    Fragment Shader Built-In Variables

## Input Values

Fragment shaders receive the iterated values of the final vertex pipeline outputs. These include the fragment's position, resolved primary and secondary colors, a set of texture coordinates, and a fog coordinate distance for the fragment. All of these values are described in Table 15-15.

| Variable | Type | Description |
|---|---|---|
| gl_FragCoord | vec4 | (Read only) Position of the fragment, including the z-component, which represents the fixed-function computed depth value |
| gl_FrontFacing | bool | (Read only) Specifies if the fragment belongs to a front-facing primitive |
| gl_Color | vec4 | Primary color of the fragment |
| gl_SecondayColor | vec4 | Secondary color of the fragment |
| gl_TexCoord[$n$] | vec4 | $n^{th}$ texture coordinates for the fragment |
| gl_FogFragCoord | float | Fragment's fog coordinate, either specified as the z-coordinate of the primitive in eye space or the interpolated fog coordinate |
| gl_PointCoord | vec2 | Fragment's location for a point sprite in the range [0.0, 1.0]. The value is undefined if the current primitive is not a point sprite or if point sprites are disabled |

**Table 15-15**   Fragment Shader Varying Global Variables

## Special Output Values

Input values are combined in a fragment program to produce the final values for fragment, as shown in Table 15-16.

| Variable | Type | Description |
|---|---|---|
| gl_FragColor | vec4 | Final color of the fragment |
| gl_FragDepth | float | Final depth of the fragment |
| gl_FragData[$n$] | vec4 | Data value written to the $n^{th}$ data buffer |

**Table 15-16**   Fragment Shader Output Global Variables

`gl_FragColor` is the final color of the fragment. While writing to `gl_FragColor` isn't required output from a fragment program, the results of the final fragment color for writing into the color buffer are undefined.

`gl_FragDepth` is the final depth of the fragment and is utilized in the depth test. While you cannot modify the *(x, y)* coordinate of a fragment, the depth value can be modified.

Finally, additional data may be written from a fragment program. The `gl_FragData` array allows for the writing of various data into extra buffers, as described below.

### Rendering to Multiple Output Buffers

A fragment shader may output values to multiple buffers simultaneously using the `gl_FragData` array. Writing a value into array element `gl_FragData[n]` will cause the color to be written into the appropriate fragment in the buffer in element *n* of the array passed to **glDrawBuffers()**.

A fragment shader may write to either `gl_FragColor` or `gl_FragData` in a shader, but not both.

# Order of Operations

This book describes all the operations performed between initial specification of vertices and final writing of fragments into the framebuffer. The chapters of this book are arranged in an order that facilitates learning, rather than in the exact order in which these operations are actually performed. Sometimes the exact order of operations doesn't matter—for example, surfaces can be converted to polygons and then transformed, or transformed first and then converted to polygons, with identical results—and different implementations of OpenGL might do things differently.

This appendix describes a possible order; any implementation is required to yield equivalent results. If you want more details than are presented here, see the *OpenGL Reference Manual*.

This appendix has the following major sections:

- "Overview"
- "Geometric Operations"
- "Pixel Operations"
- "Fragment Operations"
- "Odds and Ends"

# Overview

This section gives an overview of the order of operations, as shown in Figure A-1. Geometric data (vertices, lines, and polygons) follows the path through the row of boxes that include evaluators and per-vertex operations, while pixel data (pixels, images, and bitmaps) is treated differently for part of the process. Both types of data undergo the rasterization and per-fragment operations before the final pixel data is written into the framebuffer.

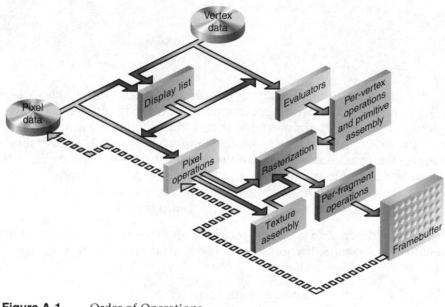

**Figure A-1**      Order of Operations

All data, whether it describes geometry or pixels, can be saved in a display list or processed immediately. When a display list is executed, the data is sent from the display list just as if it were sent by the application.

All geometric primitives are eventually described by vertices. If evaluators are used, that data is converted to vertices and treated as vertices from then on. Vertex data may also be stored in and used from specialized vertex arrays. Per-vertex calculations are performed on each vertex, followed by rasterization to fragments. For pixel data, pixel operations are performed, and the results are stored in the texture memory, used for polygon stippling, or rasterized to fragments.

Finally, the fragments are subjected to a series of per-fragment operations, after which the final pixel values are drawn into the framebuffer.

# Geometric Operations

Geometric data, whether it comes from a display list, an evaluator, or the vertices of a rectangle, or is in the form of raw data, consists of a set of vertices and the type of primitive it describes (a vertex, line, or polygon). Vertex data includes not only the $(x, y, z, w)$ coordinates, but also a normal vector, texture coordinates, an RGBA color, a color index, material properties, and edge-flag data. All these elements except the vertex's coordinates can be specified in any order, and default values exist as well. As soon as the vertex command **glVertex\*()** is issued, the components are padded, if necessary, to four dimensions (using $z = 0$ and $w = 1$), and the current values of all the elements are associated with the vertex. The complete set of vertex data is then processed. (If vertex arrays are used, vertex data may be batch processed, and processed vertices may be reused.)

## Per-Vertex Operations

In the fixed-function pipeline mode, the per-vertex operations stage of processing, each vertex's spatial coordinates are transformed by the modelview matrix, while the normal vector is transformed by that matrix's inverse transpose and renormalized if specified. If automatic texture generation is enabled, new texture coordinates are generated from the transformed vertex coordinates, and they replace the vertex's old texture coordinates. The texture coordinates are then transformed by the current texture matrix and passed on to the primitive assembly step.

Meanwhile, the lighting calculations, if enabled, are performed using the transformed vertex and normal vector coordinates and the current material, lights, and lighting model. These calculations generate new colors or indices that are clamped or masked to the appropriate range and passed on to the primitive assembly step.

For vertex shader programs, the above sequence of operations is replace by the execution of the user-defined shader, which must update the vertex's position, and may update the primary and secondary colors for the primitives front- and back-facing colors, associated texture coordinates, and fog coordinates. Additionally, the point size, and vertex position to be used with user-defined clip planes may also be updated.

## Primitive Assembly

Primitive assembly varies, depending on whether the primitive is a point, a line, or a polygon. If flat shading is enabled, the colors or indices of all the vertices in a line or polygon are set to the same value. If special clipping planes are defined and enabled, they're used to clip primitives of all three types. (The clipping-plane equations are transformed by the inverse transpose of the modelview matrix when they're specified.) Point clipping simply passes or rejects vertices; line or polygon clipping can add additional vertices, depending on how the line or polygon is clipped. After this clipping, the spatial coordinates of each vertex are transformed by the projection matrix, and the results are clipped against the standard viewing planes $x = \pm w$, $y = \pm w$, and $z = \pm w$.

If selection is enabled, any primitive not eliminated by clipping generates a selection-hit report, and no further processing is performed. Without selection, perspective division by $w$ occurs and the viewport and depth-range operations are applied. Also, if the primitive is a polygon, it's then subjected to a culling test (if culling is enabled). A polygon might convert to vertices or lines, depending on the polygon mode.

Finally, points, lines, and polygons are rasterized to fragments, taking into account polygon or line stipples, line width, and point size. Rasterization involves determining which squares of an integer grid in window coordinates are occupied by the primitive. If antialiasing is enabled, coverage (the portion of the square that is occupied by the primitive) is also computed. Color and depth values are also assigned to each such square. If polygon offset is enabled, depth values are slightly modified by a calculated offset value.

# Pixel Operations

Pixels from host memory are first unpacked into the proper number of components. The OpenGL unpacking facility handles a number of different formats. Next, the data is scaled, biased, and processed using a pixel map. The results are clamped to an appropriate range, depending on the data type, and then either written in the texture memory for use in texture mapping or rasterized to fragments.

If pixel data is read from the framebuffer, pixel-transfer operations (scale, bias, mapping, and clamping) are performed. The results are packed into an appropriate format and then returned to processor memory.

The pixel-copy operation is similar to a combination of the unpacking and transfer operations, except that packing and unpacking are unnecessary, and only a single pass is made through the transfer operations before the data is written back into the framebuffer.

## Texture Memory

OpenGL Version 1.1 provides additional control over texture memory. Texture images can be specified from framebuffer memory, as well as processor memory. All or a portion of a texture image may be replaced. Texture data may be stored in texture objects, which can be loaded into texture memory. If there are too many texture objects to fit into texture memory at the same time, the textures that have the highest priorities remain in the texture memory.

# Fragment Operations

In the fixed-function mode, if texturing is enabled, a texel is generated from texture memory for each fragment and applied to the fragment. Then fog calculations are performed, if they're enabled, followed by the application of coverage (antialiasing) values, if antialiasing is enabled.

If a fragment shader program is enabled, texture sampling and application, per-pixel fog computations, and alpha-value assignment may be done in the fragment shader. Assuming the fragment was not discarded by the fragment shader, the fragment's color will be updated with the color assigned in the fragment shader, which may include the combination of colors generated from the iterated primary and secondary colors, texture application, fog computations, or other color values. The depth value for the fragment may be also be updated and any associated fragment data may also be updated.

Next comes scissoring, followed by the alpha test (in RGBA mode only), the stencil test, and the depth-buffer test. If in RGBA mode, blending is performed. Blending is followed by dithering and logical operation. All these operations may be disabled.

The fragment is then masked by a color mask or an index mask, depending on the mode, and drawn into the appropriate buffer. If fragments are being written into the stencil or depth buffer, masking occurs after the stencil and depth tests, and the results are drawn into the framebuffer without performing the blending, dithering, or logical operation.

## Odds and Ends

Matrix operations deal with the current matrix stack, which can be the modelview, the projection, or the texture matrix stack. The commands **glMultMatrix*()**, **glLoadMatrix*()**, and **glLoadIdentity()** are applied to the top matrix on the stack, while **glTranslate*()**, **glRotate*()**, **glScale*()**, **glOrtho()**, and **glFrustum()** are used to create a matrix that's multiplied by the top matrix. When the modelview matrix is modified, its inverse transpose is also generated for normal vector transformation.

The commands that set the current raster position are treated exactly like a vertex command up until the point when rasterization would occur. At this point, the value is saved and used in the rasterization of pixel data.

The various **glClear()** commands bypass all operations except scissoring, dithering, and writemasking.

# State Variables

This appendix lists the queryable OpenGL state variables, their default values, and the commands for obtaining the values of these variables. The *OpenGL Reference Manual* contains detailed information on all the commands and constants discussed in this appendix, which contains the following major sections:

- "The Query Commands"
- "OpenGL State Variables"

## The Query Commands

In addition to the basic commands to obtain the values of simple state variables (commands such as **glGetIntegerv()** and **glIsEnabled()**, which are described in "Basic State Management" in Chapter 2), there are other specialized commands to return more complex state variables. The prototypes for these specialized commands are listed here. Some of these routines, such as **glGetError()** and **glGetString()**, have been discussed in more detail elsewhere in the book.

To find out when you need to use these commands and their corresponding symbolic constants, use the tables in the next section, "OpenGL State Variables." Also see the *OpenGL Reference Manual*.

void **glGetAttachedShaders**(GLuint *program*, GLsizei *maxCount*,
        GLsizei *\*count*, GLuint *\*shaders*);

void **glGetBufferSubData**(GLenum *target*, GLintptr *offset*,
        GLsizeiptr *size*, GLvoid\* *data*);

void **glGetBufferParameteriv**(GLenum *target*, GLenum *pname*,
        GLint *\*params*);

void **glGetBufferPointerv**(GLenum *target*, GLenum *pname*,
        GLvoid \*\**pointer*);

void **glGetClipPlane**(GLenum *plane*, GLdouble *\*equation*);

void **glGetColorTable**(GLenum *target*, GLenum *pname*, GLenum *type*,
        GLvoid *\*table*);

void **glGetColorTableParameter**{if}**v**(GLenum *target*, GLenum *pname*,
        *TYPE \*params*);

void **glGetCompressedTexImage**(GLenum *target*, GLint *lod*,
        GLvoid *\*pixels*);

void **glGetConvolutionFilter**(GLenum *target*, GLenum *format*,
        GLenum *type*, GLvoid *\*image*);

void **glGetConvolutionParameter**{if}**v**(GLenum *target*, GLenum *pname*,
        *TYPE \*params*);

GLenum **glGetError**(void);

void **glGetHistogram**(GLenum *target*, GLboolean reset, GLenum *format*,
        GLenum *type*, GLvoid *\*values*);

void **glGetHistogramParameter**{if}**v**(GLenum *target*, GLenum *pname*,
        *TYPE \*params*);

void **glGetLight**{if}**v**(GLenum *light*, GLenum *pname*, TYPE *params*);

void **glGetMap**{ifd}**v**(GLenum *target*, GLenum *query*, TYPE *v*);

void **glGetMaterial**{if}**v**(GLenum *face*, GLenum *pname*, TYPE *params*);

void **glGetMinmax**(GLenum *target*, GLboolean reset, GLenum *format*, GLenum *type*, GLvoid *values*);

void **glGetMinmaxParameter**{if}**v** (GLenum *target*, GLenum *pname*, TYPE *params*);

void **glGetPixelMap**{f ui us}**v**(GLenum *map*, TYPE *values*);

void **glGetPolygonStipple**(GLubyte *mask*);

void **glGetProgramLogInfo**(GLuint *program*, GLsizei *bufSize*, GLsizei *length*, GLchar *infoLog*);

void **glGetProgramiv**(GLuint *program*, GLenum *pname*, GLint *params*);

void **glGetQueryiv**(GLenum *target*, GLenum *pname*, GLint *params*);

void **glGetQueryObjectiv**(GLuint *id*, GLenum *pname*, GLint *params*);

void **glGetQueryObjectuiv**(GLuint *id*, GLenum *pname*, GLuint *params*);

void **glGetSeparableFilter**(GLenum *target*, GLenum *format*, GLenum *type*, GLvoid *row*, GLvoid *column*, GLvoid *span*);

void **glGetShaderInfoLog**(GLuint *shader*, GLsizei *bufSize*, GLsizei *length*, GLchar *infoLog*);

void **glGetShaderiv**(GLuint *shader*, GLenum *pname*, GLint *params*);

void **glGetShaderSource**(GLuint *shader*, GLsizei *bufSize*, GLsizei *length*, GLchar *source*);

const GLubyte * **glGetString**(GLenum *name*);

void **glGetTexEnv**{if}**v**(GLenum *target*, GLenum *pname*, TYPE *params*);

void **glGetTexGen**{ifd}**v**(GLenum *coord*, GLenum *pname*, TYPE *params*);

void **glGetTexImage**(GLenum *target*, GLint *level*, GLenum *format*, GLenum *type*, GLvoid *pixels*);

void **glGetTexLevelParameter**{if}**v**(GLenum *target*, GLint *level*, GLenum *pname*, TYPE *params*);

void **glGetTexParameter**{if}**v**(GLenum *target*, GLenum *pname*, TYPE *params*);

void **glGetUniform**{if}**v**(GLuint *program*, GLint *location*, TYPE *\*params*);

void **glGetVertexAttrib**{ifd}**v**(GLuint *index*, GLenum *pname*, TYPE *\*params*);

void **glGetVertexAttribPointerv**(GLuint *index*, GLenum *pname*, GLvoid *\*\*pointer*);

GLboolean **glIsBuffer**(GLuint *buffer*);

GLboolean **glIsList**(GLuint *list*);

GLboolean **glIsProgram**(GLuint *program*);

GLboolean **glIsQuery**(GLuint *id*);

GLboolean **glIsShader**(GLuint *shader*);

GLboolean **glIsTexture**(GLuint *texObject*);

void **gluGetNurbsProperty**(GLUnurbsObj *\*nobj*, GLenum *property*, GLfloat *\*value*);

const GLubyte * **gluGetString**(GLenum *name*);

void **gluGetTessProperty**(GLUtesselator *\*tess*, GLenum *which*, GLdouble *\*data*);

## OpenGL State Variables

The following pages contain tables that list the names of queryable state variables. For each variable, the tables list a description of it, its attribute group, its initial or minimum value, and the suggested **glGet\*()** command to use for obtaining it. State variables that can be obtained using **glGetBooleanv()**, **glGetIntegerv()**, **glGetFloatv()**, or **glGetDoublev()** are listed with just one of these commands—the one that's most appropriate given the type of data to be returned. (Some vertex-array variables can be queried only with **glGetPointerv()**.) These state variables can't be obtained using **glIsEnabled()**. However, state variables for which **glIsEnabled()** is listed as the query command can also be obtained using **glGetBooleanv()**, **glGetIntegerv()**, **glGetFloatv()**, and **glGetDoublev()**. State variables for which any other command is listed as the query command can be obtained only by using that command.

**Note:** When querying texture state, such as GL_TEXTURE_MATRIX, in an implementation where the GL_ARB_multitexture extension is defined, the values returned reference the currently active texture unit only. See "Multitexturing" on page 443 for details.

If one or more attribute groups are listed, the state variable belongs to the listed group or groups. If no attribute group is listed, the variable doesn't belong to any group. **glPushAttrib()**, **glPushClientAttrib()**, **glPopAttrib()**, and **glPopClientAttrib()** may be used to save and restore all state values that belong to an attribute group (see "Attribute Groups" in Chapter 2 for more information).

All queryable state variables have initial values; however, those that are implementation-dependent may not have an initial value listed. If no initial value is listed, you need to consult either the section where that variable is discussed or the *OpenGL Reference Manual* to determine its initial value.

# Current Values and Associated Data

| State Variable | Description | Attribute Group | Initial Value | Get Command |
|---|---|---|---|---|
| GL_CURRENT_COLOR | Current color | current | (1, 1, 1, 1) | glGetIntegerv(), glGetFloatv() |
| GL_CURRENT_SECONDARY_COLOR | Current secondary color | current | (0, 0, 0, 1) | glGetIntegerv(), glGetFloatv() |
| GL_CURRENT_INDEX | Current color index | current | 1 | glGetIntegerv(), glGetFloatv() |
| GL_CURRENT_TEXTURE_COORDS | Current texture coordinates | current | (0, 0, 0, 1) | glGetFloatv() |
| GL_CURRENT_NORMAL | Current normal | current | (0, 0, 1) | glGetFloatv() |
| GL_CURRENT_FOG_COORD | Current fog coordinate | current | 0 | glGetIntegerv(), glGetFloatv() |
| GL_CURRENT_RASTER_POSITION | Current raster position | current | (0, 0, 0, 1) | glGetFloatv() |
| GL_CURRENT_RASTER_DISTANCE | Current raster distance | current | 0 | glGetFloatv() |
| GL_CURRENT_RASTER_COLOR | Color associated with raster position | current | (1, 1, 1, 1) | glGetIntegerv(), glGetFloatv() |
| GL_CURRENT_RASTER_SECONDARY_COLOR | Secondary color associated with raster position | current | (0, 0, 0, 1) | glGetIntegerv(), glGetFloatv() |

**Table B-1** State Variables for Current Values and Associated Data

| State Variable | Description | Attribute Group | Initial Value | Get Command |
| --- | --- | --- | --- | --- |
| GL_CURRENT_RASTER_INDEX | Color index associated with raster position | current | 1 | glGetIntegerv(), glGetFloatv() |
| GL_CURRENT_RASTER_TEXTURE_COORDS | Texture coordinates associated with raster position | current | (0, 0, 0, 1) | glGetFloatv() |
| GL_CURRENT_RASTER_POSITION_VALID | Raster position valid bit | current | GL_TRUE | glGetBooleanv() |
| GL_EDGE_FLAG | Edge flag | current | GL_TRUE | glGetBooleanv() |

**Table B-1 (continued)**    State Variables for Current Values and Associated Data

## Vertex Array

| State Variable | Description | Attribute Group | Initial Value | Get Command |
| --- | --- | --- | --- | --- |
| GL_CLIENT_ACTIVE_TEXTURE | Active texture unit, for texture-coordinate array | vertex-array | GL_TEXTURE0 | glGetIntegerv() |
| GL_VERTEX_ARRAY | Vertex array enable | vertex-array | GL_FALSE | glIsEnabled() |
| GL_VERTEX_ARRAY_SIZE | Coordinates per vertex | vertex-array | 4 | glGetIntegerv() |
| GL_VERTEX_ARRAY_TYPE | Type of vertex coordinates | vertex-array | GL_FLOAT | glGetIntegerv() |
| GL_VERTEX_ARRAY_STRIDE | Stride between vertices | vertex-array | 0 | glGetIntegerv() |

**Table B-2**    Vertex-Array State Variables

| State Variable | Description | Attribute Group | Initial Value | Get Command |
|---|---|---|---|---|
| GL_VERTEX_ARRAY_POINTER | Pointer to the vertex array | vertex-array | NULL | glGetPointerv() |
| GL_NORMAL_ARRAY | Normal array enable | vertex-array | GL_FALSE | glIsEnabled() |
| GL_NORMAL_ARRAY_TYPE | Type of normal coordinates | vertex-array | GL_FLOAT | glGetIntegerv() |
| GL_NORMAL_ARRAY_STRIDE | Stride between normals | vertex-array | 0 | glGetIntegerv() |
| GL_NORMAL_ARRAY_POINTER | Pointer to the normal array | vertex-array | NULL | glGetPointerv() |
| GL_FOG_COORD_ARRAY | Fog coordinate array enable | vertex-array | GL_FALSE | glIsEnabled() |
| GL_FOG_COORD_ARRAY_TYPE | Type of fog coordinate components | vertex-array | GL_FLOAT | glGetIntegerv() |
| GL_FOG_COORD_ARRAY_STRIDE | Stride between fog coordinates | vertex-array | 0 | glGetIntegerv() |
| GL_FOG_COORD_ARRAY_POINTER | Pointer to the fog coordinate array | vertex-array | NULL | glGetPointerv() |
| GL_COLOR_ARRAY | RGBA color array enable | vertex-array | GL_FALSE | glIsEnabled() |
| GL_COLOR_ARRAY_SIZE | Color components per vertex | vertex-array | 4 | glGetIntegerv() |

**Table B-2 (continued)**   Vertex-Array State Variables

| State Variable | Description | Attribute Group | Initial Value | Get Command |
|---|---|---|---|---|
| GL_COLOR_ARRAY_TYPE | Type of color components | vertex-array | GL_FLOAT | glGetIntegerv() |
| GL_COLOR_ARRAY_STRIDE | Stride between colors | vertex-array | 0 | glGetIntegerv() |
| GL_COLOR_ARRAY_POINTER | Pointer to the color array | vertex-array | NULL | glGetPointerv() |
| GL_SECONDARY_COLOR_ARRAY | Secondary color array enable | vertex-array | GL_FALSE | glIsEnabled() |
| GL_SECONDARY_COLOR_ARRAY_SIZE | Secondary color components per vertex | vertex-array | 3 | glGetIntegerv() |
| GL_SECONDARY_COLOR_ARRAY_TYPE | Type of secondary color components | vertex-array | GL_FLOAT | glGetIntegerv() |
| GL_SECONDARY_COLOR_ARRAY_STRIDE | Stride between secondary colors | vertex-array | 0 | glGetIntegerv() |
| GL_SECONDARY_COLOR_ARRAY_POINTER | Pointer to the secondary color array | vertex-array | NULL | glGetPointerv() |
| GL_INDEX_ARRAY | Color-index array enable | vertex-array | GL_FALSE | glIsEnabled() |
| GL_INDEX_ARRAY_TYPE | Type of color indices | vertex-array | GL_FLOAT | glGetIntegerv() |
| GL_INDEX_ARRAY_STRIDE | Stride between color indices | vertex-array | 0 | glGetIntegerv() |
| GL_INDEX_ARRAY_POINTER | Pointer to the index array | vertex-array | NULL | glGetPointerv() |

**Table B-2 (continued)**    Vertex-Array State Variables

| State Variable | Description | Attribute Group | Initial Value | Get Command |
|---|---|---|---|---|
| GL_TEXTURE_COORD_ARRAY | Texture-coordinate array enable | vertex-array | GL_FALSE | glIsEnabled() |
| GL_TEXTURE_COORD_ARRAY_SIZE | Texture coordinates per element | vertex-array | 4 | glGetIntegerv() |
| GL_TEXTURE_COORD_ARRAY_TYPE | Type of texture coordinates | vertex-array | GL_FLOAT | glGetIntegerv() |
| GL_TEXTURE_COORD_ARRAY_STRIDE | Stride between texture coordinates | vertex-array | 0 | glGetIntegerv() |
| GL_TEXTURE_COORD_ARRAY_POINTER | Pointer to the texture-coordinate array | vertex-array | NULL | glGetPointerv() |
| GL_VERTEX_ATTRIB_ARRAY_ENABLED | Vertex attrib array enable | vertex-array | GL_FALSE | glGetVertexAttrib() |
| GL_VERTEX_ATTRIB_ARRAY_SIZE | Vertex attrib array size | vertex-array | 4 | glGetVertexAttrib() |
| GL_VERTEX_ATTRIB_ARRAY_STRIDE | Vertex attrib array stride | vertex-array | 0 | glGetVertexAttrib() |
| GL_VERTEX_ATTRIB_ARRAY_TYPE | Vertex attrib array type | vertex-array | GL_FLOAT | glGetVertexAttrib() |
| GL_VERTEX_ATTRIB_ARRAY_NORMALIZED | Vertex attrib array normalized | vertex-array | GL_FALSE | glGetVertexAttrib() |
| GL_VERTEX_ATTRIB_ARRAY_POINTER | Vertex attrib array pointer | vertex-array | NULL | glGetVertexAttribPointer() |

**Table B-2 (continued)**   Vertex-Array State Variables

| State Variable | Description | Attribute Group | Initial Value | Get Command |
| --- | --- | --- | --- | --- |
| GL_EDGE_FLAG_ARRAY | Edge flag array enable | vertex-array | GL_FALSE | glIsEnabled() |
| GL_EDGE_FLAG_ARRAY_STRIDE | Stride between edge flags | vertex-array | 0 | glGetIntegerv() |
| GL_EDGE_FLAG_ARRAY_POINTER | Pointer to the edge-flag array | vertex-array | NULL | glGetPointerv() |
| GL_ARRAY_BUFFER_BINDING | Current buffer binding | vertex-array | 0 | glGetIntegerv() |
| GL_VERTEX_ARRAY_BUFFER_BINDING | Vertex array buffer binding | vertex-array | 0 | glGetIntegerv() |
| GL_NORMAL_ARRAY_BUFFER_BINDING | Normal array buffer binding | vertex-array | 0 | glGetIntegerv() |
| GL_COLOR_ARRAY_BUFFER_BINDING | Color array buffer binding | vertex-array | 0 | glGetIntegerv() |
| GL_INDEX_ARRAY_BUFFER_BINDING | Index array buffer binding | vertex-array | 0 | glGetIntegerv() |
| GL_TEXTURE_COORD_ARRAY_BUFFER_BINDING | Texture-coordinate array buffer binding | vertex-array | 0 | glGetIntegerv() |
| GL_EDGE_FLAG_ARRAY_BUFFER_BINDING | Edge flag array buffer binding | vertex-array | 0 | glGetIntegerv() |
| GL_SECONDARY_COLOR_ARRAY_BUFFER_BINDING | Secondary color array buffer binding | vertex-array | 0 | glGetIntegerv() |
| GL_FOG_COORD_ARRAY_BUFFER_BINDING | Fog-coordinate array buffer binding | vertex-array | 0 | glGetIntegerv() |

**Table B-2 (continued)**     Vertex-Array State Variables

| State Variable | Description | Attribute Group | Initial Value | Get Command |
| --- | --- | --- | --- | --- |
| GL_ELEMENT_ARRAY_BUFFER_BINDING | Element array buffer binding | vertex-array | 0 | glGetIntegerv() |
| GL_VERTEX_ATTRIB_ARRAY_BUFFER_BINDING | Vertex attribute array buffer binding | vertex-array | 0 | glGetVertexAttribiv() |

**Table B-2 (continued)**    Vertex-Array State Variables

| State Variable | Description | Attribute Group | Initial Value | Get Command |
| --- | --- | --- | --- | --- |
| GL_BUFFER_SIZE | Buffer data size | — | 0 | glGetBufferParameteriv() |
| GL_BUFFER_USAGE | Buffer usage pattern | — | GL_STATIC_DRAW | glGetBufferParameteriv() |
| GL_BUFFER_ACCESS | Buffer access flag | — | GL_READ_WRITE | glGetBufferParameteriv() |
| GL_BUFFER_MAPPED | Buffer map flag | — | GL_FALSE | glGetBufferParameteriv() |
| GL_BUFFER_MAP_POINTER | Mapped buffer pointer | — | NULL | glGetBufferPointerv() |

**Table B-3**    Vertex Buffer Object State Variables

## Transformation

| State Variable | Description | Attribute Group | Initial Value | Get Command |
|---|---|---|---|---|
| GL_COLOR_MATRIX | Color matrix stack | — | Identity | glGetFloatv() |
| GL_TRANSPOSE_COLOR_MATRIX | Stack of transposed color matrices | — | Identity | glGetFloatv() |
| GL_MODELVIEW_MATRIX | Modelview matrix stack | — | Identity | glGetFloatv() |
| GL_TRANSPOSE_MODELVIEW_MATRIX | Stack of transposed modelview matrices | — | Identity | glGetFloatv() |
| GL_PROJECTION_MATRIX | Projection matrix stack | — | Identity | glGetFloatv() |
| GL_TRANSPOSE_PROJECTION_MATRIX | Stack of transposed projection matrices | — | Identity | glGetFloatv() |
| GL_TEXTURE_MATRIX | Texture matrix stack | — | Identity | glGetFloatv() |
| GL_TRANSPOSE_TEXTURE_MATRIX | Stack of transposed texture matrices | — | Identity | glGetFloatv() |
| GL_VIEWPORT | Viewport origin and extent | viewport | — | glGetIntegerv() |
| GL_DEPTH_RANGE | Depth range near and far | viewport | 0, 1 | glGetFloatv() |
| GL_COLOR_MATRIX_STACK_DEPTH | Color matrix stack pointer | — | 1 | glGetIntegerv() |

**Table B-4**     Transformation State Variables

| State Variable | Description | Attribute Group | Initial Value | Get Command |
|---|---|---|---|---|
| GL_MODELVIEW_STACK_DEPTH | Modelview matrix stack pointer | — | 1 | glGetIntegerv() |
| GL_PROJECTION_STACK_DEPTH | Projection matrix stack pointer | — | 1 | glGetIntegerv() |
| GL_TEXTURE_STACK_DEPTH | Texture matrix stack pointer | — | 1 | glGetIntegerv() |
| GL_MATRIX_MODE | Current matrix mode | transform | GL_MODELVIEW | glGetIntegerv() |
| GL_NORMALIZE | Current normal normalization on/off | transform/ enable | GL_FALSE | glIsEnabled() |
| GL_RESCALE_NORMAL | Current normal rescaling on/off | transform/ enable | GL_FALSE | glIsEnabled() |
| GL_CLIP_PLANE*i* | User clipping-plane coefficients | transform | (0, 0, 0, 0) | glGetClipPlane() |
| GL_CLIP_PLANE*i* | *i*th user clipping plane enabled | transform/ enable | GL_FALSE | glIsEnabled() |

**Table B-4 (continued)**     Transformation State Variables

## Coloring

| State Variable | Description | Attribute Group | Initial Value | Get Command |
|---|---|---|---|---|
| GL_FOG_COLOR | Fog color | fog | (0, 0, 0, 0) | glGetFloatv() |
| GL_FOG_INDEX | Fog index | fog | 0 | glGetFloatv() |
| GL_FOG_DENSITY | Exponential fog density | fog | 1.0 | glGetFloatv() |
| GL_FOG_START | Linear fog start | fog | 0.0 | glGetFloatv() |
| GL_FOG_END | Linear fog end | fog | 1.0 | glGetFloatv() |
| GL_FOG_MODE | Fog mode | fog | GL_EXP | glGetIntegerv() |
| GL_FOG | True if fog enabled | fog/enable | GL_FALSE | glIsEnabled() |
| GL_FOG_COORD_SRC | Source of coordinates for fog calculation | fog | GL_FRAGMENT_ DEPTH | glGetIntegerv() |
| GL_COLOR_SUM | True if color sum is enabled | fog/enable | GL_FALSE | glIsEnabled() |
| GL_SHADE_MODEL | glShadeModel() setting | lighting | GL_SMOOTH | glGetIntegerv() |

**Table B-5**    Coloring State Variables

## Lighting

See also Tables 5-1 and 5-3 for initial values.

| State Variable | Description | Attribute Group | Initial Value | Get Command |
|---|---|---|---|---|
| GL_LIGHTING | True if lighting is enabled | lighting/enable | GL_FALSE | glIsEnabled() |
| GL_COLOR_MATERIAL | True if color tracking is enabled | lighting | GL_FALSE | glIsEnabled() |
| GL_COLOR_MATERIAL_PARAMETER | Material properties tracking current color | lighting | GL_AMBIENT_AND_DIFFUSE | glGetIntegerv() |
| GL_COLOR_MATERIAL_FACE | Face(s) affected by color tracking | lighting | GL_FRONT_AND_BACK | glGetIntegerv() |
| GL_AMBIENT | Ambient material color | lighting | (0.2, 0.2, 0.2, 1.0) | glGetMaterialfv() |
| GL_DIFFUSE | Diffuse material color | lighting | (0.8, 0.8, 0.8, 1.0) | glGetMaterialfv() |
| GL_SPECULAR | Specular material color | lighting | (0.0, 0.0, 0.0, 1.0) | glGetMaterialfv() |
| GL_EMISSION | Emissive material color | lighting | (0.0, 0.0, 0.0, 1.0) | glGetMaterialfv() |
| GL_SHININESS | Specular exponent of material | lighting | 0.0 | glGetMaterialfv() |
| GL_LIGHT_MODEL_AMBIENT | Ambient scene color | lighting | (0.2, 0.2, 0.2, 1.0) | glGetFloatv() |
| GL_LIGHT_MODEL_LOCAL_VIEWER | Viewer is local | lighting | GL_FALSE | glGetBooleanv() |

**Table B-6**  Lighting State Variables

| State Variable | Description | Attribute Group | Initial Value | Get Command |
|---|---|---|---|---|
| GL_LIGHT_MODEL_TWO_SIDE | Use two-sided lighting | lighting | GL_FALSE | glGetBooleanv() |
| GL_LIGHT_MODEL_COLOR_CONTROL | Color control | lighting | GL_SINGLE_COLOR | glGetIntegerv() |
| GL_AMBIENT | Ambient intensity of light $i$ | lighting | (0.0, 0.0, 0.0, 1.0) | glGetLightfv() |
| GL_DIFFUSE | Diffuse intensity of light $i$ | lighting | — | glGetLightfv() |
| GL_SPECULAR | Specular intensity of light $i$ | lighting | — | glGetLightfv() |
| GL_POSITION | Position of light $i$ | lighting | (0.0, 0.0, 1.0, 0.0) | glGetLightfv() |
| GL_CONSTANT_ATTENUATION | Constant attenuation factor | lighting | 1.0 | glGetLightfv() |
| GL_LINEAR_ATTENUATION | Linear attenuation factor | lighting | 0.0 | glGetLightfv() |
| GL_QUADRATIC_ATTENUATION | Quadratic attenuation factor | lighting | 0.0 | glGetLightfv() |
| GL_SPOT_DIRECTION | Spotlight direction of light $i$ | lighting | (0.0, 0.0, −1.0) | glGetLightfv() |
| GL_SPOT_EXPONENT | Spotlight exponent of light $i$ | lighting | 0.0 | glGetLightfv() |
| GL_SPOT_CUTOFF | Spotlight angle of light $i$ | lighting | 180.0 | glGetLightfv() |
| GL_LIGHT$i$ | True if light $i$ enabled | lighting /enable | GL_FALSE | glIsEnabled() |
| GL_COLOR_INDEXES | $c_a$, $c_d$, and $c_s$ for color-index lighting | lighting | 0, 1, 1 | glGetMaterialfv() |

**Table B-6 (continued)**    Lighting State Variables

# Rasterization

| State Variable | Description | Attribute Group | Initial Value | Get Command |
|---|---|---|---|---|
| GL_POINT_SIZE | Point size | point | 1.0 | glGetFloatv() |
| GL_POINT_SMOOTH | Point antialiasing on | point/enable | GL_FALSE | glIsEnabled() |
| GL_POINT_SPRITE | Point sprite enable | point/enable | GL_FALSE | glIsEnabled() |
| GL_POINT_SIZE_MIN | Attenuated minimum point size | point | 0.0 | glGetFloatv() |
| GL_POINT_SIZE_MAX | Attenuated maximum point size | point | See Note a at end of table. | glGetFloatv() |
| GL_POINT_FADE_THRESHOLD_SIZE | Threshold for alpha attenuation | point | 1.0 | glGetFloatv() |
| GL_POINT_DISTANCE_ATTENUATION | Attenuation coefficients | point | 1, 0, 0 | glGetFloatv() |
| GL_POINT_SPRITE_COORD_ORIGIN | Origin orientation for point sprites | point | GL_UPPER_LEFT | glGetIntegerv() |
| GL_LINE_WIDTH | Line width | line | 1.0 | glGetFloatv() |
| GL_LINE_SMOOTH | Line antialiasing on | line/enable | GL_FALSE | glIsEnabled() |

**Table B-7**  Rasterization State Variables

| State Variable | Description | Attribute Group | Initial Value | Get Command |
|---|---|---|---|---|
| GL_LINE_STIPPLE_PATTERN | Line stipple | line | 1's | glGetIntegerv() |
| GL_LINE_STIPPLE_REPEAT | Line stipple repeat | line | 1 | glGetIntegerv() |
| GL_LINE_STIPPLE | Line stipple enable | line/enable | GL_FALSE | glIsEnabled() |
| GL_CULL_FACE | Polygon culling enabled | polygon/enable | GL_FALSE | glIsEnabled() |
| GL_CULL_FACE_MODE | Cull front-/back-facing polygons | polygon | GL_BACK | glGetIntegerv() |
| GL_FRONT_FACE | Polygon front-face CW/CCW indicator | polygon | GL_CCW | glGetIntegerv() |
| GL_POLYGON_SMOOTH | Polygon antialiasing on | polygon/enable | GL_FALSE | glIsEnabled() |
| GL_POLYGON_MODE | Polygon rasterization mode (front and back) | polygon | GL_FILL | glGetIntegerv() |
| GL_POLYGON_OFFSET_FACTOR | Polygon offset factor | polygon | 0 | glGetFloatv() |
| GL_POLYGON_OFFSET_UNITS | Polygon offset units | polygon | 0 | glGetFloatv() |
| GL_POLYGON_OFFSET_POINT | Polygon offset enable for GL_POINT mode rasterization | polygon/enable | GL_FALSE | glIsEnabled() |

**Table B-7 (continued)**     Rasterization State Variables

| State Variable | Description | Attribute Group | Initial Value | Get Command |
|---|---|---|---|---|
| GL_POLYGON_OFFSET_LINE | Polygon offset enable for GL_ LINE mode rasterization | polygon/enable | GL_FALSE | glIsEnabled() |
| GL_POLYGON_OFFSET_FILL | Polygon offset enable for GL_ FILL mode rasterization | polygon/enable | GL_FALSE | glIsEnabled() |
| GL_POLYGON_STIPPLE | Polygon stipple enable | polygon/enable | GL_FALSE | glIsEnabled() |
| — | Polygon stipple pattern | polygon-stipple | 1's | glGetPolygon-Stipple() |

**Table B-7 (continued)**    Rasterization State Variables

a. The initial value of GL_POINT_SIZE_MAX is the maximum of GL_ALIASED_POINT_SIZE_RANGE and GL_SMOOTH_POINT_SIZE_RANGE.

## Multisampling

| State Variable | Description | Attribute Group | Initial Value | Get Command |
|---|---|---|---|---|
| GL_MULTISAMPLE | Multisample rasterization | multisample/enable | GL_TRUE | glIsEnabled() |
| GL_SAMPLE_ALPHA_TO_COVERAGE | Modify coverage from alpha | multisample/enable | GL_FALSE | glIsEnabled() |
| GL_SAMPLE_ALPHA_TO_ONE | Set alpha to maximum | multisample/enable | GL_FALSE | glIsEnabled() |
| GL_SAMPLE_COVERAGE | Mask to modify coverage | multisample/enable | GL_FALSE | glIsEnabled() |
| GL_SAMPLE_COVERAGE_VALUE | Coverage mask value | multisample | 1 | glGetFloatv() |
| GL_SAMPLE_COVERAGE_INVERT | Invert coverage mask value | multisample | GL_FALSE | glGetBooleanv() |

**Table B-8**    Multisampling

## Texturing

| State Variable | Description | Attribute Group | Initial Value | Get Command |
|---|---|---|---|---|
| GL_COMPRESSED_TEXTURE_FORMATS | List of supported compressed texture formats | — | varies | glGetIntegerv() |
| GL_TEXTURE_x | True if x (dimensional) texturing is enabled (x is 1D, 2D, or 3D) | texture/enable | GL_FALSE | glIsEnabled() |
| GL_TEXTURE_x | x-D texture image at level of detail i (x is 1D, 2D, or 3D) | — | — | glGetTexImage() |
| GL_TEXTURE_BINDING_x | Texture object bound to GL_TEXTURE_x (x is 1D, 2D, or 3D) | texture | 0 | glGetIntegerv() |
| GL_TEXTURE_BINDING_CUBE_MAP | Texture object bound to GL_TEXTURE_CUBE_MAP | texture | 0 | glGetIntegerv() |
| GL_TEXTURE_COMPRESSED | True if texture map is stored internally in a compressed format | — | GL_FALSE | glGetTexLevelParameter*() |
| GL_TEXTURE_COMPRESSED_IMAGE_SIZE | Number of bytes in compressed texture image array | — | 0 | glGetTexLevelParameter*() |
| GL_TEXTURE_CUBE_MAP | True if cube map texturing is enabled | texture/enable | GL_FALSE | glIsEnabled() |

**Table B-9**     Texturing State Variables

| State Variable | Description | Attribute Group | Initial Value | Get Command |
|---|---|---|---|---|
| GL_TEXTURE_CUBE_MAP_POSITIVE_X | +x face cube map texture image at level of detail $i$ | — | — | glGetTexImage() |
| GL_TEXTURE_CUBE_MAP_NEGATIVE_X | -x face cube map texture image at level of detail $i$ | — | — | glGetTexImage() |
| GL_TEXTURE_CUBE_MAP_POSITIVE_Y | +y face cube map texture image at level of detail $i$ | — | — | glGetTexImage() |
| GL_TEXTURE_CUBE_MAP_NEGATIVE_Y | -y face cube map texture image at level of detail $i$ | — | — | glGetTexImage() |
| GL_TEXTURE_CUBE_MAP_POSITIVE_Z | +z face cube map texture image at level of detail $i$ | — | — | glGetTexImage() |
| GL_TEXTURE_CUBE_MAP_NEGATIVE_Z | -z face cube map texture image at level of detail $i$ | — | — | glGetTexImage() |
| GL_TEXTURE_BORDER_COLOR | Texture border color | texture | (0, 0, 0, 0) | glGetTexParameter*() |
| GL_TEXTURE_MIN_FILTER | Texture minification function | texture | GL_NEAREST_MIPMAP_LINEAR | glGetTexParameter*() |
| GL_TEXTURE_MAG_FILTER | Texture magnification function | texture | GL_LINEAR | glGetTexParameter*() |
| GL_TEXTURE_WRAP_S | Texture coord S wrap mode | texture | GL_REPEAT | glGetTexParameter*() |

**Table B-9 (continued)**    Texturing State Variables

| State Variable | Description | Attribute Group | Initial Value | Get Command |
|---|---|---|---|---|
| GL_TEXTURE_WRAP_T | Texture coord T wrap mode (2D, 3D, cube map textures only) | texture | GL_REPEAT | glGetTexParameter*() |
| GL_TEXTURE_WRAP_R | Texture coord R wrap mode (3D textures only) | texture | GL_REPEAT | glGetTexParameter*() |
| GL_TEXTURE_PRIORITY | Texture object priority | texture | 1 | glGetTexParameter*() |
| GL_TEXTURE_RESIDENT | Texture residency | texture | varies | glGetTexParameteriv() |
| GL_TEXTURE_MIN_LOD | Minimum level of detail | texture | −1000 | glGetTexParameterfv() |
| GL_TEXTURE_MAX_LOD | Maximum level of detail | texture | 1000 | glGetTexParameterfv() |
| GL_TEXTURE_BASE_LEVEL | Base texture array | texture | 0 | glGetTexParameterfv() |
| GL_TEXTURE_MAX_LEVEL | Maximum texture array level | texture | 1000 | glGetTexParameterfv() |
| GL_TEXTURE_LOD_BIAS | Texture level-of-detail bias | texture | 0.0 | glGetTexParameterfv() |
| GL_DEPTH_TEXTURE_MODE | Depth texture mode | texture | GL_LUMINANCE | glGetTexParameteriv() |
| GL_TEXTURE_COMPARE_MODE | Texture comparison mode | texture | GL_NONE | glGetTexParameteriv() |
| GL_TEXTURE_COMPARE_FUNC | Texture comparison function | texture | GL_LEQUAL | glGetTexParameteriv() |
| GL_GENERATE_MIPMAP | Automatic mipmap generation | texture | GL_FALSE | glGetTexParameter*() |
| GL_TEXTURE_WIDTH | Texture image $i$'s width | — | 0 | glGetTexLevelParameter*() |

**Table B-9 (continued)**     Texturing State Variables

| State Variable | Description | Attribute Group | Initial Value | Get Command |
|---|---|---|---|---|
| GL_TEXTURE_HEIGHT | 2D/3D texture image $i$'s height | — | 0 | glGetTexLevelParameter*() |
| GL_TEXTURE_DEPTH | 3D texture image $i$'s depth | — | 0 | glGetTexLevelParameter*() |
| GL_TEXTURE_BORDER | Texture image $i$'s border width | — | 0 | glGetTexLevelParameter*() |
| GL_TEXTURE_INTERNAL_FORMAT | Texture image $i$'s internal image format | — | 1 | glGetTexLevelParameter*() |
| GL_TEXTURE_COMPONENTS | Texture image $i$'s internal image format | — | 1 | glGetTexLevelParamter*() |
| GL_TEXTURE_RED_SIZE | Texture image $i$'s red resolution | — | 0 | glGetTexLevelParameter*() |
| GL_TEXTURE_GREEN_SIZE | Texture image $i$'s green resolution | — | 0 | glGetTexLevelParameter*() |
| GL_TEXTURE_BLUE_SIZE | Texture image $i$'s blue resolution | — | 0 | glGetTexLevelParameter*() |
| GL_TEXTURE_ALPHA_SIZE | Texture image $i$'s alpha resolution | — | 0 | glGetTexLevelParameter*() |
| GL_TEXTURE_LUMINANCE_SIZE | Texture image $i$'s luminance resolution | — | 0 | glGetTexLevelParameter*() |
| GL_TEXTURE_INTENSITY_SIZE | Texture image $i$'s intensity resolution | — | 0 | glGetTexLevelParameter*() |
| GL_TEXTURE_DEPTH_SIZE | Texture image $i$'s depth resolution | — | 0 | glGetTexLevelParameter*() |

**Table B-9 (continued)**    Texturing State Variables

| State Variable | Description | Attribute Group | Initial Value | Get Command |
|---|---|---|---|---|
| GL_TEXTURE_COMPRESSED | True, if texture image has a compressed internal format | — | GL_FALSE | glGetTexLevelParameter*() |
| GL_TEXTURE_COMPRESSED_IMAGE_SIZE | Size (in GLubyte) of compressed texture image | — | 0 | glGetTexLevelParameter*() |
| GL_COORD_REPLACE | Coordinate replacement enable | point | GL_FALSE | glTexEnviv() |
| GL_ACTIVE_TEXTURE | Active texture unit | texture | GL_TEXTURE0 | glGetIntegerv() |
| GL_TEXTURE_ENV_MODE | Texture application function | texture | GL_MODULATE | glGetTexEnviv() |
| GL_TEXTURE_ENV_COLOR | Texture environment color | texture | (0, 0, 0, 0) | glGetTexEnvfv() |
| GL_TEXTURE_LOD_BIAS | Texture level of detail bias | texture | 0.0 | glGetTexEnvfv() |
| GL_TEXTURE_GEN_x | Texgen enabled (x is S, T, R, or Q) | texture/ enable | GL_FALSE | glIsEnabled() |
| GL_EYE_PLANE | Texgen plane equation coefficients | texture | — | glGetTexGenfv() |
| GL_OBJECT_PLANE | Texgen object linear coefficients | texture | — | glGetTexGenfv() |
| GL_TEXTURE_GEN_MODE | Function used for texgen | texture | GL_EYE_LINEAR | glGetTexGeniv() |
| GL_COMBINE_RGB | RGB combiner function | texture | GL_MODULATE | glGetTexEnviv() |
| GL_COMBINE_ALPHA | Alpha combiner function | texture | GL_MODULATE | glGetTexEnviv() |

**Table B-9 (continued)**    Texturing State Variables

| State Variable | Description | Attribute Group | Initial Value | Get Command |
|---|---|---|---|---|
| GL_SRC0_RGB | RGB source 0 | texture | GL_TEXTURE | glGetTexEnviv() |
| GL_SRC1_RGB | RGB source 1 | texture | GL_PREVIOUS | glGetTexEnviv() |
| GL_SRC2_RGB | RGB source 2 | texture | GL_CONSTANT | glGetTexEnviv() |
| GL_SRC0_ALPHA | Alpha source 0 | texture | GL_TEXTURE | glGetTexEnviv() |
| GL_SRC1_ALPHA | Alpha source 1 | texture | GL_PREVIOUS | glGetTexEnviv() |
| GL_SRC2_ALPHA | Alpha source 2 | texture | GL_CONSTANT | glGetTexEnviv() |
| GL_OPERAND0_RGB | RGB operand 0 | texture | GL_SRC_COLOR | glGetTexEnviv() |
| GL_OPERAND1_RGB | RGB operand 1 | texture | GL_SRC_COLOR | glGetTexEnviv() |
| GL_OPERAND2_RGB | RGB operand 2 | texture | GL_SRC_ALPHA | glGetTexEnviv() |
| GL_OPERAND0_ALPHA | Alpha operand 0 | texture | GL_SRC_ALPHA | glGetTexEnviv() |
| GL_OPERAND1_ALPHA | Alpha operand 1 | texture | GL_SRC_ALPHA | glGetTexEnviv() |
| GL_OPERAND2_ALPHA | Alpha operand 2 | texture | GL_SRC_ALPHA | glGetTexEnviv() |
| GL_RGB_SCALE | RGB post-combiner scaling | texture | 1.0 | glGetTexEnviv() |
| GL_ALPHA_SCALE | Alpha post-combiner scaling | texture | 1.0 | glGetTexEnviv() |

**Table B-9 (continued)**　　Texturing State Variables

| State Variable | Description | Attribute Group | Initial Value | Get Command |
|---|---|---|---|---|
| GL_BLEND_EQUATION_RGB | RGB blending equation | color-buffer | GL_FUNC_ADD | glGetIntegerv() |
| GL_BLEND_EQUATION_ALPHA | Alpha blending equation | color-buffer | GL_FUNC_ADD | glGetIntegerv() |
| GL_BLEND_COLOR | Constant blend color | color-buffer | (0, 0, 0, 0) | glGetFloatv() |
| GL_DITHER | Dithering enabled | color-buffer/ enable | GL_TRUE | glIsEnabled() |
| GL_INDEX_LOGIC_OP | Color index logical operation enabled | color-buffer/ enable | GL_FALSE | glIsEnabled() |
| GL_COLOR_LOGIC_OP | RGBA color logical operation enabled | color-buffer/ enable | GL_FALSE | glIsEnabled() |
| GL_LOGIC_OP_MODE | Logical operation function | color-buffer | GL_COPY | glGetIntegerv() |

**Table B-10 (continued)**     Pixel Operations

## Framebuffer Control

| State Variable | Description | Attribute Group | Initial Value | Get Command |
|---|---|---|---|---|
| GL_DRAW_BUFFER*i* | Buffers selected for color *i* | color-buffer | — | glGetIntegerv() |
| GL_DRAW_BUFFER | Buffers selected for color 0 | color-buffer | — | glGetIntegerv() |
| GL_INDEX_WRITEMASK | Color-index writemask | color-buffer | 1's | glGetIntegerv() |
| GL_COLOR_WRITEMASK | Color write enables; R, G, B, or A | color-buffer | GL_TRUE | glGetBooleanv() |
| GL_DEPTH_WRITEMASK | Depth buffer enabled for writing | depth-buffer | GL_TRUE | glGetBooleanv() |
| GL_STENCIL_WRITEMASK | Front stencil buffer writemask | stencil-buffer | 1's | glGetIntegerv() |
| GL_STENCIL_BACK_ WRITEMASK | Back stencil buffer writemask | stencil-buffer | 1's | glGetIntegerv() |
| GL_COLOR_CLEAR_VALUE | Color-buffer clear value (RGBA mode) | color-buffer | (0, 0, 0, 0) | glGetFloatv() |
| GL_INDEX_CLEAR_VALUE | Color-buffer clear value (color-index mode) | color-buffer | 0 | glGetFloatv() |
| GL_DEPTH_CLEAR_VALUE | Depth-buffer clear value | depth-buffer | 1 | glGetIntegerv() |
| GL_STENCIL_CLEAR_VALUE | Stencil-buffer clear value | stencil-buffer | 0 | glGetIntegerv() |
| GL_ACCUM_CLEAR_VALUE | Accumulation-buffer clear value | accum-buffer | 0 | glGetFloatv() |

**Table B-11**    Framebuffer Control State Variables

## Pixels

| State Variable | Description | Attribute Group | Initial Value | Get Command |
|---|---|---|---|---|
| GL_UNPACK_SWAP_BYTES | Value of GL_UNPACK_SWAP_BYTES | pixel-store | GL_FALSE | glGetBooleanv() |
| GL_UNPACK_LSB_FIRST | Value of GL_UNPACK_LSB_FIRST | pixel-store | GL_FALSE | glGetBooleanv() |
| GL_UNPACK_IMAGE_HEIGHT | Value of GL_UNPACK_IMAGE_HEIGHT | pixel-store | 0 | glGetIntegerv() |
| GL_UNPACK_SKIP_IMAGES | Value of GL_UNPACK_SKIP_IMAGES | pixel-store | 0 | glGetIntegerv() |
| GL_UNPACK_ROW_LENGTH | Value of GL_UNPACK_ROW_LENGTH | pixel-store | 0 | glGetIntegerv() |
| GL_UNPACK_SKIP_ROWS | Value of GL_UNPACK_SKIP_ROWS | pixel-store | 0 | glGetIntegerv() |
| GL_UNPACK_SKIP_PIXELS | Value of GL_UNPACK_SKIP_PIXELS | pixel-store | 0 | glGetIntegerv() |
| GL_UNPACK_ALIGNMENT | Value of GL_UNPACK_ALIGNMENT | pixel-store | 4 | glGetIntegerv() |
| GL_PIXEL_PACK_BUFFER_BINDING | Pixel pack buffer binding | pixel-store | 0 | glGetIntegerv() |
| GL_PIXEL_UNPACK_BUFFER_BINDING | Pixel unpack buffer binding | pixel-store | 0 | glGetIntegerv() |
| GL_PACK_SWAP_BYTES | Value of GL_PACK_SWAP_BYTES | pixel-store | GL_FALSE | glGetBooleanv() |
| GL_PACK_LSB_FIRST | Value of GL_PACK_LSB_FIRST | pixel-store | GL_FALSE | glGetBooleanv() |
| GL_PACK_IMAGE_HEIGHT | Value of GL_PACK_IMAGE_HEIGHT | pixel-store | 0 | glGetIntegerv() |

**Table B-12**    Pixel State Variables

| State Variable | Description | Attribute Group | Initial Value | Get Command |
|---|---|---|---|---|
| GL_PACK_SKIP_IMAGES | Value of GL_PACK_SKIP_IMAGES | pixel-store | 0 | glGetIntegerv() |
| GL_PACK_ROW_LENGTH | Value of GL_PACK_ROW_LENGTH | pixel-store | 0 | glGetIntegerv() |
| GL_PACK_SKIP_ROWS | Value of GL_PACK_SKIP_ROWS | pixel-store | 0 | glGetIntegerv() |
| GL_PACK_SKIP_PIXELS | Value of GL_PACK_SKIP_PIXELS | pixel-store | 0 | glGetIntegerv() |
| GL_PACK_ALIGNMENT | Value of GL_PACK_ALIGNMENT | pixel-store | 4 | glGetIntegerv() |
| GL_MAP_COLOR | True if colors are mapped | pixel | GL_FALSE | glGetBooleanv() |
| GL_MAP_STENCIL | True if stencil values are mapped | pixel | GL_FALSE | glGetBooleanv() |
| GL_INDEX_SHIFT | Value of GL_INDEX_SHIFT | pixel | 0 | glGetIntegerv() |
| GL_INDEX_OFFSET | Value of GL_INDEX_OFFSET | pixel | 0 | glGetIntegerv() |
| GL_$x$_SCALE | Value of GL_$x$_SCALE; $x$ is GL_RED, GL_GREEN, GL_BLUE, GL_ALPHA, or GL_DEPTH | pixel | 1 | glGetFloatv() |
| GL_$x$_BIAS | Value of GL_$x$_BIAS; $x$ is GL_RED, GL_GREEN, GL_BLUE, GL_ALPHA, or GL_DEPTH | pixel | 0 | glGetFloatv() |
| GL_COLOR_TABLE | True if color table lookup is enabled | pixel/enable | GL_FALSE | glIsEnabled() |

**Table B-12 (continued)**    Pixel State Variables

| State Variable | Description | Attribute Group | Initial Value | Get Command |
|---|---|---|---|---|
| GL_POST_CONVOLUTION_COLOR_TABLE | True if post convolution color table lookup is enabled | pixel/enable | GL_FALSE | glIsEnabled() |
| GL_POST_COLOR_MATRIX_COLOR_TABLE | True if post color matrix color table lookup is enabled | pixel/enable | GL_FALSE | glIsEnabled() |
| GL_COLOR_TABLE | Color tables | — | empty | glGetColorTable() |
| GL_COLOR_TABLE_FORMAT | Color tables' internal image format | — | GL_RGBA | glGetColorTable Parameteriv() |
| GL_COLOR_TABLE_WIDTH | Color tables' specified width | — | 0 | glGetColorTable Parameteriv() |
| GL_COLOR_TABLE_x_SIZE | Color table component resolution; x is RED, GREEN, BLUE, ALPHA, LUMINANCE, or INTENSITY | — | 0 | glGetColorTable Parameteriv() |
| GL_COLOR_TABLE_SCALE | Scale factors applied to color table entries | pixel | (1, 1, 1, 1) | glGetColorTable Parameterfv() |
| GL_COLOR_TABLE_BIAS | Bias values applied to color table entries | pixel | (0, 0, 0, 0) | glGetColorTable Parameterfv() |
| GL_CONVOLUTION_1D | True if 1D convolution is enabled | pixel/enable | GL_FALSE | glIsEnabled() |
| GL_CONVOLUTION_2D | True if 2D convolution is enabled | pixel/enable | GL_FALSE | glIsEnabled() |

**Table B-12 (continued)**    Pixel State Variables

| State Variable | Description | Attribute Group | Initial Value | Get Command |
|---|---|---|---|---|
| GL_SEPARABLE_2D | True if separable 2D convolution is enabled | pixel/enable | GL_FALSE | glIsEnabled() |
| GL_CONVOLUTION_1D | 1D convolution filter | — | empty | glGetConvolution Filter() |
| GL_CONVOLUTION_2D | 2D convolution filter | — | empty | glGetConvolution Filter() |
| GL_SEPARABLE_2D | 2D separable convolution filter | — | empty | glGetSeparable Filter() |
| GL_CONVOLUTION_ BORDER_COLOR | Convolution border color | pixel | (0, 0, 0, 0) | glGetConvolution Parameterfv() |
| GL_CONVOLUTION_ BORDER_MODE | Convolution border mode | pixel | GL_REDUCE | glGetConvolution Parameteriv() |
| GL_CONVOLUTION_ FILTER_SCALE | Scale factors applied to convolution filter entries | pixel | (1, 1, 1, 1) | glGetConvolution Parameterfv() |
| GL_CONVOLUTION_ FILTER_BIAS | Bias values applied to convolution filter entries | pixel | (0, 0, 0, 0) | glGetConvolution Parameterfv() |
| GL_CONVOLUTION_FORMAT | Convolution filter internal format | — | GL_RGBA | glGetConvolution Parameteriv() |
| GL_CONVOLUTION_WIDTH | Convolution filter width | — | 0 | glGetConvolution Parameteriv() |

**Table B-12 (continued)**    Pixel State Variables

| State Variable | Description | Attribute Group | Initial Value | Get Command |
|---|---|---|---|---|
| GL_CONVOLUTION_HEIGHT | Convolution filter height | — | 0 | glGetConvolution Parameteriv() |
| GL_POST_CONVOLUTION_ x_SCALE | Component scale factors after convolution; x is RED, GREEN, BLUE, or ALPHA | pixel | 1 | glGetFloatv() |
| GL_POST_CONVOLUTION_ x_BIAS | Component bias values after convolution; x is RED, GREEN, BLUE, or ALPHA | pixel | 0 | glGetFloatv() |
| GL_POST_COLOR_MATRIX_ x_SCALE | Component scale factors after color matrix; x is RED, GREEN, BLUE, or ALPHA | pixel | 1 | glGetFloatv() |
| GL_POST_COLOR_MATRIX_ x_BIAS | Component bias values after color matrix; x is RED, GREEN, BLUE, or ALPHA | pixel | 0 | glGetFloatv() |
| GL_HISTOGRAM | True if histogramming is enabled | pixel/ enable | GL_FALSE | glIsEnabled() |
| GL_HISTOGRAM | Histogram table | — | empty | glGetHistogram() |
| GL_HISTOGRAM_WIDTH | Histogram table width | — | 0 | glGetHistogram Parameteriv() |
| GL_HISTOGRAM_FORMAT | Histogram table internal format | — | GL_RGBA | glGetHistogram Parameteriv() |
| GL_HISTOGRAM_x_SIZE | Histogram table component resolution; x is RED, GREEN, BLUE, ALPHA, or LUMINANCE | — | 0 | glGetHistogram Parameteriv() |

**Table B-12 (continued)**     Pixel State Variables

| State Variable | Description | Attribute Group | Initial Value | Get Command |
|---|---|---|---|---|
| GL_HISTOGRAM_SINK | True if histogramming consumes pixel groups | — | GL_FALSE | glGetHistogramParameteriv() |
| GL_MINMAX | True if minmax is enabled | pixel/enable | GL_FALSE | glIsEnabled() |
| GL_MINMAX | Minmax table | — | See Note a at the end of table. | glGetMinmax() |
| GL_MINMAX_FORMAT | Minmax table internal format | — | GL_RGBA | glGetMinmaxParameteriv() |
| GL_MINMAX_SINK | True if minmax consumes pixel groups | — | GL_FALSE | glGetMinmaxParameteriv() |
| GL_ZOOM_X | $x$ zoom factor | pixel | 1.0 | glGetFloatv() |
| GL_ZOOM_Y | $y$ zoom factor | pixel | 1.0 | glGetFloatv() |
| GL_PIXEL_MAP_x | glPixelMap() translation tables; $x$ is a map name from Table 8-1 | — | 0's | glGetPixelMap*() |
| GL_PIXEL_MAP_x_SIZE | Size of glPixelMap() translation table $x$ | — | 1 | glGetIntegerv() |
| GL_READ_BUFFER | Read source buffer | pixel | — | glGetIntegerv() |

**Table B-12 (continued)**    Pixel State Variables

a. Min table initially set to maximum representable values. Max table set to minimum representable values.

## Evaluators

| State Variable | Description | Attribute Group | Initial Value | Get Command |
|---|---|---|---|---|
| GL_ORDER | 1D map order | — | 1 | glGetMapiv() |
| GL_ORDER | 2D map orders | — | 1, 1 | glGetMapiv() |
| GL_COEFF | 1D control points | — | — | glGetMapfv() |
| GL_COEFF | 2D control points | — | — | glGetMapfv() |
| GL_DOMAIN | 1D domain endpoints | — | — | glGetMapfv() |
| GL_DOMAIN | 2D domain endpoints | — | — | glGetMapfv() |
| GL_MAP1_*x* | 1D map enables: *x* is map type | eval/enable | GL_FALSE | glIsEnabled() |
| GL_MAP2_*x* | 2D map enables: *x* is map type | eval/enable | GL_FALSE | glIsEnabled() |
| GL_MAP1_GRID_DOMAIN | 1D grid endpoints | eval | 0, 1 | glGetFloatv() |
| GL_MAP2_GRID_DOMAIN | 2D grid endpoints | eval | 0, 1; 0, 1 | glGetFloatv() |
| GL_MAP1_GRID_SEGMENTS | 1D grid divisions | eval | 1 | glGetFloatv() |
| GL_MAP2_GRID_SEGMENTS | 2D grid divisions | eval | 1, 1 | glGetFloatv() |
| GL_AUTO_NORMAL | True if automatic normal generation is enabled | eval/enable | GL_FALSE | glIsEnabled() |

**Table B-13**    Evaluator State Variables

## Shader Object State

| State Variable | Description | Attribute Group | Initial Value | Get Command |
|---|---|---|---|---|
| GL_SHADER_TYPE | Type of shader (vertex or fragment) | — | — | glGetShaderiv() |
| GL_DELETE_STATUS | Shader flagged for deletion | — | GL_FALSE | glGetShaderiv() |
| GL_COMPILE_STATUS | Last compilation status | — | GL_FALSE | glGetShaderiv() |
| — | Information log for shader objects | — | empty string | glGetShaderInfoLog() |
| GL_INFO_LOG_LENGTH | String length of shader information log | — | 0 | glGetShaderiv() |
| — | Source code for a shader | — | empty string | glGetShaderSource() |
| GL_SHADER_SOURCE_LENGTH | String length of shader source code | — | 0 | glGetShaderiv() |

**Table B-14**    Shader Object State Variables

## Program Object State

| State Variable | Description | Attribute Group | Initial Value | Get Command |
|---|---|---|---|---|
| GL_CURRENT_PROGRAM | Name of current program object | — | 0 | glGetIntegerv() |
| GL_DELETE_STATUS | Program object deleted | — | GL_FALSE | glGetProgramiv() |
| GL_LINK_STATUS | Last link attempt succeeded | — | GL_FALSE | glGetProgramiv() |
| GL_VALIDATE_STATUS | Last validate attempt succeeded | — | GL_FALSE | glGetProgramiv() |
| GL_ATTACHED_SHADERS | Number of attached shader objects | — | 0 | glGetProgramiv() |
| — | Shader objects attached | — | empty | glGetAttachedShaders() |
| — | Info log for program object | — | empty | glGetProgramInfoLog() |
| GL_INFO_LOG_LENGTH | Length of info log | — | 0 | glGetProgramiv() |
| GL_ACTIVE_UNIFORMS | Number of active uniforms | — | 0 | glGetProgramiv() |
| — | Location of active uniforms | — | — | glGetUniformLocation() |
| — | Size of active uniform | — | — | glGetActiveUniform() |
| — | Type of active uniform | — | — | glGetActiveUniform() |
| — | Name of active uniform | — | empty | glGetActiveUniform() |

**Table B-15**    Program Object State Variables

| State Variable | Description | Attribute Group | Initial Value | Get Command |
|---|---|---|---|---|
| GL_ACTIVE_UNIFORM_MAX_LENGTH | Maximum active uniform name length | — | 0 | glGetProgramiv() |
| — | Uniform value | — | 0 | glGetUniform() |
| GL_ACTIVE_ATTRIBUTES | Number of active attributes | — | 0 | glGetProgramiv() |
| — | Location of active generic attribute | — | — | glGetAttribLocation() |
| — | Size of active attribute | — | — | glGetActiveAttrib() |
| — | Type of active attribute | — | — | glGetActiveAttrib() |
| — | Name of active attribute | — | empty | glGetActiveAttrib() |
| GL_ACTIVE_ATTRIBUTES_MAX_LENGTH | Maximum active attribute name length | — | 0 | glGetProgramiv() |

**Table B-15** **(continued)**    Program Object State Variables

## Vertex Shader State

| State Variable | Description | Attribute Group | Initial Value | Get Command |
|---|---|---|---|---|
| GL_VERTEX_PROGRAM_TWO_SIDE | Two-sided color mode | enable | GL_FALSE | glIsEnabled() |
| GL_CURRENT_VERTEX_ATTRIB | Generic vertex attribute | current | (0, 0, 0, 1) | glGetVertexAttrib() |
| GL_VERTEX_PROGRAM_POINT_SIZE | Point size mode | enable | GL_FALSE | glIsEnabled() |

**Table B-16**    Vertex Shader State Variables

## Hints

| State Variable | Description | Attribute Group | Initial Value | Get Command |
|---|---|---|---|---|
| GL_PERSPECTIVE_CORRECTION_HINT | Perspective correction hint | hint | GL_DONT_CARE | glGetIntegerv() |
| GL_POINT_SMOOTH_HINT | Point smooth hint | hint | GL_DONT_CARE | glGetIntegerv() |
| GL_LINE_SMOOTH_HINT | Line smooth hint | hint | GL_DONT_CARE | glGetIntegerv() |
| GL_POLYGON_SMOOTH_HINT | Polygon smooth hint | hint | GL_DONT_CARE | glGetIntegerv() |
| GL_FOG_HINT | Fog hint | hint | GL_DONT_CARE | glGetIntegerv() |
| GL_GENERATE_MIPMAP_HINT | Mipmap generation hint | hint | GL_DONT_CARE | glGetIntegerv() |

**Table B-17**    Hint State Variables

| State Variable | Description | Attribute Group | Initial Value | Get Command |
| --- | --- | --- | --- | --- |
| GL_TEXTURE_COMPRESSION_HINT | Texture compression hint | hint | GL_DONT_CARE | glGetIntegerv() |
| GL_FRAGMENT_SHADER_DERIVATIVE_HING | Fragment shader derivative accuracy hint | hint | GL_DONT_CARE | glGetIntegerv() |

**Table B-17 (continued)**    Hint State Variables

## Implementation-Dependent Values

| State Variable | Description | Attribute Group | Minimum Value | Get Command |
| --- | --- | --- | --- | --- |
| GL_MAX_LIGHTS | Maximum number of lights | — | 8 | glGetIntegerv() |
| GL_MAX_CLIP_PLANES | Maximum number of user clipping planes | — | 6 | glGetIntegerv() |
| GL_MAX_COLOR_MATRIX_STACK_DEPTH | Maximum color matrix stack depth | — | 2 | glGetIntegerv() |
| GL_MAX_MODELVIEW_STACK_DEPTH | Maximum modelview-matrix stack depth | — | 32 | glGetIntegerv() |
| GL_MAX_PROJECTION_STACK_DEPTH | Maximum projection-matrix stack depth | — | 2 | glGetIntegerv() |
| GL_MAX_TEXTURE_STACK_DEPTH | Maximum depth of texture matrix stack | — | 2 | glGetIntegerv() |

**Table B-18**    Implementation-Dependent State Variables

| State Variable | Description | Attribute Group | Minimum Value | Get Command |
|---|---|---|---|---|
| GL_SUBPIXEL_BITS | Number of bits of subpixel precision in $x$ and $y$ | — | 4 | glGetIntegerv() |
| GL_MAX_3D_TEXTURE_SIZE | See discussion in "Texture Proxy" in Chapter 9 | — | 16 | glGetIntegerv() |
| GL_MAX_TEXTURE_SIZE | See discussion in "Texture Proxy" in Chapter 9 | — | 64 | glGetIntegerv() |
| GL_MAX_TEXTURE_LOD_BIAS | Maximum absolute texture level of detail bias | — | 2.0 | glGetFloatv() |
| GL_MAX_CUBE_MAP_TEXTURE_SIZE | Maximum cube map texture image dimension | — | 16 | glGetIntegerv() |
| GL_MAX_PIXEL_MAP_TABLE | Maximum size of a glPixelMap() translation table | — | 32 | glGetIntegerv() |
| GL_MAX_NAME_STACK_DEPTH | Maximum selection-name stack depth | — | 64 | glGetIntegerv() |
| GL_MAX_LIST_NESTING | Maximum display-list call nesting | — | 64 | glGetIntegerv() |
| GL_MAX_EVAL_ORDER | Maximum evaluator polynomial order | — | 8 | glGetIntegerv() |
| GL_MAX_VIEWPORT_DIMS | Maximum viewport dimensions | — | — | glGetIntegerv() |
| GL_MAX_ATTRIB_STACK_DEPTH | Maximum depth of the attribute stack | — | 16 | glGetIntegerv() |

**Table B-18 (continued)**     Implementation-Dependent State Variables

| State Variable | Description | Attribute Group | Minimum Value | Get Command |
|---|---|---|---|---|
| GL_MAX_CLIENT_ATTRIB_STACK_DEPTH | Maximum depth of the client attribute stack | — | 16 | glGetIntegerv() |
| GL_NUM_COMPRESSED_TEXTURE_FORMATS | Number of supported texture compression formats | — | — | glGetIntegerv() |
| GL_AUX_BUFFERS | Number of auxiliary buffers | — | 0 | glGetBooleanv() |
| GL_RGBA_MODE | True if color buffers store RGBA | — | — | glGetBooleanv() |
| GL_INDEX_MODE | True if color buffers store indices | — | — | glGetBooleanv() |
| GL_DOUBLEBUFFER | True if front and back buffers exist | — | — | glGetBooleanv() |
| GL_STEREO | True if left and right buffers exist | — | — | glGetBooleanv() |
| GL_ALIASED_POINT_SIZE_RANGE | Range (low to high) of aliased point sizes | — | 1, 1 | glGetFloatv() |
| GL_SMOOTH_POINT_SIZE_RANGE | Range (low to high) of antialiased point sizes | — | 1, 1 | glGetFloatv() |
| GL_SMOOTH_POINT_SIZE_GRANULARITY | Antialiased point-size granularity | — | — | glGetFloatv() |
| GL_ALIASED_LINE_WIDTH_RANGE | Range (low to high) of aliased line widths | — | 1, 1 | glGetFloatv() |
| GL_SMOOTH_LINE_WIDTH_RANGE | Range (low to high) of antialiased line widths | — | 1, 1 | glGetFloatv() |

**Table B-18 (continued)**    Implementation-Dependent State Variables

| State Variable | Description | Attribute Group | Minimum Value | Get Command |
|---|---|---|---|---|
| GL_SMOOTH_LINE_WIDTH_GRANULARITY | Antialiased line-width granularity | — | — | glGetFloatv() |
| GL_MAX_CONVOLUTION_WIDTH | Maximum width of convolution filter | — | 3 | glConvolution Parameteriv() |
| GL_MAX_CONVOLUTION_HEIGHT | Maximum height of convolution filter | — | 3 | glConvolution Parameteriv() |
| GL_MAX_ELEMENTS_INDICES | Recommended maximum number of glDrawRangeElement() indices | — | — | glGetIntegerv() |
| GL_MAX_ELEMENTS_VERTICES | Recommended maximum number of glDrawRangeElement() vertices | — | — | glGetIntegerv() |
| GL_MAX_TEXTURE_UNITS | Maximum number of texture units (not to exceed 32) | — | 2 | glGetIntegerv() |
| GL_SAMPLE_BUFFERS | Number of multisample buffers | — | 0 | glGetIntegerv() |
| GL_SAMPLES | Coverage mask size | — | 0 | glGetIntegerv() |
| GL_COMPRESSED_TEXTURE_FORMATS | Enumerated compressed texture formats | — | — | glGetIntegerv() |
| GL_NUM_COMPRESSED_TEXTURE_FORMATS | Number of enumerated compressed texture formats | — | 0 | glGetIntegerv() |

**Table B-18 (continued)**   Implementation-Dependent State Variables

| State Variable | Description | Attribute Group | Minimum Value | Get Command |
| --- | --- | --- | --- | --- |
| GL_QUERY_COUNTER_BITS | Number of bits in the occlusion query counter | — | — | glGetQueryiv() |
| GL_EXTENSIONS | Supported extensions | — | — | glGetString() |
| GL_RENDERER | Renderer string | — | — | glGetString() |
| GL_SHADING_LANGUAGE_VERSION | OpenGL Shading Language (GLSL) version | — | — | glGetString() |
| GL_VENDOR | Vendor string | — | — | glGetString() |
| GL_VERSION | Version string | — | — | glGetString() |
| GL_MAX_VERTEX_ATTRIBS | Number of active vertex attributes | — | 16 | glGetIntegerv() |
| GL_MAX_VERTEX_UNIFORM_COMPONENTS | Number of words for vertex shader univorm variables | — | 512 | glGetIntegerv() |
| GL_MAX_VARYING_FLOATS | Number of floats for varying variables | — | 32 | glGetIntegerv() |
| GL_MAX_COMBINED_TEXTURE_IMAGE_UNITS | Total number of texture units accessible by OpenGL | — | 2 | glGetIntegerv() |
| GL_MAX_VERTEX_TEXTURE_IMAGE_UNITS | Number of texture image units accessible by a vertex shader | — | 0 | glGetIntegerv() |

**Table B-18 (continued)**    Implementation-Dependent State Variables

| State Variable | Description | Attribute Group | Minimum Value | Get Command |
|---|---|---|---|---|
| GL_MAX_TEXTURE_IMAGE_UNITS | Number of texture image units accessible by fragment processing | — | 2 | glGetIntegerv() |
| GL_MAX_TEXTURE_COORDS | Number of texture-coordinate sets | — | 2 | glGetIntegerv() |
| GL_MAX_FRAGMENT_UNIFORM_COMPONENTS | Number of words for fragment shader uniform variables | — | 64 | glGetIntegerv() |
| GL_MAX_DRAW_BUFFERS | Maximum number of active draw buffers | — | 1+ | glGetIntegerv() |

**Table B-18 (continued)**    Implementation-Dependent State Variables

# Implementation-Dependent Pixel Depths

| State Variable | Description | Attribute Group | Minimum Value | Get Command |
|---|---|---|---|---|
| GL_x_BITS | Number of bits in x color buffer component (x is one of RED, GREEN, BLUE, ALPHA, or INDEX) | — | — | glGetIntegerv() |
| GL_DEPTH_BITS | Number of depth-buffer bitplanes | — | — | glGetIntegerv() |
| GL_STENCIL_BITS | Number of stencil bitplanes | — | — | glGetIntegerv() |
| GL_ACCUM_x_BITS | Number of bits in x accumulation buffer component (x is one of RED, GREEN, BLUE, or ALPHA) | — | — | glGetIntegerv() |

**Table B-19**    Implementation-Dependent Pixel-Depth State Variables

# Miscellaneous

| State Variable | Description | Attribute Group | Initial Value | Get Command |
|---|---|---|---|---|
| GL_LIST_BASE | Setting of glListBase() | list | 0 | glGetIntegerv() |
| GL_LIST_INDEX | Number of display list under construction; 0 if none | — | 0 | glGetIntegerv() |
| GL_LIST_MODE | Mode of display list under construction; undefined if none | — | 0 | glGetIntegerv() |

**Table B-20**    Miscellaneous State Variables

| State Variable | Description | Attribute Group | Initial Value | Get Command |
|---|---|---|---|---|
| GL_ATTRIB_STACK_DEPTH | Attribute stack pointer | — | 0 | glGetIntegerv() |
| GL_CLIENT_ATTRIB_STACK_DEPTH | Client attribute stack pointer | — | 0 | glGetIntegerv() |
| GL_NAME_STACK_DEPTH | Name stack depth | — | 0 | glGetIntegerv() |
| GL_RENDER_MODE | glRenderMode() setting | — | GL_RENDER | glGetIntegerv() |
| GL_SELECTION_BUFFER_POINTER | Pointer to selection buffer | select | 0 | glGetPointerv() |
| GL_SELECTION_BUFFER_SIZE | Size of selection buffer | select | 0 | glGetIntegerv() |
| GL_FEEDBACK_BUFFER_POINTER | Pointer to feedback buffer | feedback | 0 | glGetPointerv() |
| GL_FEEDBACK_BUFFER_SIZE | Size of feedback buffer | feedback | 0 | glGetIntegerv() |
| GL_FEEDBACK_BUFFER_TYPE | Type of feedback buffer | feedback | GL_2D | glGetIntegerv() |
| — | Current error code(s) | — | 0 | glGetError() |
| GL_CURRENT_QUERY | Active occlusion query ID | — | 0 | glGetQueryiv() |

**Table B-20 (continued)**　Miscellaneous State Variables

# OpenGL and Window Systems

OpenGL is available on many different platforms and works with many different window systems. It is designed to complement window systems, not duplicate their functionality. Therefore, OpenGL performs geometric and image rendering in two and three dimensions, but it does not manage windows or handle input events.

However, the basic definitions of most window systems don't support a library as sophisticated as OpenGL, with its complex and diverse pixel formats, including depth, stencil, and accumulation buffers, as well as double-buffering. For most window systems, some routines are added to extend the window system to support OpenGL.

This appendix introduces the extensions defined for several window and operating systems: the X Window System, the Apple Mac OS, OS/2 Warp from IBM, and Microsoft Windows. You need to have some knowledge of the window systems to fully understand this appendix.

This appendix has the following major sections:

- "Accessing New OpenGL Functions"
- "GLX: OpenGL Extension for the X Window System"
- "AGL: OpenGL Extensions for the Apple Macintosh"
- "PGL: OpenGL Extension for IBM OS/2 Warp"
- "WGL: OpenGL Extension for Microsoft Windows 95/98/NT/ME/2000/XP"

## Accessing New OpenGL Functions

OpenGL is changing all the time. The manufacturers of OpenGL graphics hardware add new extensions and the OpenGL Architecture Review Board approve those extensions and merge them into the core of OpenGL. Since each manufacturer needs to be able to update its version of OpenGL, the header files (like gl.h), and the library you use to compile (like opengl32.lib, on Microsoft Windows, for example) may be out of sync with the latest version. This would likely cause errors when compiling (or more specifically, linking) your application.

To work around this problem, a mechanism for accessing the new functions was added to each of the window system libraries. This method varies among the different window systems, but the idea is the same in all cases. You will need to get the function pointer for the function that you want to use. You need to do this only if the function is not available explicitly from your library (you'll know when it isn't; you'll get a linker error).

Each window system has its own function for getting an OpenGL function pointer; check the respective section in this appendix for specifics.

Here is an example for Microsoft Windows:

```
#include <windows.h>  /* for wglGetProcAddress() */
#include "glext.h"

PFNGLBINDPROGRAMARBPROC   glBindProgramARB;

void
init(void)
{
   glBindProgramARB = (PFNGLBINDPROGRAMARB)
     wglGetProcAddress("glBindProgramARB");
   ...
}
```

The function pointer type, in this case PFNGLBINDPROGRAMARBPROC, is defined in glext.h, as are all of the enumerants that you pass into OpenGL functions. If the returned value is zero, the function is not available in the OpenGL implementation that your program is using.

# GLX: OpenGL Extension for the X Window System

In the X Window System, OpenGL rendering is made available as an extension to X in the formal X sense. GLX is an extension to the X protocol (and its associated API) for communicating OpenGL commands to an extended X server. Connection and authentication are accomplished with the normal X mechanisms.

As with other X extensions, there is a defined network protocol for OpenGL's rendering commands encapsulated within the X byte stream, so client-server OpenGL rendering is supported. Since performance is critical in three-dimensional rendering, the OpenGL extension to X allows OpenGL to bypass the X server's involvement in data encoding, copying, and interpretation, and instead render directly to the graphics pipeline.

GLX Version 1.3 introduces several sweeping changes, starting with the new GLXFBConfig data structure, which describes the GLX framebuffer configuration (including the depth of the color buffer components, and the types, quantities, and sizes of the depth, stencil, accumulation, and auxiliary buffers). The GLXFBConfig structure describes these framebuffer attributes for a GLXDrawable rendering surface. (In X, a rendering surface is called a *Drawable*.)

GLX 1.3 provides for three types of GLXDrawable surfaces: GLXWindow, GLXPixmap, and GLXPbuffer. A GLXWindow is on-screen; a GLXPixmap or GLXPbuffer is off-screen. Because a GLXPixmap has an associated X pixmap, both X and GLX may render into a GLXPixmap. GLX may be the only way to render into a GLXPbuffer. The GLXPbuffer is intended to store pixel data in nonvisible framebuffer memory. (Off-screen rendering isn't guaranteed to be supported for direct renderers.)

The X Visual is an important data structure for maintaining pixel format information about an OpenGL window. A variable of data type XVisualInfo keeps track of pixel format information, including pixel type (RGBA or color-index), single- or double-buffering, resolution of colors, and presence of depth, stencil, and accumulation buffers. The standard X Visuals (for example, PseudoColor, and TrueColor) do not describe the pixel format details, so each implementation must extend the number of X Visuals supported.

In GLX 1.3, a GLXWindow has an X Visual, associated with its GLXFBConfig. For a GLXPixmap or a GLXPbuffer, there may or may not be a similar associated X Visual. Prior to GLX 1.3, all surfaces (windows or pixmaps) were associated with an X Visual. (Prior to 1.3, Pbuffers were not part of GLX.)

The GLX routines are discussed in more detail in the *OpenGL Reference Manual*. Integrating OpenGL applications with the X Window System and the Motif widget set is discussed in great detail in *OpenGL Programming for the X Window System* by Mark Kilgard (Addison-Wesley, 1996), which includes full source code examples. If you absolutely want to learn about the internals of GLX, you may want to read the GLX specification, which can be found at

`http://www.opengl.org/developers/documentation/glx.html`

## Initialization

Use **glXQueryExtension()** and **glXQueryVersion()** to determine whether the GLX extension is defined for an X server and, if so, which version is present. **glXQueryExtensionsString()** returns extension information about the client-server connection. **glXGetClientString()** returns information about the client library, including extensions and version number. **glXQueryServerString()** returns similar information about the server.

**glXChooseFBConfig()** returns a pointer to an array of GLXFBConfig structures describing all GLX framebuffer configurations that meet the client's specified attributes. You may use **glXGetFBConfigAttrib()** to query a framebuffer configuration about its support of a particular GLX attribute. You may also call **glXGetVisualFromFBConfig()** to retrieve the X visual associated with a GLXFBConfig.

Creation of rendering areas varies slightly, depending on the type of drawable. For a GLXWindow, first create an X Window with an X visual that corresponds to the GLXFBConfig. Then use that X Window when calling **glXCreateWindow()**, which returns a GLXWindow. Similarly for a GLXPixmap, first create an X Pixmap with a pixel depth that matches the GLXFBConfig. Then use that Pixmap when calling **glXCreatePixmap()** to create a GLXPixmap. A GLXPbuffer does not require an X Window or an X Pixmap; just call **glXCreatePbuffer()** with the appropriate GLXFBConfig.

**Note:** If you are using GLX 1.2 or earlier, you do not have a GLXFBConfig structure. Instead, use **glXChooseVisual()**, which returns a pointer to an XVisualInfo structure describing the X visual that meets the client's specified attributes. You can query a visual about its support of a particular OpenGL attribute with **glXGetConfig()**. To render to an off-screen pixmap, you must use the earlier **glXCreateGLXPixmap()** routine.

### Accessing OpenGL Functions

To access function pointers for extensions and new features in the X Window System, use the **glXGetProcAddress()** function. This function is defined in the glxext.h header file, which can be downloaded from the OpenGL Web site.

## Controlling Rendering

Several GLX routines are provided for creating and managing an OpenGL rendering context. Routines are also provided for such tasks as handling GLX events, synchronizing execution between the X and OpenGL streams, swapping front and back buffers, and using an X font.

### Managing an OpenGL Rendering Context

An OpenGL rendering context is created with **glXCreateNewContext()**. One of the arguments to this routine allows you to request a direct rendering context that bypasses the X server as described previously. (To perform direct rendering, the X server connection must be local, and the OpenGL implementation needs to support direct rendering.) **glXCreateNewContext()** also allows display-list and texture-object indices and definitions to be shared by multiple rendering contexts. You can determine whether a GLX context is direct with **glXIsDirect()**

**glXMakeContextCurrent()** binds a rendering context to the current rendering thread and also establishes two current drawable surfaces. You can draw into one of the current drawable surfaces and read pixel data from the other drawable. In many situations, the *draw* and *read* drawables refer to the same GLXDrawable surface. **glXGetCurrentContext()** returns the current context. You can also obtain the current *draw* drawable with **glXGetCurrentDrawable()**, the current *read* drawable with **glXGetCurrentReadDrawable()**, and the current X Display with **glXGetCurrentDisplay()**. You can use **glXQueryContext()** to determine the current values for context attributes.

Only one context can be current for any thread at any one time. If you have multiple contexts, you can copy selected groups of OpenGL state variables from one context to another with **glXCopyContext()**. When you're finished with a particular context, destroy it with **glXDestroyContext()**.

**Note:** If you are using GLX 1.2 or earlier, use **glXCreateContext()** to create a rendering context and **glXMakeCurrent()** to make it current. You cannot declare a drawable as a separate *read* drawable, so you do not have **glXGetCurrentReadDrawable()**.

### Handling GLX Events

GLX 1.3 introduces GLX events, which are returned in the event stream of standard X11 events. GLX event handling has been added specifically to deal with the uncertainty of the contents of a GLXPbuffer, which may be clobbered at any time. In GLX 1.3, you may use **glXSelectEvent()** to select only one event with GLX_PBUFFER_CLOBBER_MASK. With standard X event handling routines, you can now determine if a portion of a GLXPbuffer (or GLXWindow) has been damaged and then take steps, if desired, to recover. (Also, you can call **glXGetSelectedEvent()** to find out if you are already monitoring this GLX event.)

### Synchronizing Execution

To prevent X requests from executing until any outstanding OpenGL rendering is completed, call **glXWaitGL()**. Then, any previously issued OpenGL commands are guaranteed to be executed before any X rendering calls made after **glXWaitGL()**. Although the same result can be achieved with **glFinish()**, **glXWaitGL()** doesn't require a round-trip to the server and thus is more efficient in cases where the client and server are on separate machines.

To prevent an OpenGL command sequence from executing until any outstanding X requests are completed, use **glXWaitX()**. This routine guarantees that previously issued X rendering calls are executed before any OpenGL calls made after **glXWaitX()**.

### Swapping Buffers

For drawables that are double-buffered, the front and back buffers can be exchanged by calling **glXSwapBuffers()**. An implicit **glFlush()** is done as part of this routine.

### Using an X Font

A shortcut for using X fonts in OpenGL is provided with the command **glXUseXFont()**. This routine builds display lists, each of which calls **glBitmap()** for each requested character from the specified font and font size.

## Cleaning Up Drawables

Once rendering is completed, you can destroy the drawable surface with the appropriate call to **glXDestroyWindow()**, **glXDestroyPixmap()**, or **glXDestroyPbuffer()**. (These routines are not available prior to GLX 1.3, although there is **glXDestroyGLXPixmap()**, which is similar to **glXDestroyPixmap()**.)

# GLX Prototypes

### Initialization

Determine whether the GLX extension is defined on the X server:

> Bool **glXQueryExtension**( Display *dpy*, int *errorBase*,
>     int *eventBase* );

Query version and extension information for client and server:

> Bool **glXQueryVersion**( Display *dpy*, int *major*, int *minor* );

> const char* **glXGetClientString**( Display *dpy*, int *name* );

> const char* **glXQueryServerString**( Display *dpy*, int *screen*,
>     int *name* );

> const char* **glXQueryExtensionsString**( Display *dpy*, int *screen* );

Obtain available GLX framebuffer configurations:

> GLXFBConfig * **glXGetFBConfigs**( Display *dpy*, int *screen*,
>     int *nelements* );

> GLXFBConfig * **glXChooseFBConfig**( Display *dpy*, int *screen*,
>     const int *attribList*, int *nelements* );

Query a GLX framebuffer configuration for attribute or X Visual information:

> int **glXGetFBConfigAttrib**( Display *dpy*, GLXFBConfig *config*,
>     int *attribute*, int *value* );

> XVisualInfo * **glXGetVisualFromFBConfig**( Display *dpy*,
>     GLXFBConfig *config* );

Create surfaces that support rendering (both on-screen and off-screen):

GLXWindow **glXCreateWindow**( Display *dpy*,
   GLXFBConfig *config*, Window *win*, const int *attribList* );

GLXPixmap **glXCreatePixmap**( Display *dpy*, GLXFBConfig *config*,
   Pixmap *pixmap*, const int *attribList* );

GLXPbuffer **glXCreatePbuffer**( Display *dpy*, GLXFBConfig *config*,
   const int *attribList* );

Obtain a pointer to an OpenGL function:

__GLXextFuncPtr **glXGetProcAddress**(const char* *funcName*);

**Controlling Rendering**

Manage and query an OpenGL rendering context:

GLXContext **glXCreateNewContext**( Display *dpy*,
   GLXFBConfig *config*, int *renderType*, GLXContext *shareList*,
   Bool *direct* );

Bool **glXMakeContextCurrent**( Display *dpy*,
   GLXDrawable *drawable*, GLXDrawable *read*, GLXContext *context* );

void **glXCopyContext**( Display *dpy*, GLXContext *source*,
   GLXContext *dest*, unsigned long *mask* );

Bool **glXIsDirect**( Display *dpy*, GLXContext *context* );

GLXContext **glXGetCurrentContext**( void );

Display* **glXGetCurrentDisplay**( void );

GLXDrawable **glXGetCurrentDrawable**( void );

GLXDrawable **glXGetCurrentReadDrawable**( void );

int **glXQueryContext**( Display *dpy*, GLXContext *context*,
   int *attribute*, int *value* );

void **glXDestroyContext**( Display *dpy*, GLXContext *context* );

Ask to receive and query GLX events:

int **glXSelectEvent**( Display *dpy*, GLXDrawable *drawable*,
   unsigned long *eventMask* );

int **glXGetSelectedEvent**( Display *dpy*, GLXDrawable *drawable*,
   unsigned long *eventMask* );

Synchronize execution:

> void **glXWaitGL**( void );

> void **glXWaitX**( void );

Exchange front and back buffers:

> void **glXSwapBuffers**( Display *dpy*, GLXDrawable *drawable* );

Use an X font:

> void **glXUseXFont**( Font *font*, int *first*, int *count*, int *listBase* );

Clean up drawables:

> void **glXDestroyWindow**( Display *dpy*, GLXWindow *win* );

> void **glXDestroyPixmap**( Display *dpy*, GLXPixmap *pixmap* );

> void **glXDestroyPbuffer**( Display *dpy*, GLXPbuffer *pbuffer* );

## Deprecated GLX Prototypes

The following routines have been deprecated in GLX 1.3. If you are using GLX 1.2 or a predecessor, you may need to use several of these routines.

Obtain the desired visual:

> XVisualInfo* **glXChooseVisual**( Display *dpy*, int *screen*,
>     int *attribList* );

> int **glXGetConfig**( Display *dpy*, XVisualInfo *visual*, int *attrib*,
>     int *value* );

Manage an OpenGL rendering context:

> GLXContext **glXCreateContext**( Display *dpy*, XVisualInfo *visual*,
>     GLXContext *shareList*, Bool *direct* );

> Bool **glXMakeCurrent**( Display *dpy*, GLXDrawable *drawable*,
>     GLXContext *context* );

Perform off-screen rendering:

> GLXPixmap **glXCreateGLXPixmap**( Display *dpy*,
>     XVisualInfo *visual*, Pixmap *pixmap* );

> void **glXDestroyGLXPixmap**( Display *dpy*, GLXPixmap *pix* );

# AGL: OpenGL Extensions for the Apple Macintosh

This section covers the routines defined as the OpenGL extension to the Apple Macintosh (AGL). An understanding of the way the Macintosh handles graphics rendering (QuickDraw) is required. *The Macintosh Toolbox Essentials* and *Imaging with QuickDraw* manuals from the Inside Macintosh series are also useful to have at hand.

For more information (including how to obtain the OpenGL software library for the Macintosh), you may want to check out the Apple Web site for OpenGL information:

```
http://www.apple.com/opengl
```

For the Macintosh, OpenGL rendering is made available as a library that is either compiled in or resident as an extension for an application that wishes to make use of it. OpenGL is implemented in software for systems that do not offer hardware acceleration. Where acceleration is available, those capabilities that match the OpenGL pipeline are used, with the remaining functionality being provided through software rendering.

The data type AGLPixelFormat (the AGL equivalent to XVisualInfo) maintains pixel information, including pixel type (RGBA or color index); single- or double-buffering; resolution of colors; and presence of depth, stencil, and accumulation buffers.

In contrast to other OpenGL implementations on other systems (such as the X Window System), the client-server model is not used. However, you may still need to call **glFlush()**, since some hardware accelerators buffer the OpenGL pipeline and require a flush to empty it.

## Initialization

Use **aglGetVersion()** to determine which version of AGL for the Macintosh is available.

The capabilities of underlying graphics devices and your requirements for rendering buffers are resolved using **aglChoosePixelFormat()**. It returns an AGLPixelFormat structure or NULL, depending on whether or not your requirements can be accommodated.

## Rendering and Contexts

Several AGL routines are provided for creating and managing an OpenGL rendering context. You can use such a context to render into either a window or an off-screen graphics world. Routines are also provided that allow you to swap front and back rendering buffers; adjust buffers in response to a move, resize, or graphics device change event; and use Macintosh fonts. For software rendering (and, in some cases, hardware-accelerated rendering), the rendering buffers are created in the system memory space.

## Managing an OpenGL Rendering Context

An OpenGL rendering context is created (at least one context per window being rendered into) with **aglCreateContext()**. This takes the pixel format you selected as a parameter and uses it to initialize the context.

Use **aglSetDrawable()** to attach the context to the drawable and then **aglSetCurrentContext()** to make a rendering context current. Only one context can be current for a thread of control at any time. This indicates which drawable is to be rendered into and which context to use with it. It's possible for more than one context to be used (not simultaneously) with a particular drawable. Two routines allow you to determine the current rendering context and drawable being rendered into: **aglGetCurrentContext()** and **aglGetDrawable()**.

If you have multiple contexts, you can copy selected groups of OpenGL state variables from one context to another with **aglCopyContext()**. When a particular context is no longer needed, it should be destroyed by calling **aglDestroyContext()**.

## On-Screen Rendering

To render on-screen, first create a pixel format. Create a context based on this pixel format and attach the context to the window with **aglSetDrawable()**. The buffer rectangle can be modified by calling **aglSetInteger(AGL_BUFFER_RECT, ...)**.

## Off-Screen Rendering

To render off-screen, create a pixel format with the AGL_OFFSCREEN attribute. Create a context based on this pixel format and attach the context to the screen with **aglSetOffScreen()**.

## Full-Screen Rendering

To render full-screen, create a pixel format with the AGL_FULLSCREEN attribute. Create a context based on this pixel format and attach the context to the screen with **aglSetFullScreen()**.

## Swapping Buffers

For drawables that are double-buffered (as per the pixel format of the current rendering context), call **aglSwapBuffers()** to exchange the front and back buffers. The swap rectangle can be modified by calling **aglSetInteger(AGL_SWAP_RECT, ...)**. An implicit **glFlush()** is performed as part of this routine.

## Updating the Rendering Buffers

The Apple Macintosh toolbox requires you to perform your own event handling and does not provide a way for libraries to hook into the event stream automatically. So that the drawables maintained by OpenGL can adjust to changes in drawable size, position, and pixel depth, **aglUpdateContext()** is provided.

This routine must be called by your event processing code whenever one of these events occurs in the current drawable. Ideally, the scene should be re-rendered after an update call to take into account the changes made to the rendering buffers.

## Using an Apple Macintosh Font

A shortcut for using Macintosh fonts is provided with **aglUseFont()**. This routine builds display lists, each of which calls **glBitmap()** for each requested character from the specified font and font size.

## Error Handling

An error-handling mechanism is provided for the Apple Macintosh OpenGL extension. When an error occurs, you can call **aglGetError()** to get a more precise description of what caused the error.

## AGL Prototypes

### Initialization

Determine version information:

> void **aglGetVersion**( GLint *major*, GLint *minor* );

Determine available pixel formats:

> AGLPixelFormat **aglChoosePixelFormat**( const AGLDevice *gdevs*, GLint *ndev*, const GLint *attribs* );

> void **aglDestroyPixelFormat**( AGLPixelFormat *pix* );

> AGLPixelFormat **aglNextPixelFormat**( AGLPixelFormat *pix* );

> GLboolean **aglDescribePixelFormat**( AGLPixelFormat *pix*, GLint *attrib*, GLint *value* );

> AGLDevice ***aglDevicesOfPixelFormat**( AGLPixelFormat *pix*, GLint *ndevs* );

Renderer information functions:

> AGLRendererInfo **aglQueryRendererInfo**( const AGLDevice *gdevs*, GLint *ndev* );

> void **aglDestroyRendererInfo**( AGLRendererInfo *rend* );

> AGLRendererInfo **aglNextRendererInfo**( AGLRendererInfo *rend* );

> GLboolean **aglDescribeRenderer**( AGLRendererInfo *rend*, GLint *prop*, GLint *value* );

### Controlling Rendering

Manage OpenGL rendering contexts:

> AGLContext **aglCreateContext**( AGLPixelFormat *pix*, AGLContext *share* );

GLboolean **aglDestroyContext**( AGLContext *ctx* );

GLboolean **aglCopyContext**( AGLContext *src*, AGLContext *dst*,
GLuint *mask* );

GLboolean **aglUpdateContext**( AGLContext *ctx* );

Current state functions:

GLboolean **aglSetCurrentContext**( AGLContext *ctx* );

AGLContext **aglGetCurrentContext**( void );

Drawable functions:

GLboolean **aglSetDrawable**( AGLContext *ctx*, AGLDrawable *draw* );

GLboolean **aglSetOffScreen**( AGLContext *ctx*, GLsizei *width*,
GLsizei *height*, GLsizei *rowbytes*, GLvoid *\*baseaddr* );

GLboolean **aglSetFullScreen**( AGLContext *ctx*, GLsizei *width*,
GLsizei *height*, GLsizei *freq*, GLint *device* );

AGLDrawable **aglGetDrawable**( AGLContext *ctx* );

Virtual screen functions:

GLboolean **aglSetVirtualScreen**( AGLContext *ctx*, GLint *screen* );

GLint **aglGetVirtualScreen**( AGLContext *ctx* );

Configure global library option:

GLboolean **aglConfigure**( GLenum *pname*, GLuint *param* );

Swap function:

void **aglSwapBuffers**( AGLContext *ctx* );

Per context options:

GLboolean **aglEnable**( AGLContext *ctx*, GLenum *pname* );

GLboolean **aglDisable**( AGLContext *ctx*, GLenum *pname* );

GLboolean **aglIsEnabled**( AGLContext *ctx*, GLenum *pname* );

GLboolean **aglSetInteger**( AGLContext *ctx*, GLenum *pname*,
const GLint *\*params* );

GLboolean **aglGetInteger**( AGLContext *ctx*, GLenum *pname*,
GLint *\*params* );

Font function:

> GLboolean **aglUseFont**( AGLContext *ctx*, GLint *fontID*, Style *face*,
> GLint *size*, GLint *first*, GLint *count*, GLint *base* );

Error functions:

> GLenum **aglGetError**( void );

> const GLubyte ***aglErrorString**( GLenum *code* );

Soft reset function:

> void **aglResetLibrary**( void );

# PGL: OpenGL Extension for IBM OS/2 Warp

OpenGL rendering for IBM OS/2 Warp is accomplished by using PGL
routines added to integrate OpenGL into the standard IBM Presentation
Manager. OpenGL with PGL supports both a direct OpenGL context (which
is often faster) and an indirect context (which allows some integration of
Graphics Programming Interface (GPI) and OpenGL rendering).

The data type VISUALCONFIG (the PGL equivalent to XVisualInfo) maintains the visual configuration, including pixel type (RGBA or color-index);
single- or double-buffering; resolution of colors; and presence of depth,
stencil, and accumulation buffers.

To get more information (including how to obtain the OpenGL software
library for IBM OS/2 Warp, Version 3.0), you may want to start at

```
http://www.austin.ibm.com/software/OpenGL/
```

Packaged along with the software is the document *OpenGL on OS/2 Warp*,
which provides more detailed information. OpenGL support is included
with the base operating system with OS/2 Warp Version 4.

## Initialization

Use **pglQueryCapability**() and **pglQueryVersion**() to determine whether
OpenGL is supported on this machine and, if so, how it is supported
and which version is present. **pglChooseConfig**() returns a pointer to a
VISUALCONFIG structure describing the visual configuration that best

meets the client's specified attributes. A list of the particular visual configurations supported by a graphics device can be found using **pglQueryConfigs()**.

## Controlling Rendering

Several PGL routines are provided for creating and managing an OpenGL rendering context, capturing the contents of a bitmap, synchronizing execution between the Presentation Manager and OpenGL streams, swapping front and back buffers, using a color palette, and using an OS/2 logical font.

### Managing an OpenGL Rendering Context

An OpenGL rendering context is created with **pglCreateContext()**. One of the arguments of this routine allows you to request a direct rendering context that bypasses the Gpi and render to a PM window, which is generally faster. You can determine whether an OpenGL context is direct with **pglIsIndirect()**.

To make a rendering context current, use **pglMakeCurrent()**; **pglGetCurrentContext()** returns the current context. You can also obtain the current window with **pglGetCurrentWindow()**. You can copy some OpenGL state variables from one context to another with **pglCopyContext()**. When you're finished with a particular context, destroy it with **pglDestroyContext()**.

### Access the Bitmap of the Front Buffer

To lock access to the bitmap representation of the contents of the front buffer, use **pglGrabFrontBitmap()**. An implicit **glFlush()** is performed, and you can read the bitmap, but its contents are effectively read-only. Immediately after access is completed, you should call **pglReleaseFrontBitmap()** to restore write access to the front buffer.

### Synchronizing Execution

To prevent Gpi rendering requests from executing until any outstanding OpenGL rendering is completed, call **pglWaitGL()**. Then, any previously issued OpenGL commands are guaranteed to be executed before any Gpi rendering calls made after **pglWaitGL()**.

To prevent an OpenGL command sequence from executing until any outstanding Gpi requests are completed, use **pglWaitPM()**. This routine guarantees that previously issued Gpi rendering calls are executed before any OpenGL calls made after **pglWaitPM()**.

**Note:** OpenGL and Gpi rendering can be integrated in the same window only if the OpenGL context is an indirect context.

### Swapping Buffers

For windows that are double-buffered, the front and back buffers can be exchanged by calling **pglSwapBuffers()**. An implicit **glFlush()** is done as part of this routine.

### Using a Color Index Palette

When you are running in 8-bit (256-color) mode, you have to consider color palette management. For windows with a color-index visual configuration, call **pglSelectColorIndexPalette()** to tell OpenGL what color-index palette you want to use with your context. A color palette must be selected before the context is initially bound to a window. In RGBA mode, OpenGL sets up a palette automatically.

### Using an OS/2 Logical Font

A shortcut for using OS/2 logical fonts in OpenGL is provided with the command **pglUseFont()**. This routine builds display lists, each of which calls **glBitmap()** for each requested character from the specified font and font size.

## PGL Prototypes

### Initialization

Determine whether OpenGL is supported and, if so, its version number:

> long **pglQueryCapability**( HAB *hab* );

> void **pglQueryVersion**( HAB *hab*, int *\*major*, int *\*minor* );

Visual configuration selection, availability, and capability:

> PVISUALCONFIG **pglChooseConfig**( HAB *hab*, int *\*attribList* );

> PVISUALCONFIG * **pglQueryConfigs**( HAB *hab* );

### Controlling Rendering

Manage or query an OpenGL rendering context:

HGC **pglCreateContext**( HAB *hab*, PVISUALCONFIG *pVisualConfig*, HGC *shareList*, Bool isDirect );

Bool **pglDestroyContext**( HAB *hab*, HGC *hgc* );

Bool **pglCopyContext**( HAB *hab*, HGC *source*, HGC *dest*, GLuint *mask* );

Bool **pglMakeCurrent**( HAB *hab*, HGC *hgc*, HWND *hwnd* );

long **pglIsIndirect**( HAB *hab*, HGC *hgc* );

HGC **pglGetCurrentContext**( HAB *hab* );

HWND **pglGetCurrentWindow**( HAB *hab* );

Access and release the bitmap of the front buffer:

Bool **pglGrabFrontBitmap**( HAB *hab*, HPS *\*hps*, HBITMAP *\*phbitmap* );

Bool **pglReleaseFrontBitmap**( HAB *hab* );

Synchronize execution:

HPS **pglWaitGL**( HAB *hab* );

void **pglWaitPM**( HAB *hab* );

Exchange front and back buffers:

void **pglSwapBuffers**( HAB *hab*, HWND *hwnd* );

Find a color-index palette:

void **pglSelectColorIndexPalette**( HAB *hab*, HPAL, *hpal*, HGC *hgc* );

Use an OS/2 logical font:

Bool **pglUseFont**( HAB *hab*, HPS *hps*, FATTRS *\*fontAttribs*, long *logicalId*, int *first*, int *count*, int *listBase* );

# WGL: OpenGL Extension for Microsoft Windows 95/98/NT/ME/2000/XP

OpenGL rendering is supported on systems that run any modern version of Microsoft Windows (from Windows 95 and later). The functions and routines of the Win32 library are necessary to initialize the pixel format and control rendering, and for access to extensions for OpenGL. Some routines, which are prefixed by **wgl**, extend Win32 so that OpenGL can be fully supported.

For Win32/WGL, the PIXELFORMATDESCRIPTOR is the key data structure for maintaining pixel format information about the OpenGL window. A variable of data type PIXELFORMATDESCRIPTOR keeps track of pixel information, including pixel type (RGBA or color-index); single- or double-buffering; resolution of colors; and presence of depth, stencil, and accumulation buffers.

To get more information about WGL, you may want to start with technical articles available through the Microsoft Developer Network Web site.

## Initialization

Use **GetVersion()** or the newer **GetVersionEx()** to determine version information. **ChoosePixelFormat()** tries to find a PIXELFORMAT DESCRIPTOR with specified attributes. If a good match for the requested pixel format is found, then **SetPixelFormat()** should be called for actual use of the pixel format. You should select a pixel format in the device context before calling **wglCreateContext()**.

If you want to find out details about a given pixel format, use **DescribePixelFormat()** or, for overlays or underlays, **wglDescribeLayerPlane()**.

### Accessing OpenGL Functions

To access function pointers for extensions and new features in Microsoft Windows, use the **wglGetProcAddress()** function. This function is defined in the wingdi.h header file, which is automatically included when you include windows.h in your application.

## Controlling Rendering

Several WGL routines are provided for creating and managing an OpenGL rendering context, rendering to a bitmap, swapping front and back buffers, finding a color palette, and using either bitmap or outline fonts.

### Managing an OpenGL Rendering Context

**wglCreateContext()** creates an OpenGL rendering context for drawing on the device in the selected pixel format of the device context. (To create an OpenGL rendering context for overlay or underlay windows, use **wglCreateLayerContext()** instead.) To make a rendering context current, use **wglMakeCurrent()**; **wglGetCurrentContext()** returns the current context. You can also obtain the current device context with **wglGetCurrentDC()**. You can copy some OpenGL state variables from one context to another with **wglCopyContext()** or make two contexts share the same display lists and texture objects with **wglShareLists()**. When you're finished with a particular context, destroy it with **wglDestroyContext()**.

### Accessing OpenGL Extensions

Use **wglGetProcAddress()** to access implementation-specific OpenGL extension procedure calls. To determine which extensions are supported by your implementation, use **glGetString(GL_EXTENSIONS)**. **wglGetProcAddress()**, when passed the exact name of the extension returned from **glGetString()**, returns a function pointer for the extension procedure call, or returns NULL if the extension is not supported.

### OpenGL Rendering to a Bitmap

Win32 has a few routines for allocating (and deallocating) bitmaps, to which you can render OpenGL directly. **CreateDIBitmap()** creates a device-dependent bitmap (DDB) from a device-independent bitmap (DIB). **CreateDIBSection()** creates a device-independent bitmap (DIB) that applications can write to directly. When finished with your bitmap, you can use **DeleteObject()** to free it up.

### Synchronizing Execution

If you want to combine GDI and OpenGL rendering, be aware that there are no equivalents to functions such as **glXWaitGL()**, **glXWaitX()**, and **pglWaitGL()** in Win32. Although **glXWaitGL()** has no equivalent in Win32, you can achieve the same effect by calling **glFinish()**, which waits until all pending OpenGL commands are executed, or by calling **GdiFlush()**, which waits until all GDI drawing has been completed.

### Swapping Buffers

For windows that are double-buffered, the front and back buffers can be exchanged by calling **SwapBuffers()** or **wglSwapLayerBuffers()**; the latter is used for overlays and underlays.

### Finding a Color Palette

To access the color palette for the standard (nonlayer) bitplanes, use the standard GDI functions to set the palette entries. For overlay or underlay layers, use **wglRealizeLayerPalette()**, which maps palette entries from a given color-index layer plane into the physical palette or initializes the palette of an RGBA layer plane. **wglGetLayerPaletteEntries()** and **wglSetLayerPaletteEntries()** are used to query and set the entries in palettes of layer planes.

### Using a Bitmap or Outline Font

WGL has two routines, **wglUseFontBitmaps()** and **wglUseFontOutlines()**, for converting system fonts for use with OpenGL. Both routines build a display list for each requested character from the specified font and font size.

## WGL Prototypes

### Initialization

Determine version information:

```
BOOL GetVersion( LPOSVERSIONINFO lpVersionInformation );

BOOL GetVersionEx( LPOSVERSIONINFO lpVersionInformation );
```

Pixel format availability, selection, and capability:

```
int ChoosePixelFormat( HDC hdc,
    CONST PIXELFORMATDESCRIPTOR * ppfd );

BOOL SetPixelFormat( HDC hdc, int iPixelFormat,
    CONST PIXELFORMATDESCRIPTOR * ppfd );
```

int **DescribePixelFormat**( HDC *hdc*, int *iPixelFormat*, UINT *nBytes*,
    LPPIXELFORMATDESCRIPTOR *ppfd* );

BOOL **wglDescribeLayerPlane**( HDC *hdc*, int *iPixelFormat*,
    int *iLayerPlane*, UINT *nBytes*, LPLAYERPLANEDESCRIPTOR *plpd* );

Obtain a pointer to an OpenGL function:

PROC **wglGetProcAddress**(LPCSTR *funcName*);

### Controlling Rendering

Manage or query an OpenGL rendering context:

HGLRC **wglCreateContext**( HDC *hdc* );

HGLRC **wglCreateLayerContext**( HDC *hdc*, int *iLayerPlane* );

BOOL **wglShareLists**( HGLRC *hglrc1*, HGLRC *hglrc2* );

BOOL **wglDeleteContext**( HGLRC *hglrc* );

BOOL **wglCopyContext**( HGLRC *hglrcSource*, HGLRC *hlglrcDest*,
    UINT *mask* );

BOOL **wglMakeCurrent**( HDC *hdc*, HGLRC *hglrc* );

HGLRC **wglGetCurrentContext**( VOID );

HDC **wglGetCurrentDC**( VOID );

Access implementation-dependent extension procedure calls:

PROC **wglGetProcAddress**( LPCSTR *lpszProc* );

Access and release the bitmap of the front buffer:

HBITMAP **CreateDIBitmap**( HDC *hdc*,
    CONST BITMAPINFOHEADER *\*lpbmih*, DWORD *fdwInit*,
    CONST VOID *\*lpbInit*, CONST BITMAPINFO *\*lpbmi*,
    UINT *fuUsage* );

HBITMAP **CreateDIBSection**( HDC *hdc*, CONST BITMAPINFO *\*pbmi*,
    UINT *iUsage*, VOID *\*ppvBits*, HANDLE *hSection*,
    DWORD *dwOffset* );

BOOL **DeleteObject**( HGDIOBJ *hObject* );

Exchange front and back buffers:

BOOL **SwapBuffers**( HDC *hdc* );

BOOL **wglSwapLayerBuffers**( HDC *hdc*, UINT *fuPlanes* );

Find a color palette for overlay or underlay layers:

int **wglGetLayerPaletteEntries**( HDC *hdc*, int *iLayerPlane*,
    int *iStart*, int *cEntries*, CONST COLORREF *\*pcr* );

int **wglSetLayerPaletteEntries**( HDC *hdc*, int *iLayerPlane*, int *iStart*
    int *cEntries*, CONST COLORREF *\*pcr* );

BOOL **wglRealizeLayerPalette**( HDC *hdc*, int *iLayerPlane*,
    BOOL *bRealize* );

Use a bitmap or an outline font:

BOOL **wglUseFontBitmaps**( HDC *hdc*, DWORD *first*, DWORD *count*,
    DWORD *listBase* );

BOOL **wglUseFontOutlines**( HDC *hdc*, DWORD *first*, DWORD *count*,
    DWORD *listBase*, FLOAT *deviation*, FLOAT *extrusion*, int *format*,
    LPGLYPHMETRICSFLOAT *lpgmf* );

# Basics of GLUT: The OpenGL Utility Toolkit

This appendix describes a subset of Mark Kilgard's OpenGL Utility Toolkit (GLUT), which is fully documented in his book, *OpenGL Programming for the X Window System* (Addison-Wesley, 1996). GLUT has become a popular library for OpenGL programmers because it standardizes and simplifies window and event management. GLUT has been ported atop a variety of OpenGL implementations, including both the X Window System and Microsoft Windows.

This appendix has the following major sections:

- "Initializing and Creating a Window"

- "Handling Window and Input Events"

- "Loading the Color Map"

- "Initializing and Drawing Three-Dimensional Objects"

- "Managing a Background Process"

- "Running the Program"

(See "How to Obtain the Sample Code" in "About This Guide" for information about how to obtain the source code for GLUT.)

With GLUT, your application structures its event handling to use callback functions. (This method is similar to using the Xt Toolkit, also known as the X Intrinsics, with a widget set.) For example, first you open a window and register callback routines for specific events. Then you create a main loop without an exit. In that loop, if an event occurs, its registered callback functions are executed. On completion of the callback functions, flow of control is returned to the main loop.

## Initializing and Creating a Window

Before you can open a window, you must specify its characteristics. Should it be single-buffered or double-buffered? Should it store colors as RGBA values or as color indices? Where should it appear on your display? To specify the answers to these questions, call **glutInit()**, **glutInitDisplayMode()**, **glutInitWindowSize()**, and **glutInitWindowPosition()** before you call **glutCreateWindow()** to open the window.

void **glutInit**(int *argc*, char **\*\****argv*);

**glutInit()** should be called before any other GLUT routine, because it initializes the GLUT library. **glutInit()** will also process command line options, but the specific options are window system dependent. For the X Window System, -iconic, -geometry, and -display are examples of command line options, processed by **glutInit()**. (The parameters to **glutInit()** should be the same as those to **main()**.)

void **glutInitDisplayMode**(unsigned int *mode*);

Specifies a display mode (such as RGBA or color-index, or single- or double-buffered) for windows created when **glutCreateWindow()** is called. You can also specify that the window have an associated depth, stencil, and/or accumulation buffer. The *mask* argument is a bitwise ORed combination of GLUT_RGBA or GLUT_INDEX, GLUT_SINGLE or GLUT_DOUBLE, and any of the buffer-enabling flags: GLUT_DEPTH, GLUT_STENCIL, or GLUT_ACCUM. For example, for a double-buffered, RGBA-mode window with a depth and stencil buffer, use GLUT_DOUBLE | GLUT_RGBA | GLUT_DEPTH | GLUT_STENCIL. The default value is GLUT_RGBA | GLUT_SINGLE (an RGBA, single-buffered window).

void **glutInitWindowSize**(int *width*, int *height*);
void **glutInitWindowPosition**(int *x*, int *y*);

Requests windows created by **glutCreateWindow()** to have an initial size and position. The arguments (*x, y*) indicate the location of a corner of the window, relative to the entire display. *width* and *height* indicate the window's size (in pixels). The initial window size and position are hints and may be overridden by other requests.

int **glutCreateWindow**(char *\*name*);

Opens a window with previously set characteristics (display mode, width, height, and so on). The string *name* may appear in the title bar if your window system does that sort of thing. The window is not initially displayed until **glutMainLoop()** is entered, so do not render into the window until then.

The value returned is a unique integer identifier for the window. This identifier can be used for controlling and rendering to multiple windows (each with an OpenGL rendering context) from the same application.

## Handling Window and Input Events

After the window is created, but before you enter the main loop, you should register callback functions using the following routines.

void **glutDisplayFunc**(void (*\*func*)(void));

Specifies the function that's called whenever the contents of the window need to be redrawn. The contents of the window may need to be redrawn when the window is initially opened, when the window is popped and window damage is exposed, and when **glutPostRedisplay()** is explicitly called.

---

void **glutReshapeFunc**(void (*_func_)(int _width_, int _height_));

Specifies the function that's called whenever the window is resized or moved. The argument _func_ is a pointer to a function that expects two arguments, the new width and height of the window. Typically, _func_ calls **glViewport**(), so that the display is clipped to the new size, and it redefines the projection matrix so that the aspect ratio of the projected image matches the viewport, avoiding aspect ratio distortion. If **glutReshapeFunc**() isn't called or is deregistered by passing NULL, a default reshape function is called, which calls **glViewport**(_0, 0, width, height_).

---

void **glutKeyboardFunc**(void (*_func_)(unsigned char _key_, int _x_, int _y_));

Specifies the function, _func_, that's called when a key that generates an ASCII character is pressed. The _key_ callback parameter is the generated ASCII value. The _x_ and _y_ callback parameters indicate the location of the mouse (in window-relative coordinates) when the key was pressed.

---

void **glutMouseFunc**(void (*_func_)(int _button_, int _state_, int _x_, int _y_));

Specifies the function, _func_, that's called when a mouse button is pressed or released. The _button_ callback parameter is GLUT_LEFT_BUTTON, GLUT_MIDDLE_BUTTON, or GLUT_RIGHT_BUTTON. The _state_ callback parameter is either GLUT_UP or GLUT_DOWN, depending on whether the mouse has been released or pressed. The _x_ and _y_ callback parameters indicate the location (in window-relative coordinates) of the mouse when the event occurred.

---

void **glutMotionFunc**(void (*_func_)(int _x_, int _y_));

Specifies the function, _func_, that's called when the mouse pointer moves within the window while one or more mouse buttons are pressed. The _x_ and _y_ callback parameters indicate the location (in window-relative coordinates) of the mouse when the event occurred.

> void **glutPostRedisplay**(void);
>
> Marks the current window as needing to be redrawn. At the next opportunity, the callback function registered by **glutDisplayFunc**() will be called.

## Loading the Color Map

If you're using color-index mode, you might be surprised to discover there's no OpenGL routine to load a color into a color-lookup table. This is because the process of loading a color map depends entirely on the window system. GLUT provides a generalized routine to load a single color index with an RGB value, **glutSetColor**().

> void **glutSetColor**(GLint *index*, GLfloat *red*, GLfloat *green*, GLfloat *blue*);
>
> Loads the index in the color map, *index*, with the given *red*, *green*, and *blue* values. These values are normalized to lie in the range [0.0, 1.0].

## Initializing and Drawing Three-Dimensional Objects

Many sample programs in this guide use three-dimensional models to illustrate various rendering properties. The following drawing routines are included in GLUT to avoid having to reproduce the code to draw these models in each program. The routines render all their graphics in immediate mode. Each three-dimensional model comes in two flavors: wireframe without surface normals, and solid with shading and surface normals. Use the solid version when you're applying lighting. Only the teapot generates texture coordinates.

> void **glutWireSphere**(GLdouble *radius*, GLint *slices*, GLint *stacks*);
> void **glutSolidSphere**(GLdouble *radius*, GLint *slices*, GLint *stacks*);

```
void glutWireCube(GLdouble size);
void glutSolidCube(GLdouble size);
```

```
void glutWireTorus(GLdouble innerRadius, GLdouble outerRadius,
                   GLint nsides, GLint rings);
void glutSolidTorus(GLdouble innerRadius, GLdouble outerRadius,
                    GLint nsides, GLint rings);
```

```
void glutWireIcosahedron(void);
void glutSolidIcosahedron(void);
```

```
void glutWireOctahedron(void);
void glutSolidOctahedron(void);
```

```
void glutWireTetrahedron(void);
void glutSolidTetrahedron(void);
```

```
void glutWireDodecahedron(GLdouble radius);
void glutSolidDodecahedron(GLdouble radius);
```

```
void glutWireCone(GLdouble radius, GLdouble height, GLint slices,
                  GLint stacks);
void glutSolidCone(GLdouble radius, GLdouble height, GLint slices,
                   GLint stacks);
```

```
void glutWireTeapot(GLdouble size);
void glutSolidTeapot(GLdouble size);
```

## Managing a Background Process

You can specify a function that's to be executed if no other events are pending—for example, when the event loop would otherwise be idle—with **glutIdleFunc()**. This is particularly useful for continuous animation or other background processing.

---
void **glutIdleFunc**(void (*func)(void));

Specifies the function, *func*, to be executed if no other events are pending. If NULL (zero) is passed in, execution of *func* is disabled.

---

## Running the Program

After all the setup is completed, GLUT programs enter an event processing loop, **glutMainLoop()**.

---
void **glutMainLoop**(void);

Enters the GLUT processing loop, never to return. Registered callback functions will be called when the corresponding events instigate them.

---

# Calculating Normal Vectors

This appendix describes how to calculate normal vectors for surfaces. You need to define normals to use the OpenGL lighting facility, which is described in Chapter 5. "Normal Vectors" in Chapter 2 introduces normals and the OpenGL command for specifying them. This appendix goes through the details of calculating them. It has the following major sections:

- "Finding Normals for Analytic Surfaces"
- "Finding Normals from Polygonal Data"

Since normals are perpendicular to a surface, you can find the normal at a particular point on a surface by first finding the flat plane that just touches the surface at that point. The normal is the vector that's perpendicular to that plane. On a perfect sphere, for example, the normal at a point on the surface is in the same direction as the vector from the center of the sphere to that point. For other types of surfaces, there are other, better means of determining the normals, depending on how the surface is specified.

Recall that smooth curved surfaces are approximated by large numbers of small flat polygons. If the vectors perpendicular to these polygons are used as the surface normals in such an approximation, the surface appears faceted, since the normal direction is discontinuous across the polygonal boundaries. In many cases, however, an exact mathematical description exists for the surface, and true surface normals can be calculated at every point. Using the true normals improves the rendering considerably, as shown in Figure E-1. Even if you don't have a mathematical description, you can do better than the faceted look shown in the figure. The two major sections in this appendix describe how to calculate normal vectors for these two cases:

- "Finding Normals for Analytic Surfaces" explains what to do when you have a mathematical description of a surface.

- "Finding Normals from Polygonal Data" covers the case in which you have only the polygonal data to describe a surface.

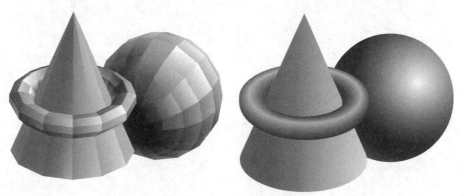

**Figure E-1**     Rendering with Polygonal Normals versus True Normals

# Finding Normals for Analytic Surfaces

An analytic surface is a smooth, differentiable surface that is described by a mathematical equation (or set of equations). In many cases, the easiest surfaces to find normals for are analytic surfaces for which you have an explicit definition in the following form:

$$\mathbf{V}(s, t) = [\; \mathbf{X}(s, t) \quad \mathbf{Y}(s, t) \quad \mathbf{Z}(s, t) \;]$$

where $s$ and $t$ are constrained to be in some domain, and $\mathbf{X}$, $\mathbf{Y}$, and $\mathbf{Z}$ are differentiable functions of two variables. To calculate the normal, find

$$\frac{\partial V}{\partial s} \text{ and } \frac{\partial V}{\partial t}$$

which are vectors tangent to the surface in the $s$- and $t$-directions. The cross product

$$\frac{\partial V}{\partial s} \times \frac{\partial V}{\partial t}$$

is perpendicular to both and, hence, to the surface. The following shows how to calculate the cross product of two vectors. (Watch out for the degenerate cases where the cross product has zero length.)

$$\begin{bmatrix} v_x & v_y & v_z \end{bmatrix} \times \begin{bmatrix} w_x & w_y & w_z \end{bmatrix} = \begin{bmatrix} (v_y w_z - w_y v_z) & (w_x v_z - v_x w_z) & (v_x w_y - w_x v_y) \end{bmatrix}$$

You should probably normalize the resulting vector. To normalize a vector $[x\; y\; z]$, calculate its length

$$\text{Length} = \sqrt{x^2 + y^2 + z^2}$$

and divide each component of the vector by the length.

As an example of these calculations, consider the analytic surface

$$\mathbf{V}(s, t) = [\; s^2 \quad t^3 \quad 3 - st \;]$$

From this we have

$$\frac{\partial V}{\partial s} = \begin{bmatrix} 2s & 0 & -t \end{bmatrix}, \quad \frac{\partial V}{\partial t} = \begin{bmatrix} 0 & 3t^2 & -s \end{bmatrix}, \text{ and } \frac{\partial V}{\partial s} \times \frac{\partial V}{\partial t} = \begin{bmatrix} 3t^3 & 2s^2 & 6st^2 \end{bmatrix}$$

For example, when $s = 1$ and $t = 2$, the corresponding point on the surface is (1, 8, 1), and the vector (–24, 2, 24) is perpendicular to the surface at that point. The length of this vector is 34, so the unit normal vector is (–24/34, 2/34, 24/34) = (–0.70588, 0.058823, 0.70588).

For analytic surfaces that are described implicitly, as $F(x, y, z) = 0$, the problem is harder. In some cases, you can solve for one of the variables, say $z = G(x, y)$, and put it in the explicit form given previously:

$$\mathbf{V}(s, t) = [\ s \quad t \quad \mathbf{G}(s, t)\ ]$$

Then continue as described earlier.

If you can't get the surface equation in an explicit form, you might be able to make use of the fact that the normal vector is given by the gradient

$$\nabla F = \left[ \frac{\partial F}{\partial x} \quad \frac{\partial F}{\partial y} \quad \frac{\partial F}{\partial z} \right]$$

evaluated at a particular point $(x, y, z)$. Calculating the gradient might be easy, but finding a point that lies on the surface can be difficult. As an example of an implicitly defined analytic function, consider the equation of a sphere of radius 1 centered at the origin:

$$x^2 + y^2 + z^2 - 1 = 0$$

This means that

$$\mathbf{F}(x, y, z) = x^2 + y^2 + z^2 - 1$$

which can be solved for $z$ to yield

$$z = +\ \sqrt{1 - x^2 - y^2}$$

Thus, normals can be calculated from the explicit form

$$\mathbf{V}(s, t) = \left[\ s \quad t \quad \sqrt{1 - s^2 - t^2}\ \right]$$

as described previously.

If you could not solve for $z$, you could have used the gradient

$$\nabla F = \begin{bmatrix} 2x & 2y & 2z \end{bmatrix}$$

as long as you could find a point on the surface. In this case, it's not so hard to find a point—for example, (2/3, 1/3, 2/3) lies on the surface. Using the gradient, the normal at this point is (4/3, 2/3, 4/3). The unit-length normal is (2/3, 1/3, 2/3), which is the same as the point on the surface, as expected.

## Finding Normals from Polygonal Data

As mentioned previously, you often want to find normals for surfaces that are described with polygonal data such that the surfaces appear smooth rather than faceted. In most cases, the easiest way to do this (although it might not be the most efficient way) is to calculate the normal vectors for each of the polygonal facets and then average the normals for neighboring facets. Use the averaged normal for the vertex that the neighboring facets have in common. Figure E-2 shows a surface and its polygonal approximation. (Of course, if the polygons represent the exact surface and aren't merely an approximation—if you're drawing a cube or a cut diamond, for example—don't do the averaging. Calculate the normal for each facet as described in the following paragraphs, and use that same normal for each vertex of the facet.)

To find the normal for a flat polygon, take any three vertices $v_1$, $v_2$, and $v_3$ of the polygon that do not lie in a straight line. The cross product

$$[v_1 - v_2] \times [v_2 - v_3]$$

is perpendicular to the polygon. (Typically, you want to normalize the resulting vector.) Then you need to average the normals for adjoining facets to avoid giving too much weight to one of them. For instance, in the example shown in Figure E-2, if $n_1$, $n_2$, $n_3$, and $n_4$ are the normals for the four polygons meeting at point P, calculate $n_1 + n_2 + n_3 + n_4$ and then normalize it. (You can get a better average if you weight the normals by the size of the angles at the shared intersection.) The resulting vector can be used as the normal for point P.

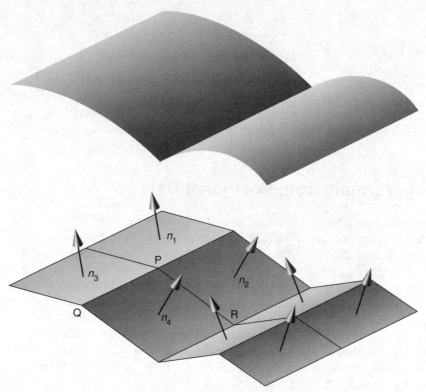

**Figure E-2**    Averaging Normal Vectors

Sometimes, you need to vary this method for particular situations. For instance, at the boundary of a surface (such as point Q in Figure E-2), you might be able to choose a better normal based on your knowledge of how the surface should look. Sometimes the best you can do is average the polygon normals on the boundary as well. Similarly, some models have some smooth parts and some sharp corners (point R is on such an edge in Figure E-2). In this case, the normals on either side of the crease shouldn't be averaged. Instead, polygons on one side of the crease should be drawn with one normal, and polygons on the other side with another.

# Homogeneous Coordinates and Transformation Matrices

This appendix presents a brief discussion of homogeneous coordinates. It also lists the forms of the transformation matrices used for rotation, scaling, translation, perspective projection, and orthographic projection. These topics are introduced and discussed in Chapter 3. For a more detailed discussion of these subjects, see almost any book on three-dimensional computer graphics—for example, *Computer Graphics: Principles and Practice*, by Foley, van Dam, Feiner, and Hughes (Addison-Wesley, 1990); or a text on projective geometry—for example, *The Real Projective Plane*, by H. S. M. Coxeter, 2nd ed. (Cambridge University Press, 1961). In the discussion that follows, the term *homogeneous coordinates* always means three-dimensional homogeneous coordinates, although projective geometries exist for all dimensions.

This appendix has the following major sections:

- "Homogeneous Coordinates"
- "Transformation Matrices"

# Homogeneous Coordinates

OpenGL commands usually deal with two- and three-dimensional vertices, but in fact all are treated internally as three-dimensional homogeneous vertices comprising four coordinates. Every column vector $(x, y, z, w)^T$ represents a homogeneous vertex if at least one of its elements is nonzero. If the real number $a$ is nonzero, then $(x, y, z, w)^T$ and $(ax, ay, az, aw)^T$ represent the same homogeneous vertex. (This is just like fractions: $x/y = (ax)/(ay)$.) A three-dimensional Euclidean space point $(x, y, z)^T$ becomes the homogeneous vertex with coordinates $(x, y, z, 1.0)^T$, and the two-dimensional Euclidean point $(x, y)^T$ becomes $(x, y, 0.0, 1.0)^T$.

As long as $w$ is nonzero, the homogeneous vertex $(x, y, z, w)^T$ corresponds to the three-dimensional point $(x/w, y/w, z/w)^T$. If $w = 0.0$, it corresponds to no Euclidean point, but rather to some idealized "point at infinity." To understand this point at infinity, consider the point $(1, 2, 0, 0)$, and note that the sequence of points $(1, 2, 0, 1)$, $(1, 2, 0, 0.01)$, and $(1, 2.0, 0.0, 0.0001)$ corresponds to the Euclidean points $(1, 2)$, $(100, 200)$, and $(10,000, 20,000)$. This sequence represents points rapidly moving toward infinity along the line $2x = y$. Thus, you can think of $(1, 2, 0, 0)$ as the point at infinity in the direction of that line.

**Note:** OpenGL might not handle homogeneous clip coordinates with $w < 0$ correctly. To be sure that your code is portable to all OpenGL systems, use only non-negative $w$-values.

## Transforming Vertices

Vertex transformations (such as rotations, translations, scaling, and shearing) and projections (such as perspective and orthographic) can all be represented by applying an appropriate $4 \times 4$ matrix to the coordinates representing the vertex. If $\mathbf{v}$ represents a homogeneous vertex and $\mathbf{M}$ is a $4 \times 4$ transformation matrix, then $\mathbf{Mv}$ is the image of $\mathbf{v}$ under the transformation by $\mathbf{M}$. (In computer-graphics applications, the transformations used are usually nonsingular—in other words, the matrix $\mathbf{M}$ can be inverted. This isn't required, but some problems arise with singular matrices.)

After transformation, all transformed vertices are clipped so that $x$, $y$, and $z$ are in the range $[-w, w]$ (assuming $w > 0$). Note that this range corresponds in Euclidean space to $[-1.0, 1.0]$.

## Transforming Normals

Normal vectors aren't transformed in the same way as vertices or position vectors are. Mathematically, it's better to think of normal vectors not as vectors, but as planes perpendicular to those vectors. Then, the transformation rules for normal vectors are described by the transformation rules for perpendicular planes.

A homogeneous plane is denoted by the row vector $(a, b, c, d)$, where at least one of $a, b, c$, and $d$ is nonzero. If $q$ is a nonzero real number, then $(a, b, c, d)$ and $(qa, qb, qc, qd)$ represent the same plane. A point $(x, y, z, w)^T$ is on the plane $(a, b, c, d)$ if $ax + by + cz + dw = 0$. (If $w = 1$, this is the standard description of a Euclidean plane.) In order for $(a, b, c, d)$ to represent a Euclidean plane, at least one of $a, b$, or $c$ must be nonzero. If they're all zero, then $(0, 0, 0, d)$ represents the "plane at infinity," which contains all the "points at infinity."

If $\mathbf{p}$ is a homogeneous plane and $\mathbf{v}$ is a homogeneous vertex, then the statement "$\mathbf{v}$ lies on plane $\mathbf{p}$" is written mathematically as $\mathbf{pv} = 0$, where $\mathbf{pv}$ is normal matrix multiplication. If $\mathbf{M}$ is a nonsingular vertex transformation (that is, a $4 \times 4$ matrix that has an inverse $\mathbf{M}^{-1}$), then $\mathbf{pv} = 0$ is equivalent to $\mathbf{pM}^{-1}\mathbf{Mv} = 0$, so $\mathbf{Mv}$ lies in the plane $\mathbf{pM}^{-1}$. Thus, $\mathbf{pM}^{-1}$ is the image of the plane under the vertex transformation $\mathbf{M}$.

If you like to think of normal vectors as vectors instead of as the planes perpendicular to them, let $\mathbf{v}$ and $\mathbf{n}$ be vectors such that $\mathbf{v}$ is perpendicular to $\mathbf{n}$. Then, $\mathbf{n}^T\mathbf{v} = 0$. Thus, for an arbitrary nonsingular transformation $\mathbf{M}$, $\mathbf{n}^T\mathbf{M}^{-1}\mathbf{Mv} = 0$, which means that $\mathbf{n}^T\mathbf{M}^{-1}$ is the transpose of the transformed normal vector. Thus, the transformed normal vector is $(\mathbf{M}^{-1})^T\mathbf{n}$. In other words, normal vectors are transformed by the inverse transpose of the transformation that transforms points. Whew!

# Transformation Matrices

Although any nonsingular matrix $\mathbf{M}$ represents a valid projective transformation, a few special matrices are particularly useful. These matrices are listed in the following subsections.

## Translation

The call **glTranslate\***(x, y, z) generates T, where

$$T = \begin{bmatrix} 1 & 0 & 0 & x \\ 0 & 1 & 0 & y \\ 0 & 0 & 1 & z \\ 0 & 0 & 0 & 1 \end{bmatrix} \text{ and } T^{-1} = \begin{bmatrix} 1 & 0 & 0 & -x \\ 0 & 1 & 0 & -y \\ 0 & 0 & 1 & -z \\ 0 & 0 & 0 & 1 \end{bmatrix}$$

## Scaling

The call **glScale\***(x, y, z) generates **S**, where

$$S = \begin{bmatrix} x & 0 & 0 & 0 \\ 0 & y & 0 & 0 \\ 0 & 0 & z & 0 \\ 0 & 0 & 0 & 1 \end{bmatrix} \text{ and } S^{-1} = \begin{bmatrix} \frac{1}{x} & 0 & 0 & 0 \\ 0 & \frac{1}{y} & 0 & 0 \\ 0 & 0 & \frac{1}{z} & 0 \\ 0 & 0 & 0 & 1 \end{bmatrix}$$

Notice that $S^{-1}$ is defined only if x, y, and z are all nonzero.

## Rotation

The call **glRotate\***(a, x, y, z) generates R as follows:

Let $v = (x, y, z)^T$, and $u = v/\|v\| = (x', y', z')^T$.

Also let

$$S = \begin{bmatrix} 0 & -z' & y' \\ z' & 0 & -x' \\ -y' & x' & 0 \end{bmatrix} \text{ and } M = uu^T + (\cos a)(I - uu^T) + (\sin a) S$$

Then

$$R = \begin{bmatrix} m & m & m & 0 \\ m & m & m & 0 \\ m & m & m & 0 \\ 0 & 0 & 0 & 1 \end{bmatrix}$$

*Appendix F: Homogeneous Coordinates and Transformation Matrices*

where $m$ represent the elements from **M**, which is the $3 \times 3$ matrix defined on the preceding page. The **R** matrix is always defined. If $x = y = z = 0$, then **R** is the identity matrix. You can obtain the inverse of **R**, $\mathbf{R}^{-1}$, by substituting $-a$ for $a$, or by transposition.

The **glRotate*()** command generates a matrix for rotation about an arbitrary axis. Often, you're rotating about one of the coordinate axes; the corresponding matrices are as follows:

$$\textbf{glRotate*}(a, 1, 0, 0): \begin{bmatrix} 1 & 0 & 0 & 0 \\ 0 & \cos a & -\sin a & 0 \\ 0 & \sin a & \cos a & 0 \\ 0 & 0 & 0 & 1 \end{bmatrix}$$

$$\textbf{glRotate*}(a, 0, 1, 0): \begin{bmatrix} \cos a & 0 & \sin a & 0 \\ 0 & 1 & 0 & 0 \\ -\sin a & 0 & \cos a & 0 \\ 0 & 0 & 0 & 1 \end{bmatrix}$$

$$\textbf{glRotate*}(a, 0, 0, 1): \begin{bmatrix} \cos a & -\sin a & 0 & 0 \\ \sin a & \cos a & 0 & 0 \\ 0 & 0 & 1 & 0 \\ 0 & 0 & 0 & 1 \end{bmatrix}$$

As before, the inverses are obtained by transposition.

## Perspective Projection

The call **glFrustum($l, r, b, t, n, f$)** generates **R**, where

$$\mathbf{R} = \begin{bmatrix} \dfrac{2n}{r-l} & 0 & \dfrac{r+l}{r-l} & 0 \\ 0 & \dfrac{2n}{t-b} & \dfrac{t+b}{t-b} & 0 \\ 0 & 0 & \dfrac{-(f+n)}{f-n} & \dfrac{-2fn}{f-n} \\ 0 & 0 & -1 & 0 \end{bmatrix} \quad \text{and } \mathbf{R}^{-1} = \begin{bmatrix} \dfrac{r-l}{2n} & 0 & 0 & \dfrac{r+l}{2n} \\ 0 & \dfrac{t-b}{2n} & 0 & \dfrac{t+b}{2n} \\ 0 & 0 & 0 & -1 \\ 0 & 0 & \dfrac{-(f-n)}{2fn} & \dfrac{f+n}{2fn} \end{bmatrix}$$

**R** is defined as long as $l \neq r$, $t \neq b$, and $n \neq f$.

## Orthographic Projection

The call **glOrtho**(*l, r, b, t, n, f*) generates **R**, where

$$
R = \begin{bmatrix} \dfrac{2}{r-l} & 0 & 0 & -\dfrac{r+l}{r-l} \\ 0 & \dfrac{2}{t-b} & 0 & -\dfrac{t+b}{t-b} \\ 0 & 0 & \dfrac{-2}{f-n} & \dfrac{f+n}{f-n} \\ 0 & 0 & 0 & 1 \end{bmatrix} \text{ and } R^{-1} = \begin{bmatrix} \dfrac{r-l}{2} & 0 & 0 & \dfrac{r+l}{2} \\ 0 & \dfrac{t-b}{2} & 0 & \dfrac{t+b}{2} \\ 0 & 0 & \dfrac{f-n}{-2} & \dfrac{n+f}{2} \\ 0 & 0 & 0 & 1 \end{bmatrix}
$$

**R** is defined as long as $l \neq r$, $t \neq b$, and $n \neq f$.

# Programming Tips

This appendix lists some tips and guidelines that you might find useful. Keep in mind that these tips are based on the intentions of the designers of OpenGL, not on any experience with actual applications and implementations. This appendix has the following major sections:

- "OpenGL Correctness Tips"

- "OpenGL Performance Tips"

- "GLX Tips"

## OpenGL Correctness Tips

- Perform error checking often. Call **glGetError()** at least once each time the scene is rendered to make certain error conditions are noticed.

- Do not count on the error behavior of an OpenGL implementation—it might change in a future release of OpenGL. For example, OpenGL 1.1 ignores matrix operations invoked between **glBegin()** and **glEnd()** commands, but a future version might not. Put another way, OpenGL error semantics may change between upward-compatible revisions.

- Check the extension string to verify that any extensions you want to use are supported. This is particularly relevant for routines that must be accessed through a function pointer retrieved by functions such as **glXGetProcAddress()** or **wglGetProcAddress()**.

- If you need to collapse all geometry to a single plane, use the projection matrix. If the modelview matrix is used, OpenGL features that operate in eye coordinates (such as lighting and application-defined clipping planes) might fail.

- Do not make extensive changes to a single matrix. For example, do not animate a rotation by continually calling **glRotate*()** with an incremental angle. Rather, use **glLoadIdentity()** to initialize the given matrix for each frame, and then call **glRotate*()** with the desired complete angle for that frame.

- Count on multiple passes through a rendering database to generate the same pixel fragments only if this behavior is guaranteed by the invariance rules established for a compliant OpenGL implementation. (See Appendix H for details on the invariance rules.) Otherwise, a different set of fragments might be generated.

- Do not expect errors to be reported while a display list is being defined. The commands within a display list generate errors only when the list is executed.

- Place the frustum's near plane as far from the viewpoint as possible to optimize the operation of the depth buffer.

- Call **glFlush()** to force all previous OpenGL commands to be executed. Do not count on **glGet*()** or **glIs*()** to flush the rendering stream. Query commands flush as much of the stream as is required to return valid data but don't guarantee completion of all pending rendering commands.

- Turn dithering off when rendering predithered images (for example, when **glCopyPixels()** is called).

- Make use of the full range of the accumulation buffer. For example, if accumulating four images, scale each by one-quarter as it is accumulated.

- If exact two-dimensional rasterization is desired, you must carefully specify both the orthographic projection and the vertices of primitives that are to be rasterized. The orthographic projection should be specified with integer coordinates, as shown in the following example:

```
gluOrtho2D(0, width, 0, height);
```

where *width* and *height* are the dimensions of the viewport. Given this projection matrix, polygon vertices and pixel image positions should be placed at integer coordinates to rasterize predictably. For example, **glRecti**(0, 0, 1, 1) reliably fills the lower left pixel of the viewport, and **glRasterPos2i**(0, 0) reliably positions an unzoomed image at the lower left of the viewport. Point vertices, line vertices, and bitmap positions should be placed at half-integer locations, however. For example, a line drawn from (*x1*, 0.5) to (*x2*, 0.5) will be reliably rendered along the bottom row of pixels into the viewport, and a point drawn at (0.5, 0.5) will reliably fill the same pixel as **glRecti**(0, 0, 1, 1).

An optimum compromise that allows all primitives to be specified at integer positions, while still ensuring predictable rasterization, is to translate *x* and *y* by 0.375, as shown in the following code fragment. Such a translation keeps polygon and pixel image edges safely away from the centers of pixels, while moving line vertices close enough to the pixel centers.

```
glViewport(0, 0, width, height);
glMatrixMode(GL_PROJECTION);
glLoadIdentity();
gluOrtho2D(0, width, 0, height);
glMatrixMode(GL_MODELVIEW);
glLoadIdentity();
glTranslatef(0.375, 0.375, 0.0);
/* render all primitives at integer positions */
```

- Avoid using negative *w* vertex coordinates and negative *q* texture coordinates. OpenGL might not clip such coordinates correctly and might make interpolation errors when shading primitives defined by such coordinates.

- Do not assume the precision of operations based on the data types of parameters to OpenGL commands. For example, if you are using **glRotated()**, you should not assume that the geometric processing pipeline maintains double-precision floating-point accuracy during its operation. It is possible that the parameters to **glRotated()** are converted to a different data type before processing.

## OpenGL Performance Tips

- Try to minimize state changes during rendering by grouping primitives of like OpenGL state.

- Use **glColorMaterial()** when only a single material property is being varied rapidly (at each vertex, for example). Use **glMaterial()** for infrequent changes or when more than a single material property is being varied rapidly.

- Use **glLoadIdentity()** to initialize a matrix, rather than load your own copy of the identity matrix.

- Use specific matrix calls such as **glRotate*()**, **glTranslate*()**, and **glScale*()**, rather than compose your own rotation, translation, or scale matrices and call **glMultMatrix()**.

- Use query functions when your application requires just a few state values for its own computations. If your application requires several state values from the same attribute group, use **glPushAttrib()** and **glPopAttrib()** to save and restore them.

- Favor the use of vertex buffers objects over display lists.

- In many cases, using indexed vertex arrays rendered with **glDrawElements()** may take advantage of hardware caching of transformed vertices.

- Use texture objects to encapsulate texture data. Place all the **glTexImage*()** calls (including mipmaps) required to completely specify a texture and the associated **glTexParameter*()** calls (which set texture properties) into a texture object. Bind this texture object to select the texture.

- If the situation allows it, use **gl*TexSubImage()** to replace all or part of an existing texture image, rather than the more costly operations of deleting and creating an entire new image.

- If your OpenGL implementation supports a high-performance working set of resident textures, try to make all your textures resident—that is, make them fit into the high-performance texture memory. If necessary, reduce the size or internal format resolution of your textures until they all fit into memory. If such a reduction creates intolerably fuzzy textured objects, you may give some textures lower priority, which will, when push comes to shove, leave them out of the working set.

- If you need to render the same pixel rectangle multiple times, store the image in a texture map and render it using a screen-aligned quadrilateral rather than calling **glDrawPixels()**.

- Use evaluators even for simple surface tessellations to minimize network bandwidth in client-server environments.

- Provide unit-length normals if it's possible to do so, and avoid the overhead of GL_NORMALIZE. Avoid using **glScale\*()** when doing lighting because it almost always requires that GL_NORMALIZE be enabled.

- Set **glShadeModel()** to GL_FLAT if smooth shading isn't required.

- Use a single **glClear()** call per frame if possible. Do not use **glClear()** to clear small subregions of the buffers; use it only for complete or nearly complete clears.

- Use a single call to **glBegin**(GL_TRIANGLES) to draw multiple independent triangles, rather than calling **glBegin**(GL_TRIANGLES) multiple times or calling **glBegin**(GL_POLYGON). Even if only a single triangle is to be drawn, use GL_TRIANGLES, rather than GL_POLYGON. Use a single call to **glBegin**(GL_QUADS) in the same manner, rather than calling **glBegin**(GL_POLYGON) repeatedly. Likewise, use a single call to **glBegin**(GL_LINES) to draw multiple independent line segments, rather than calling **glBegin**(GL_LINES) multiple times.

- Some OpenGL implementations benefit from storing vertex data in vertex arrays. Use of vertex arrays reduces function call overhead. Some implementations can improve performance by batch processing or reusing processed vertices.

- In general, use the vector forms of commands to pass precomputed data, and use the scalar forms of commands to pass values that are computed near call time.

- Avoid making redundant mode changes, such as setting the color to the same value between each vertex of a flat-shaded polygon.

- Be sure to disable expensive rasterization and per-fragment operations when drawing or copying images. OpenGL will even apply textures to pixel images if asked.

- Unless absolutely necessary, avoid having different front and back polygon modes.

- Only call **glFinish()** when you are measuring the execution time of OpenGL rendering. Remove it from your program once you're done making measurements.

- OpenGL commands are automatically flushed (as if you called **glFlush()**) when a double-buffered window is swapped.

## GLX Tips

- Use **glXWaitGL()**, rather than **glFinish()**, to force X rendering commands to follow GL rendering commands.

- Likewise, use **glXWaitX()**, rather than **XSync()**, to force GL rendering commands to follow X rendering commands.

- Be careful when using **glXChooseVisual()**, because Boolean selections are matched exactly. Since some implementations won't export visuals with all combinations of Boolean capabilities, you should call **glXChooseVisual()** several times with different Boolean values before you give up. For example, if no single-buffered visual with the required characteristics is available, check for a double-buffered visual with the same capabilities. It might be available, and it's easy to use.

# OpenGL Invariance

OpenGL is not a pixel-exact specification. It therefore doesn't guarantee an exact match between images produced by different OpenGL implementations. However, OpenGL does specify exact matches, in some cases, for images produced by the same implementation. This appendix describes the invariance rules that define these cases.

The obvious and most fundamental case is repeatability. A conforming OpenGL implementation generates the same results each time a specific sequence of commands is issued from the same initial conditions. Although such repeatability is useful for testing and verification, it's often not useful to application programmers, because it's difficult to arrange for equivalent initial conditions. For example, rendering a scene twice, the second time after swapping the front and back buffers, doesn't meet this requirement. Therefore, repeatability can't be used to guarantee a stable, double-buffered image.

A simple and useful algorithm that counts on invariant execution is erasing a line by redrawing it in the background color. This algorithm works only if rasterizing the line results in the same fragment $(x, y)$ pairs being generated in both the foreground and background color cases. OpenGL requires that the coordinates of the fragments generated by rasterization be invariant with respect to framebuffer contents; which color buffers are enabled for drawing; the values of matrices other than those on the tops of the matrix stacks; the scissor parameters; all writemasks; all clear values; the current color, index, normal, texture coordinates, and edge-flag values; the current raster color, raster index, and raster texture coordinates; and the material properties. It is further required that exactly the same fragments be generated, including the fragment color values, when framebuffer contents, color buffer enables, matrices other than those on the tops of the matrix stacks, the scissor parameters, writemasks, or clear values differ.

OpenGL further suggests, but doesn't require, that fragment generation be invariant with respect to the matrix mode, the depths of the matrix stacks, the alpha test parameters (other than alpha test enable), the stencil parameters (other than stencil enable), the depth test parameters (other than depth test enable), the blending parameters (other than enable), the logical operation (but not logical operation enable), and the pixel-storage and pixel-transfer parameters. Because invariance with respect to several enables isn't recommended, you should use other parameters to disable functions when invariant rendering is required. For example, to render invariantly with blending enabled and disabled, set the blending parameters to GL_ONE and GL_ZERO to disable blending, rather than call **glDisable**(GL_BLEND). Alpha testing, stencil testing, depth testing, and the logical operation all can be disabled in this manner.

Finally, OpenGL requires that per-fragment arithmetic, such as blending and the depth test, is invariant to all OpenGL states except the state that directly defines it. For example, the only OpenGL parameters that affect how the arithmetic of blending is performed are the source and destination blend parameters and the blend enable parameter. Blending is invariant to all other state changes. This invariance holds for the scissor test, the alpha test, the stencil test, the depth test, blending, dithering, logical operations, and buffer writemasking.

As a result of all these invariance requirements, OpenGL can guarantee that images rendered into different color buffers, either simultaneously or separately using the same command sequence, are pixel-identical. This holds for all the color buffers in the framebuffer or all the color buffers in an off-screen buffer, but it isn't guaranteed between the framebuffer and off-screen buffers.

# Built-In OpenGL Shading Language Variables and Functions

The OpenGL Shading Language, commonly called the "GLSL," defines a number of variables for matching OpenGL state and large set of convenience functions. This appendix[1] provides a complete list of GLSL built-in variables and functions.

---

[1] This appendix is adapted from *The OpenGL® Shading Language Specification* (Version 1.20) by John Kessenich.

# Variables

Much of the OpenGL state that an application can configure is also available as variables from within a GLSL shader. The next sections describe all state variables available to shaders, and any restrictions on their use.

## Vertex Shader Input Attributes Variables

Table I-1 lists the set of global attribute values reflect the per-vertex input data that can be accessed exclusively from within a vertex shader.

| Variable Name | Type | Specifiying Function | Description |
| --- | --- | --- | --- |
| gl_Vertex | vec4 | **glVertex** | Vertex's world-space coordinate |
| gl_Color | vec4 | **glColor** | Primary color value |
| gl_SecondaryColor | vec4 | **glSecondaryColor** | Secondary color value |
| gl_Normal | vec3 | **glNormal** | Lighting normal |
| gl_MultiTexCoord$n$ | vec4 | **glMultiTexCoord(** $n$, ... **)** | Texture unit $n$'s texture coordinates, with $n = 0 ... 7$. |
| gl_FogCoord | float | **glFogCoord** | Fog coordinate |

**Table I-1**     Global Vertex Shader Attribute Variables

## Vertex Shader Special Output Variables

The following variables are used in later stages of the vertex processing pipeline, and are only available in vertex shaders.

In particular, the gl_Position variable is the only required output of vertex shaders, and specifies the final, projected position of the input vertex. Generally, this is accomplished in one of two ways:

1.  Directly multiplying the input vertex by the combined modelview and projection transformations, as in:

    ```
    gl_Position = gl_ModelViewProjectionMatrix * gl_Vertex;
    ```

2.  Using the **ftransform()** function, as in:

```
gl_Position = ftransform();
```

While the first method is generally faster, use the second method if you are doing multipass rendering using a combination of the fixed-function vertex pipeline and vertex shaders rendering passes Table I-2 enumerates the special output variables of a vertex shader..

| Variable Name | Type | Description |
|---|---|---|
| gl_Position | vec4 | Transformed vertex position. |
| gl_PointSize | float | Point size (in pixels) of output vertex. This value overrides the current OpenGL setting if glEnable(GL_VERTEX_PROGRAM_POINT_SIZE); has been called. |
| gl_ClipVertex | vec4 | Vertex position to be used with user-defined clipping planes. This value must be in the same coordinate as the clipping planes: eye- coordinates, or object-coordinates |

**Table I-2**    Special Vertex Shader Output Variables

## Vertex Shader Output Varying Variables

While user-defined varying variables are shared between vertex and fragment shaders, certain OpenGL-defined varying variables are accessible only in vertex shader, with their values being assigned to a unique set of (corresponding, but differently named) varying values that are available only in fragment shaders.

Table I-3 lists the variables that are only available in vertex shaders.

| Variable Name | Type | Description |
|---|---|---|
| gl_FrontColor | vec4 | Primary color to be used for front-facing primitives |
| gl_BackColor | vec4 | Primary color to be used for back-facing primitives |
| gl_FrontSecondaryColor | vec4 | Secondary color to be used for front-facing primitives |

**Table I-3**    Varying Vertex Shader Output Variables

| Variable Name | Type | Description |
|---|---|---|
| gl_BackSecondaryColor | vec4 | Secondary color to be used for back-facing primitives |
| gl_TexCoord[n] | vec4 | $n^{th}$ Texture coordinates values |
| gl_FogFragCoord | vec4 | Fragment fog coordinate value |

**Table I-3 (continued)**     Varying Vertex Shader Output Variables

Table I-4 lists the set of input varying variables available in fragment shaders.

| Variable Name | Type | Description |
|---|---|---|
| gl_Color | vec4 | Primary color of the fragment |
| gl_SecondayColor | bool | Secondary color of the fragment |
| gl_TexCoord[n] | vec4 | $n^{th}$ Texture coordinates for the fragment. |
| gl_FogFragCoord | float | Fragment's fog coordinate |
| gl_PointCoord | vec2 | Fragment's coordinates when point sprites are enabled |

**Table I-4**     Varying Fragment Shader Input Variables

## Built-In Implementation Constants

Most implementation-dependent maximum values are reflected as constant integer variables accessible in both vertex and fragment shaders. The variables listed in Table I-5 represent the minimum capabilities of an OpenGL implementation, and all represented as a single constant integer expression.

| Variable Name | Default Value | Description |
|---|---|---|
| gl_MaxLights | 8 | Number of lights |
| gl_MaxClipPlanes | 6 | Number of user-defined clipping planes |
| gl_MaxTextureUnits | 2 | Number of texture units |

**Table I-5**     Implementation Maximum Value Variables

| Variable Name | Default Value | Description |
|---|---|---|
| gl_MaxTextureCoords | 2 | Number of texture-coordiantes supported. |
| gl_MaxVertexAttribs | 16 | Number of vec4 sets of vertex attributes |
| gl_MaxVertexUniformComponents | 512 | Number of vec4 uniform variables available for a vertex shader |
| gl_MaxVaryingFloats | 32 | Number of varying float variables |
| gl_MaxVertexTextureImageUnits | 0 | Number of texture units available from within a vertex shader |
| gl_MaxCombinedTextureImageUnits | 2 | Total number of texture units available for both vertex and fragment shaders |
| gl_MaxTextureImageUnits | 2 | Number of texture units available from within a fragment shader |
| gl_MaxFragmentUniformComponents | 64 | Number of vec4 uniform variables available from a fragment shader |
| gl_MaxDrawBuffers | 1 | Number of buffers available for simultaneous output from within a fragment shader using `gl_FragData` |

**Table I-5  (continued)**    Implementation Maximum Value Variables

## Built-In Uniform State Variables

The following sets of variables are available in both vertex and fragment shaders, and reflect the OpenGL state settings specified by the appliation.

### Transformation Matrix State

The following variables represent the matrix transformation states of OpenGL. Various matrices are derived from the values set within an OpenGL application. For example, lighting normals (see "Define Normal Vectors for Each Vertex of Every Object" in Chapter 5) are transformed by the inverse-transpose of the upper-left $3 \times 3$ part of the modelview matrix, which is automatically computed for you when changes are made to the modelview matrix and presented using the gl_NormalMatrix varaible.

Derived matrices (particularly those involving matrix inverses) may be undefined if the source matrix is ill-conditioned or singular.

Table I-6 lists the availble matrices in GLSL.

| Variable Name | Type | Description |
| --- | --- | --- |
| gl_ModelViewMatrix | mat4 | Current modelview matrix |
| gl_ProjectionMatrix | mat4 | Current projection matrix |
| gl_ModelViewProjectionMatrix | mat4 | Product of the modelview and projection matrices |
| gl_TextureMatrix[$n$] | mat4 | Texture matrix for texture unit $n$. The maximum dimension of the array is gl_MaxTextureCoords. |
| gl_NormalMatrix | mat3 | Inverse-transpose of the upper $3 \times 3$ of the modelview matrix |
| gl_ModelViewMatrixInverse | mat4 | Inverse of the modelview matrix |
| gl_ProjectionMatrixInverse | mat4 | Inverse of the projection matrix |
| gl_ModelViewProjectionMatrixInverse | mat4 | Inverse of combined modelview and projection matrices |
| gl_TextureMatrixInverse[$n$] | mat4 | Inverse of texture matrix $n$ |
| gl_ModelViewMatrixTranspose | mat4 | Transpose of the modelview matrix |
| gl_ProjectionMatrixTranspose | mat4 | Transpose of the projection matrix |
| gl_ModelViewProjectionMatrixTranspose | mat4 | Inverse of the combined modelview and projection matrix |

**Table I-6**   Transformation Matrix Variables

| Variable Name | Type | Description |
| --- | --- | --- |
| gl_TextureMatrixTranspose[$n$] | mat4 | Transpose of texture matrix $n$ |
| gl_ModelViewMatrixInverseTranspose | mat4 | Inverse-transpose of the modelview matrix |
| gl_ProjectionMatrixInverseTranspose | mat4 | Inverse-transpose of the projection matrix |
| gl_ModelViewProjection MatrixInverseTranspose | mat4 | Inverse-transpose of the combined modelview and projection matrix |
| gl_TextureMatrixInverseTranspose[$n$] | mat4 | Inverse-transpose of texture matrix $n$ |

**Table I-6     (continued)**     Transformation Matrix Variables

## Lighting Normal Normalization State

Vertex normals can be normalized within a shader by using the **normalize()** function. However, if normals were uniformly scaled (all calls to **glScale()** had the same values for *x, y,* and *z)*, they could be normalized by a simple scaling operation (thus saving the potentially expensive square root operation required by **normalize()**). The scaling factor is stored in:

```
uniform float gl_NormalScale;
```

and applied as

```
vec3 normal = gl_NormalScale * gl_Normal;
```

## Depth Range State

Access to the depth range values (as set by **glDepthRange()**) can be accessed using:

```
struct gl_DepthRangeParameters {
    float near;
    float far;
    float diff;
};

uniform gl_DepthRangeParameters gl_DepthRange;
```

Table I-7 provides descriptions for each of the depth range variables.

| Variable Name | Type | Description |
|---|---|---|
| gl_DepthRange.near | float | Depth value that vertices at the near clipping plane are mapped to |
| gl_DepthRange.far | float | Depth value that vertices at the far clipping plane are mapped to |
| gl_DepthRange.diff | float | Difference between the near and far depth range values, computed as (far - near) |

**Table I-7**      Depth Range Variables

### User-Defined Clipping Planes

Access to the user-defined clipping planes (as specified by **glClipPlane()**) can be accessed in a shader through the array:

```
uniform vec4 gl_ClipPlane[gl_MaxClipPlanes];
```

### Point Parameter

Parameters controlling the size and shading of points are controlled by the state set by calling **glPointParameter()**. The following structure allows access to all point parameter settings:

```
struct gl_PointParameters {
    float size;
    float sizeMin;
    float sizeMax;
    float fadeThresholdSize;
    float distanceConstantAttenuation;
    float distanceLinearAttenuation;
    float distanceQuadraticAttenuation;
};

uniform gl_PointParameters gl_Point;
```

The variables associated with point sizes and parameters are listed in Table I-8.

| Variable Name | Type | Description |
| --- | --- | --- |
| gl_Point.size | float | Current point-size setting |
| gl_Point.sizeMin | float | Minimum value for derived point sizes |
| gl_Point.sizeMax | float | Maximum value for derived point sizes |
| gl_Point.fadeThresholdSize | float | Thresholding value for selecting whether to fade a point's alpha value |
| gl_Point.distanceConstantAttenuation | float | Constant coefficient for point attenuation computations |
| gl_Point.distanceLinearAttenuation | float | Linear coefficient for point attenuation computations |
| gl_Point.distanceQuadraticAttenuation | float | Quadratic coefficient for point attenuation computations |

**Table I-8**     Point Size and Attenuation Variables

## Material State

Material state, as specified by calling **glMaterial()**, can be queried by utilizing the values in the following structure, which stores material properties for both the front- and back-material state:

```
struct gl_MaterialParameters {
    vec4 emission;
    vec4 ambient;
    vec4 diffuse;
    vec4 specular;
    float shininess;
};

uniform gl_MaterialParameters gl_FrontMaterial;
uniform gl_MaterialParameters gl_BackMaterial;
```

Table I-9 lists the material variables and their descriptions.

| Variable Name | Type | Description |
|---|---|---|
| gl_FrontMaterial.emission<br>gl_BackMaterial.emission | vec4 | Emission color for material |
| gl_FrontMaterial.ambient<br>gl_BackMaterial.ambient | vec4 | Ambient color for material |
| gl_FrontMaterial.diffuse<br>gl_BackMaterial.diffuse | vec4 | Diffuse color for material |
| gl_FrontMaterial.specular<br>gl_BackMaterial.specular | vec4 | Specular color for material |
| gl_FrontMaterial.shininess<br>gl_BackMaterial.shininess | float | Shininess color for material |

**Table I-9**     Lighting Material Variables

## Lighting State

The state associated with each light in OpenGL is stored in the following structure. For this section, the notation described in "The Mathematics of Lighting" on page 220 is used.

```
struct gl_LightSourceParameters {
    vec4 ambient;
    vec4 diffuse;
    vec4 specular;
    vec4 position;
    vec4 halfVector;
    vec3 spotDirection;
    float spotExponent;
    float spotCutoff;
    float spotCosCutoff;
    float constantAttenuation;
    float linearAttenuation;
    float quadraticAttenuation;
};

uniform gl_LightSourceParameters gl_LightSource[gl_MaxLights];
```

Table I-10 provides a list of the parameters associated with each light source available in a shader.

| Variable Name | Type | Description |
|---|---|---|
| gl_LightSource[n].ambient | vec4 | Ambient color for light n |
| gl_LightSource[n].diffuse | vec4 | Diffuse color for light n |
| gl_LightSource[n].specular | vec4 | Specular color for light n |
| gl_LightSource[n].position | vec4 | World-coordinate position for light n |
| gl_LightSource[n].halfVector | vec4 | Lighting half-vector for light n |
| gl_LightSource[n].spotDirection | vec3 | Spotlight direction for light n |
| gl_LightSource[n].spotExponent | float | Spotlight expoent for light n |
| gl_LightSource[n].spotCutoff | float | Spotlight cutoff angle for light n |
| gl_LightSource[n].spotCosCutoff | float | Cosine of the spotlight cutoff angle for light n |
| gl_LightSource[n].constantAttenuation | float | Constant coefficient for attenuation compuation for light n |
| gl_LightSource[n].linearAttenuation | float | Constant coefficient for attenuation compuation for light n |
| gl_LightSource[n].quadraticAttenuation | float | Constant coefficient for attenuation compuation for light n |

**Table I-10**   Light Source Variables

The following structure contains the values for the light-model parameters.

```
struct gl_LightModelParameters {
    vec4 ambient;
};

uniform gl_LightModelParameters gl_LightModel;
```

The values associated with the light model are described in Table I-11.

| Variable Name | Type | Description |
| --- | --- | --- |
| gl_LightModel.ambient | vec4 | Light model's ambient color |

**Table I-11**    Light Model Variables

To help reduce the computation required for computing the colors based on OpenGL's Phone lighting model, the non-light dependent terms of the lighting equation (the emission and ambient material terms) combined with the light model ambient value are cached in the following structure and are described in Table I-12.

```
struct gl_LightModelProducts {
    vec4 sceneColor;
};

uniform gl_LightModelProducts gl_FrontLightModelProduct;
uniform gl_LightModelProducts gl_BackLightModelProduct;
```

| Variable Name | Type | Description |
| --- | --- | --- |
| gl_FrontLightModelProduct.sceneColor<br>gl_BackLightModelProduct.sceneColor | vec4 | $\text{emission}_{material} + \text{ambient}_{material}$ $* \text{ambient}_{light\ model}$ |

**Table I-12**    Cached Light Model Value Variables

Similarly, various products of constant factors of the material and lights are cached in the following structure and described in Table I-13.

```
struct gl_LightProducts
    vec4 ambient;
    vec4 diffuse;
    vec4 specular;
};

uniform gl_LightProducts gl_FrontLightProduct[gl_MaxLights];

uniform gl_LightProducts gl_BackLightProduct[gl_MaxLights];
```

| Variable Name | Type | Description |
|---|---|---|
| gl_FrontLightProduct[$n$].ambient<br>gl_BackLightProduct[$n$].ambient | vec4 | ambient$_{material}$ * ambient$_{light}$ |
| gl_FrontLightProduct[$n$].diffuse<br>gl_BackLightProduct[$n$].diffuse | vec4 | $(\max \{\mathbf{L} \cdot \mathbf{n}, 0\})$ * diffuse$_{light}$ *<br>diffuse$_{material}$ |
| gl_FrontLightProduct[$n$].specular<br>gl_BackLightProduct[$n$].specular | vec4 | $(\max \{\mathbf{s} \cdot \mathbf{n}, 0\})^{shininess}$ *<br>specular$_{light}$ * specular$_{material}$ |

**Table I-13**    Cached Light Product Value Variables

### Texture Environment State

The texture environment color (as specified by **glTexEnv()**) for each texture unit is available by accessing:

```
uniform vec4 gl_TextureEnvColor[gl_MaxTextureImageUnits];
```

### Texture Coordinate Generation State

The user-defined planes for texture coordinate generation are availble by accessing the following sets of values, one for each set of texture coordinates.

```
uniform vec4 gl_EyePlaneS[gl_MaxTextureCoords];
uniform vec4 gl_EyePlaneT[gl_MaxTextureCoords];
uniform vec4 gl_EyePlaneR[gl_MaxTextureCoords];
uniform vec4 gl_EyePlaneQ[gl_MaxTextureCoords];

uniform vec4 gl_ObjectPlaneS[gl_MaxTextureCoords];
uniform vec4 gl_ObjectPlaneT[gl_MaxTextureCoords];
uniform vec4 gl_ObjectPlaneR[gl_MaxTextureCoords];
uniform vec4 gl_ObjectPlaneQ[gl_MaxTextureCoords];
```

### Fog

The state associated with fog and atmospheric effects (See "Fog" in Chapter 6) in OpenGL are stored in the following structure and described in Table I-14:

```
struct gl_FogParameters {
    vec4 color;
    float density;
    float start;
```

```
        float end;
        float scale;
    };

    uniform gl_FogParameters gl_Fog;
```

| Variable Name | Type | Description |
|---|---|---|
| gl_Fog.color | vec4 | Fog color |
| gl_Fog.density | float | Fog density |
| gl_Fog.start | float | Starting distance for linear fog |
| gl_Fog.end | float | Ending distance for linear fog |
| gl_Fog.scale | float | Scaling factor for linear fog. This value is computed as $scale = \dfrac{1}{end - start}$ |

**Table I-14**　　Fog Variables and Cached Values

# Built-In Functions

## Angle Conversion and Trigonometric Functions

Table I-15 describes the trigonmetric functions available in GLSL shaders. Angles are measured in radians, and the following commands operate on each component separately. *TYPE* represents one of: float, vec2, vec3, or vec4.

| Function Syntax | Description |
|---|---|
| *TYPE* **radians**(*TYPE degrees*) | Returns $\left(\dfrac{\pi}{180}\right) \cdot degrees$ |
| *TYPE* **degrees**(*TYPE radians*) | Returns $\left(\dfrac{180}{\pi}\right) \cdot radians$ |
| *TYPE* **sin**(*TYPE angle*) | Returns the sine of *angle* |
| *TYPE* **cos**(*TYPE angle*) | Returns the cosine of *angle* |
| *TYPE* **tan**(*TYPE angle*) | Returns the tangent of *angle* |

**Table I-15**　　Angle Conversion and Trigonometric Functions

| Function Syntax | Description |
|---|---|
| *TYPE* **asin**(*TYPE x*) | Returs the arcsine $(\sin^{-1})$ of $x$. The range of values returned by this function is $[-\pi/2, \pi/2]$, and the result is undefined if $|x| > 1$. |
| *TYPE* **acos**(*TYPE x*) | Returns the arccosine $(\cos^{-1})$ of $x$. The range of values returned by this function is $[0, \pi]$, and the result is undefined if $|x| > 1$. |
| *TYPE* **atan**(*TYPE y*, *TYPE x*) | Returns the arctangent $(\tan^{-1})$ of $y/x$. The signs of $x$ and $y$ are used to determine what quadrant the angle is in. The range of values returned by this function is $[-\pi, \pi]$, and the result is undefined if $x$ and $y$ are both 0. |
| *TYPE* **atan**(*TYPE y_over_x*) | Returns the arctangent $(\tan^{-1})$ of $y\_over\_x$. The range of values returned by this function is $[-\pi/2, \pi/2]$. |

**Table I-15   (continued)**    Angle Conversion and Trigonometric Functions

## Transcendental Functions

Table I-16 lists the logarithmic and exponential functions available in GLSL. The commands operate on each component separately. *TYPE* represents one of: float, vec2, vec3, or vec4.

| Function Syntax | Description |
|---|---|
| *TYPE* **pow**(*TYPE x*, *TYPE y*) | Returns $xy$. Results are undefined if $x < 0$, or if $x = 0$ and $y \leq 0$ |
| *TYPE* **exp**(*TYPE x*) | Returns $e^x$. |
| *TYPE* **log**(*TYPE x*) | Returns $\ln(x)$. Results are undefined if $x \leq 0$ |
| *TYPE* **exp2**(*TYPE x*) | Returns $2^x$. |
| *TYPE* **log2**(*TYPE x*) | Returns $\log_2(x)$. Results are undefined if $x \leq 0$. |

**Table I-16**    Transcendental Functions

| Function Syntax | Description |
|---|---|
| *TYPE* **sqrt**(*TYPE x*) | Returns $\sqrt{x}$. Results are undefined if $x \le 0$. |
| *TYPE* **inversesqrt**(*TYPE x*) | Returns $\dfrac{1}{\sqrt{x}}$. Results are undefined if $x \le 0$. |

**Table I-16 (continued)**     Transcendental Functions

## Basic Numerical Functions

Table I-17 lists the basic numerical functions that GLSL supports. Each commands operate on each component separately. TYPE represents one of: float, vec2, vec3, or vec4.

| Function Syntax | Description |
|---|---|
| *TYPE* **abs**(*TYPE x*) | Returns $\lvert x \rvert$ |
| *TYPE* **sign**(*TYPE x*) | Returns $\begin{cases} 1 & x > 0 \\ 0 & x = 0 \\ -1 & x < 0 \end{cases}$ |
| *TYPE* **floor**(*TYPE x*) | Returns a value equal to the nearest integer that is less than or equal to $x$ |
| *TYPE* **ceil**(*TYPE x*) | Returns a value equal to the nearest integer that is greater than or equal to $x$ |
| *TYPE* **fract**(*TYPE x*) | Returns $x - floor\ (x)$ |
| *TYPE* **mod**(*TYPE x*, float *y*) <br> *TYPE* **mod**(*TYPE x*, *TYPE y*) | Returns the floating-point modulus: <br> $x - y \cdot floor\ (x/y)$ |
| *TYPE* **min**(*TYPE x*, *TYPE y*) <br> *TYPE* **min**(*TYPE x*, float *y*) | Returns $x < y\ ?\ x : y;$ |
| *TYPE* **max**(*TYPE x*, *TYPE y*) <br> *TYPE* **max**(*TYPE x*, float *y*) | Returns $x > y\ ?\ x : y;$ |
| *TYPE* **clamp**(*TYPE x*, *TYPE minVal*, *TYPE maxVal*) <br> *TYPE* **clamp**(*TYPE x*, float *minVal*, float *maxVal*) | Returns <br> **min(max(x, minVal), maxVal)** |

**Table I-17**     Basic Numerical Functions

| Function Syntax | Description |
|---|---|
| TYPE **mix**(TYPE x, TYPE y, TYPE a)<br>TYPE **mix**(TYPE x, TYPE y, float a) | Returns $x \cdot (1 - a) + y \cdot a$ |
| TYPE **step**(TYPE edge, TYPE x)<br>TYPE **step**(float edge, TYPE x) | Returns $x < edge \ ? \ 0.0 : 1.0;$ |
| TYPE **smoothstep**(TYPE edge0,<br>  TYPE edge1, TYPE x)<br>TYPE **smoothstep**(float edge0,<br>  float edge1, TYPE x) | Returns $\begin{cases} 0.0 & x \le edge0 \\ t^3 - 2t^2 & edge0 < x < edge1 \\ 1.0 & x \ge edge1 \end{cases}$ <br><br> where $t = \dfrac{x - edge0}{edge1 - edge0}$ |

**Table I-17 (continued)**    Basic Numerical Functions

## Vector-Operation Functions

Table I-18 describes the vector operations in GLSL. The following commands operate on their arguments as vectors. Where not explicitly specified, *TYPE* represents one of: float, vec2, vec3, or vec4.

| Function Syntax | Description |
|---|---|
| float **length**(TYPE x) | Returns the length of vector $x$:<br>  **sqrt** $(x[0] \cdot x[0] + x[1] \cdot x[1] + ...)$ |
| float **distance**(TYPE p0, TYPE p1) | Returns the distance between $p0$ and $p1$:<br>  **length** $(p0 - p1)$ |
| float **dot**(TYPE x, TYPE y) | Returns the dot product of $x$ and $y$:<br>  $result = x[0] \cdot y[0] + x[1] \cdot y[1] + ...$ |
| vec3 **cross**(vec3 x, vec3 y) | Returns the cross product of x and y, i.e.<br>  $result.x = x[1] \cdot y[2] - y[1] \cdot x[2]$<br>  $result.y = x[2] \cdot y[0] - y[2] \cdot x[0]$<br>  $result.z = x[0] \cdot y[1] - y[0] \cdot x[1]$ |
| TYPE **normalize**(TYPE x) | Returns a vector in the same direction as $x$ but with a length of 1. |

**Table I-18**    Vector-Operation Functions

| Function Syntax | Description |
|---|---|
| vec4 **ftransform**() | Returns the transformed input vertex such that it matches the output of the fixed-function vertex pipeline. |
| TYPE **faceforward**(TYPE N, TYPE I, TYPE Nref) | Returns **dot** (Nref, I) < 0 ? N : –N |
| TYPE **reflect**(TYPE I, TYPE N) | Returns the reflection direction for incident vector I, given the normalized surface orientation vector N:<br>result = $I - 2 \cdot$ **dot**$(N, I) \cdot N$ |
| TYPE **refract**(TYPE I, TYPE N, float *eta*) | Returns the refracted vector R, given the normalized incident vector I, normalized surface normal N, and the ratio of indices of refraction *eta*. The refracted vector is computed in the following manner: |

$$k = 1 - eta^2(1 - (\hat{N} \bullet \hat{I})^2)$$

$$\vec{R} = \begin{cases} 0 & k < 0 \\ (eta \cdot \hat{I} - eta\hat{N} \bullet \hat{I} + \sqrt{k}\hat{N}) & k > 0 \end{cases}$$

**Table I-18    (continued)**    Vector-Operation Functions

## Matrix Functions

As compared to standard matrix multiplication, which is defined using the * operator, the **matrixCompMult**() routine, described in Table I-19, produces a component-wise multiplication of two, equally-dimensioned matrices.

| Function Syntax | Description |
|---|---|
| mat **matrixCompMult**(mat x, mat y) | Multiply matrix x by matrix y component-wise, i.e., $result_{ij}$ is the scalar product of $x_{ij}$ and $y_{ij}$. |

**Table I-19**    Matrix Functions

| Function Syntax | Description |
|---|---|
| mat2 **outerProduct**( vec2 *c*, vec2 *r*) <br> mat3 **outerProduct**( vec3 *c*, vec3 *r*) <br> mat4 **outerProduct**( vec4 *c*, vec4 *r*) | Generates a $c \times r$ matrix by computing the outer matrix product (also called the tensor product). |
| mat2x3 **outerProduct**( vec3 *c*, vec2 *r*) <br> mat3x2 **outerProduct**( vec2 *c*, vec3 *r*) | |
| mat2x4 **outerProduct**( vec4 *c*, vec2 *r*) <br> mat4x2 **outerProduct**( vec2 *c*, vec4 *r*) | |
| mat3x4 **outerProduct**( vec4 *c*, vec3 *r*) <br> mat4x3 **outerProduct**( vec3 *c*, vec4 *r*) | |
| mat2 **transpose**(mat2 *m*) <br> mat3 **transpose**(mat3 *m*) <br> mat4 **transpose**(mat4 *m*) | Return the transpose of the matrix *m*. The input matrix is not modified. |
| mat2x3 **transpose**(mat3x2 *m*) <br> mat3x2 **transpose**(mat2x3 *m*) | |
| mat2x4 **transpose**(mat4x2 *m*) <br> mat4x2 **transpose**(mat2x4 *m*) | |
| mat3x4 **transpose**(mat4x3 *m*) <br> mat4x3 **transpose**(mat3x4 *m*) | |

**Table I-19 (continued)** Matrix Functions

## Vector-Component Relational Functions

The following functions produce a vector of boolean values representing the results of the specified operation conducted on each pair of components from the input vectors. *TYPE* represents any of: vec2, vec3, vec4, ivec2, ivec3, or ivec4 in the prototypes below, or a boolean vector when explicitly specified. The input vectors must be of the same type, and the boolean vector returned, represented by *bvec* below, will have the same size at the input vectors.

Table I-20 describes the accepted vector functions.

| Function Syntax | Description |
|---|---|
| bvec **lessThan**(*TYPE* x, *TYPE* y) | Returns the component-wise compare of $x < y$. |
| bvec **lessThanEqual**(*TYPE* x, *TYPE* y) | Returns the component-wise compare of $x \leq y$. |
| bvec **greaterThan**(*TYPE* x, *TYPE* y) | Returns the component-wise compare of $x > y$. |
| bvec **greaterThanEqual**(*TYPE* x, *TYPE* y) | Returns the component-wise compare of $x \geq y$. |
| bvec **equal**(*TYPE* x, *TYPE* y)<br>bvec **equal**(bvec x, bvec y) | Returns the component-wise compare of $x == y$. |
| bvec **notEqual**(*TYPE* x, *TYPE* y)<br>bvec **notEqual**(bvec x, bvec y) | Returns the component-wise compare of $x\ != y$. |
| bool **any**(bvec x) | Returns true if any component of $x$ is **true**. |
| bool **all**(bvec x) | Returns true only if all components of $x$ are **true**. |
| bvec **not**(bvec x) | Returns the component-wise logical complement of $x$. |

**Table I-20**     Vector Component Operation Functions

## Texture Lookup Functions

Texture lookup functions are available to both vertex and fragment shaders if supported by the underlying OpenGL implementation.

However, level of detail is not computed by fixed functionality for vertex shaders, resulting in some differences in operation between vertex and fragment texture lookups. The functions in Tables I-21 through I-24, provide access to textures through samplers, as set up through the OpenGL API. Texture properties such as size, pixel format, number of dimensions, filtering method, number of mip-map levels, depth comparison, and so on are also defined by OpenGL API calls. Such properties are taken into account as the texture is accessed via the built-in functions defined below.

## Basic Texture Access Functions

The following functions use the provided texture coordinates to retrieve a texel from the texture map associated with *sampler*.

All forms are accepted by fragment shaders. Functions with the *bias* parameter are not accepted in vertex shaders.

The optional *bias* parameter is used to alter which mipmap is sampled (see "Calculating the Mipmap Level" in Chapter 9). If a *bias* value is provided while accessing a texture that does not contain mipmaps, the texture is accessed directly, and the value is ignored. The *bias* forms of the texture functions are only available in fragment shaders.

| Function Syntax | Description |
| --- | --- |
| vec4 **texture1D**(sampler1D *sampler*, float *coord*)<br>vec4 **texture1D**(sampler1D *sampler*, float *coord*, float *bias* ) | Samples a one-dimensional texture map, with optional mipmap-level biasing |
| vec4 **texture2D**(sampler2D *sampler*, vec2 *coord* )<br>vec4 **texture2D**(sampler2D *sampler*, vec2 *coord*, float *bias* ) | Samples a two-dimensional texture map, with optional mipmap-level biasing |
| vec4 **texture3D**(sampler3D *sampler*, vec3 *coord* )<br>vec4 **texture3D**(sampler3D *sampler*, vec3 *coord*, float *bias* ) | Samples a three-dimensional texture map, with optional mipmap-level biasing |

**Table I-21**    Basic Texture Access Functions

## Projective Texture Access Functions

The following functions retrieve a texel from the texture map associated with *sampler*. Before the texel is retrieved, all components of the input texture coordinate, *coord*, are divided by the last coordinate.

All forms are accepted by fragment shaders. Functions with the *bias* parameter are not accepted in vertex shaders.

Once again, The optional *bias* parameter is used to alter which mipmap is sampled (see "Calculating the Mipmap Level" in Chapter 9). If a *bias* value is provided while accessing a texture that does not contain mipmaps, the texture is accessed directly and the value is ignored. The *bias* forms of the texture functions are only available in fragment shaders.

| Function Syntax | Description |
|---|---|
| vec4 **texture1DProj**(sampler1D *sampler*, vec2 *coord*)<br><br>vec4 **texture1DProj**(sampler1D *sampler*, vec4 *coord*)<br><br>vec4 **texture1DProj**(sampler1D *sampler*, vec2 *coord*, float *bias*)<br><br>vec4 **texture1DProj**(sampler1D *sampler*, vec4 *coord*, float *bias*) | Samples a one-dimensional texture map, with optional mipmap-level biasing. The input texture coordinate is divided by the last texture coordinates (*coord.s* for the vec2 call; *coord.q* for the vec4 call). |
| vec4 **texture2DProj**(sampler2D *sampler*, vec3 *coord*)<br><br>vec4 **texture2DProj**(sampler2D *sampler*, vec4 *coord*)<br><br>vec4 **texture2DProj**(sampler2D *sampler*, vec3 *coord*, float *bias* )<br><br>vec4 **texture2DProj**(sampler2D *sampler*, vec4 *coord*, float *bias* ) | Samples a two-dimensional texture map, with optional mipmap-level biasing. The input texture coordinate is divided by the last texture coordinates (*coord.t* for the vec2 call; *coord.q* for the vec4 call). |
| vec4 **texture3DProj**(sampler3D *sampler*, vec4 *coord*)<br><br>vec4 **texture3DProj**(sampler3D *sampler*, vec4 *coord*, float *bias* ) | Samples a three-dimensional texture map, with optional mipmap-level biasing. The input texture coordinate is divided by the last texture coordinates (*coord.p* for the vec2 call; *coord.q* for the vec4 call). |

**Table I-22**  Projective Texture Access Functions

## Vertex Shader Texture Access Functions

Texel retrieval in vertex shaders does not include the automatic computation of a mipmap level, as happens in a fragment shader. The following functions allow for the sampling of mipmaped textures by vertex shaders by providing an mipmap level-of-detail, or *lod* value (see "Calculating the Mipmap Level" in Chapter 9 for how to compute the level-of-detail value).

The vertex shader versions of the texture access functions are available in non-projective and projective forms (those calls that include "**Proj**" in the name. The input texture coordinates for the projective forms are processed as described in "Projective Texture Access Functions" on page 786.

| Function Syntax | Description |
|---|---|
| vec4 **texture1DLod**(sampler1D *sampler,* float *coord,* float *lod)*<br><br>vec4 **texture1DProjLod**(sampler1D *sampler,* vec2 *coord,* float *lod)*<br><br>vec4 **texture1DProjLod**(sampler1D *sampler,* vec4 *coord,* float *lod)* | Samples a one-dimensional texture map by specifying the mipmap level-of-detail. |
| vec4 **texture2DLod**(sampler2D *sampler,* vec2 *coord,* float *lod)*<br><br>vec4 **texture2DProjLod**(sampler2D *sampler,* vec3 *coord,* float *lod)*<br><br>vec4 **texture2DProjLod**(sampler2D *sampler,* vec4 *coord,* float *lod)* | Samples a two-dimensional texture map by specifying the mipmap level-of-detail. |
| vec4 **texture3DLod**(sampler3D *sampler,* vec3 *coord,* float *lod)*<br><br>vec4 **texture3DProjLod**(sampler3D *sampler,* vec4 *coord,* float *lod)* | Samples a three-dimensional texture map by specifying the mipmap level-of-detail. |

**Table I-23**    Vertex Shader Texture Access Functions

## Cube-Map Texture Access Functions

Retrieve the texel at input texture coordinate, *coord,* in the cube map texture currently bound to *sampler.* The direction of *coord* is used to select which face to do a 2-dimensional texture lookup in.

| Function Syntax | Description |
|---|---|
| vec4 **textureCube**(samplerCube *sampler,* vec3 *coord)*<br><br>vec4 **textureCube**(samplerCube *sampler,* vec3 *coord,* float *bias)*<br><br>vec4 **textureCubeLod**(samplerCube *sampler,* vec3 *coord,* float *lod)* | Samples a cube-mapped texture, with optional *bias* (fragment shader only) or *lod* parameters. |

**Table I-24**    Cube-Map Texture Access Functions

## Shadow-Map Texture Access Functions

If a non-shadow texture call is made to a sampler that represents a depth texture with depth comparisons turned on, then results are undefined. If a shadow texture call is made to a sampler that represents a depth texture with depth comparisons turned off, then results are undefined. If a shadow texture call is made to a sampler that does not represent a depth texture, then results are undefined.

| Function Syntax | Description |
|---|---|
| vec4 **shadow1D**(sampler1DShadow *sampler,* vec3 *coord*) | Sample a shadow depth map. The functions utilizing the *bias* parameter are only available in fragment shaders. |
| vec4 **shadow2D**(sampler2DShadow *sampler,* vec3 *coord*) | |
| vec4 **shadow1D**(sampler1DShadow *sampler,* vec3 *coord*, float *bias*) | |
| vec4 **shadow2D**(sampler2DShadow *sampler,* vec3 *coord*, float *bias*) | The LOD and projective versions of the functions process texture coordinates similarly to other LOD and projective functions respectively. |
| vec4 **shadow1DProj**(sampler1DShadow *sampler,* vec4 *coord*) | |
| vec4 **shadow2DProj**(sampler2DShadow *sampler,* vec4 *coord*) | |
| vec4 **shadow1DProj**(sampler1DShadow *sampler,* vec4 *coord*, float *bias*) | |
| vec4 **shadow2DProj**(sampler2DShadow *sampler,* vec4 *coord*, float *bias*) | |
| vec4 **shadow1DLod**(sampler1DShadow *sampler,* vec3 *coord*, float *lod*) | |
| vec4 **shadow2DLod**(sampler2DShadow *sampler,* vec3 *coord*, float *lod*) | |
| vec4 **shadow1DProjLod**(sampler1DShadow *sampler,* vec4 *coord*, float *lod*) | |
| vec4 **shadow2DProjLod**(sampler2DShadow *sampler,* vec4 *coord*, float *lod*) | |

**Table I-25**     Shadow-Map Texture Access Functions

## Fragment Processing Functions

Table I-26 describes the functions for accessing a fragment's derivative, which are computed as the fragments of the underlying geometric primitive are rasterized.

| Function Syntax | Description |
| --- | --- |
| *TYPE* **dFdx**(*TYPE p*) | Returns the derivative in the x-direction. |
| *TYPE* **dFdy**(*TYPE p*) | Returns the derivative in the y-direction |
| *TYPE* **fwidth**(*TYPE p*) | Returns $|dFdx(p)| + |dFdy(p)|$ |

**Table I-26**    Fragment Derivative Functions

## Noise Functions

The stochastic noise functions described in Table I-27 are available in both vertex and fragment shaders. The computed noise values returned are pseudo-random, but repeatable provided the same random number seed is used.

| Function Syntax | Description |
| --- | --- |
| float **noise1**(*TYPE x*) | Returns a 1D noise value based on the input value $x$. |
| vec2 **noise2**(*TYPE x*) | Returns a 2D noise value based on the input value $x$. |
| vec3 **noise3**(*TYPE x*) | Returns a 3D noise value based on the input value $x$. |
| vec4 **noise4**(*TYPE x*) | Returns a 4D noise value based on the input value $x$. |

**Table I-27**    Random-Noise Generation Functions

# Glossary

**accumulation buffer**

Memory (bitplanes) that is used to accumulate a series of images generated in the color buffer. Using the accumulation buffer may significantly improve the quality of the image, but also take correspondingly longer to render. The accumulation buffer is used for effects such as depth of field, motion blur, and full-scene antialiasing.

**aliasing**

A rendering technique that assigns to pixels the color of the primitive being rendered, regardless of whether that primitive covers all or only a portion of the pixel's area. This results in jagged edges, or jaggies.

**alpha**

A fourth color component. The alpha component is never displayed directly and is typically used to control color blending. By convention, OpenGL alpha corresponds to the notion of opacity, rather than transparency, meaning that an alpha value of 1.0 implies complete opacity, and an alpha value of 0.0 complete transparency.

**ambient**

Ambient light is nondirectional and distributed uniformly throughout space. Ambient light falling upon a surface approaches from all directions. The light is reflected from the object independent of surface location and orientation, with equal intensity in all directions.

**animation**

Generating repeated renderings of a scene, with smoothly changing viewpoint and/or object positions, quickly enough so that the illusion of motion is achieved. OpenGL animation is almost always done using double-buffering.

### antialiasing

A rendering technique that assigns pixel colors based on the fraction of the pixel's area that's covered by the primitive being rendered. Antialiased rendering reduces or eliminates the jaggies that result from aliased rendering.

### application-specific clipping

Clipping of primitives against planes in eye coordinates; the planes are specified by the application using **glClipPlane()**.

### ARB Imaging Subset

The collection of OpenGL extensions for processing pixel rectangles. Imaging Subset operations include color table lookups, color matrix transformations, image convolutions, and image statistics.

### attenuation

The property of light that describes how a light's intensity diminishes over distance.

### attribute group

A set of related state variables, which OpenGL can save or restore together at one time.

### back faces

See *faces*.

### bit

Binary digit. A state variable having only two possible values: 0 or 1. Binary numbers are constructions of one or more bits.

### bitmap

A rectangular array of bits. Also, the primitive rendered by the **glBitmap()** command, which uses its *bitmap* parameter as a mask.

### bitplane

A rectangular array of bits mapped one-to-one with pixels. The framebuffer is a stack of bitplanes.

### blending

Reduction of two color components to one component, usually as a linear interpolation between the two components.

**buffer**

A group of bitplanes that store a single component (such as depth or green) or a single index (such as the color index or the stencil index). Sometimes the red, green, blue, and alpha buffers together are referred to as the color buffer, rather than the color buffers.

**buffer object**

A vertex array located in the GL's server memory, as opposed to the client application's memory. Vertex data and indicies stored in buffer objects may render considerably faster than the equivalent client-side versions.

**byte swapping**

The process of exchanging the ordering of bytes in a (usually integer) variable type (i.e., `int`, `short`, etc.)

**C**

God's programming language.

**C++**

The object-oriented programming language of a pagan deity.

**client**

The computer from which OpenGL commands are issued. The computer that issues OpenGL commands can be connected via a network to a different computer that executes the commands, or commands can be issued and executed on the same computer. See also *server*.

**client memory**

The main memory (where program variables are stored) of the client computer.

**clip coordinates**

The coordinate system that follows transformation by the projection matrix and precedes perspective division. View-volume clipping is done in clip coordinates, but application-specific clipping is not.

**clipping**

Elimination of the portion of a geometric primitive that's outside the half-space defined by a clipping plane. Points are simply rejected if outside. The portion of a line or polygon that's outside the half-space is eliminated, and additional vertices are generated as necessary to complete the primitive within the clipping half-space. Geometric primitives and the current raster position (when specified) are always clipped against the six half-spaces defined by the left, right, bottom, top, near, and far planes of the view volume. Applications can specify optional application-specific clipping planes to be applied in eye coordinates.

### color index

A single value that represents a color by name, rather than by value. OpenGL color indices are treated as continuous values (for example, floating-point numbers), while operations such as interpolation and dithering are performed on them. Color indices stored in the framebuffer are always integer values, however. Floating-point indices are converted to integers by rounding to the nearest integer value.

### color-index mode

An OpenGL context is in color-index mode if its color buffers store color indices, rather than red, green, blue, and alpha color components.

### color-lookup table

A one-dimensional image used to substitute RGBA color components in an image pixel.

### color map

A table of index-to-RGB mappings that's accessed by the display hardware. Each color index is read from the color buffer, converted to an RGB triple by lookup in the color map, and sent to the monitor.

### color matrix

The $4 \times 4$ matrix used to transform RGBA pixel values when passed into the Imaging Subset. Color matrices are particularly useful in color space conversions.

### components

Single, continuous (for example, floating-point) values that represent intensities or quantities. Usually, a component value of zero represents the minimum value or intensity, and a component value of one represents the maximum value or intensity, although other ranges are sometimes used. Because component values are interpreted in a normalized range, they are specified independent of actual resolution. For example, the RGB triple (1, 1, 1) is white, regardless of whether the color buffers store 4, 8, or 12 bits each.

Out-of-range components are typically clamped to the normalized range, not truncated or otherwise interpreted. For example, the RGB triple (1.4, 1.5, 0.9) is clamped to (1.0, 1.0, 0.9) before it's used to update the color buffer. Red, green, blue, alpha, and depth are always treated as components, never as indices.

### concave

A polygon that is not convex. See *convex*.

### context

A complete set of OpenGL state variables. Note that framebuffer contents are not part of OpenGL state, but that the configuration of the framebuffer is.

### convex

A polygon is convex if no straight line in the plane of the polygon intersects the polygon more than twice.

### convex hull

The smallest convex region enclosing a specified group of points. In two dimensions, the convex hull is found conceptually by stretching a rubber band around the points so that all of the points lie within the band.

### convolution filter

One- or two-dimensional images that are used for computing the weighted average of pixel images.

### convolution kernel

See *convolution filter*.

### coordinate system

In $n$-dimensional space, a set of $n$ linearly independent vectors anchored to a point (called the origin). A group of coordinates specifies a point in space (or a vector from the origin) by indicating how far to travel along each vector to reach the point (or tip of the vector).

### culling

The process of eliminating a front face or back face of a polygon so that it isn't drawn.

### current matrix

A matrix that transforms coordinates in one coordinate system to coordinates of another system. There are three current matrices in OpenGL: the modelview matrix transforms object coordinates (coordinates specified by the programmer) to eye coordinates; the perspective matrix transforms eye coordinates to clip coordinates; the texture matrix transforms specified or generated texture coordinates as described by the matrix. Each current matrix is the top element on a stack of matrices. Each of the three stacks can be manipulated with OpenGL matrix-manipulation commands.

### current raster position

A window coordinate position that specifies the placement of an image primitive when it's rasterized. The current raster position and other current raster parameters are updated when **glRasterPos()** is called.

### decal

A method of calculating color values during texture application, where the texture colors replace the fragment colors or, if alpha blending is enabled, the texture colors are blended with the fragment colors, using only the alpha value.

### depth

Generally refers to the $z$ window coordinate.

### depth buffer

Memory that stores the depth value at every pixel. To perform hidden-surface removal, the depth buffer records the depth value of the object that lies closest to the observer at every pixel. The depth value of every new fragment uses the recorded value for depth comparison and must pass the comparison test before being rendered.

### depth-cuing

A rendering technique that assigns color based on distance from the viewpoint.

### diffuse

Diffuse lighting and reflection accounts for the direction of a light source. The intensity of light striking a surface varies with the angle between the orientation of the object and the direction of the light source. A diffuse material scatters that light evenly in all directions.

### directional light source

See *infinite light source*.

### display list

A named list of OpenGL commands. Display lists are always stored on the server, so display lists can be used to reduce network traffic in client-server environments. The contents of a display list may be preprocessed and might therefore execute more efficiently than the same set of OpenGL commands executed in immediate mode. Such preprocessing is especially important for computing intensive commands such as NURBS or polygon tessellation.

### dithering

A technique for increasing the perceived range of colors in an image at the cost of spatial resolution. Adjacent pixels are assigned differing color values; when viewed from a distance, these colors seem to blend into a single intermediate color. The technique is similar to the halftoning used in black-and-white publications to achieve shades of gray.

### double-buffering

OpenGL contexts with both front and back color buffers are double-buffered. Smooth animation is accomplished by rendering into only the back buffer (which isn't displayed), and then causing the front and back buffers to be swapped. See **glutSwapBuffers()** in Appendix D.

### edge flag

A Boolean value at a vertex that marks whether that vertex precedes a boundary edge. **glEdgeFlag*()** may be used to mark an edge as not on the boundary. When a polygon is drawn in GL_LINE mode, only boundary edges are drawn.

### element

A single component or index.

### emission

The color of an object that is self-illuminating or self-radiating. The intensity of an emissive material is not attributed to any external light source.

### evaluated

The OpenGL process of generating object-coordinate vertices and parameters from previously specified Bézier equations.

### execute

An OpenGL command is executed when it's called in immediate mode or when the display list that it's a part of is called.

### extension

A new feature of OpenGL that hasn't been added into the core of OpenGL. An extension does not have to be supported by every OpenGL implementation, as compared to core OpenGL functions, which are supported for every OpenGL implementation. There are different types of extensions, based upon how broadly supported the functionality is. Generally, extensions supported only by a single company's OpenGL implementation will have a name that includes an abbreviation of the company name. If more companies adopt the extension, its name will change from the abbreviation to a string that includes the letters, EXT; for example, GL_EXT_polygon_offset. If OpenGL's governing body, the OpenGL Architecture Review Board (or ARB, for short) reviews and approves the extension, its name will change once again. For example, a reviewed extension that was approved by the ARB is GL_ARB_multitexture.

### eye coordinates

The coordinate system that follows transformation by the modelview matrix and precedes transformation by the projection matrix. Lighting and application-specific clipping are done in eye coordinates.

### faces

The sides of a polygon. Each polygon has two faces: a front face and a back face. Only one face or the other is ever visible in the window. Whether the back or front face is visible is effectively determined after the polygon is projected onto the window. After this projection, if the polygon's edges are directed clockwise, one of the faces is visible; if directed counterclockwise, the other face is visible. Whether clockwise corresponds to front or back (and counterclockwise corresponds to back or front) is determined by the OpenGL programmer.

### feedback

OpenGL's mechanism for allowing an application to retrieve information about which geometric and imaging primitives that would have rasterized to the window. No pixels are updated in feedback mode.

### filtering

The process of combining pixels or texels to obtain a higher or lower resolution version of an input image or texture.

## fixed-function pipeline

The processing model where the order of operations that OpenGL uses on vertices and fragments is fixed by the implementation. A programmer's control over its operation is limited by setting state values and enabling or disabling operations. See *programmable graphics pipeline*.

## flat shading

Refers to a primitive colored with a single, constant color across its extent, rather than smoothly interpolated colors across the primitive. See *Gouraud shading*.

## fog

A rendering technique that can be used to simulate atmospheric effects such as haze, fog, and smog by fading object colors to a background color based on distance from the viewer. Fog also aids in the perception of distance from the viewer, giving a depth cue.

## fonts

Groups of graphical character representations generally used to display strings of text. The characters may be roman letters, mathematical symbols, Asian ideograms, Egyptian hieroglyphics, and so on.

## fragment

Fragments are generated by the rasterization of primitives. Each fragment corresponds to a single pixel and includes color, depth, and sometimes texture-coordinate values.

## framebuffer

All the buffers of a given window or context. Sometimes includes all the pixel memory of the graphics hardware accelerator.

## front faces

See *fsaces*.

## frustum

The view volume warped by perspective division.

## gamma correction

A function applied to colors stored in the framebuffer to correct for the nonlinear response of the eye (and sometimes of the monitor) to linear changes in color-intensity values.

### geometric model

The object-coordinate vertices and parameters that describe an object. Note that OpenGL doesn't define a syntax for geometric models, but rather a syntax and semantics for the rendering of geometric models.

### geometric object

See *geometric model*.

### geometric primitive

A point, a line, or a polygon.

### GLSL

The short name for *The OpenGL Shading Language*.

### GLX

The window system interface for OpenGL on the X Window System.

### Gouraud shading

Smooth interpolation of colors across a polygon or line segment. Colors are assigned at vertices and linearly interpolated across the primitive to produce a relatively smooth variation in color. Also called *smooth shading*.

### group

Each pixel of an image in client memory is represented by a group of one, two, three, or four elements. Thus, in the context of a client memory image, a group and a pixel are the same thing.

### half-spaces

A plane divides space into two half-spaces.

### hidden-line removal

A technique to determine which portions of a wireframe object should be visible. The lines that comprise the wireframe are considered to be edges of opaque surfaces, which may obscure other edges that are farther away from the viewer.

### hidden-surface removal

A technique to determine which portions of an opaque, shaded object should be visible and which portions should be obscured. A test of the depth coordinate, using the depth buffer for storage, is a common method of hidden-surface removal.

## histogram

A database of the distribution of pixel values in an image. The results of the histogram process are counts of unique pixel values.

## homogeneous coordinates

A set of $n+1$ coordinates used to represent points in $n$-dimensional projective space. Points in projective space can be thought of as points in Euclidean space together with some points at infinity. The coordinates are homogeneous because a scaling of each of the coordinates by the same nonzero constant doesn't alter the point that the coordinates refer to. Homogeneous coordinates are useful in the calculations of projective geometry, and thus in computer graphics, where scenes must be projected onto a window.

## image

A rectangular array of pixels, either in client memory or in the framebuffer.

## image primitive

A bitmap or an image.

## immediate mode

Execution of OpenGL commands when they're called, rather than from a display list. No immediate-mode bit exists; the mode in immediate mode refers to use of OpenGL, rather than to a specific bit of OpenGL state.

## index

A single value that's interpreted as an absolute value rather than as a normalized value in a specified range (as is a component). Color indices are the names of colors, which are dereferenced by the display hardware using the color map. Indices are typically masked, rather than clamped when out of range. For example, the index 0xf7 is masked to 0x7 when written to a 4-bit buffer (color or stencil). Color indices and stencil indices are always treated as indices, never as components.

## indices

Preferred plural of index. (The choice between the plural forms indices or indexes—as well as matrices or matrixes and vertices or vertexes—has engendered much debate between the authors and principal reviewers of this guide. The authors' compromise solution is to use the -ices form, but to state clearly for the record that the use of indice [*sic*], matrice [*sic*], and vertice [*sic*] for the singular forms is an abomination.)

**infinite light source**

A directional source of illumination. The radiating light from an infinite light source strikes all objects as parallel rays.

**interleaved**

A method of storing vertex arrays whereby heterogeneous types of data (i.e., vertex, normals, texture coordinates, etc.) are grouped together for faster retrieval.

**interpolation**

Calculation of values (such as color or depth) for interior pixels, given the values at the boundaries (such as at the vertices of a polygon or a line).

**IRIS GL**

Silicon Graphics' proprietary graphics library, developed from 1982 through 1992. OpenGL was designed with IRIS GL as a starting point.

**jaggies**

Artifacts of aliased rendering. The edges of primitives that are rendered with aliasing are jagged, rather than smooth. A near-horizontal aliased line, for example, is rendered as a set of horizontal lines on adjacent pixel rows, rather than as a smooth, continuous line.

**jittering**

A pseudo-random displacement (shaking) of the objects in a scene, used in conjunction with the accumulation buffer to achieve special effects.

**kernel**

See *convolution kernel*.

**level of detail**

The process of creating multiple copies of an object or image with different levels of resolution. See also *mipmap*.

**lighting**

The process of computing the color of a vertex based on current lights, material properties, and lighting-model modes.

**line**

A straight region of finite width between two vertices. (Unlike mathematical lines, OpenGL lines have finite width and length.) Each segment of a strip of lines is itself a line.

**local light source**

A source of illumination that has an exact position. The radiating light from a local light source emanates from that position. Other names for a local light source are *point light source* or *positional light source* A *spotlight* is a special kind of local light source.

**local viewer mode**

An OpenGL light model mode that accurately computes the vector from a vertex to the eye. For performance reasons, *local viewer mode* is not enabled, and an approximation to the real vector is used for lighting computations.

**logical operation**

Boolean mathematical operations between the incoming fragment's RGBA color or color-index values and the RGBA color or color-index values already stored at the corresponding location in the framebuffer. Examples of logical operations include AND, OR, XOR, NAND, and INVERT.

**luminance**

The perceived brightness of a surface. Often refers to a weighted average of red, green, and blue color values that indicates the perceived brightness of the combination.

**material**

A surface property used in computing the illumination of a surface.

**matrices**

Preferred plural of matrix. See *indices*.

**matrix**

A two-dimensional array of values. OpenGL matrices are all $4 \times 4$, though when stored in client memory they're treated as $1 \times 16$ single-dimension arrays.

**minmax**

The process of computing the minimum and maximum pixel values in an image using the Imaging Subset.

**mipmap**

A reduced resolution version of a texture map, used to texture a geometric primitive whose screen resolution differs from the resolution of the source texture map.

## modelview matrix

The $4 \times 4$ matrix that transforms points, lines, polygons, and raster positions from object coordinates to eye coordinates.

## modulate

A method of calculating color values during texture application whereby the texture and the fragment colors are combined.

## monitor

The device that displays the image in the framebuffer.

## motion blurring

A technique that uses the accumulation buffer to simulate what appears on film when you take a picture of a moving object or when you move the camera while taking a picture of a stationary object. In animations without motion blur, moving objects can appear jerky.

## multitexturing

The process of applying several texture images to a single primitive. The images are applied one after another, in a pipeline of texturing operations.

## network

A connection between two or more computers that enables each to transfer data to and from the others.

## nonconvex

A polygon is nonconvex if a line exists in the plane of the polygon that intersects the polygon more than twice.

## normal

A three-component plane equation that defines the angular orientation, but not position, of a plane or surface.

## normal vectors

See *normal*.

## normalized

To normalize a normal vector, divide each of the components by the square root of the sum of their squares. Then, if the normal is thought of as a vector from the origin to the point $(nx', ny', nz')$, this vector has unit length.

factor = sqrt($nx^2 + ny^2 + nz^2$)

$nx' = nx$ / factor

$ny' = ny$ / factor

$nz' = nz$ / factor

### NURBS

Non-Uniform Rational B-Spline. A common way to specify parametric curves and surfaces. (See GLU NURBS routines in Chapter 12.)

### object

An object-coordinate model that's rendered as a collection of primitives.

### object coordinates

Coordinate system prior to any OpenGL transformation.

### The OpenGL Shading Language

The language used for authoring *shader program*. Also commonly known as the *GLSL*.

### orthographic

Nonperspective (or parallel) projection, as in some engineering drawings, with no foreshortening.

### outer product

A process that produces a matrix from two vectors. For the matrix $A$, which is the outer product of the vectors $u$ and $v$, $A_{ij} = u_i v_j$.

### pack

The process of converting pixel colors from a buffer into the format requested by the application.

### parameters

Values passed as arguments to OpenGL commands. Sometimes parameters are passed by reference to an OpenGL command.

### perspective correction

An additional calculation for texture coordinates to fix texturing artifacts for a textured geometric rendered in a perspective projection.

### perspective division

The division of $x$, $y$, and $z$ by $w$, carried out in clip coordinates.

### picking

A form of *selection* that uses a rectangular region (usually near the cursor location) to determine which primitives to select.

### pixel

Picture element. The bits at location $(x, y)$ of all the bitplanes in the framebuffer constitute the single pixel $(x, y)$. In an image in client memory, a pixel is one group of elements. In OpenGL window coordinates, each pixel corresponds to a $1.0 \times 1.0$ screen area. The coordinates of the lower left corner of the pixel are $(x, y)$, and of the upper right corner are $(x + 1, y + 1)$.

### point

An exact location in space, which is rendered as a finite-diameter dot.

### point light source

See *local light source*.

### polygon

A near-planar surface bounded by edges specified by vertices. Each triangle of a triangle mesh is a polygon, as is each quadrilateral of a quadrilateral mesh. The rectangle specified by **glRect*()** is also a polygon.

### polygon offset

A technique to modify depth-buffer values of a polygon when additional geometric primitives are drawn with identical geometric coordinates.

### positional light source

See *local light source*.

### primitive

A point, a line, a polygon, a bitmap, or an image. (Note: Not just a point, a line, or a polygon!)

### projection matrix

The $4 \times 4$ matrix that transforms points, lines, polygons, and raster positions from eye coordinates to clip coordinates.

**proxy texture**

A placeholder for a texture image, which is used to determine if there are enough resources to support a texture image of a given size and internal format resolution.

**programmable graphics pipeline**

The mode of operation where the processing of *vertices*, *fragments*, and their associated data (texture coordinates, for example) is under the control of *shader programs* specified by the programmer.

**quadrilateral**

A polygon with four edges.

**rasterization**

Converts a projected point, line, or polygon, or the pixels of a bitmap or image, to fragments, each corresponding to a pixel in the framebuffer. Note that all primitives are rasterized, not just points, lines, and polygons.

**rectangle**

A quadrilateral whose alternate edges are parallel to each other in object coordinates. Polygons specified with **glRect*()** are always rectangles; other quadrilaterals might be rectangles.

**rendering**

Conversion of primitives specified in object coordinates to an image in the framebuffer. Rendering is the primary operation of OpenGL—it's what OpenGL does.

**resident texture**

A texture image that is cached in special, high-performance texture memory. If an OpenGL implementation does not have special, high-performance texture memory, then all texture images are deemed resident textures.

**RGBA**

Red, Green, Blue, Alpha.

**RGBA mode**

An OpenGL context is in RGBA mode if its color buffers store red, green, blue, and alpha color components, rather than color indices.

**scissoring**

A fragment clipping test. Fragments outside of a rectangular scissor region are rejected.

**selection**

The process of determining which primitives intersect a 2D region or 3D volume defined by matrix transformations.

**separable filter**

A form of 2D *convolution filter* that can be represented by two 1D vectors. The 2D separable filter is determined by computing the *outer product* of the two vectors.

**server**

The computer on which OpenGL commands are executed. This might differ from the computer from which commands are issued. See *client*.

**shader program**

A set of instructions written in a graphics shading language (The OpenGL Shading Language, also called GLSL) that control the processing of graphics primitives.

**shading**

The process of interpolating color within the interior of a polygon, or between the vertices of a line, during rasterization.

**shininess**

The exponent associated with *specular* reflection and lighting. Shininess controls the degree with which the specular highlight decays.

**single-buffering**

OpenGL contexts that don't have back color buffers are single-buffered. You can use these contexts for animation, but take care to avoid visually disturbing flashes when rendering.

**singular matrix**

A matrix that has no inverse. Geometrically, such a matrix represents a transformation that collapses points along at least one line to a single point.

**smooth shading**

See *Gouraud shading*.

### specular

Specular lighting and reflection incorporates reflection off shiny objects and the position of the viewer. Maximum specular reflectance occurs when the angle between the viewer and the direction of the reflected light is zero. A specular material scatters light with greatest intensity in the direction of the reflection, and its brightness decays, based upon the exponential value *shininess*.

### spotlight

A special type of local light source that has a direction (where it points to) as well as a position. A spotlight simulates a cone of light, which may have a fall-off in intensity, based upon distance from the center of the cone.

### sprite

A screen-aligned graphics primitive. Sprites are ususally represented as either a single vertex that is expanded to cover many pixels around the transformed vertex, or as a quadralaterial its vertices specified so that it is perpendicular to the viewing direction (or put another way, parallel to the image plane).

### sRGB color space

An RGB color space standard specified by the International Electrotechnical Commission (IEC) that matches the color intensity outputs of monitors and printers better than a linear RGB space. The sRGB approximately corresponds to gamma correcting RGB (but not alpha) values using a gamma value of 2.2. See IEC standard 61966-2-1 for all of the gory details.

### stencil buffer

Memory (bitplanes) that is used for additional per-fragment testing, along with the *depth buffer*. The stencil test may be used for masking regions, capping solid geometry, and overlapping translucent polygons.

### stereo

Enhanced three-dimensional perception of a rendered image by computing separate images for each eye. Stereo requires special hardware, such as two synchronized monitors or special glasses, to alternate viewed frames for each eye. Some implementations of OpenGL support stereo by including both left and right buffers for color data.

**stipple**

A one- or two-dimensional binary pattern that defeats the generation of fragments where its value is zero. Line stipples are one-dimensional and are applied relative to the start of a line. Polygon stipples are two-dimensional and are applied with a fixed orientation to the window.

**tessellation**

Reduction of a portion of an analytic surface to a mesh of polygons, or of a portion of an analytic curve to a sequence of lines.

**texel**

A texture element. A texel is obtained from texture memory and represents the color of the texture to be applied to a corresponding fragment.

**texture mapping**

The process of applying an image (the texture) to a primitive. Texture mapping is often used to add realism to a scene. For example, you can apply a picture of a building facade to a polygon representing a wall.

**texture matrix**

The $4 \times 4$ matrix that transforms texture coordinates from the coordinates in which they're specified to the coordinates that are used for interpolation and texture lookup.

**texture object**

A named cache that stores texture data, such as the image array, associated mipmaps, and associated texture parameter values: width, height, border width, internal format, resolution of components, minification and magnification filters, wrapping modes, border color, and texture priority.

**textures**

One- or two-dimensional images that are used to modify the color of fragments produced by rasterization.

**texture unit**

When multitexturing, as part of an overall multiple pass application of texture images, a texture unit controls one processing step for a single texture image. A texture unit maintains the texturing state for one texturing pass, including the texture image, filter, environment, coordinate generation, and matrix stack. Multitexturing consists of a chain of texture units.

**transformations**

The warping of spaces. In OpenGL, transformations are limited to projective transformations that include anything that can be represented by a $4 \times 4$ matrix. Such transformations include rotations, translations, (nonuniform) scalings along the coordinate axes, perspective transformations, and combinations of these.

**triangle**

A polygon with three edges. Triangles are always convex.

**unpack**

The process of converting pixels supplied by an application to OpenGL's internal format.

**vertex**

A point in three-dimensional space.

**vertex array**

A block of vertex data (vertex coordinates, texture coordinates, surface normals, RGBA colors, color indices, and edge flags) may be stored in an array and then used to specify multiple geometric primitives through the execution of a single OpenGL command.

**vertices**

Preferred plural of vertex. See *indices*.

**viewpoint**

The origin of either the eye- or the clip-coordinate system, depending on context. (For example, when discussing lighting, the viewpoint is the origin of the eye-coordinate system. When discussing projection, the viewpoint is the origin of the clip-coordinate system.) With a typical projection matrix, the eye-coordinate and clip-coordinate origins are at the same location.

**view volume**

The volume in clip coordinates whose coordinates satisfy the following three conditions:

$-w \leq x \leq w$

$-w \leq y \leq w$

$-w \leq z \leq w$

Geometric primitives that extend outside this volume are clipped.

## VRML

VRML stands for Virtual Reality Modeling Language, which is (according to the VRML Mission Statement) "a universal description language for multi-participant simulations." VRML is specifically designed to allow people to navigate through three-dimensional worlds that are placed on the World Wide Web. The first versions of VRML are subsets of the Open Inventor file format with additions to allow hyperlinking to the Web (to URLs—Universal Resource Locators).

## window

A subregion of the framebuffer, usually rectangular, whose pixels all have the same buffer configuration. An OpenGL context renders to a single window at a time.

## window-aligned

When referring to line segments or polygon edges, implies that these are parallel to the window boundaries. (In OpenGL, the window is rectangular, with horizontal and vertical edges.) When referring to a polygon pattern, implies that the pattern is fixed relative to the window origin.

## window coordinates

The coordinate system of a window. It's important to distinguish between the names of pixels, which are discrete, and the window-coordinate system, which is continuous. For example, the pixel at the lower left corner of a window is pixel (0, 0); the window coordinates of the center of this pixel are (0.5, 0.5, $z$). Note that window coordinates include a depth, or $z$, component, and that this component is continuous as well.

## wireframe

A representation of an object that contains line segments only. Typically, the line segments indicate polygon edges.

## working set

On machines with special hardware that increases texture performance, this is the group of texture objects that are currently resident. The performance of textures within the working set outperforms the textures outside the working set.

## X Window System

A window system used by many of the machines on which OpenGL is implemented. GLX is the name of the OpenGL extension to the X Window System. (See Appendix C.)

# Index

computer-aided design
orthographic parallel projection, use of, 136

concave polygons
GLU tessellation, 506
stencil buffer, drawing with the, 618

cones, 524, 764
improving rendering of, 627

constant attenuation, 198

contours, 435

control points, 534, 538, 542, 551

convex polygons, 39

convolutions, 353–361
1d filters, 359
2d filters, 353
border modes, 360
post convolution scale and bias, 361
sample program, 355
separable filters, 357

Conway, John, 627

coordinate systems
grand, fixed, 119, 128, 153
local, 119, 128, 153, 157
simple 2D, 36

coordinates
*see* clip coordinates, depth coordinates, eye coordinates, homogeneous coordinates, normalized device coordinates, object coordinates, q texture coordinates, texture coordinates, w coordinates, or window coordinates

coverage, pixel, 247

Coxeter, H. S. M., 773

cross product, 131, 769

CSG, *see* computational solid geometry

cube maps, 441

culling, 56–57
enabling, 57
rendering pipeline stage, 12, 682
selection mode, 574

curves and curved surfaces, 41
*see also* evaluators or NURBS

*Curves and Surfaces for Computer-Aided Geometric Design*, 535

cylinders, 524

## D

data types
RGBA color conversion, 177
special OpenGL, 8
texture data, 382
warning about data type conversions, 782

decals, 477, 617
polygon offset used for, 274
texture function, 424

depth buffer, 186, 468, 469
*see also* hidden-surface removal
background, using masking for a common, 474
blending, use for three-dimensional, 243
clearing, 32, 186, 471
decals, for, 617
Dirichlet domains, for, 626
drawing static backgrounds, 625
masking, 473
near frustum plane effect on resolution, 780
pixel data, 321, 332

depth coordinates, 109, 141
perspective division, 141
picking use, 585
polygon offset, 274–276
rendering pipeline stage for depth-range operations, 12, 682
sample program with picking, 585
selection hit records, 574

depth test, 483
*see also* depth buffer
rendering pipeline stage, 14, 683

depth-cuing, *see* fog

depth-of-field effect, 497–501
sample program, 499

destination factor, *see* blending

determining object coordinates from window coordinates, 160, 163

diffuse
  contribution to lighting equation, 223
  light, 188, 196
  material properties, 189, 213
directional light source, 197
Dirichlet domains, 626
disks, 524
display lists, 29, 279
  changing mode settings, 299
  compiling, 287
  creating, 285
  deleting, 292
  disadvantages, 284, 290
  error handling, 286, 780
  executing, 285, 289
  executing multiple, 292
  font creation, 293, 309
  hierarchical, 290
  immediate mode, mixing with, 289
  indices for, obtaining, 286
  naming, 286
  nesting, 290
  nesting limit, querying, 290
  networked operation, 289
  performance tips, 782
  querying use of an index, 291
  rendering pipeline stage, 11
  sample program creating a font, 294
  sample program for creating, 279, 285
  sharing among rendering contexts, 739, 754
  state variables saved and restored, 298
  tessellation, use with, 521
  uses for, 283, 299
  vertex-array data, 289
  what can be stored in, 288
distorted images, 611
  texture images, 428
dithering, 172–173, 488, 781
  and clearing, 471
  rendering pipeline stage, 14, 683
dot product
  lighting calculations, use in, 223
  texture combiner function, 451
double-buffering, 22–23
  automatic glFlush(), 35
  changing between single-buffering and, 176

object selection using the back buffer, 610
  querying its presence, 469
drawing
  clearing the window, 30
  forcing completion of, 34
  icosahedron, 96
  points, 43
  polygons, 43, 56
  preparing for, 30
  rectangles, 40
  spheres, cylinders, and disks, 523–532
drawing pixel data, *see* pixel data
Duff, Tom, 239

# E

edge flags, 62–63
  tessellated polygons generate, 510
  vertex arrays, specifying values with, 69
emission, 188, 214, 221
enabling
  alpha test, 476
  antialiasing of points or lines, 249
  antialiasing polygons, 260
  blending, 235
  color material properties mode, 217
  color sum mode, 455
  culling, 57
  depth test, 484
  dithering, 173, 488
  evaluators, 539, 543
  fog, 261
  lighting, 211
  line stippling, 52
  logical operations, 489
  multisampling, 256
  normal vectors for evaluated surfaces, automatic generation of, 543, 551
  polygon offset, 274
  polygon stippling, 58
  rescaling normals, 65, 192
  stencil test, 478
  texture coordinate generation, 438
  texturing, 376, 379
  unit length normal vectors ensured, 65, 192

framebuffer, 170, 467
  capacity per pixel, 468
  clearing, 470–471
  copying pixel data within, 313, 321, 322
  enabling for reading, 472
  enabling for writing, 472
  minimum configuration with the X
      Window System, 468
  querying color resolution, 170
  reading pixel data from, 313, 315
  writing pixel data to, 313, 319
front-facing polygons, 56
  specifying material property for, 212
  two-sided lighting, 209
frustum, 133
ftp (file-transfer protocol) site
  GLX specification, 738
*Fundamentals of Computer Aided Geometric*
  *Design*, 535

## G

Game of Life, 627
gamma correction, 171
Gardner, Martin, 627
geometric primitives, 37–48, 680–682
  performance when specifying, 783
  rendering pipeline stage, 12
geosciences
  use of texturing in applications, 434
giraffe, 174
GL_VERTEX_PROGRAM_POINT_SIZE, 673
GL_VERTEX_PROGRAM_TWO_SIDE, 674
glActiveTexture(), 445
glAreTexturesResident(), 419
glArrayElement(), 72
  legal between glBegin() and glEnd(), 47
Glassner, Andrew S., xxxix
glAttachShader(), 640
glBegin(), 42, 43, 510
  restrictions, 46
glBeginQuery(), 486
glBindAttribLocation(), 671

glBindBuffer(), 84
glBindTexture(), 379, 416
  multitexturing, 445
glBitmap(), 303, 740
  feedback mode, 593
  fonts, used for, 310
  imaging pipeline operations, 323
  pixel-storage modes effect, 326
glBlendColor*(), 235
glBlendEquation(), 235
glBlendEquationSeparate(), 235
glBlendFunc(), 233
glBlendFuncSeparate(), 233
glBufferData(), 84
glBufferSubData(), 87
glCallList(), 282, 285, 290
  legal between glBegin() and glEnd(), 47
glCallLists(), 292
  fonts, use for, 309
  legal between glBegin() and glEnd(), 47
  sample program, 311
glClear(), 31, 471, 684
  depth buffer, clearing the, 186
glClearAccum(), 32, 471
glClearColor(), 31, 471
glClearDepth(), 31, 471
glClearIndex(), 32, 179, 471
  fog, use with, 266
glClearStencil(), 32, 471
glClientActiveTexture(), 448
glClipPlane(), 150
glColor*(), 33, 177
  legal between glBegin() and glEnd(), 46
glColorMask(), 471, 473
glColorMaterial(), 217
  performance tips, 782
glColorPointer(), 69
glColorSubTable(), 352
glColorTable(), 348
glColorTableParameter(), 350
glCompileShader(), 639
glCompressedTexImage1D(), 398

glHint()
  fog use, 261
  texture use, 380
glHistogram(), 363
glIndex*()
  fog, use with, 266
  legal between glBegin() and glEnd(), 46
glIndexMask(), 471, 473
glIndexPointer(), 69
glInitNames(), 571, 572, 573
glInterleavedArrays(), 79
glIsBuffer(), 83, 688
glIsEnabled(), 10, 49, 688
glIsList(), 291, 688
glIsProgram(), 644, 688
glIsQuery(), 485, 688
glIsShader(), 644, 688
glIsTexture(), 415, 688
glLight*(), 193, 194, 195, 200
glLightModel*(), 208
glLineStipple(), 52
glLineWidth(), 51
glLinkProgram(), 641
glListBase(), 292
  fonts, use for, 309
  sample program, 311
glLoadIdentity(), 113, 115, 125, 684
  performance tips, 782
  viewing transformations, use before, 111
glLoadMatrix*(), 114, 115, 684
glLoadName(), 572, 574
glLoadTransposeMatrix*(), 114, 116
glLogicOp(), 236
glMap*(), 538
glMap1*(), 540
glMapBuffer(), 87
glMapGrid1*(), 541
glMapGrid2*(), 545
glMaterial*(), 194, 212
  legal between glBegin() and glEnd(), 46
  performance tips, 782

glMatrixMode(), 113, 115
  use with matrix stacks, 146
glMinmax(), 366
glMultiDrawArrays(), 78
  version, 29
glMultiDrawElements(), 75
  version, 29
glMultiTexCoord*(), 447
glMultMatrix*(), 114, 115, 684
  performance tips, 782
glMultTransposeMatrix*(), 114, 116
glNewList(), 281, 285, 287
glNormal*()
  legal between glBegin() and glEnd(), 46
glNormal3*(), 64
glNormalPointer(), 69
glOrtho(), 137, 684
  picking matrix use, 579
glPassThrough(), 592, 594
glPixelMap*(), 333
glPixelStore*(), 326, 395
  cannot be stored in display lists, 289
  polygon stippling, 58
  texture image data, effect on, 382, 384,
    387, 389, 391, 394, 398, 399
glPixelTransfer*(), 330, 625
  texture image data, effect on, 382, 384,
    387, 389, 391, 394, 398, 399
glPixelZoom(), 334, 611
glPointParameter*(), 272
glPointSize(), 50, 673
glPolygonMode(), 56
  antialiasing, effect on, 260
  polygon offset, use with, 274
glPolygonOffset(), 274
glPolygonStipple(), 58
  pixel-storage modes effect, 326
glPopAttrib(), 10, 92, 298, 447, 689
glPopClientAttrib(), 10, 93, 447, 689
glPopMatrix(), 146, 157, 203, 298
  restore orientation of coordinate systems,
    159
  selection, use with, 571

**L**

Lasser, Dieter, 535
layers, drawing, 612
Life, Game of, 627
light sources, 194–207
  ambient light, 188, 196
  contribution to lighting equation, 222
  diffuse light, 188, 196
  directional, 197
  display lists cache values, 283
  infinite light source, 197
  local light source, 197
  maximum number of sources, 193
  moving along with the viewpoint, 205
  moving light sources, 201–206
  multiple light sources, 200
  performance tips, 193
  positional, 197
  rendering pipeline stage, 12, 681
  RGBA values, 189
  sample program that moves the light
     source, 204
  specifying a light source, 193
  specular light, 188
  spotlights, 199–200
  stationary, 202
lighting
  *see also* light sources, material properties
  ambient light, 187
  approximation of the real world, 187
  attenuation, 197–198
  calculations in color-index mode, 227
  color-index mode, 226–228
  default values, using, 194
  display lists cache values, 283
  enabling, 193, 194
  enabling and disabling, 211
  equation that calculates lighting, 221
  global ambient light, 208, 222
  lighting model, 207–210
  lighting model, specifying a, 193
  rendering pipeline stage, 12, 681
  sample program introducing lighting, 190
  specular color separated, 210, 225, 455
  steps to perform, 190

  two-sided materials, 209
  viewer, local or infinite, 209
line segment, 38
linear attenuation, 198
lines, 38
  antialiasing, 249–255, 624
  connected closed loop, specifying, 43, 45
  connected strip, specifying, 43, 45
  feedback mode, 593
  querying line width, 51
  sample program with wide, stippled lines,
    54
  specifying, 43, 45
  stippling, 52
  tessellated polygons decomposed into, 510
  width, 51
local light source, 197
logical operations
  rendering pipeline stage, 14, 683
  transposing images, using for, 629
lookup table, *see* color map
luminance, 315, 341
  pixel data formats for, 317, 325
  texture image data type, 422

**M**

magnifying images, 334
masking, 473
  antialiasing characters, 615
  layers, drawing, 612
  rendering pipeline stage, 14, 683
material properties, 194, 211–220
  ambient, 189, 213
  changing a single parameter with
    glColorMaterial(), 217
  changing material properties, 215
  diffuse, 189, 213
  display lists cache values, 283
  emission, 188, 214, 221
  enabling color material properties mode,
    217
  performance when changing, 782
  rendering pipeline stage, 12, 681
  RGBA values, 190

specular
  contribution to lighting equation, 224
  light, 188
  material properties, 189, 214
  secondary specular color, 210, 225, 455
sphere map, 439
spheres, 524, 763
split-screen
  multiple viewports, 139
spotlights, *see* light sources
state attributes
  perserving, 92
  preserving vertex arrays, 93
  reverting, 92
  reverting vertex arrays, 93
state machine, 9–10
state variables, 48
  attribute groups, 91–93
  display list execution, effect of, 297
  enable and disable states, 49
  list of, 688–733
  performance of storing and restoring, 782
  querying, 49
stencil buffer, 468, 469
  clearing, 32, 471
  concave polygons, for drawing, 618
  decals, for, 617
  Dirichlet domains, for, 626
  Game of Life, for the, 627
  hidden-line removal, 623
  masking, 473
  pixel data, 317, 332
stencil test, 478–483
  examples of using, 480
  interference regions found using clipping
    planes, 620
  querying stencil parameters, 479
  rendering pipeline stage, 14, 683
  sample program, 480
stereo, 469, 472
  querying its presence, 469
stippling
  display lists cache stipple patterns, 283
  enabling line stippling, 52
  enabling polygon stippling, 58

fade effect, use for, 608
line pattern reset, 53, 593, 597
lines, 52
polygons, 58
sample program with line stipple, 54
stencil test, use of, 483
translucency, use to simulate, 608
stitching, 274
stretching objects, *see* scaling
stride
  vertex arrays, 71, 79
subdivision, 94–102
  generalized, 101
  icosahedron example, 99
  recursive, 101
subimages, 387–390, 391, 394
superimposing images, 617
surface normals, *see* normal vectors
surfaces, *see* evaluators or NURBS
swapping buffers, *see* double-buffering
syntax, *see* command syntax

## T

*Terminator 2*, 439
tessellation, 40, 506–523
  backward compatibility with obsolete
    routines, 522
  begin and end callback routines, 510
  callback routines, 508–513
  combine callback routine, 510, 513
  contours, specifying, 519
  converting code to use the GLU 1.2
    tessellator, 523
  creating an object, 508
  decomposition into geometric primitives,
    510
  deleting objects, 521
  display list use, 282
  edge flag generation, 510
  error handling, 510
  evaluators used to perform, 783
  interior and exterior, determining,
    514–517
  intersecting contours combined, 510, 513

texture objects *(continued)*
  priority, 420
  rendering pipeline, 13, 683
  sample program, 377
  sample program with multiple texture
    objects, 416
  sharing among rendering contexts, 739,
    754
  steps to perform, 414
  using, 415
texturing
  *see also* texture coordinates, texture
    functions, texture images, texture
    matrix, and texture objects
  antialiasing characters, 624
  antialiasing lines, 624
  blending, 239
  border colors, treatment of, 429
  color-index mode limitations, 375, 383
  combiner functions, 449–454
  compressed textures, 397
  creating contours, 435
  cube maps, 441
  decals with alpha testing, 477
  differences among releases, 373
  enabling, 376, 379
  filtering, 411–413
  image transformations, 624
  mipmapping, 401–411, 413
  mosaic texture, 406
  multitexturing, 443–448
  perspective correction hint, 379, 380
  popping visual artifact, 406
  rendering pipeline stage, 13, 683
  sample code using point sprites, 457
  sample code with a depth texture, 460–462
  sample code with combiner functions, 453
  sample code with multitexturing, 446
  sample program, 377
  sample program with cube maps, 443
  sample program with evaluated, Bézier
    surface, 548
  sample program with mipmapping, 403
  sample program with texture coordinate
    generation, 435
  sample uses for, 624
  simulating shadows or spotlights, 458

specular color separated, 210, 225, 455
sphere map, 439
steps to perform, 375
*3D Computer Graphics: A User's Guide for
  Artists and Designers,* xxxix
3D models, rendering, 20, 763
Tiller, Wayne, 535
tips, programming, 779
  *see also* performance tips
  error handling, 780
  selection and picking, 589
  transformations, 142
transformations
  *see also* modeling transformations,
    projection transformations, viewing
    transformations, and viewport
    transformations
  combining multiple, 152–159
  display lists cache transformations, 283
  general-purpose commands, 114
  matrices, 775–778
  modeling, 117, 120–125
  ordering correctly, 117–120
  overview, 104
  performance tips, 782
  projection, 112, 133–138
  reversing the geometric processing
    pipeline, 160
  sample program, 110
  sample program combining modeling
    transformations, 154, 157
  sample program for modeling
    transformations, 125
  sample program showing reversal of
    transformation pipeline, 161
  troubleshooting, 142–144
  units, 136
  viewing, 117, 126–131
  viewport, 114, 138–140
translation, 121
  matrix, 776
translucent objects, 232, 608
  stencil test, creating with the, 483
transparent objects, 232
  creating with the alpha test, 477
transposing images, 629

triangle
    fan, specifying, 43
    specifying, 43, 45
    strip, specifying, 43, 45
    tessellated polygons decomposed into, 510
trimming
    curves and curved surfaces, 565–568
    sample program, 567
tutorials
    on-line, xl
two-sided lighting, 209

# U

up-vector, 111
Utility Library, OpenGL, *see* GLU
Utility Toolkit, OpenGL, *see* GLUT

# V

van Dam, Andries, xxxviii, 167, 171, 773
van Widenfelt, Rolf, 458
vendor-specific extensions, 605
versions, 603–605
    GLU, 604
vertex, 37
    *see also* vertex arrays
    evaluators, generating with, 536
    feedback mode, 593
    per-vertex operations pipeline stage, 12,
        681
    specifying, 41
    tessellation, specifying for, 511, 519
    transformation pipeline, 106
vertex arrays, 65–81
    dereference a list of array elements, 73, 75,
        76
    dereference a sequence of array elements,
        77, 78
    dereference a single element, 72
    differences among releases, 29
    disabling, 68
    display list use, 289
    enabling, 67
    interleaved arrays, 78

interleaved arrays, specifying, 79
multitexturing texture coordinates, 448
performance tips, 783
querying, 688
querying range values, 76
reuse of vertices, 74
specifying data, 68
steps to use, 66
stride between data, 71, 79
vertex shader
    rendering pipeline stage, 681
video
    fake, 628
    flipping an image with glPixelZoom(), 335
    textured images, 387
viewing
    camera analogy, 106–107
viewing transformations, 110, 117, 126–131
    connection to modeling transformations,
        111
    default position, 111
    different methods, 131
    pilot view, 132
    polar view, 132
    tripod analogy, 106
    up-vector, 111
viewing volume, 134
    clipping, 138, 149
    jittering, 492, 495
viewpoint
    lighting, for, 209
viewport transformations, 109, 114, 138–140
    photograph analogy, 106
    rendering pipeline stage, 12, 682
visual simulation
    fog, use of, 261
Voronoi polygons, 626

# W

w coordinates, 38, 109, 114
    avoiding negative values, 781
    lighting, use with, 197
    perspective division, 141, 682
warping images, 624

Watt, Alan, 370
web sites, xxxix
  errata list, xl
  IBM OS/2 software and documentation, 749
  Microsoft Developer Network, 753
WGL, 14, 753
  wglCopyContext(), 754, 756
  wglCreateContext(), 753, 754, 756
  wglCreateLayerContext(), 754, 756
  wglDeleteContext(), 756
  wglDescribeLayerPlane(), 753, 756
  wglDestroyContext(), 754
  wglGetCurrentContext(), 754, 756
  wglGetCurrentDC(), 754, 756
  wglGetLayerPaletteEntries(), 755, 757
  wglGetProcAddress(), 756
  wglMakeCurrent(), 754, 756
  wglRealizeLayerPalette(), 755, 757
  wglSetLayerPaletteEntries(), 757
  wglShareLists(), 754, 756
  wglSwapLayerBuffers(), 755, 757
  wglUseFontBitmaps(), 755, 757
  wglUseFontOutlines(), 755, 757
wglGetProcAddress(), 607
Williams, Lance, 401
Win32
  ChoosePixelFormat(), 753, 755
  CreateDIBitmap(), 754, 756
  CreateDIBSection(), 754, 756
  DeleteObject(), 754, 756
  DescribePixelFormat(), 753, 756
  GetVersion(), 753, 755
  GetVersionEx(), 753, 755
  SetPixelFormat(), 753, 755
  SwapBuffers(), 755, 757

winding, 57
winding rules, 514–517
  computational solid geometry, used for, 515
  reversing winding direction, 518
window coordinates, 109, 138
  feedback mode, 593
  polygon offset, 275
  raster position, 305
window management
  glViewport() called, when window resized, 139
  using GLUT, 17, 36
Windows, *see* Microsoft
working set of textures, 386, 414, 419
  fragmentation of texture memory, 421
writemask, *see* masking (buffers)
writing pixel data, *see* pixel data (drawing)
www.opengl.org, xxxix

## X

X Window System, 14, 738
  client-server rendering, 5
  minimum framebuffer configuration, 468
  X Visual, 176, 737

## Z

z buffer, *see* depth buffer
z coordinates, *see* depth coordinates
zooming images, 334
  filtered, 629

# OpenGL® Titles from Addison-Wesley

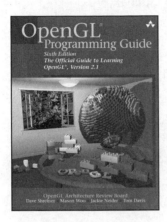

## OpenGL® Programming Guide, Sixth Edition
### The Official Guide to Learning OpenGL® Version 2.1
**OpenGL Architecture Review Board, Dave Shreiner, Mason Woo, Jackie Neider, and Tom Davis**
0-321-48100-3

*OpenGL® Programming Guide, Sixth Edition*, provides definitive, comprehensive information on OpenGL and the OpenGL Utility Library. This sixth edition of the best-selling "red book" describes the latest features of OpenGL Version 2.1.

## OpenGL® Shading Language, Second Edition
**Randi Rost**
0-321-33489-2

*OpenGL® Shading Language, Second Edition*, is the experienced application programmer's guide to writing shaders. Part reference, part tutorial, this book explains the shift from fixed-functionality graphics hardware to the new era of programmable graphics hardware and the additions to the OpenGL API that support it.

## OpenGL® Library, Fourth Edition
0-321-51432-7

This special boxed set contains both *OpenGL® Programming Guide, Sixth Edition*, and *OpenGL® Shading Language, Second Edition*.

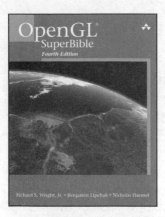

## OpenGL® SuperBible, Fourth Edition
### Comprehensive Tutorial and Reference
**Richard S. Wright Jr., Benjamin Lipchak,
and Nicholas Haemel**
0-321-49882-8

*OpenGL® SuperBible, Fourth Edition*, offers comprehensive coverage of applying and using OpenGL in your
day-to-day work. It covers topics such as OpenGL ES
programming for handhelds and OpenGL implementations
on multiple platforms, including Windows, Mac OS X, and
Linux/UNIX.

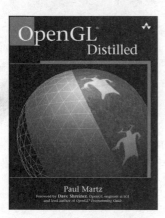

## OpenGL® Distilled
**Paul Martz**
0-321-33679-8

*OpenGL® Distilled* provides the fundamental information
you need to start programming 3D graphics, from setting up an OpenGL development environment to creating
realistic textures and shadows. Written in an engaging,
easy-to-follow style, you'll quickly learn the essential and
most-often-used features of OpenGL, along with the best
coding practices and troubleshooting tips.

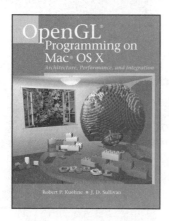

## OpenGL® Programming on Mac® OS X
### Architecture, Performance, and Integration
**Robert P. Kuehne and J. D. Sullivan**
0-321-35652-7

Apple's highly efficient, modern OpenGL implementation
makes Mac OS X one of today's best platforms for OpenGL
development. *OpenGL® Programming on Mac OS® X* is the
first comprehensive resource for every graphics programmer who wants to create, port, or optimize OpenGL
applications for this high-volume platform.